John Willis
Theatre World
1995-1996 SEASON

VOLUME 52

APPLAUSE
NEW YORK • LONDON
THEATRE BOOK PUBLISHERS
211 WEST 71ST STREET • NEW YORK NY • 10023

LIBRARY OF CONGRESS CATALOG CARD NO. 73-82953
ISBN 1-55783-322-2 (cloth)
ISBN 1-55783-323-0 (paper)

BETTY COMDEN

ADOLPH GREEN

With boundless admiration, appreciation and
gratitude, this volume is dedicated to
performers, playwrights, lyricists and
Broadway's longest-running collaborators:
Betty Comden and Adolph Green.
Their words have adorned numerous musicals,
have been rewarded with many "Tony" nominations,
and are the recipients of several.

1944-*On The Town*
1945-*Billion Dollar Baby*
1951-*Two On The Aisle*
1953-*Wonderful Town*
1954-*Peter Pan*
1956-*Bells Are Ringing*
1958-*Say Darling*
       A Party with Comden And Green
1960-*Do Re Mi*
1961-*Subways Are For Sleeping*
1964-*Fade Out! Fade In!*
1965 *Leonard Bernstein's Theatre Songs*
1968-*Hallelujah, Baby!* (2 Tonys)
1970-*Applause* (2 Tonys)
1974-*Lorelei*
1978-*On The 20th Century* (2 Tonys)
1982-*A Doll's Life*
1985-*Singin' In The Rain*
1989-*Jerome Robbin's Broadway*
1991-*The Will Rogers Follies* (Tony)

The cast of *Rent*
photograph © Joan Marcus

CONTENTS

EDITOR: JOHN WILLIS
ASSISTANT EDITOR: TOM LYNCH

Assistants: Stine Elbirk Cabrera, Alexander Dawson Herbert Hayward, Jr., Barry Monush,
Christopher Morelock, Eric Ort, John Sala, John Stachniewicz
Staff Photographers: Gerry Goodstein, Michael Riordan, Michael Viade, Van Williams
Production: Claiborne Hancock, Steve Ledezma, Julia Moberg
Paul Sugarman, Bob Ward, Sarah Weisman

BROADWAY PRODUCTIONS

Red Buttons

Red Button (and above)

BUTTONS ON BROADWAY

Musical Director, Bryan Louiselle; Sets, Nancy Thun; Lighting, Ken Billington; Sound. Lewis Mead; Technical Supervisor, Peter Fulbright; General Manager, 101 Productions; Company Manager, David Auster; Stage Managers, J.P. Elins, K. Dale White; Presented by Don Gregory; Press, Bill Evans/ Jim Randolph, Terry M. Lilly, Tom D'Ambrosio; Previewed from June 5; Opened in the Ambassador Theatre on Thursday, June 8, 1995*

CAST

RED BUTTONS

An entertainment in two acts.

Times: (Ben Brantley) "...able to command the stage for nearly two hours..does the mildly ribald burlesque routines he performed on the same stage more than 50 years ago." News: (Howard Kissel) "If Broadway is going to be a resurrection of the Borscht Belt, it should at least have some old style zest and energy." Post: (Clive Barnes) "...back among us, as bright as, well yes, a button." Newsday: (Jan Stuart) "...celebrates a very respectable career." Variety: (Greg Evans) "...isn't likely to attract anyone too young to know the Ho-Ho Dance..."

*Closed July 16, 1995 after 33 performances and three previews. Red Buttons appeared at this theatre in 1942's *Wine, Women, and Song.*

Joan Marcus Photos

CHRONICLE OF A DEATH FORETOLD

Adapted by Graciela Daniele and Jim Lewis from the novel by Gabriel Garcia Marquez; Music/Arrangements, Bob Telson; Additional Material, Michael John LaChiusa; Conceived/Directed/Choreographed by Graciela Daniele; Musical Director/Dance Arrangements, Steve Sandberg; Sets, Christopher Barreca; Costumes, Toni-Leslie James; Lighting, Jules Fisher, Beverly Emmons; Sound, Tony Meola; Associate Choreographer, Willie Rosario; Production Manager, Jeff Hamlin; General Manager, Steven C. Callahan; Company Manager, Florie Seery; Stage Managers, Leslie Loeb, Valerie Lau-Kee, Robert Castro; Presented by Lincoln Center Theater (Directors, Andre Bishop, Bernard Gersten) by arrangement with INTAR Hispanic American Arts Center; Press, Merle Debuskey/Susan Chicoine, Owen Levy; Previewed from Thursday, May 18; Opened in the Plymouth Theatre on Thursday, June 15, 1995*

Gregory Mitchell, Tonya Pinkins, Luis Perez

CAST

Santiago Nasar	George de la Pena
Cristo	Julio Monge
Placida	Yolande Bavan
Victoria	Myra Lucretia Taylor
Divina	Monica McSwain
Angela Vicario	Saundra Santiago
Pura Vicario	Ivonne Coll
Pablo Vicario	Luis Perez
Pedro Vicario	Gregory Mitchell
Bayardo San Roman	Alexandre Proia
Clotilde	Tonya Pinkins
Flora	Lisa Leguillou
Faustino	Lazaro Perez
Xius	Norberto Kerner
Col. Aponte	Nelson Roberto Landrieu
Father Amador	Jaime Tirelli
Margot	Rene M. Ceballos
Maria	Denise Faye

UNDERSTUDIES: Edgard Gallardo (Santiago/Cristo/Pablo/Pedro/Bayardo/Aponte), Julio Monge (Santiago), Colten Green (Cristo/Pablo/Pedro/Bayardo/Faustino/Xius), Susan Pilar (Placida/Victoria/Angela/Clotilde) Marina Chapa (Placida/Divina/Angela/Flora), Eyan Williams (Victoria/Pura/Clotilde/Margot/Maria), Rene M. Ceballos (Pura), Marianne Filali (Flora/Margot/Maria), Edouard DeSoto Faustino/Xius/Aponte/Amador), Nelson Roberto Landrieu (Amador)

A dance musical performed without intermission. The action takes place on an isolated Latin American town, past and present.

Saundra Santiago, Ivonne Coll

Variety tallied 4 favorable, 3 mixed and 7 unfavorable reviews. Times: (Vincent Canby) "...frequently stunning show that is less a conventional musical adaptation than a performance piece..." (Margo Jefferson) "...shallow but pretty..." News: (Kissel) "It's all very artful, all very arty..." Newsday: (Linda Winer) "...extremely admirable claptrap..." Variety: (Jeremy Gerard) "...a hash of elements that don't quite come together..."

*Closed July 16, 1995 after 37 performances and 30 previews.

Joan Marcus Photos

George de la Peña, Julio Monge

THE PLAY'S THE THING

By Ferenc Molnar; Adaptation, P.G. Wodehouse; Director, Gloria Muzio; Sets, Stephan Olson; Costumes, Jess Goldstein; Lighting, Peter Kaczorowski; Sound, Douglas J. Cuomo; Hairstylist, David H. Lawrence; General Manager, Ellen Richard; Stage Manager, Denise Yaney; Presented by Roundabout Theatre Company (Artistic Director, Todd Haimes; Founding Director, Gene Feist); Press, Chris Boneau~Adrian Bryan-Brown/Susanne Tighe; Previewed from Saturday, June 17; Opened in the Criterion Center Stage Right on Sunday, July 9, 1995*

CAST

Mansky..Joe Grifasi
Sandor Turai...Peter Frechette
Albert Adam ....Jay Goede
Johann Dwornitschek...Paul Benedict
Ilona Szabo..J. Smith-Cameron
Almady..Jeff Weiss
Mr. Mell ....Keith Reddin
STANDBYS: Jonathan Bustle (Sandor/Almady), George Hosmer (Mansky/Johann), Jared Reed (Albert/Mell), Rebecca Wisocky (Ilona)

A new production of a 1926 comedy, based on Molnar's original, in three acts. The action takes place in a castle on the Italian Riviera.

Times: (Canby) "What's missing is any sense of the securely sophisticated style that defines high comedy." News: (Kissel) "The set is tolerable, the costumes often garish, the direction seemingly nonexistent." Post: (Barnes) "When does a fashionable play become dated?...what on earth has gone so woefully wrong..." Newsday: (Stuart) "...agreeable wind-up toy of a play with enough good shtick to go around." Variety: (Gerard) "...woefully miscast and lumpish..."

*Closed August 17, 1995 after 49 performances and 22 previews.

Carol Rosegg Photos

J. Smith-Cameron, Jeff Weiss

Paul Benedict, Peter Frechette

Keith Reddin, Jeff Weiss, J. Smith-Cameron, Jay Goede

8

SOMETHING WONDERFUL

Musical Directors, Eric Stern, Catherine Matejka; Producer/Press, Bert Fink; Presented by The Rodgers & Hammerstein Organization in association with Livent (U.S.); Press, Mary Bryant/Wayne Wolfe; Presented in the Gershwin Theatre on Wednesday, July 12, 1995 for one performance only

CAST

Maureen McGovern	Doug Le Breque
Liz Calloway	Rebecca Luker
Joel Blum	Michel Bell
Garth Drabinsky	Dorothy Stanley
William Hammerstein	Jonathan Dukochitz
Audra McDonald	Schuyler G. Chapin
	Theodore S. Chapin, host

PROGRAM: A Cockeyed Optimist (from South Pacific), Oh What a Beautiful Mornin' (From Oklahoma), Can I Forget You? (from High Wide and Handsome), A Wonderful Guy (from South Pacific), Stan' Up and Fight (from Carmen Jones), All Er Nothin' (from Oklahoma), All the Things You Are (from Very Warm for May), Something Wonderful (from King and I), Suddenly Lovely (intended for South Pacific)

A celebration of lyricist Oscar Hammerstein II (1895-1960) on what would been his 100th birthday.

Oscar Hammerstein II

Carol Burnett, Philip Bosco

Robert Goulet, Lynn Redgrave

Carol Burnett

MOON OVER BUFFALO

By Ken Ludwig; Director, Tom Moore; Sets, Heidi Landesman; Costumes, Bob Mackie; Lighting, Ken Billington; Sound, Tony Meola; Fights, B.H. Barry; Production Supervisor, Steven Beckler; General Manager, 101 Productions; Production Manager, Peter Fulbright; Company Manager, Richard Biederman; Stage Managers, Steven Beckler, Tom Capps; Presented by Elizabeth Williams, Heidi Landesman, DLT Entertainment, Hal Luftig and Jujamcyn Theatres; Press, Chris Boneau~Adrian Bryan-Brown/Bob Fennell, Jackie Green, James Sapp, Clint Bond Jr.; Previewed from Wednesday, September 13; Opened in the Martin Beck Theatre on Sunday, October 1, 1995*

CAST

Ethel..Jane Connell
Rosalind..Randy Graff
Howard..Andy Taylor
George Hay ....Philip Bosco +1
Charlotte Hay...Carol Burnett +2
Eileen..Kate Miller
Paul ....Dennis Ryan
Richard Maynard..James Valentine
STANDBYS: Richard Poe (George/Richard), Jane Sell Trese (Charlotte/Ethel), Lannyl Stephens (Rosalind/Eileen), David Beach (Howard/Paul)

A comedy in two acts. The action takes place on stage and backstage at Buffalo's Erlanger Theatre, 1953

Variety tallied 4 favorable, 2 mixed and 12 unfavorable reviews. Times: (Canby) "Time hasn't tarnished Burnett's cockeyed splendor..it has enriched her comic presence." (Jefferson) "Plays that work this hard to be lightweight intend to be forgotten." News: (Kissel) "Bosco has the best part..hysteria of the stage business only underscores the play's hollowness." Post: (Barnes) "...no great comic moment but considerable farcical delight." Variety: "Relentlessly second-rate..never stops trying to please.."

*Closed June 30, 1996 after 308 performances and 20 previews.

+Succeeded by: 1. Robert Goulet 2. Lynn Redgrave

Joan Marcus Photos

Philip Bosco, Carol Burnett

Dennis Ryan, Carol Burnett, Randy Graff

11

Boyd Gaines

Veanne Cox

COMPANY

Music/Lyrics, Stephen Sondheim; Book, George Furth; Director, Scott Ellis; Musical Staging, Rob Marshall; Musical Director, David Loud; Orchestrations (reduction of originals), Jonathan Tunick; Sets, Tony Walton; Costumes, William Ivey Long; Lighting, Peter Kaczorowski; Sound, Tony Meola; Cast Recording, Angel; Projections, Wendall K. Harrington; Hair/Wigs, Paul Huntley; Stage Managers, Lori M. Doyle, Matthew T. Mundinger; Presented by Roundabout Theatre Company (Artistic Director, Todd Haimes; General Manager, Ellen Richard; Founding Director, Gene Feist); Press, Chris Boneau~Adrian Bryan Brown, Andy Shearer, Susanne Tighe, Meredith Moore, Cindy Valk; Previewed from Wednesday, August 30; Opened in the Criterion Center Stage Right on Thursday, October 5, 1995*

CAST

Robert ....Boyd Gaines +1
Sarah ....Kate Burton
Harry ....Robert Westenberg
Susan ....Patricia Ben Peterson
Peter...Jonathan Dokuchitz
Jenny ....Diana Canova
David ....John Hillner
Amy ....Veanne Cox
Paul..Danny Burstein
Joanne ....Debra Monk
Larry ....Timothy Landfield
Marta...La Chanze
Kathy ....Charlotte d'Amboise
April...Jane Krakowski

STANDBYS: James Clow (Robert/Peter/Paul), Andy Umberger (Harry/David/Larry), Colleen Fitzpatrick (Susan/Jenny/Marta/April), Nancy Hess (Amy/Kathy/April)

MUSICAL NUMBERS: Overture, Company, Little Things You Do Together, Sorry-Grateful, You Could Drive a Person Crazy, Have I Got a Girl for You, Someone Is Waiting, Another Hundred People, Getting Married Today, Marry Me a Little (not in orig. Bdwy prod.), Entr'Acte, Side By Side By Side/What Would We Do Without You, Poor Baby, Tick Tock, Barcelona, The Ladies Who Lunch, Being Alive, Finale

A new production of the 1970 musical in two acts. The action takes place in New York City. For original Broadway production see Theatre World Vol.26.

Variety tallied 5 favorable, 7 mixed and 2 unfavorable reviews. Times: (Canby) "...you'll always know it better for what it reveals over time..than for what will ever appear in a single public performance." (Jefferson) "Mr. Sondheim the composer and Mr. Sondheim the lyricist are a brilliant match. Two is all the company we need here." News: (Kissel) "...one of the quintessentially New York musicals, looks like it was done by people who had never been here." Post: "...Boyd Gaines..seemed splendid..the others, all good.." Variety: (Gerard) ..a lot of people are going to want to see this show, and they won't be disappointed..the striped-down, synthesizer-dependent (and guitarless!) orchestra sounds thin.."

*Closed December 3, 1995 after 68 performances and 43 previews.

+ 1. James Clow (during illness).

Carol Rosegg Photos

The Company

Boyd Gaines, Jane Krakowski

Elizabeth Ashley

Myra Carter, Pamela Payton-Wright

GARDEN DISTRICT

By Tennessee Williams; Directors, Theodore Mann (Something Unspoken), Harold Scott (Suddenly Last Summer), Sets/Costumes, Zack Brown; Lighting, Marc B. Weiss; Composer, Kevin Farrell; Sound, Bruce Cameron; Dialects, K.C. Ligon; Movement, Loyd Williamson; Fights, B.H. Barry; Company Managers, Gordon Forbes, Don Roe; Stage Managers, Linda Harris, Cheryl Zoldowski; Presented by Circle in the Square (Co-Artistic Directors, Theodore Mann, Josephine Abady); Press, Jeffrey Richards/Kevin Rehac; Previewed from Friday, September 22; Opened in the Circle in the Square Uptown on Tuesday, October 10, 1995*

CASTS
SOMETHING UNSPOKEN
Cornelia ....Myra Carter
Grace ....Pamela Payton-Wright

SUDDENLY LAST SUMMER
Mrs. Venable ....Elizabeth Ashley
Dr. Cukrowicz..Victor Slezak
Miss Foxhill ....Peggy Cosgrove
Mrs. Holly...Celia Weston
George Holly..Mitchell Lichtenstein
Catharine Holly...Jordan Baker
Sister Felicity ....Leslie Lyles
UNDERSTUDIES: Maeve McGuire (Mrs. Venable/Grace/Miss Foxhill), Orlagh Cassidy (Catharine), Peggy Cosgrove (Cornelia/Mrs. Holly/Felicity), Neil Maffin (Cukrowicz/George)

   A new production of a 1958 double bill of one-act plays. The action in both plays takes place in the Garden District of New Orleans, 1936.

   Variety tallied 6 favorable and 5 negative notices. Times: (Canby) "...not one of Williams's great plays but it's a very good one..Ms. Ashley and Ms. Baker are in two different hemispheres." (Jefferson) "..a violent, beautifully controlled piece of Gothic drama.." Post: (Barnes) "We are probably not going to see much better acting this season.." Variety(Gerard) "..problematic but rewarding..revelation here is Baker.."

   *Closed November 5, 1995 after 31 performances and 19 previews.

Gerry Goodstein Photos

PATTI LuPONE ON BROADWAY

Conception/Direction, Scott Wittman; Musical Director, Dick Gallagher; Arrangements, John McDaniel, Steven D. Bowen, Glen Roven, Marc Shaiman, Jonathan Tunick, Mr. Gallagher; Writer, Jeffrey Richman; Lighting, John Hastings; Sound, Otts Munderloh; General Manager, Marvin A. Krauss; Company Manager, Mark Andrews; Stage Manager, George Darveris; Presented by Jujamcyn Theatres; Press, Philip Rinaldi/James LL Morrison, Brian Rubin; Previewed from Thursday, October 5; Opened in the Walter Kerr Theatre on Thursday, October 12, 1995*

CAST

PATTI LuPONE

Byron Motley, Josef Powell,.Gene Van Buren,.John West

A musical entertainment in two parts. The first act presented a variety of songs while act II featured songs from Ms. LuPone's theatre performances: Sunset Boulevard, Evita, Les Miserables, Robber Bridegroom, Oliver, The Bakers Wife, Pal Joey and Anything Goes.

Variety tallied 7 positive and 5 mixed reviews. Times: (Stephen Holden) "...she really is a queen in exile waiting for another crown, another role of a lifetime that will mobilize all the emotional energy anxiously flung throughout her one-woman show." News: (Kissel) "The tone of irony seeps into Patti LuPone on Broadway even during the customary remarks before the show begins..enormous talent, oddly packaged." Post: (Barnes) "..don't cry for her, Lloyd Webber, she is doing just dandy. She is one of Broadway's great performers.." Variety: (Evans) "In a diva-packed Broadway season, Patti LuPone bursts front and center,.."

*Closed November 25, 1995 after 46 performances and 7 previews.

Joan Marcus Photos

Patti LuPone

Josef Powell, John West, Patti LuPone, Byron Motley, Gene Van Buren

15

Jay Garner, Florence Lacey

Carol Channing, Julian Brightman

HELLO, DOLLY!

Music/Lyrics, Jerry Herman; Book, Michael Stewart; Based on the play *The Matchmaker* by Thornton Wilder; Directed and Staged by Lee Roy Reams; Associate Choreographer, Bill Bateman; Musical Supervision, Tim Stella; Musical Director, Jack Everly; Orchestrations (original), Philip J. Lang; Set, Oliver Smith; Lighting, Ken Billington; Costumes, Jonathan Bixby; Sound, Peter J. Fitzgerald; Dance Arrangements, Peter Howard; New Cast Recording, Varese Sarabande; Production Supervisor, Jerry Herman; General Management, Niko Associates; Company Manager, Brig Berney; Stage Managers, Thomas P. Carr, Jim Semmelman; Presented by Manny Kladitis, Magic Promotions and Theatricals, Pace Theatrical Group and John B. Platt; Press, Chris Boneau/Adrian Bryan-Brown/Dennis Crowley, Miguel Tuason; Previewed from Wednesday, October 11; Opened in the Lunt-Fontanne Theatre on Thursday, October 19, 1995*

CAST

Mrs. Dolly Gallagher Levi	Carol Channing
Ernestina	Monica M. Wemitt
Ambrose Kemper	James Darrah
Horse	Sharon Moore, Michele Tibbitts
Horace Vandergelder	Jay Garner
Ermengarde	Christine DeVito
Cornelius Hackl	Michael DeVries
Barnaby Tucker	Cory English
Minnie Fay	Lori Ann Mahl
Irene Molloy	Florence Lacey
Mrs. Rose	Elizabeth Green
Rudolph	Steve Pudenz
Stanley	Julian Brightman
Judge	Bill Bateman
Court Clerk	Halden Michaels

Townspeople/Waiters/Etc. .....John Bantay, Desta Barbieri, Bill Bateman, Kimberly Bellmann, Bruce Blanchard, Stephen Bourneuf, Julian Brightman, Holly Cruikshank, Simone Gee, Jason Gillman, Milica Govich, Elizabeth Green, Donald Ives, Dan LoBuono, Jim Madden, Halden Michaels, Sharon Moore, Michael Quinn, Robert Randle, Mitch Rosengarten, Mary Setrakian, Clarence M. Sheridan, Randy Slovacek, Roger Preston Smith, Ashley Stover, Michele Tibbitts
UNDERSTUDIES/STANDBYS: Florence Lacey (Dolly), Julian Brightman (Barnaby), Steve Pudenz (Vandergelder), Mary Setrakian (Irene), Jim Madden (Cornelius), Christine DeVito (Minnie), Dan LoBuono (Ambrose), Michele Tibbitts (Ermengarde), Elizabeth Green (Ernestina), Halden Michaels (Judge), Roger Preston Smith (Rudolph/Clerk), Milica Govich (Mrs. Rose), Matthew A. Sipress (Stanley)

MUSICAL NUMBERS: Overture, I Put My Hand In, It Takes a Woman, Put on Your Sunday Clothes, Ribbons Down My Back, Motherhood, Dancing, Before the Parade Passes By, Elegance, Waiters Gallop, Hello Dolly, Polka Contest, It Only Takes a Moment, So Long Dearie, Finale

A new production of the 1964 musical in two acts. The action takes place in New York City and Yonkers, NY. For original Broaway production with Carol Channing see Theatre World Vol.20. Previous Broadway revivals include Pearl Bailey in 1975 (Theatre World Vol.32) and Carol Channing in 1978 (Theatre World Vol.34).

Times: (Canby) "There I sat with some embarrassment as if chemically stimulated: helpless with pleasure and turned into a goon, wearing a dopey, ear-to-ear grin..Ms Channing and the show, which officially opened last night, are the real thing..Celebrate her." (Jefferson) "..this ruthless, driven-and masterful-performance is as close as musical-comedy gets to Mother Courage.." News: (Kissel) "...fresh, innocent, exuberant..The ovations, of course, represent huge affection for a character almost as intersting as Dolly Levi..Channing herself." Post: (Barnes) "There is a love-fest going on at the Lunt-Fontanne..remarkable on many a count, not least for the indestructible, inextinguishable Channing." Variety(Gerard) "Channing certainly is winning them over again..a razzle-dazzle throwback to a Broadway that no longer exists. Norma Desmond's descent down a much fancier staircase two blocks and several million dollars away doesn't pack half the emotional wallop."

*Closed January 18, 1996 after 188 performances and 11 previews.

Joan Marcus Photos

Jay Garner, Carol Channing

Carol Channing

The Company

17

Michael McGrath, Kathy Fitzgerald, Lewis Cleale

SWINGING ON A STAR
THE JOHNNY BURKE MUSICAL

Lyrics, Johnny Burke; Music, Mr. Burke, Joe Bushkin, Erroll Garner, Robert Haggart, Arthur Johnston, James Monaco, Harold Spina, Jimmy Van Heusen; Writen/Directed by Michael Leeds; Choreography, Kathleen Marshall; Musical Director/Orchestrations/Vocal Arrangements, Barry Levitt; Sets, James Youmans; Costumes, Judy Dearing; Lighting, Richard Nelson; Sound, T. Richard Fitzgerald; Technical, Aurora Productions; Video/Projections, Batwin + Robin Productions; General Manager, Paul B. Berkowsky; Company Manager, Peter Bogyo; Stage Managers, Mary Porter Hall, R. Wade Jackson; Originally Produced by George Street Playhouse; Presented   by Richard Seader, Mary Burke Kramer, Paul B. Berkowsky and Angels of the Arts; Press, Keith Sherman/Jim Byk, Stuart Ginsberg, Kevin Rehac; Previewed from Friday, October 6; Opened in the Music Box Theatre on Sunday, October 22, 1995*

CAST

Terry Burrell   Lewis Cheale
Denise Faye   Kathy Fitzgerald
Eugene Fleming   Alvaleta Guess
                          Michael McGrath

MUSICAL NUMBERS: You're Not the Only Oyster in the Stew, Chicago Style, Ain't It a Shame About Mame, What's New, Dr. Rhythm, Pennies from Heaven, When Stanislaus Got Married, His Rocking Horse Ran Away, Annie Doesn't Live Here Anymore, Scatterbrain, One Two Button Your Shoe, Whoopsie Daisy Day, What Does It Take to Make You Take to Me?, Irresistible, An Apple for the Teacher, Thank Your Lucky Stars and Stripes, Personality, There's Always the Blues, Polka Dots and Moonbeams, Swinging on a Star, Don't Let That Moon Get Away, All You Want to Do Is Dance, You Danced with Dynamite, Imagination, It Could Happen to You, Road to Morocco, Apalachicola, Ain't Goy a Dime to My Name, You Don't Have to Know the Language, Going My Way, Shadows on the Swanee, Pakistan, But Beautiful, Like Someone in Love, Moonlight Becomes You, If Love Ain't There, Sunday Monday or Always, Misty, Here's That Rainy Day, Finale

A musical revue in two acts with seven sections: Speakeasy (Chicago), Depression (The Bowery), Radio Show (New York City), USO Show (Pacific Islands), Ballroom (Hotel Roosevelt-Akron, Ohio), Road to (Paramount Studios, Hollywood) and Starlight Supper Club (Manhattan-the Present).

Variety tallied 5 favorable, 2 mixed and 4 negative notices. Times: (Brantley) "...immensely likable new revue..echoes the revues celebrating fresh, individual talent that were a staple of Broadway.." (Jefferson) "The direction of Michael Leeds and the choreography of Kathleen Marshall go hand in glove." News: (Kissel) "These are not theatre songs, which fill the stage with character or ideas." Post: (Barnes) "...absolutely splendid young cast.." Variety: (Gerard) "...lots of forced audience participation..notably short on emotional wallop."

*Closed January 14, 1996 after 97 performances and 19 previews.

Diane Sobolewski Photos

Eugene Fleming, Alvaleta Guess

Julie Andrews in *Victor/Victoria*

Tony Roberts, Julie Andrews, Rachel York, Michael Nouri

Julie Andrews (c)

VICTOR/VICTORIA

Music, Henry Mancini, Frank Wildhorn; Lyrics, Leslie Bricusse; Book/Direction, Blake Edwards; Choreography, Rob Marshall; Orchestrations, Billy Byers; Musical Director/Vocal Arrangements, Ian Fraser; Sets, Robin Wagner; Costumes, Willa Kim; Lighting, Jules Fisher, Peggy Eisenhauer; Sound, Peter Fitzgerald; Dance/Incidental Music, David Krane; Fights, B.H. Barry; Hairstylist, Michaeljohn; Cast Recording, Philips; Production Supervisor, Arthur Siccardi; General Manager, Niko Associates; Company Manager, Erich Hamner; Stage Managers, Arturo E. Porazzi, Bonnie L. Becker; Presented by Blake Edwards, Tony Adams, John Scher, Endemol Theatre Productions and Polygram Broadway Ventures; Press, Peter Cromarty/Hugh Hayes, Bill Klemm; Previewed from Tuesday, October 3; Opened in the Marquis Theatre on Wednesday, October 25, 1995*

CAST

Carroll Todd..Tony Roberts
Les Boys ....Michael-Demby Cain, Angelo Fraboni, Darren Lee, Michael O'Donnell, Vince Pesce, Arte Phillips, Rocker Verastique
Richard Di Nardo..Michael Cripe
Henri Labisse...Adam Heller
Gregor/Juke..Casey Nicholaw
Madame Roget..Jennifer Smith
Victoria Grant...Julie Andrews +1
Choreographer...Christopher Innvar
Miss Selmer..Cynthia Sophiea
Andre Cassell..Richard B. Shull
Jazz Singer..Devin Richards
Jazz Hot Musicians ....Michael-Demby Cain, Arte Phillips, Rocker Verastique
Norma Cassidy ....Rachel York
King Marchan ....Michael Nouri
Squash (Mr. Bernstein)..Gregory Jbara
Chambermaid...Jennifer Smith
Street Singer...Tara O'Brien
Norma's Girls ....Roxanne Barlow, Caitlin Carter, Pascale Faye, Amy Heggins Aixa M. Rosario Medina, Cynthia Onrubia
Sal Andretti...Ken Land
Clam..Mark Lotito
Ensemble..... Roxanne Barlow, Michael-Demby Cain, Caitlin Carter, Pascale Faye, Angelo Fraboni, Amy Heggins, Darren Lee, Aixa M. Rosario Medina, Casey Nicholaw, Tara O'Brien, Michael O'Donnell, Cynthia Onrubia, Vince Pesce, Arte Phillips, Devin Richards, Jennifer Smith, Cynthia Sophiea, Rocker Verastique
UNDERSTUDIES/STANDBY: Anne Runolfsson, Tara O'Brien (Victoria), Alex Wipf, Ken Land (Todd), Christopher Innvar (King), Roxane Barlow, Caitlin Carter (Norma), Mark Lotito (Squash/Sal), Casey Nicholaw (Henri), Angelo Fraboni (Richard), Michael-Demby Cain (Jazz Singer), Jennifer Smith (Street Singer) SWINGS: Mark S. Hoebee, Elizabeth Mozer, Scott Taylor DURING PREVIEWS: Hillet Gitter (Balloon Man)

MUSICAL NUMBERS: Overture, Paris By Night, If I Were a Man, Trust Me, Le Jazz Hot, The Tango, Paris Makes Me Horny, Crazy World, Louis Says, King's Dilemma, Apache, You & Me, Almost a Love Song, Chicago Illinois, Living in the Shadows, Victor Victoria DURING TRYOUT: This Is Not Going to Change My Life, The Victoria Variations (I've No Idea Where I'm Going), Someone Else, Attitude, I Guess It's Time, I Know Where I'm Going

A musical comedy in two acts. The action takes place in Paris and Chicago.

Julie Andrews

Gregory Jbara   **Adam Heller**

Variety tallied 3 favorable, 11 mixed and 5 negative reviews. Times: (Canby) "At 60, Ms. Andrews looks terrific and sings with a sweet purity not heard on Broadway since she last played the street in *Camelot*..time has made no dent in her immaculate appearance and diction, and in her grandly funny stage presence..there's a splendidly funny, beautifully timed farcical routine in which five characters zip in and out of the doorways in adjoining duplex hotel suites.." News: (Kissel) "..a vehicle worth of Benny Hill..Andrews is in such great shape. Rachel York is sensational.." Post: (Barnes) "..the musical doesn't lack for much of anything-except for music and lyrics..She has never been more totally enchanting. To see her is to love her. Variety: (Gerard) "The lyrics are witless-they're the only truly awful aspect of the show..the songs tend to be in contralto keys that don't show off a soprano of legendary beauty."

+Succeeded by: 1. Anne Runolfsson during illness

*Closed July 27, 1997 after 734 performances and 25 previews

Carol Rosegg/Joan Marcus Photos

Bill Irwin, David Shiner

David Shiner, Bill Irwin

FOOL MOON

Created by Bill Irwin & David Shiner; Set, Douglas Stein; Costumes, Bill
Kellard; Lighting, Nancy Schertler; Sound, Tom Morse; Flying by Foy;
General Managers, Fremont Associates; Stage Managers, Nancy Harring-
ton, Tami Toon; Presented by Pachyderm Entertainment, James B. Freyd-
berg, Kenneth Feld, Jeffrey Ash and Dori Berinstein; Press, Chris
Boneau~Adrian Bryan-Brown/Meredith Moore, Jackie Green, James
Sapp; Previewed from Saturday, October 21; Opened in the Ambassador
Theatre on Sunday, October 29, 1995*

CAST

DAVID SHRINER, BILL IRWIN, Red Clay City Ramblers

A return engagement of the 1993 entertainment in two acts. For original Broadway production see Theatre World Vol.49.

Times: (Canby) "As laugh-out-loud funny as it is witty." Post:
(Barnes) "Shiner and Irwin are brilliant.."

*Closed January 7, 1996 after 80 performances and 10 previews.

Joan Marcus, Jay Thompson Photos

Bill Irwin, David Shiner

THE TEMPEST

By William Shakespeare; Director, George C. Wolfe; Sets, Riccardo Hernandez; Costumes, Toni-Leslie James; Lighting, Paul Gallo; Sound, Dan Moses Schreier; Masks/Puppets, Barbara Pollitt; Music, Carlos Valdez, Mr. Schreier; Production Manager, Rik Kaye; Company Manager, Jeffrey M. Wilson; Stage Managers, Buzz Cohen, Lisa Buxbaum; Executive Producer, Joey Parnes; Presented by the New York Shakespeare Festival (Producer, George C. Wolfe) by special arrangement with the Shubert Organization, Jujamcyn Theatres and Capital Cities/ABC; Press, Carol Fineman/Thomas V. Naro; Previewed from Tuesday, October 10; Opened in the Broadhurst Theatre on Wednesday, November 1, 1995*

Patrick Stewart

CAST

Shipmaster	Avery Glymph
Boatswain	Adam Dannheisser
Alonso, King of Naples	Miguel Perez
Gonzalo, the King's counselor	MacIntyre Dixon
Sebastian, the King's brother	Graham Winton
Antonio, Prospero's brother	Nestor Serrano
Miranda, Prospero's daughter	Carrie Preston
Prospero, the right Duke of Milan	Patrick Stewart
Ariel	Aunjanue Ellis
Caliban	Teagle F. Bougere
Ferdinand, the King's son	Paul Whitthorne
Adrian, a Neopolitan Lord	Neal Huff
Trinculo, a servingman	Ross Lehman
Stephano, a drunken butler	Mario Cantone
Iris	Midori Nakamura
Ceres	Hilary Chaplain
Juno	Sybyl Walker

Kuroko........   Hilary Chaplain, Midori Nakamura, Sybyl Walker, David Constabile, Avery Glymph, Michael McGuigan, Seamas L. O'Brien, Adam Dannheisser, Marin Hinkle, Rainn Wilson, Michelle M. Robinson

UNDERSTUDIES: Miguel Perez (Prospero), Marin Hinkle (Miranda), Sybyl Walker (Miranda/Ariel), Midori Nakamura (Ariel), Avery Glymph (Caliban/Ferdinand), Neal Huff (Ferdinand/Antonio), Adam Dannheisser (Alonso/Sebastian), David Constabile (Gonzalo/Trinculo), Rainn Wilson (Antonio/Stephano/Boatswain/Shipmaster), Michael McGuigan (Adrian), Michelle M. Robinson (Iris/Ceres/Juno) SWING: Spencer S. Barros

Aunjanue Ellis, Patrick Stewart

A new version of Shakespeare's play which was presented in Central Park's Delacorte Theater in June-July, 1995. The Tempest is #29 in the New York Shakespeare Festival Shakespeare marathon.

Variety tallied 9 favorable, 3 mixed and 4 negative reviews. News: (Kissel) "...George C. Wolfe has used New World myth and music to give the play unusual power, especially in Stewart's imaginative performance." Variety: (Evans) "Audiences drawn by Stewart won't be disappointed-his baritone reading as Prospero is as impressive as ever..extremely accessible Shakespeare.."

*Closed December 31, 1995 after 71 performances and 25 previews.

Michal Daniel Photos

Paul Whitthorne, Carrie Preston

Frank Raiter, Jane Cecil, Reno Roop, Giancarlo Esposito, Herb Foster, Damian Young

Giancarlo Esposito, Brian Tarantina, Ellen Burstyn

SACRILEGE

By Diane Shaffer; Director, Don Scardino; Sets, John Arnone; Costumes, Alvin Colt; Lighting, Howell Binkley; Sound, Aural Fixation; General Manager, Marvin A. Krauss; Company Manager, Kathy Lowe; Stage Managers, Bob Borod, Ira Mont; Associate Producer, Hildy Parks; Presented by Alexander H. Cohen and Max Cooper; Press, Merle Debuskey/Susan Chicoine, Patt Dale; Previewed from Thursday, October 26; Opened in the Belasco Theatre on Thursday, November 2, 1995*

CAST

Sister Grace ....Ellen Burstyn
Crackerjack..Brian Tarantina
Ramon ....Giancarlo Esposito
Sister Joseph ....Jane Cecil
Father Jerome ....Damian Young
Cardinal King...Herb Foster +1
Sister Virgilia...Augusta Dabney
Bishop Foley ....Reno Roop
Monsignor Frigerio ....Frank Raiter
STANDBYS/UNDERSTUDIES: Carol Fox Prescott (Sister Grace), Al Espinosa (Ramon/Crackerjack), June Squibb (Sister Virgilia/Sister Joseph)

A drama in two acts. The action takes place in and around New York City and Washington D.C. during the last six years.

Variety tallied 6 mixed and 4 negative reviews. Variety: (Gerard) "...how many plays take on such loaded issues? Even bad art can stir people..."

*Closed November 19, 1995 after 21 performances and 8 previews.

+Preceeded by: 1. John Forsythe during tryout

Joan Marcus Photos

Zoe Caldwell in *Master Class*

Zoe Caldwell

Jay Hunter Morris, Zoe Caldwell

MASTER CLASS

By Terrence McNally; Director, Leonard Foglia; Set, Michael McGarty; Costumes, Jane Greenwood; Lighting, Brian MacDevitt; Sound, Jon Gottlieb; Musical Supervisor, David Loud; General Manager, Stuart Thompson; Company Manager, Bruce Klinger; Stage Managers, Dianne Trulock, Linda Barnes; Presented by Robert Whitehead & Lewis Allen and Spring Sirkin; Press, Bill Evans/Jim Randolph, Terry M. Lilly, Tom D'Ambrosio; Previewed from Tuesday, October 26; Opened in the Golden Theatre on Sunday, November 5, 1995*

CAST

Manny ....David Loud
Maria Callas...Zoe Caldwell
Sophie...Karen Kay Cody
Stagehand..Michael Friel
Sharon ....Audra McDonald
Tony ....Jay Hunter Morris
UNDERSTUDIES: Lorraine Goodman (Sophie/Sharon), Gary Green (Manny), Matthew Walley (Stagehand/Tony)

A drama in two acts. The setting is a master class as soprano Maria Callas teaches young aspiring opera singers. Winner of the 1996 "Tony" Awards for Best Play, Leading Actress in a Play (Zoe Caldwell) and Featured Actress in a Play (Audra McDonald).

Variety tallied 15 favorable and 3 mixed reviews. Times: (Canby) "Having won the Tony Award last season, Terrence McNally now seems to have topped himself.." (Jefferson) "Ms. Caldwell glitters and gleams.." News: (Kissel) "..a valentine to theatre itself-a sometimes somber, sometimes poetic, sometimes uproariously funny meditation on why we gather in the dark." Variety: (Gerard) "This magnificent production is in exactly the right place..It is certainly an unqualified triumph for Zoe Caldwell."

*Closed June 28, 1997 after 601 performances and 12 previews.

Joan Marcus Photos

David Loud, Zoe Caldwell, Karen Kay Cody

Zoe Caldwell, Audra McDonald

Karen Kay Cody, Zoe Caldwell, David Loud

Danny Gans

DANNY GANS ON BROADWAY: THE MAN OF MANY VOICES

Production Supervisor, Chip Lightman; Lighting, John Featherstone, Fred Irish, Norm Schwab; Sound, On Stage Audio, Tom Nicks; General Manager, Leo K. Cohen; Company Manager, Steven M. Levy; Press, Pete Sanders/Glenna Freedman, Michael Hartman; Previewed from Friday, October 27; Opened in the Neil Simon Theatre on Wednesday, November 8, 1995*

CAST

DANNY GANS

An entertainment performed without intermission.

Variety: (Evans) "Boasting a repertoire of more than 200 voices, the impressionist races through what feels like nearly all of them.."

*Closed November 12 after 6 performances and 10 previews.

Tony Randall, Jennifer Harmon, Matt Bradford Sullivan, Mary Lou Rosato, Kate Forbes in *The School for Scandal*

THE SCHOOL FOR SCANDAL

By Richard Brinsley Sheridan; Director, Gerald Freedman; Sets, Douglas W. Schmidt; Costumes, Theoni V. Aldredge; Lighting, Mary Jo Dondlinger; Sound, T. Richard Fitzgerald; Music, Robert Waldman; Production Supervisor, Arthur Siccardi; General Manager, Niko Associates; Company Manager, David Richards; Stage Manager, Richard Costabile; Executive Producer, Manny Kladitis; Presented by National Actors Theatre (Tony Randall, Founder/Artistic Director) in association with Great Lakes Theatre Festival by special arrangement with The Acting Company (Margot, Harley, Producing Director); Press, Gary and John Springer/Candi Adams, Ann Guzzi; Previewed from Tuesday, November 14; Opened in the Lyceum Theatre on Sunday, November 19, 1995*

Simon Jones, Tony Randall

CAST

Lady Sneerwell	Mary Lou Rosato
Snake	Norman Snow
Sneerwell Servant	Kevin Shinick
Joseph Surface	Simon Jones
Maria	Megan Dodds
Mrs. Candour	Jennifer Harmon
Mr. Crabtree	Philip Goodwin
Sir Benjamin Backbite	Matt Bradford Sullivan
Sir Peter Teazle	Tony Randall
Rowley	
	Ron Randell
Lady Teazle	Kate Forbes
Sir Oliver Surface	Ted Sorel
Moses	Norman Snow
Trip	Richard Topol
Charles Surface	Tom Hewitt
Careless	Ray Virta
Sir Harry Bumper	Allen Gilmore
Charles Friends	Anthony M. Brown, Matthew Edwards, Kevin Shinick
Joseph's Servant	Derek Meader
Lady Teazle's Maid	Leslie Geraci

Servants... Katherine De Boda, Jennifer Chambers, Mony Damevsky, John Kinsherf, Brett LaRose, Judith Stambler, Mark C. Tatoya
UNDERSTUDIES: Ray Virta (Joseph/Charles), Richard Topol (Backbite/Snake), Matt Bradford Sullivan (Bumper/Trip), Leslie Geraci (Lady Teazle/Mrs. Candour), Heather Harlan (Maria/Maid), Matthew Edwards (Careless/Servants), Allen Gilmore (Crabtree), Derek Meader (Rowley/Moses/Charles' Friend)

Tony Randall, Kate Forbes

A new production of the 1777 comedy in two acts. The action takes place in the homes of Lady Sneerwell, Peter Teazle, Charles Surface and Joseph Surface.

Variety tallied 6 mixed and 6 negative reviews. Variety: (Gerard) "..almost completely devoid of humor.."

*Closed December 7, 1995 after 31 performances and 8 previews.

Roger Mastroianni Photos

Mary Lou Rosato, Simon Jones

Ian Staurt, George N. Martin, Richard Clarke

Josef Sommer, Kathleen Chalfant

Denis O'Hare, Brian Murray

RACING DEMON

By David Hare; Director, Richard Eyre; Sets/Costumes, Bob Crowley; Lighting, Mark Henderson; Projections, Wendall K. Harrington; Sound, Scott Myers; Music, George Fenton; Production Manager, Jeff Hamlin; General Manager, Steven C. Callahan; Company Manager, Edward J. Nelson; Stage Manager, Susie Cordon; Presented by Lincoln Center Theater (Andre Bishop, Bernard Gersten, Directors) by arrangement with the Royal National Theatre; Press, Merle Debuskey/Susan Chicoine, Charlie Siedenburg; Previewed from Tuesday, October 31; Opened in the Vivian Beaumont Theatre on Monday, November 20, 1995*

CAST

CLERGY
Rev. Lionel Espy ....Josef Sommer
Rt. Rev. Charlie Allen, Bishop of Southwark ....George N. Martin
Rev. Tony Ferris...Michael Cumpsty
Rev. Donald "Streaky" Bacon..Paul Giamatti
Rev. Harry Henderson...Brian Murray
Rt. Rev. Gilbert Heffernan, Bishop of Kingston ....John C. Vennema

LAITY
Frances Parnell ....Kathryn Meisle
Stella Marr ....Patrice Johnson
Heather Espy ....Kathleen Chalfant
Ewan Gilmour...Denis O'Hare
Tommy Adair...John Curless
Head Waiter..Richard Clarke
Waiter...Robert Gomes
Servers...Ian Stuart, Richard Clarke
Synod Delegates ....Tom Bloom, Alison Sheehy, Angela Thornton, Terri Towns

UNDERSTUDIES: Ian Stuart (Espy), Richard Clarke (Allen/Henderson), Robert Gomes (Ferris/Gilmour), Tom Bloom (Bacon/Heffernan/Adair), Alison Sheehy (Parnell), Terri Towns (Stella), Angela Thornton (Heather)

A drama in two acts. The action takes place in South London.

Variety tallied 9 favorable, 3 mixed and 6 negative reviews. Times: (Canby) "In examining the politics of the Church of England, he is also examining the nature of faith in the late 20th century." (Jefferson) "..I wish I felt that real lives and beliefs were at stake, not just the words and deeds of well-wrought characters.." Post:: (Barnes) "...what are really memorable are Hare's ideas racing around the track of our waning century." Variety: (Gerard) "...unsettling, deeply pessimistic play."

*Closed December 31, 1995 after 48 performances and 23 previews.

Joan Marcus Photos

Brian Murray, Michael Cumpsty, Paul Giamatti

Kathryn Meisle, Michael Cumpsty

John Curless, Denis O'Hare

Patrice Johnson, Josef Sommer

31

GYPSY OF THE YEAR

Director/Choreographer, Michael Lichtefeld; Stage Managers, Kenneth Hanson, Charlene Speyerer, Debora Porazzi, Produced by Michael Graziano, Tom Viola and Maria Di Dia; Press, Chris Boneau~Adrian Bryan-Brown/Miguel Tuason, Corey Moore; Presented in the Virginia Theatre on Monday November 27 and Tuesday, November 28, 1995.

CAST INCLUDES

JONATHAN HADARY (11/27 HOST), MARIO CANTONE (11/28 HOST)

Harvey Evans, Patrick Stewart, Carol Burnett, Betty Buckley, Carol Channing, Anne Runolfsson, Jon Secada and the casts of Smokey Joe's Cafe, Miss Saigon(Free Gay & Happy), Hello Dolly!(Carol's Back), Grease, Tony n' Tina's Wedding, Sunset Boulevard (the lost episode of The Greatest Star of All), Show Boat (Let Us Find Peace), Sylvia (in Praise of Cole Porter), Cats, Phantom of the Opera(Names), Victor/Victoria (Arte Phillips & Pascale Faye), How to Succeed.., The Tempest, Crazy for You, Beauty and the Beast, and Les Miserables (Remember).

GYPSY OF THE YEAR GYPSIES: James Darrah, Timothy Albrecht, Michael-Demby Cain, Gregory Garrison, Joel Goodness, Howard Kaye, Jean Laurent Martinez, Bruce Moore, Thomas Titone, Roxanne Barlow, Kris Carr, Holly Cruikshank, Sally Mae Dunn, Deanna Dys, Kimberly Hester, Shannon Lewis, Penny Ayn Maas, Elizabeth Mills, Angie L. Schworer, Joan Leslie Simms, Jenny Lynn Suckling, Jillana Urbina, Wendy Waring, Leigh-Anne Wencker, Leigh Zimmerman

The seventh annual competition for Broadway Cares/Equity Fights AIDS raised $1,213,083.

Jay Brady Photo

Kim Raver, Tony Goldwyn

Harvey Evans

HOLIDAY

By Philip Barry; Director, David Warren; Sets, Derek McLane; Costumes, Martin Pakledinaz; Lighting, Donald Holder; Sound/Score, John Gromada; Style/Movement, Loyd Williamson; Production Supervisor/Stage Manager, Frank Marino; Stage Manager, Lori Lundquist; Press, Jeffrey Richards/Kevin Rehac, Irene Gandy; Previewed from Saturday, November 18; Opened in the Circle in the Square Uptown on Sunday, December 3, 1995*

CAST

Julia Seton	Kim Raver
Henry	Jim Oyster
Charles	Reese Madigan
Johnny Case	Tony Goldwyn
Linda Seton	Laura Linney
Ned Seton	Reg Rogers
Edward Seton	Tom Lacy
Seton Cram	Rod McLachlan
Laura Cram	Becca Lish
Nick Potter	Michael Countryman
Susan Potter	Anne Lange

UNDERSTUDIES: Christopher Cousins (Johnny/Nick/Henry), Allison Daugherty (Linda/Susan), Reese Madigan (Ned/Seton), Jim Oyster (Edward), Kim Sebastian (Julia/Laura)

A new production of the 1928 comedy in three acts. The action takes place in New York City in December 1928.

Times: (Canby) "...youthful, vigorous, good-looking revival..time gives this comedy a rather darker edge than it must have possessed originally..Tony Goldwyn..elegant, serious and funny portrayal..beautiful Laura Linney is his equal..(Jefferson) "...never mind if the text was playing it safe; that's the kind of writer Philip Barry was..." News: (Kissel) "David Warren's absolutely delectable production..reminded me how much I missed plays about rich people..Reg Rogers is winsome, wickedly funny and touching.." Variety: (Gerard) "..the best production in one of New York's toughest spaces in years..unfolds with exceptional finesse."

*Closed January 14, 1996 after 49 performances and 17 previews.

Carol Rosegg Photos

Avery Brooks

PAUL ROBESON

By Phillip Hayes Dean; Director, Harold Scott; Lighting, Shirley Prendergast; Choreography, Diann McIntyre; Orchestrations, Eva C. Brooks; Musical Director, Ernie Scott; Presented by Eric Krebs and Anne Strickland Squadron; Press, David Rothenberg; Previewed from Monday, December 18; Opened in the Longacre Theatre on Wednesday, December 20, 1995*

CAST

Paul Robeson...Avery Brooks
Lawrence Brown...Ernie Scott

A drama with music. Avery Brooks previously did this play at the Golden Theatre in 1988 (see Theatre World Vol.45). For original 1978 Broadway production with James Earl Jones see Theatre World Vol. 34.

*Closed December 31, 1995 after limited run of 12 performances and 2 previews.

Adger Cowans Photos

Gail Strickland, Frank Langella

Angela Bettis, Frank Langella

THE FATHER

By August Strindberg; Adaptor, Richard Nelson; Director, Clifford Williams; Sets, John Lee Beatty; Costumes, Martin Pakledinaz; Lighting, Kenneth Posner; Sound, John Gromada; Stage Manager, Jay Adler; Presented by Roundabout Theatre Company (Todd Haimes, Artistic Director; Ellen Richard, General Manager; Gene Feist, Founding Director); Press, Chris Boneau~Adrian Bryan-Brown/Andy Shearer, Stephen Pitalo; Previewed from Tuesday, December 14; Opened in the Criterion Center Stage Right on Thursday, January 11, 1996*

CAST

The Captain..Frank Langella
The Pastor..Ivar Brogger
Orderly..William Verderber
Nojd..Garret Dillahunt
Laura ....Gail Strickland
Dr. Ostermark ....Tom Beckett
Old Margaret ....Irene Dailey
Bertha ....Angela Bettis
UNDERSTUDIES:William Verderber (Captain/Pastor), Kyle Fabel (Orderly/Nojd/Ostermark), Stephanie A. Jones (Bertha)

A new production of the 1887 drama performed without intermission. The action takes place in the Captain's house in a remote Swedish province.

Variety tallied 2 favorable, 7 mixed and 5 negative reviews. Times: (Jefferson) "...intermittently powerful and continually frustrating..Frank Langella does make a gripping Father." News: (Kissel) "In order for the play to work, the actors must make us sense the topography of the monster lurking beneath the surface..Frank Langella brings undeniable size to the stage..." Post: (Barnes) "It is a wonderfully powerful yet subtle portrait of a man first loosening the losing his grasp of himself and the world." Variety: (Gerard) "...I don't have a lot of patience for early Strindberg, who was already cracked, if not completely separated from the yolk, in the late 1880s, when he wrote his influential, so-called naturalistic plays..."

*Closed February 25, 1996 after 52 performances and 31 previews.
Joan Marcus Photos

Angela Bettis, Frank Langella in *The Father*

Faith Prince

DU BARRY WAS A LADY

Music/Lyrics, Cole Porter; Book, Herbert Fields, B.G. DeSylva; Adaptation, David Ives, Walter Bobbie; Director, Charles Repole; Musical Director, Rob Fisher; Orchestration, Hans Spialek; Set, John Lee Beatty, Choreography, Kathleen Marshall; Sound, Scott Lehrer; Lighting, Peter Kaczorowski; Stage Manager, Perry Cline; Presented by City Center Encores; Great American Musicals in Concert (Artistic Director, Walter Bobbie); Press, Philip Rinaldi; Opened in City Center on Thursday February 15, 1996*

CAST

Vi Hennessey/Mme. La Duchesse De Villardell ....Ruth Williamson
Bill Kelly/Le Duc De Choiseul ....Bruce Adler
Harry Norton/Capt. of King's Guard ....Scott Waara
Alice Barton/Mme La Marquise Alisande De Vernay..............Liz Larsen
Florian/Zamore ....Eugene Fleming
Louis Blore/His Most Royal Majesty, King of France.........Robert Morse
May Daly/Mme. La Comtesse Du Barry...............................Faith Prince
Alex Barton/Alixe..Burke Moses
Charley/His Royal Highness, Dauphin of France ....Michael McGrath
Docteur Michel..Dick Latessa
IRS Agent...Donald Trump
Singers......... Danny Burstein, Ken McMullen, Beth McVey, Karen Murphy, Susan Pfau, Clif Thorn, Elizabeth Walsh, Joseph Webster

Dancers.......Mamie Duncan-Gibbs, Sean Grant, Colton Green, Elizabeth Mills, Troy Myers, Aimee Turner
....and the Coffee Club Orchestra

MUSICAL NUMBERS: Overture, Opening, Ev'ry Day a Holiday, It Ain't Etiquette, When Love Beckoned, Come On In, Dream Song, Mesdames et Messieurs, Gavotte, But in the Morning No, Do I Love You?, Du Barry Was a Lady, Danse Tzigane, Give Him the Oo-La-La, Well Did You Evah!, It Was Written in the Stars, Katie Went to Haiti, Friendship, Finale

A staged concert of the 1939 musical which originally featured Ethel Merman, Bert Lahr and Betty Grable.   *Closed February 17, 1996 after limited run of 4 performances.

35

BUS STOP

By William Inge; Director, Josephine R. Abady; Sets, Hugh Landwehr; Costumes, Linda Fisher; Lighting, Dennis Parichy; Sound, Tom Gould; Wigs, Paul Huntley; Fights, B.H. Barry; Company Managers, Gordon Forbes, Don Roe; Stage Managers, Frank Marino, Robert Bennett; Presented by Circle in the Square (Theodore Mann, Josephine R. Abady, Co-Artistic Directors); Press, Jeffrey Richards/Scott Karpf, Steve Sunderlin, Laramie Dennis; Previewed from Saturday, February 3; Opened in the Circle in the Square Uptown on Thursday, February 22, 1996*

CAST

Elma Duckworth	Patricia Dunnock
Grace Hoyland	Kelly Bishop
Will Masters	Scott Sowers
Cherie	Mary-Louise Parker
Dr. Gerald Lyman	Ron Perlman
Carl	Michael Cullen
Virgil Blessing	Larry Pine
Bo Decker	Billy Crudup

A new production of the 1955 drama in two acts. The action takes place in a street-corner restaurant in a small town about 30 miles west of Kansas City. For original Broadway production with Kim Stanley, Albert Salmi and Elaine Stritch see Theatre World Vol.11.

Variety tallied 4 favorable, 6 mixed and 5 negative reviews. Times: (Canby) "Inge dramatized the melancholy, the humor and the unconscious gallantry of commonplace characters. He saw them mostly in economically depressed but sexually charged circumstances..." (Jefferson) "I like this because the play is about oddly matched tones and manners: conversations going on at the same time in different tempos..." News: (Kissel) "What is interesting about the 40 year-old play is that it anticipates our era's idea's about masculinity. What makes Bo attractive to his conquest is his unexpected vulnerability." Post: (Barnes) "It's a vehicle on its last legs, an old-time streetcar named commerce that has well and truly stopped." Variety: (Evans) "Does *Bus Stop* merit a cast this good, a production this solid?..Little matter-as an excuse to see an exciting young actor like Billy Crupud strut his way up the Broadway ladder..will do just fine."

*Closed March 17, 1996 after 29 performances and 21 previews.

Carol Rosegg Photos

Mary-Louise Parker, Larry Pine

Billy Crudup, Mary-Louise Parker

Mary-Louise Parker

GETTING AWAY WITH MURDER

By Stephen Sondheim and George Furth; Director, Jack O'Brien; Set, Douglas W. Schmidt; Lighting, Kenneth Posner; Costumes, Robert Wojewodski; Sound, Jeff Ladman; Special Effects, Gregory Meeh; Fights, Steve Rankin; General Manager, Marvin A. Krauss; Company Manager, Kathleen Lowe; Stage Managers, Jeff Lee, Julie Baldauff; Presented by Roger Berlind; Press, Bill Evans/Jim Randolph, Tom D'Ambrosio; Previewed from Tuesday, February 20; Opened in the Broadhurst Theatre on Sunday, March 17, 1996*

CAST

Martin Chisholm	John Rubinstein
Dossie Lustig	Christine Ebersole
Young Man	William Ragsdale
Charmaine	Michelle Hurd
Pamela Prideaux	Kandis Chappell
Vassili Laimorgos	Josh Mostel
Gregory Reed	Terrence Mann
Dan Gerard	Frankie R. Faison
Nam-Jun Vuong	Jodi Long
Roberto	Al Espinosa
Dr. Conrad Bering	Herb Foster

STANDBYS/UNDERSTUDIES: Nancy Opel (Dossie/Pamela), Chuck Cooper (Dan), Stephanie Park (Charmaine/Nam-Jun), Joel Kramer (Bering/Vassili), Jesus Ontiveros (Roberto), Eddie Castrodad, Al Espinosa (Young Man)

A comedy thriller in two acts. The action takes place on the top floor of an old New York apartment building during October. Between the first preview and opening night, the fate of the killer was completely reversed.

Variety tallied 1 favorable, 1 mixed and 14 negative reviews. News: (Phil Roura) "...suspense and thrills..." Variety: (Gerard) "...utterly thrill free and almost utterly laugh-free...I'm certain the play is full of in-jokes I missed..."

*Closed March 31, 1996 after 17 performances and 31 previews.

Joan Marcus Photos

John Rubinstein, Christine Ebersole

Christine Ebersole, Josh Mostel, John Rubinstein, Terrence Mann, Jodi Long, Frankie Faison

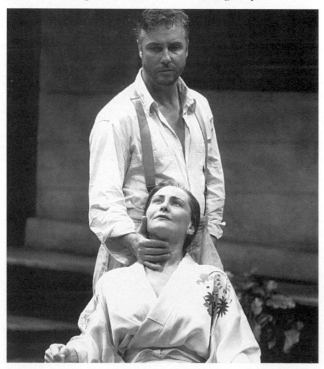

(foreground) Cherry Jones, Lawrence McCauley

(background) Williiam Petersen, Diego Lopez

THE NIGHT OF THE IGUANA

By Tennessee Williams; Director, Robert Falls; Set, Loy Arcenas; Costumes, Susan Hilferty; Lighting, James F. Ingalls; Sound, Richard Woodbury; Stage Managers, Janet Beroza, Matthew T. Mundinger; Presented by Roundabout Theatre Company (Todd Haimes, Artistic Director; Ellen Richards, General Manager; Gene Feist, Founding Director); Press, Chris Boneau~Adrian Bryan-Brown/Andy Shearer, Stephen Pitalo, Patty Onagan; Previewed from Wednesday, March 6; Opened in the Criterion Center Stage Right on Thursday, March 21, 1996*

CAST

Maxine Faulk..Marsha Mason
Pancho..Alfredo MacDonald
Pedro..Diego Lopez
Rev. Shannon ....William Petersen
Hilda..Sinje Ollen
Wolfgang ....Lawrence Woshner
Herr Fahrenkopf..Dan Frick
Frau Fahrenkopf...Betsy Freytag
Hank..Scott Jaeck
Judith Fellowes ....Mary Beth Fisher
Hannah Jelkes..Cherry Jones
Charlotte Goodall...Paula Cale
Jonathan Coffin (Nonno) ....Lawrence McCauley
Jake Latta...Dennis Predovic
UNDERSTUDIES: Karen MacDonald (Hannah/Frau/Judith), Betsy Freytag (Maxine), Scott Jaeck (Shannon), Michelle Courtney (Charlotte/Hilda), Steve Boles (Fahrenkopf/Jake), A.J. Lopez (Pedro/Pancho), Charles Huston (Hank/Wolfgang), Richard Spore (Nonno)

A new production of the 1961 drama in three acts, performed with one intermission. The action takes place at the Costa Verde Hotel in Puerto Barrio, Mexico during summer 1940. For original Broadway production with Bette Davis, Patrick O'Neal and Margaret Leighton see Theatre World Vol.18.

Variety tallied 6 favorable, 4 mixed and 6 negative notices. Times: (Canby) "...the most difficult to realize on the stage today, being the most easily misinterpreted with the help of hindsight. That's being demonstrated in the Roundabout Theater..." (Jefferson) "What Ms. Jones gives her and us is wit, authority and a sturdy generosity." News: (Kissel) "...a carnival of souls at the end of their tether..." Variety: (Gerard) "...the production makes a persuasive case for the play..incandescent Cherry Jones..three hours pass quickly and often movingly."

*Closed May 19, 1996 after 68 performances and 18 previews.
Joan Marcus, Liz Lauren Photo

Cherry Jones, William Petersen

Cherry Jones, Lawrence McCauley

LOVE THY NEIGHBOR

Written/Created by Jackie Mason; Production Design/Lighting, Neil Peter Jampolis; Sound, Charles McIntyre; Company Manager, Veronica Claypool; Stage Manager, Don Myers; Executive Producer, Jyll Rosenfeld; Presented by Abe Hirschfeld; Press, Richard Rubenstein/Mitch Zamarin; Previewed from Tuesday, March 19; Opened in the Booth Theatre on Sunday, March 24, 1996*

CAST
JACKIE MASON

An evening of comedy. Prior Mason Broadway engagements were The World According to Me (1986-88), Brand New (1990-91) and Politically Incorrect (1994-95).

Newsday(Jan Stuart) "...we do not attend a Jackie Mason performance to have our perspective broadened. We go to have it narrowed."

*Closed January 5, 1997 after 236 performances and 5 previews.

Jackie Mason

John Davidson, Ben Wright, Kathryn Crosby, Andrea McArdle

Andrea McArdle, Scott Wise

Jacquiline Rohrbacker, John Davidson, Ben Wright,
Andrea McArdle, Kathryn Crosby

Kathryn Crosby, John Davidson

STATE FAIR

Music, Richard Rodgers; Lyrics, Oscar Hammerstein; Book, Tom Briggs and Louis Mattioli based on screenplay by Mr. Hammerstein and novel by Phil Stong; Directors, James Hammerstein and Randy Skinner; Choreography, Mr. Skinner; Orchestrations, Bruce Pohamac; Musical Director/Vocal Arrangements, Kay Cameron; Sets, James Leonard Joy; Costumes, Michael Bottari, Ronald Case; Lighting, Natasha Katz; Sound, Brian Ronan; Dance Arrangements, Scot Wooley; Cast Recording, DRG; General Manager, Ralph Roseman; Company Manager, Tom Domenici; Stage Managers, Warren Crane, Donald Christy, Anita Ross; Presented by David Merrick, The Theatre Guild and Thomas Viertel; Press, Susan Schulman; Previwed from Wednesday, March 20; Opened in the Music Box Theatre on Wednesday, March 27, 1996*

CAST

Abel Frake	John Davidson
Gus	James Patterson
Melissa Frake	Kathryn Crosby
Wayne Frake	Ben Wright
Dave Miller/Judge Heppenstahl	Charles Goff
Eleanor	Susan Haefner
Margy Frake	Andrea McArdle +1
Harry	Peter Benson
Uncle Sam	Michael Lee Scott
Fair Announcer/Clay	J. Lee Flynn
Midway Cow	Kelli Barclay
Midway Pig/Violet	Jackie Angelescu
Hoop-La Barker	Tim Fauvell
Emily Arden	Donna McKechnie
Astounding Stralenko/Police Chief	Steve Steiner
Vivian	Tina Johnson
Jeanne	Leslie Bell
Mrs. Edwin Metcalf	Jacquiline Rohrbacker
Pat Gilbert	Scott Wise
Charlie	Darrian C. Ford
Lem	John Wilkerson
Hank Munson	Newton R. Gilchrist

Fairtones....Ian Knauer, James Patterson, Michael Lee Scott, Scott Willis
Roustabouts...Mr. Scott, Mr. Willis
Barkers/Vendors/Judges/Fairgoers........Kelli Barclay, Leslie Bell, Linnea Dakin, SuEllen Estey, Tim Fauvell, Amy Gage, Susan Haefner, Tina Johnson, Ian Knauer, James Patterson, Michael Lee Scott, Mary C. Sheehan, Steve Steiner, Scott Willis

UNDERSTUDIES: SuEllen Estey (Melissa), J. Lee Flynn (Abel), Ian Knauer (Wayne), Susan Haefner (Margy), Leslie Bell (Emily), Linnea Dakin (Violet/Eleanor), Mary C. Sheehan (Mrs. Metcalf), James Patterson (Harry), Tina Johnson (Hoop-La), Kelli Barclay (Vivian/Jeanne), Tim Fauvell (Hank/Lem/Dave/Judge), Steve Steiner (Clay), Scott Willis (Pat/Police/Stralenko), John Scott (Charlie/Gus/Uncle Sam/Fairtones/Roustabouts), Julie Lira (Cow/Pig) SWINGS: Julie Lira, John Scott

MUSICAL NUMBERS: Overture, Opening, It Might As Well Be Spring, Driving at Night (new-unused music from Allegro), Our State Fair, That's for Me, More Than Just a Friend (from 1962 film version), Isn't It Kinda Fun?, You Never Had It So Good (cut from Me and Juliet), When I Go Out Walking with My Baby (cut from Oklahoma), So Far (from Allegro), It's a Grand Night for Singing, Entr'acte, The Man I Used to Be (from Pipe Dream), All I Owe Ioway, That's the Way It Happens (from Me and Juliet), Boys and Girls Like You and Me (cut from Oklahoma), The Next Time It Happens (from Pipe Dream), Finale

Donna McKechnie

A musical in two acts. The action takes place in Brunswick and Des Moines, Iowa, August, 1946. This new stage adaptation uses the score of the 1945 screen musical State Fair, the 1962 musical remake, and songs (some previously unused) from other Rodgers & Hammerstein shows.

Variety tallied 6 favorable, 5 mixed and 7 negative reviews. Post: (Barnes) "The overture starts and almost immediately you feel that unmistakable surge..This is the real thing..." Newsday: (Stuart) "...a bit Twilight Zone-y at a time when the ugliest kind of political rancor and ethnic division soil the headlines." Variety: (Gerard) "Innocuous and empty headed..tries awfully hard to please..."

*Closed June 30, 1996 after 118 performances and 8 previews.

+Succeeded by: 1. Susan Haefner, Susan Egan

Carol Rosegg Photos

SEVEN GUITARS

By August Wilson; Director, Lloyd Richards; Sets, Scott Bradley; Costumes, Constanza Romero; Lighting, Christopher Akerlind; Musical Director, Dwight Andrews; Sound, Tom Clark; Technical Supervisor, Gene O'Donovan; General Manager, Marshall B. Purdy; Stage Managers, Jane E. Neufeld, Narda Alcorn; Presented by Sageworks (Benjamin Mordecai, Executive Producer), Center Theatre Group/Ahmanson (Gordon Davis, Artistic Director), Herb Alpert, Margo Lion, Scott Rudin, Paramount Pictures and Jujamcyn Theatres in association with Goodman Theatre, Huntington Theatre Company, American Conservatory Theatre and Manhattan Theatre Club; Press Chris Boneau~Adrian Bryan-Brown/Andy Shearer, Bob Fennell, Meredith Moore, Stephen Pitalo, Susanne Tighe; Previewed from Sunday, March 17; Opened in the Walter Kerr Theatre on Thursday, March 28, 1996*

CAST

Louise	Michele Shay
Canewell	Ruben Santiago-Hudson
Red Carter	Tommy Hollis
Vera	Viola Davis
Hedley	Roger Robinson
Floyd Barton	Keith David
Ruby	Rosalyn Coleman

UNDERSTUDIES: W. Allen Taylor (Floyd/Canewell)

A drama in two acts. The action takes place in the Hill District of Pittsburgh, 1948. This is the playwright's seventh play chronicling the African-American experience in the twentieth century: Joe Turner's Come and Gone (covering 1910s), Ma Rainey's Black Bottom (1920s), The Piano Lesson (1930s), Fences (1950s), Two Trains Running (1960s) and Jitney (1970s). Winner of the 1996 New York Drama Critics Circle Award for Best Play and winner of 1996 "Tony" Award for Featured Actor in a Play (Ruben Santiago-Hudson).

Variety tallied 12 favorable and 1 mixed review. Times: (Canby) "..as funny as it is moving and lyrical. It's the highlight of what now seems to be a brand-new theatre season." News: (Kissel) "...like a muted trumpet in the wee hours..this one is full of quiet truth..It is hard to imagine the play being better performed than it is under the direction of Lloyd Richards." Post: (Barnes) "...never quite magic enough, nor is its symbolism ever even remotely clear." Variety: (Gerard) "...what an ensemble Wilson and Richard have gathered, with David at the center in a fiercely moving performance."

*Closed September 8, 1996 after 187 performances and 11 previews.
Joan Marcus Photos

Keith David, Viola Davis

Viola Davis, Keith David

Tommy Hollis, Keith David, Ruben Santiago-Hudson in *Seven Guitars*

Melissa Errico

ONE TOUCH OF VENUS

Music, Kurt Weill; Lyrics, Ogden Nash; Book, S.J. Perelman, Mr. Nash; Based on The Tinted Venus by F.J. Anstey; Director/Adaptation, Leonard Foglia; Musical Director, Rob Fisher; Orchestration, Mr. Weill; Set, John Lee Beatty; Choreography, Hope Clarke; Sound, Scott Lehrer; Lighting, Peter Kaczorowski; Stage Manager, Patrick Ballard; Presented by City Center Encores!: Great American Musicals in Concert (Artistic Director, Walter Bobbie); Press, Philip Rinaldi; Opened in City Center on Thursday, March 28, 1996*

CAST

Whitelaw Savory ....David Alan Grier
Molly Grant ....Carol Woods
Taxi Black ....Danny Rutigliano
Stanley ....Kevin Chamberlin
Rodney Hatch...Andy Taylor
Venus,,,,...Melissa Errico
Mrs. Moats...,,,,,,Sheryl McCallum
Bus Starter ....Peter Flynn
Mrs. Kramer...Marilyn Cooper
Gloria Kramer...Jane Krakowski
Police Lt. ....Timothy Robert Blevins
Dr. Rook...Keith Byron Kirk
Matron...Melinda Klump
Singers....Mr. Blevins, Benjamin Brecher, Tony Capone, Mr. Flynn, John Halmi, Kimberly JaJuan, Jennifer Joan Joy, Mr. Kirk, Ms. Klump, Kim Lindsay, Ms. McCallum, Jesse Means II, Betsi Morrison, M. Alet Oury, Abe Reybold, Lucy Schaufer
Dancers..........Kristine Bendul, Michael Berresse, Jessica Michaels, Troy Myers, Michelle Robinson, Keith Thoams
....and the Cofee Club Orchestra

MUSICAL NUMBERS: Overture, New Art Is True Art, One Touch of Venus, How Much I Love You, I'm a Starnger Here Myself, West Wind, Way Out West in Jersey, That's How I Am Sick of Love, Foolish Heart, The Trouble with Women, Speak Low, Doctor Crippen, Entr'acte, Very Very Very, Catch Hatch. That's Him, Wooden Wedding, Venus in Ozone Heights Ballet, Finaletto

A staged concert of the 1943 musical which originally featured Mary Martin.

*Closed March 30, 1996 after limited run of 4 performances.

A MIDSUMMER NIGHT'S DREAM

By William Shakespeare; Director, Adrian Noble; Design, Anthony Ward; Lighting, Chris Parry; Music, Ilona Sekacz; Movement, Sue Lefton; Sound, Paul Slocombe, Duncan Edwards; Production Supervisor, Alan Hall; General Manager, Roy Gabay; Company Manager, Diana L. Fairbanks; Stage Managers, Eric Lumsden, Kate Vinnicombe; Presented by The Royal Shakespeare Company, Terry Allen Kramer, James L. Nederlander, Carole Shorenstein Hays, John F. Kennedy Center for the Performing Arts and Elizabeth Ireland McCann; Press, Chris Boneau~Adrian Bryan-Brown/Bob Fennell, Cindy Valk, Clint Bond, Jr.; Previewed from March 20; Opened in the Lunt-Fontanne Theatre on Sunday, March 31, 1996*

CAST

Theseus/Oberon	Alex Jennings
Hippolyta/Titania	Lindsay Duncan
Philostrate/Puck	Barry Lynch
Egeus	Alfred Burke
Hermia	Monica Dolan
Lysander	Daniel Evans
Demetrius	Kevin Robert Doyle
Helena	Emily Raymond
Peter Quince	John Kane
Nick Bottom	Desmond Barrit
Francis Flute	Mark Letheren
Tom Snout	Howard Crossley
Snug	Kenn Sabberton
Robin Starveling	Robert Gillespie
First Fairy	Ann Hasson

Fairies......Emily Button, Jane Colenutt, Mr. Crossley, Mr. Gillespie, Tim Griggs, Mr. Kane, Mr. Letheren, Darren Roberts, Kenn Sabberton
UNDERSTUDIES: Kevin Robert Doyle (Theseus/Oberon), Emily Button (Hippolyta/Titania), Kenn Sabberton (Philostrate/Puck), Howard Crossley (Egeus/Bottom), Ann Hasson (Hermia), Mark Letheren (Lysander), Darren Roberts (Demetrius/Snout/Snug), Jane Colenutt (Hippolyta/Titania/Helena/Fairy), Tim Griggs (Flute/Robin)

A new production of Shakespeare's comedy performed with one intermission.

Variety tallied 8 positive, 3 mixed and 3 negative reviews. Newsday "All the clowns are unusually endearing..As a bare-chested Puck, Lynch plays Oberon's magical servant as an erotic street tough..The RSC..has been much missed." Variety: (Gerard) "...great grab bag of a show, by turns warmly volopyuous and chilly..Grab bag is also the word for a company led here by a ravishing Lindsay Duncan..for all its visual elegance and keen articulation, the production mostly left me cold."

*Closed May 26, 1996 after 65 performances and 13 previews.

Mark Douet Photos

Top: Barry Lynch, Ann Hasson
Below: (center) Lindsay Duncan, Desmond Barrit

Tom Aldredge, George C. Scott, Garret Dillahunt in *Inherit the Wind*

George C. Scott, Charles Durning

Anthony Heald, Bill Corritore

INHERIT THE WIND

By Jerome Lawrence and Robert E. Lee; Director, John Tillinger; Sets, James Noone; Lighting, Ken Billington; Costumes, Jess Goldstein; Sound, Aural Fixation; Production Supervisor, Maureen F. Gibson; General Manager, Niko Associates; Company Manager, David Richards; Stage Manager, Jill Rendall; Executive Producer, Manny Kladitis; Presented by National Actors Theatre (Tony Randall, Founder/Artistic Director); Press, Gary Springer-John Springer/Candi Adams, Ann Guzzi; Previewed from Tuesday February 27; Opened in the Royale Theatre on Thursday, April 4, 1996*

CAST

Rachel Brown ....Kate Forbes
Meeker ....Tom Stechschulte
Bertram Cates ....Garret Dillahunt
Mr. Goodfellow ....Clement Fowler
Mrs. Krebs ....Marylouise Burke
Rev. Jeremiah Brown ....Tom Aldredge
Sillers ....John Griesemer
Platt ....Norman Snow
Finney ....Kevin McClarnon
Timmy ....Craig Lawlor
Cooper ....Kenneth P. Strong
Bannister ....David Dossey
Dunlap ....Fred Burrell
Howard ....Paul F. Dano
Melinda ....Allie Calnan
Mother ....Alice Connorton
Vendor ....Robert Jimenez
Mrs. McLain ....Prudence Wright Holmes
Mrs. Blair ....Joyce Lynn O'Connor
Elijah ....Ronn K. Smith
E.K. Hornbeck ....Anthony Heald
Hurdy Gurdy Man ....Bill Corritore
Matthew Harrison Brady ....Charles Durning
Mrs. Brady ....Bette Henritze
Reuter's Man ....Dominic Cuskern
Mayor...Reathel Bean
Tom Davenport...Herndon Lackey
Henry Drummond ....George C. Scott +1
Judge..Michael Lombard
Harry Y. Esterbrook ....J.R. Horne
Townspeople, jurors, scientists etc.. ......Sam Andrew, Jeff Berry, Jennifer Chambers, Bill Corry, Katherine De Boda, Brad Fairbanks, Glenn Gehweiler, Joe Gioco, Rich Heraty, William York Hyde, Dawn Jamieson, John Kinsherf, Brett LaRose, Michael Lehr, John Lenartz, Charles Prior, Timothy Sozen, Judith Stambler, Mark C. Tafoya, Sewell Whitney

A new production of the 1955 drama, based on the 1925 Scopes "Monkey" Trial in Tenn., now performed in two acts. The action takes place in a small town, not too long ago. For original Broadway production with Paul Muni, Ed Begley and Tony Randall see Theatre World Vol.11.

Variety tallied 7 favorable, 3 mixed and 3 negative reviews. Times:(Canby) "Crisp, handsome and very entertaining." News:(Kissel) "George C. Scott brings ferocious power..." Post: (Barnes) "...Scott in a role he seems almost to have been born to play. It is a performance for the record books." Variety: (Gerard) "What's missing here..was the intense claustrophobia and choking heat of the setting, the barely contained violence this conflict engendered."

*Closed May 12, 1996 after 45 performances and 30 previews.

+Succeeded by: 1. Tony Randall during illness.

Joan Marcus Photos

George C. Scott, Charles Durning

EASTER BONNET COMPETITION

Tony Randall, Julie Andrews,
Carol Channing

Director, Charles Repole; Choreography, Tony Parise; Musical Supervisor, Seth Rudetsky; Assistant Director, Scott T. Stevens; Associate Choreographer, Cynthia Thole; Stage Managers, James Harker, John M. Atherlay, Jill Larmett, M.A. Howard, Paul J. Smith; Producer, Michael Graziano; Producing Director, Tom Viola; Production Team, Carol A. Ingram, John V. Fahey, Raymond Shelton, Carla Cherry, Kevin Duncan; Press, Chris Boneau~Adrian Bryan-Brown/Miguel Tuason; Presented in the Palace Theatre on Monday, April 8 and Tuesday, April 9, 1996

CAST INCLUDES

Julie Andrews, Carol Channing, Tony Randall, Marsha Mason and Alan Campbell, Davis Gaines and Lynne Redgrave, John Cullum and Carol Woods, Judith Ivey and Keith David, Alex Jennings and Lindsay Duncan, Tony Roberts and Donna McKechnie, Anne Runolfsson, Melba Moore, Zoe Caldwell, Betty Buckley, Mark Nelson, Kathryn Crosby, Andrea McArdle, the voice of Thom Christopher and cast members from After-Play, Inherit the Wind, Master Class, Sunset Blvd., King and I, Grandma Sylvia's Funeral, Zombie Prom, Phantom of the Opera, Miss Saigon, Cats, Dancers Responding to AIDS, Tragic and Horrible Life of the Singing Nun, Beauty and the Beast (Bdwy & tour), Show Boat, Forever Plaid, Les Miserables (Bdwy & tour), Fiddler on the Roof tour, Grease, Tony N' Tina's Wedding, Midsummer Night's Dream, Funny Thing Happened..., State Fair, Picasso at the Lapin Agile, How to Succeed... and Victor/Victoria

BONNET DANCERS: Timothy Albrecht, Philip Michael Baskerville, Eric Chan, Simone Gee, Dennis Jones, Lacey Hornkohl, Brian-Paul Mendoza, April Nixon, Michelle O'Steen, Lorna Shane, Daniel Wright

BONNET SINGERS: Paul Castree, Mary Satrakian, Molly Wasserman, Andrea Bern, Russell Brown, Neil Cohen, Margery Daley, Bruce Fifer, Margo Gribb, Jason Little, Bruce Moore, Beverly Myers, Rachel Rosales, Beth Rudetsky, Tracey Lynn Thomas, Cliff Townsend, Mark Waldrop

The tenth annual Broadway Cares/Equity Fights AIDS Easter fundraiser brought in $1,304,525. Victor/Victoria won the bonnet competition and raised the most money.

Joseph Marzullo Photos

The Finale

Brandon Ngai, Amy Y. Tai
(The King and I)

47

THE KING AND I

Music, Richard Rodgers; Lyrics/Book, Oscar Hammerstein II; Director, Christopher Renshaw; Original Choreography, Jerome Robbins; Musical Staging, Lar Lubovitch; Musical Director, Michael Rafter; Musical Supervision, Eric Stern; Orchestrations, (original) Robert Russell Bennett, (new) Bruce Coughlin; Sets, Brian Thomson; Costumes, Roger Kirk; Lighting, Nigel Levings; Sound, Tony Meola, Lewis Mead; Hairstylist, David H. Lawrence; General Manager, David Strong Warner; Company Manager, Sandra Carlson; Stage Managers, Frank Hartenstein, Karen Armstrong; Presented by Dodger Productions, John F. Kennedy Center for the Performing Arts, James M. Nederlander, Perseus Productions with John Frost and the Adelaide Festival Centre in association with The Rodgers and Hammerstein Organization; Press, Chris Boneau~Adrian Bryan-Brown/Susanne Tighe, Cindy Valk; Previewed from Tuesday, March 19; Opened in the Neil Simon Theatre on Thursday, April 11, 1996*

CAST

Capt. Orton	John Curless
Louis Leonowens	Ryan Hopkins
Anna Leonowens	Donna Murphy
Interpreter	Alan Muraoka
The Kralahome	Randall Duk Kim
King of Siam	Lou Diamond Phillips
Lun Tha	Jose Llana
Tuptim	Joohee Choi
Lady Thiang	Taewon Kim
Prince Chulalongkorn	John Chang
Fan Dancer	Kelly Jordan Bit
Princess Yaowlak	Lexine Bondoc
Sir Edward Ramsey	Guy Paul

Royal Wives/Slaves/Guards/Guests.. ....Tito Abeleda, John Bantay, Camille M. Brown, Benjamin Bryant, Meng-Chen Chang, Kam Cheng, Vivien Eng, Lydia Gaston, Margaret Ann Gates, C. Sean Kim, Shawn Ku, Doan Mackenzie, Paolo Montalban, Alan Muraoka, Paul Nakauchi, Tina Ou, Andrew Pacho, mami Saito, Lainie Sakakura, Carol To, Yolanda Tolentino Tran T. Thuc Hanh, Yan Ying, Kayoko Yoshioka, Greg Zane

Royal Children............. Kelly Jordan Bit, Lexine Bondoc, Kailip Boonrai, Jacqueline Te Lem, Erik Lin-Greenberg, Kenji Miyata, Brandon Marshall,.Ngai, Amy Y. Tai, Jenna Noelle Ushkowitz, Shelby Rebecca Wong, Jeff G. Yalun

Small House of Uncle Thomas Ballet:

Eliza	Yan Ying
Simon of Legree	Tito Abeleda
Angel George	Meng-Chen Chang
Little Eva	Tran T. Thuc Hanh
Topsy	Tina Ou
Uncle Thomas	Mami Saito
Dogs	John Bantay, Doan Mackenzie, Greg Zane
Guards	Andrew Pacho, C. Sean Kim, Shawn Ku
Propmen	Benjamin Bryant, Paolo Montalban, Alan Muraoka, Paul Nakuuchi

Archers...........Camille M. Brown, Vivien Eng, Lainie Sakakura, Kayoko Yoshioka

Singers... Kam Cheng, Margaret Ann Gates, Carol To, Yolanda Tolentino STANDBYS/UNDERSTUDIES:Raul Aranas (King), Barbara McCulloh (Anna), Paul Nakauchi (King/Kralahome), Benjamin Bryant, Paolo Montalban (Lun Tha), Alan Muraoka (Kralahome), John Curless (Ramsey), Kam Chneg, Carol To (Tuptim), Jonathan Giordano (Louis), Guy Paul (Orton), Lydia Gaston, Yolanda Tolentino (Lady Thiang) SWINGS: Mr. Giordano, Devanand N. Janki, Susan Kikuchi, Joan Tsao

MUSICAL NUMBERS: Overture (shortened), I Whistle a Happy Tune, Royal Dance Before the King, My Lord and Master, Hello Young Lovers, March of the Siamese Children, A Puzzlement, Getting to Know You, We Kiss in a Shadow, Shall I Tell You What I Think of You?, Something Wonderful, I Have Dreamed, Small House of Uncle Thomas, Song of the King, Shall We Dance, Procession of the White Elephant, Finale, NOTE: Western People Funny cut during previews; Production also omits the Price/Louis "Puzzlement" duet.

Top: Lou Diamond Phillips, John Chang
Below: Donna Murphy, John Curless, Ryan Hopkins, Ensemble

A new production of the 1951 musical in two acts. The action takes place at the Royal Palace in Bangkok, 1860s. Winner of 1996 "Tony" Awards for Revival of a Musical, Leading Actress in a Musical (Donna Murphy), Best Scenic Design and Best Costume Design. For original Bdwy production with Yul Brynner and Gertrude Lawrence see Theatre World Vol.7.

Variety tallied 18 positive, 4 mixed and 1 negative review. Times: (Canby) "...a Rodgers and Hammerstein classic which is not always evident in the new production.." (Jefferson) "...endlessly rich and endlessly provocative. Let us not forget that the ballad of forbidden longing that Lun Tha sings to Tuptim has gone on to become an emblem for every kind of love..." News: (Kissel) "Lou Diamond Phillips..has a disarming boyishness..He is a marvelous, resourceful actor..Donna Murphy is elegance itself..Everything about this revival bespeaks consumate intelligence and craft." Post: (Barnes) "It is like a canvas cleaned..staging for the 21st century." Variety: (Gerard) "Two additional, heavily Eastern-influenced dances..with music pieced together from different Rodgers sources and choreographed by Lar Lubovitch, have been added..some dialogue bits from Ernest Lehman's screenplay for the 1956 20th Century Fox film..have found their way into the revival.."

*Closed February 22, 1998 after 807 performances and 27 previews

Joan Marcus Photos

Donna Murphy and Royal children

Donna Murphy, Lou Diamond Phillips

49

THE APPLE DOESN'T FALL...

Florence Stanley, Margaret Whitton

By Trish Vradenburg; Director, Lenoard Nimoy; Sets/Projections, Kenneth Foy; Costumes, Gail Cooper-Hecht; Lighting, Ken Billington; Sound, Tom Clark; Music, David Lawrence; General Manager, Leonard Soloway; Company Manager, Steven M. Levy; Stage Managers, K. Lee Harvey, Robert Collins; Presented by Chase Mishkin and Jennie Blackton; Press, Bill Evans/Jim Randolph, Tom D'Ambrosio; Previewed from Friday, March 29; Opened in the Lyceum Theatre on Sunday, April 14, 1996

CAST

Kate Griswald	Margaret Whitton
Selma Griswald	Florence Stanley
Jack Griswald	Lee Wallace
Madge Wellington	Janet Sarno
Dr. Sam Gordon	Richard Cox
Lorna	Madeline Miller

A comedy in two acts. The action takes place in New York, Tenafly, Grand Canyon, Miami, L.A., and Washington, D.C.

Variety tallied 9 negative reviews. Times: (Canby) "...sitcom prototypes, characterized entirely by dialogue that's either sarcastic or sentimental." News: (Kissel) "To write a comedy about Alzheimer's disease suggests a lack of taste.." Post: (Barnes) "...Nimoy's staging nimbly prevented the actors from bumping into the screens.." Variety: (Gerard) "...excrutiating awfulness..several fine actors appear to be having at least as terrible a time onstage as we are in the audience.."

*Closed April 14, 1996 after 1 performance and 19 previews.

Joan Marcus, Craig Schwartz Photos

Nathan Lane, Mark Linn-Baker, Ernie Sabella, Lewis J. Stadlen in *A Funny Thing Happened on the Way to the Forum*

50

Ernie Sabella, Nathan Lane

Mary Testa, Mark Linn-Baker

A FUNNY THING HAPPENED ON THE WAY TO THE FORUM

Music/Lyrics, Stephen Sondheim; Book, Burt Shevelove and Larry Gelbart; Director, Jerry Zaks; Choreography, Rob Marshall; Orchestrations, Jonathan Tunick; Musical Supervision, Edward Strauss; Set/Costumes, Tony Walton; Dance Arrangements, David Chase; Hairstylist, David H. Lawrence; Cast Recording, Broadway Angel; Production Manager, Peter Fulbright; General Management, Dodger Productions; Company Manager, Marcia Goldberg; Stage Managers, Arthur Gaffin, Michael Pule; Presented by Jujamcyn Theatres, Scott Rudin/Paramount Pictures, Viertel-Baruch-Frankel Group, Roger Berlind, and Dodger Productions; Press, Chris Boneau~Adrian Bryan-Brown/Jackie Green, Susanne Tighe, Amy Jacobs, Stephen Pitalo, Stefanie Kastel; Previewed from Monday, March 18; Opened in the St. James Theatre on Thursday, April 18, 1996*

CAST

Prologus(an actor)/Pseudolus ....Nathan Lane
Proteans ....Brad Aspel, Cory English, Ray Roderick
Hero ....Jim Stanek
Philia ....Jessica Boevers
Senex ....Lewis J. Stadlen
Domina..Mary Testa
Hysterium..Mark Linn-Baker
Lycus...Ernie Sabella
Tintinabula ,,,Pamela Everett
Panacea...Leigh Zimmerman
The Geminae..Susan Misner, Lori Werner
Vibrata ....Mary Ann Lamb
Gymnasia..Stephenie Pope
Erronius ....William Duell
Miles Gloriosus...Cris Groenendaal
UNDERSTUDIES: Bob Amaral (Psedolus/Hysterium/Lycus), Cory English, Kevin Kraft (Hero), Jennifer Rosin (Philia), Macintyre Dixon (Senex/Erronius), Kenneth Kantor (Senex/Miles/Lycus), Ruth Gottschall (Domina), Patrick Garner (Hysterium/Lycus/Erronius), Leigh Zimmerman (Gymnasia) SWINGS: Michael Arnold, Kevin Kraft, Kristin Willits

MUSICAL NUMBERS: Comedy Tonight, Love I Hear, Free, House of Marcus Lycus, Lovely, Everybody Ought to Have a Maid, I'm Calm, Impossible, Bring Me My Bride, That Dirty Old Man, That'll Show Him, Funeral Sequence, Finale NOTE: Production omits Pretty Little Picture.

A new production of the 1962 musical in two acts. The action takes place on a street in Rome, 200 years before the Christian era. Winner of 1996 "Tony" Award for Leading Actor in a Musical (Nathan Lane). For original Bdwy production with Zero Mostel see Theatre World Vol.18. For 1972 revival with Phil Silvers see Theatre World Vol.28.

Variety tallied 11 favorable, 5 mixed and 2 negative notices. Times: (Canby) "...smart, cheeky, buoyant..Mr. Lane is welcome back on Broadway where he belongs, at the top of the bill." (Jefferson) "...deftly rambunctious book,,witty and sly score.." News: (Kissel) "...little more than a diversion for tired businessmen..the lowest of low comedy..when he wrote *Funny Thing*, Sondheim still wanted to entertain audiences rather than enlighten or afflict them." Post: (Barnes) "Nathan Lane remains a national treasure..It's a great performance, a great show.." Variety: (Gerard) "...a romp with pretentions..Brad Aspel, Cory English and Ray Roderick are wonderful as the Proteans..Sondheim has altered some of the lyrics..cheering crowds applauding Lane's very entrance.."

*Closed January 4, 1998 after 715 peformances and 35 previews

Joan Marcus Photos

Elaine Stritch, George Grizzard

A DELICATE BALANCE

By Edward Albee; Director, Gerald Gutierrez; Sets, John Lee Beatty; Costumes, Jane Greenwood; Lighting, Pat Collins; Sound, Aural Fixation; General Manager, Steven C. Callahan; Stage Managers, Michael Brunner, Richard Hester; Presented by Lincoln Center Theater (Andre Bishop, Artistic Director; Executive Producer, Bernard Gersten); Press, Philip Rinaldi, Merle Debuskey/Susan Chicoine; Previewed from Thursday, March 28; Opened in the Plymouth Theatre on Sunday, April 21, 1996*

CAST

Agnes	Rosemary Harris
Tobias	George Grizzard
Claire	Elaine Stritch
Harry	John Carter
Edna	Elizabeth Wilson +1
Julia	Mary Beth Hurt

STANDBYS: Patricia Kilgarriff (Agnes/Edna), William Cain (Tobias/Harry), Barbara Andres (Claire/Edna), Charlotte Maier

A new production of the 1966 drama in three acts. The action takes place in a large and well-appointed suburban house. Winner of 1996 "Tony" Awards for Revival of a Play, Best Direction of a Play and Leading Actor in a Play (George Grizzard). For original Bdwy production with Jessica Tandy and Hume Cronyn see Theatre World Vol.23. Variety tallied 14 favorable and 1 mixed review. Times: (Canby) "...has the impact of entirely new work..now revealed to be almost as ferocious and funny as-and far more humane than-*Who's Afraid of Virginia Woolf?*" (Jefferson) "...dared us, seduced us into questioning every piety we had ever held dear about Marriage and Family..Mr. Albee is the real thing, and his words were built to last." News: (Kissel) "Rosemary Harris has her customary reserve and elegance..George Grizzard is triumphant..Elaine Stritch..never sacrifices the character to get the laughs..it seems to have the stature and eloquence of a classic." Post: (Barnes) "...manages to explore every nuance, finding thrills in crooks and depths in crannies."

Closed September 29, 1996 after 186 performances and 27 previews.

Succeeded by: 1. Rosemary Murphy

Joan Marcus Photos

Rosemary Harris

JACK

A NIGHT ON THE TOWN WITH JOHN BARRYMORE

Devised by Nicol Williamson and Leslie Megahey; Director, Mr. Megahey; Set, Bethia Jane Green; Lighting, Richard Winkler; Sound, Christopher Bond; General Manager, Richard Martini; Company Manager, Joann Swanson; Stage Managers, Thomas P. Carr, Newton Cole; Presented by John Heyman in association with Freddie Hancock, Meridian Theatrical and Geffen Playhouse; Press, Peter Cromarty/Alice Herrick, Hugh Hayes; Previewed from Saturday, April 20; Opened in the Belasco Theatre on Wednesday, April 24, 1996*

CAST

NICOL WILLIAMSON

A one-man play on the life of actor John Barrymore in two acts. The action takes place on Broadway and in Hollywood.

Variety tallied 2 favorable, 4 mixed and 4 negative reviews. Times: (Brcantley) "...an unexpectedly easygoing portrait of a vulnerable, pleasure-loving and perpetually disappointed man..." News: (Kissel) "What actor is noted for his alcoholism, his arrogance, his habit of slugging other actors?..there is something courageous about the way Williamson incorporates his own notoriety.." Post: (Barnes) "...it's Williamson's triumph..Williamson apologized to the audience for his poor performance early in last night's premiere..went on to explain that he tried to make up for his erratic showing in the first act by giving the second act "all I could"..known for his flamboyant behavior on and off stage..." Variety: (Evans) "...Williamson's reputation precedes him, and the actor doesn't shy away from it or anything else during his energetic two-hours-plus onstage. That the actor outshines the character in this one-man show says as much about Williamson's commanding theatrical control as it does about the serviceable but unexceptional play..."

*Closed May 5, 1996 after 12 performances and 4 previews.

Craig Schwartz Photos

Top and Below: Nicol Williamson

Jimmy Tate, Savion Glover, Baakari Wilder, Vincent Bingham

Raymond King, Jared Crawford

BRING IN 'DA NOISE
BRING IN 'DA FUNK

Conceived/Directed by George C. Wolfe; Choreography, Savion Glover; Based on an idea by Mr. Glover and Mr. Wolfe; Music, Daryl Waters, Zane Mark, Ann Duquesnay; Book, Reg E. Gaines; Sets, Riccardo Hernandez; Costumes, Paul Tazewell; Lighting, Jules Fisher, Peggy Eisenhauer; Musical Supervision/Orchestration, Daryl Waters; Musical Director, Zane Mark; Vocal Arrangements, Ann Duquesnay; Cast Recording, RCA; Production Manager, Bonnie Metzgar; Stage Manager, Bonnie Panson; Presented by the Joseph Papp Public Theatre/New York Shakespeare Festival (George C. Wolfe, Producer); Press, Carol Fineman, Thomas Naro, Bill Coyle; Previewed from Tuesday, April 9; Opened in the Ambassador Theatre on Thursday, April 25, 1996*

CAST

Savion Glover	Baakari Wilder
Vincent Bingham	Jimmy Tate
Jared Crawford	Jeffrey Wright
	Anne Duquesnay
	Raymond Hill
	Dule Hill

UNDERSTUDIES/STANDBYS: Baakari Wilder (for Mr. Glover), Lynette G. DuPre (For Ms. Duquesnay), Mark Gerald Douglas (For Mr. Wright), Dule Hill (for Mr. Wilder), Omar A. Edwards, Derick K. Grant, Joseph Monroe Webb (For Mr. Bingham, Mr. Hill, Mr. Tate, Mr. Wilder), David Peter Chapman (for Mr. Crawford, Mr. King)

PROGRAM: IN 'DA BEGINNING: Bring in 'da Noise Bring in 'da Funk, Door to Isle Goree, Slave Ships, SOM'THIN' FROM NUTHIN': Som'thin' from Nuthin'/Circle Stomp, Pan Handlers, URBANIZATION: Lynching Blues, Chicago Bound, Shifting Sounds, Industrialization, Chicago Riot Rag, I Got the Beat/Dark Tower, Whirligig Stomp, WHERE'S THE BEAT?: Now That's Tap, Uncle Huck-a buck Song, Kid Go!, Lost Beat Swing, Green Chaney Buster Slyde, STREET CORNER SYMPHONY: 1956-Them Conkheads, 1967-Hot Fun, 1977-Blackout, 1987-Gospel/Hip Hop Rant, NOISE/FUNK: Drummin', Taxi, Conversations, Hittin', Finale

A dance musical in two acts telling the story, through tap, of black history from slavery to the present. Winner of 1996 "Tony" Awards for Direction of a Musical, Best Choreography, Featured Actress in a Musical (Ann Duquesnay) and Best Lighting Design. The production originated earlier in the season at the Public Theatre.

Variety tallied 13 favorable and 3 mixed reviews. Times: (Brantley) "...it now seems clear that Broadway is its natural and inevitable home. And it is speaking to its audiences with an electricity and immediacy that evoke the great American musicals..." (Jefferson) "...shows us things we need to know-about our history, about our art, about grace, grit and invention under pressure." News: (Kissel) "...demonstrated the extraordinary versatility of tap as a way to express anger, defiance, resignation and sometimes just plain joy." Post: (Barnes) "Glover, seemingly despising the old buck and wing of historic showbiz tap-he's a little too satirically tough here on Bojanges Robinson and the Nicholas Brothers..He moves into a world of rhythm, noise and feeling taht conveys a sense of the purest, barest poetry." Variety: (Gerard) "George C. Wolfe..confirms his status as a producer and director of unsurpassed gifts..Savion Glover-at 22 already a Broadway veteran-emerges as a tremendous, bankable, exciting star.

*Still playing May 31, 1996.

Michal Daniel Photos

Jared Crawford, Savion Glover

Ann Duquesnay

BIG

Music, David Shire; Lyrics, Richard Maltby Jr.; Book, John Weidman; Based on the 1988 film written by Gary Ross and Anne Spielberg; Director, Mike Ockrent; Choreography, Susan Stroman; Orchestrations, Douglas Besterman; Musical Director, Paul Gemignani; Dance Music, David Krane; Sets, Robin Wagner; Costumes, William Ivey Long; Lighting, Paul Gallo; Cast Recording, Universal; Sound, Steve Canyon Kennedy; Hair/Wigs, David Brian Brown; Special Effects, Gregory Meeh; Production Supervisor, Arthur Siccardi; General Management, Fremont Associates/Robert Kamlot; Company Manager, Steven Zweigbaum; Stage Managers, Steven Zweigbaum, Clifford Schwartz; Presented by James B. Freydberg, Kenneth Feld, Laurence Mark, Kenneth D. Greenblatt, in association with FAO Schwartz Fifth Avenue; Press, Chris Boneau~Adrian Bryan-Brown/Bob Fennell, Patrick Paris, Susanne Tighe, Clint Bond Jr., Susan Moodie; Previewed from Monday, April 8; Opened in the Shubert Theatre on Sunday, April 28, 1996*

CAST

Cynthia Benson	Lizzy Mack
Young Josh	Patrick Levis
Tiffany	Samantha Robyn Lee
Maggie	Lori Aine Bennett
Mrs. Baskin	Barbara Walsh
Mr. Baskin/Derelict/Larry Johnson/Tom	John Sloman
Mr. Kopecki/Panhandler/Nick	Ray Wills
Billy	Brett Tabisel
Mrs. Kopecki/Diane	Donna Lee Marshall
Carnival Man/Barrett	Clent Bowers
Derek	Alex Sanchez
Zoltar	Himself
Voice of Zoltar	Michel Bell
Josh Baskin	Daniel Jenkins
Arcade Man/Lipton	Frank Mastrone
Matchless/Birnbaum	Frank Vlastnik
Paul	Gene Weygandt
Susan	Crista Moore
MacMillan	Jon Cypher
Starfighter	Brandon Espinoza
FAO Sales Executive	Joan Barber
Miss Watson	Jan Neuberger
Deathstarettes	Joyce Chittick, CJay Hardy
Abigail	Jill Matson
Skatephone	Spencer Liff
Kid with Walkman	Enrico Rodriguez
Skateboard Romeo	Graham Bowen
Parents, Shoppers, Executives, Office Staff	The Company

UNDERSTUDIES: Graham Bowen (Young Josh/Billy), Spencer Liff (Young Josh), Donna Lee Marshall (Mrs. Baskin/Susan), Joan Barber (Mrs. Baskin), Brandon Espinoza (Billy), Stacey Todd Holt, Frank Vlastnik (Josh), Ray Wills (Paul), Frank Mastrone (Paul/MacMillan/Nick/Tom), Jill Matson (Susan), Clent Bowers (MacMillan)

Top: Patrick Levis

MUSICAL NUMBERS: Can't Wait, Talk to Her, The Carnival, This Isn't Me, I Want to Go Home, Time of Your Life, Fun, Dr. Deathstar, Josh's Welcome, Here We Go Again, Stars Stars Stars, Tavern Foxtrot, Cross the Line, It's Time, Stop Time, Happy Birthday Josh, Dancing All the Time, I Want to Know, Coffee Black, The Real Thing, One Special Man, When You're Big, Skateboard Romance, Finale DURING TRYOUT: Thirteen, Big, I'll Think About It Later, Isn't It Magic?, Dish at the Dance, Your Wish Is Granted

A musical in two acts. The action takes place in New Jersey and New York City.

Variety tallied 4 favorable, 6 mixed and 6 negative reviews. Times: (Canby) "...bright, shiny, larger-than-life toy of a show..so exuberantly gifted that it gives you the helium high of a balloon flight..Mr. Jenkins is beguiling..other standout performances are those of Patrick Levis..and pint-sized Brett Tabisel.." News: (Kissell) "All the songs are intelligently conceived, but few have any emotional impact..Susan Stroman's choreography has great energy." Post: (Barnes) "Everything is busy but also pointless.." Variety: (Gerard) "One scene actually improves on the film, because it looks at the story in theatrical terms..little Josh emerges to sing, in a haunting falsetto, the lovely I Want to Know..Moore does sing beautifully, and Maltby and Shire have given her a nice anthem, Dancing All the Time, as well as a lovely duet with Jenkins, Stars Stars Stars..the show only comes together in the final scene."

*Closed October 13, 1996 after 192 performances and 22 previews.

Joan Marcus/Carol Rosegg Photos

Daniel Jenkins, Crista Moore

Daniel Jenkins, Jon Cypher

The Kids

Brett Tabisel, Patrick Levis, Lizzy Mack

RENT

Music/Lyrics/Book by Jonathan Larson; Director, Michael Greif; Arrangements, Steve Skinner; Muiscal Supervision/Additional Arrangements, Tim Weill; Choreography, Marlies Yearby; Original Concept/Additional Lyrics, Billy Aronson; Set, Paul Clay; Costumes, Angela Wendt; Lighting, Blake Burba; Sound, Kurt Fischer; Cast Recording, Dreamworks; General Management, Emanuel Azenberg, John Corker; Stage Managers, John Vivian, Crystal Huntington; Presented by Jeffrey Seller, Kevin McCollum, Allan S. Gordon, and New York Theatre Workshop; Press, Richard Kornberg/Don Summa, Ian Rand; Previewed from Tuesday, April 16; Opened in the Nederlander Theatre on Monday, April 29, 1996*

CAST

Mark Cohen ....Anthony Rapp
Roger Davis...Adam Pascal
Tom Collins ....Jesse L. Martin
Benjamin Coffin III ....Taye Diggs
Joanne Jefferson ....Fredi Walker
Angel Schunard ....Wilson Jermaine Heredia
Mimi Marquez ....Daphne Rubin-Vega
Maureen Johnson ....Idina Menzel
Mark's Mom/Alison/Others ....Kristen Lee Kelly
Christmas Caroler/Mr. Jefferson/Pastor/ Others ....Byron Utley
Mrs. Jefferson/Woman with Bags/Others ....Gwen Stewart
Gordon/The Man/Mr. Grey/Others ....Timothy Britten Parker
Man with Squeegee/Waiter/Others ....Gilles Chiasson
Paul/Cop/Others ....Rodney Hicks
Alexi Darling/Roger's Mom/Others....................Aiko Nakasone
UNDERSTUDIES: Gilles Chiasson, David Driver (Roger/Mark), Darius de Haas (Tom/Benjamin/Angel), Byron Utley (Tom), Rodney Hicks (Benjamin), Shelly Dickinson (Joanne), Simone (Joanne/Mimi), Mark Setlock (Angel), Yassmin Alers (Mimi/Maureen), Kristen Lee Kelly (Maureen)
SWINGS: Ms. Allers, Mr. de Haas, Ms. Dickinson, Mr. Driver, Mr. Setlock, Simone

MUSICAL NUMBERS: Tune Up, Voice Mail (#1-#5), Rent, You Okay Honey?, One Song Glory, Light My Candle, Today 4 U, You'll See, Tango: Maureen, Life Support, Out Tonight, Another Day, Will I?, On the Street, Santa Fe, We're Okay, I'll Cover You, Christmas Bells, Over the Moon, La Vie Boheme/I Should Tell You, Seasons of Love, Happy New Year, Take Me or Leave Me, Without You, Contact, Halloween, Goodbye Love, What You Own, Finale/Your Eyes

A musical in two acts. The action takes place in New York City's East Village. This production originated at Off-Bdwy's New York Theatre Workshop earlier in the season. Winner of 1996 "Tony" Awards for Best Musical, Best Original Score, Best Book of a Musical and Featured Actor in a Musical (Wilson Jermaine Heredia). Winner of the New York Drama Critics Circle Award for Best Musical. Winner of the 1996 Pulitzer Prize for Drama. Tragedy occured when the 35 year old author,Jonathan Larson, died of an aortic aneurysm after watching the final dress rehearsal of his show January 24, 1996.

Top: Fredi Walker, Idina Menzel
Right: Wilson Jermaine Heredia,
Jesse L. Martin

Variety tallied 11 favorable, 2 mixed and 2 negative reviews. Times: (Brantley/original review) "...exhilarating, landmark rock opera..the unflaggingly focused Mr. Rapp gives the show its energentic motor; the golden-voiced Mr. Pascal its meditative soul and Ms. Rubin-Vega its affirmative sensuality..People who complain about the demise of the American musical have simply been looking in the wrong places." (Bdwy transfer) "What makes Rent so wonderful is not its hipness quotient but its extraordinary spirit of hopeful defiance and humanity." (Jefferson) Jonathan Larson..had talent and idealism. Its cast does too, and they reach out to the audience again and again." (Frank Rich) "...lovingly merging the musical theatre traditions of past generations..with rock.. At so divisive a time in our country's culture, Rent shows signs of revealing a large, untapped appetite for something better." News: (Kissel/orig review) "...often funny, invariably coarse..leaves you frazzled." (Bdwy transfer) "...as a barometer of the ongoing comedy of middle-class America trashing itself, it's a major landmark." Post: (Barnes/orig. review) "...full of heart, passion and wit..where it scores heavily is with its score..." (Bdwy transfer) "...Michael Greif has done a great job in giving the show more focus than it had downtown..deepening performances of its actors..Larson has achieved the hope marked out by his seize-this-day hero..." Variety: (Gerard/orig. review) "...the most sensational musical in maybe a decade..points the Anerican musical toward the future." (Bdwy transfer) "..bigger, bolder, louder, sadder, wilder, and every bit as powerful as it was in the East Village..makes the musical theatre joyously important again."

*Still playing May 31, 1996.

Joan Marcus/Carol Rosegg Photos

Right: Anthony Rapp

Below: Adam Pascal, Daphne Rubin-Vega

Above and Top: The cast of *Rent*

BURIED CHILD

By Sam Shepard; Director, Gary Sinise; Sets, Robert Brill; Costumes, Allison Reeds; Lighting, Kevin Rigdon; Sound, Rob Milburn; General Manager, Robert Cole; Company Manager, Rob Wallner; Stage Managers, Laura Koch, Franklin Keysar; Presented by Frederick Zollo, Nicholas Paleologos, Jane Harmon, Nina Keneally, Gary Sinise, Edwin Schloss, Liz Oliver, and the Steppenwolf Theatre Company; Press, Chris Boneau~Adrian Bryan-Brown/Andy Shearer, Clint Bond Jr., Jackie Green, Erin Dunn; Previewed from Tuesday, April 16; Opened in the Brooks Atkinson Theatre on Tuesday, April 30, 1996*

CAST

Bradley	Leo Burmester
Dodge	James Gammon
Tilden	Terry Kinney
Father Dewis	Jim Mohr
Shelly	Kellie Overbey
Halie	Lois Smith
Vince	Jim True

UNDERSTUDIES: Patricia Jones (Shelly), Darrie Lawrence (Halie), Barton Tinapp (Tilden/Bradley), Connor Trinneer (Vince), Christopher Wynkoop (Dodge/Dewis)

A new production of the 1978 drama in three acts. The action takes place in Central Illinois, 1978. Original Off-Bdwy production (see Theatre World Vol 35) won the 1979 Pulitzer Prize.

Variety tallied 10 favorable, 4 mixed and 1 negative review. Times (Brantley) "This fierce testimony to the theory that you really can't go home again (and if you try, be prepared for the consequences) actually appears to have grown more resonant, funnier and far more accessible..." News: (Kissel) "..the playwright has substantially revised..it also has an adolescent's primal, raw energy." Post (Barnes) "What it all means specifically I have no idea..it lingers with you like the scent of strange poetry or the taste of strident radishes. It won't be easily forgotten the next morning." Variety: (Gerard) "...bristles with its own eccentric humor, much of which is at least in evidence here. Yet the play is overwhelmed by the imposing spectacle of this production, and its black heart has been obscured."

*Closed June 30, 1996 after 71 performances and 16 previews.

T. Charles Erickson Photos

Jim True
Below: James Gammon, Terry Kinney,
Kellie Overby, Jim True

AN IDEAL HUSBAND

By Oscar Wilde; Director, Peter Hall; Design, Carl Toms; Lighting, Joe Atkins, Mike Baldassari; General Manager, Stuart Thompson; Company Manager, Lisa M. Poyer; Stage Managers, David Hyslop, Greg Schanuel; Presented by Bill Kenwright; Press, Philip Rinaldi/Eugenie Hero; Previewed from Thursday, April 25; Opened in the Ethel Barrymore Theatre on Wednesday, May 1, 1996*

CAST

Sir Robert Chiltern ....David Yelland
Lady Chiltern...Penny Downie
Miss Mabel Chiltern...Victoria Hasted
Earl of Caversham ....Michael Dennison
Lord Goring ....Martin Shaw
Mrs. Cheveley...Anna Carteret
Lady Markby ....Dulcie Gray
Vicomte De Nanjac ....Dominic Hawksley
Lady Bilsildon ....Valerie Leonard
Mrs. Marchmont ....Allsion Daugherty
Mr. Montford/Phipps ....Dennis Holmes
Mason ....Edmund C. Davys
James/Mr. Barford ....J. Paul Boehmer
Duchess of Maryborough ....Angela Thornton
Lady Jane Barford ....Cheryl Gaysunas
STANDBYS/UNDERSTUDIES: Edmund C. Davys (Chiltern/Montford/Phipps), Allison Daugherty (Lady Chiltern), Cheryl Gaysunas (Mabel/Mrs. Marchmont), Denis Holmes (Caversham), Dominic Hawksley (Goring), Valerie Leonard (Mrs. Cheveley), Angela Thornton (Lady Markby/Lady Basildon), J. Paul Boehmer (Vicomte/Mason).

A new production of the 1895 comedy in four acts, performed with one intermission. The action takes place in various houses in London, 1895.

Variety tallied 12 positive and 2 mixed reviews. Times: (Canby) "This gleaming production celebrates not only itself, the genius of Wilde and the strengths of the contemporary English theatre but also the potential vitality of Broadway." News: (Kissel) "...Goring seems a stand-in for the author, and his plea for charity, written presumably before Wilde's own need for it was patent, adds poignancy to the play." Post: (Barnes) "...a warm, loving, funny, humane play to be cherished..." Variety (Gerard) "...rich with contemporary resonance..what Wilde saw as the utter foolishness of moral absolutism."

*Closed January 26, 1997 after 309 performances and 7 previews.

+Succeeded by: Mark Douet,

Joan Marcus Photos

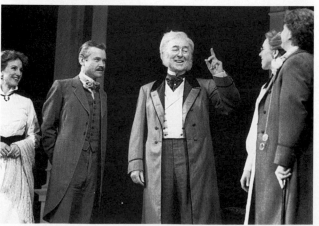

Top: Penny Downie, Dulcie Gray, Anna Carteret

Center: Martin Snow, Victoria Hasted

Right: Penny Downie, David Yelland,

Michael Dennison, Victoria Hasted, Martin Shaw

CHICAGO

Music, John Kander; Lyrics, Fred Ebb; Book, Mr. Ebb, Bob Fosse; Based on the play by Maurine Dallas Watkins; Adaptation, David Thompson; Director, Walter Bobbie; Orchestrations, Ralph Burns; Choreography Ann Reinking in the style of Bob Fosse; Set, John Lee Beatty; Sound, Scott Lehrer; Lighting, Daryl Bornstein; Lighting, Ken Billington; Stage Manager, Clayton Phillips; Presented by City Center Encores!: Great American Musicals in Concert (Artistic Director, Walter Bobbie); Press, Philip Rinaldi; Opened in City Center on Thursday, May 2, 1996*

CAST

Velma Kelly	Bebe Neuwirth
Roxie Hart	Ann Reinking
Fred Casely	Michael Berresse
Sgt. Fogarty	Michael Kubala
Amos Hart	Joel Grey
Liz	Denise Faye
Annie	Mamie Duncan-Gibbs
June	Lisa Leguillou
Hunyak	Tina Paul
Mona	Caitlin Carter
Matron "Mama" Morton	Marcia Lewis
Billy Flynn	James Naughton
Mary Sunshine	D. Sabella
Go-to-Hell Kitty	Mary Ellen Stuart
Harry	Rocker Verastique
Aaron	David Gibson
Martin Harrison	Bruce Anthony Davis
Judge	Jim Borstelmann
Court Clerk	John Mineo

MUSICAL NUMBERS: All That Jazz, Funny Honey, Cell Block Tango, When You're Good to Mama, Tap Dance, All I Care About, A Little Bit of Good, We Both Reached for the Gun, Roxie, I Can't Do It Alone, Chicago After Midnight, My Own Best Friend, Hot Honey Rag, I Know a Girl, Me and My Baby, Mister Cellophane, When Velma Takes the Stand, Razzle Dazzle, Class, Nowadays/Finale

A staged concert of the 1975 musical which originally featured Gwen Verdon, Chita Rivera and Jerry Orbach. This concert returned as an open run in the 1996-97 season.

*Closed May 4, 1996 after a limited run of 4 performances.

John Glover, Haviland Morris

**Tina Paul, Denise Faye, Mamie Duncan-Gibbs,
Ann Reinking, Bebe Neuwirth,
Caitlin Canter, Mary Ellen Stewart**

TARTUFFE: BORN AGAIN

By Moliere; Adaptation, Freyda Thomas; Director, David Saint; Sets, Allen Moyer; Costumes, Jess Goldstein; Lighting, Jeff Davis; Sound, John Kilgore; Video, Ben Rubin; Dialects, K.C. Ligon; Production Supervisor, Frank Marino; Company Manager, Don Roe; Stage Managers, Mr. Marino, Robert Bennett; Presented by Circle in the Square (Theodore Mann, Josephine R. Abady, Co-Artistic Directors); Press, Jeffrey Richards/Mark Cannistraro, Laramie Dennis, Irene Gandy; Previewed from Tuesday, May 7; Opened in the Circle in the Square Uptown on Thursday, May 30, 1996*

CAST

Cleante	Richard Bekins
Mrs. Pernell	Patricia Conolly
Elmire	Haviland Morris
Dorine	Alison Fraser
Damis	Kevin Dewey
Maryann	Jane Krakowski
Orgon	David Schramm
Valere	T. Scott Cunningham
Tartuffe	John Glover
Ms. De Salle	Susie Duff
Visitor	Peter Rini
Production Assistant	Jeanne Hime

UNDERSTUDIES: Susie Duff (Elmire/Dorine), Jeanne Hime (Maryann), Tom Ligon (Orgon/Visitor), Peter Rini (Valere/Damis), Angela Pietropinto (Mrs. Pernell/Ms/ DeSalle)

A new version of the 1664 satire performed in two acts. The action now takes place in a tv studio in the American South where Tartuffe is a deposed televangelist.

Times: (Brantley) "...this Tartuffe has a hysterical, psychosexual side that is way out of kilter..." News: (Kissel) "In Memphis, it might seem gutsy. In New York, an attack on the Religious Right only reinforces the audience's smugness..." Post: (Barnes) "...something more dangerous at play here than with transposed Shakespeare-language..John Glover..is marvelous..."

*Closed June 23, 1996 after 29 performances and 26 previews.

Gerry Goodstein Photos

63

BROADWAY PRODUCTIONS FROM PAST SEASONS

BEAUTY AND THE BEAST

Music, Alan Menken; Lyrics, Howard Ashman, Tim Rice; Book, Linda Woolverton; Director, Robert Jess Roth; Orchestrations, Danny Troob; Musical Supervision/Vocal Arrangements, David Friedman; Musical Director/Incidental Arrangements, Michael Kosarin; Choreography, Matt West; Sets, Stan Meyer; Costumes, Ann Hould-Ward; Lighting, Natasha Katz; Sound, T. Richard Fitzgerald; Hairstylist, David H. Lawrence; Illusions, Jim Steinmeyer, John Gaughan; Prosthetics, John Dods; Fights, Rick Sordelet; Cast Recording, Walt Disney Records; General Manager, Dodger Productions; Production Supervisor, Jeremiah J. Harris; Company Manager, Kim Sellon; Stage Managers, James Harker, John M. Atherlay, Pat Sosnow, Kim Vernace; Presented by Walt Disney Productions; Press, Chris Boneau/Adrian Bryan-Brown, Patty Onagan, Brian Moore, Michael Tuason; Previewed from Wednesday, March 9, 1994; Opened in the Palace Theatre on Monday, April 18, 1994*

Jeff McCarthy, Sarah Uriarte

CAST

Enchantress	Wendy Oliver
Young Prince	Tom Pardoe
Beast	Jeff McCarthy +1
Belle	Sarah Uriarte +2
Lefou	Harrison Deal
Gaston	Marc Kudisch
Three Silly Girls	Alisa Klein, Sarah Solie Shannon, Linda Talbott
Maurice	Kurt Knudson
Cogsworth	Heath Lamberts +3
Lumiere	Lee Roy Reams +4
Babette	Stacey Logan
Mrs. Potts	Beth Fowler +5
Chip	Andrew Keenen-Bolger, Pattrick Lavery
Madame de la Grande Bouche	Eleanor Glockner
Monsieur D'Arque	Gordon Stanley
Townspeople/Enchanted Objects	Anna Maria Andricain, Kevin Berdini, Andrea Burns, Christophe Caballero, Sally Mae Dunn, Barbara Folts, Elmore James, Alisa Klein, Anna McNeely, Beth McVey, Bill Nabel, Wendy Oliver, Tom Pardoe, Joseph Savant, Sarah Solie Shannon, Matthew Shepard, Steven Sofia, Gordon Stanley, Linda Talcott, David A. Wood, Wysandria Woolsey
Prologue Narrator	David Ogden Stiers

MUSICAL NUMBERS: Overture, Prologue (Enchantress), Belle, No Matter What, Me, Home, Gaston, How Long Must This Go On?, Be Our Guest, If I Can't Love Her, Entr'acte/Wolf Chase, Something There, Human Again, Maison des Lunes, Beauty and the Beast, Mob Song, The Battle, Transformation, Finale

A musical in two acts. An expanded, live action version of the 1992 animated film musical with additional songs. Winner of 1994 "Tony" for Best Costume Design.

*Still playing May 31, 1996.

+Succeeded by: 1. Steve Blanchard 2. Christianne Tisdale, Kerry Butler 3. Peter Bartlett 4. Patrick Quinn 5. Cass Morgan, Beth Fowler

(Joan Marcus/Marc Bryan-Brown/Walt Disney Theatrical Photos)

Cast of *Beauty and the Beast*

CATS

Music, Andrew Lloyd Webber; Based on *Old Possum's Book Of Practical Cats* by T.S. Eliot; Orchestrations, David Cullen, Lloyd Webber; Prod. Musical Director, David Caddick; Musical Directors, Edward G. Robinson, Patrick Vaccariello; Sound, Martin Levan; Lighting, David Hersey; Design, John Napier; Choreography/Associate Director, Gillian Lynne; Director, Trevor Nunn; Cast Recording, Polydor; Casting, Johnson-Liff Associates; Company Manager, James G. Mennen; Stage Managers, Peggy Peterson, Tom Taylor, Suzanne Viverito; Executive Producers, R. Tyler Gatchell, Jr., Peter Neufeld; Presented by Cameron Mackintosh, The Really Useful Co., David Geffen, and The Shubert Organization; Press, Fred Nathan/Michael Borowski; Opened in the Winter Garden Theatre on Thursday, October 7, 1982*

Ken Prymus

CAST

Alonzo	Hans Kriefall
Bustopher/Asparagus/Growltiger	Richard Poole
Bombalurina	Marlene Danielle
Cassandra	Isa Gilliams
Coricopat	James Hadley
Demeter	Mercedes Perez
Grizabella	Liz Callaway
Jellylorum/Griddlebone	Nina Hennessey
Jennyanydots	Carol Dilley
Mistoffolees	Lindsay Chambers +1
Mungojerrie	Roger Kachel
Munkustrap	Keith Bernardo
Old Deuteronomy	Ken Prymus
Plato/Macivity/Rumpus Cat	Philip Michael Baskerville +2
Pouncival	Jacob Brent
Rum Tum Tiger	David Hibbard
Rumpleteazer	Kristi Sperling +3
Sillabub	Bethany Samuelsohn +4
Skimbleshanks	Eric Scott Kincaid
Tantomile	Jill Nicklaus
Tumblebrutus	Levansky Smith
Victoria	Nadine Isenegger
Cat Chorus	Joel Briel, Susan Powers, Peter Samuel, Heidi Stallings

STANDBYS/UNDERSTUDIES: Alaine Kashian (+5), David E. Liddell, Joe Locaro, Jack Magradey (+6), Rusty Mowery, Naomi Naughton (+7), Susan Somerville, Lynn Sterling, Owen Taylor, Suzanne Viverito

MUSICAL NUMBERS: Jellicle Songs for Jellicle Cats, Naming of Cats, Invitation to the Jellicle Ball, Old Gumbie Cat, Rum Tum Tugger, Grizabella the Glamour Cat, Bustopher Jones, Mungojerrie and Rumpleteazer, Old Deuteronomy, Aweful Battle of the Pekes and Pollicles, Jellicle Ball, Memory, Moments of Happiness, Gus the Theatre Cat, Growltiger's Last Stand, Skimbleshanks, Macavity, Mr. Mistoffolees, Journey to the Heavyside Layer, Ad-dressing of Cats

A musical in two acts with 20 scenes.

Liz Callaway

*Still playing May 31, 1996. The production celebrated its thirteenth birthday during the season and has now played more than 5,500 performances. Winner of 1983 "Tonys" for Best Musical, Score, Book, Direction, Costumes, Lighting, and Featured Actress in a Musical (Betty Buckley as Grizabella). For original 1982 production see *Theatre World* Vol.39.
+Succeeded by: 1. Steve Ochoa, Gen Horiuchi 2. Karl Wahl 3. Maria Jo Ralabate 4. Alaine Kashian, Bethany Samuelson 5. Lisa Mayer, Alaine Kashian 6. Steve Dahlem 7. Angel Caban

Carol Rosegg Photos

**Nadine Isenegger, Bethany Samuelson,
David Hibbard, Kristi Sperling**

A CHRISTMAS CAROL

Music, Alan Menken; Lyrics, Lynn Ahrens; Book, Mike Ockrent, Lynn Ahrens; Based on the story by Charles Dickens; Director, Mike Ockrent; Choreography, Susan Stroman; Orchestrations, Michael Starobin; Musical Director, Paul Gemignani; Sets, Tony Walton; Costumes, William Ivey Long; Lighting, Jules Fisher, Peggy Eisenhauer; Sound, Tony Meola; Projections, Wendall K. Harrington; Flying by Foy; Dance Arrangements, Glen Kelly; Cast Recording, Columbia; Production Supervisor, Gene O'Donovan; Company Manager, Steven H. David; Stage Managers, Steven Zweigbaum, Clifford Schwartz; Producers, Dodger Productions, Tim Hawkins; Presented by Nickelodeon Family Classics and Madison Square Garden; Press, Chris Boneau/Adrian Bryan-Brown, Patty Onagan, Jamie Morris, Craig Karpel; Original Production opened in the Paramount Theatre on Thursday, December 1, 1994-January 1, 1995; Seasonal re-opening in the Paramount Theatre on Thursday, November 30, 1995*

CAST

Scrooge ....Terrence Mann
Ghost of Christmas Past ....Ben Vereen
Bob Cratchit..Nick Corley
Ghost of Christmas Past ....Ken Jennings
Ghost of Jacob Marley ....Paul Kandel
Mr. Smythe..James Judy
Blind Hag ....Nicole Arrington
Mrs. Cratchit...Robin Baxter
Fred ....Steve Blanchard
Fezziwig...Michael Cone
Mrs. Fezziwig ....Joy Hermalyn
Scrooge's Mother ....Barbara Marineau
Scrooge's Father..Michael X. Martin
Mrs. Mops ....Karen Murphy
Emily ....Emily Skinner
Scrooge at 18 ....Tom Stuart
Ghost of Christmas Future ....Theara J. Ward
Young Marley ....Ken Barnett
Sally...Stephanie Bast
Scrooge at 12 ....Paul Franklin Dano, Christopher Mark Petrizzo
Jonathon ....Jason Fuchs, Evan J. Newman
Grace Smythe ....Cara Horner, Joanna Howard
Judge..Michael H. Ingram
Tiny Tim ....Zach London, Chris Marquette
Old Joe/Hawkins..Kenneth McMullen
Charity Man...Robert Ousley
Charity Man...Wayne W. Pretlow
Charity Man/Poulterer...Walter Willison
Ensemble Farah Alvin, Matthew Baker, Rachel Black, Amy B. Blake, Brad Bradley, Candy Cook, Rob Donohoe, Donna Dunmire, Peter Gregus, Melissa Haizlip, Jeffrey Hankinson, Dana Leigh Jackson, Don Johanson, David Lowenstein, Dana Lynn Mauro, Carol Lynn Meadows, Sean Thomas Morrissey, Tom Pardoe, Gail Pennington, Angela Piccinni, Josef Reiter, Pamela Remler, Sam Reni, Eric Riley, Rommy Sandhu, Erin Stoddard, Tracy Terstriep, Cynthia Thole, Matthew J. Vargo, Jeff Williams, Matthew Ballinger, Julia Bowen, Eliza Atkins Clark, Anthony Roth Costanzo, Mathis M. Fender, Nicholas Gould, Jack Ingram, Nicole Napolitano, Olivia Oguma, Nathalie Paulding, Zachary Petkanas, Diana Mary Rice, Bobby Steggert, Christian Stuck

MUSICAL NUMBERS: A Jolly Good Time (new this season), Nothing to Do With Me, You Mean More to Me (new this season), Street Song, Link By Link, Lights of Long Ago, God Bless Us Everyone, A Place Called Home, Mr. Fezziwig's Annual Christmas Ball, Abundance and Charity, Christmas Together, Dancing on Your Grave, Yesterday Tomorrow and Today, London Town Carol (new this season), Final Medley

A musical performed without intermission. The action takes place in London, 1880.

*Closed December 31, 1995 after seasonal run of 88 performances.

George Kalinsky Photos

Terrence Mann (on ladder)

Joy Hermalyn, Walter Willison

Terrence Mann (center), Ben Vereen and Company

Karen Ziemba, James Brennan

Pia Zadora

CRAZY FOR YOU

Music, George Gershwin; Lyrics, Ira Gershwin, Gus Kahn, Desmond Carter; Book, Ken Ludwig; Conception, Mr. Ludwig and Mike Ockrent, inspired by material by Guy Bolton and John McGowan; Director, Mr. Ockrent; Choreography, Susan Stroman; Orchestrations, William D. Brohn, Sid Ramin; Musical Director, Paul Gemignani; Musical Consultant, Tommy Krasker; Dance/Incidental Arrangements, Peter Howard; Sets, Robin Wagner; Costumes, William Ivey Long; Lighting, Paul Gallo; Sound, Otts Munderloh; Casting, Julie Hughes, Barry Moss; Cast Recording, Broadway Angel; Fights, B.H. Barry; Hairstylist, Angela Gari; General Manager, Gatchell & Neufeld; Prod. Manager, Peter Fulbright; Company Manager, Richard Biederman; Stage Manager, John Bonanni; Associate Producers, Richard Godwin, Valerie Gordon; Presented by Roger Horchow and Elizabeth Williams; Press, Bill Evans/Jim Randolph, Susan L. Schulman, Erin Dunn; Previewed from Friday, January 31, 1992; Opened in the Shubert Theatre on Wednesday, February 19, 1992*

CAST

Tess	Beth Leavel +1
Patsy	Jill Matson +2
Bobby Child	James Brennan
Bela Zanger	John Jellison +3
Sheila	Judine Hawkins Richard
Mitzi	Wendy Waring
Susie	Ida Gilliams +4
Louise	Jean Marie
Betsy	Angel L. Schworer +5
Margie	Kimberly Hester
Vera	Shannon Lewis
Elaine	Paula Legett Chase +6
Irene Roth	Kay McClelland +7
Mother	Jane Connell +8
Perkins/Custus	James Young
Moose	Gary Douglas
Mingo	Branch Woodman
Sam	Michael Duran +9
Junior	John M. Wiltberger
Custus	James Young
Pete	Fred Anderson +10
Jimmy	Michael Kubala
Billy	Ray Roderick
Wyatt	Sean Martin Hingston +11
Harry	Joel Goodness
Polly Baker	Karen Ziemba
Everett Baker	Carleton Carpenter +12
Lank Hawkins	John Hillner +13
Eugene	Stephen Temperley
Patricia	Colleen Smith Wallnau

MUSICAL NUMBERS: Original sources follow in parentheses: K razy for You (*Treasure Girl,* 1928), I Can'ts Be Bothered Now (Film: *A Damsel in Distress,* 1937), Bidin' My Time (*Girl Crazy,* 1930), Things Are Looking Up (*A Damsel in Distress,*), Could You Use Me (*Girl Crazy*), Shall We Dance (Film: *Shall We Dance,* 1937), Someone to Watch Over Me (*Oh Kay,* 1926), Slap That Bass (*Shall We Dance*), Embraceable You (*Girl Crazy*), Tonight's the Night (previously unused), I Got Rhythm (*Girl Crazy*), The Real American Folk Song is a Rag (*Ladies First,* 1918), What Causes That? (*Treasure Girl*), Naughty Baby (previously unused), Stiff Upper Lip (*A Damsel in Distress*), They Can't Take That Away From Me (*Shall We Dance*), But Not for Me (*Girl Crazy*), Nice Work If You Can Get It (*A Damsel in Distress*), Finale

A musical comedy, inspired by *Girl Grazy* (1930), in two acts with 17 scenes. The action takes place in New York City and Deadrock, Nevada in the 1930's.

*Closed January 7, 1996 after 1,622 performances and 21 previews. Winer of 1992 "Tonys" for Best Musical, Best Choreography and Best Costumes.

+Succeeded by: 1. Melinda Buckley 2. Rebecca Downing 3. Bruce Adler, Sandy Edgerton 4. Angie L. Schworer 5. Leigh Zimmerman 6. Elizabeth Mills 7. Pia Zadora 8. Ann B. Davis 9. Alan Gilbert 10. James Doberman 11. Stephen Reed 12. Roger Horchow, Carleton Carpenter, John Jellison, Al Checco, John Jellison 13. Darren Kelly STANDBY: Karen Culp

Joan Marcus Photos

Rob Becker

DEFENDING THE CAVEMAN

By Rob Becker; Music, R.B. & Michael Barrow; Company Manager, Todd Grove; Stage Manager, Jason Lindhorst; Presented by Contemporary Productions; Press, Merle Frimark and Marc Thibodeau/Erin Dunn, Colleen Brown; Previewed from Wednesday, March 1, 1995; Opened in the Helen Hayes Theatre on Sunday, March 26, 1995*

CAST

ROB BECKER

A one-man comedy performed without intermission.

*Still playing May 31, 1996.

Joan Marcus Photos

Rob Becker

68

GREASE

Music/Lyrics/Book by Jim Jacobs and Warren Casey; Director /Choreography, Jeff Calhoun; Orchestrations, Steve Margoshes; Musical Director/Vocal and Dance Arrangements, John McDaniel; Musical Coordinator, John Monaco; Sets, John Arnone; Costumes, Willa Kim; Lighting, Howell Binkley; Hairstylist, Patrik D. Moreton; Sound, Tom Morse; Associate Choreographer, Jerry Mitchell; Cast Recordings, RCA; General Manager, Charlotte W. Wilcox; Casting, Stuart Howard, Amy Schecter; Company Manager, Barbara Darwall; Stage Managers, Craig Jacobs, David Hyslop; Presented in associated with PACE Theatrical Group, TV Asahi; The Tommy Tune Production presented by Barry & Fran Weissler, Jujamcyn Theatres; Press, Pete Sanders/Ian Rand, Bruce Laurienzo, Meredith Oritt; Previewed from Saturday, April 23, 1994; Opened in the Eugene O'Neill Theatre on Wednesday, May 11, 1994*

CAST

Vince Fontaine	Brian Bradley +1
Miss Lynch	Mimi Hines +2
Sonny Latierri	Brad Kane +3
Kenickie	Jason Opsahl +4
Frenchy	Monica Lee Gradischek +5
Doody	Ray Walker +6
Danny Zuko	Adrian Zmed +7
Marty	Sherie Rene Scott +8
Roger	Hunter Foster
Jan	Heather Stokes +9
Betty Rizzo	Joley Fisher +10
Sandy Dumbrowski	Susan Wood +11
Patti Simcox	Christine Toy +12
Eugene Florczyk	Paul Castree
Straight A's	Clay Adkins, Brad Aspel, Paul Castree, Denny Tarver
Dream Mooners	Brad Aspel, Katy Grenfell
Heartbeats	Katy Grenfell, Janice Lorraine Holt, Lorna Shane
Cha-Cha Degregorio	Jennifer Cody
Teen Angel	Jennifer Holliday +13

Ensemble.......Clay Adkins, Brad Aspel, Gregory Cunneen, Jeff Edgerton, Katy Grenfell, Janice Lorraine Holt, Allison Metcalf, Connie Ogden, Lorna Shane, Denny Tarver

A new production of the 1972 musical in two acts with 13 scenes. The action takes place in and around Rydell High, 1950s. For original Broadway production see *Theatre World* Vol. 29.

*Closed January 25, 1998 after 1,503 performances and 20 previews

+Succeeded by: 1. Mickey Dolenz, Brian Bradley , Joe Piscopo 2. JoAnne Worley, Dody Goodman, Marcia Lewis 3. Nick Cavarra, Danny Cistone, Carlos Lopez 4. Douglas Crawford 5. Beth Lipari 6. Ty Taylor 7. Ricky Paull Goldin, Jon Secada, Jeff Trachta, Joseph Barbara 8. Leah Hocking, Deirdre O'Neill 9. Marissa Jaret Winokur 10. Tia Riebling, Susan Moniz, Jody Watley 11. Susan Moniz, Lacy Hornkohl 12. Carrie Ellen Austin 13. Charles Gray, Al Jarreau, Chubby Checker

Carol Rosegg, Stan Schnier/Carmen Schiavone Photos

Jessica Stone, Sam Harris, Ricky Paull Goldin, Megan Mullally, Hunter Foster

JoAnne Worley   **Jennifer Holliday**

Jon Secada   **Sally Struthers**

HOW TO SUCCEED IN BUSINESS WITHOUT REALLY TRYING!

Matthew Broderick, Sarah Jessica Parker

Megan Mullally, John Stamos

Music/Lyrics, Frank Loesser; Book, Abe Burros, Jack Weinstock and Willie Gilbert; Based on the book by Shepard Mead; Director, Des McAnuff; Choreography, Wayne Cilento; Musical Director/Vocal Arrangements, Ted Sperling; Orchestrations, Danny Troob, David Siegel, Robert Ginzler; Sets, John Arnone; Costumes, Susan Hilferty; Lighting, Howell Binkley; Video, Batwin + Robin; Sound, Steve Canyon Kennedy; Hairstylist, David H. Lawrence; Cast Recording, RCA Victor; Company Manager, Marcia Goldberg; Stage Managers, Frank Hartenstein, Diane DiVita; Presented by Dodger Productions, Kardana Productions, John F. Kennedy Center for the Performing Arts; and the Nederlander Organization; Press, Chris Boneau/Adrian Bryan-Brown, John Barlow, Susanne Tighe; Previewed from Thursday, March 9, 1995; Opened in the Richard Rodgers Theatre on Thursday, March 23, 1995*

CAST

Voice of the Narrator	Walter Cronkite
J. Pierpont Finch	Matthew Broderick +1
Milt Gatch	Tom Flynn
Jenkins	Jay Aubrey Jones
Davis	John MacInnis
Bert Bratt	Jonathan Freeman
Tackaberry	Martin Moran
J.B. Biggley	Ronn Carroll +2
Rosemary Pilkington	Megan Mullally +3
Smitty	Victoria Clark
Bud Frump	Jeff Blumenkrantz +4
Miss Krumholtz	Kristi Lynes
Office Boy/Ovington/TV Announcer	John Bolton
Security Guard	Kevin Bogue
Henchmen	Jack Hayes, Jerome Vivona
Miss Jones	Lillias White
Twimble	Gerry Vichi
Hedy La Rue	Luba Mason
Toynbee	Tom Flynn
Scrubwomen	Rebecca Holt, Carla Renata Williams
Dance Soloist	Susan Misner

Wickets and Wickettes ....Kevin Bogue, Maria Calabrese, Jack .....Hayes, JoAnn M. Hunter, Kristi Lynes, Susan Misner, Jerome Vivona, Carla ....Renata Williams
Wally Womper ....Gerry Vichi
Ensemble...Kevin Bogue, John Bolton, Maria .Calabrese, Tom Flynn, Jack Hayes, Rebecca Holt, JoAnn M. Hunter, Jay Aubrey Jones, Kristi Lynes, John MacInnis, Susan Misner, Martin Moran, Jerome Vivona, Carla Renata Williams

UNDERSTUDIES: Martin Moran (Finch), John Bolton (Finch), Randl Ask (Finch/Frump), Jay Aubrey Jones (Twimble/Womper), Tom Flynn (Bratt), Carla Renata Williams (Smitty/Miss Jones), Pamela Gold, Rebecca Holt (Hedy), Kristi Lynes (Rosemary), William Ryall (Biggley)
SWINGS: Jeffry Denman, Tom Flagg, Pamela Gold, Jerold Goldstein, Andrew Palermo, Jennifer Prescott

MUSICAL NUMBERS: Overture, How to Succeed, Happy to Keep His Dinner Warm, Coffee Break, The Company Way, A Secretary Is Not a Toy, Been a Long Day, Grand Old Ivy, Paris Original, Rosemary, Entr'acte, Love from a Heart of Gold, I Believe in You, Pirate Dance, Brotherhood of Man, Finale

A new production of the 1961 musical in two acts. The action takes place at the World Wide Wicket Company in NYC, 1961. For original Broadway production with Robert Morse and Rudy Vallee see *Theatre World* Vol. 18.

*Closed July 14, 1996 after 548 performances and 16 previews.

+Succeeded by: 1. Martin Moran (during vacation), John Stamos, Matthew Broderick 2. William Ryall 3. Jessica Stone, Sarah Jessica Parker 4. Brooks Ashmanskas 4.Tina Fabrique

Joan Marcus Photos

LES MISERABLES

By Alain Boublil and Claude-Michel Schonberg; Based on the novel by Victor Hugo; Music, Mr. Schonberg; Lyrics, Herbert Kretzmer; Original French Text, Mr. Boublil and Jean-Marc Natel; Additional Material, James Fenton; Direction/Adaptation, Trevor Nunn and John Caird; Orchestral Score, John Cameron; Musical Supervisor, Robert Billig; Musical Director, Tom Helm; Design, John Napier; Lighting, David Hersey; Costumes, Andreane Neofitou; Casting, Johnson-Liff & Zerman; Original Cast Recording, Geffen; General Manager, Alan Wasser; Company Manager, Robert Nolan; Stage Managers, Marybeth Abel, Mary Fran Loftus, Brent Peterson; Executive Producer, Martin McCallum; Presented by Cameron Mackintosh; Press, Marc Thibodeau/Merle Frimark; Previewed from Saturday, February 28; Opened in the Broadway Theatre on Thursday, March 12, 1987* and moved to the Imperial Theatre on October 16, 1990.

CAST

PROLOGUE: Donn Cook +1(Jean Valjean), Merwin Ford +2 (Javert), J.C. Sheets, Joel Robertson, Tom Zemon, Kipp Marcus, Richard Vida, Drew Eshelman, Ron Bohmer, John Cudia, Tom Donohue (Chain Gang), Bryan Landrine (Farmer), Mr. Vida (Labourer), Lucille DeCristofaro (Innkeeper's Wife), Gary Lynch (Innkeeper), Kevin McGuire (Bishop), Marsh Hanson, Paul Avedidian (Constables)

MONTREUIL-SUR-MER 1823: Paige O'Hara +3 (Fantine), Mr. Robertson (Foreman), Mr. Landrine, Mr. Marcus (Workers), Liz McCartney, Jessica Sheridan, Madeleine Doherty, Kristen Behrendt (Women Workers), Audrey Klinger (Factory Girl), Mr. Cudia, Mr. Sheets, Mr. Marcus (Sailors), Ms. DeCristofaro, Ms. Doherty, Ms. Behrendt, Tamara Hayden, Audrey Klinger, Jessica-Snow Wilson, Dana Meller, Tammy Jacobs (Whores), Ms. McCartney (Old Woman), Ms. Sheridan (Crone), Kevin McGuire (Pimp/Fauchelevent), Mr. Sheets (Bamatabois)

MONTFERMEIL 1823: Lea Michele, Crysta Macalush, Kimberly Hannon (Young Cosette/Young Eponine), Gina Ferrall(Mme. Thenardier), Drew Eshelman (Thenardier), Mr. Landrine (Drinker), Mr. Vida, Ms. Jacobs (Young Couple), Mr. Lynch (Drunk), Paul Avedisian, Ms. Doherty (Diners), Mr. McGuire, Mr. Zemon, Mr. Sheets, Ms. McCartney, Ms. DeCristofaro (Drinkers), Mr. Cudia (Young Man), Ms. Behrendt, Ms. Meller (Young Girls), Ms. Sheridan, Mr. Marcus (Old Couple), Mr. Robertson, Mr. Hanson (Travelers)

PARIS 1832: Simon Pearl, Michael Zeidman (Gavroche), Ms. DeCristofaro (Beggar Woman), Ms. Klinger (Young Prostitute), Mr. Lynch (Pimp), Jessica Snow-Wilson +4 (Eponine), Mr. Vida (Montparnasse), Mr. Hanson (Babet), Mr. Sheets (Brujon), Mr. McGuire (Claquesous), Ron Bohmer +5 (Enjolras), Craig Rubano +6 (Marius), Tamra Hayden (Cosette), Mr. Robertson (Combeferre), Mr. Cudia (Feuilly), Mr. Landrine (Courfeyrac), Mr. Marcus (Joly), Mr. Zemon (Grantaire), Mr. Avedisian (Lesgles), Mr. Lynch (Jean Prouvaire)

UNDERSTUDIES: Joel Robertson, Bryan Landrine, Nicholas F. Saverine, Dave Clemmons (Valjean), Gary Lynch, Michael X. Martin (Javert), Paul Avedisian, Joseph Kolinski, Wayne Scherzer (Bishop), Jean Fitzgibbons, Kerrianne Spellman (Fantine), Ken Krugman, Mr. Saverine (Thenardier), Ms. Fitzgibbons, Nicola Boyer (Mme. Thenardier), Jessica Snow-Wilson, Jodie Langel (Eponine/Cosette), Tom Donoghue, Matt McClanahan (Marius), Mr. Avedisian, Michael Berry (Enjolras), Lacey Chabert (Gavroche) SWINGS: Christa Justus, Joseph Kolinski, Wayne Scherzer, Kerrianne Spellman

MUSICAL NUMBERS: Prologue, Soliloquy, At the End of the Day, I Dreamed a Dream, Lovely Ladies, Who Am I?, Come to Me, Castle on a Cloud, Master of the House, Thenardier Waltz, Look Down, Stars, Red and Black, Do You Hear the People Sing?, In My Life, A Heart Full of Love, One Day More, On My Own, A Little Fall of Rain, Drink with Me to Days Gone By, Bring Him Home, Dog Eats Dog, Soliloquy, Turning, Empty Chairs at Empty Tables, Wedding Chorale, Beggars at the Feast, Finale

A dramatic musical in two acts with four scenes and prologue.

Frederick C. Inkley, David Masenheimer

Melba Moore

*Still playing May 31, 1996. The production began its tenth year on Broadway during the season. Winner of 1987 "Tonys" for Best Musical, Best Score, Best Book, Best Featured Actor and Actress in a Musical (Michael Maguire, Frances Ruffelle), Direction of a Musical, Scenic Design and Lighting.

+ Succeeded by: 1. Frederick C. Inkey, Craig Schulman 2. David Masenheimer 3. Jacqueline Piro, Melba Moore, Susie McMonagle 4. Christina Michelle Riggs 5. Gary Mauer 6. Tom Donohue, Ricky Martin

Joan Marcus Photos

71

MISS SAIGON

Music, Claude-Michel Schonberg; Lyrics, Richard Maltby, Jr., Alain Boublil; Adapted from Boublil's French Lyrics; Book, Mr. Boublil, Mr. Schonberg; Additional Material, Mr. Maltby, Jr.; Director, Nicholas Hytner; Musical Staging, Bob Avian; Orchestrations, William D. Brohn; Musical Supervisors, David Caddick, Robert Billig; Associate Director, Mitchell Lemsky; Design, John Napier; Lighting, David Hersey; Costumes, Andreane Neofitou, Suzy Benzinger; Sound, Andrew Bruce; Conductor, Edward G. Robinson; Stage Managers, Tom Capps, Sherry Cohen, Beerly Jenkins; Cast Recording (London), Geffen; Presented by Cameron Mackintosh; Press, Marc Thibodeau/Merle Frimark~Erin Dunn; Previewed from Saturday, March 23, 1991; Opened in the Broadway Theatre on Thursday, April 11, 1991*

CAST

SAIGON - 1975
The Engineer ....Raul Aranas +1
Kim..Joan Almedilla, Roxanne Taga
Gigi ....Imelda De Los Reyes
Mimi ....Zoie Lam
Yvette ....Chloe Stewart
Yvonne ....Mirla Criste
Bar Girls ....Margaret Ann Gates, Ai Goeku, Emily Hsu,
....Elizabeth Paw, Roxanne Taga
Chris..Eric Kunze +2
John..Norm Lewis
Marines ....Donnell Aarone, Erik Bates, Robert Bartley, C.C.
....Brown, Jay Douglas, Leonard Joseph, Norman Kauahi, Howard Kaye,
Kevin Neil ....McCready, Matthew Pedersen, Jeff Reid, Robert Weber,
....Welly Yang
Barmen..........................Zar Acayan, Alan Ariano, Eric Chang, Ming Lee
Vietnamese Customers...Tito Abeleda, Francis J. Cruz, Darrell Autor, Jim
....Harrison, Juan P. Pineda, Ray Santos
Army Nurse..Heidi Meyer
Thuy ....Yancey Arias
Embassy Workers, Vendors, etc...Company
HO CHI MINH CITY (Formerly Saigon)-April 1978
Ellen ....Misty Cotton
Tam..Melanie Carabuena, Justin Lee Wong
Guards ....Mr. Cruz, Mr. Pineda
Dragon Acrobats ....Mr. Autor, Mr. Harrison, Mr. Weber
Asst. Commissar..Mr. Yang
Soldiers......Mr. Abeleda, Mr. Acayan, Mr. Ariano, Mr. Kauahi,Mr. Santos
Citizens, Refugees ....Company
USA - September 1978
Conference Delegates ....Company
BANGKOK - October 1978
Hustlers .....Mr. Acayan, Mr. Harrison, Mr. Kauahi, Mr. Santos, Mr. Yang
Moulin Rouge Owner ....Mr. Cruz
Inhabitants, Bar Girls, Vendors, Tourists....................................Company
SAIGON - April 1975
Shultz ....Howard Kaye
Doc ....Erik Bates
Reeves ....C.C. Brown
Gibbons ....Kevin Neal McCready
Troy ....Leonard Joseph
Nolen ....Donnell Aarone
Huston ....Matthew Pederson
Frye ....Jay Douglas
Marines, Vietnamese..Company
BANGKOK - October 1978
Inhabitants, Moulin Rouge Customers ....Company

UNDERSTUDIES: Norman Kauahi, Ming Lee, Ray Santos (Engineer), Imelda de los Reyes, Elizabeth Paw, Chloe Stewart, Roxanne Taga (Kim), Erik Bates, Robert Bartley, Jay Douglas (Chris), Donnell Aarone, C.C. Brown, Leonard Joseph (John), Heidi Meyer (Ellen), Zar Acayan, Jim Harrison, Marc Oka, Juan P. Pineda, Welly Yang (Thuy) SWINGS: Eric Chan, Sylvia Dohi, Frank J. Maio, Marc Oka, Fay Rusli, Jeff Siebert

Raul Aranas

MUSICAL NUMBERS: The Heat is on in Saigon, Movie in My Mind, The Transaction, Why God Why?, Sun and Moon, The Telephone, The Cere-mony, Last Night of the World, Morning of the Dragon, I Still Believe, Back in Town, You Will Not Touch Him, If You Want to Die in Bed, I'd Give My Life for You, Bui-Doi, What a Waste, Please, Guilt Inside Your Head, Room 317, Now That I've Seen Her, Confrontation, The American Dream, Little God of My Heart

A musical in two acts. The action takes place in Saigon, Bangkok, and the USA between 1975-79.

*Still playing May 31, 1996. The production passed the 2000 performance mark during the season. Winner of 1991 "Tonys" for Leading Actor in a Musical (Jonathan Pryce), Leading Actress in a Musical (Lea Salonga) and Featured Actor in a Musical (Hinton Battle).

+ Succeeded by: 1. Luoyong 2. Tyley Ross

Joan Marcus Photos

THE PHANTOM OF THE OPERA

Music, Andrew Lloyd Webber; Lyrics, Charles Hart; Additional Lyrics, Richard Stilgoe; Book, Mr. Stilgoe, Mr. Lloyd Webber; Director, Harold Prince; Musical Staging/Choreography, Gillian Lynne; Orchestrations, David Cullen, Mr. Lloyd Webber; Based on the novel by Gaston Leroux; Design, Maria Bjornson; Lighting, Andrew Bridge; Sound, Martin Levan; Musical Direction/Supervision, David Caddick; Conductor, Jack Gaughan; Cast Recording (London), Polygram/Polydor; Casting, Johnson-Liff & Zerman; General Manager, Alan Wasser; Company Manager, Michael Gill; Stage Managers, Steve McCorkle, Bethe Ward, Richard Hester, Barbara-Mae Phillips; Presented by Cameron Mackintosh and The Really Useful Theatre Co.; Press, Merle Frimark, Marc Thibodeau; Previewed from Saturday, January 9, 1988; Opened in the Majestic Theatre on Tuesday, January 26, 1988*

CAST

The Phantom of the Opera	Davis Gaines
Christine Daae	Tracy Shayne
	Laurie Gayle Stephenson, Teri Bibb (alternates)
Raoul, Vicomte de Chagny	Brad Little
Carlotta Giudicelli	Elena Jeanne Batman
Monsieur Andre	Jeff Keller
Monsieur Firmin	George Lee Andrews
Madame Giry	Leila Martin
Ubaldo Piangi	Frederic Heringes
Meg Giry	Tener Brown
M. Rever	Thomas James O'Leary
Auctioneer	Richard Warren Pugh
Porter/Marksman	Gary Lindemann
M. Lefevre	Kenneth Waller
Joseph Buquet	Philip Steele
Don Attilio/Passarino	Peter Atherton
Slave Master/Solo Dancer	Thomas Terry
Flunky/Stagehand	Jack Hayes
Policeman	Thomas Sandri
Page	Patrice Pickering
Porter/Fireman	Maurizio Corbino
Spanish Lady	Marci DeGonge-Manfredi
Wardrobe Mistress/Confidante	Mary Leigh Stahl
Princess	Raissa Katona
Madame Firmin	Melody Johnson
Innkeeper's Wife	Teresa Eldh

Ballet Chorus of the Opera Populaire..Harriet M. Clark, Alina Hernandez, ...Cherylyn Jones, Lori MacPherson, Tania Philip, Kate Solmssen, Christine Spizzo

UNDERSTUDIES: Jeff Keller, (Phantom), Raissa Katona, Laurie Gayle Stephenson (Christine), Gary Lindemann, James Romick (Raoul), Peter Atherton, Paul Laureano (Firmin), Richard Warren Pugh (Firmin/Piangi), George Lee Andrews, James Thomas O'Leary,Mr. Romick (Andre), Marcy DeGonge-Manfredi, Teresa Eldh, Melody Johnson (Carlotta), Patrice Pickering, Mary Leigh Stahl (Giry), Maurizio Corbino (Piangi), Cherilyn Jones, Kate Solmssen, Lori MacPherson (Meg), Thomas Terry (Master) Paul B. Sadler, Jr. (Dancer)

MUSICAL NUMBERS: Think of Me, Angel of Music, Little Lotte/The Mirror, Phantom of the Opera, Music of the Night, I Remember/Stranger Than You Dreamt It, Magical Lasso, Notes/Prima Donna, Poor Fool He Makes Me Laugh, Why Have You Brought Me Here?/ Raoul I've Been There, All I Ask of You, Masquerade/Why So Silent?, Twisted Every Way, Wishing You Were Somehow Here Again, Wandering Child/Bravo Bravo, Point of No Return, Down Once More/Track Down This Murderer, Finale

A musical in two acts with nineteen scenes and a prologue. The action takes place in and around the Paris Opera house, 1881-1911.

*Still playing May 31, 1996. Winner of 1988 "Tonys" for Best Musical, Leading Actor in a Musical (Michael Crawford), Featured Actress in a Musical (Judy Kaye), Direction of a Musical, Scenic Design and Lighting. The title role has been played by Michael Crawford, Timothy Nolen, Cris Groendaal, Steve Barton, Jeff Keller, Kevin Gray, Marc Jacoby and Marcus Lovett and Davis Gaines.

Joan Marcus/Clive Barda Photos

Davis Gaines and Tracy Shayne

Cast of *The Phantom of the Opera*

SHOW BOAT

Music, Jerome Kern; Lyrics/Book, Oscar HammersteinII; Based on the novel by Edna Ferber; Director, Harold Prince; Choreography, Susan Stroman; Orchestrations, (original) Robert Russell Bennett, (new) William David Brohn; Musical Supervisor, Jeffrey Huard; Design, Eugene Lee; Costumes, Florence Klotz; Lighting, Richard Pilbrow; Sound, Martin Levan; Dance Music Arrangements, David Krane; Mr. Prince's Assistant, Ruth Mitchell; Cast Recording, Livent Music; General Manager, Frank P. Scardino; Company Manager, Jim Brandeberry; Stage Managers, Randall Buck, Betsy Nicholson; Presented by Livent (U.S.); Press, Mary Bryant/Wayne Wolfe; Previewed from Thursday, Sept.22; Opened in the Gershwin Theatre on Sunday, October 2, 1994*

CAST

Steve	Doug LaBrecque +1
Queenie	Gretha Boston
Pete	David Bryant
Parthy	Elaine Stritch +2
Windy	Ralph Williams
Cap'n Andy	John McMartin +3
Ellie	Dorothy Stanley +4
Frank	Joel Blum
Julie	Lonette McKee +5
Gaylord Ravenal	Mark Jacoby +6
Vallon	Jack Dabdoub
Magnolia	Rebecca Luker +7
Joe	Michel Bell +8
Dealer/Jake	Bob Walton
Balcony Soloist	Lorna Hampson
Jeb	David Earl Hart
Backwoodsman/Jim	Michael O'Carroll
Young Kim	Larissa Auble
Ethel	Danielle Greaves
Landlady	Lorraine Foreman
Mother Superior/Old Lady(on the Levee)	Sheila Smith
Charlie/Radio Announcer	Michael Scott
Lottie	Louise-Marie Mennier
Dottie	Karen Curlee
Drunk	David Bryant
Fan (on the Levee)	Kim Lindsay
Kim	Tammy Anderson

ENSEMBLE: Van Abrahams, Timothy Albrecht, Derin Altay, Kevin Bagby, hal Beasley, Timothy Robert Blevens, David Bryant, Joseph Cassidy, Roosevelt Andre Credit, Karen Curlee, Jack Dabdoub, Debbie de Coudreaux, Steve Elmore, Lorraine Foreman, Jose Garcia, Ron Gibbs, Steve Girardi, Danielle Greaves, Jeff Hairston, Lorna Hampson, Linda Hardwick, Pamela Harley, David Earl Hart, Richard L. Hobson, Edwin Hodge, Michael LaFleche, Karen Lifshey, Kim Lindsay, Jesse Means II, Louise-Marie Mennier, Kiri-Lyn Muir, Panchali Null, Mike O'Carroll, Amy Jo Phillips, Catherine Pollard, Jimmy Rivers, Michael Scott, Jill Slyter, Bob Walton, Laurie Walton, Cheryl Warfield, Jo Ann Hawkins White, Dathan B. Williams, Gay Willis, Lionel Woods, Darlene B. Young
SWINGS: Dennis Daniels, David Dannehl, Tari Kelly, Ritchie McCall, Kimberley Michaels, Louise St. Cyr
CHILDREN: Larissa Auble, Kimberly Jean Brown, Joran Corneal, Edwin Hodge, Imani Parks
STANDBYS/UNDERSTUDIES: Sheila Smith (Parthy), Ralph Williams (Cap'n Andy), Andre Solomon-Glover (Joe), Mike O'Carroll (Cap'n Andy), Lorraine Foreman (Parthy/Mother Superior/Old Lady), Kim Lindsay, Gay Willis (Magnolia), Doug LaBrecque, Joseph Cassidy (Ravenal), Derin Altay, Debbie de Coudreaux (Julie), Pamela Harley, Jo Ann Hawkins White (Queenie), Richard L. Hobson, Jose Garcia (Joe), Michael Scott (Steve/Backwoods/Vallon/Jim), David Earl Hart (Steve/Windy/Pete/Drunk), Bob Walton, Steve Girardi, Ronn Gibbs (Frank), Karen Curlee, Tari Kelly (Ellie), Kiri-Lyn Muir, Karen Lifshey (Kim), Kimberly Jean Brown (young Kim), David Dannehl (Windy/Pete/Backwoods/Vallon/Jim/Jake/Jeb/Dealer/Charlie/Drunk), Dennis Daniels (Jake/Jeb/Dealer/Charlie), Kimberley Michaels, Louise St. Cyr (Ethel), Panchali Null (Landlady/Mother Superior/Old Lady), Laurie Walton, Tari Kelly (Lottie/Dottie)

Carole Shelley, John Cullum

Sarah Pfisterer, Hugh Panaro

MUSICAL NUMBERS: Overture, Cottton Blossom, Cap'n Andy's Ballyhoo, Where's the Mate for Me?, Make Believe, Ol' Man River, Can't Help Lovin' Dat Man, Till Good Luck Comes My Way, Mis'ry's Comin' Aroun', I Have the Room Above Her, Life Upon the Wicked Stage, Queenie's Ballyhoo, You Are Love, Wedding Celebration, Why Do I Love You?, Dandies on Parade, Alma Redemption Mater, Bill, Goodbye My Lady Love, After the Ball, Dance Away the Night, Kim's Charleston, Final

A new production of the 1927 musical in two acts. The action takes place along the Mississippi River and in Chicago, 1887-1927. This production uses material from previous revivals and film adaptations in addition to the 1927 original.

*Closed January 5, 1997

+Succeeded by: 1. Fred Love 2. Carole Shelley 3. John Cullum 4. Beth Leavel 5. Marilyn McCoo, Lonette McKee 6. Hugh Panaro 7. Sarah Pfisterer 8. Andre Solomon Glover

Catherine Ashmore, Michael Cooper Photos

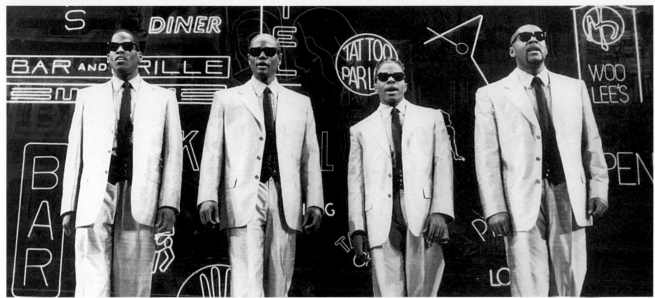

SMOKEY JOE'S CAFE

Adrian Bailey, Ken Ard, Victor Trent Cook, Frederick B. Owens

Music/Lyrics, Jerry Leiber and Mike Stoller; Director, Jerry Zaks; Musical Staging, Joey McKneely; Orchestrations, Steve Margoshes; Conductor/Arranger, Louis St. Louis; Music Coordinator, John Miller; Sets, Heidi Landesman; Costumes, William Ivey Long; Lighting, Timothy Hunter; Sound, Tony Meola; Hair/Make-up, Randy Houston Mercer; Production Supervisor, Steven Beckler; Production Manager, Peter Fulbright; Original Concept, Stephen Helper, Jack Viertel; Cast Recording, Atlantic; General Management, Richard Frankel; Company Manager, Laura Green; Stage Managers, Kenneth Hanson, Maximo Torres; Presented by Richard Frankel, Thomas Viertel, Steven Baruch, Jujamcyn Theatres/Jack Viertel, Rick Steiner, Frederic H. Mayerson and Center Theatre Group/Ahmanson/Gordon Davidson; Press, Chris Boneau/Adrian Bryan-Brown, Jackie Green, Patty Onagan, Meredith Moore, Ari Cohn, Scott Walton; Previewed from Wednesday, February 8; Opened in the Virginia Theatre on Thursday, March 2, 1995*

CAST

Ken Ard	Adrian Bailey
	Brenda Braxton
Victor Trent Cook	B.J. Crosby
	Pattie Darcy Jones
DeLee Lively	Frederick B. Owens
	Michael Park

STANDBYS· Bobby Daye, April Nixon, Kevyn Morrow, Monica Page

MUSICAL NUMBERS: Neighborhood, Young Blood, Falling, Ruby baby, Dance with Me, Keep on Rollin', Searchin', Kansas City, Trouble, Love Me/Don't, Fools Fall in Love, Poison Ivy, Don Juan, Shoppin' for Clothes, I Keep Forgettin', On Broadway, D.W. Washburn, Saved, That is Rock & Roll, Yakety Yak, Charlie Brown, Stay a While, Pearl's a Singer, Teach Me How to Shimmy, You're the Boss, Smokey Joe's Cafe, Loving You, Treat Me Nice, Hound Dog, Little Egypt, I'm a Woman, There Goes My baby, Love Potion #9, Some Cats Know, Jailhouse Rock, Fools Fall in Love, Spanish Harlem, I Who Have Nothing, Stand By Me, Finale

A musical revue in two acts.

*Still playing May 31, 1996.

Joan Marcus Photos

Brenda Braxton, B. J. Crosby, DeLee Lively, Pattie Darcy Jones

SUNSET BLVD.

Betty Buckley

John Barrowman

Music, Andrew Lloyd Webber; Lyrics/Book, Don Black and Christopher Hampton; Based on the 1950 Billy Wilder film; Director, Trevor Nunn; Musical Staging, Bob Avian; Orchestrations, David Cullen, Lloyd Webber; Musical Supervision, David Caddick; Musical Director, Paul Bogaev; Design, John Napier; Costumes, Anthony Powell; Lighting, Andrew Bridge; Sound, Martin Levan; Cast Recording, Polydor; Production Supervisor, Peter Lawrence; Technical, Peter Feller, Arthur Siccardi; General Manager, Nina Lannan; Company Manager, Abbie M. Strassler; Stage Managers, Peter Lawrence, John Brigleb, Jim Woolley, Lynda J. Fox; Presented by The Really Useful Company; Press, Chris Boneau/Adrian Bryan-Brown/John Barlow; Previewed from Tuesday, November 1; Opened in the Minskoff Theatre on Thursday, November 17, 1994*

CAST

Norma Desmond	Betty Buckley
Joe Gillis	Alan Campbell +1
Max von Mayerling	George Hearn
Betty Schaefer	Alice Ripley
Cecil B. DeMille	Alan Oppenheimer
Artie Green	Vincent Tumeo
Harem Girl/Beautician	Sandra Allen
Young Writer/Salesman/DeMilles's Asst.	Bryan Batt
Heather/2nd Masseuse	Susan Dawn Carson
Cliff/Salesman/Young Guard	Matthew Dickens
Jean/Beautician/Hedy Lamarr	Colleen Dunn
Morino/Salesman/Hog Eye	Steven Stein-Grainer
Lisa/Doctor	Kim Huber
1st Financeman/Film Actor/Salesman	Rich Herbert
Katherine/Psychiatrist	Alicia Irving
Harem Girl/Beautician	Lada Boder
Mary/1st Masseuse	Lauren Kennedy
Sheldrake/Police Chief	Sal Mistretta
John/alesman/Victor Mature	Mark Morales
Myron/Manfred	Rick Podell
Financeman/Salesman/Party Guest	Tom Alan Robbins
Jonesy/Sammy/Salesman	David Eric
Choreographer/Salesman	Rick Sparks
Joanna/Astrologer	Wendy Walter

STANDBYS/UNDERSTUDIES: Karen Mason (Norma), Susan Dawn Carson (Norma), Bryan Batt, Matthew Dickens (Joe), Kim Huber, Lauren Kennedy (Betty), Steven Stein-Grainger(DeMille), David Eric (De-Mille/Sheldrake), Matthew Dickens, Darrin Baker, Harvey Evans (Writer/Salesman/Asst./Cliff/Morino/Hog Eye/Financeman/Film Actor/Police/John/Sammy/Jonesy/Choreographer), Darrin Baker (Artie), Rosemary Loar, Darlene Wilson (Harem Girls, Beauticians/Lisa/Doctor/Heather/Masseuses/Hedy/Joanna/Astrologer/Katherine/Psychiatrist/Mary)

MUSICAL NUMBERS: Overture, Prologue, Let's Have Lunch, Surrender, With One Look, Salome, The Greatest Star of All, Every Movie's a Circus, Girl Meets Boy, New Ways to Dream, The Lady's Paying, The Perfect Year, This Time Next Year, Sunset Boulevard, As If We Never Said Goodbye, Eternal Youth Is Worth a Little Suffering, Too Much in Love to Care, Finale

A musical in two acts. The action takes place in Los Angeles, 1949-50.

*Closed March 22, 1997 after 977 performances and 17 previews.

+Succeeded by: 1. John Barrowman

Francesco Scavullo Photos

OFF-BROADWAY PRODUCTIONS FROM PAST SEASONS

THE FANTASTICKS

Music, Harvey Schmidt; Lyrics/Book, Tom Jones; Director, Word Baker; Original Musical Director/Arrangements, Julian Stein; Design, Ed Wittstein; Musical Director, Dorothy Martin; Stage Managers, Kim Moore, James Cook, Steven Michael Daly, Christopher Scott; Presented by Lore Noto; Associate Producers, Sheldon Baron, Dorothy Olim, Jules Field, Cast Recording, MGM/Polydor; Opened in the Sullivan Street Playhouse on Tuesday, May 3, 1960*

CAST

The Boy	Josh Miller +1
The Girl	Lisa Mayer +2
The Girl's Father	William Tost
The Boy's Father	Gordon G. Jones
Narrator/El Gallo	Robert Vincent Smith +3
Mute	Paul Blankenship
Old Actor	Bryan Hull
Man Who Dies	Joel Bernstein

UNDERSTUDIES: Paul Blankenship (Boy), Jill Colgan (Girl), William Tost, Gordon G. Jones (Both Fathers)

MUSICAL NUMBERS: Overture, Try to Remember, Much More, Metaphor, Never Say No, It Depends on What You Pay, Soon It's Gonna Rain, Abduction Ballet, Happy Ending, This Plumb is Too Ripe, I Can See It, Plant a Radish, Round and Round, They Were You, Finale

A musical in two acts suggested by *Les Romanesques* by Edmond Rostand.

*Still playing May 31, 1996. The world's longest running musical.

+Succeeded by: 1. Darren Romeo, Eric Meyersfield 2. Jennifer Westfeldt, Christine Long 3. John Savarese

(Chuck Pulin Photo)

Cast of *The Fantasticks*

Grandma Sylvia's Funeral

GRANDMA SYLVIA'S FUNERAL

Conceived by Glenn Wein and Amy Lord Blumsack; Created by Wein, Blumsack and the original company; Director, Mr. Wein; Design, Leon Munier; Lighting, David J. Lander; Costumes, Peter Janis; Choreography, Joanna Rush; Stage Manager, Margaret Bodrighian; Press, John and Gary Springer/Sharon Rothe; Opened at the Playhouse on Vandam on Sunday, October 2, 1994*

CAST

Dave Schildner	Paul Eagle
Rabbi Michael Wolfe	David Ellzey, Bill Kraus
Elise Duey	Holgie Forrester
Jerry Grossman	Ron Gilbert
Dori Grossman	Karen Ginsburg
Marlena Weiss Grossman	Sheri Goldner
Helen Krantz	Sondra Gorney
Ava Gerard	Brooke Johnson
Mark Grossman	Marc Kamhi
Vlad Helsenrott	Morgan Lavere
Dr. Rachel Rosenbaum	Simone Lazer
Melinda Franklin	Janice Mautner
Dr. Byron Franklin	Brocton Pierce
Sky Boy/Stuart Grossman	David Eric Rosenberg
Natalie Chasen	Joanna Rush
Fredo Iannuzzi	Tom Darpi
Harvey Grossman	Stanley Allan Sherman
Helga Helsenrott	Helen Siff
Rita Iannuzzi	Justine Slater
Gary Grossman	Glenn Wein
Todd Grossman	Barry Weinberger

A theatrical funeral in two acts. The action takes place at the Helsenrott Jewish Mortuary and includes a "mitzvah Meal."

Succeeding Cast Members: Jaid Barrymore, Carol Shaya

*Still Playing May 31, 1996.

PARTY

By David Dillon; Set, James Noone; Costumes, Gail Cooper-Hecht; Lighting, Ken Billington; Sound, Tom Clark; Stage Manager, Bruce Greenwood; Press, Bill Evans/Jim Randolph, Terry M. Lily, Tom D'Ambrosio; Opened in the Douglas Fairbanks Theater on Friday, April 14, 1995*

CAST

Kevin ....David Pevsner +1
Ray ....Ted Bales +2
Philip...Larry Alexander +3
Brian...Kellum Lewis +4
Peter ....Tom Stuart +5
James...Jay Corcoran
Andy ....Vince Gatton +6

A New York-set comedy involving a truth-or-dare game in which everyone ends up naked.

*Closed March 24, 1996 after 342 performances and 31 previews,

+Succeeded by: 1. Marc Wolf 2. Craig Dawson 3. Tom Humphreys 4. Tony Meindl 5. Achilles Tsakirdis 6. Jason Mauro

Nigel Teare Photo

Catherine Russell in *Perfect Crime*

Achilles Tsakirdis, Tom Humphreys, Jason Mauro, Craig Dawson, David Pevsner, Tony Meindl, Jay Corcoran in *Party*

PERFECT CRIME

By Warren Manzi; Director, Jeffrey Hyatt; Set, Jay Stone; Costumes, Nancy Bush; Lighting, Jeff Fontaine; Sound, David Lawson; Stage Manager, Joseph Millett; Presented by The Actors Collective in association with the Methuen Company; Press, Michelle Vinvents, Paul Lewis, Jeffrey Clarke; Opened in the Courtyard Playhouse on April 18, 1987* and later transferred to the Second Stage, 47th St. Playhouse, Intar, Harold Clurman Theatre, Theatre Four, and currently The Duffy Theatre.

CAST

Margaret Thorne Brent ....Catherine Russell
Inspector James Ascher ....Gene Terinoni
W. Harrison Brent..David Butler
Lionel McAuley...J. A. Nelson
David Breuer..Dean Gardner

UNDERSTUDIES: Lauren Lovett (Females), J. R. Robinson (Males)

A mystery in two acts. The action takes place in Windsor Locks, Connecticut.

*Still playing May 31, 1996.

STOMP

Created/Directed by Luke Cresswell and Steve McNicholas; Lighting, Mr. McNicholas, Neil Tiplady; Production Manager, Pete Donno; General Management, Richard Frankel/Marc Routh; Presented by Columbia Artists Management, Harriet Newman Leve, James D. Stren, Morton Wolkowitz, Schuster/Maxwell, Galin/Sandler, and Markley/Manocherian; Press, Chris Boneau/Adrian Bryan-Brown, Jackie Green, Bob Fennell; Previewed from Friday, February 18, 1994; Opened in the Orpheum Theatre on Sunday, February 27, 1994*

CAST

Luke Cresswell ....Nick Dwyer
Sarah Eddy ....Theseus Gerard

Fraser Morrison..David Olrod
Carl Smith ....Fiona Wilkes
SWINGS: Everett Bradley, Allison Easter

An evening of percussive performance art. The ensemble uses everything but conventional percussion to make rhythm and dance.

*Still playing May 31, 1996.

(Stuart Morris, Steve McNicholas Photos)

Luke Cresswell, Theseus Gerard in *Stomp*

TONY N' TINA'S WEDDING

By Artificial Intelligence; Conception, Nancy Cassaro (Artistic Director); Director, Larry Pellegrini; Supervisory Director, Julie Cesari; Musical Director, Lynn Portas; Choreography, Hal Simons; Design/Decor, Randall Thropp; Costumes/Hairstyles/Makeup, Juan DeArmas; General Manager, Leonard A. Mulhern; Company Manager, James Hannah; Stage Managers, Bernadette McGay, W. Bart Ebbink; Presented by Joseph Corcoran & Daniel Cocoran; Press, David Rothenberg/Terence Womble; Opened in the Washington Square Church & Carmelita's on Saturday, February 6, 1988*

CAST

Valentia Lynne Nunzio, the bride ....Justine Rossi
Anthony Angelo Nunzio, the groom ....
....Tony Meola
Connie Mocogni, maid of honor ....Susan Laurenzi
Barry Wheeler, best man ....Timothy Monagan
Donna Marsala, bridesmaid ....Susan Campanero
Dominick Fabrizzi, usher ....Joseph Barbara
Marina Gulino, bridesmaid ....Cheryl Giuliano
Johnny Nunzio, usher/brother of groom..........................Nick Gambella
Josephine Vitale, mother of the bride ....Victoria Barone
Joseph Vitale, brother of the bride ....Richard Falzone
Luigi Domenico, great uncle of the bride ....Stan Winston
Rose Domenico, aunt of the bride.......................................Cayte Thorpe
Sister Albert Maria, cousin of bride ....Fran Gennuso
Anthony Angelo Nunzio, Sr., father of groom ....Dan Grimaldi
Madeline Monroe, Mr. Nunzio's girlfriend...........................Karen Cellini
Grandma Nunzio, grandmother to groom...........................Elaine Unnold
Michael Just, Tina's ex-boyfriend ....Anthony T. Lauria
Father Mark, parish priest ....Gary Schneider
Vinnie Black, caterer ....Tom Karlya
Loretta Black, wife of the caterer ....Victoria Constan
Mick Black, brother of the caterer ....Robert R. Oliver
Nikki Black, daughter of the caterer ....Jodi Grant
Mikie Black, son of the caterer ....John Walter
Pat Black, sister of the caterer ....Maria Gentile
Rick Demarco, the video man ....Kerry Logan
Sal Antonucci, the photographer...Tony Patellis

An environmental theatre production. The action takes place at a wedding and reception.

*Still playing May 31, 1996 after moving to St. John's Church and Vinnie Black's Coliseum.

(Blanche Mackey Photo)

Theseus Gerard, Fiona Wilkes in *Stomp*

TUBES

Created and Written by Matt Goldman, Phil Stanton, Chris Wink; Director, Marlene Swartz; Artistic Coordinator; Caryl Glaab; Sets, Kevin Joseph Roach; Lighting, Brian Aldous; Costumes, Lydia Tanji, Patricia Murphy; Sound, Raymond Schilke; Computer Graphics, Kurisu-Chan; Stage Manager, Kevin Cunningham; Press, David Rothenberg; Opened at the Astor Place Theatre on Thursday, November 7, 1991*

CAST

Blue Man Group (Matt Goldman, Phil Stanton, Chris Wink)

An evening with the performance group, performed without intermission.

*Still playing May 31, 1996.

Blue Man Group

PRODUCTION THAT CLOSED– PRIOR TO SCHEDULED BROADWAY PREMIERE

Phillip Huber, Tommy Tune

BUSKER ALLEY

Music/Lyrics, Richard M. Sherman and Robert B. Sherman; Book, A.J.

Carothers; Based on the 1938 British film St. Martin's Lane by Clemence Dane; Director/Choreography, Jeff Calhoun; Musical Director, John McDaniel; Orchestrations, William David Brohn; Sets, Tony Walton; Costumes, Willa Kim; Lighting, Richard Pilbrow; Sound, Brian Ronan; Stage Manager, Mark S. Krause; Presented by Barry and Fran Weissler, Jujamcyn Theatres/TV Asahi in association with PACE Theatrical Group; Press,

Peter Cromarty/Hugh Hayes; Opened in Macauley Theatre in Louisville Kentucky on Friday, April 7, 1995 and closed Sunday, October 8, 1995 at the Tampa Bay Performing Center in Tampa Florida after Tommy Tune broke his left foot.

CAST

Tommy Tune (Charley Baxter), Darcie Roberts (Libby), Brent Barret, Marcia Lewis, Robert Nichols, Lee Mark Nelson, Drew Eliot, Laurie Gamache, Huber Marionettes, David S. Alexander, Michael Arnold, Brad Aspel, Michael Berresse, Philip Huber, Jeffrey James, Regi Jennings, Dennis Jones, Bruse Moore, Paige Price, George Riddle, Mark Santoro,

Abe Sylvia, Richard Vida, David Warren-Gibson

A musical comedy set in London's West End theatre district just before the Second World War. Previously performed under the titles *Stage Door Charley* and *Buskers*

Martha Swope Photo

Tommy Tune

PRODUCTIONS FROM PAST SEASONS THAT CLOSED DURING THIS SEASON

PRODUCTION	OPENED	CLOSED	PERFORMANCES
After-Play	1/10/95	4/28/96	283 (Theatre Four)
			59 & 24 previews MTC
Arcadia	3/30/95	8/27/95	173 & 31 previews
Crazy For You	2/29/92	1/7/96	1,622 & 21 previews
Damn Yankees	3/3/94	8/6/95	510 & 35 previews
Death Defying Acts	2/24/95	2/25/96	407
Hamlet (Ralph Fiennes)	5/2/95	7/22/95	91 & 19 previews
Having Our Say	4/6/95	12/31/95	308 & 24 previews
The Heiress	3/9/95	12/31/95	340 & 31 previews
Indiscretions	4/27/95	11/4/95	220 & 28 previews
Kiss of the Spider Woman	5/3/93	7/2/95	906 & 16 previews
London Suite	3/28/95	9/3/95	169 & 15 previews
Love! Valour! Compassion!	2/14/95	9/17/95	249 & 28 previews Bdwy
			72 & 24 previews MTC
The Only Thing Worse...	3/26/95	9/16/95	175 & 9 previews
Party	4/14/94	3/24/96	342 & 31 previews
The Rose Tattoo	4/30/95	7/2/95	73 & 10 previews
Swingtime Canteen	2/24/95	11/26/95	294
Three Tall Women	1/27/94	8/26/95	582 Promenade
			4 7 Vineyard
The Who's Tommy	4/22/93	6/17/95	899 & 28 previews

John Glover, Randy Becker, Mario Cantone, Justin Kirk, Anthony Heald, John Benjamin Hickey, Stephen Bogardus in
Love! Valour! Compassion!

Charlotte d'Amboise in *Damn Yankees*

Anne Meara, Larry Keith, Merwin Goldsmith,
Barbara Barrie in *After-Play*

AMERICAN JEWISH THEATRE

Twenty-second Season

Artistic Director, Stanley Brechner; Chief Sponser, Raymond J. Greenwald; Counsel, Walter Gidaly; House Manager, Richard Germain; Press, Jeffrey Richards/Scott Karpf, Kevin Rehac, Stephen Sunderlin

Saturday, Nov.4-Dec.3, 1995 (21 performances and 16 previews)
THE WARM-UP by Sammy Shore and Rudy DeLuca; Director, Martin Landau; Set, Kent Hoffman; Sound, Bruce Ellman; Lighting, Herrick Goldman CAST: Sammy Shore (Himself)
A comedy performed without intermission.

Saturday, Jan.6-Feb.25, 1996 (38 performances and 17 previews)
THE YIDDISH TROJAN WOMEN by Carole Braverman; Director, Richard Sabellico; Set, James Wolk; Lighting, Herrick Goldman; Costumes, Gail Baldoni; Sound, Bruce Ellman; Stage Manager, Paul A. Kochman CAST: Laura Esterman (Tess Brodsky), Marilyn Pasekoff (Brenda Brodsky), Lori Wilner (Abigail Brodsky), Joanna Merlin (Devorah Brodsky), Hugh O'Gorman (Luke Harris)
A drama in two acts. The action takes place in Brooklyn, early 1980s.

Lori Wilner, Laura Esterman, Marilyn Passekof
in *Yiddish Trojan Women*

Saturday, March 9-Apr.17, 1996 (26 performances and 9 previews)
WORKING TITLE by Andrew Bergman; Director, Max Mayer; Set, Peter Harrison; Lighting, Jeff Croiter; Costumes, Laura Cunningham; Sound, Aural Fixation; Stage Manager, Julie Hyman CAST: Susan Blackwell (Laura Teichman), David Chandler (Alan Teichman), Jerry Grayson (Bobby Teichman), Stephen O'Reilly (Donnie DiNardo), John Seitz (Harry Crane), Gia Carides (Marie Oldam), Douglas Weston (Sandy Littweiler)
A comedy in two acts. The action takes place at a Long Island beach house.

Saturday, Apr.27-June 23, 1996 (49 performances and 17 previews), transferred July 27, 1996 to American Place Theatre
THE COCOANUTS; Music/Lyrics, Irving Berlin; Book, George S. Kaufman; Director/Choreography, Richard Sabellico; Music Director, Andrew Gerle; Set, Jeff Modereger; Costumes, Jonathan Bixby; Lighting, Herrick Goldman; Stage Manager, Jason Brouillard CAST: Michael Waldron (Jamison), Brad Bradley (Bellboy), Laurie Gamache (Penelope Martyn), Celia Tackaberry (Mrs. Potter), Becky Watson (Polly Potter), Richard Roland (Bob Adams), Kirby Ward (Harvey Yates), Michael McGrath (Henry W. Schlemmer-Groucho), Peter Slutsker (Willie the Shill-Chico), Robert Sapoff (Silent Sam-Harpo), Michael Mulheren (Hennessey)
MUSICAL NUMBERS: Florida by the Sea, The Bellhop, Pack Up Your Sins and Go To the Devil (not in orig.), A Little Bungalow, With a Family Reputation, Lucky Boy, We Should Care, Always(cut from orig.), Five O'Clock Tea, Tango Melody, We Work While You Sleep (not in orig.), When My Dreams Come True (from 1929 film version), Shaking the Blues Away (not in orig.), Tale of a Shirt, Finale
A revised version of a 1925 musical comedy in two acts. The action takes place in Florida.

Gerry Goodstein, Carol Rosegg Photos

Sammy Shore in *The Warm Up*

Right: David Chandler, Gia Canides, John Seitz,
Jerry Grayson *in Working Title*

BROOKLYN ACADEMY OF MUSIC

Chairman, Bruce C. Ratner; President/Executive Producer, Harvey Lichtenstein

(Opera House) Wednesday, June 7-10, 1995 (4 performances)
MADAME SE SADE by Yukio Mishima; Translations, Gunilla Lindberg-Wada, Per Erik Wahlund, Donald Keene; Director, Ingmar Bergman; Sets/Costumes, Charles Koroly; Choreography, Donya Feuer CAST: Stina Ekblad (Renee, Madame de Sade), Anita Bjork (Madame de Montreuil), Elin Klinga (Anne), Agneta Ekmanner (Countess de Saint-Fond)
   Presented by the Royal Dramatic Theater of Sweden.

(Majestic) Tuesday, Oct.17-21, 1995 (5 performances)
SALOME by Oscar Wilde; Director, Steven Berkoff; Set, Robert Ballagh; Costumes, David Blight; Lighting, Brian Knox, Trevor Dawson; Music, Roger Doyle CAST: Zigi Ellison (Salome), Jolyon Baker (Jokanaan), Carmen Du Sautoy (Herodias), Steven Berkoff (Herod), Richard Clothier (Narraboth), Peter Brennan (Naaman), Christopher Brand (Page), Jeremy Peters (Tigellinus)
   This version sets the action at a 1920s cocktail party.

(Majestic) Wednesday, Dec.6-16, 1995
THE DUCHESS OF MALFI by John Webster; Director, Declan Donnellan; Design, Nick Ormerod; Music/Music Director, Catherine Jayes; Movement, Jane Gibson; Lighting, Judith Greenwood CAST: Anastasia Hille (Duchess), Matthew Macfadyen (Antonio), George Anton (Bosola), Paul Brennen (Cardinal), Scott Handy (Ferdinand), Nicola Redmond (Julia), Shaun Parkes (Delio), Avril Clark (Cariola), Matthew Boyer, Sean Hannaway, Christopher Kell, Terence Maynard, Guy More, Peter Moreton
   Performed by London's Cheek by Jowl company.

Agneta Ekmanner, Anita Bjork, Margaretha Bystrom
in *Madame de Sade*

(Opera House) Friday, Feb.23-Mar.3, 1996
IN THE LONELINESS OF THE COTTON FIELDS by Bernard-Marie Koltes; Director, Patrice Chereau; Sets, Richard Peduzzi; Choreography, Christophe Bernard; Costumes, Moidele Bickel; Lighting, Jean Luc Chanonat; Sound, Philippe Cachia CAST: Patrice Chereau (Dealer), Pascal Greggory (Client)
   A French drama

(Opera House) Tuesday, Apr.30-May 5, 1996 (5 performances)
DON JUAN by Moliere; Director, Jacques Lassalle; Set/Costumes, Rudy Sabounghi; Lighting, Franck Thevenon; Sound, Jean Lacornerie; Fights, Francois Rostain CAST: Jacques Sereys (Don Louis), Isabelle Gardien (Mathurine), Eric Ruf (Don Carlos), Andrzej Seweryn (Don Juan), Bruno Raffaelli (Gusman/Franciscan/Dimanche), Gerard Giroudon (Pierrot), Olivier Dautrey (Don Alonse), Eric Theobald (La Violette), Roland Bertin (Sganarelle), Jeanne Balibar (Elvire), Enrico Horn (Commander statue), Catherine Sauval (Charlotte)
   The 1665 comedy performed by Paris' Comedie Francaise.

(Majestic) Tuesday, May 7-12, 1996 (5 performances)
THE INCONSTANT LOVERS by Marivaux; Director/Lighting, Jean-Pierre Miquel; Set, Pancho Quilici; Costumes, Patrice Cauchetier CAST: Claire Vernet (Flaminia), Claude Mathieu (Lisette), Michel Favory (Lord), Philippe Torreton (Harlequin), Alain Lenglet (Prince), Michel Robin (Trivelin), Silvia (Coraly Zahonero), Mario Costa, Patrice Colombe (Footmen), Florence Wasserman, Eine Riviere, Nathela Davrichewy (Maids)
   Presented by France's Theatre du Vieux Colombier.

Laurencine Lot, Martine Voyeux, Bengt Wanselius Photos

Philippe Torreton, Coraly Zahonero
in *Inconstant Lovers*

CIRCLE REPERTORY THEATER (COMPANY)

Twenty-seventh Season

Artistic Director, Austin Pendleton; Executive Director, Milan Stitt; Managing Director, Andrew Chipok; Literary Manager, Mimi Kramer; Business Manager, Daniel M. Stadler; Press, Jeffrey Richards/Peter Eramo Jr., Kevin Rehac, Scott Karpf, Stephen Sunderlin

Friday, June 23-July 23, 1995
LONELY PLANET by Steven Dietz; Director, Leonard Foglia; Set, Michael McGarty; Lighting, Howard Werner; Costumes, Markas Henry; Sound, One Dream; Stage Manager, Deborah Heimann CAST: Denis O'Hare (Carl), Mark Shannon (Jody)
   A revised and restaged version of a two act drama performed at the Perry St. Theatre in 1994. The action takes place at a map store on the oldest street in an American city. Produced in association with the Barrow Group.

Wednesday, Oct.18-Dec.3, 1995 (34 performances and 13 previews)
RIFF RAFF; Written/Directed by Laurence Fishburne; Set, Edward T. Gianfrancesco; Costumes, Michael Krass; Lighting, Dennis Parichy; Sound, Darron L. West; Fights, Rick Sordelet; Stage Manager, Greta Minsky CAST: Laurence Fishburne ("20/20" Mike Leon), Titus Welliver (Billy "Torch" Murphy), Heavy D (Tony "The Tiger" Lee)
   A drama performed without intermission. The action takes place in an abandoned building on the Lower East Side.

Wednesday, Dec.20, 1995-Feb.4, 1996 (28 performances and 13 previews)
THE HOPE ZONE by Kevin Heelan; Director, Richard Jenkins; Set, Eugene Lee; Costumes, Walker Hicklin; Lighting, Russell Champa; Stage Manager, Tom Stone CAST: Olympia Dukakis (Countess), Barbara Caren Sims (Fern), Anne Scurria (Maureen), Craig Bockhorn (Newton), George Morfogen (Veeche)
   A drama in two acts. The setting is a seedy Maryland resort.

Friday, Jan.12-Feb.3, 1996 (12 performances)
THIS IS WHERE I GET OFF; Written/Performed by Beth Littleford; Co-Written/Directed by Warren Etheredge; Set, Shaun Motley; Lighting, Anne Duston Cheney; Stage Manager, Leah Priceman
   A late night comic monologue.

Wednesday, Mar.6-Apr.7, 1996 (20 performances and 14 previews)
THE SIZE OF THE WORLD by Charles Evered; Director, Austin Pendleton; Set, Jeff Pajer; Lighting, Tom Sturge; Costumes, Walker Hicklin; Sound, Raymond D. Schilke; Stage Manager, Tom Stone CAST: Frank Whaley (Peter Hogancamp), Louis Zorich (Stan Merkle), Rita Moreno (Vivian Merkle)
   A play in two acts. The action takes place in New Jersey.

Gerry Goodstein, Marcia Allert Photos

Top: Rita Moreno, Frank Whaley, Louis Zorich
in *Size of the World*
Center: Beth Littleford in *This Is Where I Get off*
Left: Titus Welliver Laurence Fishburne, in *Riff Raff*

ENSEMBLE STUDIO THEATRE

Artistic Director, Curt Dempster; Managing Director, Susan Jonas; Executive Producer, Jamie Richards; Marathon Producer, Mark Roberts; Lighting Designer, Greg MacPherson; Sound Designer, Jeffrey Taylor; Press, Jim Baldassare

Wednesday, May 8-19, 1996 (12 performances)
MARATHON '96:SERIES A; Sets, Michael Allen; Costumes, David Kay Mickelsen
Cats and Dogs by Cherie Vogelstein; Director, Jamie Richards CAST: Anne O'Sullivan (Annette), Brad Bellamy (Michael), Alison Fraser (Dini), Joseph Lyle Taylor (Guy), Ellen Mareneck (Waitress), Thomas McHugh (Head Teamster), Marc Romeo, Denny Bess, Rick Reardon, Tony Tucci (Teamsters)
Geliebteh by Howard Korder; Director, Matthew Penn CAST: Lynn Cohen (Woman)
Degas C'est Moi by David Ives; Director, Shirley Kaplan CAST: Donald Berman (Ed), Susan Greenhill (Doris), Chris Lutkin (Man 1-7), Ilene Kristem (Woman (1-7)
Elegy for a Lady by Arthur Miller; Director, Curt Dempster CAST: Christina Haag (Propriestress), James Murtaugh (Man)

Wednesday, May 22-June 2, 1996 (12 performances)
MARATHON'96:SERIES B; Sets, Mark Symczak; Costumes, Andy Wallach; Fights, Jake Turner; Stage Managers, Greg W. Brevoort, David P. Smith, Babette M. Roberts, Joe Sharkey
Slice of Life by Stuart R. Brown; Director, Pirie MacDonald CAST: Richmond Hoxie (C.C.), Paul Austin (Earl)
English (It's Where the Words Are) by Peter Basch; Director, Susann Brinkley CAST: Joseph Lyle Taylor (Joey), Stephanie Cannon (Suzy)
Bel Canto by Will Scheffer; Director, Brian Meltes CAST: Phyllis Somerville (Ma), Elizabeth Berridge (Phil), Fiona Gallagher (Vinnie)
Love Like Fire (Part I); Written/Directed by Romulus Linney CAST: John-Martin Green (Chamberlain), Chris Ceraso (King), Thomas Schall (Duke), Melinda Page Hamilton (Princess), Bill Cwikowski (Prince)

Wednesday, June 5-16, 1996 (12 performances)
MARATHON '96:SERIES C; Sets, Bruce Goodrich; Costumes, Murell Horton; Stage Managers, Kirstin Mooney, Kim Donovan, John Handy, Eileen Myers, Alicina Vilankulu
Home by Laura Cahill; Director, Jace Alexander CAST: Helen Gallagher (Olivia), Janet Zarish (Mary Jane)
Slide Show; Written/Performed by Paul Selig
The Adoption by Joyce Carol Oates; Director, Kevin Confoy CAST: Dan Daily, Cecilia deWolf, Donna Marvin, Tara Sands, Margo Skinner
The Observatory by Greg Germann; Director, Jim Simpson CAST: Dennis Boutsikaris (Roman), Diana LaMar (Alice)
The nineteenth annual festival of one-act plays.

Craol Rosegg Photos

Top: Bill Cwikowski, Melinda Page Hamilton, Tom Schall
in *Love Like Fire*
Center: Cecilia deWolf, Margo Skinner, Dan Daily in *The Adoption*
Left: Stephanie Cannon, Joseph Lyle Taylor in *English....*

IRISH REPERTORY THEATRE

Artistic Director, Charlotte Moore; Producing Director, Ciaran O'Reilly; Development Director, Fran Reinhold; Press, Philip Rinaldi/James L.L. Morrison

Thursday, Sept.14-Oct.15, 1995 (26 performances and 7 previews)
SAME OLD MOON by Geraldine Aron; Director, Charlotte Moore; Set, Bryan Johnson; Lighting, Gregory Cohen; Costumes, David Toser; Sound, Aural Fixation; Choreography, Barry McNabb; Stage Manager, Sandra M. Bloom   CAST: Madeleine Potter (Brenda Barnes), Aideen O'Kelly (Peace), Terry Donnelly (Bridie/Granny), Risteard Cooper (Desmond), John Keating (Barman/Priest/Kevin/Trevor/Mark), Ciaran O'Reilly (Mooney/Caruso/Postman/Mullen), Paddy Croft (Mother Superior/Cafe Daphne/Geeny), Aedin Moloney (Bella/Di/Nurse)
A comedy in two acts. The action takes place in Ireland and England, 1941-1980s.

Friday, Nov.10-Dec.10, 1995 (22 performances and 10 previews)
JUNO AND THE PAYCOCK by Sean O'Casey; Director, Charlotte Moore; Set, Michael Todd Potter; Lighting, Ken davis; Costumes, Victor Whitehurst   CAST: WB Brydon (Capt. Boyle), Risteard Cooper (Joxer Daly), Pauline Flanagan (Juno Boyle), Aedin Moloney (Mary), John Keating (Johnny Boyle), Terry Donnelly (Mrs. Madigan), Michael Judd, Jim Cunningham Jr.
A drama set in Dublin, 1922.

Thursday, Nov.30-Dec.17, 1995 (12 performances and 4 previews)
SHIMMER by John O'Keefe; Director, David Elliott; Lighting, Robert Williams; Stage Manager, Jessica Lynch   CAST: Jud Meyers
A monodrama performed on the second stage.

Tuesday, Jan.23-Feb.18, 1996 (24 performances and 7 previews)
FRANK PIG SAYS HELLO by Pat McCabe; Director, Joe O'Byrne; Set, Ian McNicholl; Stage Manager, Connor Smith   CAST: David Gorry (Piglet), Sean Rocks (Frank)
A black comedy set in Co. Monaghan, Irelenad. Presented with The Co-Motion Theatre Company.

Saturday, Feb.24-Mar.31, 1996 (38 performances and 5 previews)
A WHISTLE IN THE DARK by Thomas Murphy; Director, Charlotte Moore; Set, David Raphel; Lighting, Gregory Cohen; Costumes, Monica Russell; Stage Manager, Kathe Mull   CAST: James Beecher (Iggy), Ciaran O'Reilly (Harry), Jim Cunningham Jr. (Hugo), Jean Parker (Betty), Denis O' Neill (Mush), Chris O'Neill (Michael), David Leary (Dada), Dara Coleman (Des)
A drama in two acts. The action takes place in Coventry, England.

Carol Rosegg, Eric Baer, Susan Johann, Co-Motion Photos

Top: Terry Donnelly, Madeleine Potter, Aideen O'Kelly
in *Same Old Moon*
Center: Jud Meyers in *Shimmer*
Right: David Gorry, Sean Rocks in *Frank Pig Says Hello*

JEWISH REPERTORY THEATRE

Twenty-second Season

Artistic Director, Ran Avi; Managing Director, Damond Gallagher; House Manager, Cathleen Cintron; Press, Shirley Herz/Wayne Wolfe, Sam Rudy, Miller Wright

(All Productions at Playhouse 91) Saturday, Oct.28-Nov.26, 1995 (21 performances and 10 previews)
OLD WICKED SONGS by Jon Marans; Director, Seth Barrish; Set/Costumes, Markas Henry; Lighting, Howard Werner; Sound, One Dream; Stage Manager, D.C. Rosenberg CAST: Hal Robinson (Professor Josef Mashjan), Michael Stuhlbarg (Stpehen Hoffman)
A drama in two acts. The action takes place in Vienna, 1986. Produced with The Barrow Group and Daryl Roth.

Thursday, Jan.11-Mar.24, 1996 (63 performances and 9 previews)
SHEBA; Music, Gary William Friedman; Lyrics/Book, Sharleen Cooper Cohen; Director/Choreography, Tony Stevens; Musical Director, Christopher McGovern; Sets, Gregory Hill; Costumes, Jonathan Bixby; Lighting, Tom Sturge; Sound, One Dream; Stage Manager, Ruth E. Kramer CAST: Brent Black (Hiram), Lynda Divito (Leah), Tony Gilbert (Zadok), Jonathan Giordano (Rheoboam), Michael Goz (Benaiah), Jonathan Hadley (Shem), Cynthia Leigh Heim (Cherna), Jonathan Todd Horenstein (Abner), Ernestine Jackson (Makela), Joe Langworth (Zaku), Rose McGuire (Maat), Elizabeth Moliter (Mizpah), Lisa Morris (Irit), Natasha Rennalls (Nadi), Michael Sangiovanni (Mitra), Nandita Shenoy (Tiza), Joseph Siravo (Solomon), Jane Strauss (Widow Huldah), Tamara Tunie (Ni-Caul), Andrew Varela (Jeroboam), Carrie Wilshusen (Mera)
MUSICAL NUMBERS: Begging the Question, Song of Solomon, We Praise the Lord, Entrance of the Sabaens, I Question You, How Does a King Decide, You'll Be King, Day in the Jerusalem, Water Wears the Stone, Opinions in Public, The Names, Give and Take, Pas de Deux, You Are the One, Invitation, Night of Love, This Is the Day/Shema Ysrael, Moment in the Sun, Advice for a Friend, Who Is This Man/Woman to Me, The Announcement, God of Our Fathers, Mysteries, Ballet, The Warning, Child of Mine, Come with Me, Solomon Decide, Finale: You Fill My Arms
A two-act musical set in Jerusalem, 960 B.C.

Saturday, Apr.13-June 2, 1996 (43 performances and 8 previews)
TOVAH: OUT OF HER MIND: Conceived/Performed by Tovah Feldshuh; Chief Writers, Larry Amoros, Ms. Feldshuh; Director/Musical Staging, Sara Louise Lazarus; Musical Director, Scott Cady; Visual Consultant, Tony Walton; Costumes, William Ivey Long; Lighting, Matt Berman; Sound, Robert Campbell; Stage Manager, Ruth E. Kramer
A one-woman show featuring characters aged 8 to 80.

Joan Marcus, Carol Rosegg Photos

Top: Michael Stuhlbarg, Hal Robinson in *Old Wicked Songs*
Center: TamaraTunie, Joseph Sinaro in *Sheba*
Right: Tovah Feldshuh in *Tovah: Out of Her Mind*

LINCOLN CENTER THEATER

Eleventh Season

Artistic Director, Andre Bishop; Executive Producer, Bernard Gersten; General Manager, Steven C. Callahan; Production Manager, Jeff Hamlin; Development Director, Hattie K. Jutagir; Production Manager, Jeff Hamlin; Musical Theatre Program Director, Ira Weitzman; Press, Merle Debuskey/Susan Chicoine, Charlie Siedenburg

(Off-Bdwy Productions at Mitzi E. Newhouse Theater) Thursday, Oct.5, 1995-Jan.5, 1996 (81 performances and 28 previews)
NORTHEAST LOCAL by Tom Donaghy; Director, Gerald Gutierrez; Sets, John Lee Beatty; Costumes, Jane Greenwood; Lighting, Brian MacDevitt; Music, Louis Rosen; Sound, Otts Munderloh; Stage Manager, Marjorie Hamlin CAST: Mary Elizabeth Mastrantonio (Gi), Anthony LaPaglia (Mickey), Eileen Heckart (Mair), Terry Alexander (Jesse)
A drama tracing a blue-collar family's lives from 1963 to the present

Top: Anthony LaPagalia, Terry Alexander, Eileen Heckart, Mary Elizabeth Mastrontonio
Right: Mary Elizabeth Mastrantonio, Anthony LaPaglia

Thursday, Feb.1-June 30, 1996 (153 performances and 21 previews) **A FAIR COUNTRY** by Jon Robin Baitz; Director, Daniel Sullivan; Sets, Tony Walton; Costumes, Jane Greenwood; Lighting, James F. Ingalls; Music, Robert Waldman; Sound, Scott Lehrer; Stage Manager, Roy Harris CAST: Matt McGrath (Gil Burgess), Judith Ivey succeeded by Joyce Van Patten (Patrice Burgess), Teagle F. Bougere (Hilton), Laurence Luckinbill (Harry Burgess), Jack Davidson (Ellsworth Hodges), Maduka Steady (Victor), Dan Futterman (Alec Burgess), Richard Clarke (Gerrit Van Elder), Katie Finneran (Carly Fletcher)

A drama in two acts. The action takes place in southern Mexico, South Africa , West Africa and Holland.

For other Lincoln Center Theater productions: *Chronicle of a Death Foretold*, *Racing Demon* and *A Delicate Balance*, see BROADWAY CALENDAR.

Ken Howard Photos

Right: Judith Ivey, Matt McGrath
Bottom Left: Judith Ivey
Bottom Right: Matt McGrath, Judith Ivey, Dan Futterman, Laurence Luckinbill

MCC THEATER
(MANHATTAN CLASS COMPANY)

Tenth Season

Executive Directors, Robert LuPone, Bernard Telsey; Associate Director, W.D. Cantier; Administrative Director, Lynne McCreary; Development Director, Donna Moreau-Cupp; Literary Manager, Stephen Willems; Press, Merle Frimark & Marc Thibodeau/Erin Dunn, Chris Boneau~Adrian Bryan-Brown

Friday, Sept.29-Dec.23, 1995 (55 performances and 4 previews) transferred to Westside Theater/Downstairs Tuesday, Mar.5-May 12, 1996 (70 performances and 9 previews)
NIXON'S NIXON by Russell Lees; Director, Jim Simpson; Sets/Lighting, Kyle Chepulis; Costumes, Daniele Hollywood; Sound, Mike Nolan; Projections, Abigail Simon, Tal Yarden; Stage Manager, Erica Blum CAST: Gerry Bamman (Richard M. Nixon), Steve Mellor (Henry Kissinger)
A play performed without intermission. The action takes place in the White House on Aug.7, 1974, the eve of President Nixon's resignation.

Friday, Jan.5-Feb.24, 1996 (47 performances and 4 previews)
THE GREY ZONE by Tim Blake Nelson; Director, Douglas Hughes; Sets, Neil Patel; Costumes, Catherine Zuber; Lighting, Michael Chybowski; Music/Sound, David Van Tieghem; Stage Manager, Bernadette McGay CAST: Christopher McCann (Dr. Miklos Nyiszli), Edward Dougherty (Old Man/Moll), Gus Rogerson (Rosenthal), Matthew Sussman (Schlermer), Michael Stuhlbarg (Hoffman), David Chandler (Abramowics), Henry Stram (Muhsfeldt), Abigail Revasch (Girl)
A drama set in Auschwitz concentration camp, 1944.

Monday, May 13-June 8, 1996 (23 performances and 5 previews)
THREE IN THE BACK, TWO IN THE HEAD by Jason Sherman; Director, Pamela Berlin; Sets, Neil Patel; Costumes, Michael Krass; Lighting, Howard Werner; Music/Sound, David Van Tieghem; Stage Manager, Elaine Bayless CAST: Ben Shenkman (Paul Jackson), Byron Jennings (John Doyle), Fred Burrell (Ed Sparrow), Nick Wyman (Donald Jackson), Alma Cuervo (Anna Jackson)
A thriller performed without intermission. The setting is the CIA's Langley, Virginia offices.

Joan Marcus Photos

Top: Steve Mellon, Gerry Bamman in *Nixon's Nixon*
Center: Michael Stuhlbarg, Gus Rogerson, David Chandler
in *Grey Zone*
Left::Alma Cuervo, Nick Wyman, Ben Shenkman in *Three in the*
Bank

MANHATTAN THEATRE CLUB

Twenty-fifth Season

Artistic Director, Lynne Meadow; Executive Producer, Barry Grove; General Manager, Victoria Bailey; Associate Artistic Director, Michael Bush; Production Manager, Michael R. Moody; Play Development, Kate Loewald; Musical Theatre Program Director, Clifford Lee Johnson III; Press, Helene Davis, Barbara Carroll

(Stage II) Tuesday, Sept.26-Nov.19, 1995 (31 performances and 25 previews)
FULL GALLOP by Mark Hampton and Mary Louise Wilson; Director, Nicholas Martin; Set, James Noone; Costumes, Michael Krass; Lighting, David F. Segal; Sound, Bruce Ellman; Stage Manager, John Handy CAST: Mary Louise Wilson (Diana Vreeland)
A monodrama in two acts. The action takes place in Vreeland's Park Ave. apartment, 1971.

(Stage I) Tuesday, Oct.17-Dec.22, 1995 (53 performances and 24 previews)
NEW ENGLAND by Richard Nelson; Director, Howard Davies; Set, Santo Loquasto; Costumes, Jennifer von Mayrhauser; Lighting, Richard Nelson; Sound, Mark Bennett; Stage Manager, Franklin Keysar CAST: Larry Bryggman (Harry Baker/Alfred Baker), Penny Fuller (Alice Berry), Tom Irwin (Tom Berry), Mia Dillon (Elizabeth Baker), T. Scott Cunningham (Paul Baker), Allison Janney (Gemma Baker), Margaret Whitton (Sophie Baker)
A drama performed without intermission. The action takes place in a western Connecticut farmhouse.

(Stage II) Tuesday, Nov.28, 1995-Jan.21, 1996 (48 performances and 25 previews) re-opened on (Stage I) Tuesday, April 23-June 23, 1996 (73 performances)
VALLEY SONG; Written/Directed by Athol Fugard; Set/Costumes, Susan Hilferty; Lighting, Dennis Parichy; Music, DiDi Kriel; Stage Manager, Sandra Lea Carlson CAST: Athol Fugard succeeded by Marius Weyers for return(The Author/Abraam Jonkers), Lisa Gay Hamilton (Veronica Jonkers)
A drama performed without intermission. The action takes place in South Africa.

(Stage I) Tuesday, Jan.16-Mar.24, 1996 (56 performances and 24 previews)
BLUE WINDOW by Craig Lucas; Director, Joe Mantello; Set, Robert Brill; Costumes, Laura Cunningham; Lighting, Brian MacDevitt; Sound, John Gromada; Stage Manager, William Joseph Barnes CAST: David Aaron Baker (Norbert), Johanna Day (Emily), John Benjamin Hickey (Griever), Allison Janney (Boo), Ellen McLaughlin (Alice), J. Smith-Cameron (Libby), David Warshofsky (Tom)
A 1984 drama performed without intermission. The action takes place in New York City.

Mary Louise Wilson in *Full Gallup*

Lisa Gay Hamilton, Athol Fugard in *Valley Song*

(Stage II) Tuesday, Feb.13-Apr.14, 1996 (48 performances and 24 previews)
OVERTIME by A.R. Gurney; Director, Nicholas Martin; Set, John Lee Beatty; Costumes, Michael Krass; Lighting, Brian MacDevitt; Sound, Aural Fixation; Stage Manager, Ed Fitzgerald CAST: Joan McMurtrey (Portia), Dennis Parlato (Antonio), Jere Shea (Bassanio), Michael Potts (Gratiano), Marissa Chibas (Nerissa), Jill Tasker (Jessica), Willis Sparks (Lorenzo), Robert Stanton (Salerio), Nicholas Kepros (Shylock)
A modern comic sequel to Shakespeare's *Merchant of Venice*. The action takes place in Belmont, outside Venice.

(Stage II) Tuesday, Apr.30-June 30, 1996 (42 performances and 30 previews)
BY THE SEA, BY THE SEA, BY THE BEAUTIFUL SEA by Joe Pintauro (Act I), Lanford Wilson (Act II), Terrence McNally (Act III); Director, Leonard Foglia; Set, Michael McGarty; Costumes, Laura Cunningham; Lighting, Brian MacDevitt; Sound, One Dream; Stage Manager, Jill Cordle CAST: Lee Brock, Timothy Carhart, Mary Beth Fisher
Three one-acts set at a beach during summer.

Joan Marcus, Ken Howard, T. Charles Erickson Photos

Lee Brock, Mary Beth Fisher, Timothy Carhart in
By the Sea, By the Sea, By the Beautiful Sea

NEW YORK SHAKESPEARE FESTIVAL

Patrick Stewart, Carrie Preston in *Tempest*

Forty-first Season

Producer, George C. Wolfe; Artistic Producer, Rosemarie Tichler; Executive Producer, Joey Parnes; Executive Director, Laurie Beckelman; Associate Producer, Kevin Kline; Production Manager, Rik Kaye; Development Director, Margaret M. Lioi; Press, Carol Fineman/Tom Naro, Eugenie Hero, Bill Coyle

(Delacorte/Central Park) Thursday, June 22-July 19, 1995 (22 performances)
THE TEMPEST by William Shakespeare; Director, George C. Wolfe; Sets, Riccardo Hernandez; Costumes, Toni-Leslie James; Lighting, Paul Gallo; Sound, Dan Moses Schreier; Masks/Puppets, Barbara Pollitt; Music, Carlos Valdez, Mr. Schreier; Choreography, Hope Clarke; Stage Manager, Buzz Cohen CAST: Tyrone Mitchell Henderson (Shipmaster), Nathan Hinton (Boatswain), Larry Bryggman (Alonso), MacIntyre Dixon (Gonzalo), Liev Schreiber (Sebastian), Nestor Serrano (Antonio), Carrie Preston (Miranda), Patrick Stewart (Prospero), Aunjanue Ellis (Ariel), Teagle F. Bougere (Caliban), Kamar De Los Reyes (Ferdinand), Neal Huff (Adrian), Bill Irwin (Trinculo), John Pankow (Stephano), Midori Nakamura (Iris), Hilary Chaplain (Ceres), Akwesi Asante (Juno), Adam Dannheisser, Michael McGuigan, Seamas L. O'Brien, Jodi Somers, Paul Whitthorne

Performed with one intermission. This production is #28 in the ongoing Shakespeare Marathon. The production re-opened at the Broadhurst Theatre in October (see BROADWAY CALENDAR).

**Elizabeth Marvel, Steven Spinella, Neal Huff
in *Troilus and Cressida***

(Delacorte/Central Park) Friday, Aug.4-Sept.3, 1995 (16 performances and 11 previews)
TROILUS AND CRESSIDA by William Shakespeare; Director, Mark Wing-Davey; Sets, Derek McLane; Costumes, Catherine Zuber; Lighting, Christopher Akerlind; Sound, Dan Moses Schreier; Music, Mark Bennett; Choreography, Daniel Banks; Stahe Manager, Ron Nash CAST: Paul Calderon (Achilles), Bill Camp (Paris), Phillip Christian (Patroclus), Elaina Davis (Andromache/Hecuba), Jeffrey Donovan (Diomedes), Herb Foster (Nestor), Avery Glymph (Helenus), Neal Huff (Troilus), Peter Francis James (Aeneas), Catherine Kellner (Cassandra), Elizabeth Marvel (Cressida), Boris McGiver (Hector), Eddie Mitchell Morris (Antenor), Tim Blake Nelson (Thersites), Daniel Oreskes (Agamemnon), Steven Skybell (Ulyssses), Mark Kenneth Smaltz (Ajax), Stephen Spinella (Pandarus), Henry Stram (Priam/Menelaus/Servant), Tamara Tunie (Helen), Victor L. Williams (Prologue), Joel Carino, David Costabile, Robert Dolan, Olase Freeman, Wood Harris, Morley Kamen, Timothy McCracken, Klea Scott, Nathaniel Trice

Performed with one intermission. This production is #29 in the Shakespeare Marathon.

(Delacorte/Central Park) Friday, Sept.8-10, 1995 (3 performances)
TAKIGI-NOH '95; FEATURED CAST: Umewaka Rokuro, Hosho Wan, Yamamoto Takashi, Yamamoto Noritoshi, Ron Nakahara

Japan's Noh Theater presents a double bill of comedy and tragedy. Noh blends poetry, drama, dance, vocal and instrumental music. Takigi means firewood and refers to bonfires that light the stage.

(Public/Newman) Friday, Nov.3, 1995-Jan.28, 1996 (85 performances and 13 previews)
BRING IN 'DA NOISE BRING IN 'DA FUNK: *A Tap/Rap Discourse on the Staying Power of the Beat*; Conceived/Directed by George C. Wolfe; Based on idea by Savion Glover and Mr. Wolfe; Text, Reg E. Gaines; Music, Ann Duquesnay, Zane Mark, Daryl Waters; Orchestrations, Mr. Waters; Music Direction, Mr. Mark; Sets, Riccardo Hernandez; Costumes, Karen Perry; Lighting, Jules Fisher, Peggy Eisenhauer; Sound, Dan Moses Schreier; Projections, Batwin + Robin; Stage Manager, Gwendolyn M. Gilliam CAST: Savion Glover, Baakari Wilder, Jimmy Tate, Vincent Bingham, Reg E. Gaines, Ann Duquesnay, Jared Crawford, Raymond King, Dule Hill
A dance musical in two acts. Re-opened at the Ambassador Theatre on April 25, 1996. See BROADWAY CALENDAR for details.

(Public/LuEsther Hall) Friday, Nov.9-26, 1995 (9 performances and 3 previews)
WAKE UP, I'M FAT; Written/Performed by Camryn Manheim; Director, Mark Brokaw; Set, Allen Moyer; Lighting, Kenneth Posner; Sound, Janet Kalas; Stage Manager, Michael F. Ritchie
A comic monologue on the journey of being overweight.

Camryn Manheim in *Wake Up, I'm Fat*

(Public/Martinson Hall) Thursday, Nov.30, 1995-Jan 7, 1996 (25 performances and 21 previews)
WASP AND OTHER PLAYS by Steve Martin; Director, Barry Edelstein; Sets, Thomas Lynch; Lighting, Donald Holder; Costumes, Laura Cunningham; Sound, Red Ramona; Stage Manager, James Latus
Guillotine CAST: Nesbitt Blaisdell (Salesman), Don McManus (Customer), Carol Kane (Maid)
The Zig-Zag Woman CAST: Amelia Campbell (Woman), Peggy Pope (Toni), Nesbitt Blaisdell (Older Man), Don McManus (Middle Man), Kevin Isola (Billy Boy)
Patter for the Floating Lady CAST: Don McManus (Magician), Amelia Campbell (Angie), Carol Kane (Assistant)
WASP CAST: Don McManus (Dad), Carol Kane (Mom), Amelia Campbell (Sis), Kevin Isola (Son), Peggy Pope (Female Voice), Nesbitt Blaisdell (Premier/Choirmaster/Roger)
Four one-act plays. *Zig-Zag Women* was cut during the run. An earlier version of *Wasp* played Ensemble Studio Theatre in May-June 1994.

(Public/Anspacher) Tuesday, Jan.9-Feb.18, 1996 (28 performances and 17 previews)
KING LEAR by William Shakespeare; Director, Adrian Hall; Sets, Eugene Lee; Costumes, Catherine Zuber; Lighting, Natasha Katz; Sound, Dan Moses Schreier; Music, Richard Cumming; Fights, J. Steven White; Stage Manager, Ruth Kreshka CAST: F. Murray Abraham (Lear), Scott Brasfield (Servant/Gentleman), Brienin Bryant (Cordelia), Rob Campbell (Edgar), Mel Duane Gionson (Curan/Old Man/Gentleman), Margaret Gibson (Goneril), Jared Harris (Edmund), Thomas Hill (Earl of Gloucester), Francis Jue (Oswald), Paul Kielar (Doctor), Ezra Knight (Duke of Cornwall), Elizabeth Marvel (Regan), Chris McKinney (Duke of Burgundy), Lee Mark Nelson (King of France), Armand Schultz (Duke of Albany), Jeff Stafford (Gentleman/Herald), John Woodson (Earl of Kent), Jeffrey Wright (Fool), Joe Zaloom (Knight)
A drama performed with one intermission. The action takes place in Gloucester, Cornwall and Dover, pre-history.

Muchael Daniel Photos

**F. Murray Abraham, Brienin Bryant in King Lear
Above: Jared Harris, Rob Campbell in King Lear**

(Public/LuEsther Hall) Tuesday, Feb.13-Mar.17, 1996 (22 performances and 18 previews)
DANCING ON HER KNEES by Nilo Cruz; Director, Graciela Daniele; Set, Riccardo Hernandez; Costumes, Toni-Leslie James; Lighting, Peggy Eisenhauer; Sound, Scott Stauffer; Music, Carlos Valdez; Stage Manager, Buzz Cohen CAST: Luis Ramos (Francine), Franca Barchiesi (Ramona), Paul Calderon (Federico), Marianne Filali (Rosario Del Cielo), Julio Monge (Anuncio), Henry Stram (Matthias)

A drama performed without intermission. The action takes place in Miami Beach, All Souls' Day, late 1980s.

(Public/Anspacher) Friday, Mar.15-Apr.28, 1996 (29 performances)
NUDE NUDE TOTALLY NUDE; Written/Performed by Andrea Martin; Director, Walter Bobbie; Set, Loren Sherman; Costumes, Jane Greenwood; Lighting, Brian MacDevitt; Sound, John Gromada; Special Material, Bruce Vilanch; Musical Director, Seth Rudetsky

A comic monologue.

(Public/Anspacher) Friday, Mar.22-Apr.28, 1996 (29 performances)
A LINE AROUND THE BLOCK; Written/Performed by Marga Gomez; Director, Corey Madden; Set, Loren Sherman; Costumes, Candace Cain; Lighting, Brian MacDevitt; Sound, John Gromada

A monologue set in Manhattan's Latino community during the 1960s.

(Public/Martinson Hall) Tuesday, Apr.16-May 19, 1996 (22 performances and 18 previews)
VENUS by Suzan-Lori Parks; Direction/Sets, Richard Foreman; Costumes, Paul Tazewell; Lighting, Heather Carson; Songs, Phillip Johnson; Stage Manager, Lisa Porter CAST: Adina Porter (Sartje Baartman/Venus Hottentot), Peter Francis James (Man/Baron Docteur), Sandra Shipley (Brother/Mother Showman/School Chum), Mel Johnson Jr. (Negro Resurrectionist), Cedric Harris (Fat Man), Ben Shenkman, Kevin Isola, Lynn Hawley, Thomas Jay Ryan, Adriane Lenox, Rainn Wilson, John Lathan

A drama based on the life of an early nineteenth century African woman exhibited in an English circus. Co-produced with Yale Repertory Theatre.

Henry Stram, Luis Ramos in *Dancing On Her Knees*

(Public/Newman) Tuesday, Apr.23-May 26, 1996 (17 performances and 23 previews)
THE SKRIKER by Caryl Churchill; Director, Mark Wing-Davey; Choreography, Sara Rudner; Set/Costumes, Marina Draghici; Lighting, Christopher Akerlind; Music, Judith Weir; Sound/Music, John Gromada; Musical Director, Martin Goldray; Stage Manager, James Latus CAST: Jayne Atkinson (The Skriker), Angie Phillips (Lily), Caroline Seymour (Josie), April Armstrong (Lost Girl), Marc Calamia (Fair Fairy), Rene M. Ceballos (Green Lady), Torrin T. Cummings (Black Dog), Kate Egan (Hag), Philip Seymour Hoffman (RawHeadAndBloodyBones), Jodi Melnick (Passerby), Ric Oquita (Dark Fairy), Diana Rice (Dead Child), Valda Setterfield (Black Annis), Jack Shamblin (Man with Bucket), Doug Van Nessen (Kelpie), Sturgis Warner (Johnny Squarefoot)

A drama performed without intermission. The action takes place mostly in London.

(Public/LuEsther Hall) Tuesday, Apr.30-June 2, 1996 (23 performances and 17 performances)
THE CHANG FRAGMENTS by Han Ong; Director, Marcus Stern; Set/Costumes, James Schuette; Lighting, Scott Zielinski; Sound, John Huntington; Stage Manager, Kristen Harris CAST: Darren Lee (Ivan), Ernest Abuba (Chang/james Takashi), Tom Aulino (Flophouse Resident/Betty/Rita), Robin Miles (Roshumba/Flophouse Resident/Ghost), Stuart Rudin (Flophouse Resident/Ghost), Tina Chen (Mrs. Chang), Jennifer Kato (Lily), Daniel Dae Kim (Bruce)

A drama in two acts.

Michal Daniel Photos

Diana Rice, Jayne Atkinson in *The Skriker*

NEW YORK THEATRE WORKSHOP

Artistic Director, James C. Nicola; Managing Director, Nancy Kassak Diekmann; Associate Artistic Director, Linda S. Chapman; Literary Manager/Dramaturg, Jerry Manning; General Manager, Esther Cohen; Development Director, Jill A. Clark; Press, Richard Kornberg/Don Summa

Friday, Nov.3-Dec.22, 1995 (26 performances and 25 previews)
QUILLS by Doug Wright; Director, Howard Shalwitz; Set, Neil Patel; Costumes, James Schuette; Lighting, Blake Burba; Sound, Darron L. West; Stage Manager, Kate Broderick CAST: Daniel Oreskes (Dr. Royer-Collard), Kirk Jackson (M. Prouix/Lunatic), Lola Pashalinski (Renee Pelagie), Jefferson Mays (Abbe de Coulmier), Rocco Sisto (Marquis), Katy Wales Selverstone (Madeleine LeClerc/Madame Royer-Collard)
A drama in two acts. The action takes place at Charenton Asylum, on the outskirts of Paris, 1807.

Friday, Jan.26-Mar.31, 1996 (49 performances and 19 previews)
RENT; Music/Lyrics/Book by Jonathan Larson; Director, Michael Grief; Musical Director, Tim Weil; Choreography, Marlies Yearby; Set, Paul Clay; Costumes, Angela Wendt; Lighting, Blake Burba; Sound, Darron L. West; Stage Manager, Crystal Huntington CAST: Anthony Rapp (Mark Cohen), Adam Pascal (Roger Davis), Jesse L. Martin (Tom Collins), Taye Diggs (Benjamin Coffin III), Fredi Walker (Joanne Jefferson), Wilson Jermaine Heredia (Angel Schunard), Daphne Rubin-Vega (Mimi Marquez), Idina Menzel (Maureen Johnson), Kristen Lee Kelly (Mark's Mom/Alison), Byron Utley (Christmas Caroler/Mr. Jefferson/Pastor), Gwen Stewart (Mrs Jefferson), Timothy Britten Parker (Gordon)/The Man), Gilles Chiasson (Man with Squeegee/Cop), Rodney Hicks (Paul/Cop), Aiko Nakasone (Alexi Darling/Roger's Mom)
MUSICAL NUMBERS: Tune Up, Voice Mail #1-5, Rent, You Okay Honey?, One Song Glory, Light My Candle, Today 4 U, You'll See, Tango: Maureen, Life Support, Out Tonight, Another Day, Door/Wall, On the Street, Santa Fe, I'll Cover You, Will I?, We're Okay, Christmas Bells, Over the Moon, La Vie Boheme, I Should Tell You, Seasons of Love, Happy New Year, Take Me or Leave Me, Without You, Contact, Halloween, Goodbye Love, What You Own, Finale/Your Eyes
A musical drama in two acts. The action takes place in New York City's East Village. The first public preview, Jan.25, 1996, was cancelled due to the tragic death of author Jonathan Larson earlier that a.m. In place of the preview, the company sang the score for Mr. Larson's friends and family. The production re-opened at the Nederlander Theatre on Apr.29, 1996-see BROADWAY CALENDAR for details.

Anthony Rapp, Adam Pascal in *Rent*

Katy Wales Selverstone, Jefferson Mays, Rocco Sisto in *Quills*

Sunday, April 6 1996
JUST ADD WATER FESTIVAL: NOTHING FOREVER and **YESTERDAY'S WINDOW** by Chiori Miyagawa; Director, Karin Coonrod; Sets/Lighting, Darrel Maloney; Costumes, Myung Hee Cho; Music/Sound, Fabian Obispo; Lyrics, Mark Campbell CAST: Dawn Akemi Saito, Lenora Champagne, Bobby Daye
A studio production of two new plays-in-progress.

Friday, May 24-June 30, 1996 (26 performances and 14 previews)
A PARK IN OUR HOUSE by Nilo Cruz; Director, Loretta Greco; Set, Robert Brill; Costumes, Anne Patterson; Lighting, Allen Lee Hughes; Sound, Stephen G. Smith; Stage Manager, Janet M. Clark CAST: Vanessa Aspillaga (Pilar), Joe Quintero (Camilo), Franca Barchiesi (Ofelina), Gary Perez (Fifo), Shawn Elliott (Hilario), James Colby (Dimitri)
A drama in two acts. The action takes place in Cuba, 1970.

Joan Marcus Photos

Franca Barchiese, Shawn Elliot, James Colby, Vanessa Aspillaga in *A Park in Our House*

PEARL THEATRE COMPANY

Twelfth Season

Artistic Director, Shepard Sobel; Managing Director, Parris Relkin; Development Director, Mona Z. Koppelman; Artistic Associate, Joanne Camp; Resident Set Designer, Robert Joel Schwartz; Press/Marketing Director, Liz Parish

Tuesday, Sept.5-Oct.21, 1995 (35 performances and 13 previews)
A DOLL'S HOUSE by Henrik Ibsen; Translation, William Archer; Director, Grey Johnson; Lighting, Stephen Petrilli; Costumes, Deborah Rooney; Sound, Donna Riley; Stage Manager, Dale Smallwood CAST: Michael Butler (Torvald Helmer), Robin Leslie Brown (Nora), Robert Hock (Dr. Rank), Carol Schultz (Mrs. Linde), Kurt Ziskie (Nils Krogstad), Tyler Flagg, Rebecca Pollack (Ivar), Olivia Kinter, Heather Maxie Federman (Emmy), Anna Minot (Anna), Joanne Comerford (Ellen), Robert English (Porter)
Ibsen's 1879 drama in three acts. The action takes place in Christiania (Oslo), Norway.

Friday, Oct.27-Dec.9, 1995 (35 performances and 10 previews)
ANTIGONE by Sophocles; Translation, Dudley Fitts, Robert Fitzgerald; Director, Shepard Sobel; Set, Eric Lowell Renschler; Costumes, Leslie Yarmo; Lighting, Stephen Petrilli; Stage Manager, Kay Foster CAST: Robin Leslie Brown (Antigone), Candace Taylor (Ismene), Robert Hock (Creon), Kurt Ziskie (Sentry), Bradford Cover (Teiresias/Haimon), Carol Schultz (Eurydice/Chorus), Robert English, Lavern Summers
This version replaces the traditional Greek Chorus with the single figur of Eurydice.

Friday, Dec.15, 1995-Jan.27, 1996 (35 performances and 10 previews)
WHEN LADIES BATTLE by Eugene Scribe and Ernest Legouve; Translation, Michael Feingold; Director, John Rando; Costumes, Murell Horton; Lighting, Phil Monat; Sound, Donna Riley; Music, Thomas Cabaniss; Stage Manager, Kelley Kirkpatrick CAST: Bradford Cover (Charles), Patricia Jones (Leonie), Joanne Camp (Countess of Autreval), Arnie Burton (Gustave de Grignon), Mark La Mura (Baron de Montrichard), William Stiles (Officer of Dragoons), Dustin Longstreth, Eric McNaughton (Dragoons), Mr. Longstreth, Maja Wampuszyc, Petra Wright (Dancers)
An 1851 comedy in three acts. The action takes place in a chateau near Lyon, 1817.

Friday, Feb.2-Mar.16, 1996 (35 performances and 10 performances)
THE WINTER'S TALE by William Shakespeare; Director, Kathryn Long; Costumes, Sarah Eckert; Lighting, A.C. Hickox; Music, Mike Yionoulis; Stage Manager, Darcy Stephens CAST: John Wylie (Time/Antigonus/Autolycus), Julie Oda (Mamillius/Perdita), Maja Wampuszyc (Sicilian/Mopsa), Robert English (Tutor/Shepard), Tom Bloom (Camillo), Bradford Cover (Archidamus/Clown), Arnie Burton (Leontes), Patricia Jones (Hermione/Shepard), Allen Gilmore (Polixenes/Mariner), Petra Wright (Emilia/Dorcas), William Stiles (Cleomentes/Servant), Dustin Longstreth (Lord/Shepard), Edward Seasmon (Lord/Old Shepard), Brett Camp (Dion/Soldier/Shepard), Sean Pratt (Soldier/Florizel), Joanne Camp (Paulina), Tom Bloom (Gaoler)
A drama performed with one intermission. The setting is the Kingdoms of Sicilia and Bohemia.

Friday, Mar.22-May 5, 1996 (36 performances and 10 previews)
LIFE IS A DREAM by Calderon De La Barca; Translation, Edwin Honig; Director, Rob Bundy; Costumes, Murell Horton; Lighting, Stephen Petrilli; Sound, Brian Hallas; Stage Manager, Dale Smallwood CAST: Joanne Camp (Rosura), Bradford Cover (Clarin), Sean Pratt (Segismundo), Robert Hock (Clotaldo), Joshua Gordon, Chris Dylewski, Michael Moran (Servant/Soldier), Darrell Carey (Astolfo), Patricia Jones (Estrella), John Wylie (Basilio), Erika Gimbel (Lady-in-Waiting)
A Spanish drama set in and around the Polish court.

Tom Bloom, Janice Fett Photos

Robin Leslie Brown, Candace Taylor, Robert Hock in *Antigone*

Joanne Camp, Bradford Cover, Patricia Jones in *When Ladies Battle*

Allen Gilmore, Patricia Jones, Arnie Burton in *The Winter's Tale*

PLAYWRIGHTS HORIZONS

Twenty-fifth Season

Artistic Directors, Don Scardino, Tim Sanford; Managing Director, Leslie Marcus; General Manager, Lynn Landis; Musical Theatre Program Director, Dana Williams; Production Manager, Christopher Boll; Press, Philip Rinaldi/James Morrison, Brian Rubin

(Studio) Tuesday, June 13-July 30, 1995 (46 performances and 10 previews)
THE SPRINGHILL SINGING DISASTER; Written/Performed by Karen Trott; Directed/Developed by Norman Rene; Set, Loy Arenas; Costumes, Walker Hicklin; Lighting, Debra J. Kletter; Voice-Overs, Willie Reale; Sound, Joseph Robinson; Stage Manager, Andrea J. Testani
    A comic solo play with music.

Friday, Oct.20-Nov.26, 1995 (22 performances and 24 previews)
THE MONOGOMIST by Christopher Kyle; Director, Scott Elliott; Set, Derek McLane; Costumes, Eric Becker; Lighting, Peter Kaczorowski; Sound, Raymond D. Schilke; Video, Mark McKenna; Stage Manager, John J. Harmon   CAST: Caroline Seymour (Jasmine Stone), Arliss Howard (Dennis Jensen), Lisa Emery (Susan Barry), Timothy Olyphant

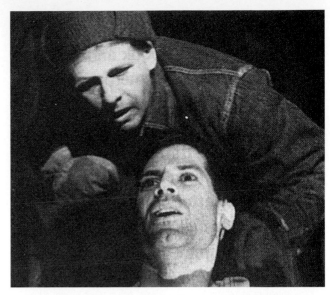

Martin Moran, Christopher Innvar in Floyd Collins

(Studio) Tuesday, Nov.28-Dec.10, 1995 (9 performances and 7 previews)
BLACK INK; Sets, David Harwell; Lighting, Annie Padien; Costumes, Mimi O'Donnell; Sound, Michael Clark; Stage Managers, Mic McCormack, Caroline Ranald   CASTS: Ray Aranha, Ellen Bethea, Anne Bobby, Chad Coleman, David Eisenberg, Kevin Geer, Stephen Mendillo, Keith Randolph Smith, Melinda Wade, Liza Weil
PROGRAM: *Cover* by Beverly Smith-Dawson; Director, Gilbert McCauley
The Bodhisattva Locksmith by Lynn Martin; Director, Pamela Berlin
Man in Polyester Suit by Ed DuRante; Director, Pam Berlin
Life By Asphyxiation by Kia Corthron; Director, Gilbert McCauley
    Four one-act plays by members of the theatre's African American playwright's unit.

Karen Trott in *The Springhill Singing Disaster*

Friday, Feb.9-Mar.24, 1996 (25 performances and 28 previews)
FLOYD COLLINS: Music/Lyrics, Adam Guettel; Book/Direction, Tina Landau; Musical Director, Ted Sperling; Orchestrations, Bruce Coughlin; Set, James Schuette; Costumes, Melina Root; Lighting, Scott Zielinski; Sound, Dan Moses Schreier; Cast Recording, Nonesuch; Stage Manager, Erica Schwartz   CAST: Christopher Innvar (Floyd Collins), Stephen Lee Anderson (Bee Doyle), Rudy Roberson (Ed Bishop), Jesse Lenat (Jewell Estes), Don Chastain (Lee Collins), Cass Morgan (Miss Jane), Theresa McCarthy (Nellie Collins), Jason Danieley (Homer Collins), Martin Moran (Skeets Miller), Michael Mulheren (H.T. Carmichael), Brian d'Arcy James (Cliff Roncy/Reporter), Matthew Bennett (Dr. Hazlett/Reporter), James Bohanek (Reporter/Con Man)
MUSICAL NUMBERS: The Call, 'Tween a Rock 'an a Hard Place, Lucky, Daybreak, I Landed on It, Blue Eyes, Heart an' Hand, Riddle Song, Is That Remarkable?, The Carnival, Through the Mountain, Git Comfortable, Family Hymn, The Dream, How Glory Goes, Ballad of Floyd Collins
    A musical in two acts. Based on actual events, the action takes place in Barren County, Kentucky, 1925.

Friday, April 26-June 9, 1996 (25 performances and 28 previews)
ARTS & LEISURE by Steve Tesich; Director, JoAnne Akalaitis; Set, Douglas Stein; Costumes, Susan Hilferty; Lighting, Frances Aronson; Sound, Bruce Odland; Stage Manager, Alan Fox   CAST: Harris Yulin (Alex Chaney), Randy Danson (Maria), Mary Diveny (Mother), Frances Conroy (Lenore), Elizabeth Marvel (Daughter)
    A drama performed without intermission.

Frances Conroy, Harris Yulin in *Arts & Leisure*

Joan Marcus Photos

PRIMARY STAGES

Eleventh Season

Artistic Director, Casey Childs; Associate Producer, Seth Gordon; General Manager, Margaret Chandler; Literary Manager, Andrew Leynse; Public Relations Director, Anne Einhorn; Associate Artistic Director, Janet Reed; Press, Tony Origlio/Michael Cullen

Wednesday, Oct.11-Nov.12, 1995 (21 performances and 13 previews)
THE MODEL APARTMENT by Doanld Margulies; Director, Lisa Peterson; Set, Neil Patel; Costumes, Katherine Roth; Lighting, Paul Clay; Music/Sound, David Van Tieghem; Fights, Jake Turner; Stage Manager, Christine Lemme CAST: Lynn Cohen (Lola), Paul Stolarsky (Max), Roberta Wallach (Debby), Akili Prince (Neil)
A drama performed without intermission. The action takes place at a condominium development in Florida, 1985.

Wednesday, Jan.10-Feb.11, 1996 (22 performances and 12 previews)
THE PRESERVATION SOCIETY by Wm. S. Leavengood; Director, Casey Childs; Set, Bob Phillips; Lighting, Deborah Constantine; Costumes, Rodney Munoz; Sound, Jim van Bergen; Stage Manager, Christine Catti CAST: Laurie Kennedy (Jeanette), Nina Humphrey (Marsha), Deidre Lovejoy (Lewis), Bryan Clark (George), Larry Pine, Robert Hogan (Howard), Kevin Geer (Richard)
A comedy in two acts. The action takes place in the mountains of western No. Carolina.

Tuesday, Jan.16-Mar.31, 1996 (62 performances and 8 previews) transferred to Atlantic Theatre Friday, Apr.12-June 30, 1996 (74 performances)
VIRGINS AND OTHER MYTHS; Written/Performed by Colin Martin; Developed/Directed by Bruce Blair; Co-Producer, Ted Snowden
A life voyage from All-American boy to gay hustler. Performed in two acts.

Wednesday, Mar.6-Apr.27, 1996 (41 performances and 13 previews)
SABINA by Willy Holtzman; Director, Melia Bensussen; Set, Judy Gailen; Costumes, Claudia Stephens; Lighting, Dan Kotlowitz; Music/Sound, David Van Tieghem; Stage Manager, Bridget Murray Edwards CAST: Marin Hinkle (Sabina), David Adkins (Binswanger), Kenneth L. Marks (Jung), George Bartenieff (Freud)
A drama in two acts. The action takes place in Zurich, 1906-38.

Wednesday, May 8-June 23, 1996 (35 performances and 13 previews)
ANCIENT HISTORY and **ENGLISH MADE SIMPLE** by David Ives; Director, John Rando; Set, Loren Sherman; Costumes, Rodney Munoz; Lighting, Deborah Constantine; Sound, Jim van Bergen; Stage Manager, Christine Catti CAST: *English...* Megan Dodds (Jill), Kyle Fabel (Jack), Michael Rupert (Loudspeaker Voice) *History* Vivienne Benesch (Ruth), Michael Rupert (Jack)
Two plays performed without intermission.

James Leynse, Paul Gregory Photos

Top: Deirdre Lovejoy, Bryan Clark, Nina Humphey, Larry Pine, Laurie Kennedy in *The Preservation Society*
Center: Megan Dodds, Kyle Fabel in *English Made Simple*
Left: Colin Martin in *Virgins & Other Myths*

PUERTO RICAN TRAVELING THEATRE
Twenty-ninth Season

Artistic Director/Producer, Miriam Colon Valle; Managing Director, Geoff Shales; Community Coordinator, Lissette Montolio; Development Director, Philip Langer; Company Manager, Fernando Quinn; Press, Max Eisen/Michele Gotham, Laurel Factor NOTE: Performances are given in both English and Spanish.

Thursday, Aug.3-27, 1995 (25 performances in City/NJ Parks)
ENTREMESES by Miguel De Cervantes; Director, Jose Cheo Oliveras; Choreography, Carmelo Santana; Musical Director, Axel Cintron; Set/Costumes, Harry Nadal; Stage Manager, Tata Canuelas CAST: Wanda Arriaga, Anabel Lopez, Luis Felipe Melendez, Loret Ramirez, Roberto Rodriguez, Eva Vasquez, Juan Villarreal, Edgardo Zayas, Axel Cintron, Jose Cheo Oliveras
Three Spanish classical comedy/musical plays.

Wednesday, Mar.13-Apr.21, 1996 (33 performances and 8 previews)
BOMBER JACKETS by Rob Santana; Director, Alba Oms; Translation, Sandra Garcia; Set, Richard Harmon; Lighting, Peter Greenbaum; Stage Manager, F. Quinn CAST: Luis Caballero (Eric-Spanish), Alex Furth (Patrick), Marc Geller (Eric-English), Louie Leonardo (Torch/Lopez), Francisco Lorite (Detective Cohen), Marcos Muniz (Rapallo)
A drama set in Bay Ridge, Brooklyn.

Wednesday, May 8-June 30, 1996 (48 performances and 8 performances)
ONE HOUR WITHOUT TELEVISION by Jaime Salom; Director, Miriam Colon Valle; Translation, Jack Agueros; Set, G.W. Mercier; Lighting, Peter Greenbaum; Sound, Yolanda Wright; Stage Manager, F. Quinn CAST: Christina SanJuan (Patricia), Alfredo Huereca (Eduardo)
A comedy in two acts. The action takes place at the home of a city couple.

Top: Alfredo Huerca, Christina San Juan in *One Hour Without Television*
Bottom Left: Wanda Arriaga, Anabel Lopez, Eva Vasquez in *Entremeses*
Bottom Right: Alex Furth, Marcos Muniz, Louis Leonardo in *Bomber Jacket*

101

ROUNDABOUT THEATRE COMPANY

odd Haimes; General Manager, Ellen Richard; Founding Director, Gene Feist; Development/Public Affairs Director, Julia C. Levy; Artistic Associate, Jim Carnahan; Marketing Director, David B. Steffen; Press, Chris Boneau~Adrian Bryan-Brown/Andy Shearer, Stephen Pitalo, Bob Fennell, Jackie Green, Craig Karpel, Jamie Morris, Patty Onagan, Miguel Tuason, Erin Dunn

(Off Broadway productions at Criterion Center/Laura Pels Theatre) Wednesday, Sept.27-Dec.17, 1995 (95 performances and 23 previews) **MOONLIGHT** by Harold Pinter; Director, Karel Reisz; Sets, Tony Walton; Costumes, Mirena Rada; Lighting, Richard Pilbrow; Sound, Tom Clark; Stage Manager, Jay Adler CAST: Melissa Chalsma (Bridget), Jason Robards (Andy), Blythe Danner (Bel), Barry McEvoy (Fred), Liev Schreiber (Jake), Kathleen Widdoes (Maria), Paul Hecht (Ralph)
A drama performed without intermission. Set in two bedrooms.

Tuesday, Dec.26, 1995-May 12, 1996 (145 performances and 15 previews)
MOLLY SWEENEY; Written/Directed by Brian Friel; Set/Costumes, Joe Vanek; Lighting, Mick Hughes; Produced in association with The Gate Theatre Dublin and Emanuel Azenburg CAST: Catherine Byrne (Molly Sweeney), Jason Robards (Mr. Rice), Alfred Molina (Frank Sweeney)
A drama in two acts.

Joan Marcus, Carol Rosegg Photos

Catherine Byrne in *Molly Sweeney*

Paul Hecht, Kathleen Widdoes, Jason Robards, Blythe Danner in *Moonlight*

Top Left: Scott Glenn, Jennifer Esposito in *Dark Rapture*
Top Right: Tony Gillan, Mary Beth Hurt, David Aaron Baker,
John Glover in *Oblivion Postponed*

SECOND STAGE THEATRE

Seventeenth Season

Artistic Director, Carole Rothman; Producing Director, Suzanne Schwartz Davidson; Associate Producer, Carol Fishman; Marketing Director, Harold Marmon; Development Director, Waddy Thompson; Business Manager, C. Barrack Evans; Literary Manager/Dramaturg, Erin Sanders; Production Manager, Allen Bernard; Press, Richard Kornberg/Ian Rand, Don Summa, William Finnegan, Gail Parenteau, Frank Vigliotti

Tuesday, Sept.12-Oct.29, 1995 (23 performances and 33 previews)
SIN by Wendy MacLeod; Director, David Petrarca; Set, Scott Bradley; Lighting, Robert Christen; Costumes, Allison Reeds; Music/Sound, Rob Milburn; Stage Manager, Nancy Harrington   CAST: Bruce Norris (Michael), Kelly Coffield (Avery), Julio Monge (Louis), Steve Carell (Jonathan), Camryn Manheim (Helen), Tom Aulino (Fred), John Elsen (Jason), Jeffrey Hutchinson (Gerard)
A two-act comedy of resistance and temptation. The setting is San Francisco, 1989.

Tuesday, Nov.14, 1995-Jan.6, 1996 (35 performances and 26 previews)
OBLIVION POSTPONED by Ron Nyswaner; Director, Nicholas Martin; Set, Allen Moyer; Costumes, Michael Krass; Lighting, Michael Lincoln; Sound, Randy Freed; Stage Manager, Elise-Ann Konstantin CAST: David Aaron Baker (david), John Glover (Jeffrey), Tony Gillan (Vincenzo), Mary Beth Hurt (Patti), James Rebhorn (Kyle)
A drama in two acts. The action takes place on a hotel terrace in Rome.

Tuesday, Apr.23-June 16, 1996 (30 performances and 34 previews)
DARK RAPTURE by Eric Overmyer; Director, Scott Ellis; Set, Santo Loquasto; Lighting, Natasha Katz; Costumes, Jennifer von Mayrhauser; Sound, Tony Meola; Music, Jeremy Grody; Fights, David Leong; Stage Manager, Elise-Ann Konstantin CAST: Scott Glenn (Ray), Dan Moran (Babcock/Nizam), Marisa Tomei (Julia), Derek Smith (Danny/Tony), Joseph Siravo (Lexington/Mathis), Conan McCarty (Vegas/Bartender), Bruce MacVittie (Ron/Waiter/Scones/Lounge Singer), Jennifer Esposito (Renee/Waitress), Ellen McElduff (Max)
A mystery in two acts.

Susan Cook Photos

John Elsen, Kelly Coffield in *Sin*

103

Tim Michael, Jennifer Gibbs, Sanaa Lathan in
A Movie Star Has to Star in Black and White

Ellen Bethea, Cleve Lamison in *Funnyhouse of a Negro*

SIGNATURE THEATRE COMPANY

Fifth Season

Artistic Director, James Houghton; Managing Director, Thomas C. Proehl; Associate Director, Elliot Fox; Development Director, Ellen Barker; Resident Set Designer, E. David Cosier; Resident Lighting, Designer, Jeffrey S. Koger; Resident Costume Designer, Teresa Snider-Stein; Press, Philip Rinaldi/James L.L. Morrison, Anne Lowrie

(In residence at Public/Shiva Theatre) Friday, Sept.22-Oct.22, 1995 (32 performances)
FUNNYHOUSE OF A NEGRO and **A MOVIE STAR HAS TO STAR IN BLACK AND WHITE** by Adrienne Kennedy; Costumes, Teresa Snider-Stein, Jonathan Green; Music, Cathy Elliot; Sound, Bruce Ellman; Stage Managers, Christopher De Camillis, Jennifer N. Rogers
Funnyhouse Director, Caroline Jackson Smith CAST: Alta Withers (Mother), Candy Buckley (Landlady), Troy Ruptash (Raymond), Ellen Bethea (Negro/Sarah), Caroline Clay (Queen Victoria Regina), Lisa Renee Pitts (Duchess of Hapsburg), Robert Jason Jackson (Patrice Lamumba), Cleve Lamison (Jesus), Aisha Benoir (Cellist)
Movie Star Director, Joseph Chaikin CAST: Wendy vanden Heuvel (Jean Peters/Columbia Pictures Lady), Bruce Faulk (Wallace), Sanaa Lathan (Clara), Joyce Lynn O'Connor (Bette Davis), Simon Jutras (Paul Henreid), Joan Harris (Mother), Robert Colston (Father), Michael Early (Eddie), Wayne Maughans (Marlon Brando), Tim Michael (Montgomery Clift), Jennifer Gibbs (Shelly Winters)
Two one-act drama.

Friday, Nov.10-Dec.10, 1995 (32 performances)
JUNE AND JEAN IN CONCERT by Adrienne Kennedy; Adapted from the autobiography *People Who Led to My Plays*; Director, James Houghton; Music, Loren Toolajian; Costumes, Mary Myers; Sound, Jim van Bergen; Stage Manager, Renee Lutz CAST: Angela Bullock (Mother), Eisa Davis (June), Max DeLisi (Jackie), Mike Hodge (Minister), Ken LaRon (Dr. Mays/Nat King Cole), Sean McCourt (Frank Sinatra/Bing Crosby/Mr. Davis), Joann Merhaut (Judy Garland/Wee Bonnie Baker/Nurse), Nicole Parker (Aunt Ella), Lisa Renee Pitts (June's Ghost/Wings Over Jordan), Cedric Turner (Father), Alicia Rene Washington (Jean)
A drama performed without intermission. The action takes place in Ohio and Georgia, 1941-74.

Friday, Feb.23-Mar.24, 1996 (32 performances)
SLEEP DEPRIVATION CHAMBER by Adam Kennedy and Adrienne Kennedy; Director, Michael Kahn; Costumes, Teresa Snider-Stein, Jonathan Green; Sound, Jim van Bergen; Fights, David Leong; Stage Manager, Donald Fried CAST: Glynis Bell (Mrs. Wagner), Trazana Beverley (Suzanne), Willie C. Carpenter (David), Kevin T. Carroll (Teddy), Jonathan Fried (Holzer), Paul Geier (Edelstein), Ben Hersey (Donald Jr.), Leslie Silva (Patrice), Grafton Trew (March), Mark Gorman, Bo Smith, Jacques Henri Taylor (Ensemble)
A drama performed without intermission.

Friday, April 19-May 19, 1996 (32 performances)
THE ALEXANDER PLAYS...SUZANNE IN STAGES by Adrienne Kennedy; Director, Robbie McCauley; Costumes, Teresa Snider-Stein, Jonathan Green; Sound, Jim van Bergen; Stage Manager, Monique Martin CAST: Leon Addison Brown, Tom Gerard, Jake-Ann Jones, Sanaa Lathan, Seret Scott, Ned Van Zandt, Jennifer Wiltsie, Craig Wroe
Three plays: *Dramatic Circle*(1991), *Ohio State Murders*(1990) and *Motherhood 2000*(1993).

Left: Jonathan Fried, Kevin T. Carroll, Trazana Beverley
in *Sleep Deprivation Chamber*

Top Left: Afemo Amilami, Sanaa Lathan in *Por'Knockers*
Top Right: Steven Skybell, Ned Eisenberg in *AntigoneNew York*

VINEYARD THEATRE

Fifteenth Season

Artistic Director, Douglas Aibel; Executive Director, Barbara Zinn Krieger; Managing Director, Jon Nakagawa; Production Manager, Mark Lorenzen; General Manager, Michael A. Buchanan; Artistic/Administrative Associate, Bob Swee; Press, Shirley Herz/Sam Rudy

Wednesday, Nov.8-Dec.10, 1995 (22 performances and 12 previews)
POR'KNOCKERS by Lynn Nottage; Director, Michael Rogers; Set, G.W. Mercier; Lighting, Phil Monat; Costumes, Candice Donnelly; Sound, Aural Fixation; Stage Manager, Robin C. Gillette CAST: Ray Ford (Lance), Sanaa Lathan (Tamara), Ramon Melindez Moses (James), earl Nash (Ahmed), Afemo Omilami (Kwami), Daniel Zelman (Lewis)
A drama performed without intermission. The setting is East New York.

Tuesday, Jan.16-Mar.10, 1996 (40 performances and 16 previews)
BED AND SOFA; Music, Polly Pen; Libretto, Laurence Klavan; Based on the 1926 silent film by Abram Room; Director, Andre Ernotte; Orchestrations, John McKinney; Musical Director, Alan Johnson; Set/Costumes, G.W. Mercier; Lighting, Phil Monat; Sound, Aural Fixation; Movement, Loni Ackerman; Cast Recording, Varese Sarabande; Stage Manager, Eileen Myers CAST: Terri Klausner (Ludmilla), Michael X. Martin (Nikolai-Kolya), Jason Workman (Volodya), Martin Moran, Polly Pen (Radio Voices)
A musical performed without intermission. The action takes place in Moscow, 1926.

Wednesday, Apr.10-May 12, 1996 (21 performances and 13 performances)
ANTIGONE IN NEW YORK by Janusz Glowacki; Director, Michael Mayer; Set, William Barclay; Costumes, Michael Krass; Lighting, Christopher Akerlind; Music/Sound, David Van Tieghem; Fights, J. Steven White; Stage Manager, Robin C. Gillette CAST: Monti Sharp (Police), Priscilla Lopez (Anita), Steven Skybell (Sasha), Ned Eisenberg (Flea), Michael Ringler (Pauli)
A drama in two acts. The setting is a New York City park.

Terri Klausner, Jason Workman, Michael Martin in *Bed and Sofa*

Carol Rosegg Photos

Josh Hamilton, Daniel Zelman in *Wonderful Time*

**Bill Porter, Brooks Ashmanskas, Jessica Molaskey,
Andrea Burns in *Songs for a New World***

WPA THEATRE
(WORKSHOP OF THE PLAYERS ART)
Nineteenth Season

Artistic Director, Kyle Renick; Managing Director, Lori Sherman; Business Manager, Mark Merriman; Production Manager, Alistair Wandesforde-Smith; Press, Jeffrey Richards/Kevin Rehac, Kitty Coyne, Laramie Dennis

Wednesday, Oct.11-Nov.5, 1995 (12 performances and 15 previews)
SONGS FOR A NEW WORLD; Music/Lyrics, Jason Robert Brown; Director, Daisy Prince; Orchestrations, Brian Besterman, Mr. Brown; Choreography, Michael Arnold; Set, Stephan Olson; Lighting, Craig Evans; Costumes, Gail Brassard; Sound, Jim Bay, John Curvan; Cast Recording, RCA; Stage Manager, Kristen Harris CAST: Brooks Ashmanskas, Andrea Burns, Jessica Molaskey, Billy Porter
MUSICAL NUMBERS: The New World, On the Deck of a Spanish Sailing Ship 1492, Just One Step, I'm Not Afraid of Anything, The River Won't Flow, Stars and the Moon, She Cries, The Steam Train, The World Was Dancing, Surabaya-Santa, Christmas Lullaby, King of the World, I'd Give It All for You, Flagmaker 1775, Flying Home, Hear My Song
A musical revue in two acts.

Thursday, Dec.28, 1995-Jan.31, 1996 (21 performances and 14 previews)
WONDERFUL TIME by Jonathan Marc Sherman; Director, Tim Vasen; Set, Henry Dunn; Lighting, Jeremy Stein; Costumes, Mimi Maxmen; Sound, Aural Fixation; Stage Manager, Gwendolyn D. Burrow CAST: Josh Hamilton (Linus Worth), Anney Giobbe (Robin/Waitress), Silas Weir Mitchell (Ernie/Peter), Marin Hinkle (Betsy Flynn), Daniel Zelman (Clyde)
A romantic comedy performed without intermission. The action takes place in California and New York City.

Tuesday, Mar.5-31, 1996 (20 performances and 8 previews)
BRINE COUNTY WEDDING; Written/Performed by Christopher V. Alessi; Director, Henry Polic II; Set, Alistai Wandesforde-Smith; Lighting, Jack Mehler; Sound, Kurt B. Kellenberger; Stage Manager, Ruth E. Kramer
A one-man comedy performed without intermission.

Carol Rosegg, John Waroff Photos

OFF-BROADWAY PRODUCTIONS
(JUNE 1, 1995-MAY 31, 1996

(Miranda Theatre) Thursday, June 1-18, 1995 Serendipity Productions in association with Georgia Buchanan presents:
THE SOUL OF AN INTRUDER by Steve Braunstein; Director, Frank Cento; Set, William F. Moser; Costumes, Harry Nadal; Lighting, Ed McCarthy; Sound, Dean Cama; Stage Manager, Colleen Marie Davis; Press, Jeffrey Richards/Kevin Rehac, Richard Guido CAST: Darby Townsend (Mabel Codd), Patrick Skelton (Jack Amsterdam), Jeffrey Spolan (Eddie Dixon)

A thriller in two acts.

(Samuel Beckett Theatre) Thursday, June 1-11, 1995 (12 performances and 1 preview)
GERMAN GAMES/EVANGELINE AND GOD by Berrilla Kerr; Director, Alex Dmitriev; Sets, Richard Harrison; Lighting, Mary Ann Long; Costumes, Deborah J. Edelman; Sound, Christopher Cronin; Stage Manager, Robert Moss; Press, Howard & Barbara Atlee CASTS: *German Games*: Bella Jarrett (Helga), Jennifer Thomas (Young Helga), Lucille Patton, Jan Buttram (Frieda), Kathleen Manikowski (Young Frieda), Ray Atherton (Father), Janine L. Miskulin (Lisbeth Schmidt), Billy Ray Tyson (Henry Clay Washington) *Evangeline*: Jane Cronin (Evangeline), Paul Barry (Godfrey), Donald Scott Smyth (Attendant)

Two one-act dramas.

Jeffrey Spolan, Patrick Skelton, Darby Townsend
in Soul of an Intruder

Jennie Crotero, Jason McKay in *Homo Americanus* (Lynn Kanter)

(Bouwerie Lane Theatre) Friday, June 2-25, 1995 (13 performances and 2 previews) Purgatorio Ink Theatrer presents:
HOMO AMERICANUS by Assurbanipal Babilla; Costumes, John Calvin; Set, Mr. Babilla; Lighting, Jason Boyd; Sound, One Dream; Stage Manager, Sue Patino; Press, Shirley Herz/Stephen Barry CAST: Laurie Wickens (Liliwhite), Bill Martin (Jedediah Krappe), Leyla Ebtehadj (Eulalie Krappe), David Cote (Shedrach Krappe), Andrew Costell (Mishach Krappe), Jason McKay (Abednego Krappe), Georgia Hodes (Molly Krappe), Jennie Crotero (Dolly Krappe), Suzanne E. Fletcher (Eleonora), Lynne Kanter (Godiva Ubralles), Assurbanipal Babilla (Jackson)

A four-act drama performed with one intermission. The action takes palce on a mythical future frontier at Thanksgiving, Christmas, Fourth of July and Halloween.

(46 Walker St.) Saturday, June 3-25, 1995 (20 performances) New Georges presents:

FRANK , FRANK; Written/Directed/Choreographed by Randolyn Zinn and Jennifer McDowall; Set/Costumes, James Schuette; Lighting, Jeanne Koenig Rubin; Sound, Chris Todd; Stage Manager, Kelly O'Rourke; Press, Shirley Herz/Wayne Wolfe CAST: Randolyn Zinn (Frankie), Doug Krizner (Dad), Maria Lakis, Jean McDade (Tone Ladies), Susan Hall (Shelly)

A dance/theatre work performed with intermission. Set to a score of Frank Sinatra music, the action revolves around a father and daughter relationship from the 1950s to the present.

(Judith Anderson Theatre) Sunday, June 4-18, 1995 (11 performances and 2 previews) Emerging Artist Theatre Company presents:
SISTERS' DANCE by Sarah Hollister; Director, Yana Landowne; Sets, William F. Moser; Lighting, Craig R. Ferraro; Costumes, David Robinson; Music/Sound, Lewis Flinn; Stage Manager, Marylou Lynn; Press, Tony Origlio/Stephen Murray, David Powell Smith CAST: Robin Poley (Alice), Blanche Cholet (Mother), Carter Mac Inskeep (Roy), Susan Finch (Fleur), Paul Lima (Duncan)

A drama in two acts. The action takes place in a country farmhouse

Doug Krizner, Randolyn Zinn in *Frank, Frank*

(Theatre at St. Peter's) Monday, June 5-10, 1995 (7 performances) The Directors Company and the Harold Prince Musical Theatre Program present:

CAMILA with Music/Lyrics/Book by Lori McKelvey; Director, Melia Bensussen; Choreography, Janet Bogardus; Musical Director, Deborah R. Lapidus; Set, John Conklin; Lighting, Allen Lee Hughes; Costumes, Beba Shamash; Sound, Randy Freed; Stage Managers, Anne Marie Padlucci, Allison Somers; Press, Guy Giarrizzo   CAST: Philip Anthony (Dancer/Mariano), Mimi Bessette (Marcia O'Gorman), Virginia Billia (Marcia O'Gorman), Geoffrey Blaisdell (Fr. Gannon), David Brummel (Senor O'Gorman), Maurizio Corbino (Eduardo O'Gorman), Anthony Crivello (Fr. Ladislao Gutierrez), Cynthia Farrell (Lieutenant's Wife), Marcy Harriell (Lucia), Dena Moore (Dancer/Mariano's Wife), Judith Roberts (Grandmother), Marla Schaffel (Camila O' Gorman), Matthew Thibideau (Ignacio), Todd Thurston (Officer), Tom Treadwell (Jose Maria Rodriguez), Michael-Leon Wooley (Lieutenant/Rancher).

MUSICAL NUMBERS: Tango, La Luna, Ave Maria, I Had a Dream, Dance for Me, Long Live the Holy Federation, Twenty Drops of Blood/Requiem, Did You Hear?, Convent or Marriage, Man That I'll Marry, What I Recommend, I Love Him, Into the Night, For the Innocent, Finale. An unfinished musical set in mid-19th Century Argentina. with **THE BALLAD OF LITTLE JO** with Music by Mike Reis; Lyrics, Sara Schlesinger; Book, Ms. Schlesinger, Mike Kaats; Based on Maggie Greenwald's film; Director, Rod Kaats; Musical Director, Stan Tucker; Sets, John Conklin; Lighting, Allen Lee Hughes; Costumes, David Brooks; Sound, Randy Freed; Stage Managers, Marjorie Horne, Jill Larmett CAST: Anne Allgood (Kate Ryan), Christopher Eaton Bailey (Lawrence Ryan), Kathryn Blake (Debutante), Don Chastain (Thomas Harrison), John Haggerty (Salesman), James Hindman (Lee Gibbs), Patricia G. Kennedy (Marion), Tucker McCrady (Horner), Rob Narita (Tin Man Wong), Ingrid Olsen (Photographer's Wife), Rex Robbins (James Monaghan), Rodney Scott (Conductor), Richard L. Smith (Photographer), Jon Vanderholen (Charles Ryan), Barbara Walsh (Josephine Monaghan)

MUSICAL NUMBERS: Lead Me Home, Passing Through, No Price Could Ever Be Too Much To Pay, Night Song, Everything That Touched Her, To Winter, Unbuttoning the Buttons

An unfinished musical set in the Wild West, 1865-1903.

(55 Grove St.) Tuesday, June 6-16, 1995 (8 performances) Playwrights' Preview Productions presents:

BLUES FOR MISS BUTTERCUP by L.E. McCullough; Director, Patricia R. Floyd; Design, Bob Lott; Lighting, Curtis "Chel" Hodge; Costumes, Kenneth J. Wyrtch, Roxanne Bevel; Stage Manager, Karimah CAST: Inga Ballard, Damon Chandler, Damien Leake, Sandy Moore, Gloria Sauve, Judy Tate, Daniel Whitner

A drama set in Indianapolis' Knocka Jug Cafe, 1935.

(Wall & Broad Streets) Tuesday, June 6-July 16, 1995 En Garde Arts presents:

J.P. MORGAN SAVES THE NATION; Music, Jonathan Larson; Lyrics/Book, Jeffrey M. Jones; Director, Jean Randich; Musical Director, Jules Cohen; Choreography, Doug Elkins; Sound, Dave Meschter/Applied Audio; Sets, Kyle Chepulis; Lighting, Pat Dignan; Costumes, Kasha Maimone; Press, David Rothenberg CAST INCLUDES: James Judy (J.P. Morgan), Stephen DeRosa (Uncle Sam), Buzz Bovshow (G. Washington, Esq.), Julie Fain Lawrence (Liberty), Robin Miles (A Devil)

A site-specific musical tracing J.P. Morgan's life performed in front of Federal Hall, the J.P. Morgan Bank Building and the New York Stock Exchange.

(Joyce Theatre) Tuesday, June 6-16, 1995 (16 performances)

AMERICAN BALLROOM THEATRE; Artistic Directors, Pierre Dulaine and Yvonne Marceau; Choreography, Peter diFalco, Geoffrey Holder, Gary Pierce, John Roudis, Geoffrey Holder; Press, Peter Cromarty/Philip Thurston CAST: Gary Pierce and Gaye Bowidas, Victor Kanevsky and Dee Quinones, Alex Tchassov and Natasha Bragarnik, Louis Brockman and Sarah White, Lars Rosager and Anna de Pagan, Yoshi Yano and Katya Surrence

Anthony Crivello, Marla Schaffel in *Camila* (Carol Rosegg)

Barbara Walsh, Rob Nanita in *Ballad of Little Joe* (Carol Rosegg)

Lars Rosager, Anna de Pagan in
American Ballroom Theatre (Jack Mitchell)

(HERE) Friday, June 9-July 1, 1995 (18 performances) igLoo presents:
GANGSTER APPAREL by Richard Venture; Director, Ethan Silverman; Set, Keith Ian Raywood; Costumes, April Bulla; Lighting, Stan Presser; Sound, Tony Meola; Press, Philip Rinaldi CAST: Anthony De Sando (Joey), Christopher Peditto (Louie)
   A comedy in two acts.

(Harold Clurman Theatre) Friday, June 9-25, 1995 (12 performances) Love Creek Productions presents:
THE FASHION POLICE by Fred Gormley; Director, Sharon Fallon; Set, Viola Bradford; Lighting, Richard Kent Green; Stage Manager, Lisa Mackie; Press, Annie Chadwick CAST: Alan Denny (Harlan Zukovsky), Chuck Simone (Sarge Smith), Wende O'Reilly (Teresa Maytag), Stephen Roman (Jan Troxel), Kirsten Walsh (Jess Drinan), Bob Manus (Eduardo Vittelone), Kevin Finan
   A comedy set in New York City.

(One Dream) Friday, June 9-July 2, 1995 (15 performances and 3 previews) One Dream in association with Machine Full presents:
A CANDLE IN THE WINDOW by Tom Gilroy; Director, Michael Imperioli; Set, John Farrell; Lighting, Russell Champa; Costumes, Lili Taylor; Press, Shirley Herz/Wayne Wolfe CAST: Tom Gilroy (Johnny), Maggie Low (Maddy)
   A drama involving an ex-marine and a middle-aged school teacher.

(One Dream) Friday, June 9-July 1, 1995 (10 performances and 1 preview) One Dream and Zena Group present;
THE MUSEUM OF CONTEMPORARY ART; Written/Performed by Stephen Rappaport; Director, Hope Alexander Willis; Lighting, Russell H. Champa; Press, Shirley Herz/Wayne Wolfe
   A monodrama in one-act.

(Playhouse 91) Wednesday, June 14-July 9, 1995 (16 performances and 9 previews) The Eclectic Theatre Company in association with Peralta Productions presents:
IDENTICAL TWINS FROM BALTIMORE; Music/Lyrics, Dan Alvy; Book, Marc Mantell; Director/Choreographer, Bill Castellino; Musical Director, Christopher McGovern; Orchestrations, Mr. McGovern, Sande Campbell; Set/Projections, Michael Bottari and Ronald Case; Costumes, Tzili Charney; Lighting, Mathew J. Williams; Sound, Tom Clark; Stage Manager, Eve Clulow; Press, Pete Sanders/Glenna Freedman, Michael Hartman CAST: Rose McGuire (Madonna), Rob Roznowski (Max Pulian), T. Robert Rigott (Tony Dilema), Neil Schleifer (Manny Gelt), Colleen Durham (Fritzie), Lisa McMillan (Hedy Harlowe), Jeremy Czarniak (Cedric), Bill Whitefield (Randy Bachelor), Jill Locnikar (Sheila), Robert Cary (Baby Boy Bruce), Adriane Lenox (Jill Undergrowth), Mary Stout (Jane Undergrowth)
MUSICAL NUMBERS: Take the Picture, New York Get Ready for Us, Famous for Fifteen Minutes, This Night, One Sided Love, I'm on Your Side, Movie Moguls, Love Gets in the Way, Everyone's Here, Interrogation, Another Chance, The Girls Are Back, I Made It to the Top, Finale
   A musical comedy in two acts. The action takes place in New York and Los Angeles. The time is Distant/Present.

(Altered Stages) Thursday, June 15-July 2, 1995 (13 performances and 1 preview) Anchor Theatre Company presents:
ROCKET TO THE MOON by Clifford Odets; Director, John McDonough; Sets, Mary E. Houston; Lighting, Chuck Cameron; Costumes, Sang-Jin Lee; Press, Denise Robert CAST: Paige Witte (Cleo Singer), Maggie Silcoff (Belle Stark), William Stiles (Willy Wax), Edward Yankie (Ben Stark), Leo Bertelsen, David Tillistrand, J. Barrett Lindgren
   A 1938 drama set in a dentist's office.

(Trocodero Cabaret) Friday, June 16-November, 1995 The New York Actors' Alliance presents:
BEYOND THERAPY by Christopher Durang; Director, Mark Cannistraro; Set, Katherine L. Spencer; Stage Manager, Karl Martini; Press, Elizabeth Thompson CAST: Ben Hodges (Bob), Jack Lewis (Bruce), Claudia Orenstein, Laura Craig (Prudence), Paul Powell (Dr. Stuart Framingham), Victoria Bell (Mrs. Charlotte Wallace), Peter Fasanelli (Andrew)
   A 1981 comedy performed without intermission.

Maggie Low, Tom Gilroy, in *A Candle in the Window* (Lisa Maizliah)

Adriane Lenox, Mary Stout in *Identical Twins From Baltimore* (Carol Rosegg)

Ben Hodges, Claudia Orenstein, Jack Lewis in *Beyond Therapy* (Ron Peaslee)

Kevin Shine, Stephanie Jones in *Autumn House*
(Carl Sturmer)

Patrice Johnson, Catrina Ganey, Tamika Lamison, Dorcas Johnson,
Yvette Ganier, Deidra Johnson, Brenda Phillips in *For Colored Girls*
Who Have Considered Suicide When the Rainbow is Enuf

Jennifer Lee Andrews, Suzanne Ishee, Denis Lawson, Janet Aldrich,
Judith Moore in *Lust* **(Gerry Goodstein)**

(Samuel Beckett Theater) Friday, June 16-25, 1995 (6 performances) IRT's New Directions Theatre presents:
MEASURED HONESTY by Chris Shaw Swanson; Director, Jenny Psaki; Set, Steve Capone; Lighting, Paul Ziemer; Costumes, Lisa Tracy CAST: Frances Ford (Annie Mack), Nina Ciancio (Bridget Mason), Charles Loffredo (George Troy), Carl Sturmer (Terry Andrews), Christopher Lucey (Peter Sands)
   A comedy in two acts. The setting is a Cleveland ad agency.

(Samuel Beckett Theater) Saturday, June 17-24, 1995 (6 performances) IRT's New Directions Theatre presents:
THE AUTUMN HOUSE by John Attanas; Director, Jonathan Fluck; Set, Steve Capone; Lighting, Paul Ziemer; Costumes, Lisa Tracy CAST: Steve Dane (Tom MacDougal), Matt Tomasino (Louis Heller), Jonquil Saleheen (Carla Geller), Debra Funkhouser (Jennifer Ryan), Kevin Shine (Andy Stevens), Dory Binyon (Amy Carson), Stephanie A. Jones (Kara West), Bruce Barney (Jared Berkowitz)
   A drama in two acts. The action takes place in a Long Island beach house.

(Prism Playhouse) Monday, June 19, 1995 (1 limited performance) Prism Playhouse presents:
DORMEZ VOUS by Chris Collet; Director, Lauren Lovett CAST: Haynes Thigpen (Robert), Stephanie Berry (Felice), Ann Talman (Karen), Joseph Cappelletti (Stuart), Kevin Orton (Stage Directions)
   A drama exploring modern romance.

(Vineyard 26th St.) Wednesday, June 21-July 9, 1995 (16 performances and 2 previews) The National Asian American Theatre Company presents:
THE SCHOOL FOR WIVES by Moliere; Translation, Richard Wilbur; Director, Stephen Stout; Set, Sarah Lambert; Costumes, Ronna Rothenberger; Lighting, Jennifer Tanzer; Stage Manager, John Roque; Press, Shirley Herz/Stephen Barry CAST: Ron Nakahara (Arnolphe), Mel Duane Gionson (Chrysalde), Jojo Gonzalez (Alain), Eileen Rivera (Georgette), Arloa Reston (Agnes), Daniel Dae Kim (Horace), Ching Gonzalez (Notary/Enrique), Richard Eng (Oronte)
   A 1662 comedy.

(New Federal Theatre) Thursday, June 22-July 16 transferred to Tribecca Performing Arts Center Wednesday, Aug.16-Sept.24, 1995 Nw Federal Theatre presents:
FOR COLORED GIRLS WHO HAVE CONSIDERED SUICIDE WHEN THE RAINBOW IS ENUF...; Written/Directed by Ntozake Shange; Music, Craig Harris; Choreography, Mickey Davidson; Lighting, William H. Grant III; Set, Chris Cumberbatch; Costumes, Judy Dearing; Sound, Tim Schellenbaum; Stage Manager, Jacqui Casto; Press, Max Eisen/Michele Gotham CAST:Catrina Ganey (Lady in Violet), Yvette Ganier (Lady in Aqua), Deidra LaWan Johnson (Lady in Gold), Dorcas M. Johnson (Lady in Pink), Patrice Johnson (Lady in Mint), Tamika Lamison (Lady in Rose), Brenda Phillips (Lady in Orange)
   A 1976 poetry drama.

(John Houseman Theatre) Friday, June 23-Aug.5, 1995 (27 performances and 23 previews) Eric Krebs, Frederic B. Vogel, Anne Strickland Squadron and the Walnut Street Theatre present:
LUST; Music/Lyrics/Book by The Heather Brothers(Neil, Lea, John, Charles); Freely adapted from William Wycherley's *The Country Wife*; Director, Bob Carlton; Musical Director, John Johnson; Design, Rodney Ford; Lighting, F. Mitchell Dana; Musical Staging, Barry Finkel; Stage Manager, Frank Anzalone; Press, David Rothenberg/David Lotz, David Gersten, Peter Webb, Tim Flaherty, Meg Gordean CAST: Denis Lawson (Horner), Robert McCormick (Quack), David Barron (Pichwife), Jennifer Lee Andrews (Margery Pinchwife), Lee Golden (Jasper Fidget), Judith Moore (Lady Fidget), Janet Aldrich (Mistress Dainty), Suzanne Ishee (Mistress Squeamish), Jenifer Piech (Alithea Pinchwife), A.J. Vincent (Harcourt), Dan Schiff (Dorilant), Barry Finkel (Sparkish), Michael Babin, Leslie Castay, James Javore (Servants/Townspeople)
MUSICAL NUMBERS: Lust, Art of Deceiving, Serve the Dog Right, I Live for Love, A Pox on Love and on Wenching, Somewhere Out There, Ladies of Quality, Husbands Beware, Why Did You Have to Come Into My Life, What a Handsome Little Fellow, Captain's Jig, Wait and See, Dear Sir, Ode to the One I Love, China, Come Tomorrow, Master Class, One of You, Vengeance, We Thank You/Finale
   A musical in two acts. The action takes place in London, 1661.

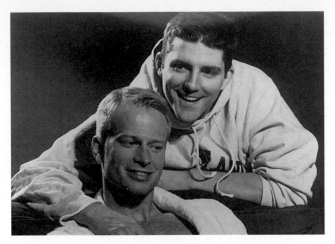

**Michael Curry, Robert Gomes in *2 Boys in a Bed on a
Cold Winter's Night* (Robert Discalfani)**

Caroline Seymour in *Ecstasy* (Ron Reeves)

**William Zariello, Mercury, Melissa Ritz, Alexia Rane in
Triumph of the West (Kymm Zuckert)**

(Manhattan Center) Saturday, June 24, 1995 (2 performances) International Dragfest Group presents:
LYPSINKA! AS I LAY LIP-SYNCHING; Created/Performed by John Epperson; Director, Kevin Malony; Press, Shirley Herz/Sam Rudy
The latest in a series of musical evenings with the lip-synching songstress.

(Synchronicity Space) Friday, June 30-July 16, 1995 (12 performances and 3 previews) The No-Pants Theatre Company presents:
TROY; Written/Directed by Dominic Orlando; Set/Costumes, Jay Durrwachter; Lighting, Roma Flowers; Music, Randy Redd; Fights, Matthew Baker; Stage Manager, Jaqui Lynch; Press, Patricia Story/Leigh Brodsky CAST: Jim Cronin (Fortunato Bova), Sean Weil (Odysseus), Sila Agavale (Guard/Apollo/Justice/Hector), Inger Tudor (Doctor/Kalypso), Karin Bowersock (Athena/Liberty/Helen/Penelope), Stephan Alexander (Dionysus/Freedom), Jeffrey Edward Peters (Diomedes/Mac), Frank Spinelli (Patrocles/Mayflower/Homer), Madison Cowan (Achilles), Hope Garland (Iphegenia/Orestes), Mary Neufeld (Menelaus/Smith), Soomi Kim (Paris/Elektra), Mark Poppleton (Agememnon/Pomp), Victoria Linchon (Polyxena/Hahn), Andy Mulcahy (Deiphobus/Telemachos)
A war drama performed with one intermission.

(Alice Tully Hall) Thursday, July 6-8, 1995 (3 performances) Alley Theatre and Lincoln Center Productions present:
HAMLET: A MONOLOGUE; Directed/Designed/Performed by Robert Wilson; Adapted by Wolfgang Wiens and Mr. Wilson from Shakespeare's play; Music/Sound, Hans Peter Kuhn; Costumes, Frida Parmeggiani; Lighting, Stephen Strawbridge; Stage Manager, Abbie H. Katz
Presented as part of Lincoln Center's Serious Fun festival.

(Theatre Off Park) Friday, July 7-Sept.17, 1995 (64 performances and 10 previews) Rattlestick Productions and Theatre Off Park present:
2 BOYS IN A BED ON A COLD WINTER'S NIGHT by James Edwin Parker; Director, Thomas Caruso; Set/Costumes, Paul Weimer; Lighting, Ed McCarthy; Stage Manager, Rita L. Williams; Press, Bill Evans/Jim Randolph CAST: Robert Gomes (Daryl), Michael Curry (Peter)
A drama performed without intermission.

(Judith Anderson Theater) Friday, July 7-Oct.7, 1995 (101 performances) The New Group and Axis in association with Michael Lang present:
ECSTASY by Mike Leigh; Director, Scott Elliott; Set, Kevin Price, Zaniz; Costumes, Eric Becker; Lighting, Benjamin Pearcy; Sound, Raymond D. Schilke; Music, Tom Kochan; Stage Manager, John J. Harmon; Press, Philip Rinaldi CAST: Francis Hope (Roy), Caroline Seymour (Jean), Marian Quinn succeeded by Toby Poser (Dawn), Zaniz Jakubowski (Val), Jared Harris succeeded by Neal Jones(Len), Patrick Fitzgerald (Mick)
A two-act drama set in Northwest London. This is a return engagement of last season's John Houseman Studio production.

(Harold Clurman Theatre) Tuesday, July 11-23, 1995 (8 performances) Love Creek Productions present:
THE TRIUMPH OF THE WEST by Michael T. Folie; Director/Sound, Geoffrey Tangeman; Set, Viola Bradford; Lighting, Richard Kent Green; Stage Manager, Sean Kering Deming; Press, Annie Chadwick/Colin Campbell CAST: Philip Albanese, Lillian Garcia, Mercury, Alexia Rane, Melissa Ritz, Matthew Solari, Forest Thomas, William Zarriello
An evening of eighteen short comedies.

(Mint Theater) Wednesday, July 12-29, 1995 (15 performances and 1 preview) Mint Theater and Annette Moskowitz/Alexander E. Racolin present:
KING JAMES AND THE INDIAN by Tony Howarth; Director, William Roudebush; Set, Christopher Jones; Lighting, William Kneissl; Costumes, Tom McAlister; Stage Manager, Mazerati Nieves; Press, David Rothenberg CAST: Gil Silverbird (Namontack), Jim Sterling (Capt. Newport), Gabriel Barre (James I), William Groth (Harry Whitfield), Mark Schulte (Henry), Vincent Barrett, Tercio Bretas (Soldiers), Kristin Flanders (Queen Anne), Sioux Madden (Katrina), Mark Alan Gordon (Robert Carr), Bob Emmett (William Bancroft), Patricia Kelley (Masquer)
A drama in two acts. The action takes place in England, 1610.

(Westside Repertory Theatre) Wednesday, July 12-30, 1995 (12 performances and 3 previews) Westside Repertory presents:

FANNY FIRST PLAY by George Bernard Shaw; Director, Kathleen Powers; Lighting, Jennifer E. Tanzer; Costumes, Mary Marsicano; Set, David Zyla, Ms. Powers; Stage Manager, Kim Marie T. Jones; Press, Mr. Zyla CAST: Rayna Baker (Mr. Gunn/Mrs. Knox), Tom Biglin (Savoyard/Duvallet), Munro Bonnell (Billy Burjoyce/Gilbey), Melody Cooper (Darling Dora), Creme O. Dooply (Maid), Ruthanne Geréghty (Mr. Vaughn/Mrs. Gilbey), Timothy Jeffryes (Trotter/Bobby), Andrew Rothkin (Bannal/Juggins), Peter Ruffett (Count O'Dowda/Knox), Seana Lee Wyman (Fanny/Margaret)

A rarely performed Shaw comedy.

(IBIS Supper Club) Thursday, July 13-Aug.31, 1995 (15 performances and 12 previews) Sidney Productions present:

OFF THE WALL by Brian Jaffe; Director, Grey Johnson; Design, David Ortlieb; Stage Manager, Don Myers; Press, Peter Cromarty/Sara Chaiken, Hugh Hayes CAST: David Johnston (Edward Chump III), Carol Brooks (Theresa), Tracey Wagner (Heidi Hoe), Sam Josephson (Arthur Treacle), Erik Engstrom (Jean-Paul Georges-Ringeau), Brian Jaffe (Frederick Kahnman)

An interactive comedy set in an auction house in which audience members bid on art.

(McGinn/Cazale Theatre) Friday, July 14-Aug.13, 1995 (27 performances and 4 previews) Deborah S. Thomas and Mark Rozzano present:

BONHOEFFER 1945 by D. Paul Thomas; Director, Albert Sinkys; Lighting, Russell Pyle; Costumes, Louise Frogley; Stage Manager, John Hagen; Press, Chris Boneau~Adrian Bryan-Brown/Patty Onagan CAST: D. Paul Thomas (Dietrich Bonhoeffer), Nicholas Hormann (Judge Advocate)

A drama in two acts. The action takes place in Tegel, the Wehrmacht Military Prison in Berlin, 1943-45.

**D. Paul Thomas, Nicholas Hormann in *Bonhoeffer 1945*
(Bill Youngblood)**

**Neil Necastro, David Mogentale, Tim Cocoran
in *Breast Men* (Bob Drefendorf)**

Brian Jaffe, Tracey Wagner, Eric Engstrom, Sam Josephson, Carol Brooks, David Johnston, in *Off the Wall* (Carol Rosegg)

`(Harold Clurman Theatre) Monday, July 17-29, 1995 (13 performances) Love Creek Productions presents:

OBJECTIVELY YOURS by Theresa Wozunk; Director, Geoffrey Tangeman; Set, Viola Bradford; Lighting, Richard Kent Green; Stage Manager, Sean Wahl; Press, Annie Chadwick/Colin Campbell CAST: Henry Marsden Davis, John Dougherty, Jennifer Ann Hall, Jackie Jenkins, Bill Johnson, Mark Macken, David M. Pincus, Devin Quigley, Sherri Ann Rose, Gregg David Shore, Bart Tangredi, J.D. Walters, Kymm Zuckert

Seven short plays.

(29th St. Repertory Theater) Monday, July 17-Aug.19, 1995 (30 performances) The 29th St. Repertory presents:

THE SIXTH ANNUAL SUMMER ONE-ACT FESTIVAL; Sets, Mark Bloom (A), Mary Houston (B); Lighting, Robert Perry; Stage Managers, Rob Volk (A), Brad Rohrer (B); Press, John and Gary Springer/Candi Agams EVENING A: *Single and Proud* by Frederick Stroppel; Director, Michael Hillyer CAST: Lois Raebeck (Sylvia), Charles Willey (Steve), Elizabeth Elkins (Jackie), Alysia Reiner (Jeanette) *Marmalade Tears* by Ann Elizabeth Miller; Director, Vivian Sorenson CAST: Bernadette Frankel (Greta), Alice O'Neill (Fatima), Peter Basch (Otto Teaworth) *Breast Men* by Bill Bozzone and Joe DiPietro; Director, James Abar CAST: Tim Corcoran (Lloyd), David Mogentale (Stuart), Neil Necastro (Gene)

EVENING B: *The Mamet Women* by Frederick Stroppel; Director, Katy Bolger CAST: Ritamarie Kelly (Sally), Sani Klein, Lee Heinz (Polly) *Ever After* by T.S. Stobart; Director, Leslie Lynn Meeker CAST: Iris Paldiel (A), Leo Farley (B) *Baptists* by Bill Nave; Director, Vera Beren CAST: Colin Campbell (Fern Alton Sr.), Tom Martins (Wally), Leah Posey (Gladys), Paula Ewin (Sally) *The Hand of God* by Bill Nave; Director, Vera Beren CAST: Paula Ewin (Gail), Arpine Tcholakian (Marietta), Brad Rohrer (Bob)

(Theatre East) Wednesday, July 19-Sept.24, 1995 (68 performances and 11 previews) Leahy Productions in association with Arthur B. Brown present:
PETS; Conceived/Directed/Choreographed by Helen Butleroff; Writers/Music/Lyrics, Marion Adler, Adele Ahronheim, Raphael Crystal, Rick Cummins, Richard Enquist, Faye Greenberg, Alison Hubbard, Dan Kael, Kim Oler, Jimmy Roberts, Ben Schaechter, June Siegel, Carolyn Sloan, Thomas Tierney, Thomas Edward West, Greer Woodward, Jane Broady Zales; Musical Director/Orchestrations, Albert Ahronheim; Set, Holger; Costumes, Gail Cooper-Hecht; Lighting, Phil Monat; Sound, Ray Schilke; Stage Manager, D.C. Rosenberg; Press, Peter Cromarty CAST: Michelle Azar, Barbara Broughton, Christopher Harrod, Christopher Scott, Jenifer Simard
MUSICAL NUMBERS: Pets, Take Me Home with You, Don't Worry 'Bout Me, I Walk Ze Dogs, Just Do It Without Me, Cat in the Box, There's a Bagel on the Piano, Perpetual Care, Cool Cats, Dear Max, First Cat, What About Us?, Peculiar, Bonus #1-3, Franklin, Mice of Means, Night of the Iguana, If You Can Stay, All in a Day's Work, Finale
A musical revue in two acts.

(Synchronicity Space) Thursday, July 20-Aug.6, 1995 (14 performances) Synchronicity Space and Flip Productions present:
THE ALL-NUDE COLLEGE-GIRL REVUE by Lisa Faith Phillips; Direction/Set, Todd Stuart Phillips; Lighting, David Alan Comstock; Costumes, Ms. Phillips, Cast; Sound, Ms. Phillips, Philip Goetz CAST: Carissa Ashley (Carlotta), Dede Kinerk (Ginger), Pam Wilterdink (Babydoll), Megan Schmidt (Suzy), Laura McLauchlin (Rusty), Tiffany Phillips (Cat), Yvonne Lewis (Eve), Christina Lahera (Annie)
A drama in two acts. The action takes place at the Peek-A-Boo Club in Boston's "Combat Zone", 1986.

Ron Bagden, Ben Shenkman, Johanna Schmidt in *Moose Mating*

Johnetta Alston, Carl Hall in *Time and the Wind* **(Blanche Macket)**

Jennifer Simard, Christopher Harrod, Michelle Azar, Christopher Scott, Barbara Broughton in *Pets* **(Carol Rosegg)**

(HERE) Thursday, July 20-Aug.13, 1995 (15 performances) HERE presents:
MOOSE MATING by David Grae; Director, Annie Loui; Set/Lighting, Leonel C. Valle; Costumes, Melissa Toth; Music, Andy Boehmke; Stage Manager, Emily Orr; Press, Shirley Herz/Wayne Wolfe, Heather Eckhaus CAST: David Greenspan, (Narrator), Johnna Schmidt (Betsy), Ben Shenkman (Lonnie), Ron Bagden (Michael), Lydia Radziul (Josie)
A comedy performed without intermission. The action takes place in New York City.

(Chicago City Limits) Thursday, July 20, 1995-June 22, 1996 (293 performances) Chicago City Limits presents:
THAT'S WHAT YOU SAID; Director, Paul Zuckerman; Musical Director, Gary Adler; Stage Manager, Nicole J. Baker; Press, Keith Sherman/Jim Byk, Stuart Ginsberg CAST: Gary Adler, Carl Kissin, John Cameron Telfer, Leslie Upson, John Webber
An improvisational musical revue.

(John Houseman Studio) Thursday, July, 27-Sept.2, 1995 (27 performances and 12 previews) Eric Krebs and John Houseman Theatre Center in association with AMAS Musical Theatre present:
TIME AND THE WIND; Music/Arrangements/Musical Director, Galt MacDermot; Lyrics, Norman Matlock; Director/Choreography, Louis Johnson; Costumes, Bernard Johnson; Lighting, Deborah Constantine; Stage Manager, Christine Catti; Press, David Rothenberg CAST: Johnetta Alston, Russell Brown, Carol Denise, Suzanne Griffin, Carl Hall, Chris Jackson
MUSICAL NUMBERS: Time and the Wind, Mais Oui, I Came to Town, Gentle Rain, By the Time I Forget Her, Now I Am Ready (Flustered), My Key Don't Fit the Lock, I Am Not Gone, There Are Times, Should I Tell Him, If What I Saw, They Didn't Ask, Quittin' Time, What Can I Say, I've Seen People Like Them Before, Ah It's Love, When You Love Really, Tell Her You Care, Send Me You, Funky Dance, When I Was a Child, Level with You, I Was Taught to Love, Flowers for Her Hair, What You Looked Like, I Love You, True Love's Hand, Wanted to Dine, There Are Girls, Goodbye, According to Plan, Finale
A musical in two acts. The action takes place in New York City.

(45th St. Theatre) Saturday, July 22-Oct.1, 1995 (77 performances and 6 previews) re-opened by York Theatre Company (Theatre at St. Peter's) Thursday, May 23-June 30, 1996 (40 performances) Michael & Barbara Ross and Lois Teich present:

WE'LL MEET AGAIN; Conceived/Directed by Johnny King; Writer, Vicki Stuart; Additional Material, Ivan Menchell; Set, James Morgan; Lighting, Daniel Ettinger; Sound, One Dream; Costumes, Oleg Cassini; Musical Director/Arrangements, Paul Katz; Stage Manager, Michael J. Chudinski; Press, Penny Landau (45th St.), Keith Sherman (York) CAST: Vicki Stuart, Paul Katz

MUSICAL NUMBERS: Remember, Look for the Silver Lining, Beyond the Blue Horizon, The Army the Navy & the Air Force, They'll Always Be an England, A Nightingale Sang in Berkeley Square, Stick It on the Wall Mrs. Riley, Underneath the Arches, All Our Tomorrows, The Thingummybob, Dancing with My Shadow, Wish Me Luck, Deepest Shelter, Love Letters, P.S. I Love You, Don't Sit Under the Apple Tree, Don't Get Around Much Anymore, They're Either Too Young or Too Old, You'll Never Know, Long Ago and Far Away, I'll Be Seeing You, These Foolish Things, Luverly Bunch of Coconuts, White Cliffs of Dover, London By Night, Yours, You'd Be So Nice to Come Home To, Lili Marlene, Auf Wiedersehn, We'll Meet Again

A musical journey through England during World War II performed without intermission.

(Harold Clurman Theatre) Tuesday, Aug.1-6 (7 performances) Love Creek Productions present:

BUBBLING by Le Wilhelm; Director, Diane Hoblit; Set, Viola Bradford; Lighting, Richard Kent Green; Stage Manager, Michael James Fry CAST: Melissa Ritz (Julie), Donna Davidge (Monique), Edythe Davis (Zoe Ann), Carol Ratnoff (Becky), Alexandra Williamson (Susie), Sharon Lee Prince (Zelda), Lori Brown-Niang (Shirley)

(Vineyard/Dimson Theatre) Tuesday, Aug.8-26, 1995 (20 performances) MA-YI Theatre Ensemble presents:

THE CAUCASIAN CHALK CIRCLE by Bertolt Brecht; Director, Chito Jao Garces; Music, Fabian Obispo; Set, Clint Ramos; Costumes, Mr. Ramos, Chris Glasgow; Lighting, Kristabelle Munson; Choreography, Max Luna III; Music Director, Robert Lee; Stage Manager, Victoria Epstein; Press, Francine L. Trevins CAST: Rona Figueroa (Grusha), Behn Cervantes (Singer/Azdak), Arthur Acuna (Aide-de-Camp), Boni B. Alvarez (Fat Prince's Nephew), Anthony Arzaga (Michael), Christina Canon (Ludovika), Marshall Factora (Prince/Lawyer/Lord etc..), Stephenie Ann Paulate La Torre (Michael), Lilah Kan (Cook/Defendant/Peasant), Mehr Mansuri (Governor's Wife), Tom Matsusaka (Grand Duke/Old Man), Sol Oca (Aniko/Nurse/Architect), Ralph Pena (Lavrenti/Shauva, etc..), Rio Puertollano (Rider/Ironshirt), Sam Ramirez (Yussup), Al D. Rodriguez (Corporal/Blackmailer), Danny Swartz (Simon), Virginia Wing (Singer/Mother-in-Law), Maria Aggabao (Ensemble)

MUSICAL NUMBERS: Dapat Bawiin, Mercy Your Grace, Down to the Abyss, I Shall Be Waiting, To the War My Weary Way I'm Wending, I Shall Have to Take You, Song of the Rotten Bridge, Stay in the Middle of the War, Battle Began Gray of Dawn, Cry Goes Unheard, Song of Injustice, When with Flames the Skies Were Glowing, Every Pleasure Costs Full Measure, Times When Masters Fight with Masters, If He Walked in Golden Shoes

(HERE) Tuesday, Aug.8-23, 1995 and Nov.1-4, 1995 New Georges and HERE present:
LOVE IN THE VOID; Conceived/Directed by Elyse Singer; Co-Adapted by Ms. Singer and Carolyn Baeumler; Set, Martin Fahrer; Sound, Lewis Flinn; Video/Lighting, Daniel Sollinger; Costumes, Kaye Voyce; Stage Manager, Margaret Bodriguian CAST: Carolyn Baeumler

A multimedia adaptation of Courtney Love's internet posts, 1994-95.

(Intar Theatre) Wednesday, Aug.9-13, 1995 (7 performances)
TWO ONE-ACTS; Director, Madison Michaels; Lighting, Lisa Cameron; Stage Manager, Susan Coulombe; Press, Michael Weiss BUDDHA by Katharine Houghton CAST Diana Henry, Mark Niebuhr; PRELUDE AND LIEBESTOD by Terrence McNally CAST: John Bergdahl, Luvada Harrison, Ms. Henry, Scott Hudson, Eric Lueck

Vicki Stuart in *We'll Meet Again* (Carol Rosegg)

Marshall Factora, Behn Cervantes in *Caucasian Chalk Circle* (Nigel Teare)

Carolyn Baeumler in *Love in the Void* (Daniel Sollinger)

(Westside Theatre/Upstairs) Monday, Aug.7, 1995-June 9, 1996 (352 performances) Robert V. Straus, Randall L. Wreghitt, Annette Niemtzow, Michael Jackowitz in association with Evangeline Morphos and Nancy Richards present:

THE FOOD CHAIN by Nicky Silver; Director, Robert Falls; Set, Thomas Lynch; Costumes, William Ivey Long; Lighting, Kenneth Posner; Sound, Duncan Edwards/Ben Rubin; Stage Manager, Allison Sommers; Press, Richard Kornberg/Ian Rand, Don Summa, William Finnegan CAST: Hope Davis succeeded by Marsha Dietlein, Katie MacNichol, Veanne Cox (Amanda), Phyllis Newman succeeded by Joy Behar (Bea), Rudolph Martin (Ford), Patrick Fabian succeeded by Spencer Rochfort (Serge), Tom McGowan succeeded by Rob Leo Roy (Otto)

A three-scene comedy performed without intermission. The action takes place in New York City.

Top: Tom McGowan, Patrick Fabian
Bottom Left: Phyllis Newman
Bottom Center: Patrick Fabian, Rudolf Martin, Hope Davis
Bottom Right: Spencer Rochfort
(Carol Rosegg)

(Trocadero Cabaret) Thursday, Aug.10-Sept.28, 1995 (8 performances) SourceWorks Theatre presents:

BEIRUT by Alan Browne; Director, Mark Cannistraro; Music, Dean Meyers; Set, Alex Dewez; Press Scott Taylor CAST: Shawn Batten, Jack Lewis, Aaron Williams
A new production of a 1986 drama set in the near future.

(Bessie Schonberg Theater) Wednesday, Aug.16-19, 1995 (4 performances) MVineyard Entertainment presents:
CRUISIN ON THE QE2; Music/Lyrics/Book/Directed/Performed by Joseph Wise; Lighting, Phil Sandstrom
A one-man show set on an imaginary cruise.

(Prospect Park) Thursday, Aug.24-Sept.3, 1995 Kings County Shakespeare Company present:
TWELFTH NIGHT by William Shakespeare; Director, K.G. Wilson; Set, Tom Crisp; Lighting, Bill Bradford; Stage Manager, William Doyle; Press, Jonathan Slaff CAST: Esquizito (Musician), Renee Bucciarelli (Viola), Allan Styer (Captain/Priest), Michael Oberlander (Orsino), Toru Ohno (Curio), Brad Thomas (Valentine), Lynn Marie Macy (Maria), Ron Sanborn (Toby Belch), Nick Dantos (Andrew Augecheek), Deborah Wright Houston (Feste), Karen Eterovich (Fabianne), Lisa M. Bostnar (Olivia), Vicki Hirsch (Malvolia), Randy Aromando (Sebastian), Herb Downer (Antonio)

(Theatre 22) Thursday, Aug.31-Sept.10, 1995 (10 performances) Terese Hayden presents:
SEASCAPE by Edward Albee; Director, Terese Hayden; Design, Fred Kolo; Lighting, George Kodar; Stage Manager, Stephen Brian Jones; Press, Max Eisen/Laurel Factor CAST: Jacqueline Brookes (Nancy), James Stevenson (Charlie), Charles D. Cissel (Leslie), Vanessa Parise (Sarah)
A 1975 drama in two acts. The action takes place on a sand dune.

(HERE) Tuesday, Sept.5-30, 1995 (13 performances and 7 previews) HOME for Contemporary Theatre and Art present:
FLOATING RHODA AND THE GLUE MAN by Eve Ensler; Director, Ariel Orr Jordan; Set, Mark Beard; Costumes, Donna Zakowska; Lighting, Jason Boyd; Music, Andy Teirstein; Violence, Daniel Kucan; Stage Manager, Bern Gautier; Press, Shirley Herz/Sam Rudy CAST: Myriam Cyr (Rhoda), Dylan McDermott (Barn), Priscilla Shanks (Storm), Matthew Dixon (Barn's Stand-In), Tara B. Hauptman (Terrace), Debbon Ayer, Shauna Lewis (Rhoda's Stand-In), Harry O'Reilly (Coyote), Joseph Lyle Taylor (Waiter), Matthew Pierce (Violin), Dina Emerson (Singer)
A comedy of bonding and bondage in two acts.

(Miranda Theatre) Wednesday, Sept.6-30, 1995 (15 performances and 5 previews) Miranda Theatre Company presents:
A GREATER GOOD by Keith Huff; Director, Mark Hunter; Set/Lighting, Sound, Bryon Winn; Costumes, Carol Lane; Stage Manager, David Smith; Press, Jim Baldassare CAST:Liz Davis (Lynn Quisnie), Christopher Hurt (Peter/Randy/Poshwurst/Marine/Sam Kessel/Everett), Jerry Mettner (Arlo), Jerry Mayer (Damen/Lou/Fez/Eldon/Jerry/Rufus), Annette Hunt (Bernice/Donna/Agnes/Hapgood/Janine/Lucy/Marjorie), Connie Winston (Kay/Elena/EMT/Karen), Geneva Carr (Melissa/Teresa/Holly), Joel Goldes (Bartender/Larry/Karl)
A comedy/drama in three acts. The action takes place in Chicago, Lake Superior, and Rochester, MN. The time spans 1987 to 2010.

(Greenwich St. Theatre) Wednesday, Sept.6-23, 1995 (17 performances) Villar-Hauser Theatre Compnay and Play Producers present:
IMPROPRIETY by Ron Elisha; Director, Ludovica Villar-Hauser; Set/Costumes, Christopher Lione; Lighting, Stewart Wagner; Sound, Raymond Schilke, Mary Anne Mundy; Stage Manager, Greg Dratva; Press, MAYA/Penny M. Landau CAST: Barbara Gruen (Ada Speidel), Richard Michael Hughes (Dirk Brauer), Owen S. Rackleff (Ernst Hagen), Manuel Brown (Max Speidel)
A drama in two acts. The action takes place in Berlin, 1991.

Shawn Batten, Aaron Williams in *Beirut* (Ron Peaslee)

Jacqueline Brooks, Vanessa Parise, Charles Cissel, James Stevenson in *Seascape* (Susan Johann)

Jerry Mettner, Liz Davis Chris Hunt in *A Greater Good* (Carol Rosegg)

(INTAR Theatre) Wednesday, Sept.6-10, 1995 (6 performances) Red Light District Theatre presents:
FAUSTUSA RITUAL; Adapted from Christopher Marlowe's play; Director/Set/Costumes, Marc Geller; Lighting, Frank DenDanto III CAST: Elizabeth Bove (Augur/Lucifer), Marilyn Duryea (Good Angel), Bill Roulet (Evil Angel), Jack DiMonte (Faustus), Marc Geller (Mephostophilis), Andrew Zechman (Pride/Friend/Whore), Christina Lisi (Covetousness/Whore), Gregg Dubner (Envy/Friend), Jimmy Holder (Wrath/Friend), Tracey Gilbert (Gluttony), Joseph Ditmyer (Sloth/Friend), Colleen Ward (Lechery/Helen of Troy)

(Harold Clurman Theatre) Wednesday, Sept.6-24, 1995 (23 performances) Annette Moskowitz and Alexander E. Racolin, Le Wilhelm and Love Creek Productions present:
THE WALLENBERG MISSION by Nicholas Wenkheim; Director, Francine L. Trevens; Set, Viola Bradford; Lighting, Richard Kent Green; Sound, George Jacobs; Stage Manager, Robert Villianovia; Press, Annie Chadwick/Colin Campbell CAST: Scott Sparks (Actor 1), Larry Weissman (Actor 2), Philip Albanese (Actor 3), Gil Grail (Actor 4), Roslyne Hahn (Actress), Jeff P. Weiss (Raoul Wallenburg), T.L. Reilly (Voice), Michael James Fry, Frank Marzullo, Vesna Tolomanska
A drama in two acts. The action takes place in Hungary, Sweden and Russia, 1944-73.

Larry Weissman, Bryan King, Gil Grail in
Wallenberg Mission **(Carl Sturmer)**

(Synchronicity Space) Thursday, Sept.7-24, 1995 (16 performances) Lightning Strikes Theatre Company presents:
TONS OF MONEY by Will Evans and Valentine; Adaptation, Alan Ayckbourn; Director, Liz Sipes; Set/Lighting, David Macfarlane; Costumes, Lauren Pytel; Fights, Ron Piretti; Press, Gary and John Springer/Candi Adams CAST: John McDermott (Sprules), Holly Greif (Simpson), Francine Julian (Benita Mullett), Kathleen Bloom (Louise Allington), Fred Harlow (Aubrey Henry Maitland Allington), Patrick McCaffrey (Giles), Martin Everall (James Chesterman), Rochelle Stempel (Jean Everard), D.L. Shroder (Henery), Atli Kendall (George Maitland)
A 1986 adaptation of a 1922 comedy in three acts. The action takes place in Marlow, England, 1922.

Kathleen Bloom, Fred Harlow in *Tons of Money* **(Scott Newirth)**

(Westside Theatre/Downstairs) Thursday, Sept.7, 1995-Feb.18, 1996 The New York Minyan L.P., R.E.L. Productions, Judith Resnick, Paul Morer, Norman Kurtz and Steve Harris present:
TOO JEWISH?; Written/Performed by Avi Hoffman; Musical Director, Ben Schaechter; Set, Leonard Hoffman; Lighting, Robert Bessoir; Stage Manager, Robert Lemieux; Press, Richard Kornberg/Ian Rand, Don Summa
Return engagement of last season's revue presenting songs and comedy from Jewish vaudeville.

(NADA) Thursday, Sept.7-10, 1995 (4 performances) NADA and Pierce Group present:
THE DREAM CANVAS by Sharr White; Director, Ron Bashford; Set, Chris Cardinale; Costumes, Ka Miller; Lighting, Jason Sturm; Sound, Bert Fasbender; Music, Harold Meltzer; Press, Carol Fineman CAST: Katherine Freedman, Guiesseppe Jones, Sharr White
A drama about a homeless artist.

(Camilla's Theatre Gallery) Friday, Sept.8-30, 1995 Harland Productions presents:
MATH AND AFTERMATH by Jim Grimsley; Director, Dean Gray; Music/Sound, Michael Keck; Lighting, Jack Mehler; Set, Daniel Ettinger; Costumes, Fabio Toblini, Stage Manager, Kim Marie T. Jones; Press, Elisabeth Lewis Corley CAST: Kernan Bell (Grip), David Duffield (Best Boyd), Jeff Burchfield (Pug Montreat), John-Michael Lander (Hugh Young), Elisabeth Lewis Corley (Voiceover), Sheri Galan (Dawn Stevens), Joe Heffernan (Joe Lube Cool), Antonia Beamish (Blue Donna Morgan), David Morgan O'Connor (Ghost of Hugh Young)
A drama about the unauthorized filming of a gay porn movie in the Marshall Islands, Feb.28, 1953 the day before the experimental explosion of an atomic bomb.

Jeff Burchfield, John-Michael Lander in
Math and Aftermath **(Susan Johann)**

Cynthia Watros, Gregg Edelman in *Standing By* (Carol Rosegg)

Maia Danziger, Michael MacCauley in *Measure for Measure*

Hamilton Clancy, Eliza Ventura, Michael Collins in
The Window (Joan Marcus)

(Playhouse 91) Friday, Sept.8-24, 1995 (16 performances and 4 previews) The Secret Annex LLC presents:
THE SECRET ANNEX; Music, William Charles Baton; Lyrics/Book, Robert K. Carr; Director/Staging, Dom Ruggiero; Musical Directors, Edward R. Conte, Jeffrey Buchsbaum; Set, Ellen Waggett; Christopher Landy; Costumes, Tracy Dorman; Sound, Simon Matthews; Stage Manager, Renee Rimland; Press, Max Eisen/Michele Gotham CAST: Lydia Gladstone (Edith Frank), Don Frame (Otto Frank), Rhonda Merritt (Margot Frank), Patricia Ann Gardner (Anne Frank), Steve Robbins (Mr. Van Pels), Nancy Ward (Mrs. Van Pels), Kevin Berthiaume (Lars Peters), Jan Austell (Mr. Kleinman), Karin Reed Bamesberger (Marleuse), Jim Straz (Sargent), Glen Badyna (Peter Van Pels), Reggie Barton (Dr. Pfeffer), Ingrid Olsen (Clerk), Joseph DiGennaro, Julie Halpern, Carse David Parker (Ensemble)
MUSICAL NUMBERS: Montage, We Are God's Forgotten People, Recitative, Forever Friends, War, Knights and Kings, Lullaby, Day and Night, The Final Hour, Pieces of My Life, Anne's Song, Evening Prayer, World Beyond the Pane, Peas, Mother's Love, Reprise, These Four Walls, On My Side, My Darling Close Your Eyes, Summer Afternoons, Living in New York, Man I've Become, Power of Dreams, Finale
    A two-act musical based on Anne Frank's story. The action takes place in the Frank family home and the secret annex during WWII.

(St. Peter's) Friday, Sept.8-Oct.8, 1995 (26 performances and 6 previews) The York Theatre Company presents:
STANDING BY by Norman Barasch; Director, Alex Dmitriev; Set, James Morgan; Costumes, Beba Shamash; Lighting, Jerold R. Forsyth; Sound, Jim van Bergen; Stage Manager, Colleen Marie Davis; Press, Keith Sherman/Jim Byk, Stuart Ginsberg CAST: Gregg Edelman (Jeffrey Miller), Cynthia Watros (Ellen Henry)
    A romantic comedy performed without intermission.

(Chelsea Playhouse) Tuesday, Sept.12-Oct.1, 1995 (15 performances and 1 preview) Lark Theatre Company presents:
MEASURE FOR MEASURE by William Shakespeare; Director, John Clinton Eisner; Sets, Larry Gruber; Lighting, Ed McCarthy; Costumes, Carol Brys; Choreography, Kayla Schwartz; Music, Frank Schiro; Stage Manager, Christopher De Camillis; Press, Chris Boneau~Adrian Bryan-Brown/Patty Onagan, Meredith Moore CAST: Michael Boyle (Elbow/Barnadine), Gary Bryan Budoff (Claudio), Maia Danziger (Isabella), Christopher Delaney (Pompey), Elan Evans (Gentleman/Friar Peter/Officer), C.M. Gampel (Escalus), Davis Hall (Duke), Margaret Howard (Julietta/Servant/Boy), Laura E. Johnston (Varrius/Gentleman/Francisca/ Justice/Froth/Officer), Susan Knott (Mariana), Michael MacCauley (Angelo), Marshall McGehee (Officer/Messenger), David Snizek (Lucio), John Thomas Waite (Provost), Olivia Williams (Mistress Overdone/Abhorson/Officer)
    Performed with one intermission.

(ATA Theatre) Wednesday, Sept.13-Oct.22, 1995 (33 performances and 8 previews) Andrew R. Sackin in association with Michelle Marceau and Adam R. Mattessich present:
THE WINDOW and **IN AN INFINITE UNIVERSE** by Sheldon Woodbury; Director, Sue Lawless; Sets, Tim Craig; Lighting, Jack Lush; Sound, Alex Sarmiento; Costumes, Dana Maczuga; Stage Manager, Gene Crespo; Press, Tony Origlio/Michael Cullen CASTS: *Window* Hamilton Clancy (Ozzie), Michael Collins (Kid), Eliza Ventura (Secretary) *Universe* Ms. Ventura (Mother), Mr. Collins (Father), Mr. Clancy (Doctor)
    Two one-act comedies.

(Kraine Theater) Wednesday, Sept.13-Oct.7, 1995 (16 performances) Cooper Square Workshop presents:
COLUMBUS IN THE AGE OF GOD by Paul Peditto; Director, Frank Licato; Choreography, Alicia Harding; Music, Donald Stark; Costumes, Beth Suhocki; Projections, Adrian Wattenmaker; Stage Manager, Rebecca Wilson CAST: Royanna Black, Paul D'Amato

Richard Hoehler in *Working Class* (Flash Rosenberg)

John Fedele, Tara Leigh, Robert Arcaro in *Brotherly Love* (Blanche Mackey)

Suzanne Fletcher, Jerry Jaffee in *Any Place But Here* (Amnon Ben Norris)

(Image Theatre) Wednesday, Sept.13-24, 1995 (10 performances) MJT Productions presents:
CHILDE BYRON by Romulus Linney; Director, Michael Hunold; Set, William F. Moser; Costumes, Joelyn R. Draut; Lighting, Jason Livingston; Sound, Michael Keck; Choreography, Lesly Countryman; Stage Manager, Julie Burton; Press, Howard and Barbara Atlee CAST: Lynne McCollough (Ada), Mark McDonough (Byron), Tim Deak (Boy), Maggie Lacey (Girl), Chase Booth (Young Man), Katherine Obrecht (Young Woman), John O'Creagh (Man), Julia McLaughlin (Woman)
A "dream play" in two acts. The action takes place in London, 1852.

(Mint Theater) Wednesday, Sept.13-Oct.8, 1995 (23 performances and 1 preview) returned Wednesday, Jan.17-Feb.18, 1996 (30 performances) Mint Theater Company presents:
WORKING CLASS; Written/Performed by Richard Hoehler; Press, David Rothenberg
A one-man portrait of eight American men. Earlier version titles *Out of the Blue*.

(Samuel Beckett Theatre) Thursday, Sept.14-Oct.8, 1995 (18 performances and 5 previews) Italian American Repertory Theatre presents:
BROTHERLY LOVE by John Fedele; Director, Robert Mariah; Set, Sal Perrotta; Lighting, Jeremy Kumin; Costumes, Peter Janis; Stage Manager, Margaret Bodriguian; Press, Tony Origlio/David Powell Smith CAST: Robert Arcaro (Mark), John Fedele (Vincent), John LaGioia (Uncle Tony), Tara Leigh (Mary), Rosalina Macisco
A comedy drama in two acts.

(HERE) Monday, Sept.18-25, 1995 (2 performances) HOME for Contemporary Theatre and Art presents:
FALLEN ANGLES; Written/Choreographed/Performed by Martin Moran; Staged in collaboration with Catherine Coray; Sound, Michael Butler; Lighting/Sound, Alexandra Avens, Lawrence Clayton
One lapsed Catholic hoofs for clues and sings for help.

(Don't Tell Mama) Wednesday, Sept.20-Oct.20, 1995 (11 performances and 3 previews)
BORN WITH TEETH; Written/Performed by Lynda Lyday and Heidi Oringer; Director, Sheila Head; Lighting/Sound, Shawn Moninger and Bob Kneeland; Press, Judy Jacksina
12 "small plays".

(Theater for the New City) Thursday, Sept.21-Oct.8, 1995 (12 performances) Theater for the New City/Crystal Field presents:
ANYPLACE BUT HERE by Caridad Svitoht Director, Marie Irene Fornes; Lighting, Tyler Micoleau; Press, Jonathan Slaff CAST: Joseph Goodrich (Chucky), Mary Forcade (Lydia), Suzanne E. Fletcher (Veronica), Jerry Jaffe (Tommy)
A drama set in working-class New Jersey.

(Theatre Row Theatre) Thursday, Sept.21-Oct.1, 1995 (12 performances) Reckless Theatre Compnay presents:
THE MADERATI by Richard Greenberg; Director, Frank Pisco; Set, Doug Huszti; Lighting, Jarrett Mager; Sound, Bart Fasbender; Stage Manager, Bradley Moates CAST: Lisa Harris (Rena deButts), Richard Munroe (Chuck deButts), Wendell Laurent (Ritt Overlander), Karin Sibrava (Dewy Overlander), Tim Hodgin (Martin Royale), John Rowell (Keene Esterhazy), Marisa Zalabak (Cuddles Molotov), Barbara Beach (Charlotte Ebbinger), Robert Duncan (Danton Young)
A play in two acts.

(Vineyard 26th St.) Thursday, Sept.21-Oct.8, 1995 (9 performances and 3 previews) Immigrant's Theatre Project presents:
ODYSSEUS' HOMECOMING by Ben-Hur Carmona; Director, Marcy Arlin; Set, Luba Lukova; Lighting, Zdenek Kriz; Costumes, Werner Stadler; Songs, Linda Samet; Stage Manager, Deborah Ratelle; Press, Shirley Herz/Miller Wright CAST: Murielle Borst (Blue Penelope), Edythe Davis (Red Penelope), Samantha Cintron (Yellow Penelope), Francisco Rivela (Odysseus), Christine Penney (Calypso), Eran Bohem (Oz), Ron Jones (X32), Paige Churchman (Rose), Edgard Nau (Robert), Nicholson Billey (Dalton), Cheryl Belkin (Vasilisa)
A drama set in NYC and "Latin America".

(Theatre Off Park) Saturday, Sept.23-Oct.15, 1995 (16 performances and 2 previews) Rattlestick Productions presents:
reinventing daddy by Gary Bonasorte; Director, Susana Tubert; Set, Narelle Sissons; Lighting, Ed McCarthy; Costumes, Kim Krumm Sorenson; Sound, Roy B. Yokelson; Music, Neil Benezra; Stage Manager, Rita L. Williams; Press, Peter Cromarty/Hugh hayes CAST: Jeff Robins (Daddy), Meg Kelly (Honey/Baby Doll), Crayton Robey (Brain Scanner/Therapist)

A surreal comedy set in suburbia.

(Playhouse 91) Tuesday, Sept.26-Oct.15, 1995 Atlantic Arts presents:
RADICAL RADIO; Conceived/Created/Performed by Jerry Sanders, Steve Underwood and Karmo Sanders; Director, Brian P. Allen; Orchestration/Musical Director, Steve Underwood; Costumes, Karmo Sanders; Press, Kevin P. McAnarney
MUSICAL NUMBERS: Radically Me, Walking in the Jungle, Badlands Texas, The Lucky One, Dancing Shoes, Everybody Here Knows How to Rock & Roll, I Like Traveling, Planet Z, More Than Enough Love, Funk Town, Rockin' in the Nursery Rhymes, Dancing in the Moonlight

A musical revue.

(CSC Theatre) Tuesday, Sept.26-Oct.29, 1995 (23 performances and 9 previews) Classic Stage Company presents:
ENDGAME by Samuel Beckett; Director/Set, David Esbjornson; Costumes, Elizabeth Hope Clancy; Lighting, Kenneth Posner; Stage Manager, Crystal Huntington; Press, Denise Robert CAST: John Seitz (Hamm), Kathleen Chalfant (Clov), Alan Manson (Nagg), Irma St. Paule (Nell)

Performed without intermission.

Mark Gorman, Richard Sisk, Bob Heitman, Joseph Edwards, David Warren in *Acts of Contrition* **(Chris DeLazzero)**

Sarah Ford, Denise Dumaine in
Edith Wharton's Manhattan **(Scott Wynn)**

Jeff Robins, Crayton Robey, Meg Kelly in
reinventing daddy **(Carol Rosegg)**

(Synchronicity Space) Wednesday, Sept.27-Oct.15, 1995 (13 performances and 2 previews) Present Tense Productions presents:
ACTS OF CONTRITION by Timothy Nolan; Director, Celia Braxton; Set, Van Santvoord; Costumes, Leslie Bernstein; Lighting, David Alan Comstock; Sound, Michael Chimenti; Stage Manager, Bess Eckstein; Press, Jed Canaan CAST: David Warren (Fr. Steve Pernicone), Mark Gorman (Fr. Tom Kerner), Joseph Edwards (Fr. Joe Beckett), Bob Heitman (Daniel Cardinal Brennan), Richard Sisk (Bishop Edward Sweeney)

A drama set at a Catholic retreat house on Cape May Point, NJ.

(Pulse Theatre) Thursday, Sept.28-Oct.14, 1995 (12 performances and 3 previews) Pulse Ensemble Theatre presents:
EDITH WHARTON'S MANHATTAN by Paul Minx; Based on *The House of Mirth*; Additional Material/Director, Alexa Kelly; Set, Mikhail Garakanidze and Valentin Volkov; Costumes, Fran Cole; Lighting, Kevin Lock; Sound, Mitchell Simchowitz; Music, Bruce Cohen; Stage Manager, Dana Ortiz; Press, Pete Sanders/Michael Hartman CAST: Susan Barrett (Gerty), Tom Dennis (Rosedale), Denise Du Maine (Grace Stepney/Maid), Mark Eis (Selden), Sarah Ford (Mrs. Peniston), Patrick Hillian (Percy Gryce/George Dorset), Christine Jones (Judy Trenor/Louisa Bry), Matty McFadden (Mrs. Haffen/Evie Van Osburgh/Mrs. Kilroy), Laura Patrick (Lily Bart), Luisa Sermol (Mrs. Dorset), Judy Turkisher (Carrie Fisher/Maid), James K. Wuensch (Augustus Trenor/Lawyer)

A drama in two acts. The action takes place in NYC and Monte Carlo.

(New Perspectives Theatre) Friday, Sept.29-Oct.17, 1995 (15 performances) New Perspectives Theatre Compnay presents:
ADMISSIONS by Tony Vellela; Director, Austin Pendleton; Set, Jeff Pajer; Lighting, Jason A. Cina; Costumes, Crystal Thompson; Press, Merle Frimark/Erin Dunn CAST: Aaron Harpold (Rob), Kim Dooley (Melanie), LaTonya Borsay (Arletta), Edward Tully (Hank), Jules Graciolett (Ricardo), Ken Leung (Thomas), Chad L. Coleman (Julian), Randy Bourne (Lance Curtis), Amy Sloane (Voice of Aide), Sam Waterston (Governor's Voice)

A drama performed without intermission. The action takes place on an American college campus.

(John Houseman Theatre) Friday, Sept.29, 1995-Jan.28, 1996 (140 performances) Manhattan Theatre Club presents:
SYLVIA by A.R. Gurney; Director, John Tillinger; Set, John Lee Beatty; Costumes, Jane Greenwood; Lighting, Ken Billington; Sound, Aural Fixation; Stage Manager, Roy Harris; Press, Helene Davis, Kevin McAnarney CAST: Jan Hooks (Sylvia), John Cunningham (Greg), Mary Beth Peil (Kate), Derek Smith (Tom/Phyllis/Leslie)

A comedy in two acts. The action takes place in New York City. Presented for 167 performances last season at Manhattan Theatre Club with Sarah Jessica Parker, Charles Kimbrough and Blythe Danner.

(Atlantic Theater) Saturday, Sept.30-Dec.31, 1995 (87 performances and 10 previews) Atlantic Theater Company presents:
DANGEROUS CORNER by J.B. Priestley; Adapted/Directed by David Mamet; Sets, James Wolk; Costumes, Laura Cunningham; Lighting, Howard Werner; Sound, Douglas Jaffe; Stage Managers, Matthew Silver, Michelle Bosch; Press, Chris Boneau~Adrian Bryan-Brown/Andy Shearer, Stephen Pitalo CAST: Hilary Hinckle (Maud Mockridge), Rebecca Pidgeon (Olwen Peel), Felicity Huffman (Freda Chatfield), Mary McCann (Betty Whitehouse), David Pittu (Charles Stanton), Robert Bella (Gordon Whitehouse), Jordan Lage (Robert Chatfield)

A 1932 mystery in two acts. The action takes place at the Chatfield country home, 1930s.

(New York Historical Society) Monday, Oct.2-16, 1995 (2 performances) David Merrick Arts Foundation and The Actors' Company Theatre present:
THE MAN WHO CAME TO DINNER by Moss Hart and George S. Kaufman; Director, Scott Alan Evans; Music, Andrew Evan Cohen; Stage Manager, Babette Lloyd; Press, Alma Viator/Bill Schelble CAST: Hayley Barr (June Stanley), Ryan Bowker (John), Maia Danzinger (Maggie Cutler), Francesca Di Mauro (Sarah), Delphi Harrington (Miss Preen), Cynthia Harris (Lorraine Sheldon), Stephen Harrison (Mr. Stanley), David Edward Jones (Mr. Baker/Westcott), Larry Keith (Sheridan Whiteside), Elise Knight (Mrs. Dexter/Choirboy), Liz Martin (Mrs. McCutcheon/Choirboy), Gabe Olds (Richard Stanley), Dennis Carlo Patella (Prof. Metz/Choirboy), Guy Paul (Beverly Carlton), Gregory Salata (Bert Jefferson), Jo-Ann Salata (Harriet Stanley), Scott Schafer (Banjo), Jim Shue (Michaelson/Expressman/Deputy), Tom Stewart (Dr. Bradley), Shane Stevens (Sandy/Henderson/Deputy), Lynn Vogt (Mrs. Stanley)

A staged reading of a three-act comedy performed with one intermission. The action takes place in a small Ohio town, 1939.

John Cunningham, Jan Hooks, Mary Beth Peil in *Sylvia* (Joan Marcus)

Rebecca Pidgeon, Felicity Hoffman in *Dangerous Corner* (Gerry Goodstein)

(45th St. Theatre/Bos) Wednesday, Oct.4-22, 1995 (15 performances) VagaBOND Theatre Company presents:
BAD LANGUAGE by Dusty Hughes; Director, Kent Paul; Set, Michael Lasswell; Lighting, Ellen E. Bone; Costumes, Vern Malone; Stage Managers, Lorn Eisen, Terry Kelsey; Press, Alma Viator/Eileen Weiss CAST: Charles Clough (Phil Kirby), Nicholas Coster (Tim Sargesse), Julie Entwisle (Davina Scott), ej ndeto (Suelene), Dino Scopas (Stanley Waters), Jason Tendell (Dr. Robert Thomas), John Wallace (Alastair Yonge)

A drama in two acts. The action takes place at England's Cambridge University, 1983.

(Public/Martinson Hall) Wednesday, Oct.4-29, 1995 (31 performances) Young Playwrights Inc. (Sheri M. Goldhirsch, Artistic Director; Brett W. Reynolds, Managing Director) presents:
THE 1995 YOUNG PLAYWIGHTS FESTIVAL; Sets, Narelle Sissons; Costumes, Karen Perry; Lighting, Donald Holder; Sound, Janet Kalas; Production Manager, Michael Cote; Stage Managers, Elise-Ann Konstantin, James Latus; Press, Serio Coyne/Terence Womble
Guyworld by Bret LaGree; Director, Michael Breault CAST:Jim Bracchitta (Tom), Robert Montano (Ray), Gary Perez (bartender), Ray Wills (Dave)
The King by Denise Ruiz; Director, Susana Tubert CAST: Benny Nieves (Ishmel), Vincent Laresca (Miguel), Robert Montano (Rolando), Al D. Rodriguez (Tuto), David Wolos-Fonteno (Guard/Priest), Gary Perez (Dito), Jim Bracchitta (Julio), Ray Wills (Prison Trustee), Divina Cook (Mother)
Proof Through the Night by Clarence Coo; Director, Richard Caliban CAST: Aleta Mitchell (Mavis), Sean Runnette (Toby)
This Is About a Boy's Fears by Shaun Neblett; Director, Mark Brokaw CAST: Sharif (Marc), Sean Thomas (Enis), Aleta Mitchell (Angela), David Wolos-Fonteno (Jerry)

Four plays by seventeen-year-old playwrights make up the fourteenth annual edition of this series.

(Grove St. Playhouse) Wednesday, Oct.4-29, 1995 (20 performances) The Glines presents:
IF THIS ISN'T LOVE! by Sidney Morris; Director/Set, John Wall; Lighting, David Jensen; Costumes, Mark D. Sorensen; Stage Manager, William H. "Pete" Miller CAST: Martin Outzen (Eric), Bob Merckel (Adam)

A gay romantic comedy in three acts. The action takes place in New York City.

Charles Clough, Jason Tendell, Julie Entwisle in *Bad Language*

(Public/Martison Hall) Wednesday, Oct.4-29, 1995 (31 performances) Young Playwrights Inc. (Sheri M. Goldhirsch, Artistic Director; Brett W. Reynolds, Managing Director) presents:

THE 1995 YOUNG PLAYWRIGHTS FESTIVAL; Sets; Narelle Sissons; Costumes, Karen Perry; Lighting, Donald Holder; Sound, Janet Kalas; Production Manager, Michael Cote; Stage Managers, Elise-Ann Konstantin, James Latus; Press, Serio Coyne/Terence Womble

Guyworld by Bret LaGree; Director, Michael Breault CAST:Jim Bracchitta (Tom), Robert Montano (Ray), Gary Perez (bartender), Ray Wills (Dave)

The King by Denise Ruiz; Director, Susana Tubert CAST: Benny Nieves (Ishmel), Vincent Laresca (Miguel), Robert Montano (Rolando), Al D. Rodriguez (Tuto), David Wolos-Fonteno (Guard/Priest), Gary Perez (Dito), Jim Bracchitta (Julio), Ray Wills (Prison Trustee), Divina Cook (Mother)

Proof Through the Night by Clarence Coo; Director, Richard Caliban CAST: Aleta Mitchell (Mavis), Sean Runnette (Toby)

This is About a Boy's Fears by Shaun Neblett; Director, Mark Brokaw CAST: Sharif (Marc), Sean Thomas (Enis), Aleta Mitchell (Angela), David Wolos-Fonteno (Jerry)

Four plays by seventeen-year-old playwrights make up the fourteenth annual edition of this series.

Ray Willis, Jim Bracchitta, Robert Montano in
Guyworld **(Gerry Goodstein)**

Laila Robins, Uta Hagen, Amy Wright in *Mrs. Klein* **(Carol Rosegg)**

(Union Square Theatre) Thursday, Oct.5-Nov.26, 1995 (37 performances and 9 previews) Julian Schlossberg, Brian Brolly, with Alan J. Schuster, Mitchell Maxwell present:
MOSCOW STATIONS; Adapted by Stephen Mulrine from the novel *Moscow to Petushki* by Venedikt Yerofeev; Director, Ian Brown; Set/Costumes, Tim Hatley; Lighting, Ian Sommerville; Sound, John Irvine; Stage Manager, John Vivian; Press, Bill Evans/Tom D'Ambrosio, Terry M. Lilly, Jim Randolph CAST: Tom Courtenay (Venichka Yerofeev)
A one-man drama in two acts. The action takes place in Russia during the Brezhnev years.

(Chelsea Playhouse) Thursday, Oct.5-29, 1995 (12 performances and 6 previews) Gilgamesh Theatre Group presents:
TWO, NIKITA by Jeffrey Hatcher; Director, John Morrison; Set, Roger Hanna; Costumes, Crystal Thompson; Lighting, Jason Livingston; Sound, David P. Earle; Stage Manager, Valerie A. Gramling; Press, Jeffrey Richards/Kevin Rehac CAST: Richard Mover (Producer/Feets Disperbio/Khrushchev), Michael MacCauley (Grace), Mark Hattan (Stevie Parsons/Dresden/Mouse), Dan Daily (Overton/Dr. Brettel), Matt Higgins (Benton/Paul), Suzanne Von Eck (Mrs. Bryden), T. Ryder Smith (Shepkin), Oliver Dixon (Angler/Earl), Susan Orem (Mrs. dancer/Pauline), John Greene, St. Clair Ripley (G-Men)
A comedy thriller in two acts. The action takes place all over the U.S.A. and the Soviet Union, 1960.

(Lucille Lortel Theatre) Friday, Oct.6-June 29, 1996 David Richenthal, Lucille Lortel, Anita Howe-Waxman, Jeffrey Ash present:
MRS. KLEIN by Nicholas Wright; Director, William Carden; Set, Ray Recht; Costumes, David C. Woolard; Lighting, Chris Dallos; Sound, Robert Auld; Stage Manager, Lloyd Davis Jr.; Press, Jeffrey Richards/Kevin Rehac, Roger Bean, Laramie Dennis CAST: Uta Hagen (Mrs. Klein), Amy Wright (Paula), Laila Robins (Melitta)
A drama in two acts. The action takes place in London, 1934.

(Promenade Theatre) Friday, Oct.6, 1995-May 26, 1996 (249 performances and 19 previews) Stephen Eich, Joan Stein, Levitt/Fox Theatricals/Mages present:
PICASSO AT THE LAPIN AGILE by Steve Martin; Director, Randall Arney; Set, Scott Bradley; Costumes, Patricia Zipprodt, Lighting, Kevin Rigdon; Sound, Richard Woodbury; Wigs/Hairstylist, David H. Lawrence; Stage Manager, Mark Cole; Press, Alma Viator/Michael S Borowski, William Schelble CAST: Mark Nelson (Albert Einstein), Harry Groener succeeded by Robert Ari (Freddy), Carl Don succeeded by William Keeler, Richard Kuss (Gaston), Rondi Reed (Germaine), Susan Floyd succeeded by Rebecca Creskoff (Suzanne/Countess/Female Admirer), John Christopher Jones succeeded by Bill Buell (Sagot), Tim Hopper succeeded by Paul Provenza (Pablo Picasso), Peter Jacobson (Charles Dabernow Schmendiman), Gabriel Macht (A Visitor)

A comedy performed without intermission. The action takes place at a bar in Paris, 1904.

Top: Tim Hopper, Mark Nelson
Left: Susan Floyd, Paul Provenza

Joan Marcus Photos

(Mint Theatre) Saturday, Oct.7, 1995-Mar.2, 1996 (6 limited performances) Mint Theatre Company presents:
AT WAR WITH THE DINOSAURS; Written/Performed by David Paul Rothenberg; Press, David Gersten
   A solo performance.

(Ubu Rep. Theater) Wednesday, Oct.11-22, 1995 (13 performances) Ubu Repertory Theater presents:
NIGHT JUST BEFORE THE FOREST by Bernard-Marie Koltes; Translation, Timothy Johns; Director, Susan Einhorn; Set, Watoku Ueno; Lighting, Greg MacPherson; Costumes, Carol Ann Pelletier; Sound, David Margolin Lawson; Stage Manager, Eileen Myers; Press, Jonathan Slaff
CAST: David Weynand
   A one-man drama performed without intermission. The action takes place in Paris.

(Judith Anderson Theatre) Wednesday, Oct.11-28, 1995 (14 performances) The Playful Repertory Company presents:
HUNTING HUMANS by Richard Thompson; Director, Mike Wills; Set, Lauren Helpern; Press, Manuel Igrejas   CAST: Dean Bradshaw (Rev), Todd Butera (Fick), Paul Singleton (Jay-Mac), J.B. McLendon (Lump), Mark Skinner
   A comedy in two acts. The action takes place in Atlantic City.

(Players Theatre) Wednesday, Oct.11-Dec.24, 1995 Colin Cabot presents:
ZOMBIES FROM THE BEYOND; Music/Lyrics/Book by James Valcq; Director/Choreography, Pam Kriger; Musical Director, Andrew Wilder; Sets/Costumes, James Schuette; Lighting, Ken Billington; Sound, Ivan Pokorny; Stage Manager, Lisa Jean Lewis; Press, Shirley Herz/Sam Rudy
CAST: Michael Shelle (Major Malone), Robert Boles (Rick Jones), Suzanne Graff (Charlene "Charlie" Osmanski), Jeremy Czarniak (Billy Krutzik), Claire Morkin (Mary Malone), Matt McClanahan (Trenton Corbett), Susan Gottschalk (Zombina)
MUSICAL NUMBERS: Sky's the Limit, The Rocket-Roll, Second Planet on the Right, Blast Off Baby, Atomic Feet, Big Wig, In the Stars, Secret Weapon, Zombies from the Beyond, Dateline: Milwaukee, The American Way, I Am a Zombie, Last Man on Earth, Breaking the Sound Barrier, Keep Watching the Skies
   A musical spoof in two acts. The action takes place at the Milwaukee Space Center and environs, 1955.

(Mint Space) Wednesday, Oct.11-Nov.5, 1995 (23 performances) The Next Stage! presents:
COLOMBINA'S SUITE by Ludmilla Petrushevskaya; Director, Linda Lees; Press, Gary and John Springer/Candi Adams   CAST: Ludmila Bokievsky, Antoinette LaVecchia, Alice O'Neil, Michael Rudko, Stephen Turner
   Four one-act plays.

(66 Wooster St.) Thursday, Oct.12-29, 1995 (12 performances and 4 previews) Watermark Theater presents:
WAITER, WAITER by David Simpatico; Director, Nela Wagman; Set, Sarah Lambert; Sound, Christopher A. Granger; Lighting, Joe Saint; Costumes, Kitty Leach, David Matwijkow; Stage Manager, Emily Orr; Press, Richard Kornberg/Ian Rand, Don Summa, William Finnegan   CAST: Marie Dame (Betty), Karl Herlinger (Fang), Amy Lammert (Margo), Chris Prizzi (Fred), Patricia Randell (Rocky), M.W. Reid (Whip), Cheryl Rogers (Crystal), Melissa Schaffer (Mimi), D.L. Shroder (Dean), Jane Young (Diva) (28th St. Theater) Thursday, Oct.12-29, 1995 (14 performances) Africa Arts Theatre Company presents:
HER MAJESTY'S VISIT by Onukaba A. Ojo; Director, Loni Berry; Set, Michael Moore; Lighting, Zdeneck Kriz; Costumes, Kimberly Jones; Press, Jonathan Slaff   CAST: Louise Mike (Mother), Todd Anthony-Jackson (Doctor), Lynne-Marie Brown (Wife)   A comedy set in New York City

David Rothenberg in *At War with the Dinosaurs*

Jeremy Czarniak, Robert Boles, Susan Gottschalk, Suzanne Graff, Michael Shelle in *Zombies from the Beyond* **(T. L. Boston)**

Louise Mike, Todd Anthony-Jackson, Lynne-Marie Brown in *Her Majesty's Visit* **(Jonathan Slaff)**

(Triad) Thursday, Oct.12-Nov.11, 1995 (13 performances and 1 preview) Mark Christian Subias presents:**CHRIS DURANG & DAWNE**; Director, Deborah Lapidus; Musical Director, Bruce Coyle; Costumes, Harriet Walle, Harrison Morgan; Stage Manager, Simone Harrison; Press, Chris Boneau~Adrian Bryan-Brown/Miguel Tuason, Corey Moore CAST: Chris Durang, Sherry Anderson, John Augustine A musical revue.

(Fools Company Space) Friday, Oct.13-21, 1995 Aurora Stage Company presents:
HEARTBREAK HOUSE by George Bernard Shaw; Director, Deb Guston; Set/Lighting, Walter Ulasinski; Stage Manager, George Seylaz CAST: Laura Fois (Ellie Dunn), Sharon Watroba (Nurse), Bob Sonderskov (Capt. Shotover), Paula Eschweiler (Ariadne Utterword), Vicki Meisner (Hesione Hushabye), Michael Walczak (Hector Hushabye), Barry Ford (Mazzini Dunn), Carter Inskeep (Boss Mangan), Anthony John Lizzul (Randall Uterword), James Ashcraft (Billy Dunn)
   Performed in three acts. The action takes place in the English countryside, 1913.

(Actors' Playhouse) Friday, Oct.13, 1995-Jan.14, 1996 (72 performances and 9 previews) The Ridiculous Theatrical Company presents:
MURDER AT MINSING MANOR: A NANCY BOYS MYSTERY by Michael Simon and Richard Simon; Director, Chuck Brown; Set, Tom Greenfield; Costumes, Kaye Voyce; Lighting, Richard Currie; Sound, Raymond D. Schilke; Wigs/Makeup, Zsamira Ronquillo; Fights, Steven Satta; Stage Manager, Bill Nobes; Press, Philip Rinaldi/James Morrison CAST: Grant Neale (Marius Minsing/Buck Arnge), Cory Lippiello (Bob Andreson), Christa Kirby (Buddy Brady), Tom Deroesher (Officer Joe McCarty), Everett Quinton (Glory Holden), Kyle Kennedy (Father Pat), Jason Williams (Pig Marrano), Lenys Sama (Zarah Zine), Wilfredo Medina (Eddie), Dave Murray (Marty)
   A mystery satire set in Levittown, NY in the 1950s (outrageous anachronisms notwithstanding).

Christa Kirby, Everett Quinton, Cory Lipiello in *Murder at Missing Manor: A Nancy Boys Mystery* (Susan Johann)

(Metropolitan Playhouse) Monday, Oct.16-Nov.18, 1995 (17 performances each) Parsifal's Productions presents:
ROUND TRIP by Oliver Hailey; Director, Mark Hirschfield and **JOANNA'S HUSBAND AND DAVID'S WIFE** by Elizabeth Forsythe Hailey; Director, Rebecca Taylor; Sets, Vincent Li; Lighting, Brian Orter; Costumes, Linette Delmonico; Stage Managers, Babette M Lloyd, Donna DeRosa, Press, Diana Walker CASTS: *Round Trip*: Steve Boles, William Driscoll, Robin Poley, William Pract, Lisbeth Zelle *Joanna's Husband...*: Michael Hobbs (David), Mary Wadkins (Joanna)
   Two comedies in repertory.

(Crane Theatre) Tuesday, Oct.17, 1995- Crossover Productions presents:
PAINTING X'S ON THE MOON by Richard Vetere CAST: Teddy Coluca, Jennifer Esposito, Vincent Pastore, Sean Patrick Reilly, Celia Schaefer, Charlie Yanko
   A drama set in L.A. and NYC.

(American Place Theatre) Wednesday, Oct.18 Dec.10, 1995 (52 performances and 4 previews) American Place Theatre Presents:
SPOONBREAD AND STRAWBERRY WINE by Norma Jean Darden; Director, Josh Broder; Set, Ken Rothchild; Press, Denise Robert CAST: Norma Jean Darden, Jou Jou Papailler
   Return engagement of last season's evening of food, songs and family discoveries.

(West Park Presbyterian) Thursday, Oct.19-Nov.12, 1995 (16 performances) Frog & Peach Theatre Company presents:
KING JOHN by William Shakespeare; Director, Lynnea Benson; Design, Kim Owens; Costumes, Jonathan Green; Fights, Kathy Keil CAST: Michael McFadden, Bryant Fraser, Marc Goodman, Karen Lynn Gorncy, Mervyn Haines Jr., Maureen Hayes, Leone Hechler, Steve Kaiser, Sylva Kelegian, Howard I. Laniado, Wilma Mondi, Jill O. Stanevich, Doug Stone, Carolyn Sullivan-Zinn, Richard B. Watson, Raymond Yust, Ted Zukowski

(Synchronicity Space) Thursday, Oct.19-Nov.5, 1995 (14 performances) Jewish Theatre of New York presents:
LIKE TWO EAGLES by Tuvia Tenenbom; Director, Robert Kalfin; Set, Alexander Solodhuko; Music, John Clifton; Costumes, Sarah Jablon; Lighting, Chris Dallos; Press, Ed Callaghan/Jared Hart CAST: Jon Avner, June Ballinger, Lee Beltzer, Robert Andrew Bonnard, Robert Carin, Funda Duyal, David Hirsh, Eric Kuttner, Ronnie Newman, Manos Pantelidis, Foster Solomon, Debra Sperling, Matthew Wallis
   A drama set in Jerusalem.

Sherry Anderson, Christopher Durang, John Augustine in *Chris Durang and Dawne* **(Allison Leach)**

Tony Meindl, T. L. Reilly, David Jacob Ryder
in *Like A Brother* (Carl Sturmer)

Kristin Griffith, Brad Bellamy, Tristin Skyler, in
Crocodiles in the Potomac (Martha Holmes)

(224 Waverly Place) Thursday, Oct.19-Nov.12, 1995 (21 performances and 4 previews) The Rufus Company presents:
LIKE A BROTHER by T.E. Klunzinger; Director, Jeff Brenner; Set, Anthony J. Bellomo; Lighting, Ted Daniel; Costumes, Lark Burger, DJ Krogol; Sound, Russell Willard; Stage Manager, Thomas McCurdy; Press, Francine L. Trevens CAST: T.L. Reilly (William), David Jacob Ryder (Henry), Richard Welton (Robert), Tony Meindl succeeded by Gil Grail (FitzHaimo), Peter Johnson (Anselm/DeLisle), Wesley Stevens (Flambard/Bristol), Waldemar Kannenberg (Oxford/Lanfranc/Peasant), Steve Kolbo (Bedford/Tyrrell).
A drama about the sons of William the Conqueror. The action takes place from 1087-1100.

(Theatre Row Theatre) Thursday, Oct.19-Nov.12, 1995 (22 performances and 6 previews) Women's Project & Productions presents:
CROCODILES IN THE POTOMAC by Wendy Belden; Director, Suzanne Bennett; Set/Lighting, Roger Hanna; Costumes, Elizabeth Fried; Sound, Mark Bruckner; Stage Manager, Shelli Aderman; Press, Shirley Herz/Miller Wright CAST: Kristin Griffith (Bev Lehr), Gretchen Egolf (Jackie Crayton), Tristine Skyler (Becky Lehr), Firdous Bamji (Constantin Xanthos), Brad Bellamy (Richard Nixon)
A comedy set in Washington, D.C., 1974.

(St. Clement's) Tuesday, Oct.24-Nov.18, 1995 (25 performances and 3 previews) Pan Asian Repertory presents:
PRIVATE LIVES by Noel Coward; Director, Ron Nakahara; Sets, Robert Klingelhoefer; Lighting, Richard Schaefer; Costumes, Terry Leong; Sound, Ty Sanders; Press, Denise Robert CAST: Elizabeth H. Piccio (Amanada), Michael Gee (Elyot), Fay Rusli (Sibyl), Sam Ardeshir (Victor), Christine Villamor
An Asian-American cast in the Coward comedy.

(IBIS) Tuesday, Oct.24, 1995-still playing May 31, 1996 Samiha Koura D'Aiuto presents:
THE MAGIC CARPET REVUE; Conceived/Directed by Samiha Koura-D'Aiuto; Lighting, Laurent Legal; Costumes, Jose "Angel" Garcia, Raafat Haggar, Ahmad Kahl; Sound, John Perez; Choreography, Serena Wilson, Laura Stilwell, Stephen N. Kontansky; Press, Peter Cromarty/Hugh Hayes CAST: Chappy Brazil, Jose "Angel" Garcia, Coleen McMahon, Sayed Reda, Terence Clowe, Stephen J. Izzard, Cathy Lubash, Lisa-Marie Panagos, Dina Rivera, Megan Smith, IBIS Dancers
A supper club revue.

(City Center) Wednesday, Oct.25-28, 1995 (3 performances) Sir Andrew Lloyd Webber and National Youth Music Theatre present:
PENDRAGON; Music/Lyrics/Book/Direction by Peter Allwood, Joanna Horton, Jeremy James Taylor and Frank Whately; Musical Director, Mr. Allwood; Design, Alison Darke; Lighting, Richard House; Sound, Simon Baker; Press, Philip Rinaldi CAST: Nick Saich (Uther Pendragon/Sir Malaigaunce), Shula Keyte (Ygraine/Lady of the Lake), Kyriacos Messios (Merlin), Neil Abrahamson (Priest), Louise Potter (Nurse), Hayley Gelling (Young Morgan Le Fay), Hannah Spearritt (Young Guinevere), Sheridan Smith (Young Elaine), Richard Stacey (Young Arthur Pendragon), James Hoare (Sir Kay), Tom Chambers(King Pellinore), Sonell Dadral (Will), Hugo Sheppard (Thomas), Lara Pulver (Kelemon), Irfan Ahmad (Monk), Helen Power (Raven), Daniel Beckett (Matt), Joshua Deutsch (Luke), Katie Wilson (Older Morgan Le Fay), Timothy Fornara (Older Arthur Pendragon), Angharad Reece (Lady Angharad), Michelle Thomas (Lady Alice), Sarah McMillan (Lady Margaret), Adam Knight (Gawain), Maurice MacSweeney (Sir Caradoc), Rebecca Lock (Older Guinevere), Charlotte Hoare (Older Elaine), Reuben Jones (King Leodegraunce), Tom Sellwood (King Lot of Orkney), Edmund Comer (Ulfius), Christian Coulson (Sir Gaynor), Paul Cattermole (Sir Lancelot)
A musical in two acts. The action takes place in Britian during the Dark Ages.

Pendragon Cast

Paula Hoza, Joseph Small, Lynn Warie Macy in
Playboy of the Western World **(Lee Snider)**

Peter Herrick, Pamela Paul, Carole Monferdini
in *Glory Girls* **(Jonathan Slaff)**

(INTAR Theater) Wednesday, Oct.25-Dec.3, 1996 (29 performances and 13 pewviews) INTAR Hispanic American Arts Center presents:
CUBAN LIBRE; Conceived/Directed by Max Ferra; Musical Director, Meme Solis; Choreography, Alberto Alonso; Sets, Donald Eastman; Costumes, Caryn Neman; Lighting, Frances Aronson; Projections, Elaine McCarthy; Sound, Richard Jansen; Stage Manager, Sergio Cruz; Press, Shirley Herz/Miller Wright CAST: Sonia Calero, Annia Linares, Meme Solis, Eduardo Oliva
A musical revue.

(City Center) Thursday, Oct.26-28, 1995 (3 performances) Sir Andrew Lloyd Webber and National Youth Music Theatre present:
THE THREEPENNY OPERA by Bertolt Brecht and Kurt Weill, Director, Mark Pattenden; Movement, Wendy Cook; Musical Director, Alison Berry; Design, Jason Denvir; Lighting, Chris Davey; Sound, Simon Baker; Press, Philip Rinaldi CAST: Nick Dutton, Catherine Simmonds (Ballad Singers/Narrators), Tim Steeden (Jeremiah Peachum), Kate Chesworth (Mrs. Peachum), Kevin Pamplin (Filch), Laurence Taylor (Macheath), Jessica Watson (Polly Peachum), Esther Shanson (Lucy Brown), Jonathan Chesworth (Matt of the Mint), James Capewell (Crooked Fingered Jake), Barney Dillon (Bob the Saw), Jean-Paul Pfluger (Ned), Delroy Atkinson (Jimmy Twitcher), Alex Bourne (Dreary Walter), Matthew Walton (Rev. Kimball), David Oyelowo (Tiger Brown), Matthew Gough (Smith), Chris Swift (Constable), Tiffany Gore (Jenny Diver), Emma Sharnock (Vixen), Kelly Brett (Dolly), Johanna Hewitt (Coaxer), Carryl Thomas (Brazen), Hong-Van Laffer (Suky Tawdry), Joanna Dunn (Betty), Fiona Finlow (Divine)
The 1928 musical set in London on the eve of a Royal Coronation.

(Theatre 1010) Thursday, Oct.26-Nov.19, 1995 (16 performances and 1 preview) Ten Ten Players present:
THE PLAYBOY OF THE WESTERN WORLD by J.M. Synge; Director, Celia Braxton CAST: Kevin Connell, Lynn Marie Macy, Joseph Small, Alan Scott, Paula Hoza, Mike Timoney, Michael Gnat, Karen Eterovich, Andre Brennan, Jeryl Ann Costell, Georgianna Guevara, E. Kyle Minor, Karl Dyner

(Samuel Beckett Theatre) Friday, Oct.27-Nov.12, 1995 (16 performances) Abingdon Theatre Company presents:
GLORY GIRLS by Jan Buttram; Director, Cathey Crowell Sawyer; Set, Richard Harrison; Lighting, David Castaneda; Costumes, Crystal Thompson; Sound, Jeff Ward; Musical Director, Philip Cunningham; Press, Randy Lichtenwalner CAST: Carole Monferdini (Pauline), Peter Brouwer (Peter), Pamela Paul (Patsy), Kate Bushmann (Pepper), Peter Herrick (Dee)
A comedy with hymns in two acts. The action takes place in NYC and Houston.

(28th St. Theater) Friday, Oct.27-Nov.11, 1995 (9 performances)
KNEE DEEP; Written/Performed by Eric Slovin and Leo Allen; Director, Jeremy Dobrish; Press, Gary and John Springer
An evening of comedy.

(Kraine Theatre) Friday, Oct.27-Nov.18, 1995 (10 performances)
THE BERT FERSHNERS; Written/Performed by Dan Berrett, Dan Fleming, Joey Garfield, Mark Hervey, Josh Lewis, Mike Rock, Chris Tullman; Press, Chris Boneau~Adrian Bryan-Brown/Bob Fennell
An evening of sketch comedy.

***Threepenny Opera* Cast**

Mike Rock of the *Bert Fershners*

(Folksbiene Playhouse) Saturday, Oct.28, 1995-Jan.14, 1996 Folksbiene Playhouse presents:
DOUBLE IDENTITY; Music, Ben Schaechter; Lyrics/Book, Miriam Hoffman; Based on Sholom Aleichem's comedy *Hard to Be a Jew*; Director, Bryna Wasserman; Press, Richard Kornberg/Gail Parenteau, Ian Rand CAST: Steve Sterner (Vanya), Jennifer Bern-Vogel (Betty Shapiro), Harry Peerce (Shneyerson), Zypora Spaisman (Sore), Ino Toper (Mr. Shapiro), Norman Kruger, Sam Josephson
   A musical set in Russia, 1913.

(Theatre Off Park) Sunday, Oct.29-30, 1995 (2 performances) Theatre Off Park & Millennial Arts Productions/Paula Heil Fisher present:
I MARRIED AN ANGEL; Music, Richard Rodgers; Lyrics, Lorenz Hart; Book, Rodgers and Hart from a play by John Vaszary; Director, Albert Harris; Musical Director, James Stenborg; Staging, Joey McKneely; Lighting, Herrick Goldman; Narration, Laurence Holzman, Felicia Needleman; Stage Manager, Alex Nicholas; Press, Bill Evans/Jim Randolph CAST: Brent Barrett (Harry Mischka Szigetti), Victoria Clark (Anna Murphy), Robert Creighton (Peter Mueller), Kim Criswell (Peggy Palaffi), Jason Graae (Willie Palaffi), Edmund Lyndeck (Narrator/Gen. Lucash), Marin Mazzie (Angel), Viola Harris (Duchess/Modiste), Susan Owen (Olga), Scott Beck, Matthew Burnett, Karen Culp, Lauren Ward (Ensemble)
MUSICAL NUMBERS: Overture, Opening Ballet, Did You Ever Get Stung?, I Married an Angel, The Modiste, Honeymoon Ballet, I'll Tell the Man in the Street, How to Win Friends and Influence People, Spring Is Here, Angel Without Wings, A Twinkle in Your Eye, Roxie Routine (I'm Ruined), At the Roxy Music Hall, Finale
   A staged conect of the 1938 musical in two acts. The action takes place in Budapest, 1938.

Robert Creighton, Brent Barrett, Victoria Clark, Jason Graae, Kim Criswell, Marin Mazzie in *I Married an Angel* (Joan Marcus)

(American Place Theatre) Wednesday, Nov.1-19, 1995 (14 performances and 9 previews) Bay Street Theatre presents:
SPLENDORA; Music, Stephen Hoffman; Lyrics, Mark Campbell; Book, Peter Webb; Based on the novel by Edward Swift; Director, Jack Hofsiss; Musical Staging, Robert La Fosse; Orchestrations, Michael Gibson; Musical Director, Sariva Goetz; Set, Eduardo Sicangco; Costumes, William Ivey Long; Lighting, Richard Nelson; Sound, Randy Freed; Press, David Rothenberg/David J. Gersten, David Lotz, Meg Gordean CAST: Evalyn Baron (Sue Ella Lightfoot), KT Sullivan (Maga Dell Spivy), Laura Kenyon (Zeda Earl Goodrich), Kathy Robinson (Agnes Pullens), Susan Rush (Lucille Monroe), Nancy Johnston (Jessica Gatewood), Michael Moore (Timothy John Coldridge), Ken Krugman (Brother Leggett)
MUSICAL NUMBERS: In Our Hearts, How Like Heaven, Don't Get Me Started, Pretty Boy, Home/Say Goodnight, Poor Sad Thing, Hymn to Her, Up at Dawn, In Small and Simple Ways, Warms My Soul, Dear Heart, How Little I Know, Had He Kissed Me Tonight, If He Knew, Good Hearts Rejoice, What Is Ain't, Promise Me One Thing, I Got Faith in You, All the Time in the World, Man Named Dewey, I Am Beauty, Miss Crepe Myrtle, Grateful, My Name Is Timothy John, Finale
   A musical in two acts. The action takes place in a small town in east Texas, not so long ago.

(La Mama) Thursday, Nov.2-11, 1995 (5 performances and 1 preview) Purgatorio Ink presents:
ALL ABOUT JEEZ OR THE SACRED SQUIRT; Written/Directed by Assurbanipal Babilla; Lighting, Howard Thies; Sound, One Dream; Press, Shirley Herz/Wayne Wolfe, Lauren Rosenblum CAST INCLUDES: Assurbanipal Babilla, David Cote, Jennie Crotero, Leyla Ebtehadj, Suzanne Elizabeth Fletcher, Lynne Kanter, Bill Martin
   A comedy incorporating dance and puppetry.

Michael Christopher Moore, Nancy Johnston
in *Splendora* (G. J. Mamay)

(Worth St. Theater) Thursday, Nov.2-Dec.3, 1995 (29 performances)
Worth St. Theater Ensemble presents:
THE COYOTE BLEEDS by Tony DiMuro; Director, R. Jeffrey Cohen; Set, Julie Melton; Costumes, Helena Prince; Lighting, Pat Dias; Stage Manager, Francys Olivia Burch; Press, Carol Fineman, Tom Gammino CAST: Peter Appel (Detective Hunt Moore), Joyce Ann Lee (Asst. D.A. Robinson), Stewart Steinberg (Detective Colm McShane), Anthony Mangano (Detective Mitchell Confer), Chauncey de Leon Gilbert (McKinley Greene)

A drama set in a New York City precinct house.

(Phil Bosakowski Theatre) Thursday, Nov.2-19, 1995 (16 performances) Peccadillo Theater Company presents:
THE LOOPHOLE by James Kahn; Director, Dan Wackerman; Set/Lighting, Katherine Spencer; Costumes, Susan Soetaert; Stage Manager, Michael Palmer; Press, Howard and Barbara Atlee CAST: Christine Mosere (Jane McCall), William Steel (Harry Spindell), Bill Corsair (Ronzo Fantasia), Cris Parker (Erica Gouda), Dale Carman (Paul Gorchnow), Herman O. Arbeit (Leo Gouda), Gayle Kelly Landers (Diane Rose)

A farce in two acts.

(Chelsea Playhouse) Sunday, Nov.5-Dec.3, 1995 (22 performances and 3 previews) The National Shakespeare Company presents:
TRUE WEST by Sam Shepard; Director, Alan Langdon; Set, C.H. Jones; Lighting, James McClure; Costumes, Sue M. McLaughlin; Sound, Paul Aston; Stage Manager, Laura Ma; Press, Jeffrey Richards/Kevin Rehac, Peter Eramo Jr. CAST: Chris Juell (Lee), Greg Lombardo (Austin), Gary Lamadore (Saul Kimmer), Grace Pettijohn (Mom)

A 1980 play set in a Southern California suburb.

(Don't Tell Mama) Monday, Nov.6-Dec.18, 1995 (7 performances) Bobbie Kraus presents:
LIFE IS NOT LIKE THE MOVIES; Music/Lyrics, Francesca Blumenthal; Director, Hope Hardcastle; Musical Director, Lanny Meyers; Press, David Rothenberg CAST: Kat Cogswell, Michael Marotta, Deborah Tranelli

(Ubu Rep Theater) Tuesday, Nov.7-19, 1995 (13 performances and 1 preview) Ubu Repertory presents:
THE CASE OF KASPAR MAYER by Jean-Yves Picq; Translation, Michael Feingold; Director, Andre Ernotte; Set, Watoku Ueno; Lighting, Greg MacPherson; Costumes, Carol Ann Pelletier; Sound, David Margolin Lawson; Stage Manager, Eileen Myers; Press, Jonathan Slaff CAST: Ian Kahn (Kaspar Mayer Junior), Kurt Rhoads (Artmann), Brad Morris, Stelio Savante (Male Nurses), Erika Petersen (voice only)

A French drama.

(Minetta Lane Theatre) Tuesday, Nov.7, 1995-Feb.11, 1996 (90 performances and 10 previews) Mitchell Maxwell, Alan Schuster, Margaret Selby in association with International Management Group present:
JAM ON THE GROOVE;Conceived/Created/Written/Composed /Choreographed by GhettOriginal Productions; Set, Andrew Jackness; Murals, Erni Vales; Lighting, Peter Kaczorowski; Sound, One Dream; Press, Richard Korberg/Don Summa, Ian Rand, Gail Parenteau, William Finnegan, Frank Vigliotti CAST: Peter "Bam Bam" Arizmendi, Leon "Mr. Popper" Chesney, Steve "Mr. Wiggles" Clemente, Zoraya "Zee Boogie" Clemente, "Crazy Legs", Gabriel "Kwikstep" Dionisio, Kenny "Ken Swift" Gabbert, Tamara Gaspard, Scott "D.J. Skribble" Ialacci, Antoine "Doc" Judins, Risa Kobatake, Adesola "D'Incredible" Osakalumi, Jorge "Fabel" Pabon, "Q-Unique", Jerry "Flow Master" Randolph, Roger "Orko" Romero, Ereina "Honey Roc Well" Valencia

A hip-hop musical performed without intermission.

(Musical Theatre Works) Wednesday, Nov.8-19, 1995 (13 performances) Musical Theatre Works, the Pasadena Playhouse and Michael Jackson present:
SISTERELLA; Music/Lyrics/Book by Larry Hart; Director, David Simmons; Musical Director, Matthew Sklar; Choreography, Raymond G. del Barrio; Press, Jeffrey Richards/Kevin Rehac CAST INCLUDES: Rain Pryor

A musical that resets the Cinderella story in an African-American context.

(Theatre 603) Wednesday, Nov.8-19, 1995 (10 performances) NMR Group presents:
THE GREAT KHAN and **THE GIFT OF THE SPICE PEOPLE** by Ty Adams; Director, Frank Pisco CASTS: *Kahn*: Jim Abele, Colleen Davenport, Andrea Maulella *Gift*: Ms. Davenport, Mr. Abele, Stewart Clarke

Two plays.

(Henry St. Settlement) Thursday, Nov.9-Dec.10, 1995 (29 performances) New Federal Theatre presents:
BLACK GIRL by J.E. Franklin; Director, Anderson Johnson; Set, Kent Hoffman; Lighting, Antoinette E. Tynes; Costumes, Vassie Welback-Browne; Sound, Genji Ito; Stage Manager, Malik; Press, Max Eisen/Laurel Factor CAST: Sabrina DePina (Billie Jean), Justin West (Little Earl), TraLynn Husbands (Sheryl), Lynn Dandridge (Norman Faye), Maggie Henderson (Ruth Ann), Leslie Uggams (Mama Rosie), Marlene Chavis (Mu'Dear), Arthur French (Mr. Herbert), Adam Wade (Earl), Cheray O'Neal (Netta)

A 1970 drama in two acts.

129

Terry Greiss, Kathryn Grant in *A Family Affair* (Gerry Goodstein)

Brett Hamilton, Jennifer Little, Henry Grossman in
***A Musical: Madame Bovary* (William Pierce)**

(Hudson Guild Theatre) Thursday, Nov.9-Dec.3, 1995 (16 performances) Blue Herron Theatre presents:
RESCUERS by Elizabeth Striker; Based on the book *Rescuers: Portraits of Moral Courage* by Gay Block and Malka Drucker; Director, Joe Banno; Set, Scott A. Perich; Lighting, D.M. Wood; Costumes, Loren Bevans; Choreography, Andrea Borak; Stage Manager, James Pelegano CAST: Jim Chance, Mary Eastman, Kateri Eastman, Merle Eisenberg, Emma Friedman, Dale Fuller, Edward Henzel, Paul McCarren, Matt Kowalski, Madigan Ryan, Paul Sado, Ben Siegel, Elizabeth Striker, Nancy Walsh, Rik Walter, Tim Zay
   A two-act drama about Christians who risked their lives to save Jews during the Holocaust.

(Sagi) Thursday, Nov.9-22, 1995 (13 performances) re-opened Thursday, April 18-20 (3 performances) Solo Arts Group Inc. presents:
JUMPING OFF THE FRIDGE; Written/Performed by Ellen Hulkower; Director, Maria Mileaf; Press, Kevin Mazuzan
   A one-woman comedy.

(Theatre for the New City) Friday, Nov.10-Dec.16, 1995 (25 performances and 2 previews) The Irondale Ensemble Project presents:
A FAMILY AFFAIR by Alexander Ostrovsky; Adaptation, Nick Dear; Director, Jim Niesen; Set, Ken Rothchild; Costumes, Hilarie Blumenthal; Lighting, A.C. Hickox; Music, Johan Petri; Press, Tony Origlio/Michael Cullen   CAST: Terry Greiss (Bolshov), Kathryn Grant (Agrafena), Georgina Corbo (Lipochka), Steven Satta (Lazar), Jacqueline Klee (Ustinya), Michael-David Gordon (Rispolozhensky), Yvonne Brechbuler (Fominishna), Alain Hunkins (Tishka)
   A Russian comedy in two acts.

(New York Historical Society) Monday, Nov.13-20, 1995 (2 performances) David Merrick Arts Foundation and The Actors' Company Theatre present:
FASHION by Anna Cora Mowatt; Adaptation/Direction, Scott Alan Evans; Music, Glen Cortese; Stage Manager, Babette Lloyd; Press, Alma Viator/Bill Schelble   CAST: Ryan Bowker (T.Tennyson Twinkle), Francesca DiMauro (Millinette), Delphi Harrington (Prudence), Cynthia Harris (Mrs. Tiffany), Jodi Jinks (Seraphina Tiffany), Larry Keith (Mr. Adam Trueman), Bill Kux (Augustus Fogg), James Murtaugh (Tiffany), Alec Phoenix (Col. Howard), Gregory Salata (Snobson), Scott Schafer (Mac), David Staller (Count Jolimaitre), Lyn Wright (Gertrude), Tom Stewart (Stage Directions)
   A staged reading of a five-act play performed with one intermission. The action takes place in New York City, 1845.

(Judith Anderson Theatre) Thursday, Nov.16-26, 1995 (10 performances and 1 preview) Passajj Productions presents:
A MUSICAL: MADAME BOVARY; Music/Lyrics/Adaptation by Paul Dick; Based on the novel by Gustave Flaubert; Director, Ed Setrakian; Choreography, Artemis Preeshl; Set/Lighting, Jack Mehler; Costumes, Dave Esler; Press, Shirley Herz/Wayne Wolfe, Lauren Rosenblum CAST: Jennifer Little, Henry Grossman, Brett Hamilton, David Jordan, Patrick Sullivan, Janet Momjian, Heidi K. Eklund, Colleen T.C. Martin, Larry French, Laurence Lucaro, C. Anson Hedges
   A musical based on the classic novel.

(John Houseman Theatre) Sunday, Nov.19, 1995-February 1996 (48 performances) Eric Krebs presents:
WASTING TIME WITH HARRY DAVIDOWITZ; Director, Julia Carey; Press, David Rothenberg CAST: Dani Maseng
   The musical journey of a Jewish soul.

Left: Dani Maseng in *Wasting Time with Harry Davidowitz* (Barry Burns)

(45th St. Theater) Sunday, Nov.19-Dec.16, 1995 (21 performances and 10 previews) Blue Light Theater Company presents:
GOLDEN BOY by Clifford Odets; Director, Joanne Woodward; Set, Michael Schweikardt; Costumes, Laurie Churba; Sound, Raymond D. Schilke; Lighting, Deborah Constantine; Stage Manager, Colleen Marie Davis; Fights, B.H. Barry; Press, Gary and John Springer/Candi Adams CAST: James Naughton (Tom Moody), Angie Phillips (Lorna Moon), Greg Naughton (Joe Bonaparte), Joe Grifasi (Tokio), Yusef Bulos (Mr. Carp), Peter Gregory (Siggie), Spiro Malas (Mr. Bonaparte), Emily Wachtel (Anna), James Matthew Ryan (Frank Bonaparte), Lee Wilkof (Roxy Gottlieb), Bruce MacVittie (Eddie Fuseli), P.J. Brown (Pepper/Drake/Driscoll), Alex Draper (Mickey/Lewis/Barker), Jon Rothstein (Sam/Call Boy)
    A 1937 drama in two acts.

(Atlantic Theater) Monday, November 20, 1995 (1 limited performance) Atlantic Theater Company presents:
THE MONDAY NIGHT STOP: THE TIES THAT BIND; Director, Mark Patton; Music, Roman Fruge; Press, Chris Boncau~Adrian Bryan-Brown/Amy Jacobs CAST: Tammy Grimes, John Cameron Mitchell, Guy Stroman, Mark Patton, Roman Fruge
PROGRAM: *The Short History of a Small Place* by T.R. Pearson, *Barn Burning* by William Faulkner, *Notes Towards a Performance of Jean Racine's Tragedy Athalie* by Neil Bartlett, and *A Short Story* by Tennessee Williams
    Stories of family separation.

(Theatre Row Theatre) Monday, Nov.20-Dec. 1995 Tamar Climan presents:
SIX CHARACTERS IN SEARCH OF AN AUTHOR by Luigi Pirandello; Translation, Felicity Firth; Director, Timothy Childs; Set, Ted Simpson; Costumes, Amela Baksic; Lighting, Robert Williams; Press, Pete Sanders CAST: Sally Burtenshaw, John Cates, Leigh Frillici, Earl Hagan, Roslyne Hahn, Greg Longenhagen, Andrea Masters, Julie Mazzarella, Cameron Meyer, Matthew Jason Picheny, Jeanine Pugh, Karen Zippler
    The 1921 drama

(Theatre Off Park) Tuesday, Nov.21-Dec.31, 1995 (42 performances) Positive Image Theatre Compnay presents:
DIRTY TALK! by Joe Pintauro; Director, Kevin Crowe; Lighting, Herrick Goldman; Costumes, Martha Majsak; Stage Manager, Carlos Monge; Press, Pete Sanders CAST: Hayden Adams, Christine Caleo, Michael Feigin, Jill Jackson, Jonathan Stewart
    Ten one-acts performed without intermission.

Laurie Graff, Michael Reilly, Corbin Bleu in
Tiny Tim is Dead **(Carol Rosegg)**

Greg Naughton, Joe Grifasi in *Golden Boy* (Joan Marcus)

(St. Peter's) Friday, Nov.24-Dec.31, 1995 (39 performances and 7 previews) Broadway Arts Theatre for Young Audiences presents:
A CAPTURED CLAUS; Music, Joe Raposo; Lyrics/Book, Nick Raposo; Director, Michael John Murnin; Musical Director/Arrangements, Steve Steiner; Choreography, Jennifer Roth; Sets, Perry Arthur Kroeger; Lighting, Helen A. McCullagh; Costumes, Sara Jablon; Press, David Lotz/David Gersten CAST: John Funk, Doreen Montalvo, Steve Steiner, Susan Stringer, Robert Zanfini, Jonathan Giordano, James P. Wisniewski
    A Christmas musical based on an L. Frank Baum short story.

(Harold Clurman Theatre) Friday, Nov.24-Dec.9, 1995 (14 performances) Love Creek Productions presents:
MADAME, MADMEN, AND MAYHEM by Tom Reilly; Director, Sharon Fallon; Set, Viola Bradford; Lighting, Richard Kent Green; Sound, Henry Marsden Davis; Choreography, Roberta Montuori; Fights, James R. Robinson; Stage Manager, Stephen Shearer; Press, Annie Chadwick CAST: Jackie Jenkins (Madame Grizelda), Sam Street (Dr. Wesson), Bob Celli (Albert), Bart Tangredi (Mr. X)
    A comedy involving a medium and mafioso.

(Currican Theatre) Saturday, Nov.25-Dec.10, 1995 (14 performances and 2 previews) Playwrights' Preview Productions presents:
TINY TIM IS DEAD by Barbara Lebow; Director, Frank Wittow; Set, Jeff Cowie; Lighting, Jason Boyd; Costumes, Alan Michael Smith; Stage Manager, Liz Reddick; Press, Keith Sherman/Stuart Ginsberg, Jim Byk CAST: Laurie Graff (Verna), Corbin Bleu, Jason Edwards Townes (Boy), Michael Reilly (Charlie), Cortez Nance Jr. (Otis Pope), Delores Martin (Azalee Hodge), A J Lopez (Filomeno Cordero)
    A drama in two acts. The action takes place on a dead-end city street, Dec.24-25.

(Nada) Saturday, Nov.25-Dec.23, 1995 (62 performances) Target Margin Theater presents:
TARGET MARGIN FESTIVAL: THE BLIZZARD; Press, Shirley Herz/Sam Rudy
Cymbeline by William Shakespeare; Director, David Herskovits CAST INCLUDES: Rinne Groff, Will Badgett, Steven Rattazzi, Lenore Pembrook, Mary Meufeld
The Nutcracker by E.T.A. Hoffman; Adaptation, David Herskovits and Douglas Langworthy; Director, Mr. Herskovits CAST INCLUDES: Jacqueline Gregg, Gretchen Kritch, Randolph Curtis Rand, Mark Setlock
My Dinner with Goethe by Johann Wolfgang von Goethe; Adapted/Directed by Douglas Langworthy CAST INCLUDES: Aaron Beall, Gary Brownlee, Don Carter
No Xit; Written/Directed by Lyndel Moore; *Whirligig* by Jean Genet; Adapted/Directed by Elizabeth Stevens; *Feast;* Adapted/Directed by Emma Griffin; *The Ozone Advisory* by Eva Mantell; *Bradley Glenn, Suburban Poet*; *The Poison Jelly Episode* by Gans and Register; *Try! Try!* by Frank O'Hara; Director, Gretchen Griffin

(HERE) Tuesday, Nov.28-Dec.22, 1995 Tiny Mythic Theatre Company presents:
7; A HAUNTED DECONSTRUCTION OF NATHANIEL HAWTHORNE'S THE HOUSE OF THE SEVEN GABLES; Conceived/Directed by Tim Maner; Adaptation, Elizabeth Banks; Texts, Britt Coles, David Greenspan, Anita Liberty, Ruth Margraff; Music, Matthew Pierce, Steven Day, Stephen Streuber; Sets, Darrel Maloney; Costumes, Nancy Brous; Lighting, Allen Hahn; Press, Eugenie Hero CAST: Joanna P. Adler, Rachelle Anthes, Alan Benditt, Kate Benson, Lindsay Bishop, John Chaneski, Benjamin Davis, James Ferguson, Kimberly Gambino, Lea Gulino, Roberta Kastelic, Mariana Newhard, Thomas Pasley, Jan-Peter Pedross, Suzanne Schuckel, Emme Shaw, Sam Turich, Todd Van Voris
 Inspired by Hawthorne's story of the last living members of a cursed New England family.

(CSC Theatre) Tuesday, Nov.28-Dec.23, 1995 (20 performances and 6 previews) Falstaff Presents Productions presents:
THE MISANTHROPE by Moliere; Adaptation, The Company; Director, Peter Francis James; Set, Debra Booth; Costumes, Tonya M. Peck; Lighting, Adam Silverman; Music, Peter Alex Orlov; Stage Manager, Martha Donaldson; Press, Tony Origlio/Michael Cullen CAST: Matt Servitto (Philinte), Murphy Guyer (Alceste), Jay Patterson (Oronte), Bridgit Ryan (Celimene), Tim Artz (Basque), Gwendolyn Lewis (Eliante), Ben Gotlieb (Acaste), Mark Feurerstein (Clitandre), Olivia Birkelund (Arsinoe), Mark Feuerstein (Dubois)
    A new translation sets the action in Paris, 1920s. Performed with one intermission.

Aaron Beall, Gary Brownlee, Don Carter in *Target Margin Festival: The Blizzard* (Jamey O'Quinn)

Bridgit Ryan, Olivia Birkelund in *The Misanthrope* (Blance Mackey)

(The Acting Studio) Thursday, Nov.30-Dec.16, 1995 (12 performances) Chelsea Repertory Company presents:
KNOXVILLE, 1915; Adapted/Directed by John Grabowski; from James Agee's novel *A Death in the Family*; Set, Hong Jiwakanon; Lighting, Colin D. Young; Costumes, Judith Lundberg; Sound, Gregory Fensterman; Music, Tom Adelman, Robin Goldwasser; Stage Manager, Rhoda Cosme CAST: Shane Blodgett (Agee/Bartender/Clerk), James Price (Jay Follet), Wendy Ward (Mary Follet), Io Tillet Wright (Rufus Follet), Michael Ryan (Joel Lynch), Sandra Booth (Catherine Lynch), Diane Pulzello (Hannah Lynch), Curtis Harwell (Andrew Lynch), Leo Farley (Walter Starr), Robert Brown (Fr. Jackson), Alexander Mintz, Jonathan Bleicher, Eliav Mintz, Ryan Paylor (Boys), John Hubbard, Brent George, Mike Rutowski (Pall Bearers), Bill Brunkhurst (John-Henry Folllet), Virginia E. Forst (Jessie Follet), R.J. Chesney (Ralph Follet), Sarah Becker (Sally), Chris Valdes (Jim-Wilson Follet), Yvone Adrian (Sadie Follet), Esther Leeming (Great Granmaw)
    A drama in two acts. The action takes place in and around Knoxville, Tennessee, 1915. Tad Mosel's 1960 play *All the Way Home* is based on the same material.

(St. Clement's) Friday, Dec.1-23, 1995 (27 performances) Stone Apparel and The Actors Shakespeare Compnay presents:
MOLIERE'S SHORTS; Created/Directed by John Plummer; Songs, Ray Bokhour; Press, Patricia Buckley CAST: Ray Bokhour, Patricia Buckley, Oliver Field, Peter Gaitens, Peter Greenberg, Maia Guest, Jenny Langsam, John Plummer
    A remodeling of Moliere's one-act plays.

Jenny Langsam, Peter Gaitens, John Plummer in *Moliere's Shorts*

(Gene Frankel Theatre) Friday, Dec.1-17, 1995 (9 performances) Kevin Leslie, John Lynch and Diana Takata present:
TIBET DOES NOT EXIST by Don Thompson; Director, John Thompson; Set/Lighting, Joel Giguere; Costumes, Loren Bevans; Design, Joel Giguere; Stage Manager, Jodi Lynn Finkel CAST: Marshall Factora, Nicholas Haylett, Tiffany Marshall, Tim Rankin, Jonathan Uffelman, Karen Wright

A drama involving the meeting of Tibetan Buddhist monks and Yale University professors.

(44th St. Theatre) Tuesday, Dec.5-17, 1995 (12 performances) Crisis Theatre presents:
THE AMERICAN DREAM by Edward Albee; Director, Sebastian Tejeda; Press, Gary and John Springer/Candi Adams CAST: Cooley (Grandma), Scott Brasfield (Young Man), Cheryl Hedges (Mommy), Tina Stafford (Mrs. Barker), Alexis Woutas (Daddy)

A comedy/drama in one act.

(Mint Theater) Tuesday, Dec.5-30, 1995 (15 performances) Mint Theater Company presents:
THE GRABELSKI CONCERTOS by Tommy Swerdlow with Michael Goldberg; Director, Stephen DiMenna; Set, William Kneissl; Lighting, Mark T. Simpson; Costumes, John Kristiansen; Sound, Raymond D. Schilke; Stage Manager, Bradley Moates; Press, David Rothenberg CAST: Mark Lake (Jonah Jonestown), Sam Seder (Stein Steinman)

A coming of age story.

(Samuel Beckett Theatre) Tuesday, Dec.5, 1995-Feb.18, 1996 (78 performances and 10 previews) The Negro Ensemble Company and Theatre Legend present:
DICK GREGORY LIVE; Set, Michael Green; Lighting, Marshall Williams; Press, Jeffrey Richards/Irene Gandy

A solo performance.

(Chelsea Playhouse) Thursday, Dec.7-24, 1995 (11 performances and 3 previews) The Invisible Theatre in collaboration with Groundwerx Dance Theatre presents:
THE FALL OF THE HOUSE OF USHER by Edgar Allan Poe; Adapted by Linda Manning with Douglas Wagner; Director/Music/Lighting/Sound, Mr. Wagner; Choreography, Groundwerx Dance Theatre; Set, Deborah L. Jensen; Costumes, Marilyn Salvatore; Stage Manager, Tina Juul; Press, Shirley Herz/Sam Rudy CAST: Linda Manning (Madeline Usher), Michael Pinney (Roderick Usher), Derek Stearns (William Hawken), Heather Ahern, Peter Bramante, Donna Meierdiercks, Cathy Nicoli (House of Usher)

A drama in two acts.

Cheryl Hedges, Tina Stafford; Scott Brasfield, Cooley, Alexis Woutas in *American Dream* (Kipling Berger)

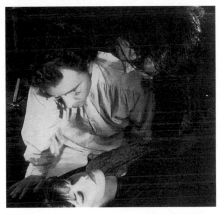

Linda Manning, Derek Stearns, Michael Pinney in *Fall of the House of Usher* (Tom Nolan)

(Theatre Off Park) Sunday, Dec.10-11, 1995 (2 performances) Theatre Off Park and Millennial Arts Productions/Paula Heil Fisher present:
AMERICA'S SWEETHEART; Music, Richard Rodgers; Lyrics, Lorenz Hart; Book, Herbert Fields; Director, Albert Harris, Musical Director, John McDaniel; Musical Restoration, James Stenborg; Lighting, A.C. Hickox; Stage Manager, Alex Nicholas, Press, Bill Evans/Jim Randolph CAST: Ed Dixon (S.A. Dolan), Jarrod Emick (Michael Perry), Alison Fraser (Denise Torel), Liz Larsen (Madge Farrell), Darcie Roberts (Geraldine March), Guy Stroman (Larry Pitkin), Kerry O'Malley (Dorith), Susan Owen (Paula), Cordell Stahl (Eddie Lynch/Radio Voice), David Jordan (Man at Radio), Matthew Burnett, Jennifer Piech, Jonathon Stewart, Clif Thorn (Ensemble)
MUSICAL NUMBERS: Overture, Mr. Dolan Is Passing Through, In Californ-i-a, My Sweet, I've Got Five Dollars, Sweet Geraldine, There's So Much More, We'll Be the Same, How About It, Innocent Chorus Girls of Yesterday, A Lady Must Live, You Ain't Got No Savoir Faire, Two Unfortunate Orphans, I Want a Man, Finale

A staged concert of a 1931 musical in two acts. The action takes place in Hollywood. A planned series of Rodgers-Hart revivals(*I Married An Angel* was presented earlier in the season) was aborted after this production due to the death of Albert Harris.

(47th St. Theater) Sunday, Dec.10, 1995-Jan.7, 1996 Jerry Hammer and Pat DeRosa in association with Harold J. Newman present:
RENDEZ-VOUS WITH MARLENE; Written/Performed by Torill; Musical Director, Stan Freeman; Set, Bruce Goodrich; Costumes, Wong, Goff, Rodriguez

A Norwegian entertainer recreates Marlene Dietrich.

Jarrod Emick, Guy Stroman, Darcie Roberts in
America's Sweethearts (Joan Marcus)

(Mint Theater) Tuesday, Dec.12, 1995-Jan.7, 1996 (15 performances)
Mint Theater Company presents:
KIND EYES by S.W. Stout; Director, K.G. Wilson; Set, William Kneissl; Lighting, Mark T. Simpson; Costumes, John Kristiansen; Sound, Raymond D. Schilke; Stage Manager, Michelle Colletti; Press, David Rothenberg CAST: Lisa M. Bostnar (Hallie), Lynn Niederman Silver (Joyce)

A tale of two women.

(La Mama) Thursday, Dec.14-23, 1995 (7 performances) La Mama E.T.C. presents:
TINY TIM AND THE SIZE QUEEN; Written/Directed by Daniel Haben Clark; Music, Ned Parkhouse; Set, Ian Gordon; Costumes, Lisa Zinni; Lighting, Yun Young Koo; Press, Jonathan Slaff CAST: Joe Pichette (Haspel Preminuce), Brad Chandler (Tim Vida), Diane Bradshaw (Mother/Bunny/Stefka), Jay Bonnell (Andrew Hande/K. Sera/Pussyman), Barry Ford (Cop/Ducky/Dr. Colorado), Nicholas Van Eeden (Cash McBoy/Florian/Leo)

A modern re-telling of *A Christmas Carol*.

(Theater for the New City) Thursday, Dec.14-Jan.7, 1995 (16 performances) Theater for the New City presents:
RUBY AND PEARL: A CLASS ACT by Laurence Holder; Director, Rome Neal; Music, Christopher Cherney; Set, Anie Blackburn; Lighting, Zdenek Kriz; Costumes, Marcel Christian; Sound, David Wright; Press, Jonathan Slaff CAST: Randy Pannell (Ruby), Arlana Blue (Pearl)

A drama about two strippers in the 1960s.

(Theatre Row Theatre) Friday, Dec.15, 1995-Jan.13, 1996 (18 performances and 13 previews) Pure Orange Productions presents:
THE PRINCIPALITY OF SORROWS by Keith Bunin; Director, Elizabeth Gottlieb; Set, Henry Dunn; Lighting, Jeff Croiter; Costumes, Angelina Avallone; Sound, Red Ramona; Stage Manager, Alex Lyu Volckhausen; Press, Richard Kornberg/Troy Hollar CAST: Robert Sean Leonard (Teddy), Joanna Going (Iris/Lucinda/Holly), David Lansbury (Marc)

A drama in three acts. The action takes place in a castle garden in Belgium during 1923, 1934 and 1947.

(Harold Clurman Theatre) Friday, Dec.15, 1995-Jan.7, 1996 (23 performances and 5 previews) Willow Cabin Theatre Company presents:
A CHILD'S CHRISTMAS IN WALES by Dylan Thomas; Adaptation, Jeremy Brooks and Adrian Mitchell; Director, Edward Berkeley; Set, John Kasarda; Costumes, Dede Pochos, Tasha Lawrence; Lighting, Matthew McCarthy; Musical Director, Christine Radman; Press, Jim Baldassare CAST: Laurence Gleason (Dylan Thomas), Fiona Davis (Mother), Ken Forman (Father), Robert Harryman (Postman/Gwyn), Angela Nevard (Hannah), Cynthia Besteman (Elieri), Maria Radman (Glenda), Dede Pochos (Brenda), Zachary Ansley, John Billeci, Rus Blackwell, Ken Favre, Anthony Gelsomino, Verna Lowe, Christine Radman

The action takes place in Swansea, Wales.

(New Victory Theater) Sunday, Dec.17-31, 1995 (16 performances and 1 preview) The New 42nd St. presents:
CIRQUE ELOIZE; Music, Claude St.-Jean, Tabou, Gerard Cyr; Lighting, Louis Landry; Sound, Stephane Gariepy; Press, Anita Duga-Carroll/Stacey Clement CAST: Alain Boudreau, Damien Boudreau, Daniel Cyr, Sylvain Drolet, Marc Gauthier, Roch Jutras, Lise Lepine, Jean Painchaud

A group of young circus performers inaugurates the restored New Victory, which opened in 1900 as the Theatre Republic.

(Judith Anderson Theatre) Wednesday, Dec.20, 1995-Jan.14, 1996 (28 performances) Do Gooder Productions presents:
THE MAGIC FORMULA by Sidney Morris; Director, Gareth Hendee; Set, Eilat Rimon; Costumes, Misha Kuchta; Lighting, Raymond Cullom; Stage Manager, Terry Mac; Press, Bryan Lee Utman CAST: Dominic Cuskern (Dr. Buber), Michael Dunn Litchfield (David), Mark Robert Gordon (Rubin)

A drama in two acts. The action takes place in Los Angeles, 1947. Presented last season at the Wings Theatre.

Joanna Going, Robert Sean Leonard, David Lansbury in *The Principality of Sorrows*

Calista Flockhart, Austin Pendleton in *The Imposter* (Jessica White)

(Theater for the New City) Thursday, Dec.28, 1995-Jan.21, 1995 (13 performances and 3 previews) Theater for the New City presents:
TRUE CRIMES; Written/Directed by Romulus Linney; Sets, E. David Cosier; Lighting, Jeffrey S. Koger; Costumes, Jonathan Green; Stage Manager, Anthony Pick; Press, Jonathan Slaff CAST: David Johnson (Logan Lovel), Heather Melton (Jennie Notree), Cheryl Haas (Mary Sparks), Christine Parks (Vangey Lovel), Daniel Martin (Ab Lovel), Fred Burrell (Soony Sparks), Rebecca Harris (Nancy Sparks), Mark Alan Gordon (Sawdust), Erin Hill (Voice in Wind)
A drama set in the Appalachian mountains, 1900.

(Workhouse Theatre) Friday, Dec.29, 1995 Jan20, 1996 (14 performances and 2 previews) Alice's Fourth Floor presents:
THE IMPOSTER by J. Dakota Powell; Director, John David Coles; Set, Rob Odorisio; Lighting, Michael Gottlieb; Costumes, Kim Krumm Sorenson; Sound, Jessica Murrow; Music, Richard Einhorn; Stage Manager, David P. Smith; Press, Richard Kornberg/Don Summa CAST: Austin Pendleton (Eric), Calista Flockhart (Sidra), Melinda Wade (Dell), Clark Gregg (Hank), Richard Bekins (Ron), Katherine Leask (Elizabeth), Matthew Weiss (Ethan)
A drama in two acts. The action takes place in New York City, Sag Harbor and New Jersey.

(SoHo Rep) Thursday, Jan.4-Feb.3, 1996 (25 performances) SoHo Repertory presents:
DARK RIDE by Len Jenkin; Director, Julian Webber; Set, Anthony MacIlwaine; Lighting, Adam Silverman; Sound, Chris Todd; Choreography, Dan Hurlin CAST: Joanna P. Adler (Waitress), Reed Birney (Translator), Marylouise Burke (Mrs. Lammle), Frank Deal (Mr. Zendavesta), Leslie Lyles (Deep Sea Edna), Bruce MacVittie (Thief), Joseph McKenna (Deep Sea Ed), Angie Phillips (Margo), Keith Reddin (General), Frank Wood (Jeweler), Ray Norberto, Michael La Feyta
A new production of a 1981 play.

(New Victory Theater) Friday, Jan.5-21, 1996 (17 performances and 4 previews) The New 42nd St. and Crossroads Theatre Company present:
SHEILA'S DAY by Duma Ndlovu, Mbongeni Ngema and Ebony Jp-Ann; Based on idea by Duma Ndlovu; Director, Mbongeni Ngema; Restaging, Kenneth Johnson; Set, Charles McClennehan; Lighting, Victor En Yu Tan; Costumes, Toni-Leslie James; Musical Direction, Irene Datcher, Thuli Dumakude; Stage Manager, Patreshettarlini Adams; Press, Serino Coyne/Terence Womble CAST: Stephanie Alston, Debbi Blackwell-Cook, Gina Breedlove, Carla Brothers, Irene Datcher, Thuli Dumakude, Ebony Jo-Ann, Letta Mbulu, Denise Morgan, Linda Sithole, Fuschia Walker
A play with music performed without intermission. The action takes place in Alabama and South Africa, 1965-72.

(St. Clement's) Tuesday, Jan.9-Feb.17, 1996 (25 performances and 11 previews) Theatre for a New Audience presents:
MEASURE FOR MEASURE by William Shakespeare; Director, Barry Kyle; Set, Christine Jones; Costumes, Constance Hoffman; Lighting, Donald Holder; Music, Michael Ward; Stage Manager, David Sugarman; Press, Merle Debuskey/Susan Chicoine CAST: Bill Camp (Duke), Nicholas Kepros (Escalus), Frank Lowe (Justice/Friar Peter/Abhorson), John Campion (Angelo), Michael Louden (Lucio), Claire Eye (Mistress Overdone), Mark Niebuhr (Pompey), Trellis Stepter (Provost), Firdous Bamji (Claudio), Ketuta Meskhishvili (Juliet), Jacqueline Kim (Isabella), Kristine Nielsen (Francisca/Mariana), Tom Aulino (Elbow), David Dossey (Froth/Barnadine), Anthony Manganiello (Boy), David Barlow, Tom Biglin, Richard Cavan, Sadie Chrestman, Adrienne Dreiss, Christopher Moore (Ensemble)
Performed with one intermission.

(HERE) Wednesday, Jan.10-Feb.4, 1996 (29 performances) Mabou Mines and Gertrude Stein Repertory Theatre present:
AN EPIDOG; Written/Directed by by Lee Breuer; Sets/Lighting/Puppets, Julie Archer; Costumes, Mary pat Bishop; Sound, Edward Cosla; Music, Ushio Torakai; Press, Ellen Jacobs CAST: Ruth Maleczech, Frederick Neumann, Clove Galilee, Leslie Mohn, Xin Zhang, Barbara Pollitt, Terry O'Reilly, Basil Twist, Bina Sharif, Samantha Hack, Kathy Shaw, Carrie Cantor, Emily Weiner, Marymay Impastato, Crystal Scott, Maria Hurley, Jessica Smith, Jenny Sunjack, Lute Ramblin'.
Third part of a trilogy about a dog named Rose.

(Vineyard 26th St. Theatre) Wednesday, Jan.10-Feb.11, 1996 (25 performances) The Living Theatre presents:
utopia by Hanon Reznikov; Director, Judith Malina; Music, Raaja Fischer; Lighting, Gary Brackett; Press, Mark Hall Amitin CAST: Alan Arenius, Amber, Gary Brackett, Jerry Goralnick, Joanie Fritz, Johnson Anthony, Judi Rymer, Lois Kagan Mingus, Marlene Lortev, Martin Reckhaus, Rhasaan Manning, Robert Hieger, Rob Schmidt, Silas Inches
   A play including audience participation.

(Theatre Off Park) Wednesday, Jan.10-Feb.4, 1996 (16 performances and 4 preview) Rattlestick Productions present:
A TRIP TO THE BEACH by David Van Asselt; Director, David A. Dorwart; Set, Van Santvoord; Lighting, Ed McCarthy; Stage Manager, Courtney Halliday; Press, Peter Cromarty/Hugh Hayes CAST: Kristina Lear (Linda Gardner), Mick Weber (Tom), Jack Koenig (Gabe Riplowe), Chris Hietikko (Joe Baum), Stuart Zagnit (Morris Muddflatt), Arija Bareikis (Mary)
   A drama in two acts. The action takes place within an advertising agency.

(Intar Theatre) Thursday, Jan.11-21, 1996 (12 performances) Red Light District Theatre Company presents:
BOX OFFICE POISON by Marc Geller and Bill Roulet; Director/Lyrics/Set/Costumes, Mr. Geller; Music, Daniel T. Denver; Lighting, Frank DenDanto III; Choreography, D.J. Salisbury; Stage Manager, Patrick McGowan CAST: Gregg Dubner (Slats Stewicky), Tracey Gilbert (Newscaster), Alan Denny (Pice Pilkington), Thomas F. Walsh (Irving Botsweenick/Amazing Latrine), Jackob Hoffmann (Butch "Stinky" Burger), Seth Allman (Ben Dover), Peter Floris (Buddy Booth), Robert Barbagallo (Buck Beetenoff), Elizabeth Bove (Lynn Burger), Jerry Vermilye (Rory Brocade), Beth Dodye Bass (Belva Brocade), Marilyn Duryea (Romaine Smaile), Tom Morrissey (Ricketts Bouvier), Bill Roulet (Nova Kane), Marc Geller (Lana Kane), Melissa Osborn (Pansy Pilkington), Kenton Reid (Biff Malibu)
   A mystery-comedy set in Pocatello, Idaho, 1956.

(Synchronicity Space) Thursday, Jan.11-28, 1996 The Actors Studio and Sanctuary Theatre Workshop present:
STRANGERS IN THE LAND OF CANAAN by Paul Alexander; Director, Rip Torn; Set, Tom and Steven Glisson; Lighting, Stewart Wagner; Costumes, Daniel James Cole; Stage Manager, Ed Strum; Press, Bobby Zarem/Dick Guttman CAST: David John Dean (Hunter), David P. Juergens (Worth), Stephen Largay (Tiny), Angelica Torn (Candy), Jon Leon Torn (Worth), Tim Williams (Powell)
   A drama in two acts. The action takes place in Tennessee.

(St. Peter's) Friday, Jan.12-Feb.4, 1996 (12 performances and 13 previews) York Theatre Compnay presents:
MATI HARI; Music, Edward Thomas; Lyrics/Director, Martin Charnin; Book, Jerome Coopersmith; Choreography, Michele Assaf; Orchestration/Music Direction, Keith Levenson; Sets, James Morgan; Costumes, Jennifer Arnold; Lighting, Mary Jo Dondlinger; Sound, Jim van Bergen; Stage Manager, Anne Marie Paolucci; Press, Keith Sherman/Jim Byk CAST: John Anthony (Pollinaire/Soldier), Allen Fitzpatrick (Henri La Farge), Jack Fletcher (Major Bonnard/Wounded Soldier), Jim Jacobson (Masson/Gen. Delacorte/Zauberhand/Fr. DuPre/Sergeant/French President), Marguerite MacIntyre (Mata Hari), Kirk McDonald (Young Soldier), Julia K. Murney (Pistolette/Claudine), Stephanie Seeley (Tamil/Young Lady/Michele), Robin Skye (Paulette), Judith Thiergaard (Countess/Madame DuPre/Nun), Tom Treadwell (Officer/ Duvalier/ Philipe/ Grant)
MUSICAL NUMBERS: Gone, Is This Fact?, Dance at the Salon, Everyone Has Something to Hide, How Young You Were Tonight, I'm Saving Myself for a Soldier, Choice Is Yours, Fritzie, No More Than a Moment, This Is Nice, Maman, Not Now Not Here, Hello Yank, I Don't See Him Very Much Amy More, You Have No Idea, What Might Have Been, Finale
   A revised version of a 1967 musical in two acts. The action takes place in France during World War I. For original production, which closed out-of-town in Washington, D.C., see *Theatre World* Vol.24.

Chris Hietikko, Jack Koenig, Kristina Lear, Stuart Zagnit, Arija Barekis in *Trip to the Beach* (Carol Rosegg)

Allen Fitzpatrick, Marguerite MacIntyre, (top) Kirk McDonald in *Mata Hari* (Carol Rosegg)

(Performing Garage) Wednesday, Jan.17-Feb.18, 1996 The Wooster Group presents:
THE HAIRY APE by Eugene O'Neill; Director, Elizabeth LeCompte; Music, John Lurie; Set, Jim Clayburgh; Lighting, Jennifer Tipton; Press, Alexandra Paxton CAST: Willem Dafoe, Peyton Smith, Kate Valk, Jill Clayburgh, Elizabeth LeCompte, Roy Faudree, Paul Lazar, Dave Shelly
   A comedy of ancient and modern life in eight scenes.

(Chelsea Playhouse) Wednesday, Jan.17-Feb.11, 1996 (11 performances and 9 previews) The Lark Theatre Company presents:
DOG AND HIS MASTER by Luoyong Wang and Michael Johnson-Chase; Adapted from the play *Uncle Dog's Nirvana* by Liu Jinyun; Set, Larry Gruber; Lighting, Ed McCarthy; Costumes, Carol Brys; Music, Frank Schiro; Stage Manager, Elizabeth Dickerson; Press, Chris Boneau~Adrian Bryan-Brown/Patty Onagan, Meredith Moore CAST: Jon Lee (Dog), Jaime Sanchez (Landlord Hau), Marc Jason Wong (Tiger), David Johann (Big River Lee), Les J.N. Mau (Barber Su), Ann Harada (Little Dream), Kim Miyori (Jasmine Feng), Erin Quinn, Richela Fabian
   A drama in two acts.

(Greenwich St. Theatre) Thursday, Jan.18-Feb.11, 1996 (13 performances and 3 previews) Chain Lightning Theatre presents:
THE BEAUTIFUL PEOPLE by William Saroyan; Director, Kricker James; Lighting, Scott Clyve; Set, Bill Kneissl; Costumes, Meganne George; Stage Manager, Raina Alysse Stern; Press, Jim Baldassare CAST: Max Faugno (Owen Webster), Blainie Logan (Harmony Blueblossom), Brandee Graff (Agnes Webster), Munro Bonnell (Jonah Webster), Jim Siatkowski (Prim), Frank Nastasi (Dan Hillboy), Michael Hobbs (Fr. Hogan), Frank Bradley (Harold Webster), Brian Van Flandern (Steve)
   A drama set in San Francisco, 1941.

(Theatre Row Theatre) Thursday, Jan.18-Feb.11, 1996 (28 performances) Gypsy Road Company presents:
THE 21ST CENTURY PLAYWRIGHTS FESTIVAL; Sets, John Mercurio; Lighting, Chris Gorzelnik; Costumes, Shelley Norton; Sound, Richard Rose, Shirley Herz/Miller Wright*Oh That Wily Snake!* by Martin Dockery; Director, Beth Lincks CAST: Alison Fraser, Arthur Hanket
Where I'm Headed by Leah Ryan; Director, John Rue CAST: Cerris Morgan-Moyer, Jason Tyler White, Moira Gentry, Jane Kimmel, Michael Garr, Christina Cabot, Mark Greenfield, Bart Tangredi, Robert Kilbridge, Will Crawford
Finding Rose by Bonnie Morgan; Director, Thomas Edward West CAST: Carol Higgins Clark, Jim Fantone, Mary Bacon, Aaron Harpold, Jay Devlin, Anita Keal
   Three plays by university and college playwrights.

**(top) Frank Bradley , Munro Bonnell
(bottom) Brandee Graff, Blainie Logan, Max Faugno
in *The Beautiful People* (Daisy Taylor)**

Kim Miyori, David Johann in *Dog and His Master* (Joan Marcus)

(Creative Voices Theatre) Tuesday, Jan.23-Feb.4, 1995 (14 performances) The Flock Theatre Company presents:
BARBED WIRES by Carla Johnston; Director, Shira Piven; Set, Danila Korogodsky; Sound, Robert Auld; Stage Manager, Rebecca Cammisa; Press, Scotty Rhodes CAST: Irene Glezos (Barbara June), Christopher May (Johnny), Robert Alexander (Danny), David Van Pelt (Jack)
   A dark comedy set in a trailer and a hospital room.

(Intar Theatre) Sunday, Jan.28-Feb.17, 1996 (17 performances and 2 previews) Emerging Artists Theatre Compnay presents:
THE PRICE OF MADNESS by Catherine Filloux; Director, Donna Moreau-Cupp; Set, William F. Moser; Lighting, Brian Haynsworth; Costumes, Anne Marino, Cathy Small; Music/Sound, Lewis Flinn; Stage Manager, Marylou Lynn; Press, Tony Origlio/David Powell Smith CAST: Thomas Schall (Henri), Nicola Sheara (Aloise), Liza O'Keeffe (Samantha), Simon Jutras (Paul), Jane Altman (Charlotte)
   A drama set in NYC and Baltimore.

(NY Historical Society) Monday, Jan.29-Feb.5, 1996 (2 performances) David Merrick Arts Foundation and The Actors' Company Theatre presents:
THE BEAUTY PART by S.J. Perelman; Director, Scott Alan Evans; Music, Yuzuru Sadashige; Stage Manager, Babette Lloyd; Press, Alma Viator/Bill Schelble CAST: Ivy Austin (Octavia Weatherwax/Rowena Inchcape), Ivar Brogger (Bunce/Maurice Blount/Wormser/Hennepin /Bailiff), Merwin Goldsmith (Sam Fussfeld/Seymore Krumgold/Judge Rinderburst), Cynthia Harris (Gloria Krumgold/Mrs. Younghusband/Mrs. Mifflin), Marc Kudisch (Rob Roy Fruitwell/Vishne/Poteat), Greg McFadden (Lance Weatherwax), James Murtaugh (Milo Weatherwax/Goddard Quagmeyer), Gregory Salata (Mike Mulroy/Harry Hubris/Nelson Smedley/Joe Gourielli), Jo-Ann Salata (Chenille Schreiber/Roxana De Vilbiss), Scott Schafer (Van Lennep/Vernon Eqinox/Wagnerian/Cameraman), David Staller (Hyacinth Beddos Laffoon/Boris Pickwick/Emmett Stagg/Gorilla), Tom Stewart (Hagedorn/Curtis Fingerhead/Rukeyser/Hanratty), Lynn Vogt (Kitty Entrail/Grace Fingerhead/Sherry Quicklime), Lyn Wright (April Monkhood), Maia Danziger
   A staged reading of a 1962 comedy in two acts. The action takes place in NYC and L.A.

Tim McCracken, Celeste Holm, Wendy Monz
in *The Brooch* (Carol Rosegg)

Lona Scavone, Kezia Norton in *Criminals in Love*

John Delvecchio, Jeremy Klavens, Mark Giordano in *One Way Street*

(Triad) Monday, Jan.29-Feb.26, 1996 (5 performances)
BIG CITY RHYTHMS; Music/Lyrics by Barry Kleibort CAST: Marcia Lewis, Melanie Vaughn, Lewis Cleale, Eric Michael Gillett
  A musical revue.

(Harold Clurman Theatre) Tuesday, Jan.30-Mar.3, 1996 Negro Ensemble Company presents:
NORTH SEVENTEENTH STREET by Clay Goss; Director, Susan Watson Turner; Set, Michael Odell Green; Lighting, Marshall Williams; Costumes, Harriet Michell Green; Sound, Richard Tucker CAST: Lori Brown-Niang (Mother), Regge Allan Bruce (Father), Cornelius Bruce Butler (Grandfather), Richard Craven (Leon), Zenzele J. Scott (Grandmother), Adrienne D. Williams, Oyafunmike Ogunlano (Conjurewoman), Sean Rector (Young Male Voice), Laynie Woods (Young Female Voice), Nicole Bush
  A family drama.

(Miranda Theatre) Wednesday, Jan.31-Feb.25, 1996 (20 performances) The Miranda Theatre Company presents:
THE BROOCH by Emily Whitesell; Director, A.C. Weary; Set, Katerina Fiore; Lighting, William Kneissl; Costumes, Kelly Yelton; Stage Manager, David Steinhart; Press, Jim Baldassare CAST: Celeste Holm (Harriet Wilson), Chris Hurt (Lawrence), Geneva Carr (Louise Wilson), Timothy McCracken (Georgie Wilson), Donald Symington (Nicholaus Harbour), Wendy Moniz (Maggie), David Cheaney (Teddy Horace), Pamela Jean Shaffer (Tippy Horace), Jenny Sterlin (Willemena Horace), Earle Hugens (Daniel Wylie), Charles May (Commissioner), Richard Johnston (Officer March)
  A comedy in two acts. The action takes place in New York City, January 1, 1929.

(Sargent Theatre) Wednesday, Jan.31-Feb.17, 1996 (12 performances) Home Free Theatre and Judith Gray present:
OF MICE AND MEN by John Steinbeck; Director, Robert Burton; Set, Steven Cobb; Lighting/Sound, Scott A. Bray; Costumes, Amanda Whidden; Stage Manager, Michael Foster CAST: David Higlen (George), Casey Hendershot (Lennie), William Preston (Candy), Tim McDonnell (Boss), Duff Dugan (Curley), Whitney Allen (Curley's Wife), Terry Londeree (Slim), Jeff Kronson (Carlson), Edward J. Cunningham (Whit), William Charles Mitchell (Crooks), Allan Pollack (Ranch Hand)
  A three-act drama performed with one intermission. The action takes place in Northern California, 1937.

(Kraine Theater) Thursday, Feb.1-18, 1996 (16 performances) Cooper Square Workshop and Tunney Productions present:
REQUIEM FOR A HEAVYWEIGHT by Rod Serling; Director, Frank Licato; Set, Jon Maass; Costumes, Beth Suhocki; Lighting, Paul D'Amato; Music, William Sloat; Sound, Jeff Howard CAST: Nick Sandow (Mountain), Joel Rooks (Maish), Bill Brady, Paul D'Amato, Joseph Dandry, Nick Discenza, Tony Hoty, Ernest Mingione, Julia Mueller, Michael Ornstein, Charles Jean Pierre
  A drama, originally done on tv, set in the world of prizefighting.

(Judith Anderson Theater) Friday, Feb.2-11, 1996 (8 performances and 3 previews) Breaking Ground Theatre Company presents:
CRIMINALS IN LOVE by George F. Walker; Director, Christina Burz; Design, David C. Harwell; Lighting, Joe Saint; Sound, Kate Levy; Fights, Joseph Travers; Stage Manager, John J. Harmon; Press, Francine L. Trevens CAST: Lona Scavone (Gail), Kevin Cristaldi (Junior), Peter Brets (William), James Carroll (Henry), Kezia Norton (Sandy), Deann Halper (Wineva)
  A dark comedy performed without intermission. The action takes place in dark alleys, school yards, a diner and jail.

(Theatre on Three) Tuesday, Feb.6-Mar.3, 1996 (24 performances) One Way Productions presents:
ONE WAY STREET; Written/Directed by Peter Eramo, Jr.; Sets, Arthur Adair, Greg Guarnaccia; Lighting, Mr. Guarnaccia; Stage Manager, Holly Drastal; Press, Donna Lynn Schibani CAST: John DelVecchio (David), Rebecca DuMaine (Suzanne), Mark Giordano (Kevin), Meredith Bergman (Vicki), Jeremy Klavens (Martin), Samantha Brown (Barbara)
  A drama in two acts.

(Union Square Theatre) Tuesday, Feb.6-Mar.3, 1996 (21 performances and 9 previews) Mitchell Maxwell and Victoria Maxwell in association with Workin' Man Theatricals and Fred H. Krones present:
THE AMAZING METRANO by Art Metrano and Cynthia Lee; Director, David Warren; Set, James Youmans; Lighting, Donald Holder; Projections, Wendall K. Harrington; Music/Sound, John Gromada; Stage Manager, Maureen F. Gibson; Press, Pete Sanders/Michael Hartman CAST: Art Metrano
An "accidental comedy" (dealing with the actor's fight back from paralysis) performed without intermission.

(New Victory Theater) Wednesday, Feb.7-18, 1996 (13 performances) New Victory Theater presents:
DIFFERENT FIELDS; Music, Mike Reid; Libretto, Sarah Schlesinger; Director, Mel Marvin; Sets/Costumes, Sarah G. Conly, John Michael Deegan; Orchestrations, Michael Ching; Musical Director, Joshua Rosenblum; Press, Serino Coyne/Terence Womble CAST: Judith Engel, Steven Goldstein, Theresa Hamm-Smith, Joseph Mahowald, William Walker, James Harris Wiggins III, Amir Jamal Williams
A new opera about a sports hero, on and off the field.

(Sanford Meisner Theatre) Thursday, Feb.8-25, 1996 (12 performances) Perkasie Productions presents:
HABEAS CORPUS by Allan Bennett; Director, Steven Keim; Costumes, Blythe Columbo; Stage Manager, Fran Feil; Press, Gary and John Springer/Candi Adams CAST: George Millenbach (Dr. Wicksteed), Mary Aufman (Muriel), Alan Walker, Janice Hoffman, Patrick Fitzpatrick, Susan Romanoff, Ed Smith, Tina Zaremba, Jennifer Gordon, Steve Viola, Scott Wood
A 1975 farce about a Brighton physician.

(78th St. Theatre Lab) Friday, Feb.9-Mar.17, 1996 The 78th St. Theatre Lab presents:
METESKY by Paul Limbert Allman; Director, Eric Nightengale CAST INCLUDES: Mark Zeller
(Westbeth Theater Center) Monday, Feb.12-25, 1996 (13 performances) Delsener/Slater Enterprises and James L. Nederlander present:
20TH CENTURY MAN: AN EVENING WITH RAY DAVIES; Conceived/Written/Performed by Ray Davies; Accompanied by Pete Mathison; Lighting, Timothy Hunter, Rob Odorisio; Press, Chris Boneau~Adrian Bryan Brown/Craig Karpel
A musical autobiography.

Neil Maffin, Ellen Parker in *Entertaining Mr. Sloan*
(T. Charles Erickson)

Joseph Mahowald, Amir Jamal Williams in
***Different Fields* (Joan Marcus)**

(Ubu Rep Theater) Tuesday, Feb.13-25, 1996 (12 performances and 2 previews) re-opened June 11-23 (14 performances) Ubu Repertory presents:
ALWAYS TOGETHER by Anca Visdei; Translation, Stephen J. Vogel; Director, Francoise Kourilsky; Set, Watoku Ueno; Lighting, Greg MacPherson; Music/Sound, Genji Ito; Costumes, Carol Ann Pelletier; Stage Manager, Robin Gillette; Press, Jonathan Slaff CAST: Maria Deasy (Alexandra), Thea Mercouffer (Ioana)
A drama involving two sisters from opposite sides of the Iron Curtain.

(CSC Theatre) Tuesday, Feb.13-Mar.24, 1996 (29 performances and 9 previews) Classic Stage Company presents:
ENTERTAINING MR. SLOANE by Joe Orton; Director, David Esbjornson; Set, Narelle Sissons; Costumes, Michael Krass; Lighting, Frances Aronson; Sound, John Kilgore; Stage Manager, Linda Harris; Press, Denise Robert CAST: Ellen Parker (Kath), Neil Maffin (Sloane), George Hall (Dadda), Brian Murray (Ed)
A 1964 three-act comedy performed with one intermission. The action takes place in London, 1964.

(Musical Theatre Works) Wednesday, Feb.14-25, 1996 (12 performances) Musical Theatre Works in association with the John Harms Theatre presents:
TOPPER; Music/Lyrics, Cole Porter; Book, Jerry Sterner; Director, Anthony J. Stimac; Choreography, Michele Assaf; Musical Director/Arrangements, Frank Lindquist; Set, Rafael Castanera; Costumes, Gail Baldoni; Lighting, Richard Latta; Stage Manager, Elizabeth Ann Larson; Press, Jeffrey Richards/Scott Karpf CAST: Angel Caban (Beatrice), Kathleen Rowe-McAllen (Marion), Danny Rutigliano (Ernst), Mia Sneden (Rosalie), Bart St. Clair (Roger), Kirby Ward (Topper), Richard White (George), Michael Biondi, Shawnda James, Karen Millard, Sean Gregory Palmer, Laurelle Rethke, Kristin Tudor, Michael Walkup
MUSICAL NUMBERS: Ours, I Know It's Not Meant for Me, Let's Not Talk About Love, Take Me Back to Manhattan, Let's Misbehave, Down with Everybody But Us, Queen of Terre Haute, Let's Be Buddies, You've Got That Thing, I Want to Go Home, Get Out of Town, Experiment, I Love You, It's Bad for Me, My Heart Belongs to Daddy, Rap Tap on Wood, What Are Little Husbands Made Of, Find Me a Primitive Man, Down in the Depths, Do I Love You?, Riding High
A new two-act musical based on the *Topper* film and tv series using vintage songs Porter songs.

(Judith Anderson Theatre) Wednesday, Feb.14-25, 1996 (10 performances and 1 preview) Onyx Theatre Company presents:
A LAYING OF HANDS by Michele Maureen Verhoosky; Director, Veona Thomas; Set, Cornell Riggs; Lighting, Alan Baron; Sound, David Wright; Stage Manager, Paula Syhrett; Press, Jonathan Slaff CAST: Laura Bowman (Young Louella/Yvonne Hendricks), Kai M. Reevey (Rita Mae), Patrice Joyner (Sheba), Dee Dixon (Grandma), Timothy Joyner (Tyler), David Hoxter (Ben Coleman/Dwayne), Anthea Seaman (Glory Coleman), DeVernie Winston (Willie Coleman), Jeffrey Collins (Rev. Moses/Dr. Johnson/Bro. Simon), Benjamin Henderson (Dr. Harrelson/Rex Harrelson/KKK), Nicole Greevy (Sandy Campbell/Adult Lanie/KKK), Leslie Browne (Vivian Harrelson/KKK), Lenore Pemberton (Adult Rita Mae)
A drama in two acts. The action takes place in Georgia during the depression. Performances given in English and American Sign Language.

(One Dream Theatre) Wednesday, Feb.14-24, 1996 (10 performances) The Rudy Dog Theatre Company presents:
NUT MAGNET and **LAS RAFAELLAS** by Mario Moreno; Director, David Troup; Choreography, Shannon Hobbs CASTS: Mario Moreno, Margaret Mendelson, Ellen Hulkower, Judith George
Two one-act plays.

(29th St. Rep Theater) Thursday, Feb.15-Mar.17, 1996 (15 performances and 5 previews) 29th St. Repertory Theater in association with Play Producers presents:
LION IN THE STREETS by Judith Thompson; Director, Abby Epstein; Set, Luke Cantarella; Lighting, Joel Moritz; Sound, Kurt Kellenberger; Costumes, Dana Bauer; Choreography, Peter Carpenter; Music, Canton Becker; Stage Manager, Patrice Ellison; Press, Gary and John Springer/Candi Adams CAST Alexandria Sage (Isobel), Elizabeth Elkins (Nelly/Laura/Christine/Sherry), Lisa Pierotti (Rachel/ Lily/Rhonda/ Ellen/ Scarlett),Charles Willey (Martin/George/Maria/David/Man/Edward), Tim Corcor (Scalato/Father/Bill/Ron/Michael/Ben), Leo Farley (Guy/Timmy /Carl/ Fr. Hayes/Rodney), Paula Ewin (Sue/Jill/Joanne)
A drama in two acts.

(Cherry Lane Theatre) Thursday, Feb.15-Mar.31, 1996 (24 performances and 4 previews) Axis Theatre Company presents:
ROCKLAND COUNTY NO VAUDEVILLE by Randy Sharp and Michael Gump; Director, Mr. Sharp; Set/Costumes, Ian Falconer; Lighting, Michael Gilliam; Films, Roberto Espinosa; Choreography, Laurie Kilmartin; Stage Manager, Chris Deitner; Press, Jonathan Slaff CAST: Robert Ierardi (Mr. Krispi), Michael Gump (Mr. Ogle), Paul Dawson (Marion Rasher), Maximiliano Hernandez (Blackface Minstrel Boy/Erik Estrada), Sue Ann Molinell (Cunty Pink/Cripple), Wren Arthur (Miss), Vivian R. Jordan (Piss Shit)
A vaudeville pastiche performed without intermission.

(Synchronicity Space) Friday, Feb.16-Mar.3, 1996 (13 performances) Synchronicity Theatre Group presents:
CERCEAU by Viktor Slavkin; Director, Nora Colpman; Press, Scott Karpf CAST: Nelson Avidon, Thomas Barbour, Bill Dante, Dean Harrison, Cappy Lyons, John Moraitis, Ilse Petersen
A drama set in Russia.

(Triad) Friday, Feb.16-Sept.1, 1996 (201 performances and 28 previews) John Freedson, Harriet Yellin and Jon B. Platt present:
FORBIDDEN HOLLYWOOD; Created/Written by Gerard Alessandrini; Directed/Choreographed by Mr. Alessandrini and Phillip George; Costumes, Alvin Colt; Set, Bradley Kaye; Wigs, Teresa Vuoso; Musical Director, Fred Barton; Stage Manager, Elise-Ann Konstantin; Press, Pete Sanders/Glenna Freedman CAST: Fred Barton, Toni DiBuono, Michael McGrath, Christine Pedi, Lance Roberts
Musical spoofs of Hollywood performers and films.

Kai Reevey, Dee Dixon, Patrice Joyner, (back) Ben Henderson, Laura Bowman in *A Laying of Hands* (Jonathan Slaff)

Robert Ierardi, Michael Gump in *Rockland County No Vaudeville* (Jonathan Slaff)

Christine Pedi, Lance Roberts, Michael McGrath, Toni Di Buono in *Forbidden Hollywood* (Henry Grossman)

(Atlantic Theater) Saturday, Feb.17-Mar.17, 1996 (21 performances and 4 previews) Blue Light Theater Compnay and Potomac Theatre Project present:

SCENES FROM AN EXECUTION by Howard Barker; Director, Richard Romagnoli; Costumes, Jule Emerson, Lin Waters; Set/Lighting, Mark Evancho; Stage Manager, Gary and John Springer/Candi Adams CAST: Naomi Jacobson (Galactia), Greg Naughton (Carpeta), Alex Draper (Urgentino), James Slaughter (Suffici), Francesca Di Mauro (Gina Rivera), Alan Wade (Prodo/Ostensible), Elizabeth Swain (Sketchbook), Donna Jean Fogel (Supporta), Aidan Sullivan (Dementia/Official), James Matthew Ryan (Sordo/Man in Next Cell), Jon Sherman (Lasagna/Sailer/Gaoler/Piave Man), Jon Rothstein (Sailor/Workman), Nick Toren (Pastaccio)

A drama in two acts. The action takes place in Venice during the 15th century.

Greg Naughton, Naomi Jacobson in
Scenes from an Execution **(Ken Cobb)**

(John Houseman Studio Too) Monday, Feb.19, 1996 (1 performance only) Abingdon Theatre Company presents:

COMEBACK by Claris Nelson; Director, Elaine Smith CAST: Ray Atherton, Kate Bushman, Stephen Huff, Carole Monferdini, Moss Roberts, Scott Rymer

(American Place Theatre) Wednesday, Feb.21-Mar.24, 1996 (19 performances and 11 previews) The American Place Theatre presents:

SPOKE MAN; Written/Performed by John Hockenberry; Director, Wynn Handman; Set, Joel Reynolds; Lighting, Chad McArver; Stage Manager, Judith M. Tucker; Press, Denise Robert

A monologue by an author and broadcast journalist confined to a wheelchair.

(T. Schreiber Studio) Thursday, Feb.22-Mar.24, 1996 (20 performances) T. Schreiber Studio Directors Unit presents:

AN IDEAL HUSBAND by Oscar Wilde; Director, David S. Macy; Music, Andrew Markus; Set, Ted Simpson; Lighting, Joe Saint; Costumes, Leslie Bernstein; Sound, Joseph Furnari; Stage Manager, Jennifer Murray CAST: Mark R. Ahlman (James/Harold), Nicole Alifante (Mabel Chiltern), Rick Forstmann (Lady Markby), Edward Franklin (Earl of Caversham), David A. Green (Vicomte de Nanjac/Phipps), Jane Knox (Lady Chiltern/Gertrude), Hulie Leeds (Mrs. Marchmont/Margaret), Sam McPherson (Mason), Suzy Michels (Countess of Basildon/Olivia), Jeff Mulligan (Mr. Montford/Footman), Zoey O'Toole (Mrs. Laura Cheveley), Mike Timoney (Sir Robert Chiltern), Stephen Waldrup (Viscount Goring/Arthur)

An 1895 four-act comedy performed with three intermissions. The action takes place in London, 1893.

***An Ideal Husband* Cast**

(Ohio Theatre) Thursday, Feb.22-Mar.3, 1996 (14 performances) The Magellan Project presents:

IVANOV by Anton Chekhov; Adaptation, Howard Pflanzer and Kati Kormendi; Director, Dunstan Cormack; Music, Boris Berlin; Sets, Sarah Lambert; Costumes, Mary Meyer; Lighting, Betsy Adams; Sound, Robert Auld; Press, David Rothenberg CAST: Lee Richardson, Jillian Bach, Jolie Dechey, David Fuhrer, Michael Glumicich, Michael Halliday, Kati Kormendi, Anne MacMillan, Rik Nagel, Tricia Paoluccio, Milly Schoenbaum, Kevin Svetlitch, Ray Trail, Patrick Tull, Wendy Walker

(28th St. Theater) Tuesday, Feb.27-Mar.10, 1996 (14 performances) Night & Erebus Productions presents:

DR. JEKYLL AND MR. HYDE by Brandon Long; Based on the story by Robert Louis Stevenson; Director, Caryl Butterley; Set, Anne Brahic; Lighting, Anthony Costa; Costumes, Christopher Glasgow; Music, Roger Butterley; Choreography, Staci Cobb CAST: Erik Bryan (Jekyll/Hyde), Redman Maxfield (Gabriel James), Larry Merritt (Carew/Thomas Jekyll/Priest), Michael Walczak (Hastie Lanyon), Mark Costanzi (Charles Newcomen), Jeff Macauley (Richard Enfield), Marilyn Beck (Emma Poole), Gwendolyn Thorne (Mary Chadwick), Jessie Matrullo (Young Woman/Patient/Prostitute), Pamela J. Nigro (Michelle Barton Jeklyy), Abby Imber (Dr. Klaussen), Lynne M. Nonnenmacher (Daisy Whittaker)

A new adaptation in two acts.

Jillian Bach, Lee Richardson, Kati Kormendi in *Ivanov* **(Carol Rosegg)**

(Pulse Theatre) Wednesday, Feb.28-Mar.30, 1996 (30 performances)
Pulse Ensemble Theatre presents:
MURDER MYSTERY SERIES; Sets, Mikhail Garakanidze, Valentin Volkov; Costumes, Sue Jane Stoker; Lighting, Jeffrey S. Koger; Music, Bruce Cohen; Stage Managers, Russ Marisak, Dana Ortiz, Keith Gottlieb; Press, Judy Jacksina
Night Must Fall by Emlyn Williams; Director, Robyn Lee CAST: Betty Winsett (Mrs. Bramson), Kate Mailer (Olivia Grayne), Tim Farley (Hubert Laurie), Sally Andrews (Nurse Libby), Sloane Bosniak (Mrs. Terrace), Colette Duvall (Dora Parkoe), Brian Richardson (Inspector Belsize), Patrick Hillian (Dan)
The Hollow by Agatha Christie; Director, Alexa Kelly CAST: Lee Steinhardt (Henrietta Angkatell), Frank Nicolo (Henry Angkatell), Jan Wallace (Lady Angkatell), Sydney Davolos (Midge Harvey), Brian Richardson (Gudgeon), John Howard (Edward Angkatell), Karen Lawrence (Doris), Elaine Smith (Gerda Cristow), David Sitler (John Cristow), Arley Tapir (Veronica Graye), Howell Mayer succeeded by Patrick Hillan (Inspector Colquhoun), Russell Oakes (Sgt. Penny)
Sherlock Holmes & the Speckled Band by Sir Arthur Conan Doyle; Adaptation, Alexa Kelly; Director, Paul Moss CAST: Susan Walker (Mrs. Hudson), Denise Casey (Helen Stoner), Tucker McCready (Sherlock Holmes), Frank Nicolo (Watson), Tim Farley (Dr. Roylett), Quentin Crisp (Richards), Patrick Hillan (John Armitage), Sally Andrews (Mrs. Stanton)
    Performed in repertory.

(New Victory Theater) Friday, Mar.1-24, 1996 (21 performances and 5 previews) The New 42nd St. and Theatre for a New Audience present:
THE GREEN BIRD by Carlo Gozzi; Translation, Albert Bermel and Ted Emery; Directed and Co-Designed by Julie Taymor; Music, Elliot Goldenthal; Sets, Christine Jones; Costumes, Constance Hoffman; Lighting, Donald Holder; Sound, Bob Belecki; Stage Manager, Michele Steckler; Press, Merle Debuskey/Susan Chicoine, Terence Womble; CAST: Didi Conn (Smeraldina), Myriam Cyr (Barbarina), Ned Eisenberg (Truffaldino), Lee Lewis (Pompea), Kristine Nielsen (Ninetta), Sebastian Roche (Renzo), Sophia Salguero (Aplle Soloist), Priscilla Shanks (Tartgliona), Derek Smith (Tartaglia), Trellis Stepter (Brighella), Bruce Turk (Green Bird), Erico Villanueva (Dancing Water), Andrew Weems (Pantalone)
    A philosphical comedy in two acts.

Didi Conn, Miriam Cyr in *Green Bird* (Gerry Goodstein)

Judd Hirsch, Robert Sean Leonard in *Below the Belt* (Joan Marcus)

(John Houseman Theatre) Friday, Mar.1-May 12, 1996 (68 performances and 16 previews) Julian Schlossberg, Meyer Ackerman and Anita Howe-Waxman present:
BELOW THE BELT by Richard Dresser; Director, Gloria Muzio; Sets, Stephen Olson; Costumes, Jess Goldstein; Lighting, Peter Kaczorowski; Sound, Martin R. Desjardins; Fights, Steve Rankin; Stage Manager, Denise Yaney; Press, Bill Evans/Jim Randolph CAST: Robert Sean Leonard (Dobbitt), Judd Hirsch (Hanrahan), Jude Ciccolella (Merkin)
    A comedy in two acts. The action takes place in an industrial compound in a distant land.

(Paramount Theatre) Friday, Mar.1-10, 1996 (14 performances) Ken Wydro and Vy Higgensen present:
BORN TO SING! MAMA 3; Music/Lyrics/Book/Direction by Vy Higginsen and Ken Wydro; Press, Cathy Del Priore, Sue Harrison CAST INCLUDES: CeCe Winans, Shirley Caesar, Stacy Francis, Shanna
    The third in a series of musical dramas.

(Theatre Row Theatre) Friday, Mar.1-24, 1996 (18 performances and 4 previews) Willow Cabin Theatre Company presents:
THE ENDS OF THE EARTH by Morris Panych; Director, Edward Berkeley; Set, John Kasarda; Lighting, Jane Reisman; Costumes, Dede Pochos, Tasha Lawrence; Press, Jim Baldassare CAST: John Bolger (Frank Gardner), Laurence Gleason (Henry Walker/Reggie), Angela Nevard (Willie/Libby/Astrid/Millie), Maria Radman (Alice/June/Mag/Mona), Ken Forman (Finn/Homeowner/Clayton/Jack/Lawrence/Sergio/Eduardo/Lewis/Ferryman)
    A comedy in two acts. The setting moves from place to place, we never really know where we are.

(Wings Theatre) Saturday, Mar.2-May 4, 1996 (26 performances and 3 previews) Wings Theatre Company presents:

THE CAPTAIN'S BOY; Music, Christopher Jackson; Lyrics/Book, Clint Jeffries; Director, Jeffery Corrick; Musical Director, Paul L. Johnson; Musical Staging, Robin Reseen; Design, Jason Sturm; Costumes, Betty LaRoe; Lighting, Ken Morelandd; Stage Manager, Robert Hurrell; Press, Mr. Corrick, Robert Mooney CAST: Steve Kolbo (Renard), George Brouillette (Cookie), Bill Wheeler (Bart), Garry Novikoff (Mr. Samuels), Tony Sicuso (Johnny Cheever), John Cantwell (Michael Johnson), Scott Ahearn (Jim Putnam), Jonathan Hova succeeded by Michael Dunn Litchfield (Jeremy), Celia Grinwald succeeded by Angela Della Ventura (The Lady)

A pirate musical suggested by the book *Sodomy and the Pirate Tradition.*

(INTAR Theatre) Saturday, Mar.2-31, 1996 (27 performances) INTAR Hispanic American Arts Center presents:
NEW LATINO VOICES; Sets, Van Santvoord; Costumes, Mirena Rada; Lighting, Traci Klainer-McDonnell; Sound, Johnna L. Doty; Press, Shirley Herz/Miller Wright
Inkarri's Return by Henry Guzman; Director, Paulo Nunes-Ueno CAST: Victor Argo, Blanca Camacho, Maria Cellario, Ruben Gonzalez, Adriana Inchaustegui, Joe Quintero, Hechter Ubarry
Forever in My Heart by Oscar A. Colon; Director, Michael John Garces CAST: Maria Cellario, Miriam Cruz, Doris Difarnecio
In the Land of Giants by Roger Arturo Durling; Director, Eduardo Machado CAST: Victor Argo, Blanca Camacho, Miriam Cruz, Doris Difarnecio, Michael John Garces, Adriana Inchaustegui, Joe Quintero, Hechter Ubarry
Performed in repertory.

Ger Campbell in *In a Different Light* (Jeff Sauger)

Hitomi Ozawa Kazuki Takase, Ako in *Two Cities* (Barry Burns)

Scott Ahearn, John Cantwell in *Captain's Boy* (Clint Jeffries)

(Weill Recital Hall) Monday, Mar.4, 1996 (1 performance only)
RUTH DRAPER'S NEW YORK LADIES; Director, David Kaplan; Press, Chris Boneau~Adrian Bryan-Brown/Bob Fennell, Amy Jacobs CAST: Patricia Norcia
Ms. Norcia performs Ruth Draper monologues.

(Playquest Theater) Wednesday, Mar.6-31, 1996 (16 performances and 5 previews) Playquest Theater Company presents:
IN A DIFFERENT LIGHT by Robert Fannin; Director, Hilary Fannin; Set/Lighting, Damon Hartley; Costumes, Danielle Murphy; Press, Peter Cromarty/Alice C. Herrick CAST: Ger Campbell (Vincent)
A one-man drama based on the letters of Vincent Van Gogh.

(Irish Rep Theatre) Wednesday, Mar.6-June 2, 1996 (72 performances and 8 previews) Dublin Jackeen Productions and Edmund Gaynes present:
BEIN' WITH BEHAN; Written/Performed by Michael L. Kavanagh; Director/Set, Bruce Heighley; Lighting, Lawrence Oberman; Music/Sound, Tom Rinker; Press, David Rothenberg
A one-man peformance based on the writings of Brendan Behan. The setting is McDaid's Pub in Dublin, mid-1960s.

(30th St. Theatre) Thursday, Mar.7-24, 1996 (16 performances) Spectrum Stage presents:
TWO CITIES by Ernest Ferlita; Director, Ken Lowstetter; Choreography, Ako; Music, Yukio Tsuji; Sets, William F. Moser; Costumes, Elly Van Horne; Lighting, Marcia Sheridan; Stage Manager, Elizabeth H. Reeves; Press, David Rothenberg
The Bells of Nagasaki CAST: Novel Idea (Chorus Leader), Mark Hattan (Chimoto-san), Gregory Zaragoza (Dr. Nagai), Kazuki Takase (Ichitaro Yamada), Lena Immamura (Kayano), Hitomi Ozawa, Matsuo Shimada, Kayoko Mizutani (Chorus)
The Mask of Hiroshima CAST: Novel Idea (Chorus Leader), Mark Hattan (Okuma), Kazuki Takase (Shinji Ishikawa), Ako (Hisa Ishikawa), Gregory Zaragoza (Doctor), Lena Immamura, Kayoko Mizutani, Hitomi Ozawa, Matsuo Shimada (Chorus)
Two related short plays.

**Brian Boone, Rockets Redglare, Michele Matheson,
Dana Discordia in** *Valhalla* **(Ivanhoe Gadpaille)**

Karen Lynn Gorney, Ted Zurkowski in *Hamlet*

Kristin Hughes, Christian Anderson in *Take it Easy*

(Theatre for the New City) Thursday, Mar.7-17, 1996 (8 performances) Theatre for the New City presents:
VALHALLA; Written/Directed by Jake Torem; Press, Judy Jacksina/John Piccirillo, Kevin Kennison CAST: Rockets Redglare (Mama), Michele Matheson (Daisy), Brian Boone, Dana Discordia
A drama about a modern day Fagin.

(West Park Church) Thursday, Mar.7-31, 1996 (16 performances) Frog & Peach Theatre Company presents:
HAMLET by William Shakespeare; Director, Lynnea Benson; Costumes, Vicki Gellman; Sets, John Kelly; Fights, Kathy Keil; Stage Manager, John W. Evans; Press, Gary and John Springer/Candi Adams CAST: Stephenanie Bosl (Marcellus/Fortinbras), Bryant Fraser (Claudius), Karen Lynn Gorney (Gertude), Mervyn Haines Jr. (Polonious), Leone Fogle Hechler (Guilderstern), Stephen Kaiser (Ghost), Kathy Keil (Rosencrantz), Tom Knutson (Orsic), Howard I. Laniado (Player King), Michael McFadden (Laertes), Jill O. Stanevich (Ophelia), Richard B. Watson (Horatio), Ted Zurkowski (Hamlet)

(Synchronicity Space) Thursday, Mar.7-24, 1996 (11 performances and 4 previews) The Jewish Theater of New York presents:
THE BEGGAR OF BOROUGH PARK by Tuvia Tenenbom; Director, Sasha Nanus; Set/Costumes, George Xenos; Lighting, David Alan Comstock; Music, John Beltzer; Press, Richard Kornberg CAST:Russell Costen, Steven Flum, Sally Frontman, Mark Jupiter, Herb Klinger, Jeff Kronson, Jaimi B. Williams
A comedy set in Brooklyn.

(Judith Anderson Theatre) Friday, Mar.8-June 30, 1996 (104 performances and 13 previews) New Village Productions presents:
TAKE IT EASY; Music/Lyrics/Book by Raymond Fox; Director, Collette Black; Musical Director, Bill Zeffiro; Orchestration, Mario E. Sprouse; Choreography, Tom Ribbink; Press, Mark Simmons CAST:Emmet Murphy (John Graham), Isaac Rockoff (Fred Brown), Christian Anderson (Joe Goldman), Stephanie Kurtzuba (Susan Bradshaw), Julianna Hahn (Mary Taylor), Kristin Hughes (Becky Winslow), Carrie Pollack (Winifred Taylor), Tom Nigh (Lt. Col. Davidson), Cindy Messer, Bob McGrath, Adam Turner, Robert Higginbotham, Suzanne Lindenblatt
MUSICAL NUMBERS: Overture, We're in the Army, Who Cares, Take It Easy, An Old Time Girl, Just One More Time, It's All Right, I Think I'm Falling for You, I'll Remember Spring, Funny, The Night When We Were Young, Say Farewell, Worry about the Blues Tomorrow, Home Front Farm Brigade, Home for Christmas, Our Yesterday, Looking for the Sunshine
A musical in two acts. The action takes place on a college campus, 1944.

(Town Hall) Monday, March 11, 1996 (1 limited performance) Town Hall, Andrew Barrett & Chris Burney in association with Townhouse Communications and Howard Danziger present:
archy & mehitabel; Music, George Kleinsinger; Lyrics, Joe Darion; Book, Mr. Darion, Mel Brooks; Based on the stories of Don Marquis; Director, Kirsten Sanderson; Choreography, Michael Lichtefeld; Musical Directors, Albin Konopka, James Stenborg; Stage Manager, Alexander Carney CAST: Ted Neustadt (Newspaper Man), Lee Wilkof (Archy), Taylor Dayne (Mehitabel), Timothy Warmen (Big Bill), Bill Buell (Tyrone T. Tattersall), James Darrah (Broadway the Lightning Bug), Jennifer George, Melissa Haizlip, Sharon Moore, Tina Stafford (Ladybugs), Michael Berglund, James Darrah, Erich McMillan-McCall (Mehitabel Cohorts)
MUSICAL NUMBERS: Prologue, What Do We Care, Toujours Gai, Queer Little Insect, Bragging Flea, Trio, My Real Romance, Lightning Bug Song, Flotsam and Jetsam, Come to Me-ow, Suicide Song, Actor Cat, Romeo & Juliet, A Woman Wouldn't Be a Woman, Lullaby, The Rescue, Pretty Kitty, The Way She Use to Be, Roun' in a Circle, Ladybug Song, Song of the Moth, Finale
A musical in two acts. The action takes place on the seamy side of the Big Town, in and around a newspaper office, and Shinbone Alley. The original 1957 Broadway production was titled *Shinbone Alley*.

Reed Birney, Charlie Hofheimer in *Minor Demons* **(Carol Rosegg)**

Mather Zickel, Gretchen Egolf in *Cardenio* **(Andrew Greenspan)**

Riverdance **Cast (Michael LePoer Trench)**

(Ubu Rep Theater) Tuesday, Mar.12-24, 1996 (13 performances and 1 preview) Ubu Repertory presents:
BONDS OF AFFECTION by Loleh Bellon; Translation, Barbara Bray; Director, Shirley Kaplan; Set, Watoku Ueno; Lighting, Greg MacPherson; Costumes, Carol Ann Pelletier; Sound, Robert Gould; Stage Manager, Eileen Myers; Press, Jonathan Slaff CAST: Kathryn Rossetter (Charlotte), Kristin Griffith (Jeanne), Paul Hoover (Pierre), George Hosmer (Jacques)

A drama set during World War II.

(Currican Theatre) Tuesday, Mar.12-31, 1996 (16 performances) Playwrights' Preview Productions presents:
MINOR DEMONS by Bruce Graham; Director, Richard Harden; Set, Patrick Mann; Lighting, Jeffrey McRoberts; Costumes, Alan Michael Smith; Sound, Michael Keck; Music, Matt Balitsaria; Stage Manager, Liz Reddick; Press, Keith Sherman/Charlie Siedenburg, Jim Byk, Kevin Rehac CAST: Reed Birney (Deke Winters), Amelia Marshall (Diane Gardner), Charlie Hofheimer (Kenny Simmonds), Susan Pellegrino (Carmella Delgatto), Steve Ryan (Vince Delgatto), Alexandra O'Karma (Mrs. Simmonds), Michael Cannis (Mr. Simmonds), Gil Pacheco (Victor Alvarez)

A drama set in a small town outside Pittsburgh during winter.

(Musical Theatre Works) Wednesday, Mar.13-30, 1996 (12 performances and 4 previews) Kermit Christman & Jacqueline Anne Siegel and Kathleen Etherington in association with Palm Beach Shakespeare Festival and Musical Theatre Works presents:
CARDENIO by William Shakespeare; Adaptation, Kermit Christman and Kevin Crawford; Based on the authenticated text by Charles Hamilton; Director, Kermit Christman; Set, Charles Kirby; Costumes, Ilona Somogyi; Lighting, Chris Dallos; Sound, Geoff Shearing; Stage Manager, Jennifer Hall; Press, Jeffrey Richards/Roger Bean CAST: William D. Michie (Tyrant), Mather Zickel (Cardenio), Cristine McMurdo-Wallis (Memphonia), Gretchen Egolf (The Lady), William Meisle (Helvetius), Rob Sedgwick (Votarius), Troy Ruptash (Anselmus), Arnie Quigley (Wife), Jodi Stevens (Leonella), Jamie Callahan (Bellarius), Franz Jones (Stormtrooper)

A "modern world premiere" of a possible "lost" Shakespeare play.

(Theatre at 224 Waverly Place) Wednesday, Mar.13-31, 1997 (12 performances and 5 previews) Lost Tribe Theatre Company presents:
SHAYGUAN'S PICTURE; Written/Directed by Stephen F. Kelleher; Set, Jennifer Campbell; Music, Andrew Hollander; Lighting/Sound, Casey Kearns; Stage Manager, Marko Stifanic; Press, Jim Baldassare CAST: Deann Halper (Jesse), Kofi (Father), Erik Kraus (Little Joe), Joe Masi (Marcus), Minerva Scelza (Demeri), Cezar Williams (Sam)

A drama in two acts. The action takes place in a bad section of New York City.

(American Theater of Actors) Wednesday, Mar.13-16, 1996 (4 performances) Jim Jennings presents:
BLOOD DUES by Edward Musto; Based on the book by Dotson Rader; Director, Richard Galgano; Lighting, William Kradlak II CAST: Christopher Rydman (Dotson Rader), Danette Bock (Kristin Thorn/Germaine Greer), Mick Hilgers (Tennessee Williams), Blaine Lee Holtkamp (Christopher/Andy Warhol), Joanna McEvoy (Barbara), Frank Avoletta (Hank/Arkansas), Ben Golden (Tom/Abbie Hoffman), Dana Watkins (Jann Eller)

A two-act drama that takes place in the memory of Dotson Rader, post-Watergate.

(Radio City Music Hall) Wednesday, Mar.13-17, 1996 (8 performances) returned Wednesday, Oct.2-20, 1996 (23 performances) Abhann Productions and Moya Doherty present:
RIVERDANCE; Music, Bill Whelan; Director, John McColgan; Press, Merle Frimark/Marc Thibodeau

A company of over 100 dancers and musicians celebrate Irish dance, music and song.

(Theatre East) Thursday, Mar.14-23, 1996 (8 performances) Montauk Theatre Productions presents:
SPLIT ENDS; Written/Composed by Bonnie Lee Sanders and Mark Barkan; Directors, Anita Brown and Bill Galerno; Musical Director, Woody Regan; Costumes/Choreography, Mary Ponsini; Press, Mimi Scott CAST:Jack Drummond, Alison Grambs, Michael Colby Jones, Joanna Lange, Sidney Myer, Paula Newman, Mimi Scott, David Tornabene, Morrow Wilson

A murder mystery musical.

(Mint Space) Thursday, Mar.14-31, 1996 (16 performances) Annette Moskowitz and Alexander E. Racolin on behalf of Play Producers present:
MURPHY by Jack Frankel; Director, Herman Babad; Set, Chris Jones; Lighting, Mark T. Simpson; Costumes, Karen Gerson; Stage Manager, Bradley Moates; Press, David Rothenberg CAST: Jack Frankel (Murphy), Jonathan Halyalkar (Issac Rosen), Lenore Wolf (Bebe Rosen), Jasper McGruder (Robert Washington)

A drama in two acts.

(St. Clement's) Thursday, Mar.14-30, 1996 (11 performances) Tectonic Theater Project presents:
MARLOWE'S EYE by Naomi Iizuka; Director, Moises Kaufman; Set, Sarah Lambert; Costumes, Kaye Voyce; Lighting, Mark Barton; Video, Christopher Kondek; Sound, Geoff Sitter; Press, David Rothenberg CAST: Jerry Ball, Jermaine Chambers, Sarah Gunnell, Bruce McKenzie, Maude Mitchell, Maria Striar, John Douglas Thompson, Wallace Wilhoit Jr.

A drama interweaving three historical characters: Christopher Marlowe, Pier Paolo Pasolini and Branch Davidian Ruth Riddle.

(Workhouse Theater) Thursday, Mar.14-23, 1996 (10 performances) Seraphim presents:
THE USERS WALTZ by Todd Alcott; Director, Lothaire Bluteau; Set, Brad Stokes; Lighting, Robert Perry; Costumes, Laura Cunningham CAST: Chris Bauer, Gil Bellows, Rya Kihlstedt, Brooke Smith

(Tribeca Performing Arts Center) Friday, Mar.15-17, 1996 (3 performances) Artsgenesis Productions in association with Shari Upbin present:
GHOST CAFE by James P. Mirrione; Director, Andre De Shields; Musical Director, Terry Waldo; Lighting, Susan A. White; Stage Manager, Dwight R.B. Cook; Press, Jeff Oppenheim CAST: Andre De Shields (Louis Armstrong), Mary Bond Davis (Bessie Smith)

A two-act play set in an imaginary cafe where the ghosts of Armstrong and Smith tell their tales.

Jonathan Halyakar, Jasper McGruder in *Murphy* (Barry Burns)

Robert Hogan, Marge Redmond in *The Shattering* (Carol Rosegg)

(Players Theatre) Friday, Mar.15-Apr.14, 1996 (16 performances and 22 previews) Shelmar Productions presents:
THE SHATTERING by Mark R. Shapiro; Director, Kenneth Elliott; Set, Edward T. Gianfrancesco; Costumes, Robert Mackintosh; Lighting, Phil Monat; Sound, Fox & Perla; Stage Manager, D.C. Rosenberg; Press, Peter Cromarty/Hugh Hayes, Alice Herrick CAST: Marge Redmond (Bea), Patricia Randell (Peg), Robert Hogan (Harry), Frank Vohs (Sid), Owen Hollander (Walt), Ray Aranha (Lester)

A drama in two acts. The action takes place in a lower- middle class suburb, 1992.

(Lamb's Theatre) Tuesday, Mar.19-May 12, 1996 (52 performances and 11 previews) Arthur Cantor presents:
I DO! I DO!; Music, Harvey Schmidt; Lyrics/Book, Tom Jones; Based on *The Fourposter* by Jan de Hartog; Director, Will Mackenzie; Musical Director, Tim Stella; Choreography, Janet Watson; Set, Ed Wittstein; Costumes, Suzy Benzinger; Lighting, Mary Jo Dondlinger; Stage Manager, Ira Mont; Press, Arthur Cantor CAST: David Garrison (Michael), Karen Ziemba (Agnes)
MUSICAL NUMBERS: The Wedding: All the Dearly Beloved/Together Forever/I Do I Do, Goodnight, I Love My Wife, Something Has Happened, Love Isn't Everything, Nobody's Perfect, It's a Well Known Fact, Flaming Agnes, The Honeymoon Is Over, Where Are the Snows?, My Cup Runneth Over, When the Kids Get Married, Father of the Bride, What Is a Woman?, Someone Needs Me, Roll Up the Ribbons, This House

A musical in two acts. The action spans fifty years of a marriage beginning in 1898.

David Garrison, Karen Ziemba in *I Do I Do* (Carol Rosegg)

Mary Murfitt, Lori Fischer, Mary Ehlinger in *Cowgirls* (T. Charles Erickson)

(Minetta Lane Theatre) Tuesday, Mar.19, 1996-Jan.5, 1997 (321 performances and 16 previews) Denise Cooper, Susan Gallin, Rodger Hess, Suki Sandler present:
COWGIRLS; Conception/Music/Lyrics, Mary Murfitt; Book, Betsy Howie; Director/Choreography, Eleanor Reissa; Musical Director, Pam Drews Phillips; Sets, James Noone; Costumes, Catherine Zuber; Lighting, Kenneth Posner; Sound, Scott Stauffer; Arrangements, Mary Ehlinger; Stage Manager, William Joseph Barnes; Press, Shirley Herz/Sam Rudy CAST: Rhonda Coullet (Jo Carlson), Mary Ehlinger (Rita), Lori Fischer (Lee), Mary Murfitt (Mary Lou), Betsy Howie (Mo), Jackie Sanders (Mickey)
MUSICAL NUMBERS: Overture, Three Little Maids, Jesse's Lullaby, Ode to Connie Carlson, Sigma Alpha Iota, Ode to Jo, From Chopin to Country, Kingdom of Country, Songs My Mama Sang, Heads or Tails, Love's Sorrow, Looking for a Miracle, Don't Call Me Trailer Trash, Honky Tonky Girl, Every Saturday Night, Don't Look Down, They're All Cowgirls to Me, Saddle Tramp Blues, It's Time to Come Home, We're a Travelin' Trio, Sunflower, Concert Medley, House Rules, Cowgirls
A musical comedy in two acts. The action takes place at Hiram Hall, country music hall in Rexford, Kansas.

(Ensemble Studio Theatre) Wednesday, Mar.20-April 7, 1996 (17 performances and 1 preview) The Ensemble Studio Theatre presents:
NO ONE WILL BE IMMUNE by David Mamet; Director, Curt Dempster; Set, Kert F. Lundell; Costumes, Barbara A. Bell; Lighting, Greg MacPherson; Stage Manager, Christine Lemme; Press, Jim Baldassare
A Sermon CAST: David Rasche; *Sunday Afternoon* CAST: David Margulies, David Rasche, Elaine Bromka; *Joseph Dintenfass* CAST: James Murtaugh, Kristina Lear; *Almost Done* CAST: Elaine Bromka; *No One Will Be Immune* CAST: David Rasche, Byron Jennings
Five pieces for theatre.

(Ohio Theatre) Thursday, Mar.21-Apr.14, 1996 Arden Party Theatre Company presents:
VICTOR OR CHILDREN TAKE OVER by Roger Vitrac; Translation, Aaron Etra; Director, Karin Coonrod; Lighting, Darrel Maloney; Costumes, Sonia Simon; Set, Sarah Edkino; Music/Sound, Tony Geballe; Press, Denise Robert CAST: Steven Rattazzi (Victor), T. Ryder Smith (Charles Paumelle), Jan Leslie Harding (Emilie Paumelle), Mary Christopher (Lili), Paula Cole (Esther), Patrick Morris (Antoine Magneau), Gretchen Krich (Therese Magneau), Randolph Curtis Rand (Gen. Lonsegur/Doctor), Linda Donald (Ida Mortemart/Mysterious Visitor)
A 1928 French "bourgeois comedy" in three acts. (Theater for the New City) Thursday, Mar.21-Apr.6, 1996 (10 performances and 2 previews) Theater for the New City presents:

WILDERNESS OF MIRRORS by Ralph Pezzullo; Director, Mark Marcante; Set, John Paino; Lighting, Ian Gordon; Sound, David Adrian Scott; Stage Manager, Anthony Pick; Press, Jessica Crystal CAST: Claudia J. Arenas, Chris De Oni, John Doman, Craig Meade, Valentina Quinn, Jesse Sparks, Catalina Lago
A drama set in a Honduran rain forest.

(Chelsea Playhouse) Thursday, Mar.21-Apr.13, 1996 (11 performances and 4 previews) Gilgamesh Theatre Group presents:
OEDIPUS AT COLONUS by Sophocles; Director, Alex Roe; Set, Katerina Fiore; Costumes, Kelly Lee Gregson; Lighting, William Kneissl; Music, Alex Roe; Stage Managers, Louisa Benton, Jennifer Lauren Lack; Press, Gary and John Springer CAST: Ken Bolden (Oedipus), Dee Pelletier (Antigone/Ismene), Jason Hauser (Stranger/Theseus/Creon/Polyneices), Shaula Chambliss, Tom Nolan, St. Clair Ripley (Chorus)
A new adaptation of the classic play.

147

(Fool's Company) Thursday, Mar.21-24, 1996 (6 performances) The DeSisto School presents:
INAPPROPIATE; Conceived by A. Michael DeSisto and Lonnie Mc-Neil; Adapted from creative memoirs of DeSisto School alumni; Director/Choreography/Adaptation, Lonnie McNeil; Music, Ben Baze, Shelton Becton, Debra Byrd, Seth Jaslow, Mr. McNeil, Andy Russell; Musical Director, Jim Trainor; Sets, Caroline Allanthus, Moira Moreta, Alex Mutnick, Jennifer Porterfield, Jesse Robins; Stage Manager, Laura Hamilton; Press, Tony Origlio/Jan Dobris CAST: Gage Fairey, Jonathan Hall, Ali Jeffers-Cook, Lee Kalt, Jamie Kehnie, Devin Kirby, Liam Leahy, Julia Mariani, Jesse Osborn, Melissa Richmond, Andy Russell, Rian Speakes, Bridget Stafford

A life experience musical performed without intermission.

(Variety Arts Theatre) Friday, Mar.22-Apr.19, 1996 (11 performances and 17 previews) Nat Weiss in association with Randall L. Wreghitt presents:
ZOMBIE PROM; Music, Dana P. Rowe; Lyrics/Book, John Dempsey; Based on a story by Mr. Dempsey and Hugh M. Murphy; Director, Philip Wm. McKinley; Choreography, Tony Stevens; Musical Director, Darren R. Cohen; Orchestrations, Michael Gibson; Sets, James Youmans; Costumes, Gregg Barnes; Lighting, Richard Nelson; Sound, Abe Jacob; Stage Manager, Joel P. Elins; Press, Jeffrey Richards/Roger Bean, Laramie Dennis, Mark Cannistraro CAST: Karen Murphy (Delilah Strict), Jessica-Snow Wilson (Toffee), Cathy Trien (Coco), Natalie Toro (Ginger), Rebecca Rich (Candy), Marc Lovci (Joey), Stephen Bienskie (Jake), Jeff Skowron (Josh), Richard Roland (Jonny), Richard Muenz (Eddie Flagrante)
MUSICAL NUMBERS: Enrico Fermi High, Ain't No Goin' Back, Jonny Don't Go, Good as It Gets, The C Word, Rules Regulations and Respect, Blast from the Past, That's the Beat for Me, Voice in the Ocean, It's Alive, Where Do We Go from Here, Trio (Case Closed), Then Came Jonny, Come Join Us, How Can I Say Good-Bye, Easy to Say, Expose, Isn't It?, Forbidden Love, The Lid's Been Blown, Zombie Prom

A musical comedy in two acts. The action takes place in and around Enrico Fermi High School during the "nuclear fifties".

(Chelsea Playhouse) Saturday, Mar.23-Apr.14, 1996 (10 performances and 3 previews) Gilgamesh Theatre Group presents:
SENSELESS; Conceived/Directed by Ralph Buckley; Set, Katerina Fiore; Costumes, Kelly Lee Gregson; Lighting, William Kneissl; Sound, John W. Ralston; Stage Manager, Bryan Hart; Press, Gary and John Springer CAST: Ayfer, Barry Boehm, Kevin Alfred-Brown, Tom Burnett, Cynthia Chapman, Cathy Cross, Alice Gordon, James Grattan, Matt Higgins, Gemma Kochis, Jack Levin, Nicholas Little, Jeff Petrou, Jay Rhoderick, Kevin Scott, Elizabeth Warner

Improv based political comedy written and performed by 16 Gilgamesh actors.

(Japan Society) Tuesday, Mar.26-28, 1996 (3 performances) Japan Society presents:
A CATALOGUE OF CITY LIFE; Written/Performed by Issey Ogata; Director, Yuzo Morita; Simultaneous Translation, M. Hart Larrabee IV; Press, Peter Cromarty/Hugh Hayes

An evening of comedy in two acts.

(Vineyard 26th St.) Wednesday, Mar.27-Apr.14, 1996 (16 performances and 2 previews) National Asian American Theatre Company presents:
SHAW SPRING THAW: *Two One-Acts by George Bernard Shaw*; Director, Stephen Stout; Sets, Alistair Wandesforde-Smith; Costumes, Elly van Horne; Lighting, Jennifer E. Tanzer; Stage Managers, Sue Jane Stoker, Michael Zorn; Press, Shirley Herz/Sam Rudy
How He Lied to Her Husband CAST: David Kimo Ige (He), Mia Katigbak (She), Mel Duane Gionson (Her Husband)
Village Wooing CAST: Mel Duane Gionson (A), Mia Katigbak (Z)

***Inappropriate* Cast**

Natalie Toro, Karen Murphy, Stephen Bienski, Rebecca Rich, Jessica-Snow Wilson in *Zombie Prom* (Gerry Goodstein)

**Mel Duane Gionson, David Kimo Ige in
Shaw Spring Thaw (Bec Marquez Litchfield**

(Greenwich St. Theatre) Thursday, Mar.28-Apr.21, 1996 (14 performances and 2 previews) Chain Lightning Theatre presents:
THE BEAU DEFEATED by Mary Pix; Director, Geoffrey Jangeman; Costumes, Misty Halliday; Sets, Bill Kneisl; Lighting, Mark Simpson; Stage Manager, Francys Olivia Burch; Press, Claire Higgins CAST: Elizabeth Arnold (Mrs. Fidget), Munro M. Bonnell (Elder Clerimont), Jeff Casper (jack), Steve Deighan (John Roverhead), Jack DiMonte (Younger Clerimont), Carol Emshoff (Mrs. Rich), Janet Geist (Lady La Basset), Ginger Grace (Lady Landsworth), Brandee Graff (Lucinda), Kathryn Graybill (Mrs. Clerimont), William Laney (Various Roles), Blainie Logan), Mark McGriff (Belvoir), John C. Muntone (Mr. Rich), Pamela J. Nigro (Governess), Ean O'Donoghue (Toby), Scott Wood (Chris), Sheila York (Mrs. Trickwell)

A 1700 comedy in two acts. The action takes place in London.

(New Victory Theater) Friday, Mar.29-31, 1996 (5 performances) New Victory Theater presents:
SNOWFLAKE; Written/Performed by Gale LaJoye; Press, Serino Coyne/Gina Jarrin

The story of a day in the life of a street person.

(Alice's Fourth Floor) Tuesday, Apr.2-6, 1996 (6 performances)
AIMEE & HOPE; Written/Directed by Chris Van Groningen; Sound, David Christenberry CAST: Olivia Birelund (Aimee), Anita Keal (Brit/Dot), Virginia Downing (Older Aimee/Nurse/Britty Two), Amy Stiller (Ellen/Oksana), Cathy Curtin (Jenny/Doctor), Michael James Reed (Jack)

(Center Stage) Tuesday, Apr.2-14, 1996 (16 performances) Ivy Productions presents:
CLOSE ENOUGH FOR JAZZ AND OTHER SHORT PLAYS by Joe Lauinger; Director/Design, Christopher Sanderson; Stage Manager, Connie Tarbox; Press, Gary and John Springer/Candi Adams CAST: Bill Migliore, Christina Cabot
PROGRAM: *The Box, High-Risk Giving, Close Enough for Jazz, Half in Love*

Four one-act plays.

(American Place Theatre) Tuesday, Apr.2-May 5, 1996 (23 performances and 17 previews) American Place Theatre presents:
THE SLOW DRAG by Carson Kreitzer; Director, Elise Thoron; Music Director, James Mcel Waine; Set, Joel Reynolds; Lighting, Jane Reisman; Costumes, Mirena Rada; Choreography, Stormy Brandenberger; Consultant, Pepsi Bethel; Sound, David Lawson; Stage Manager, Kate Broderick; Press, Denise Robert CAST: Peggy Shaw (Johnny Christmas), Ann Crumb (June Wedding), Vernel Bagneris (Chester Kent)

A "jazz play" performed without intermission.

Peggy Shaw in *Slow Drag* (Eva Weiss)

Gale LaJoye in *Snowflake*

William Hulings (seated) and Cast in King Henry V (T. Charles Erickson)

(Sylvia and Danny Kaye Playhouse) Thursday, April 4, 1996 (1 performance only) The Acting Company presents:
KING HENRY V by William Shakespeare; Director, Mary Lou Rosato; Set, Christine Jones; Costumes, Jeanne Button; Lighting, Brian Nason; Sound, Darron L. West; Musical Director, Lawrence Yurman; Press, Alma Viator/Michael Borowski CAST: C.J. Wilson (Francis), Kevin Dwyer (Michael Williams), Carl Jay Cofield (Peto), William Hulings (Fluellen), Mercedes Herrero (Doll), Kevin Orton (Louie), Matthew Greer (Alexander Court), Kathleen Christal (Kate), Marc Damon Johnson (Nym), Anthony Ward (Pistol), Candace Taylor (Nell), Erin J. O'Brien (Jane)

An adaptation of Shakespeare's history play performed with one intermission.

(HERE) Friday, Apr.5-28, 1996 (10 performances and 2 previews) The Mesopotamian Opera presents:
SUNSET SALOME; Music, Max Kinberg; Libretto, Peter Wing Healey; Director, Laurence J. Geddes; Costumes, Willa Kim; Sets, Ann Patterson; Lighting, Chenault Spence; Choreography, Priscilla Waldoef; Press, Shirley Herz/Sam Rudy CAST: Michael McQuary (Norma Desmond/Toyotakawa), Chris Knoblock (Exhausted Peasant/Dead Prophet), Janie Brendel (Nurse/Memnhet/Dancer), Robin Thomas Morale (Zilpah), Jim Boutin (Asphenez), Joe Gately (David), Frederick Redd (Herod Antipas), Rebekah Wilshire (Aunt Salome), Rochelle Mancini, Donna Darden-Spangler (Zadok), Peter Wing Healey (Herodias), Janet Norquist (Virgin Mary), Felicia Norton (Salome), John Heginbotham (John the Baptist), Brannon Hall-Garcia (Yahweh)

A musicalization of *Salome* as rewritten by Norma Desmond. The action takes place at Whispering Sands Hospital for the Criminally Insane in Palm Springs.

Ellen Dolan, Mischa Barton, Armand Schultz
in *Where the Truth Lies* (Carol Rosegg)

Arthur French , Amy-Monique Waddell, Roby Dee,
Peter Jay Fernandez in *Checkmates*

(Trocadero Cabaret) Friday, Apr.5-May 11, 1996 (10 performances)
SLAP! *Or, School for Slaves* by John Chatterton; Director, Ted Mornel; Costumes, Carla Gant; Set, John Velardi; Lighting/Sound, George Cameron; Stage Manager, Mark A. Mindicino; Press, Howard and Barbara Atlee CAST: Mark Hamlet (Jack), Lissa Moira (Jill)
A two-character S&M fantasy.

(St. Peter's) Tuesday, Apr.9-28, 1996 (17 performances and 7 previews) New American Stage Company and Cindy Webster present:
THE BOAR'S CARCASS by Stephanie Dickinson; Director, David Calvitto; Set, Teresa Stroh; Lighting, Jeff Segal; Costumes, Moira Shaughnessy; Sound, Rick Beenders; Press, Shirley Herz/Miller Wright CAST: Sean Cullen (Pete), Nadine Stenovitch (Ashley), Michael Cambden Richards (Dario), Diane Grotke (Lorna)
A thriller in two acts. The action takes place at the New Jersey shore.

(Irish Rep Theatre) Tuesday, Apr.9-May 5, 1996 (21 performances and 7 previews) Weissberger Theater Group presents:
WHERE THE TRUTH LIES by Catherine Butterfield; Director, Evan Yionoulis; Set, David Gallo; Costumes, Teresa Snider-Stein; Lighting, Chris Dallos; Sound, Janet Kalas; Stage Manager, Press, Gary and John Springer CAST: Catherine Butterfield (Elaine Flanagan), Brittany Boyd (Wendy Flanagan), Ellen Dolan (Leslie Camden), Mischa Barton (Cindy Camden), Taylor Stanley (Melissa Flanagan), Michael Countryman (Dan Flanagan), Armand Schultz (Vic Camden)
A drama in two acts. The action takes place in a small Vermont town.

(CSC Theatre) Tuesday, Apr.9-May 4, 1996 (31 performances and 3 previews) Classic Stage Company presents:
DON JUAN COMES BACK FROM THE WAR by Odon von Horvath; Translation, Ralph Manheim, Sean Allen; Directors, Annie-B Parson, Paul Lazar; Set, Joanne Howard; Lighting, David Moodey; Costumes, Claudia Stephens; Musical Director, Christopher Berg; Press, Denise Robert CAST: Chris McNally (Don Juan), Katya Brue, Stacy Dawson, Lauren Hamilton, Deidre Harrison, Molly Hickok, Anna Kohler, Gwen Snyder, Irma St. Paule, Stephanie Weyman, Rebecca Wisocky
Co-produced with the Cucharacha Theater.

(Miranda Theatre) Wednesday, Apr.10-28, 1996 (11 performances and 4 previews) The Invisible Theatre presents:
DO SOMETHING WITH YOURSELF, *The Life of Charlotte Bronte* by Linda Manning; Director, Douglas Wagner; Press, Shirley Herz/Sam Rudy CAST: Linda Manning (Charlotte Bronte), Michael Pinney (The Men)
An expressionistic look at the author's life.

(Harry De Hur Playhouse) Wednesday, Apr.10-May 12, 1996 (25 performances) New Federal Theatre presents:
CHECKMATES by Ron Milner; Director, Woodie King Jr.; Lighting, Antoinette Tynes; Costumes, Vassie Welback-Browne; Set, Felix E. Cochren; Sound, Tim Schellenbaum; Stage Manager, Malik; Press, Max Eisen/Laurel Factor CAST: Peter Jay Fernandez (Syl Williams), Ruby Dee (Mattie Cooper), Arthur French (Frank Cooper), Amy-Monique Waddell (Laura McClellan-Williams)
A comedy in three acts. The action takes place in Detroit.

(Samuel Beckett Theater) Wednesday, Apr.10-May 12, 1996 (22 performances and 2 previews) Power Play Enterprises presents:
GENDER WARS by Joseph P. Krawczyk; Director, Vincent Apollo; Set, P.P. Associates; Lighting, Jason A. Cina; Stage Manager, Terry Mac; Press, Francine L. Trevens CAST: Candice Rose (Angela), Tom Biglin (Nick), John Borras (Mike), Jodi Stevens (Marilyn), Denise Tomasetti (Denise)
A romantic comedy in two acts.

(Mint Space) Wednesday, Apr.10-20, 1996 (10 performances and 1 preview) Six Figures presents:
ALABAMA RAIN by Heather McCutchen; Director, Rachel Wineberg; Set, Anthony Costa; Lighting, Jeff Croiter; Costumes, Christina Lynn Whited; Sound, Blake Edwards; Stage Manager, Tracy Jackson; Press, Tony Origlio/Michael Cullen CAST: Suzanne Bradbeer (Pheenie), Kate Hoffman (Laurie Laurie), Ellen Bernfeld (Monty Louise), Susan P. Vaughn (Rachel), Andria Laurie (Dallas)
A drama in two acts. The action takes place in a southern county during the past, the present and the future.

(rear) Candice Rose, Tom Biglin, John Borras,
(front) Denise Tomasetti, Jodi Stevens in *Gender Wars*
(Barbara Efthymiou)

Ellen Bernfeld, Suzanne Bradbeer, Kate Hoffman
in *Alabama Rain* (Barbara Vaughn)

Robert Bowen Jr., Laura Lamson in
Successful Strategies **(Liana Muccio)**

Eddie Kehler, Jennifer Matt, Jacqueline Sidney, Jill Helene,
Robert Manganaro in *Shpinnen Un Shpinnen*
(Spinning andSpinning) **(Jonathan Slaff)**

(Bottom Line) Thursday, Apr.11-14, 1996 (6 performances)
DISGRACEFULLY YOURS; Written/Performed by Richard O'Brien; Press, Chris Boneau~Adrian Bryan-Brown/Craig Karpel, Stephen Pitalo
An outrageous concert in Hell.

(Theatre Off Park) Thursday, Apr.11-May 5, 1996 (16 performances and 3 previews) Rattlestick Productions presents:
CARPOOL by Laura Hembree; Director, Laura Josepher; Set, Van Santvoord; Lighting, Chad McArver; Music/Sound, Michael Whalen; Stage Manager, Meta Goforth; Press, Peter Cromarty/Hugh Hayes CAST: William Severs (Arthur Binford), David Csizmadia (Carl Vitali), Frank Girardeau (Gene Dikeman), John Tormey (Raymond Bloch), Bob Dillon (Willard Burkey)
A drama in two acts. The action takes place in various cars traveling through America's suburbs.

(Altered Stages) Thursday, Apr.11-28, 1996 (13 performances and 1 preview) Anchor Theatre Company presents:
SUCCESSFUL STRATEGIES by Marivaux; Translation, Timberlake Wertenbaker; Director, John McDonough; Set, Mary E. Houston; Costumes, Eli Katz; Lighting, Charles Cameron; Stage Manager, Fred Velez; Press, Denise Robert CAST: David Grillo (Dorante), J. Barrett Lindgren (Blaise), Greg Steinbruner (Arlequin), Kathy Pope (Lisette), Laura Lamson (La Comtesse), Kristi Wedemeyer (La Marquise), Todd Wilkerson (Frontin), Robert Bowen Jr. (Le Chevalier)
A comedy performed without intermission. The action takes place on a French country estate, 1730s.

(Ontological Theatre) Thursday, Apr.11-May 12, 1996 (20 performances and 4 previews) Target Margin Theatre presents:
MOTHER COURAGE by Bertolt Brecht; Translation, Ralph Manheim; Director, David Herskovits; Music, Thomas Cabaniss; Sets, Erika Belsey; Costumes, David Zinn; Lighting, Lenore Doxsee; Press, Shirley Herz/Sam Rudy CAST INCLUDES: Mary Neufeld (Mother Courage), Will Badgett (Cook), David Eye, Caroline Clay, Nicole Halmos

(Theater for the New City) Thursday, April 11-28, 1996 (11 performances and 1 preview) Theater for the New City and Annette Moskowitz/Alexander E. Racolin present:
SHPINNEN UN SHPINNEN (SPINNING AND SPINNING) by Beverly Taylor; Director, Walter Cohen; Set, Iosif Yusupov; Lighting, Alsion Brummer; Costumes, Seth Hanson; Stage Manager, Stacy Zinke; Press, Jonathan Slaff CAST: Amy Braverman (Becky-age 10), Robert Manganaro (phillip), Jacqueline Sydney (Ettel), Dennis Horvitz (landau), Jennifer Maxx (Becky-age 17 to 30), Jill Helene (Elsie/Soldier), Andy Bruno (Tony), Phil Hochman (Goldfarb), Eddie Kehler (Leon), John Schmerling (Announcer/Devil)
A two-act panorama of Jewish life, 1930-1953.

(Theater for the New City) Thursday, Apr.11-May 19, 1996 (18 performances and 6 previews) Theater for the New City presents:
JIM THE LIONHEARTED by Rene Kalisky; Translation, David Willinger, Luc Deneulin, Director, Mr. Willinger; Music, Arthur Abrams; Set, Clark Fidelia, Lighting, Thaddeus Strassberger; Costumes, E. Shura Pollatsek; Press, Jonathan Slaff CAST: Tony Greenleaf (Jim the Lionhearted), Donald Brooks (Adolph Hitler), Caesar Paul Del Trecco (Karl Haushofer/Heinrich Himmler), Mark Lang (Lanz Von Liebenfels/Otto Ohlendorf), Kevin M. Martin (Dietrich Eckart/Reinhardt Heydrich), Jerry Jaffe (Dr. Theodore Morell), Mari Prentice (Geli Raubal), Katy Winn (Eva Braun)
A black comedy in two acts. The action takes place in and around Jim's bed as well as throughout Europe. The time is before, during and after World War II.

(Synchronicity Space) Friday, Apr.12-28, 1996 (12 performances and 1 preview) Fifth Business in association with Red Earth Ensemble and Synchronicity Space presents:
PROMISED LAND by Harvey Huddleston; Director, Mark Roberts; Lighting/Set, Richard Lichte; Stage Manager, Kimberly I. Kefgen; Press, Jonathan Slaff CAST: Jerry Ball (F.L. Sullins), Janet Girardeau (Robby Mae Sullins), Tristan Fitch (Charlie Parker), William Hill (Elmer Brown), Kezia Norton (Betty Sweeney), Edward Cannan (Hiram Sweeney)
A drama in two acts. The action takes place in Arkansas' Ozark Mountains, 1986.

Mary Neufeld in *Mother Courage* **(Jamey O'Quinn)**

Donald Brooks, Anthony Greenleaf in
Jim the Lionhearted **(Jonathan Slaff)**

151

David Cale, Laura Esterman, Janet Haynes, Frederick Weller,
Lisa Emery, Kathleen Claypool, Betty Miller,
John Henry Cox in *Curtains* (Carol Rosegg)

Mitchell Lichtenstein, Albert Macklin in
Wally's Ghost (Byrne Guarnotta)

Len Cariou in *Papa* (Suzanne Karp Krelos)

(Theatre Row Theatre) Friday, Apr.12-28, 1996 (17 performances)
Abigdon Theatre Company presents:
BRINGING MOTHER DOWN by Lanie Robertson; Director, Craig
Fols; Set/Costumes, Bruce Goodrich; Lighting, David Castaneda; Stage
Manager, Joe Reid; Press, MediaBlitz/Beck Lee CAST: JoAnn Mariano
(Helen), Michael Deep (Cyril), Vera Cox (Stella), Ray Virta (Frankie), Al-
ice Barden (May), Scott Rymer (Jack), David Van Pelt (Jimi)
    A sex farce in two acts. The action takes place in Cherry Hill, NJ.

(Theater for the New City) Friday, Apr.12-May 25, 1996 (26 perfor-
mances and 6 previews) The Irondale Ensemble Project presents:
THE BUNDLE by Edward Bond; Director, Jim Niesen; Set, Ken
Rothchild; Costumes, Hilarie Blumenthal; Lighting, A.C. Hickox; Music,
Tyler Kent; Press, Tony Origlio/David Powell Smith CAST: Steven Satta
(Ferryman/Pu-Toi/Cracker Man), Michael-David Gordon (Basho/Old
Man/Water Seller), Georgina Corbo (Wang), Alain Hunkins (Keeper/Tor-
Quo/Soldier/Gow), Terry Greiss (Keeper/Kaka/Soldier/Husband/San-Ko),
Yvonne Brechbuhler (Old Woman/Tiger/Tuan), Kathryn Grant (Ferry-
man's Wife/Woman/Sheoul), Jacqueline Klee (Lu/Kung-Tu/Water
Seller/Soldier/To-Si)
    A drama in two acts.

(Intar Theatre) Saturday, April 13-May 12, 1996 (23 performances and
3 previews) transferred to John Houseman Theatre Tuesday, May21-July
16, 1996 (64 performances) The New Group presents:
CURTAINS by Stephen Bill; Director, Scott Elliott; Set, Kevin Price;
Costumes, Eric Becker; Lighting, Peter Kaczorowski; Sound, Raymond
D. Schilke; Stage Manager, John J. Harmon; Press, James L.L. Morrison
CAST: Janet Haynes (Margaret), Kathleen Claypool (Ida), Frederick
Weller (Michael), Laura Esterman (Katherine), John Henry Cox (Geof-
frey), David Cale (Douglas), Betty Miller (Mrs. Jackson), Lisa Emery (Su-
san)
    A drama in two acts. The action takes place in Birmingham, England,
Spring 1987.

(Soho Rep Theatre) Saturday, Apr.13-May 19, 1996 (36 performances)
Soho Rep in association with the Pick Up Performance Company presents:
WALLY'S GHOST by Ain Gordon; Directors, Mr. Gordon and Michael
Sexton; Set, Neil Patel; Lighting, John-Paul Szczepanski; Costumes, Mr.
Gordon; Stage Manager, Christine Lemme; Press, David Rothenberg
CAST: Chris De Oni (Customer/Others), Norma Fire (Norma), Michelle
Hurst (Henry James), Mitchell Lichtenstein (Tommy), Albert Macklin
(Wally), John McAdams (Mrs. Astor), Tim Michael (Jeff), Mara Stephens
(Waiter), Alison Tatlock (Marti), Oliver Wadsworth (Realtors/Others)
    A comedy in two acts. The action takes place in New York City.

(Douglas Fairbanks Theater) Tuesday, April 16-July 13, 1996 (73 per-
formances and 20 previews) Eric Krebs, Anne Strickland Squadron and
Brian C. Smith present:
PAPA by John deGroot; Director, John Henry Davis; Set, Santo Loquasto;
Lighting, F. Mitchell Dana; Sound, John Gromada, Christopher Todd;
Stage Manager, James Fitzsimmons; Press, David Rothenberg/David Ger-
sten CAST: Len Cariou (Ernest Hemingway)
    A one-man drama in two acts. The setting is Finca Vigia, Heming-
way's Cuban home, 1959.

(The Next Stage) Tuesday, Apr.16-May 5, 1996 (9 performances and 6
previews) The Next Stage Company presents:
WHITE PEOPLE by J.T. Rogers; Director, Gus Reyes; Lighting, David
Castaneda; Set, Jana and Steven Thompson; Costumes, Lorraine Ander-
son; Sound, Sheafe B. Walker; Stage Manager, Hilary Adams; Press, Tony
Origlio/Kevin P. McAnarney CAST: John L. Bader (Alan Harris), Cyn-
thia Vance (Mara Lynn Doddson), John Ottavino (Martin Bahmueller)
    A play performed without intermission. The action takes place in
NYC, No. Carolina and St. Louis, MO.

**Colette Berge, Ronald Guttman, Genevieve Schartner
in *No Exit* (Jonathan Slaff)**

**Jacqueline Pennington, Margie Rynn, Louise Martin, Kevin Mambo
in *Paradise is Closing Down* (Jonathan Slaff)**

**Angela Parks, Bradley Reynolds, Paula Betlem, Robert Hunt,
Marisa Diotalevi in *Have a Nice Day* (Carol Rosegg)**

(St. Clement's Theatre) Tuesday, Apr.16-May 11, 1996 (24 performances and 4 previews) Pan Asian Repertory presents:
FRIENDS by Kobo Abe; Translation, Donald Keene; Director, Ron Nakahara; Sound, Peter Griggs; Lighting, Richard Schaefer; Set, Robert Klingelhoefer; Stage Manager, Lisa Ledwich CAST: Dawn Akiyama, Philip Balthazar, Monique Holt, Eleonora Kihlberg, Kati Kuroda, Matthew Lai, Alvin Lum, Les J.N. Mau, Raplee Nobori, James Saito, Christen Villamor

(Ubu Rep Theater) Tuesday, Apr.16-May 5, 1996 (13 English and 8 French performances)Ubu Repertory presents:
NO EXIT by Jean-Paul Sartre; Translation, Richard Miller; Director, Francoise Kourilsky; Set, Watoku Ueno; Lighting, Greg MacPherson; Costumes, Carol Ann Pelletier; Sound, Genji Ito; Stage Manager, Eileen Myers; Press, Jonathan Slaff CAST: Ronald Guttman (Garcin), Michel Moinot (Attendant), Colette Berge (Inez), Genevieve Schartner (Estelle)
A new translation of the French drama.

(Center Stage) Wednesday, Apr.17-28, 1996 (10 performances) L.A.F. Productions presents:
LU ANN HAMPTON LAVERTY OBERLANDER by Preston Jones; Director, Lyle Feigenbaum; Set, Julia Randall, Rob Dew CAST: Reggie Barton, Marilyn Brett, Lyle Feigenbaum, Mark Gerow, Tom Gray, Christopher Peterson, Laura Poe, Timothy Rail, Laura Rose, William Short, Paul Tigue
One of three plays compromising *A Texas Trilogy*.

(Currican Theatre) Thursday, Apr.18-May 5, 1996 (16 performances) Currican presents:
RED RABBIT by Kevin Hincker; Director, Andrew Miller; Set, Mark Symczak; Sound, Michael Keck; Costumes, Constance Hoffman; Lighting, Jack Mehler; Fights, B.H. Barry; Press, Manuel Igrejas CAST: Jill Brennan, Monique Vukovic, George Ryan, Craig Bockhorn
A dark comedy about a less than typical Nielsen family.

(28th St. Theater) Thursday, Apr.18-May 5, 1996 (15 performances) Africa Arts Theater Company presents:
PARADISE IS CLOSING DOWN by Pieter-Dirk Uys; Director, George Ferencz; Design, Bill Stabile; Costumes, Sally Lesser; Lighting, Jeff Tapper; Sound, Genji Ito; Stage Manager, Kevin G. Ewing III; Press, Jonathan Slaff CAST: Margie Rynn (Molly), Louise Martin (Mouse), Jacqueline Pennington (Anna), Kevin Mambo (William)
A comedy about middle-class white women living under apartheid.

(Theatre East) Thursday, Apr.18-May 26, 1996 (31 performances and 5 previews) Select Entertainment Productions presents:
HAVE A NICE DAY!; Conceived/Written/Arranged by Rick Lewis; Director, Farnk H. Latson; Choreography, Susan Streater; Lighting, Maria Rosenblum; Costumes/Set, Bruce Goodrich; Stage Manager, Immanuel Simmons; Press, David Rothenberg/David Lotz, David Gersten CAST: Paula Betlem (Holly), Marisa Diotalevi (Ronda), Robert Hunt (Kitt), Angela Parks (Lori Anne), Bradley Reynolds (Brian)
A musical spoof of Nixon-era youth travelling shows.

(Public/Shiva Theater) Friday, April 19-May 19, 1996 (32 performances) Signature Theatre Company presents:
THE ALEXANDER PLAYS...SUZANNE IN STAGES by Adrienne Kennedy; Director, Robbie McCauley; Sets, E. David Cosier; Costumes, Teresa Snider-Stein, Jonathan Green; Lighting, Jeffrey S. Koger; Sound, Jim van Bergen; Stage Manager, Monique Martin; Press, James L.L. Morrison CAST: Leon Addison Brown, Tom Gerard, Jake-Ann Jones, Sanaa Lathan, Seret Scott, Ned Van Zandt, Jennifer Wiltsie, Craig Wroe
Three plays: *Dramatic Circle*(1991), *Ohio State Murders*(1990) and *Motherhood 2000*(1993).

(Producer's Club) Wednesday, Apr.24-June 15, 1996 (21 performances) Odilon Redon Theatre Company presents:
BLANCA AND OTHER SHORT PLAYS by Nitza Henig; Directors, Ms. Henig, Ching Valdes Aran; Design, Gabriela Chistik; Stage Manager, Jeff Cunha; Press, Jonathan Slaff *Blanca: Monologue for Mice* CAST: Nitza Henig; *A Twitch in the Sun* CAST: Joniruth White (Adella Was), Brad Chandler (RexX); *Hamlet Variations* CAST: Alexander Stephano (Hamilton), Diane Bradshaw (Olympia), Allison Baker (Hamlet), Joe A. Serpa (Reynaldo)

Performed in repertory.

(Chelsea Playhouse) Thursday, Apr.25-May 12, 1996 (16 performances) Spectrum Stage Company presents:
WHEN THE BELL TOLLS; Sets, William F. Moser; Press, Gary and John Springer
The Rose and the Crown by J.B. Priestley; Director, Clinton Bond Jr. CAST: Matthew Bower, Don Christopher, Kelly Deadmon, Stephanie Fybel, Douglas Manes, Margaret Ritchie, Geraldine Teargarden
Riders to the Sea by J.M. Synge; Director, Joan Matthiessen CAST: Helen Gallagher, Karla Hendrick, Tony O'Donoghue, Patti Specht

Two one-act plays dealing with living in the face of mortality.

(One Dream Theatre) Friday, Apr.26-still playing May 31, 1996 (Friday nights only)
NIAGARA FOLLIES; Conceived/Written by Robert Whaley and Tony Grimaldi; Press, Judy Jacksina/John Piccirillo CAST: The Niagaras

A wild night of comedy and song.

(New York Historical Society) Monday, Apr.29-May 6, 1996 (2 performances) David Merrick Arts Foundation and the Actors' Company Theatre present:

THE WOMEN by Calare Boothe Luce; Director, Scott Alan Evans; Music, David MacDonald; Stage Manager, Tercio Bretas; Press, Alma Viator/Bill Schelbe CAST: Kim Hunter (Mrs. Morehead), Joan Buddenhagen (Crystal Allen), Nora Chester (Mrs. Wagstaff/Maggie/Dowager), Maia Danziger (Nancy Blake), Cynthia Darlow (Olga), Francesca Di Mauro (Peggy Day), Delphi Harrington (Countess de Lage), Elyse Knight (Instructress/Model Girl), Elizabeth Martin (Cook/Nurse/Society Woman), Mary Alice McGuire (Miss Fordyce/Salesgirl), Cameron Meyer (Hairdresser/Saleswoman), Lauren Mitchell (Sylvia Fowler), Erin Brooke Rakow (Little Mary), Joyce Reehling (Lucy), Tresha Rodriguez (Pedicurist/Model/Debutante), Jo-Ann Salata (Miss Shapiro/Sadie), Tom Stewart (Stage Directions), AnneSwift (Edith Potter), Rebecca Tilney (Hairdresser/Model/Distressed Woman), Lynn Vogt (Mary Haines), Kay Walbye (Miriam Aarons), Jessica Weglein (Miss Trimmerback/MudMask), Lyn Wright (Jane)

A staged reading of the 1937 comedy in two acts.

Amo Gulinello, Mark Greenfield, Christina Cabot in *Round Trip* (Deborah Raven)

Allison Baker, Tom Martin, Diane Bradshaw in *Hamlet Variations* (Jonathan Slaff)

Francesco Di Mauro, Maia Danziger, Lynn Vogt, Lauren Mitchell, Anne Swift in *The Women* (Diane Silverman)

(Miranda Theatre) Wednesday, May 1-12, 1996 (9 performances and 2 previews) Merlin Entertainment presents:
EMPTY ROOMS by Gary Garrison; Director, Michael Walling; Sets, Scott A. Perich; Lighting, Wendy Luedtke; Stage Manager, Beth Hyjek; Press, Francine L. Trevens
Tender Salvation CAST: Brian O'Sullivan (Duane)
Scream with Laughter CAST: Michael Moon (Daniel), Michael Serratore (Benny), Victor Barbella (Victor), Dean Conroy (Marty)
The Big Fat Naked Truth CAST: Susan Barrett (Twinks), Kelly Champion (Margaret), Kate Fitzgerald (Reilly), Julia Sheridan Langham (Tanya), Mary Purdy (Dussey)

Three one-act plays.

(NADA) Wednesday, May 1-5, 1996 (5 performances) H2O Theater Company presents:
ROUND TRIP by Tena Cohen; Director, Christopher Sanderson; Music, Nick Didkovsky, Ian McGrath; Puppets, Basil Twist; Press, Gary and John Springer CAST: Christina Cabot, Amo Gulinello, Mark Greenfield

A drama contrasting Mexican and North American culture.

(ArcLight Theatre) Thursday, May 2-24, 1996 (14 performances and 4 previews) Alchemy Theatre Company presents:
SPEED-THE-PLOW by David Mamet; Director, Robert Saxner; Set, John Farrell; Costumes, Sam Hamilton; Lighting, Jimmy Vermuellen; Sound, Dallas Roberts; Fights, Rick Sordolet; Press, Kevin P. McAnarney CAST: Rick Kaplan (Bobby Gould), Michael Daly (Charlie Fox), Gretchen Egolf (Karen)
A black comedy set in a Hollywood development office.

(Camilla's) Thursday, May 2-25, 1996 (13 performances and 2 previews) Camilla's presents:
BRUTALITY OF FACT by Keith Reddin; Director, Casey Childs; Lighting, Chris Dallos; Set/Projections, B.T. Whitehill; Sound, Roy Trejo; Costumes, Misha Kuchta; Stage Manager, Marylou Lynn; Press, Cheryl Haas CAST: Leslie Lyles (Maggie), Rebecca Nelson (Jackie), Scotty Bloch (Valerie), Samantha Brown (Judy/Kate), Greg Stuhr (Chris), Kathryn Meisle (Corinne), Marcus Giammati (Janet/Amy), Beatrice Rose (Marlene)
A dark comedy.

(Theatre Ten Ten) Thursday, May 2-26, 1996 (15 performances and 1 preview) Ten Ten Players presents:
ENGAGED by W.G. Gilbert; Director, Alan Gilbert; Set/Lighting, Mark Simpson; Costumes, Suzan Perry; Press, Jonathan Slaff CAST: Hal Blankenship, Joanna Brown, Janet Anderson, Diana Lynn Drew, Jeffrey Eiche, David Kroll, Jason Hauser, Judith Jarosz, Jay Nickerson, Dana White
An 1877 comedy.

(Fools Company Space) Thursday, May 2-19, 1996 (13 performances and 1 preview) Judith Shakespeare Company presents:
MACBETH by William Shakespeare; Director, Joanne Zipay; Fights, Dan O'Driscoll; Lighting/Effects, Jason Ardizzone, Carolyn Sarkis; Costumes, Tom Augustine; Music, Ronny Gotler; Press, Candi Adams CAST: Neil Larson (Macbeth), Kate Konigsor (Lady Macbeth), John Carroll (Banquo), Jeffrey Shoemaker (Duncan), Kevin Elden (Macduff), H. Kevin Opela (Malcolm), Alithea H. Hages (Lady Macduff), Joyia D. Bradley, Kelli M. Cruz, Joy Dixon, Jeffrey Baxter Dunston, Don Garrity, Keith Greer, Jeanette Horn, Brian Kustrup, Kevin LeCaon, C. Amanda Maud, Kevin Reifel, Sarah Thurmond, Angela Tom, Craig Victor, Ari Brand, Juliana Stevens

(Theatre Row Theatre) Friday, May 3-26, 1996 (18 performances and 3 previews) Willow Cabin Theatre Company presents:
THE KILLING OF SISTER GEORGE by Frank Marcus; Director, Jimmy Bohr; Set, William F. Moser; Costumes, Mary Nemeck Peterson; Lighting, Howard Werner; Choreography, James Horvath; Press, Jim Baldassare CAST: Maria Radman (Sister George), Tasha Lawrence (Childie), Fiona Davis (Mercy Croft), Christine Radman (Madame Xenia)
A comedy in two acts. The action takes place in London, 1965.

Leslie Lyles, Kathryn Meisle in *Brutality of Fact* (Julie Brimberg)

Dylan Chalfy, Elizabeth Rossa, Erika Burke
in *Cross Your Heart* (Carol Rosegg)

(Hamlet of Bank Street) Friday, May 3-23, 1996 (16 performances)
CROSS YOUR HEART by Brian Connors; Director, A. Dean Irby; Set, Kent S. McFann; Lighting, John McKernon; Press, Shirley Herz/Wayne Wolfe CAST: Dylan Chalfy, Erika Burke, Jonathan Teague Cook, Alice McLane
An Irish-American family drama.

(Center Stage) Friday, May 3-26, 1996 Center Stage NY and Running Sun Theatre Company presents:
WILLIAMS' GUIGNOL by Tennessee Williams; Director, John Uecker; Sets, Myrna Duarte; Lighting, Zdenek Kriz
The Traveling Companion CAST: Bill Rice, Michael Harrigan
The Chalky White Substance CAST: Sam Trammell, Greg Cornell
Two previously unproduced one-acts.

Maria Radman, Christine Radman, Tasha Lawrence, Fiona Davis
in *Killing of Sister George* (Carol Rosegg)

(Ohio Theater) Sunday, May 5-19, 1996 Blue Light Theater Company presents:
TREASURE ISLAND; Adapted by Vernon Morris from the Robert Louis Stevenson novel; Director, B.H. Barry; Set, John Kasarda; Costumes, Laurie Churba; Lighting, Deborah Constantine; Sound, Raymond D. Schilke; Press, Gary and John Springer CAST: Katherine Beck, Patrick Boll, William Charlton, Kevin Crawford, Alex Draper, Joe Grifasi, Charlie Hofheimer, Jason Kuschner, Jordan Lund, Ian Marshall, Greg Naughton, Larry Pine, Jon Rothstein, James Matthew Ryan, Lee Wilkof, Paul Witte

(Westbeth Theater Center) Tuesday, May 7-June 2, 1996 (21 performances and 6 previews) Merry Enterprises Theatre presents:
DAMMIT SHAKESPEARE! by Seth Panitch; Director, Matt Conley; Set/Costumes, Don Jensen; Lighting, Jeremy Kumin; Music, David Wolfson; Press, David Rothenberg CAST: Rainard Rachele (Shakespeare), Michael Medeiros (Richard Burbage), David Snizek (Edward Alleyn/Philip Henslowe/Ben Johnson/Others), Eva Lowe (Barmaid/Woman/Anne Shakespeare/Sarah Corax)
   A play that takes place in and around London's Globe Theatre, somewhere between Elizabethan times and the present.

Rainard Rachele, Eva Lowe in *Dammit Shakespeare* (Barry Burns)

(La MaMa) Thursday, May 9-19, 1996 (10 performances) La MaMa E.T.C. and the Otrabanda Company present:
THE FAIRGROUND BOOTH by Alexander Blok; Translation, Michael Green; Directors, Roger Babb, Rocky Bornstein; Music, Neal Kirkwood; Set, Ralph Lee; Costumes, Gabriel Berry; Lighting, Pat Digan; Sound, Bob Kirschner, City Sound; Press, Jim Baldassare CAST: Nancy Alfaro, Roger Babb, Tim Cummings, Dan Hurlin, Jennifer Miller, Lenard Petit, Mary Shultz
   A 1906 Russian drama.

(Primary Stages) Friday, May 10-26, 1996 (16 performances) Here's Broadway presents:
BOB'S BUTCH BAR by Leo Rost; Director, Don Price; Set/Lighting, Jack Mehler; Costumes, Carla Gant; Stage Manager, John Greenbaum; Press, Les Schecter CAST: David Phillip Brooks (Kenny/Candice), Eric Cohen (Dennis/Delivery Man), Jeremy Scott Johnson (Sammy), Ron Johnston (Mr. Churchill), John-Michael Lander (Patrick), Rocky Noel (Fred/Officer), Joe Pichette (Bobby), James Rudnick (Dave/Biff), Sharon Talbot (Mrs. C)
   A play in two acts. The action takes place in a Florida gay bar.

Mary Shultz, Jennifer Miller, Lenard Petit, Tim Cummings, Nancy Alfaro in *Fairground Booth* (Suzanne Option)

(Theatre Off Park) Saturday, May 11-June 2, 1996 (16 performances and 8 previews) Lynn Wolf Enterprises in association with The Sagitaurus Group and James H. Ellis present:
THE WILDE SPIRIT; Written/Performed by Kerry Ashton; Director, Robert Kalfin; Set, Mina Albergo; Lighting, Robert Williams; Costumes, Austin K. Sanderson; Sound/Score, John Clifton; Projections, Ian Cadenhead; Stage Manager, Peter Cromarty/Hugh Hayes
  Wilde's spirit returns in a dream to settle scores and examine the 1990s.

(Harold Clurman Theatre) Monday, May 13-26, 1996 Love Creek Productions presents:
VLADIVOSTOCK BLUES by Jocelyn Beard; Director, Sharon Fallon; Press, Patricia Story CAST: Annemarie Downey (Sophia de la Cruz), Mark E. Maken (Piotr), Chuck Simone (Stu), Kirsten Walsh (Tasha), Sal Brienza (Miguel)
  A dark comedy set in Russia.

(Chelsea Playhouse) Tuesday, May 14-June 2, 1996 (18 performances) National Shakespeare Company presents:
HAMLET and **TWELFTH NIGHT** by William Shakespeare; Directors, James B. Nicola (*Hamlet*) Gregory Lombardo (*Twelfth Night*) CASTS: Mia Barron, Rachel Botchan, Jeb Berrier, Robert Corddry, Logan Ernstthal, Geoffrey Gilbert, Mary Frances Miller, John Slagle
   Performed in repertory.

Anne Marie Downey, Mark E. Maken in *Vladivostock Blues*

(Altered Stages) Thursday, May 16-June 2, 1996 (12 performances and 2 previews) Wolf Fang Productions in association with Richard Falklen and Light Hearted Productions:
POT AT THE END OF YOUR ELBOW by Robb Pruitt; Director, Rick Zieff; Special Effects, Park Borchert; Press, Judy Jacksina/John Piccirillo CAST:Robb Pruitt (Braden Collins), Joan Crowe, Park Borchert, Billy Serow, Miriam Serow, Rick Zieff, Judy Nunn

A multi-media-interactive-comedy.

(One Dream Theatre) Thursday, May 16-June 2, 1996 (13 performances and 1 preview) Deep Ellum presents:
WOLF AT THE DOOR by Erik Ehn; Director/Set/Costumes/Sound, Matthew Earnest; Lighting, Alex Radocchia; Stage Manager, Routh Chadwick; Press, Jonathan Slaff   CAST: Karen Lee Pickett (Holly), Grant James Varjas (Taylor), Trish Hawkins (Mel), Walton Wilson (Dad), John DiBenedetto (Charlie Bear), Kathryn Graybill (Jac), Trae Hicks (Collection Agent/Grandfather Tree/Editor)

A drama performed without intermission. The action takes place in a small upstate city.

(Mint Space) Thursday, May 16-June 2, 1996 (13 performances and 3 previews)
WILLIAM SHAKESPEARE'S THE RED ROSE; Adapted by Tom Loback from Shakespeare; Director, Tony Torn; Lighting, Colin Young; Costumes, Mimi O'Donnell; Stage Manager, Jim Pelegano; Press, Patt Dale   CAST: Madigan Ryan (Queen Margaret), Robert Alexander (Richard III), Anders Bolang (Duke of York), Chet Carlin (Somerset), Jim Chance (Earl of Warwick), Rufus Collins (Henry VI), Stacey Ference (Lady Bona), Dylan Green (Duke Humphrey), Matt Kowalski (Lord Clifford), Neil Martin (Buckingham), Jason McKay (Prince Edward), William D. Michie (Edward IV), Ennis Smith (Warwick), Nancy Walsh (Queen Elizabeth/Dame Eleanor), Rik Walter (Suffolk)

A play in two acts adapted from Shakespeare's dramatization of the War of the Roses.

Trae Hicks, Trish Hawkins in *Wolf at the Door* (Susan Johann)

Madigan Ryan in *The Red Rose* (Pedro Moreno)

Troy Ruptash, Jacqueline Bowman in *Orpheus Descending*

(T. Schreiber Studio) Thursday, May 23-June 23, 1996 (14 performances and 6 previews)
ORPHEUS DESCENDING by Tennesee Williams; Director, Terry Schreiber; Music, Laurie Altman; Sound, Joseph Furnari; Lighting, Joe Saint; Set, Hal Tine; Costumes, David Toser; Stage Manager, Jonathan Gershon CAST: Ellen Orchid (Dolly Hamma), Valorie Hubbard (Beulah Binnings), Shawn Brentham (Pee Wee), Gib Von Bach (Dog Hamma), Jacqueline Bowman (Carole Cutrere), Edith Larkin (Eva Temple), Cam Kornman (Sister), William Charles Mitchell (Uncle Pleasant), Troy Ruptash (Val Xavier), Elaine Bradbury (Vee Talbott), Marine Jahan (Lady Torrance), Jonathan Smit (Jabe Torrance), Robert Pusilo (Sheriff), Carl Bradford (Dubinsky), Eve Alexander (Woman), Brent Erdy (David Cutrere), Judith Astroff (Nurse), Fountain Yount (Man)

A 1957 drama in three acts.

(INTAR Theatre) Thursday, May 23-June 23, 1996 (34 performances and 1 preview) INTAR Hispanic American Arts Center presents:
RADIO MAMBO: CULTURE CLASH INVADES MIAMI; Written/Performed by Culture Clash (Richard Montoya, Ric Salinas, Herbert Siguenza); Director, Roger Guenveur Smith; Sets, Herbert Siguenza; Lighting, Lonnie Alcaraz; Sound, Mark Friedman; Choreography, Lettie Ibarra; Costumes, Elena Prietto; Press, Shirley Herz/Miller Wright

A farce performed without intermission. The action takes place in Miami.

(Synchronicity Space) Thursday, May 23-June 9, 1996 (14 performances and 1 preview) Lightning Strikes Theatre Company presents:

GOD'S COUNTRY by Steven Dietz; Director, Stephen Roylance; Set, Dick Carpenter; Costumes, Jean Brookman; Lighting, David Macfarlane; Sound, Patrick McCaffrey; Stage Manager, Faye Jackson; Press, Gary and John Springer/Candi Adams CAST: Matthew Halder, Bunky Hubbard (Boy), Rochelle Stempel (Mueller), John McDermott (Denver Parmenter), Peter Palazzo (Bob Matthews), D.L. Shroder (Alan Berg), Victor Truro (Farrell/Richard Butler/David Lane/Others), Atli Kendall (Elliot/Ward/Tom Metzger/Others), Lou Kylis (Ms. Chappel/Mother), Michael Moon (Halprin/Greg Withrow/Patrick Connor), Marie Dame (Anath White/Believer/Zillah Craig/Others), Jeff Buckner (Voice of Court/Candidate/Jones/Ruark), Dennis Kyriakos (Skinhead), Kate Flatland (Leatherman/Judith Berg)

A drama set in Seattle, Denver and across the U.S., 1983 to present.

(West End Theatre) Friday, May 24-June 17, 1996 (16 performances) West End Theatre and Centerfold Productions present:
SAY, DARLING by Richard Bissell, Abe Burrows and Marian Bissell; Songs, Jule Styne, Betty Comden, Adolph Green; Director, Robert Armin; Set/Lighting, Kevin Ash; Musical Director, Michael Lavine; Choreography, Sven Toorvald; Costumes, Breck Sullivan-Carpenter; Stage Manager, Rebecca Erin Craig CAST: Paul Amodeo (Rudy Lorraine), Charles Black (Boris Reshevsky), Lynn Bowman (Irene Lovelle), Donald Brennan (Morty Krebs), John Canary (Rex Dexter), Rebecca Erin Craig (Arlene McKee), Steve Gibbons (Ted Snow), Randy Lake (Roy/Pilot/Charlie Williams), Peggy Lu (June), Charles Luxenberg (Earl Jorgeson), Lucy McMichael, Kristine Nevins (Cheryl Merrill), Bonnie Perlman (Schatzie Harris), Max Perlman (Sammy Miles), Todd Phillips-Huyck (Photographer/Waiter), Marni Ratner (Jennifer Stevenson), Jami Simon (Mrs. Schneider), Bill Tatum (Jack Jordan), David Vogel (Richard Hackett)
MUSICAL NUMBERS: Chief of Love, Try to Love Me, It's Doom, Husking Bee, It's the Second Time You Meet That Matters, Let the Lower Lights Be·Burning, If You Hadn't But You Did, Say Darling, Carnival Song, Hold Me, Give a Little Get a Little, Dance Only with Me, Something Always Happening on the River
A revised version of the 1958 comedy with songs based on the original *Pajama Game* production. This version also uses songs from *Two on the Aisle.*

Victor Truro, Matthew Halder, Peter Palazzo in *God's Country* (Scott Newirth)

Bill Tatum, Lynn Bowman, Paul Amodeo in *Say Darling*

(Phebe's '74) Wednesday, May 29-June 16, 1996 (13 performances and 1 preview) MollyHouse Theatre presents:
KENNEDY'S CHILDREN by Robert Patrick; Director, Mark Owen; Set, Michael Perelman; Costumes, Audrey Fisher; Lighting, Joe Saint; Press, Peter Cromarty/Hugh Hayes CAST: Suzanne O'Neill (Wanda), Amy Stiller (Rona), Richard Freda (Mark), Maggie Moore (Carla), Craig Archibald (Sparger)
A 1975 drama performed in a defunct bar.

(78th St. Theatre Lab) Thursday, May 30-June 22, 1996 (12 performances) 78th St. Theatre Lab presents:
THE ADDING MACHINE by Elmer Rice; Director, Renee Philippi; Set/Costumes, Greco; Music, David Pinkard CAST: Rene Alberta, Jenny Bass, Daniel Berlfein, Denis Gawley, Eunkyung Lee, Jonathan Lopez, John George Marino, Nicholas Martin-Smith, Catherine Porter, Elizabeth Stearns
A 1923 drama.

(Workhouse Theater) Thursday, May 30-31, 1996 (2 performances)

FIFTH PLANET by David Auburn; Director, Elizabeth Gottlieb CAST: Michael Ian Black, Christina Kirk

(clockwise from bottom) Richard Freda, Suzanne O'Neill, Maggie Moore, Amy Stiller, Craig Archibald in *Kennedy's Children*

ACTORS THEATRE OF LOUISVILLE

Louisville, Kentucky
Thirty-Second Season

Producing Director, Jon Jory; Executive Director, Alexander Speer; Associate Director, Marilee Hebert-Slater; Set Designers, Paul Owen, Virginia Dancy, Elmon Webb, Neil Patel; Costume Designers, Hollis Jenkins-Evans, Myra Colley-Lee, Marcia Dixcy, Gabriel Berry, Laura Patterson, Lewis D. Rampino, James Schuette, Maria E. Marrero, Nanzi J. Adzima, Delmar L. Rinehart Jr.; Lighting Designers, T.J. Gerckens, Mimi Jordan Sherin, Michitomo Shiohara, Karl E. Haas, Brian Scott; Public Relations Director, James Seacat; Public Relation Associates, Magaret Costello, Jennifer McMaster, Joseph W. Hans.

PRODUCTIONS & CASTS

SLEUTH by Anthony Shaffer; Director, Kenneth L. Albers. CAST: William McNulty, V. Craig Heidenreich, Stanley Rushton, Robin Mayfield, Liam Mitchell.

THE PLAY'S THE THING by Ferenc Molnar; Adaptation. P.G. Wodehouse; Director, Jon Jory. CAST: William McNulty, Milton Carney, Sean Cullen, Elizabeth Heflin, V Craig Heidenreich, Luke Sickle, Patrick Husted, Ben Mazzotta, Jonathan Gibson Wan.

OLYMPIA by Ferenc Molnar; Adaptation, Sidney Howard; Director, Lazslo Marton CAST: Karen Grassle, Luke Sickle, Adale O'Brien, William McNulty, Sevanne Martin, James Farmer, V Craig Heidenreich, Briton Green, Rick Silverman.

DRACULA by Bram Stoker; Adaptation, Hamilton Deane & John L. Balderston; Director, Frazier W. Marsh. CAST: Deborah Elz, John Littlefield, Mark Sawyer-Dailey, Fred Major, Bob Burrus, Adam Lang, Libby Christophersen, James Horan.

A CHRISTMAS CAROL by Charles Dickens; Adaptation, Jon Jory & Marcia Dixcy; Director, Frazier W. Marsh. CAST: Bob Burrus, William McNulty, Ann Hodapp, Marcial Howard, Elizabeth Heflin, Adale O'Brien, Fred Major, Mark Sawyer-Dailey, David Bishins, V Craig Heidenreich, Sean McNall, Michelle Enfield, John Littlefield, James Farmer, Libby Christophersen, Ana Mercedes Torres, Suzan Mikiel, Linda Green, Justin Hagen, Allen Jeffrey Rein, Jennifer Bohler, Larry Barnett, David A. Baecker, Brent Bauer, Robert G. Cui, Mark Burns.

THE GIFT OF THE MAGI by O. Henry; Adaptation/Music/Lyrics, Peter Ekstrom; Director, Jennifer Hubbard. CAST: Deanne Lorette, Bart Shatto.

ADVENTURES OF HUCKLEBERRY FINN by Mark Twain; Adaptation/Director, Randal Myler. CAST: Leo Marks, Bernard Addison, Jennifer Hubbard, Adale O'Brien, Hamish Linklater, Libby Christophersen, Deborah Elz, Trapper Michael, Bob Burrus, Mark Sawyer-Dailey, Fred Major, Gavin C. Whitsett, William McNulty, Milton Carney, Phillip Cherry.

A PERFECT GANESH by Terrence McNally; Director, Mladen Kiselov. CAST: Faran Tahir, V Craig Heidenreich, Marion McCorry, Karen Grassle.

BLUES IN THE NIGHT Conceived and Originally Directed by Sheldon Epps; Director/Choreography, Kent Gash; Original Vocal Arrangements/Musical Direction, Chapman Roberts; Orchestrations/Additional Vocal Arrangements, Sy Johnson. CAST: Steven Cates, Sheila Gibbs, Kena Tangi Dorsey, Shelley Dickinson. MUSICIANS: Scott Kasbaum, Gary Falk, Tyrone Wheeler, Gary Hicks, Thomas E. Jolly III, Darryel Cotten.

James Farmer, Sevanne Martin in *Olympia*

The Comedy of Errors

ALL I REALLY NEED TO KNOW I LEARNED IN KINDERGARTEN by Robert Fulghum; Conception/Adaptation/Director, Ernest Zulia; Original Songs/Additional Lyrics/Original Underscoring/Piano, David Caldwell. CAST: Ray Fry, Bob Burns, Ronald Wyche, Dee Hoty.

THE COMEDY OF ERRORS by William Shakespeare; Director, Jon Jory; Choreography, Karma Camp. CAST: Helmar Augustus Cooper, William McNulty, V Craig Heidenreich, Mark Sawyer-Dailey, Tab Baker, Leo Marks, Elizabeth Meadows Rouse, Twyla Hafermann, Mark Kenneth Smaltz, Fred Major, Suzan Mikiel, Robert Montano, Lyle Kanouse, Sharon Nordlinger, Adale O'Brien, Rick Silverman, Silvia Aruj, Elaine C. Bell, Mark Burns, Robert Fowler, Adam Lang, Christopher A.T. Martin, Desiree Parkman, Leslie Stevens, Ana Mercedes Torres.

FOREVER PLAID by Stuart Ross; Director/Choreographer, Karma Camp; Musical Director, Scott Kasbaum. CAST: Jamison Stern, Sean Frank Sullivan, Ric Ryder, Matt McClanahan.

Charles Lanyer, Julie Boyd in *Gaslight*

David Patrick Kelly, David Strathairn in *Tempest*

Ken Ruta, Jean Stapleton in *The Matchmaker*

AMERICAN CONSERVATORY THEATER

Tuscon and Phoenix, Arizona
Twenty-ninth Season

Artistic Director, Carey Perloff; Administrative Director, Thomas W. Flynn; Producing Director, James Haire.

PRODUCTIONS & CASTS

Oct. 12, 1995 - Dec. 3, 1995.
ARCADIA by Tom Stoppard; Director, Carey Perloff; Scenery, Kate Edmunds; Costumes, Walker Hicklin; Lighting, Peter Maradudin; Music, Michael Roth; Sound, Stephen LeGrand; Movement, Ellie Klopp. CAST: Nineteenth Century - Tina Jones, Daniel Cantor, Gerald Hiken, Tom Lenoci, Charles Lanyer, Kimberly King, Warren D. Keith, Christopher Hickman. Twentieth Century - Katherine Borowitz, Mollie Stickney, Graham Beckel, Matthew Boston, Christopher Hickman.
A two act comedy set on the garden front of a large country house in Derbyshire.

Nov. 9, 1995 - Dec. 23, 1995.
SEVEN GUITARS by August Wilson; Director, Lloyd Richards; Scenery, Scott Bradley; Costumes, Constanza Romero; Lighting, Christopher Akerlind; Musical Direction, Dwight Andrews; Sound, Tom Clark; Casting, Meg Simon Casting. CAST: Michele Shay, Ruben Santiago-Hudson, Tommy Hollis, Viola Davis, Zakes Mokae, Keith David, Rosalyn Coleman.

Dec. 14, 1995 - Jan. 28, 1996.
GASLIGHT by Patrick Hamilton; Director, Albert Takazauckas; Scenery, J.B. Wilson; Costumes, Deborah Nadoolman; Lighting, Peter Maradudin; Sound, Stephen LeGrand; Stage Manager, Donna Rose Fletcher/Elisa Guthertz. CAST: Julie Boyd, Charles Layner, Mollie Stickney, Sharon Lockwood, William Paterson, Dana Lee, Doug Sept.
A thriller in three acts set in a house on Angel Street in the Pimlico district of London.

THE TEMPEST by William Shakespeare; Director, Carey Perloff; Original Music, David Lang; Scenery, Kate Edmunds; Lighting, Peter Maradudin; Costumes, Deborah Dryden; Sound, James LeBrecht. CAST: David Strathairn, Vera Farmiga, David Patrick Kelly, Graham Beckel, Daniel Cantor, James Carpenter, L. Peter Callender, Gerald Hiken, Michael Santo, Leith Burke, Christopher Moseley, Michael Tucker, Geoff Hoyle, Hector Correa, Drew Khalouf, Mairead Cathlin Donahey, Emmanuela Prigioni.

DARK RAPTURE by Eric Overmyer; Director, David Petrarca; Scenery, Adrianne Lobel; Costumes, Sandra Woodall; Lighting, Peter Maradudin; Sound and Original Music, Rob Milburn. CAST: Richard Snyder, Shawn Elliott, Deirdre Lovejoy, Matt DeCaro, Rod Gnapp, Mark Feuerstein, Mark Rosenthal, Jossara Jinaro, Zachary Barton, Umit Celebi.

CHERRY ORCHARD by Anton Chekov; Translation, Paul Schmidt; Director, Barbara Damashek; Scenery, Kate Edmunds; Lighting, Peter Maradudin; Costumes, Beaver Bauer; Sound, Stephen Legrand; Dance, Kathryn Roszak. CAST: Gordan Rashovich, Tina Jones, Michelle Morain, Ken Ruta, Jack Wetherall, Matthew Boston, Luis Oropeza, Sharon Lockwood, Dan Hiatt, Adria Woomer-Stewart, Gerald Hiken, Daniel Cantor, Will Marchetti, George Killingsworth, Ben Cleaveland, David Jacobs, Steven Philip Nordberg, Michael Ronin, Matthew Troncone, Mike Vaughn.

THE MATCHMAKER by Thornton Wilder; Director, Richard Seyd; Scenery, Loy Arcenas; Lighting, Peter Maradudin; Costumes, Beaver Bauer; Sound, Stephen LaGrand. CAST: Ken Ruta, Matthew Boston, Will Marchetti, Roberta Callahan, Dan Hiatt, Tina Jones, Gerald Hiken, Jean Stapleton, Ben Cleaveland, Michelle Morain, Adria Woomer-Stewart, Jack Wetherall, Daniel Cantor, Luis Oropeza, Daniel Hoffman, Gordana Rashovich, Sharon Lockwood.

**Jeremy Geidt, Mary Beth Peil, Pamela Hart,
J. Smith-Cameron in *The Naked Eye***

AMERICAN REPERTORY THEATRE

Cambridge, Massachusetts

Artistic Director, Robert Brustein; Managing Director, Robert J. Orchard; Associate Artistic Director, Ron Daniels

THE TEMPEST by William Shakespeare; Director, Ron Daniels; Sets, John Conklin; Costumes, Gabriel Berry; Lighting, Chris Parry CAST: Jonathan Hammond, D'metrius Conley-Williams, Jeremy Geidt, Will LeBow, Alvin Epstein, Remo Airaldi, Scott Ripley, Paul Freeman, Jessalyn Gilsig, Benjamin Evett, Jack Willis, Todd Kozan, Thomas Derrah, Charles Levin, Wendy Frank, Samantha Phillips, Kemba Francis
BURIED CHILD by Sam Shepard; Director, Marcus Stern; Set, Allison Koturbash; Costumes, Catherine Zuber; Lighting, John Ambrosone CAST: Jeremy Geidt, Georgine Hall, Jack Willis, Charles Levin, Benjamin Evett, Phoebe Jonas, Remo Airaldi
TARTUFFE by Moliere; Adaptation, Robert Auletta; Director, Francois Rochaix; Set, Robert Israel; Costumes, Catherine Zuber; Lighting, Mimi Jordan Sherin CAST: Francine Torres, Georgine Hall, Michelle Dahmer, Yanna McIntosh, Jessalyn Gilsig, Will LeBow, Nat DeWolf, Kevin Bergen, Thomas Derrah, Scott Ripley, Alvin Epstein, Remo Airaldi, Anthony Cistaro
SLAUGHTER CITY by Naomi Wallace; Director, Ron Daniels; Set/Costumes, Ashley Martin-Davis; Lighting, John Ambrosone CAST: Phoebe Jonas, S.J. Scruggs, Starla Benford, Jay Boyer, Judith Hawking, Terry Alexander, Remo Airaldi, Alvin Epstein
ALICE IN BED by Susan Sontag; Director, Bob McGrath; Set, Laurie Olinder, Fred Teitz; Costumes, Susan Anderson; Lighting, John Ambrosone CAST: Stephanie Roth, Steve Harper, Thomas Derrah, Will LeBow, Deborah Breitman, Blair Sams, Erica Yoder, Kwana Martinez, Kevin Bergen, Brian Lamphier
THE NAKED EYE by Paul Rudnick; Director, Christopher Ashley; Set, Derek McLane; Costumes, Catherine Zuber; Lighting, Don Holder CAST: Mary Beth Peil, Pamela Hart, Neil Maffin, Francine Torres, Thomas Derrah, Jeremy Geidt, J.Smith-Cameron, Cheryl Kenan, John Andrew Morrison, Brian Kinney
LONG DAY'S JOURNEY INTO NIGHT by Eugene O'Neill; Director, Ron Daniels; Set, Michael H. Yeargan; Costumes, Catherine Zuber; Lighting, Frances Aronson CAST: Jerome Kilty, Claire Bloom, Bill Camp, Michael Stuhlbarg, Emma Roberts

Richard Feldman, T. Charles Erickson Photos

Benjamin Evett, Alvin Epstein in *The Tempest*

Claire Bloom, Jerome Kilty, Bill Camp in *Long Day's Journey Into Night*

Stephanie Roth, Will LeBow in *Alice in Bed*

David Pichette, R. Hamilton Wright, Sally Wingert,
Katie Forgette in *Private Eyes*

Betsy Palmer, Penelope Windust, David
Paul Francis in *A Perfect Ganesh*

Sharon Leal, John Allee, Bambi Jones, Kimberly Hawthorne
in *Little Shop Of Horrors*

ARIZONA THEATRE COMPANY

Tuscon and Phoenix, Arizona
Twenty-ninth season

Artistic Director, David Ira Goldstein; Managing Director, Jessica L. Andrews.

PRODUCTIONS & CASTS

A MIDSUMMER NIGHT'S DREAM by William Shakespeare; Director, David Ira Goldstein; Choreography, Barbea M. Williams; Scenery, Bill Forrester; Costumes, Laura Crow; Lighting, Tracy Odishaw; Composer, Roberta Carlson; Sound, Scott W. Edwards; Stage Manager, Jay Rabins. CAST: Michael Kevin, Molly Mayock, Gary Briggle, Francis Jue, Corliss Preston, Jordan Lee Williams, David Scully, Tracey A. Leigh, David Pichette, Michael Woodson, Bob Sorenson, Roberto Guajardo, Mike Lawler, Gregory Colburn, Jamie Lynn Hines, Becky La Vietes, Wesley Landson.

LITTLE SHOP OF HORRORS; Book and Lyrics, Howard Ashman; Music, Alan Menken; Director, David Ira Goldstein; Choreography and Musical Staging, Patricia Wilcox; Musical Director, Jerry Wayne Harkey; Scenery, Tom Butsch; Costumes, Christine Dougherty; Lighting, Don Darnutzer; Sound, Jeff Ladman; Stage Manager, Elizabeth Stephens. CAST: Sharon Leal, Kimberly Hawthorne, Bambi Jones, Benjamin Stewart, Debby Rosenthal, John Allee, Ed Fusco, John Schiappa, Ed Fusco, Dennis Rowland, Jerry Wayne Harkey, Bill Holcomb, Robin Horn, Lisa Meneley, Robin Vining.

FIRES IN THE MIRROR; Conceived, Written and Originally Performed by Anna Deavere Smith; Director, Matthew Wiener; Scenery, R. Michael Miller; Costumes, Rose Pederson; Lighting, Tracy Odishaw; Music and Sound, Michael Roth; Stage Manager. CAST: Angela Bullock, Cheryl Rogers, Laurine Towler.

CANDIDA by George Bernard Shaw; Director, Penny Metropulos; Scenery, Norm Spencer; Costumes, Deborah Trout; Lighting, Rick Paulsen; Sound, Steven M. Klein; Stage Manager, Dawn Fenton. CAST: Terri McMahon, Mark Capri, Michael Tassoni, James J. Lawless, Robin Goodrin Nordli, Raymond L. Chapman.

A PERFECT GANESH by Terrence McNally; Director, Andrew J. Traister; Scenery, Ralph Funicello; Costumes, Clare Henkel; Lighting, Michael Gilliam; Sound, Jeff Ladman; Stage Manager, Jay Rabins. CAST: David Paul Francis, John Walcutt, Betsy Palmer, Penelope Windust.

PRIVATE EYES by Steven Dietz; Director, David Ira Goldstein; Scenery, Scott Weldin; Costumes, Rose Pederson; Lighting, Rick Paulsen; Sound, Steven M. Klein; Dramaturg, Rebecca Million; Stage Manager, Dawn Fenton. CAST: R. Hamilton Right, Sally Wingert, David Pichette, Katie Forgette, Jeff Steitzer.

CALDWELL THEATRE COMPANY

Boca Raton, Florida

Artistic and Managing Director, Michael Hall; Director of Design, Frank Bennett; Company Manager, Patricia Burdett; Development Director, William McCarthy.

PRODUCTIONS & CASTS

YOU SHOULD BE SO LUCKY by Charles Busch; Director, Michael Hall; Scenery, Tim Bennett; Costumes, Penny Koleos Williams; Lighting, Thomas Salzman; Stage Manager, Lisa Lamont. CAST: Dea Lawrence, Becky London, Charlotte Maier, Gary Nathanson, Kraig Swartz, Tom Wahl.

BUT NOT FOR ME by Christopher Cooper, Michael Hall, Dana P. Rowe and Avery Sommers; Director, Michael Hall; Musical Director, Dana P. Rowe; Scenery, Frank and Tim Bennett; Costumes, Patricia Bowes; Lighting, Thomas Salzman; Sound, Steve Shapiro; Stage Manager, Bill Oleson. CAST: Avery Sommers, Dana P. Rowe. MUSICIANS: Dana P. Rowe, Rupert Ziawinski, Jean J. Bolduc.

AN ENEMY OF THE PEOPLE by Henrik Ibsen; Adaptation, Arthur Miller; Director, Michael Hall; Scenery, Frank and Tim Bennett; Costumes, Penny Koleos Williams; Lighting, Thomas Salzman; Sound, Kenneth Melvin; Stage Manager, Bill Oleson/Lisa Lamont. CAST: Chris Clavelli, John Felix, John Gardiner, Max Gulack, Kenneth Kay, Michael Medico, Pat Nesbit, Suzanne O'Donnell, Tom Wahl, Joe Warik, Marc Ross Blumsack, Greg Roman, Michael Fernandez, Peter Fernandez.

THE UNEXPECTED GUEST by Agatha Christie; Director, Michael Hall; Scenery, Frank and Tim Bennett; Costumes, Penny Koleos Williams; Lighting, Thomas Salzman; Stage Manager, Bill Oleson. CAST: Ned Coulter, John Gardiner, Peter Haig, David Kroll, Pat Nesbit, Harriet Oser, Ellen Simmons, Kraig Swartz, Joe Warik.

LOVE! VALOUR! COMPASSION! by Terrence McNally; Director, Michael Hall; Scenery, Frank and Tim Bennett; Costumes, Penny Koleos Williams; Lighting, Thomas Salzman; Sound, Steve Shapiro; Stage Manager, Bill Oleson. CAST: Robert Cary, Michael Curry, Stephen Joseph, Tony Meindl, Alex Montesino, Anthony Newfield, Kraig Swartz, Thomas Titone.

TERRA NOVA by Ted Tally; Director, Kenneth Kay; Scenery, Frank and Tim Bennett; Costumes, Penny Koleos Williams; Lighting, Thomas Salzman; Original Music and Sound, Steve Shapiro; Stage Manager, Bill Oleson. CAST: Trevor Anthony, Mark Cronogue, Dan Leonard, Gordon McConnell, Leila Sbitani, Ronald H. Siebert, John Unruh., Ebony Jo-Ann, Harriett

Ned Coulter, Ellen Simmons, Kraig Swartz in *The Unexpected Guest*

Michael Curry, Stephen Joseph in *Love! Valour! Compassion!*

Avery Sommers in *But Not for Me.*

163

Melinda Mullins, Tom Hewitt in *Private Lives*

Stanley Wayne Mathis, Harriet D. Foy, Clayton LeBoeuf in
Spunk: Three Tales by Zora Neale Hurston

CENTER STAGE

Baltimore, Maryland

Artistic Director, Irene Lewis; Managing Director, Peter W. Culman.

PRODUCTIONS & CASTS

May 10 - June 9, 1996
PRIVATE LIVES by Noel Coward; Director, Irene Lewis; Sets, Tony Straiges; Woman's Costumes, David Burdick; Lighting, Ken Posner; Sound, John Gromada; Choreographer, Ken Roberson; Dramaturg, Charlotte Stoudt; Pianist, George F. Spicka; Stage Manager, Keri Muir. CAST: Nancy Bell, Tom Hewitt, Boris McGiver, Melinda Mullins, Ruth F. Henry.

March 22 - April 28, 1996.
SPUNK by Zora Neale Hurston; Adaptation, George C. Wolfe; Director, Seret Scott; Choreographer, Ken Roberson; Music, Chic Street Man; Sets, Neil Patel; Costumes, Susan Mickey; Lighting, Peter Maradudin; Sound, Janet Kalas; Dramaturg, James Magruder; Stage Manager, Michael B. Paul. CAST: Chic Street Man, Ebony Jo-Ann, Harriett D. Foy, Clayton LeBouef, Stanely Wayne Mathis, Glenn Turner.

Feb. 16 - March 31, 1996.
THE LOVER by Elizabeth Egloff; Director, Irene Lewis; Sets, Christopher Barreca, Costumes, Paul Tazewell; Lighting, Pat Collins; Sound, David Budries; Dramaturg, Jill Rachel Morris; Stage Manager, Keri Muir. CAST: Colleen Quinn, James Noah, William Youmans, Jefferson Mays, Kali Rocha, Patricia Hodges, Reg Rogers, Janel Bosies, Kathryn Falcone, Liam Hughes, Brad Reiss.

Jan. 5 - Feb. 11, 1996.
THE TAMING OF THE SHREW by William Shakespeare; Director, Jackson Phippin; Sets, Tony Straiges; Costumes, Paul Tazewell; Lighting, James F. Ingalls; Sound, Mark Bennett; Dramaturg, Jane Ann Crum/Jill Rachel Morris; Stage Manager, Michael B. Paul. CAST: Thomas McCarthy, Conan McCarty, Evalyn Baron, Kate Skinner, Annie Meisels, Michael Rudko, Scott Rabinowitz, Ruth F. Henry, James McDonnell, Steve Routman, Patrick Tull.

Oct. 6 - Nov. 5, 1995.
DON JUAN by Moliere; Translation, Christopher Hampton; Director, Irene Lewis; Sets, Kate Edmunds; Costumes, Candice Donnelly; Lighting, Mimi Jordan Sherin; Composition, Sound, John Gromada; Dramaturg, Catherine Sheehy; Stage Manager, Glenn Brunner. CAST: Robert Dorfman, Laurence O'Dwyer, J. Kenneth Campbell, Anne Torsiglieri, Deirdre Lovejoy, Douglas Weston, Suzanne Cryer, Rene Rivera, Matte Osian, James J. Lawless, Maren E. Rosenberg, Kathleen McMullen.

Reg Rogers in *The Lover*

Steve Routman, Kate Skinner in
The Taming of the Shrew

CENTER THEATRE GROUP
AHMANSON THEATRE

Los Angeles, California
Twenty-ninth Season

Artistic Director/Producer, Gordon Davidson; Managing Director, Charles Dillingham; General Manager, Douglas Baker; Press & Advertising Director, Tony Sherwood.

CANDIDE; Music, Leonard Bernstein; Book, Hugh Wheeler; Lyrics, Richard Wilbur; Additional Lyrics, Leonard Bernstein, John LaTouche, Dorothy Parker, Lillian Hellman, Stephen Sondeim; Director, Gordon Davidson; Choreography, Yehuda Hyman; Sets, Peter Wexler; Costumes, Lewis Brown; Lighting, Tharon Musser. CAST: Kenn Chester, Nancy Dussault, Constance Hauman, William Schallert, Sean Smith, Jeff Austin, Christopher Paul Eid, David Eric, Alayne Faraone, Nmon Ford-Livene, Alex Guerrero Jr., Ellen Harvey ,Susan Hoffman, Caryn E. Kaplan, Dawn Kehret, Michele Murlin, Jani Neuman, Christina Marie Norrup, Gabriel Pasos, Grant Rosen, Roland Rusinek, Timothy Smith, David Thome, Jennifer Wallace, Scott Watande, Ann Winkowski.

SEVEN GUITARS by August Wilson; Director, Lloyd Richards; Sets, Scott Bradley; Costumes, Constanza Romero; Lighting, Christopher Akerlind. CAST: Keith David, Rosalyn Carter, Viola Davis, Tommy Hollis, Roger Robinson, Ruben Santiago-Hudson, Michele Shay.

KISS OF THE SPIDER WOMAN; Book, Terrence McNally; Music, John Kander; Lyrics, Fred Ebb; Based on the novel by Manuel Puig; Director, Harold Prince; Choreography, Vincent Paterson; Sets, Jerome Sirlin; Costumes, Florence Klotz; Lighting, Howell Binkley. CAST: Chita Rivera, Juan Chioran, Dorian Harewood, Merle Louise, Michael McCormick, Lauren Goler-Kosarin, Wade Williams, Robert Jensen, Julio Agustin, Richard Amaro, Robert Ashford, Lloyd Culbreath, Mark Dovey, Joshua Finkel, Pete Herber, Allen Hidalgo, Todd Hunter, Richard Montoya, Gary Moss, Bonnie Schon, Gary Schwartz, Sergio Trujillo.

AN INSPECTOR CALLS by J.B. Priestley; Director, Stephen Daldry; Sets, Ian MacNeil; Lighting, Rick Fisher. CAST: Stacy Keach, Kenneth Cranham, Susan Kellermann, Harry Carnahan, Jane Fleiss, Kaye Kingston, David Andrew Macdonald, Zachary Freed, Alex Chester, Joan Chodorow, Brandon Gauvin, Donald MacKechnie, Randal McEndree, Edwin Owens, Rich Remedios, Demetra Tseckares, V.J. Wells, Alice White, Eric Woodall, Jamison Yang.

CAROUSEL; Music, Richard Rodgers; Book & Lyrics, Oscar Hammerstein II; Director, Nicholas Hytner; Set/Costumes, Bob Crowley; Lighting, Paul Pyant; Choreography, Sir Kenneth MacMillan. CAST: Patrick Wilson, Sarah Uriarte, Sherry D. Boone, Sean Palmer, Rebecca Eichenberger, Brett Rickaby, Kate Buddeke, William Metzo, Dana Stackpole, Joseph Woelfel, Kristenelle Coronado, B.J. Crockett, Jasmine Ricketts, Marty Benn, Ilene Bergelson, Duane Boutte, Leslie Anne Cardona, Eric Christian, Jeffrey Elsass, Thursday Farrar, Christopher Freeman, John Frenzer, Katie Hugo, Jeffrey James, Holly Kinaird, Keri Lee, David MacGillivray, Heather McFadden, George Merrick, Joseph Ricci, Craig Ricks, Rhea Roderick, Donna Rubin, Janet Saia, Rommy Sandhu, Jennifer Laura Thompson, Weslie Webster.

Patrick Wilson, Sarah Uriarte in *Carousel*

**Stacy Keach, Susan Kellerman
in *An Inspector Calls***

**Sean Smith, Constance Hauman, William Schallert,
Kenn Chester, Caryn E. Kaplan in *Candide***

Talia Balsam, Park Overall in *Psychopathia Sexualis*

Gerrit Graham, Dominic Hoffman, George Stephen
in *Blade to the Heat*

Michael Learned, Marian Seldes, Christina Rouner
in *Three Tall Women*

David Gordon, Ain Gordon in *The Family Business*

CENTER THEATRE GROUP
MARK TAPER FORUM

Los Angeles, California
Twenty-ninth Season

Artistic Director, Gordon Davidson; Managing Director, Charles Dillingham; Producing Director, Robert Egan; General Manager, Douglas C. Baker; Press Director, Nancy Hereford.

SLAVS!: Thinking About the Longstanding Problems of Virtue and Happiness; by Tony Kushner; Director, Michael Greif; Sets/Costumes, Mark Wendland; Lighting, James F. Ingalls. CAST: John Campion, Randy Danson, Barbara eda-Young, Jonathan Fried, Jill Jaffe, Jennie Reid Huston, Calliope Thorne.

THE FAMILY BUSINESS; Written/Directed and Choreographed by Ain Gordon and David Gordon; Lighting, Stan Pressner. CAST: Ain Gordon, David Gordon, Valda Setterfield.

THREE TALL WOMEN by Edward Albee; Director, Lawrence Sacharow; Sets, James Noone; Costumes, Muriel Stockdale; Lighting, Phil Monat. CAST: Michael Learned, Christina Rouner, Marian Seldes, Michael Rhodes.

BLADE TO THE HEAT by Oliver Mayer; Director, Ron Link; Sets, Yael Pardess; Costumes, Candice Cain; Lighting, Anne Militello. CAST: Raymond Cruz, Hassan El-Amin, Gerrit Graham, Dominic Hoffman, Sal Lorez, Justina Machado, Ray Oirel, Ellis E. Williams.

PSYCHOPATHIA SEXUALIS by John Patrick Shanley; Director, Daniel Sullivan; Sets, Andrew Wood Boughton; Costumes, Jane Greenwood; Lighting, Pat Collins. CAST: John Aylward, Talia Balsam, Gregory Itzin, Park Overall, Matt Servitto.

CINCINNATI PLAYHOUSE IN THE PARK

Cincinnati, Ohio
Thirty-sixth Season

Producing Artistic Director, Edward Stern; Executive Director, Buzz Ward; Production Manager, Phil Rundle; Director of Public Relations, Peter Robinson; Production Stage Manager, Bruce E. Coyle.

THE MOUSETRAP by Agatha Christie; Director, Timothy Near; Sets, Robert Barnett; Costumes, Derek Duarte; Lighting, David B. Smith. CAST: Kathleen Mahony-Bennett, Ezra Barnes, Chris Hietikko, Beverly May, Richard Russell Ramos, Leslie Beatty, Keith Jochim, Kavik Harum.

SOMEONE WHO'LL WATCH OVER ME by Frank McGuinness; Director, Paul Shortt; Sets, Gordon DeVinney; Costumes, James Sale; Lighting, David B. Smith. CAST: Greg Thornton, Scott Whitehurst, Philip Pleasants.

MISS EVERS' BOYS by David Feldshuh; Director, Martin L. Platt; Sets, Bill Clarke; Costumes, Holly Poe Durbin; Lighting, Robert Wierzel. CAST: Lorey Hayes, Gustave Johnson, Tab Baker, Lee Simon Jr., Allie Woods, Craig Wroe, Chuck Patterson.

A TUNA CHRISTMAS by Jaston Williams, Joe Sears and Ed Howard; Director, Kenneth Elliott; Sets, Edward Gianfrancesco; Costumes, Robert Mackintosh; Lighting, James Sale. CAST: Bill Nolte, Mark Allen Flesher.

A CHRISTMAS CAROL adapted and written by Howard Dallin; Director, Michael Haney; Sets, James Leonard Joy; Costumes, David Murin; Lighting, Kirk Bookman. CAST: Alan Mixon (Scrooge), Danny Swartz, David Haugen, Robert Elliott, Gordon Brode, Gregory Procaccino, Raye Lackford, Miles Lindahl, Emily Bissonnette, Michael Pemberton, Dale Hodges, Jay Snyder, Jennifer Marshall, Kristen Schwarz, Annie Gill, Andrew Chaney, Richard Jackson II, Regina Pugh, Lisa Dapper Butts, Chuck Leonard, Tammy Lynn Schaff, Reeves Blevins, Colin Martin, Jason White, Morgan A. Nixon, Katt Masterson.

AN ASIAN JOCKEY IN OUR MIDST by Carter W. Lewis; Director, Brian Kulick; Sets/Costumes, Mark Wendland; Lighting, Kevin Adams. CAST: Daryl Edwards, Pamela Isaacs, Kaipo Schwab, Ray Xifo.

SHE LOVES ME; Book, Joe Masteroff; Music, Jerry Bock; Lyrics, Sheldon Harnick; Director, Victoria Bussert; Sets, John Ezell; Costumes, James Scott; Lighting, Daniel Stewart. CAST: Gibby Brand, Christopher Windom, Dorothy Stanley, Brian Sutherland, Robin Haynes, Joneal Joplin, Donna English, Marci Reid, Eric van Baars, Laurent Giroux, Hunter Bell, Ethan Stanley, Kelly Yurko, Gavan Pamer, M. Kathryn Quinlan, Sharon Kay White.

GHOSTS by Henrik Ibsen, adapted by Anthony Clarvoe; Director, Madeleine Pabis; Sets, Marie Anne Chiment; Costumes, Barbra Kravitz; Lighting, Jackie Manassee. CAST: Penny Balfour, William Whitehead, Maeve McGuire, Timothy Altmeyer.

ARMS AND THE MAN by George Bernard Shaw; Director, Edward Stern; Sets, Karen TenEyck; Costumes, Kirk Bookman; Lighting, David B. Smith. CAST: Katherine Heasley, Mikel Sarah Lambert, Corliss Preston, Sam Gregory, Aaron Serotsky, Patrick Husted, Alan Mixon, John Wojda.

ALL IN THE TIMING by David Ives; Director, Stephen Rothman; Sets, Thomas C. Umfrid; Costumes, Kavid Kay Mickelsen; Lighting, Betsy Adams. CAST: Patrick Frederic, Kathy Fitzgerald, Tim McGee, Duffy Hudson, Alison Lenox.

THE CAINE MUTINY COURT-MARTIAL by Herman Wouk; Director, Steven Woolf; Sets, Michael Ganio; Costumes, Max DeVolder; Lighting, Suann Pollock. CAST: R. Ward Duffy, Jim Abele, Paul DeBoy, Joneal Joplin, Robert Elliott, Anderson Matthews, Dana Snyder, Chris Hietikko, Jon Farris, Gregory Procaccino, Mark Mocahbee, Jay Paul Smith, Alastar Brown, Michael Botuchis, Jeffrey J. Jackson, John Jameson, Arny Stoller

Gibby Brand, Christopher Windom, Dorothy Stanley in *She Loves Me*

Lorey Hayes, Tab Baker in *Miss Evers' Boys*

Chris Hietikko, Kathleen Mahony-Bennett in *The Mousetrap*

Carter Calver, Ron Taylor in *It Ain't Nothin' But the Blues*

THE CLEVELAND PLAY HOUSE

Artistic Director, Peter Hackett; Managing Director, Dean Gladden; Marketing Director/Public Relations, Peter Cambariere; Production Manager, Joe Martin.

A GRAND NIGHT FOR SINGING ; Music, Richard Rodgers; Lyrics, Oscar Hammerstein II; Conceived by Walter Bobbie; Director, Loretta Greco; Costumes, Heather Ockler; Scenic/Lighting Design, Andrea Bechert. CAST: Trent Bright, Carter Calvert, Carol Dunne, Valerie Fagan, Fabio Polanco.

UNSUNG COLE...AND CLASSICS TOO; Music/Lyrics, Cole Porter; Conceived/Compiled and with Additional Music by Norman L. Berman; Director, Scott Kanoff; Musical Director, Robert J. Wilder; Costumes, Heather Carey; Scenic/Lighting Design, Andrea Bechert. CAST: Carter Calvert, Michael J. Farina, Maryann Nagel, Scott Plate, Ellen Zachos.

THE HARRIGANS SANG by William Hoffman; Music Arrangements, Marge Adler; Stage Director, William Hoffman; Musical Director/Arrangements, Marge Adler; Sets, Andrea Bechert. CAST: Kenneth Kacmar, Maryann Nagel, Greg Violand.

IT AIN'T NOTHIN' BUT THE BLUES by Charles Bevel, Lita Gaithers, Randal Myler, Ron Taylor, Dan Wheetman; Based on an original idea by Ron Taylor; Director, Randal Myler; Musical Director, Dan Wheetman; Sets, Andrew V. Yelusich; Lighting, Don Darnutzer; Costumes, Patricia A. Whitelock. CAST: "Mississippi" Charles Bevel, Carter Calvert, Lita Gaithers, Eloise Laws, Chic Street Man, Ron Taylor, Dan Wheetman.

THE GRAPES OF WRATH by Frank Galati; Based on the novel by John Steinbeck; Director, Peter Hackett; Sets, Carlyn Ross; Costumes, Elizabeth Novak; Lighting, Don Darnutzer. CAST: Randall Bame, Tonya Beckman, Tom Blair, Paul Blankenship, Ed Blunt, Dan Patrick Brady, Ali Burke, Ashley Butler, Donald Christopher, Cathy S. Clifford, Triste Crawford, Lisa Druckman, Carol Dunne, Katie Elder, Edan Evans, Richard Farrell, Mike Hartman, Daniel J. Katula, Darrie Lawrence, John R. Magaro, Evie McElroy, Kevin Miller, Roy Mills, John Nelson, Laura Perrotta, Fabio Polanco, Alann Janell Romansky, Michael J. Ross, Kyle Shanahan, Timothy L. Thilleman, W. Francis Walters, Dave Valent.

THE TRIUMPH OF LOVE by Pierre Carlet de Marivaux; Translated by James Magruder; Director, Kent Thompson; Sets, David Crank; Costumes, Kristine Kearney; Lighting, Rachel Budin. CAST: Michael Booth, Robin Chadwick, Tara Falk, Jacqueline Knapp, Philip Lehl, Elizabeth Long, Michael Mandell, James Magruder.

PRIVATE LIVES by Noel Coward; Director, Michael Bloom; Sets, Peter Harrison; Costumes, Barbra Kravitz; Lighting, Richard Riddell. CAST: Ali Burke, James Colby, J. Michael Flynn, Twyla Hafermann, Greta Lambert.

THE AFRICAN COMPANY PRESENTS RICHARD III by Carlyle Brown; Director, Peter Francis James; Sets, Vicki Smith; Costumes, Kaye Voyce; Lighting, Don Darnutzer. CAST: Denise Burse, Peter Jay Fernandez, Gary DeWitt Marshall, John Nelson, Chuck Patterson, Jared Sakren, Mone Walton. **THE ENCHANTED MAZE** by Murphy Guyer; Director, Peter Hackett; Sets/Costumes/Lighting, Pavel Dobrusky. CAST: Donald Berman, Donald Christopher, Michael Connor, Nancy Franklin, Murphy Guyer, Mike Hartman, John R. Magaro, Perrry Laylon Ojeda, Alanna Janell Romansky, Evan Thompson, Kay Walbye, Rebecca Waxman.

THE FRONT PAGE by Ben Hecht, Charles MacArthur; Director, Jeffrey Hayden; Sets/Lighting, Kent Dorsey; Costumes, Christine Dougherty. CAST: Randall Bame, Jennifer Bill, Beeson Carroll, Jim Chance, Lee Chew, Cathy S. Clifford, David Colacci, Art Evans, David O. Frazier, John Joseph Gallagher, Nick Jolley, Dan Katula, David Lipman, David Moynihan, John Nelson, Laura Perrotta, David Shatraw, Dolores Sutton, Dudley Swetland, Rohn Thomas.

THE LADY FROM THE SEA by Henrik Ibsen; Translated by Rolf Fjelde; Sets, Tony Straiges; Costumes, Lindsay W. Davis; Lighting, Kent Dorsey; Director, Jackson Phippin. CAST: Vanessa Aspillaga, James Colby, Peter Davies, Thomas F. Honeck, John Nelson, Jared Reed, Bridgit Ryan, Kate Skinner.

QUILTERS by Molly Newman & Barbara Damashek; Music/Lyrics, Barbara Damashek; Based on *The Quilters: Women and Domestic Art* by Patricia Cooper and Norma Bradley Allen; Sets, Robert Brill; Costumes, Lindsay W. Davis; Lighting, Allen Lee Hughes; Director, Loretta Greco; Choreographer, Frank Chaves. CAST: Evalyn Baron, Kim Bey, Susan Ericksen, Sheila Gibbs, Trisha M. Gorman, Angela Lockett, Louise Mike.

James Fry, Roger Mastroianni Photos

Perry Laylon Ojeda, Donald Christopher in *The Enchanted Maze*

Dawn Sobczak, Jaclyn Iassogna, Kim Hunter in *The Children's Hour*

CONNECTICUT REPERTORY THEATER

Artistic Director, Gary M. English; Managing Director, Robert Wildman.

THE CHILDREN'S HOUR by Lillian Hellman; Director, Pamela Hunt; Sets, Crystal Tiala; Lighting Stephen Hills; Costumes, Charlene McCabe. CAST: Laura M. Celentano, David A. Cooper, Samantha Cosmas, Shea Cremer, Eric J. Dean, Kim Hunter, Jaclyn Iassogna, Jennifer A. Larkin, Allison Lebonitte, Erin Logemann, Sarah Peterson, Sandee L. Rollins, Theresa M. Rutz, Dawn Sobczak, Renea C. Stanchfield, M.J. Tomsic.

FIVE WOMEN WEARING THE SAME DRESS by Alan Ball; Director, Kathleen Powers; Sets/Costumes, Susan J. Slack; Lighting, Scott A. Morris. CAST: Robin Aronson, Claire Castel, Michael Czeczotka, Karen Giles, Reay Alwyn Kaplan, LeeAnna Lambert.

THE THREE MUSKETEERS by Alexandre Dumas; Adapted by Charles Morey; Director, Michael Montel; Sets, Campbell Baird; Lighting, Alan Keen. CAST: Mark Adams, Nicole Blake, Carrie Brewer, Matt Brooks, David A. Cooper, Samantha Cosmas, Eric J. Dean, Emily Ann Donnelly, Steven Fales, Oliver Frates, M.F. Green, Matt Greene, Mingo Long, Ian A. Pfister, Richard Ruiz, Jason Turner, William Walsh; Ensemble: Robert Cameron, Kelly Lafferty, Christian Levatino, Moe Pomerantz, Jim Rose, Christopher Rosol, Dustin Schellinkhout, Aaron C. Truax.

THE GRAPES OF WRATH by Frank Galati; Based on the novel by John Steinbeck; Director, Eric Hill; Sets, Eric Renschler; Lighting, Scott A. Morris; Costumes, Susan J. Slack. CAST: Mark Adams, Robin Aronson, Joe Beaudin, Robert Biggs, Jim Brennan, Matt Brooks, Robert Cameron, Emily Ann Donnelly, Steven Fales, Robert Gil, Claire Gregoire, Steven Guyette, C. Mingo Long, Ian A. Pfister, Elizabeth Vermilyea; Ensemble: Kennth S. Clark, Margaret Colburn, David A. Cooper, Michael Czecztoka, Eric J. Dean, Matt Greene, Jennifer A. Larkin, Sheila Logan, Emer McKenna, Kimberly Nordling, Sandee L. Rollis, Travis Richards, Richard Ruiz, Sawn Sobczak.

STAGES by Tania L. Katan; Director, Robert McDonald; Sets, Gary M. English; Lighting, Debra Leigh Siegel; Costumes, David T. Howard. CAST: Carrie Brewer, Karen Giles, Matthew T. Heron, Gina Norman, M.J. Tomsic; Ensemble: Laura Celentano, Jaclyn Iassogna, Clare O'Connor, Christopher Rosol, Theresa M. Rutz, Aaron C. Truax, Bill Wildman, Jr.

A CONNECTICUT YANKEE IN KING ARTHUR'S COURT by Brad Korbesmeyer; Adapted from Mark Twain; Director, Stephen Krasser; Puppet Director, Bart P. Roccoberton Jr.; Sets, David Regan; Lighting, Alan Keen; Costumes/Puppet Design, Joyce L. Fritz. CAST: Mark Adams, Robin Aronson, Robert Cameron, Claire Castel, Michael Czeczotka, Eric J. Dean, Oliver P. Frates, Melanie Ann Hitt, Reay Alwyn Kaplan, Tom Keegan, Jennifer A. Larkin, Ian A. Pfister, Jim Rose, Richard Ruiz, Carole Simms, William Walsh; Ensemble: Julie Morrison, Mary Petillo, Jen Watson.

THE PIRATES OF PENZANCE by Gilbert and Sullivan; Director/Choreographer, B. Pete Westerhoff; Sets, Crystal Tiala; Lighting, Tim Hunter; Costumes, Peg Carbonneau. CAST: Mark Adams, Robin Aronson, Kirsti Carhahan Steven Fales, Emily Loesser, Emily Pearson, Richard Ruiz, Terry Runnels, Phil Simmons, Nicole Blake, Danielle Conroy, Meredith Parker, Deanne Wood; Adam Abernathy, Matt Brooks, Matt Greene, Matt LaBanca, Ian A. Pfister, Patrick Reed, David Rossmer, Phil Simmons, William Walsh.

COMPANY; Music/Lyrics, Stephen Sondheim; Book, George Furth; Director, Gary M. English; Choreographer, B. Peter Westerhoff; Sets, Eric Renschler; Lighting, Kendall Smith; Costumes, Debra Stein. CAST: Adam Abernathy, Mark Adams, Robin Aronson, Shea Cremer, Steven Fales, Marcus Neville, Meredith Parker, Angela Parks, Emily Pearson, Richard Ruiz, Terry Runnels, Dorothy Stanley, B. Peter Westerhoff, Deanne Wood, Mairzy Yost.

YOU CAN'T TAKE IT WITH YOU by Moss Hart & George S. Kaufman; Director, Michael Montel; Sets, Dick Block; Costumes, Lesley Neilson-Bowman; Lighting, Marilyn Rennagel. CAST: Mark Adams, Robin Aronson, Matt Brooks, Shea Cremer, Steven Fales, David Green, Claire Gregoire, Nafe Katter, Judy Kaye, Jerry Stephen Krasser, Carol O'Shaughnessy, Angela Parks, Ian A. Pfister, Richard Ruiz, Terry Runnels, Mairzy Yost, Derek Egerman, Joe Zaccaro.

Gerry Goodstein, Peter Crowley Photos

Judy Kaye in *You Can't Take It With You*

169

Carla Brothers, Letta Mbulu in Sheila's Day

Kim Yancey Moore, David Wolos-Fonteno in *Fear Itself*

CROSSROADS THEATRE COMPANY

New Brunswick, NJ
Eighteenth Season

Artistic Director/Co-Founder, Ricardo Khan; Managing Director, Steven Warnick; Director of Marketing, Grey Johnson.

THE PIANO LESSON by August Wilson; Director, A. Dean Irby; Sets, Felix E. Cochren; Lighting, John McKeron; Costumes, Pamela L. Johnson. CAST: Gwendolyn Bartlett, Willis Burks II, Barry Shabaka Henley, Joy DeMichelle Moore, David Rainey, Roger Robinson, Elizabeth Van Dyke, Charles Weldon.

SHEILA'S DAY by Duma Ndlovu; Conceived and Created by Duma Ndlovu, Mbongeni Ngema; Ruby Lee Conceived and Co-Written by Ebony Jo-Ann; Stage/Director, Mbongeni Ngema; Restaged by Kenneth Johnson; Sets, Charles McClennehan; Lighting, Victor En Yu Tan; Costumes, Toni-Leslie James. CAST: Stephanie Alston, Gina Breedlove, Irene Datcher, Ebony Jo-Ann, Denise Morgan, Debbi Blackwell-Cook, Carla Brothers, Thuli Dumakude, Letta Mbulu, Linda Sithole, Fuschia Walker.

JELLY ROLL!: THE MUSIC AND THE MAN; Created by Vernel Bagneris; Director, A. Dean Irby; Music/Lyrics, Jelly Roll Morton; Musical Direction/Arrangements, Morten G. Larsen; Lighting, John McKernon; Sets, Michael Fish. CAST: Paul Asaro.

FEAR ITSELF by Eugene; Director, Imani; Sets/Costumes, Felix E. Cochren; Lighting, Melody Beal. CAST: Richarda Abrams, Kim Yancey Moore, Ramon Melindez Moses, Donn Swaby, David Wolos-Fonteno.

NOMATHEMBA; Book/Lyrics, Ntozake Shange, Joseph Shabalala, Eric Simonson; Music/Based on a song by Joseph Shabalala; Director, Eric Simonson; Sets, Loy Arcenas; Lighting, Natasha Katz; Costumes, Karin Kopischke. CAST: Ladysmith Black Mambazo, Cheryl Lynn Bruce, Bernadette L. Clarke, Leelai Demoz, La Tonya Hagans, Cee-Cee Harshaw, Erika L. Heard, Michael T. Kachingwe, Ntare Mwine, Tania Richard, Michael WIlliams.

THE SCREENED-IN PORCH by Marian X; Director, Judyie Al-Bilali; Sets, John Ezell; Lighting, Curtis V. Hodge; Costumes, Myrna Colley-Lee. CAST: Chad L. Coleman, Leila Danette, Erika Ewing, Lynda Gravatt, Eleanor McCoy, Tina Tyler.

Rich Pipeling Photos

Lynda Gravatt, Eleanor McCoy in *The Screened In Porch*

Matt Bradford Sullivan, Jennifer Rohn in *Arms and the Man*

DALLAS THEATER CENTER

Artistic Director, Richard Hamburger; Press Director, Richard Franco; Managing Director, Robert Yesselman.

THE INVISIBLE CIRCUS; Created and Performed by Victoria Chaplin & Jean Baptiste Thierree; Lighting, Laura De Bernardis.

OHIO TIP-OFF by James Yoshimura; Director, Kenny Leon; Sets, Christopher Barreca; Costumes, Susan E. Mickey; Lighting, Kenneth Posner. CAST: Billy Eugene Jones, Khary Payton, Robert Weldon, Spence White, Victor Williams, Charles Malik Whitfield, Adrian Roberts, Michael Cullen

A CHRISTMAS CAROL by Charles Dickens; Adapted by Gerald Freedman; Director, Jonathan Moscone; Sets, John Ezell; Costumes, Giva Taylor; Lighting, Robert Wierzel. CAST: Raphael Parry, Liz Piazza Kelley, Steven Eng, Kathryn Daniels, Lewis Flanagan, Ashley Sheahan, Katherine Thomas, Weston Self, Charles Dean, Dolores Godinez, Akin Babatunde, Steven Breese, Billy Eugene Jones, Bob Hess, Edmund Coulter, Ted Davey, Arien Elizondo, Jesse Elizondo, Liz Mikel, Gwen Templeton, Kelley Davies.

THE STERNHEIM PROJECT (The Unmentionables/The Snob) by Carl Sternheim; Translated by Paul Lambert and Kate Sullivan; Adapted by Melissa Cooper, Paul Lampert, Kate Sullivan; Director, Richard Hamburger; Sets, Christopher Barreca; Costumes, Katherine B. Roth; Lighting, Mark I. McCullough. CAST: Norman Browning, Jurian Hughes, Charis Leos, Reno Roop, Bruce DuBose, David Manis, Leslie Hendrix, Joan Buddenhagen

ARMS AND THE MAN by George Bernard Shaw; Director, Jonathan Moscone; Sets, Neil Patel; Costumes, Katherine B. Roth; Lighting, Jeremy Stein. CAST: Jennifer Rohn, Connie Nelson, Dolores Godinez, Geoffrey Owens, Bruce DuBose, Norman Browning, Matt Bradford Sullivan

ANGLES IN AMERICA: MILLENIUM APPROACHES by Richard Hamburger; Sets, Ming Cho Lee; Costumes, Katherine B. Roth; Lighting, Howell Binkley. CAST: Sheriden Thomas, Stephen Marle, Robert Gomes, Kathleen Dennehy, Tyrone Mitchell Henderson, Joseph Fuqua, Todd Weeks, Sally Nystuen

Carl Davis Photos

Khary Payton in *Ohio Tip-Off*

Sally Nystuen, Todd Weeks in *Angels in America*

DETROIT REPERTORY THEATRE

Detroit, Michigan
Thirty-eighth Season

Artistic/Managing Director, Bruce E. Millan; Production Manager, Richard Smith; Sets, Richard Smith, Bruce E. Millan; Lighting, Kenneth R. Hewitt,Jr.; Costumes, B.J. Essen.

STILL WATERS by Claudia Allen; Director, Dee Andrus. CAST: Sandra Love Aldridge, Ruth Allen, Sakuna De Laney, Henrietta Hermelin, Jeffry Chastang, Maggie Patton, William Boswell, John W. Pulchalski

PASSED OVER by Alexandra Branyon; Director, J. Center. CAST: Sakunah DeLaney, Barbara Busby.

OLEANNA by David Mamet; Director, Bruce E. Millan. CAST: Chris Ann Voudoukis, Harry Wetzel.

IF WE ARE WOMEN by Joanna McClelland Glass; Director, Lonnie Fleischer. CAST: Dee Andrus Shirley Benyas, Loretta Higgins, Catherine Worth.

Sandra Love Aldridge in *Still Waters*

Catherine Worth, Dee Andrus, Loretta Higgins, Shirley Benyas in *If We Are Women*

Roger Serbagi in *Cheap Sentiment* at George Street Playhouse

172

Angela Robinson, Alberto Cruz, Jr. in *Twist*

GEORGE STREET PLAYHOUSE

New Brunswick, New Jersey

Artistic Director, Gregory S. Hurt; Managing Director, Diane Claussen; Production Manager, Edson Womble; Marketing/Public Relations Director, Rick Engler

THE MOUSETRAP by Agatha Christie; Director, Susan Kerner; Sets, R. Michael Miller; Costumes, Deirdre Sturges Burke; Lighting, F. Mitchell Dana. CAST: Gordon Brode, Terrence Currier, Kaleo Griffith, Katherine Heasley, Jurian Hughes, Joe Palmieri, Bray Poor

LOVE COMICS; Book, Sarah Schlesinger, David Evans; Music, David Evans; Lyrics, Sarah Schlesinger; Director, Rod Kaats; Choreographer, Danny Herman; Sets/Costumes, Eduardo Sicangco; Lighting, Phillip Monat. CAST: Liz Larsen, Clif Thorn, Jennifer Simar, Peter Reardon, Terry Layman.

ARMS AND THE MAN by George Bernard Shaw; Director, Mark Rucker; Sets, Christine Jones; Costumes, Barbara Forbes. CAST: Erin O'Brien, Mercedes Herrero, Kathleen Christal, Anthony Ward, Joseph Andrew Mills III, Kevin Orton, Kevin Dwyer, C.J. Wilson

ENTRIES by Bernardo Solano; Director, Lou Jacob; Sets, G.W. Mercier; Costumes, Caryn Neman; Lighting, Frances Aronson. CAST: Candy Buckley, Johnny Garcia, Ric Oquita, T. Ryder Smith

THE MIRACLE WORKER by William Gibson; Director, Wendy Liscow; Sets, Atkin Pace; Costumes, Barbara Forbes. CAST: Judith Blazer, Gordon Brode, Patricia R. Floyd, Nathalie Paulding, Michael Pemberton, Elizabeth Perry, Rose Stockton, Christopher Wynkoop, Virginia Bosch, Heather Hodder, Jena Tesse Fox, Donovon Ian Hunter McNight, Danielle Morgan, Sparky.

CHEAP SENTIMENT by Bruce Graham; Director, Thomas Bullard; Sets, Richard Hoover; Costumes, Kim Krumm Sorenson; Lighting, Donald Holder. CAST: Evan Pappas, Mary Fogarty, Reiko Aylesworth, Roger Serbagi, Allen Swift.

TWIST; Book, William F. Brown; Music, Tena Clark, Gary Prim; Lyrics, Tena Clark; Director, Gregory S. Hurst; Choreographer, Mercedes Ellington; Sets, Atkin Pae; Costumes, Teresa Snider-Stein; Lighting, Donald Holder. CAST: Tamara Baron, Angela Robinson, Lynn Halverson, Lawrence Hamilton, Eugene Fleming, Luke Sickle, Alberto Cruz Jr., Nancy R. Braun, Jasmine Harrison, Amanda Harrison, Amanda Johnson, Jamaal Maynard, Renee Stocker, Natalie Van Kleef, Laura Wagman, Clarence Leggett, John Jellison, Larry Marshall, Monica Pege, Ivar Brogger.

Miguel Pagliere Photos

Nathalie Paulding, Judy Blazer in *The Miracle Worker*

Liz Larson, Clif Thorn in *Love Comics*

Brian Dennehy, Pamela Payton-Wright in *A Touch of the Poet*

Regina Taylor in *Escape From Paradise*

Bruno Campos, Julia Gibson in *All's Well That Ends Well*

GOODMAN THEATRE

Chicago, Illinois

Artistic Director, Robert Falls; Executive Director, Roche Schulfer; Press, Cindy Bandle, Rachel Allard.

ALL'S WELL THAT ENDS WELL by William Shakespeare; Director, Mary Zimmerman; Sets, Riccardo Hernandez; Costumes, Nan Cibula-Jenkins; Lighting, T.J. Gerckens. CAST: Mary Ann Thebus, Bruno Campos, Del Close, Jerry Saslow, Julia Gibson, Raymond Fox, John Ellison Conlee, Howard Witt, Scott Haven, Michael J. Cargill; Lee Sellars, Marc Vann, L.D. Barrett, Tom Dougherty, Cheryl Lynn Bruce, Meredith Zinner, Shannon Branham, Darryl Alan Reed.

A CHRISTMAS CAROL by Charles Dickens; Adapted, Tom Creamer; Director, Chuck Smith; Sets, Joseph Niemsinksi; Lighting, Robert Christen. CAST: Tom Mula (Scrooge), John Reeger, Paul Amandes, Jeff Parker, Brian Lynch, Christopher Vasquez, Mary Ernster, Dale Morgan, Beau Ashton Butherus, Marquita Brim, Dwain A. Perry, James Sie, David Girolmo, E. Faye Butler, Gregory Hirte, Manao DeMuth, Jaye Tyrone Stewart, Aisha deHaas, Molly White, Alyson Horn, Eli Oberlander, Malissa Strong, Cheryl Hamada, Maulik Pancholy, William Schwartz, Jordan Loperena, Jan Nisbet.

BLACK STAR LINE by Charles Smith; Director, Tazewell Thompson; Sets, Joseph P. Tilford; Costumes, Kay Kurta Silva; Lighting, T.J. Gerckens. CAST: Crystal Laws Green, Rick Worthy, Jacson Laroc, Leonard Roberts, Lynn M. House, Ora Jones, A. Benard Cummings, Ron Cephas Jones, Ernest Perry Jr., Paul Oakley Stovall, Craig Spidle, A.C. Smith, Cheryl Lynn Bruce, Dan Mooney, Todd Anthony-Jackson, Shanesia Davis, Allan Louis, Joe Van Slyke, Christopher B. Duncan, Tim Decker.

ARCADIA by Tom Stoppard; Director, Michael Maggio; Sets, Linda Buchanan; Costumes, Nan Cibula-Jenkins; Lighting, Robert Christen. CAST: Fleur Phillips, Steve Cell, Kyle Colerider-Krugh, Christopher Donahue, James McCance, Kate Collis, Dan Mooney, Kristine Thatcher, Patrick Clear, Guy Adkins, Eric Conley.

A TOUCH OF THE POET by Eugene O'Neill; Director, Robert Falls; Sets, Derek McLane; Costumes, Birgit Rattenborg Wise; Lighting, Kennth Posner. CAST: Thomas Kelly, Chris O'Neill, Jenny Bacon, Pamela Payton-Wright, Brian Dennehy, Rob Riley, Brad Armacost, Kevin Henry, Deanna Dunagan, John William Cooke.

THE HOUSE OF MARTIN GUERRE; Music/Lyrics, Leslie Arden; Book, Leslie Arden, Anna Theresa Cascio; Director, David Petrarca; Choreography, David Marques; Sets. Robert Brill; Costumes, Susan Hilferty; Lighting, James F. Ingalls. CAST: Cecily Strong, Hollis Resnik, Kevin Gudahl, Guy Adkins, John W. Eskola, Norman Moses, Jeff Dumas, Jeff Parker, Craig Bennett, David Girolmo, Cheryl Sylvester, Kelly Anne Clark, Marnie Nicolella, Tina Gluschenko, Julain Molnar, Frances Limoncelli, Willie Malnati, Allan Chambers, Anthony Crivello, Genevieve Ven-Johnson, Kingsley Leggs, Mary Ernster, Tim Rezash, Bryan P. Brems, Stephanie Swanson.

CLOUD TECTONICS by Jose Rivera; Director, Henry Godinez; Sets, Robert C. Martin; Costumes, Sharon Sachs; Lighting, Robert Shook. CAST: Maricela Ochoa, Mark D. Espinoza, Anthony Diaz-Perez.

ESCAPE FROM PARADISE; Written and Performed by Regina Taylor; Director, Shirley Jo Finney; Sets, Scott Cooper; Lighting, Robert Christen.

UNJUSTIFIABLE ACTS by Aaron Iverson; Director, Harry J. Lennix; Sets, Robert C. Martin; Costumes, Laura Cunningham; Lighting, Diane Ferry Williams. CAST: Rengin Altay, Mark Wohlgenant, Ellis Foster, Tim Rhoze, Amy Morton, David New, Sylvia Carter.

A PIRATE'S LULLABY by Jessica Litwak; Director, Susan V. Booth; Sets, John Culbert; Costumes, Linda Roethke; Lighting, Michael S. Philippi. CAST: Cynthia Orthal, Ann Stevenson Whitney, Paula Killen, Lusia Strus, Jeffrey Hutchinson.

Liz Lauren Photos

Willie Malnati, Anthony Crivello, Julian Molnar in *The House of Martin Guerre*

Todd Anthony-Jackson, Christopher B. Duncan in *Black Star Line*

Kate Collins, Steve Cell in *Arcadia*

Donna English, Michael McCormick in *The Gig*

**Sean McCourt, Erin Hill, Kevin Fox, Rick Leon,
David M. Lutken in** *Honky-Tonk Highway*

Fletcher's American Cheese Choral Society in *Strike Up the Band*

GOODSPEED OPERA HOUSE

East Haddam, Connecticut
Thirty-second Season

Excutive Director, Michael P. Price; Associate Producer, Sue Frost; Casting Director, Warren Pincus; General Manager, Howard Sherman; Director of Marketing/Public Relations, Jennifer Wislocki.

SWINGING ON A STAR; Lyrics, Johnny Burke; Music, Johnny Burke, Erroll Garner, Robert Haggart, Arthur Johnston, James Monaco, Harold Spina, Jimmy Van Heusen; Director/Writer, Michael Leeds; Choreography, Kathleen Marshall; Sets, James Youmans; Costumes, Judy Dearing; Lighting, Richard Nelson. CAST: Michael McGrath, Terry Burrell, Lewis Cleale, Alvaleta Guess, Lori Hart, Kathy Fitzgerald, Eugene Fleming.

CAN-CAN; Music/Lyrics, Cole Porter; Book, Abe Burrows; Director/Book Revised by Martin Charnin; Choreographer, Michele Assaf; Sets, Kenneth Foy; Costumes, Gail Brassard; Lighting, Ken Billington. CAST: Silvia Aruj, Pascal Benichou, Jim Borstelmann, Belle Calaway, Jamie Chandler-Torns, Michelle Chase, Eric L. Christian, Jack Cirillo, Ed Dixon, Madeleine Ehlert, Michael E. Gold, Larry Kleiber, Jennifer Lamberts, Julia K. Murney, Monica L. Patton, Dale Radunz, Jamie Ross, Tina Stafford, Todd Thurston, Barbara Tirrell, Bill Ullman, Courtney Young.

STRIKE UP THE BAND; Music/Lyrics, George Gershwin, Ira Gershwin; Book, George S. Kaufman; Director/Musical Staging, Charles Repole; Choreography, Linda Goodrich; Sets, James Noone; Costumes, John Carver Sullivan; Lighting, Kirk Bookman. CAST: Robert M. Armitage, Kristin Chenoweth, Jim Corti, Jason Danieley, Timothy Ellis, Therese Friedemann, John Halmi, Bryan Harris, Ron Holgate, Michael Hollick, Angela Howell, Gary Kilmer, Melinda Klump, Emily Loesser, Tanny McDonald, Joel Newsome, Leslie Stroud, Alex Sanchez, Bill Szobody, David Titus, Yvette Tucker.

Norma Terris Theatre

HONKY-TONK HIGHWAY; Books, Richard Berg; Music/Lyrics/Additional Dialogue, Robert Nassif-Lindsey; Director, Gabriel Barre; Sets, Sets, Charles E. McCarry; Costumes, Robert Strong Miller; Lighting, Phil Monat. CAST: Kevin Fox, Erin Hill, Rick Leon, David M. Lutken, Sean McCourt.

THE GIG; Book/Music/Lyrics, Douglas J. Cohen; Based on the motion picture *The Gig* by Frank D. Gilroy; Director, Victoria Bussert; Choreography, Daniel Stewart; Sets, James Morgan; Costumes, Tom Reiter; Lighting, Mary Jo Dondlinger. CAST: Stephen Berger, Alison Bevan, David Brummel, Donna English, James Judy, Ilene KRisten, Don Mayo, Michael McCormick, William Parry, Charles Pistone, Stuart Zagnit.

SILVER DOLLAR; Book/Lyrics, Mary Bracken Phillips; Music, Jack Murphy; Director, John Schuck; Choreography, Karen Azenberg; Sets, Peter Harrison; Costumes, Charlotte Yetman; Lighting, Victor En Yu Tan. CAST: George Ball, Tom Demenkoff, Bob Freschi, Jeff Gurner, Nick Jolley, Mary Bracken Phillips, Elizabeth Richmond, Don Stephenson.

Diane Sobolewski Photos

GREAT LAKES THEATRE FESTIVAL

Cleveland, Ohio

Tony Randall, Kate Forbes in *The School for Scandal*

Artistic Director, Gerald Freedman; Managing Director, Anne B. DesRosiers; Associate Artistic Director, John Ezell; Associate Director, Victoria Bussert; Production Manager, Anthony M. Forman.

THE SCHOOL FOR SCANDAL by Richard Brinsley Sheridan; Director, Gerald Freedman; Sets, Douglas W. Schmidt; Costumes, Theoni V. Aldredge; Lighting, Mary Jo Dondlinger. CAST: Patrick Carroll, Megan Dodds, Kate Forbes, Renee Gatien, Allen Gimore, Philip Goodwin, Jennifer Harmon, Tom Hewitt, Simon Jones, Tony Randall, Ron Randell, Mary Lou Rosato, Morgan Rowe, Joseph Schultz, Matt Shea, Norman Snow, Ted Sorel, Matt Bradford Sullivan, Richard Topol, Ray Virta.

A CHRISTMAS CAROL ; Adapted and Directed, Gerald Freedman; Stage by Rob Ruggiero; Sets, John Ezell, Gene Emerson Friedman; Costumes, James Scott; Lighting, Mary Jo Dondlinger. CAST: William Leach (Scrooge), Michael Krawic, Sally Nystuen, Kelly Murphy, Matt Shea, Rachel Kiwi, Phillip Carrroll, Josh Harvey, Hayley Samerigo, Tommy Krecic, Kali Woodside, Kevin McCarty, Maryann Nagel, Jeremy Webb, Bill Busch, Michaeljohn McGann, Jeffries Thaiss, John Buck Jr., Charles Tuthill, Katrina Cain, Patrick Bittel, Elizbaeth Leisek, Rachel Kiwi, Sandra Simon, Justin Cain, Kelly Strand, Maria Weybrecht.

AS YOU LIKE IT by William Shakespeare; Director, Michael Breault; Sets, John Ezell; Costumes, James Scott; Lighting, Mary Jo Dondlinger. CAST: Ed Blunt, John Buck Jr., Billy Busch, Jeffrey Cox, Michael Hollick, Ken Kliban, Jamie Koeth, Tommy Krecic, Peter Kybart, Mark Mineart, Kelly Murphy, Larry Nehring, Michelle O'Neill, Ron Randell, Cynthia Ruffin, Hayley Samerigo, Michael Strickland, Rohn Thomas, Charles Tuthill, Jonathan Wade, Lauren Ward.

THE DYBBUK by S. Ansky; Adapted and Director, Gerald Freedman; Choreographer, Mauricio Wainrot; Sets, John Ezell; Costumes, Barbara Kessler; Lighting, Mary Jo Dondlinger. CAST: Michael Berresse, Jonathan Brody, John Buck Jr., Jeanette L. Buell, Evangelia Constantakos, Nina Goldman, Danny Gurwin, Anita Intrieri, Max Jacobs, Dennis Johnston, Edwina King, John Lagioia, Richard Lear, Alex Lubliner, Daniel Pardo, Dorothy Silver, Reuben Silver, Amy Tarachow, Mark Tomasic, O.V. Vargas, Susana Weingarten De Evert, Daniel Wright, The Tom Evert Dance Company.

BLITHE SPIRIT by Noel Coward; Director, Victoria Bussert; Sets, John Ezell; Costumes, James Scott; Lighting, Phil MOnat. CAST: Catherine L. Albers, Brooks Almy, Alison Bevan, John Buck Jr., Carol Dunne, Laura Stitt, Charles Tuthill.

Roger Mastroianni, Bruce Zake Photos

Charles Tuthill, Brooks Almy in *Blithe Spirit*

Michael Berresse, Nina Goldman in *The Dybbuk*

Robert Stattel, Calista Flockhart in *Romeo + Juliet*

Michele Morgan in *I Ain't Yo' Uncle*

Robert Stattel, Marina Sirtis In *Loot*

Phylicia Rashad, Deidrie N. Henry in *Blues for an Alabama Sky*

HARTFORD STAGE

Hartford, Connecticut

Artistic Director, Mark Lamos; Managing Director, Stephen J. Albert; Public Relations Director, Jenni French.

ROMEO + JULIET by William Shakespeare; Director, Mark Lamos; Sets, Michael Yeargan; Costumes, Peter J. Hall; Lighting Design, David Budries; Choreographer, Robert LuPone. CAST: Dylan McCormick, David Alan Basche, Patrick Reed, Eric Evenson, John Lathan, Rick Stear, Jack Davidson, Mary Layne, Nafe Katter, Ezra Knight, Robert Petkoff, Cedric Harris, Hayden Reed Sakow, Sewell Whitney, Roberta Maxwell, Calista Flockhart, Bill Camp, Robert Stattel, Jason Karadimas, Lanie Bergin, Tony Bonsignore, Jim Bozzi, Walter Corbiere, Philip Cuomo, Barbara Dodd, Tara Sullivan.

I AIN'T YO' UNCLE: THE NEW JACK REVISIONIST UNCLE TOM'S CABIN by Robert Alexander; Director, Reggie Montgomery; Sets, Edward Burbridge; Costumes, Karen Perry; Lighting, Donald Holder; Mask and Puppet Design,Barbara Follitt. CAST: Sam Wellington, Michele Morgan, Simi Junior, Marylouise Burke, Byron Utley, Jesse L. Martin, Edward J. Hyland, Kena Tangi Dorsey, Mace Perlman, Kristin Flanders, Alva Nelson.

THE RIVALS by Richard Brinsley Sheridan; Director, Mark Lamos; Sets, Michael Yeargan; Costumes, Jess Goldstein; Lighting, Stephen Strawbridge. CAST: John Michael Higgins, David Margulies, Robert Petkoff, Alec Phoenix, Margaret Welsh, Bellina Logan, Pamela Payton-Wright, Adam LeFevre, Robert Newton, Denis Holmes, Suzanen Cryer, Denis Holmes, Eric Evenson, Tony Bonsignore, Christopher Williams.

LOOT by Bartlett Sher; Sets, Douglas Stein; Costumes, Kim Krumm Sorneson; Lighting, Robert Wierzel. CAST: Robert Stattel, Marina Sirtis, Justin Theroux, Kyle Fabel, Nick Wyman, Eric Evenson.

GHOSTS by Henrik Ibsen; Translation by Gerry Bamman, Irene B. Berman; Director, Mark Lamos; Sets, Christopher Barreca; Costumes, Susan Hilferty; Lighting, Christopher Akerlind. CAST: Fiona Gallagher, Robert Breuler, Richard Easton, Kathleen Chalfant, Ian Kahn.

BLUES FOR AN ALABAMA SKY by Pearl Cleage; Director, Kenny Leon; Sets, Marjorie Bradley Kellogg; Costumes, Susan Mickey; Lighting, Ann G. Wrightson. CAST: Phylicia Rashad, Mark Young, Gary Yates, Deidrie N. Henry, Wendell W. Wright.

T. Charles Erickson, Jennifer Lester Photos

Carlin Glynn, Ralph Waite in *The Young Man from Atlanta*

Campbell Scott, Mary Beth Peil in *Hamlet*

HUNTINGTON THEATRE COMPANY

Boston, Massachusetts
Fourteenth Season

Producing Director, Peter Altman; Managing Director, Michael Maso; Press and Public Relations Representative, Martin Blanco.

TO KILL A MOCKINGBIRD by Christopher Sergel, based on the novel by Harper Lee; Director, Charles Towers; Sets, Bill Clarke; Costumes, Elizabeth Novak; Lighting, Jackie Manassee. CAST: Seana McKenna, Catherine Epstein, Myra Lucretia Taylor, Gustave Johnson, Caleb Mayo, Deena Mazer, Gabriel Levinson, Ross Bickell, Tom Stechschulte, Neshitt Blaisdell, Baxter Harris, Danny Johnson, Jack Willis, Blakely Braniff.

HAMLET by William Shakespeare; Director, Eric Simonson; Sets, Robert Brill; Costumes, Allison Reeds; Lighting, Nancy Schertler. CAST: Jamison Selby, Peter Crook, Rene Rivera, Dominic Fumusa, Jack Willis, Jordan Charney, Justin Heneveld, Tom McCarthy, David Cromwell, Campbell Scott, Mary Beth Peil, Natacha Roi, Kirsten Potter, Robert Devaney, Jason Ma, Robert Walsh.

IOLANTHE by W.S. Gilbert and Arthur Sullivan; Director, Larry Carpenter; Choreography, Daniel Pelzig; Sets, James Leonard Joy; Costumes, Mariann Verheyen; Lighting, Marcia Madeira. CAST: Brigid Brady, Roxann Parker, Jeanine Bowman, Marie-Laurence Danvers, Patti Allison, Ann Kittredge, Robert Gallagher, Cheryl Martin, Marc Heller, James Coelho, Brian Anderson, James Javore, Ashley Howard WIlkinson, Ed Dixon.

THE YOUNG MAN FROM ATLANTA by Horton Foote; Director, Peter Masterson; Sets, E. David Cosier; Costumes, Teresa Snider-Stein; Lighting, Christopher Akerlind. CAST: Ralph Waite, Devon Abner, Christina Burz, Seth Jones, Carlin Glynn, James Pritchett, Lynda Gravatt, Michael Lewis, Beatrice Winde.

SEVEN GUITARS by August Wilson; Director, Lloyd Richards; Sets, Scott Bradley; Costumes, Constanza Romero; Lighting, Christopher Akerlind. CAST: Michele Shay, Ruben Santiago-Hudson, Tommy Hollis, Viola Davis, Zakes Mokae, Keith David, Rosalyn Coleman.

Brigid Brady, Jeanine Bowman, Marie-Laurence Danvers,
Roxann Parker in *Iolanthe*

Pete Thelen, Stephanie Bettman in *Sweet and Low Down*

ILLINOIS THEATRE CENTER

Park Forest, Illinois
Twentieth Season

Artistic Director, Steve S. Billig; Managing Director, Etel Billig; Artistic Associates, Wayne Adams, Ta-Tanisha Payne, Jonathan Roark; Sets, Wayne Adams; Costumes, Mary Ellen O'Meara, Pat Decker; Lighting, Jonathan Roark.

FALSETTOS by William Finn & James Paline; Director, Steve S. Billig; Musical DIrector, Jonathan Roark; Choreography, Pete Thelen. CAST: Marc Moritz, Pamela Turlow, Mark Gerrard, Pete Thelen, Shelley Crosby, Erin Annarella, Adam Matasar, Bobby Schmidt.

VOICES IN THE DARK by John Pielmeier; Director, Wayne Adams. CAST: Kathlyn Miles, Martin Bedoian, Tony Carsella, Kevin Kennedy, Don Pohlhammer, Kathy Paradise, Diane Gaul.

SWEET AND LOW DOWN: THE SONGS OF GEORGE & IRA GERSHWIN ; Director, Steve S. Billig; Musical Director, Jonathan Roark; Choreography, Pete Thelen. CAST: Erin Annarella, Stephanie Bettman, Sonya Seng, Rob Langeder, Jay Johnson, Peter Thelen.

PARK YOUR CAR IN HARVARD YARD by Israel Horovitz; Director, Wayne Adams. CAST: Steve S. Billig, Judy McLaughlin, Morgan Fitch.

JAR THE FLOOR by Cheryl L. West; Director, Steve S. Billig. CAST: Irma P. Hall, Laura Collins, Paulette McDaniels, Bernadette Clarke, Diane Gaul, Juanita D. Wilson.

A THOUSAND CLOWS by Herb Gardner; Director, Etel Billig. CAST: Alan Kopischke, Sandy Morris, Bobby Schmidt, Adam Matasar, Wayne Adams, Howard Hahn, Steve S. Billig.

HEARTBEATS by Amanda McBroom; Director, Steve S. Billig; Musical Director, Jonathan Roark; Choreography, Pete Thelen. CAST: Shelley Crosby, Pete Thelen, Rebecca Kolber, Erin Annarella, Steven Anderson, Pat Fitch, Jay Johnson, Christopher Ptack.

Pamela Turlow, Adam Matasar, Mark Gerrard in *Falsettos*

Bernadette L. Clarke, Irma P. Hall, Paulette McDaniels
in *Jar the Floor*

Judy McLaughlin, Steve S. Billy in *Park Your Car in Harvard Yard*

LA JOLLA PLAYHOUSE

San Diego, California

Artistic Director, Michael Greif; Managing Director, Terrence Dwyer; Associate Artistic Director, Robert Blacker; Director-in-Residence, Des McAnuff; Communications Director, Joshua Ellis.

THE INVISIBLE CIRCUS; Created and Performed by Victoria Chaplin & Jean Baptiste Thierree; Lighting, Laura De Bernardis; Wardrobe & Properties, Chantal Ravaud, Olivier Ernoult.

CLOUD TECTONICS by Jose Rivera; Director, Tina Landau; Sets, Riccardo Hernandez; Costumes, Brandin Baron; Lighting, Anne Militello. CAST: Javi Mulero, Luis Antonio Ramos, Camilia Sanes.

A MIDSUMMER NIGHT'S DREAM by William Shakespeare; Director, Marion McClinton; Sets, Robert Brill; Costumes, Paul Tazewell; Lighting, Christopher Akerlind. CAST: Duane Boutte, Joshua W. Coleman, Kent Davis, Loretta Devine, Carla Harting, Matthew Hoverman, Lisa Louise Langford, Mark Christopher Lawrence, Marissa Perez, Wendell Pierce, Akili Prince, Giovanni Pucci, Angela Reed, Erin Ryan, Keith Randolph Smith, Malcolm-Jamal Warner.

SLAVS!: THINKING ABOUT THE LONGSTANDING PROBLEMS OF VIRTUE & HAPPINESS by Tony Kushner; Director, Michael Greif; Sets/Costumes, Mark Wendland; Lighting, James F. Ingalls. CAST: Robin Bartlett, John Campion, Randy Danson, Jonathan Fried, Cristina Hussong, Callie Thorne.

AN ALMOST HOLY PICTURE by Heather McDonald; Director, Michael Mayer; Sets, Michelle Riel; Costumes, Norah L. Switzer; Lighting, Kevin Adams. CAST: David Morse.

FAUST; Music/Lyrics/Book, Randy Newman; Director, Michael Greif; Choreography, Lynne Taylor-Corbett; Sets, James Youmans; Costumes, Mark Wendland; Lighting, Christopher Akerlind; Orchestrations, Michael Roth CAST: H. Clent Bowers, Jonathan Brody, Andre Carthen, Joshua W. Coleman, Kurt Deutsch, Shelley Dickinson, Brian Evers, David Garrison, Melissa Haizlip, Erin Hill, Michael Hune, Melissa Jones, Ken Page, Marissa Perez, Michael Potts, Daphne Rubin-Vega, Erin Ryan, Lindsay Marie Sablan, Sherie Rene Scott, Christopher Sieber, Bellamy Young.

Ken Howard Photos

David Garrison, Kurt Deutsch, Ken Page in *Faust*

Jean Baptiste Thierrée, Victoria Chaplin in *The Invisible Circus*

David Morse in *An Almost Holy Picture*

Duane Boutté, Lisa Louise Langford, Malcolm-Jamal Warner in
A Midsummer's Night 's Dream

LONG WHARF THEATRE

New Haven, Connecticut
Thirty-first Season

Artistic Director, Arvin Brown; Executive Director, M. Edgar Rosenblum; Artistic Adminstrator, Janice Muirhead; General Manager, John Conte; Director of Marketing & Development, Pamela Tatge; Press, Jeffrey Fickes.

AS YOU LIKE IT by William Shakespeare; Director, John Tillinger; Sets, Ming Cho Lee; Costumes, Marcia Dixcy; Lighting, Brian Nason. CAST: Bernard K. Addison, Steve Bassett, Helmar Augustus Cooper, Edmund C. Davys, Tim Donohue, Patrick Garner, Sean Haberle, Denis Holmes, David Kear, Barry McMurtrey, Kathleen McNenny, Annie Meisels, Ntare Mwine, Kristine Nielsen, James Michael Nolan, Ylonda Powell, Pedro Porro, Elizabeth Meadows Rouse, John Gould Rubin, Lori J. Weaver.

DENIAL (World Premiere) by Peter Sagal; Director, Arvin Brown; Sets, Marjorie Bradley Kellogg; Costumes, David Murin; Lighting, Richard Nelson. CAST: Starla Benford, Geoffrey P. Cantor, Bonnie Franklin, Sol Frieder, Alan Mandell, Max Wright.

THE AMEN CORNER by James Baldwin; Director, Seret Scott; Sets, Michael Yeargan; Costumes, Karen Perry; Lighting, Pat Collins. CAST: Mary Alice, Rosanna Carter, Caroline Stefanie Clay, Victoria Dancy, Brenda Denmark, Lloyd Goodman, Jackie Miller, Aleta Mitchell, Barbara Montgomery, Tony Moss, Gregorie Mouning, Ron O'Neal, Ylonda Powell, Petie Trigg Seale, Charles Turner, Glenn Turner.

A SONG AT TWILIGHT by Noel Coward; Director, Arvin Brown; Sets, Hugh Landwehr; Costumes, Jess Goldstein; Lighting, Dennis Parichy. CAST: Joyce Ebert, Rochelle Oliver, Stephen Turner, Fritz Weaver.

ALMOST IN THE TIMING by David Ives; Director, Gordon Edelstein; Sets, James Youmans; Costumes, Candice Donnelly; Lighting, Donald Holder. CAST: Tim Choate, Martin Garcia, Julia Gibson, Ann McDonough, Eve Michelson, Richard Nagel, Robert Sella.

I LOVE YOU, YOU'RE PERFECT, NOW CHANGE; Book/Lyrics, Joe DiPietro; Music, Jimmy Roberts; Director, Joel Bishoff; Sets, Neil Peter Jampolis; Costumes, Candice Donnelly; Lighting, Mary Louise Geiger. CAST: Jordan Leeds, Robert Roznowski, Jennifer Simard, Melissa Weil.

TWILIGHT: LOS ANGELES, 1992; Conceived, Written and Performed by Anna Deavere Smith; Director, Sharon Ott; Sets, Christopher Barreca; Costumes, Candice Donnelly; Lighting, Pat Collins.

Stage II

ROBBERS by Lyle Kessler; Director, Marshall W. Mason; Sets, Loren Sherman; Costumes, Laura Crow; Lighting, Richard Nelson. CAST: Kira Arne, Paul Ben-Victor, Katherine Hiler, Judd Hirsch, Robert Hogan, Peter Rini.

LET'S DO IT (Workshop Production); Music/Lyrics, Cole Porter; Book, A.R. Gurney; Director, John Tillinger; Choreography, David Marques. CAST: Steve Barton, Robert Cary, Jennifer Clippinger, Jennifer Frankel, Donald Grody, Sean Martin Hingston, Shannon Lewis, Kimberly Lyon, Caroline McMahon, Gregory Mitchell, Maureen Moore, Ruth Williamson.

T. Charles Erickson Photos

Bonnie Franklin, Max Wright in *Denial*

Rochelle Oliver, Fritz Weaver, Joyce Ebert in *A Song at Twilight*

Jennifer Clippinger, Shannon Lewis, Maureen Moore,
Jennifer Frankel, Kimberly Lyon in *Let's Do It*

Tim Choate, Julia Gibson in *Almost All in the Timing*

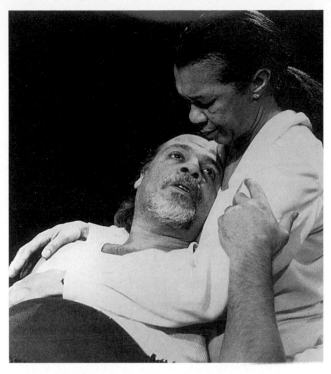

Ron O'Neal, Mary Alice in *The Amen Corner*

Anna Deavere Smith in *Twilight: Los Angeles*

Kathleen McNenny, Kristine Nielson in *As You Like It*

Kira Arné, Peter Rini in *Robbers*

Robert Roznowski, Jennifer Simard, Jordan Leeds, Melissa Weil
in *I Love You, You're Perfect, Now Change*

183

Kathryn Jaeck, David Studwell in *The New Yorkers*

MARRIOTT'S LINCOLNSHIRE
THEATRE

Lincolnshire, Illinois

Artistic Director, Dyanne Earley; Executive Producer, Kary M. Walker; Associate Producer, Terry James; Sets, Thomas M. Ryan; Costumes, Nancy Missimi; Lighting, Diane Ferry Williams, Kenneth Moore.

THE NEW YORKERS; Book, Herbert Fields; Music/Lyrics, Cole Porter; Based on a story by Peter Arno and E. Ray Goetz; Directors, Anthony J. Stimac, Dyanne Earley; . CAST: Kathryn Jaeck, David Studwell, Paula Scrofano, Ray Frewen, Kelli Cramer, Alan Ball, Angela Berra, Todd Petersen, Stephen P. Full, Brian Herriott, Pamela Harden, Ronald Heaton, Leisa Mather, Kelly Etter, Jennifer Lupp, Tait Runnfeldt, Rob Rahn, Brian Herriott, Paul Sullenger, Matthew Orlando, Danny Vacarro.

AND THE WORLD GOES 'ROUND; Music, John Kander; Lyrics, Fred Ebb; Conceived by Scott Ellis, Susan Stroman, David Thompson; Director/Choreography, David H. Bell. CAST: Rick Boynton, Mary Ernster, Heather Headley, Kingsley Leggs, Alene Robertson, Kathy Santen, Ron Sharpe.

MS. CINDERELLA; Book, Sean Grennan, Kathy Santen; Music, Michael Duff; Lyrics, Cheri Coons; Director, Joe Leonardo. CAST: Nancy Voigts, Rick Boynton, James FitzGerald, Carol Kuykendall, David New, Bradley Mott, Iris Lieberman, Catherine Lord, Jill Walmsley, Iris Leiberman, Jill Walmsley, Kevin Earley, Julie Ann Emery, Kelli Crmaer, Mark G. Hawbecker, Aaron Thielen, Blake Hammond, Scott Calcagno, Stephen P. Full, Elizabeth Gelman, Joan Krause, Sophia Thomas.

ELEANOR: AN AMERICAN LOVE STORY; Book, Jonathan Bolt; Music, Thomas Tierney; Lyrics, John Forster; Director, Joe Leonardo; Choreography, Rob Rahn. CAST: Anne Kanengeiser, Larry Yando, Joel Hatch, Ann Whitney, Don Forston, Kelly Prybycien, Kathy Santen, Jessie Fisher, Alene Robertson, Bernie Yvon, Ronald Keaton, Judy Dery, Robert C. Torri, Stephen P. Full, Roberta Duchak, Kevin Earley, Aaron Thielen, David Kreppel, Kim Mallery.

HEARTBEATS; Book, Music and Lyrics, Amanda McBroom; Created by Amanda McBroom and Bill Castellino; Additional Music, Gerald Sternbach, Michele Brourman, Tom Snow, Craig Safan; Director, Dyanne Earley; Choreography, Robin Kersey-Dickerson. CAST: Shannon Cochran, Brian Robert Mani, Jessica Boevers, Bernie Yvon, Joan Krause, Kelli Cramer, Aaron Thielen, Rob Rahn.

HELLO, DOLLY!; Book, Michael Stewart; Music/Lyrics, Jerry Herman; Director, Dominic Missimi; Choreography, Karen Azenberg. CAST: Alene Robertson, Todd Petersen, Susan Moniz, Jeff Dumas, Debbie Laumand, Joel Hatch, Iris Lieberman, Kevin Earley, Rachel Rockwell, Don Forston, Terrance L. Barber, Stacey Flaster, Ron J. Hutchins, Robin Kersey-Dickerson, Simon Lewis, Joseph M. Killilea, Philip Masterton, Robn Rahn, Jennifer Rosin, Aaron Thielen, Annette Thurman.

184

Carol Kuykendall, Nancy Voigts in *Ms. Cinderella*

Anne Kanengeiser, Joel Hatch, Larry Yando in *Eleanor*

Aaron Thielen, Shannon Cochran, Kelli Cramer in *Heartbeats*

MCCARTER THEATRE

Princeton, New Jersey

Artistic Director, Emily Mann; Managing Director, Jeffrey Woodward; General Manager, Kathleen Kund Nolan; Marketing Director, David Mayhew; Publicist/Press Director, Daniel Y. Bauer.

PRIVATE LIVES by Noel Coward; Director, Stephen Wadsworth; Sets, Thomas Lynch; Costumes, Candice Donnelly; Lighting, Peter Kaczorowski. CAST: Jennifer Dundas, Jeff Woodman, Mark Capri, Margaret Welsh, Marceline Hugot.

VALLEY SONG by Athol Fugard; Director, Fugard; Sets/Costumes, Susan Hilferty; Lighting, Dennis Parichy. CAST: Lisa Gay Hamilton, Athol Fugard.

A CHRISTMAS CAROL by Charles Dickens; Adaptation, David Thompson; Director, Padraic Lillis (based on original direction by Scott Ellis); Composer, Louis Rosen; Choreography, Williamichael Badolato; Sets, Michael Anania; Costumes, Lindsay W. Davis; Lighting, Peter Kaczorowski. CAST: Robin Chadwick, Kim Brockington, Donna Davis, Anthony Fusco, Erika L. Heard, John Hickok, Polly Pen, Jared Reed, Mary Testa, Karen Tsen Lee, Peter Van Wagner, Gordon Joseph Weiss, Michael Winther.

GREENSBORO (A REQUIEM) (World Premiere) by Emily Mann; Director, Mark Wing-Davey; Sets, Robert Brill; Costumes, Catherine Homa-Rocchio; Lighting, Pat Collis. CAST: Michael Countryman, Jeffrey DeMunn, Jon DeVries, Lisa Eichhorn, Deborah Hedwall, Philip Seymour Hoffman, Robert Jason Jackson, Stanley Wayne Mathis, Angie Phillips, Myra Lucretia Taylor, Carol Woods.

THE MISANTHROPE by Moliere; Translator, Richard Wilbur; Director, Andre Ernotte; Choreography, Williamichael Badolato; Sets, Douglas Stein; Costumes, Martin Pakledinaz; Lighting, Michael Chybowski. CAST: Jim Abele, Stephen Lang, John Ellison Conlee, Nancy Bell, Ted Rooney, Anne Torsiglieri, Rod McLachlan, Chris Hietikko, Gilbert Cruz, Valerie Leonard, Wally Dunn.

A DOLL HOUSE by Henrik Ibsen; Translators, Gerry Bamman, Irene B. Berman; Director, Emily Mann; Sets, Thomas Lynch; Costumes, Jennifer von Mayrhauser; Lighting, Pat Collins. CAST: Cynthia Nixon, David Lansbury, Deborah Hedwall, Mark Zeisler, Nicholas Hormann, Barbara Lester, Nina Humphrey.

AN ALMOST HOLY PICTURE by Heather McDonald; Director, Michael Mayer. CAST: David Morse.

PLAYING BY EAR: THREE PLAYS FOR RADIO:
TWO SISTERS AND A PIANO (World Premiere) by Nilo Cruz; Director, Loretta Greco. CAST: Gilbert Cruz, Adriana Inchaustegui, Judy Reyes, Maritza Rivera, Yul Vazquez.
THE BABY IN THE ICEBOX by James M. Cain; Adapter and Director, Ellen Sandler. CAST: Mark Deakins, Richard Thompson, Margaret Welsh.
THE DUMB CAKE (World Premiere) by Polly Pen; Director, Andre Ernotte. CAST: Alma Cuervo, Philip Lehl, Theresa McCarthy.

T. Charles Erickson, Gerry Goodstein Photos

Jeff Woodman, Margaret Welsh in *Private Lives*

Stephen Lang, Nancy Bell, Wendy Young in *The Misanthrope*

Cynthia Nixon, David Lansbury in *A Doll House*

185

MEADOW BROOK THEATRE

Rochester, Michigan

Artistic Director, Geoffrey Sherman; Managing Director, Gregg Bloomfield; Associate Director, Philip Locker; Public Relations Director, Michael C. Vigilant; Set Design, Peter W. Hicks, Carol Stavish; Lighting Design, Reid G. Johnson, Paul Wonsek; Costume Design, Barbara Jenks, Carol Wells-Day

THE THREE MUSKETEERS; Adapted by Charles Morey from Alexandre Dumas' novel; Director, Mr. Morey CAST: Timothy Altmeyer, Spencer Beckwith, Paul Hopper, Phillip Locker, Matthew Loney, Thomas D. Mahard, John Michael Manfredi, Richard Marlatt, Richard Matthews, Kathleen McCall, Maureen McDevitt, Christopher Mixon, Richard A. Schrot, Diana Van Fossen
LEND ME A TENOR by Ken Ludwig; Director, Geoffrey Sherman CAS: Alison Edwards, Phillip Locker, Laurie V. Logan, John Patrick Lowrie, Thomas D. Mahard, Kathleen McCall, Scott Mikita, Diana Van Fossen
A CHRISTMAS CAROL by Charles Dickens; Adapted/Directed by Geoffrey Sherman CAST: Mary Benson, Terry Heck, Nina Kircher, Phillip Locker, John Patrick Lowrie, Richard Marlatt, Thomas D. Mahard, John Michael Manfredi, Scott Mikita, Richard A. Schrot, Diana Van Fossen
CAMPING WITH HENRY AND TOM by Mark St. Germain; Director, T. Newell Kring CAST: Arthur J. Beer, Booth Colman, John Michael Manfredi, William J. Norris
THE PIANO LESSON by August Wilson; Director, Debra L. Wicks CAST: Ron Bobb-Semple, Danny Robinson Clark, Elain Graham, Tamika Lamison, Anthony Lamont, Eric A. Payne, Daniel Whitner
SHADOWLANDS by William Nicholson; Director, Geoffrey Sherman CAST: Arthur J. Beer, Laurie Brown, Bruce Burkhartsmeier, David Duchene, Joseph Haynes, Thomas D. Mahard, Richard Thomsen, Daina Van Fossen
CORPSE by Gerald Moon; Director, Phillip Locker CAST: Donald Ewer, Thomas D. Mahard, Patti Perkins, Peter Gregory Thomson

Rick Smith Photos

Timothy Altmeyer, Kathleen McCall in *The Three Musketeers*

Donald Ewer, Peter Gregory Thomson in *Corpse!*

Mary Benson, John Patrick Lowrie in *A Christmas Carol*

**William J. Norris, Booth Colman, Arthur J. Beer
in *Camping With Henry and Tom***

NEW JERSEY SHAKESPEARE FESTIVAL

Madison, New Jersey

Artistic Director, Bonnie J. Monte; Managing Director, Michael Stotts; Artistic Associate, Joe Discher; Press/Marketing Director, Mark Rossier

PRODUCTIONS (1996)

TWO GENTLEMEN OF VERONA; Music, Galt MacDermot; Lyrics, John Guare; Adapted by Mr. Guare and Mel Shapiro from Shakespeare's play; Director, Robert Duke; Sets, Rob Odorisio; Costumes, Ivan Ingermann; Lighting, Michael Giannitti; Musical Director, F. Wade Russo; Choreography, Carol Schuberg CAST: Andy Paterson, Todd Rosen, Keith Byron Kirk, Philip Hernandez, Dana M. Reeve, Barbara McCrane, Paul Mullins, John Cleary, Don Mayo, Tamara Tunie, Antonio del Rosario, Kim Barron, Clark S. Carmichael, Donna Hazel de Mesa, Cole Freeman, Simone Gordon, Jack Rose, Craig Skelton, Stephen Travis Wilson

OUR TOWN by Thornton Wilder; Director, Dylan Baker; Sets, Michael Vaughn Sims; Costumes, Maggie Morgan; Lighting, Scot Zielinski CAST: Dylan Baker, Kevin Cooney, Todd Rosen, Brian Taylor, Becky Ann Baker, Lisbeth Bartlett, Talmadge Lowe, Meg DeFoe, David Finkel, Jennifer Dundas, Paul Mullins, Edmont Genest, Karla Mason, John Derderian, Allison Krizner, Kate Schlesinger, Justin J. Steeve, Josh Adler, John Cleary

RICHARD III by William Shakespeare; Director, Daniel Fish; Sets, Christine Jones; Costumes, Kaye Voyce; Lighting, Scott Zielinski CAST: Michael Rudko, Robert Stattel, David Chandler, Jack Moran, Christopher Moran, Allison Krizner, Yolande Bavan, Judith Anna Roberts, Claire Lautier, Kate Skinner, Steve Wilson, Michael Rogers, Craig Wallace, Mark Nieblhur, Ian Helter, Matthew Daly

THE WINTER'S TALE by William Shakespeare; Director, Scottt Wentworth; Sets, Shelley Barclay; Costumes, Murell Horton; Lighting, Ken Moreland CAST: Josh Adler, Marion Adler, George Braun, Michael Buster, Philippe Chang, John Cleary, Vanessa Hidary, Walker Jones, Colette Kilroy, Allsion Krizner, Karla Mason, Paul Mullins, Andy Paterson, Herman Petras, Todd Rosen, Scott Whitehurst, Steve Wilson, Peter Zazzali

LEOCADIA by Jean Anouilh; Translation, Timberlake Wertenbaker; Director, Bonnie J. Monte; Sets, Rob Odorisio; Costumes, Murell Horton; Lighting, Steve Rosen CAST: Susan Cremin, Yolande Bavan, Ken Kliban, Meg DeFoe, Sanaz Hojreh, Justin J. Steeve, Thomas Barbour, Brian N. Taylor, Tom Brennan, Gregory Jackson, Robert LuPone, Ian Helfer

THE COMPLEAT WORKS OF WLLM SHKSPR (abridged) by Jess Borgeson, Adam Long, Daniel Singer; Director, Joe Discher; Sets, Michelle Malavet; Costumes, Hillary Guenther Wittich; Lighting, Charles Cameron CAST: Bradford Cover, Tom Delling, James Michael Reilly

Gerry Goodstein, Curtis Henderson Photos

Thomas Barbour, Yolande Bavan, Susan Cremin in *Leocadia*

Dylan Baker in *Our Town*

Philippe Chang, Allison Krizner in *The Winter's Tale*

OLD GLOBE THEATRE

San Diego, California
Sixty-first Season

Artistic Director, Jack O'Brien; Executive Producer, Craig Noel; Managing Director, Thomas Hall; Press, Ken Novice, David Tucker, Laura Lee Juliano

DANCING AT LUGHNASA by Brian Friel; Director, Andrew J. Traister; Sets, Ralph Funicello; Costumes, Marianna Elliott; Lighting, Barth Ballard CAST: Joel Anderson, Michael Learned, Katherine McGrath, Robin Pearson Rose, Sally Smythe, Erika Rolfsrud, James O'Neil, Richard Easton

OVERTIME by A.R. Gurney; Director, Nicholas Martin; Sets, Robert Morgan; Costumes, Michael Krass; Lighting, Kenneth Posner CAST: Joan McMurtrey, Bo Foxworth, Angela Lanza, Sterlin Macer Jr., Wendy Kaplan, David Aaron Baker, Tom Lacy, Nicholas Kepros, David Ledingham

THE DOCTOR IS OUT by Stephen Sondheim and George Furth; Director, Jack O'Brien; Sets, Douglas W. Schmidt; Costumes, Robert Wojewodski; Lighting, Kenneth Posner CAST: John Rubinstein, Becky Ann Baker, William Ragsdale, Elisa Llamido, Nestor G. Carbonell, Crystal Allen, Kandis Chappell, Josh Mostel, Terrence Mann, Chuck Cooper, Takayo Fischer, Nestor G. Carbonell, F.J. O'Neil

PUDDIN 'N PETE: FABLE OF A MARRIAGE by Cheryl L. West; Director, Gilbert McCauley; Sets, Greg Lucas; Costumes, Yslan Hicks; Lighting, Michael Gilliam CAST: Elizabeth Ommilami, Kevin E. Jones, Robert Barry Fleming, Cara Rene, Lisa Louise Langford, Jonathan Earl Peck, Mark Hutter

HEDDA GABLER by Henrik Ibsen; Adaptation, Christopher Hampton; Director, Sheldon Epps; Sets, Ralph Funicello; Costumes, Marianna Elliott; Lighting, Ashley York Kennedy CAST: Patricia Fraser, Trina Kaplan, John Leonard Thompson, CCH Pounder, Dawn Saito, Ron Glass, John Campion

PILGRIMS by Stephen Metcalfe; Director, Thomas Bullard; Sets, Greg Lucas, Robin Sanford Roberts; Costumes, Michael Krass; Lighting, Ashley York Kennedy CAST: William Anton, Tracey Middendorf, David Mann, Gregory Vignolle, Dann Florek, John Paul Saurine, Gary Brownlee, Elisa Llamido

UNCOMMON PLAYERS; Created/Directed by Dakin Matthews; Sets, Robin Sanford Roberts; Costumes, Andrew V. Yelusich; Lighting, Ashley York Kennedy CAST: Jonathan McMurtry, Lillian Garrett-Groag, Katherine McGrath, Richard Easton

HENRY IV by William Shakespeare; Director, Jack O'Brien; Adapted by Dakin Matthews; Sets, Ralph Funicello; Costumes, Lewis Brown; Lighting, Michael Gilliam CAST: Richard Easton, David Lansbury, Michael Brandt, Henry J. Jordan, James R. Winker, Vaughn Armstrong, Dakin Matthews, Katherine McGrath, Mark Harelik, Erika Rolsrud, James Joseph O'Neil, Russell Edge, Melissa Friedman, John Worley, David Natale, Leonard Stewart, Jonathan McMurtry, Eric Almquist, John Goodman, Steve Rankin, Don Sparks, Christopher Whenry, Mark Hill, Anna Cody, Crystal Allen, Tracey Atkins, Scott Eberlein, Scott Ferrara, Paul Fitzgerald, Andee Mason, Lina Patel, David Prentiss, Henny Russell

MISTER ROBERTS by Thomas Heggen and Joshua Logan; Director, Craig Noel; Sets, Ralph Funicello; Costumes, Andrew V. Yelusich; Lighting, Michael Gilliam CAST: Jack Winans, Robert Hays, William Roesch, Andrew J. Traister, Ramon Bieri, David Mann, Leo Stewart, David Natale, Paul Fitzgerald, Eric Almquist, James O'Neil, David Prentiss, John Walcutt, Larry Raben, Mark Hill, Michael Brandt, Andee Mason, Scott Ferrara, John Worley, Russell Edge, Scott Eberlein, Russell Edge, Scott Ferrara, Robert J. Ford, John Worley, Robert Adams, Chad M. Brockbrader, Glen A. Cook, Harold J. Kover, David F. Ronzello

John Goodman in *Henry IV*

Joan McMurtry, Nicholas Kepros in *Overtime*

Mary Ehlinger, Mary Murfitt, Lori Fischer, Jackie Sanders in *Cowgirls*

Takayo Fischer, Becky Ann Baker, John Rubinstein, Chuck Cooper, Kandis Chappell, Josh Mostel, Terrence Mann in *The Doctor is Out*

COWGIRLS; Conception/Music/Lyrics, Mary Murfitt; Book, Betsy Howie; Director/Choreographer, Eleanor Reissa; Musical Director, Pam Drews Phillips; Sets, James Noone; Costumes, Catherine Zuber; Lighting, Ken Posher CAST: Rhonda Coullet, Jackie Sanders, Betsy Howie, Mary Ehlinger, Lori Fischer, Mary Murfitt

THE GATE OF HEAVEN by Lane Nishikawa and Victor Talmadge; Director, Benny Sato Ambush; Sets, Ralph Funicello; Costumes, Susan Snowden; Lighting, Kevin Rigdon CAST: Lane Nishikawa, Victor Talmadge, Eric Almquist, James O'Neil, Erika Rolfsrud

TIME AND AGAIN; Music/Lyrics, Walter Edgar Kennon; Book, Kack Viertel based on Jack Finney's novel; Sets, John Conklin; Costumes, Catherine Zuber; Lighting, Peter Kaczorowski; Orchestrations, Chris Walker; Musical Director, Tom Helm CAST Anne Allgood, Terry Burrell, Danny Burstein, John Carpenter, Susan Cella, George Dvorsky, Sean Grant, Marc Heller, Nancy Hess, JoAnn M. Hunter, Joseph Kolinski, Jessica Molaskey, Roxann Parker, William Parry, Luis Perez, Jacqquelyn Piro, KT Sullivan, Andy Umberger, John Leslie Wolfe

THE SUBSTANCE OF FIRE by John Robin Baitz; Director, Andrew J. Traister; Sets, Robin Sanford Roberts; Costumes, Dione Lebhar; Lighting, Barth Ballard CAST: Melissa Friedman, Brian Drillinger, Harold Gould, Maury Ginsberg, Katherine McGrath

VOIR DIRE by Joe Sutton; Director, Craig Noel; Sets, Robin Sanford Roberts; Costumes, Dione Lebhar; Lighting, Barth Ballard CAST: Yolanda lloyd Delgado, Bill Geisslinger, Anne O'Sullivan, Robin Pearson Rose, Kimberly Scott, Andee Mason, Russell Edge, John Worley

PRIVATE LIVES by Noel Coward; Director, Sheldon Epps; Sets, Ralph Funicello; Costumes, Marianna Elliot; Lighting, Ashley York Kennedy CAST: Andee Mason, Robert Foxworth, Granville Van Dusen, Kandis Chappell, Lina Patel

Ken Howard, T. Charles Erickson Photos

Victor Talmadge, Lane Nishikawa in *The Gate of Heaven*

Leslie Uggams in *Call Me Madam*

Nancy Ringham, Clint Holmes, Adam Wade, Scott Irby-Rannier, LaChanze in *Comfortable Shoes*

Jan Neuberger, Judy McLane, Stephanie Pope, Paul Schoeffler, Glory Crampton, Judith McCauley in *Nine*

PAPER MILL PLAYHOUSE

Millburn, New Jersey
Sixty-sixth Season

Executive Producer, Angelo Del Rossi; Artistic Director, Robert Johanson; General Manager, Geoffrey Cohen; Set Design, Michael Anania; Costume Design, Gregg Barnes; Lighting Design, Tim Hunter, Tom Sturge, Mark Stanley, Richard Winkler; Press, Richard Kornberg

NINE; Music/Lyrics, Maury Yeston; Book, Arthur Kopit; Adaptation, Mario Fratti; Director, Robert Johanson; Musical Director, Jim Coleman; Choreography, D.J. Salisbury CAST: Gregory Butler, Glory Crampton, Celeste DiSimone, Matthew Fasano, Robin Irwin, Lauren Kennedy, Judith McCauley, Judy McLane, Jan Neuberger, Stephanie Pope, Paul Schoeffler, Sally Ann Tumas, Cheryl Allsion, Andrea Szucs, Pamela Jordan, Betsi Morrison, Renee Lawless-Orsini, Carol Denise, Adam Resnick, Ronald R. Dwenger, Tony Lehmenkuler, Paolo Montalban, Connie Pearson, Michael Oberlander, Kathy Robinson, Valerie Cutko, Kristine Zbornik, Wendelin Lockett, Anthony DeFilippo, Ivon Dominguez, Jonathan Giordano, Jason Daniel Kus, Brent Samuel Loree, Evan Newman, Christopher Spencer, Brandon Tee

DREAMGIRLS; Music, Henry Krieger; Lyrics/Book, Tom Eyen; Direction/Staging, Mark S. Hoebee; Choreography, Kenny Ingram CAST: Curtiss I' Cook, Herb Downer, LaTonya Holmes, Deirdre Lang, Angela Robinson, Marshall Titus, Alton Fitzgerald White, David A. White, Sharon Wilkins, Enga Davis, Monica L. Patton, Debra M. Walton, Cjay Hardy, Sondra M. Bonitto, Orlando Powers, Tyrone Grant, Edgard Gallardo, Kevyn Haile, Jay Poindexter, Dean A. Anderson, Steve Campanella, Simon Lewis, Michael Gerhart, Danielle Du Fore

YOU NEVER KNOW; Music/Lyrics, Cole Porter; Original Play, Sigfried Geyer, karl Farkas, Robert Katscher; Adaptation, Rowland Leigh; Additional Adaptation, Paul Lazarus; Director, Charles Repole; Choreography, Michael Lichtefeld; Musical Director, John Mulcahy CAST: Stephanie Douglas, Nancy Hess, Tom Ligon, Michael O'Steen, John Scherer, KT Sullivan

COMFORTABLE SHOES; Music/Lyrics, Clint Holmes and Nelson Kole; Book, Mr. Holmes; Director, Robert Johanson; Choreography, John Carrafa; Musical Director/Arrangements, Mr. Kole CAST: Cheryl Allison, Clint Holmes, Scott Irby-Ranniar, LaChanze, Natalie Dawn Oliver, Nancy Ringham, Adam Wade, David A. White

CALL ME MADAM; Music/Lyrics, Irving Berlin; Book, Howard Lindsay, Russel Crouse; Director, Charles Repole; Choreography, Daniel Stewart; Musical Director, Jim Coleman CAST: Leslie Uggams, Michael James Leslie, Hal Robinson, MichaelJohn McCann, J.B. Adams, Jonathan Hadley, Nancy Johnston, Neal Benari, Mark Baker, Dan LoBuono, Mark Manley, Jay Stuart, Vanessa Dorman, Seth Swoboda, James Allen Baker, Krissy Richmond, Gregory Butler, Elizabeth Green, Heather Laws, Deborah Leamy, Dana Lynn Mauro, Robin O'Leary, David Parker, Andrew Parkhurst, David Alan Quart, Andrea Szucs, Sarah Laine Terrell

EVITA; Music, Andrew Lloyd Webber; Lyrics, Tim Rice; Director/Choreography, Larry Fuller; Musical Director, Tim Stella CAST: Judy McLane, Christine Kienzle, Daniel C. Cooney, Raymond McLeod, Adelaide Mestre, Scott Hayward, Lenny Daniel, Kevin M. Burrows, David Roberts, Ronald L. Brown, Michael J. Farina, Russ Jones, David Lowenstein, Eric Knitel, R. Kim Jordan, Anna Marie Gutierrez, Jane Brockman, Lili Calahan, Christine Kienzle, Melissa Swender, Melissa Bell, Jane Brockman, Sterling Clark, Bill E. Dietrich, Scott Hayward, Jeremy Koch, Kelli Kruger, Adelaide Mestre, Denene Mulay, Stephen Nachamie, Josh Rhodes, Vincent Sandoval, Melissa Swender, Tara Tyrrell

Gerry Goodstein, Jerry Dalia, Joan Marcus Photos

PLAYHOUSE ON THE SQUARE

Memphis, Tennessee

Executive Producer, Jackie Nichols; Artistic Director, Ken Zimmerman; Lighting/Sound Design, Steve Crick; Costumes, Lisa Phillips-Phillips; Publicity Director, Natalie Jalenak

RESIDENT COMPANY: Josephine Hall, Kevin Jones, Jim Ostrander, DeJon Mayes, Jenny Odle
GUEST ARTISTS: Frederick Strother, John Pierce

PRODUCTIONS: *Keely and Du, From the Mississippi Delta, Five Guys Named Moe, Angels in America, Miss Evers' Boys, Tapestry, Beehive, Othello, The Lion The Witch And The Wardrobe, Free To Be You And Me, Month in the Country, The Sisters Rosensweig, Holiday Memories, Joined at the Head, Peter Pan, Forever Plaid, Waiting For Godot/Endgame, Broken Glass, Fantasticks*

Annalee Jeffries, Keir Dullea in *The Seagull*

Gwendolyn Mulamba, Kimberly Hawthorne, Crystal Laws Green

Angels in America at Playhouse on the Square

PLAYMAKERS REPERTORY COMPANY

Chapel Hill, North Carolina

Producing Director, Milly S. Barranger; Associate Producing Director, David Hammond; Managing Director, Zannie Giraud Voss; Production Manager, Kenneth J. Lewis; Sets/Costumes, Judy Adamson, Judith Chang, McKay Coble; Marketing/Press Director, Pam O'Connor

RESIDENT COMPANY: David Adamson, Michael Babbitt, David M. Brooks, Kevin M. Butler, Thomas D. Carr, Bostin Christopher, Kim Clay, Jennifer Blair Cornell, Dede Corvinus, Peter Dillard, Ray Dooley, Julie Fishell, Matt Fleming, Heather Grayson, Michelle Hendrick, Michael Hunter, David Jung, Timothy Klein, Rob Kramer, Nancy Lane, Brent Landgon, Julie Padilla, Susanna Rinehart, Shannon Roberts, Bruce Romans, John Rosenfeld, Sarah Shively, Joey Strimling, Joshua Tower, Craig Turner
GUEST ARTISTS/ACTORS: Timothy Altmeyer, Earl Baker Jr., Alyssa Bresnahan, Richard Burgwin, Celeste Ciulla, Keir Dullea, Joel Forsythe, Bo Foxworth, Crystal Laws Green, Kimberly Hawthorne, Annalee Jefferies, Conan McCarty, DeAnn Mears, Gwendolyn Mulamba, Mark Niebuhr, Patricia O'Connell, Kurt Rhoads, Nance Williamson, Rex Young
PRODUCTIONS: *Othello* by William Shakespeare; Director, David Hammond; *A Perfect Ganesh* by Terrence McNally; Director, Daniel Fish; *Beauty and the Beast* by Tom Huey; Conceived/Directed by Michael Wilson; Staged by Christopher R. Baker; *The Seagull* by Anton Chekhov; Translation, Paul Schmidt; Director, Michael Wilson; *From the Mississippi Delta* by Dr. Endesha Ida Mae Holland; Director, Tazewell Thompson; *Arcadia* by Tom Stoppard; Director, David Hammond

Will Owens Photos

Alma Cuervo, Paul Deboy, Brooks Almy in The Sisters Rosensweig

Michael James Reed, Keith Jochim in *The Life of Galileo*

REPERTORY THEATRE OF ST. LOUIS

Artistic Director, Steven Woolf; Managing Director, Mark D. Bernstein; Associate Artistic Director, Susan Gregg; Production Manager, Edward M. Coffield; Public Relations Manager, Judy Andrews

TO KILL A MOCKINGBIRD by Harper Lee; Adaptation, Christopher Sergel; Director, Charles Towers; Sets, Bill Clarke; Costumes, Elizabeth Novak; Lighting, Jackie Manassee CAST: Greta Lambert, Patrick Justin Vaughn, Stevia Wren Haller, Alan Mixon, Tom Stechschulte, Conni Blair, Zoe Vonder Haar, Gabriel Levinson, Whit Reichert, Ross Bickell, Darrell Rutlin, Rodney Clark, Deirdre Madigan, Danny Johnson
THE SISTERS ROSENSWEIG by Wendy Wasserstein; Director, Melia Bensussen; Sets, Linda Buchanan; Costumes, Dorothy L. Marshall; Lighting, Max De Volder CAST: Anne Devereaux Vega, Alma Cuervo, Judith Roberts, Paul DeBoy, Stan Lachow, Brooks Almy, Nathan Cummings, Joneal Joplin
SHE LOVES ME; Music, Jerry Bock; Lyrics, Sheldon Harnick; Book, Joe Masteroff; Director, Victoria Bussert; Choreography, Daniel Stewart ; Sets, John Ezell; Costumes, James Scott; Lighting, Peter E. Sargent CAST: Gibby Brand, Christopher Windom, Dorothy Stanley, Brian Sutherland, Robin Haynes, Joneal Joplin, Donna English, Eric van Baars, Laurent Giroux, Hunter Bell, Gavan Palmer, M. Kathryn Quinlan, Marci Reid, Sharon Kay White
THREE TALL WOMEN by Edward Albee; Director, Susan Gregg; Set, John Wright Stevens; Costumes, James Scott; Lighting, Phillip Monat CAST: Judith Roberts, Darrie Lawrence, Susan Ericksen, Brian A. Peters
THE LIFE OF GALILEO by Bertolt Brecht; Translation, David Hare; Director, Steve Woolf; Sets, John Ezell; Costumes, Dorothy L. Marshall; Lighting, Phillip Monat CAST: Keith Jochim, Gabriel Levinson, Carol Schultz, Robert Fente, Eric Forsythe, Joe Palmieri, Susan Ericksen, Drew Sobey, Whit Reichert, John Grassilli, Alan Knoll, Philip M. Coffield, Anderson Matthews, Norbert Butz, Michael James Reed, Richard Esvang, Brian A. Peters, Gary Glasgow, Scott De Broux, St. Louis Arches
MISALLIANCE by George Bernard Shaw; Director, John Going; Set, James Wolk; Costumes, J. Bruce Summers; Lighting, Howard Werner CAST: Michael Booth, Timothy Reynolds, Katherine Leask, June Gibbons, Richard Ooms, Charles Antalosky, Bob Kirsh, Corinna May, Timothy Gulan
MISSISSIPPI SUGAR by Randy Redd; Conceived/Adapted from stories by Lewis Nordan; Director, Martin LaPlatney; Set, Arthur Ridley; Costumes, Clyde Ruffin; Lighting, Glenn Dunn CAST: Randy Redd, Paula Newsome, Ken Triwush, Lori Putnam, Bernie Sheredy, Spike McClure
SCOTLAND ROAD by Jeffrey Hatcher; Director, Tom Martin; Set, William F. Schmiel; Costumes, Louis Bird; Lighting, Mark Wilson CAST: Bruce Longworth, Beirdre Madigan, Cheryl Gaysunas, Billie Lou Watt
GHOSTS by Henrik Ibsen; Adaptation, Anthony Clarvoe; Director, John Dillon; Set/Costumes, Lindsay W. Davis; Lighting, Max De Volder CAST: Pilar Witherspoon, Robert Elliott, Joneal Joplin, Peggy Friesen, Matthew Rauch

Judy Andrews Photos

Randy Redd, Spike McClure in *Mississippi Sugar*

Pamela Tyson, Matte Osian in *A Streetcar Named Desire*

(clockwise from top right), **Melinda Gilb, Susan Mosher, Sharon Murray, Linda Libby, Vanessa Townsell-Crisp, Kate Kiley** in *Six Women with Brain Death*

SAN DIEGO REPERTORY THEATRE

San Diego, California
Twentieth Season

SUDS by Melinda Gilb, Steve Gunderson, Will Roberson, Bryan Scott; Director/Choreography, Javier Velasco; Musical Director, William Doyle; Sets, Alan Okazaki; Costumes, Gregg Barnes; Lighting, Scott O'Donnell CAST: Melinda Gilb, Steve Gunderson, Susan Mosher, Shana Wride
THE TRUE HISTORY OF COCA-COLA IN MEXICO by Patrick Scott and Aldo Velasco; Director, Amy Gonzalez; Set, Victoria Petrovich; Costumes, Cheryl Lindley, Lighting, Brenda Berry CAST: Ron Campbell, Herbert Siguenza
A CHRISTMAS CAROL by Charles Dickens; Adaptation, Douglas Jacobs; Director, Mr. Jacobs, Javier Velasco; Sets, Michelle Riel; Costumes, Nick Reid; Lighting, John Philip Martin CAST: Priscilla Allen, Lisa Martinez Archibeque, Katherine Richards Brunson, Darla Cash, Doren Elias, Steve Gouveia, Steve Gunderson, Paul James Kruse, Michele McConnell, Megan Nimura, Kellie Evans-O'Connor, Dewain Michell Robinson, Jenny Selner, James R. Winker, Shana Wride
A STREETCAR NAMED DESIRE by Tennessee Williams; Director, Sam Woodhouse; Sets, Nya Patrinos, Michelle Riel; Costumes, Mary Larson; Lighting, John Philip Martin CAST: Fred Biven, Bill Dunnam, Ruben Flores, Sabrina LeBeauf, Wendel Lucas, Catalina Maynard, Stan Mott, Matte Osian, Sylvia M'Lafi Thompson, Pamala Tyson
6 WOMEN WITH BRAIN DEATH or *Expiring Minds Want to Know!* by Cheryl Benge, Christy Brandt, Rosanna E. Coppedge, Valerie Fagan, Ross Freese, Mark Houston, Sandee Johnson, Peggy Pharr Wilson; Music/Lyrics, Mr. Houston; Director, Sam Woodhouse; Music Director, William Doyle; Choreography, Steve Anthony; Sets, Victoria Petrovich; Costumes, Cheryl Lindley; Lighting, Scott O'Donnell CAST: Melinda Gilb, Kate Kiley, Linda Libby, Susan Mosher, Sharon Murray, Vanessa Townsell-Crisp

Ken Jacques Photos

Harry Groener, Nike Doukas in *Arms and the Man*

SOUTH COAST REPERTORY

Costa Mesa, California

Producing Artistic Director, David Emmes; Artistic Director, Martin Benson; Managing Director, Paula Tomei; Production Manager, Michael Mora; Marketing/Communications Director, Naomi Grabel

DIRECTORS: Martin Benson, David Chambers, Barbara Damashek, David Emmes, Jose Cruz Gonzalez, John-David Keller, Sharon Ott, Mark Rucker, David Warren, Diane Wynter

ACTORS: Hope Alexander-Willis, Edna Alvarez, Christine Avila, Marco Barricelli, Robert Patrick Benedict, Fran Bennett, Bibi Besch, Ron Boussom, Amanda Carlin, Jane Carr, Jefrey Alan Chandler, Emily Chase, Tom Chick, Steven Culp, Nike Doukas, Richard Doyle, John Ellington, David Fenner, Patricia Fraser, Julie Fulton, George Galvan, Lillian Garrett-Groag, Lynne Griffin, Harry Groener, Cissy Guerrero, Julie Hagerty, Sala Iwamatsu, John-Fredrick Jones, Jane Kaczmarek, Cindy Katz, Matt Keeslar, John-David Keller, Sally Kemp, Dian Kobayashi, Art Koustik, Emily Kuroda, Hal Landon Jr., Michael McFall, Katherine McGrath, Matt McGrath, Kate McLaughlin, Ben Livingston, Bill Mondy, Richard Montoya, James Newcomb, Scott Nielson, Lane Nishikawa, Jim Norton, Deirdre O'Connell, Michael O'Hagan, Jennifer Parsons, Melinda Peterson, Phil Proctor, Devon Raymond, Daniel Reichert, Douglas Rowe, Ricardo Salinas, Mikael Salazar, Susannah Schulman, Howard Shangraw, Douglas Sills, Sab Shimono, Laurel Smith, Richard Soto, Eric Steinberg, Hisa Takakawa, Barbara Tarbuck, Jodi Thelen, Dan Took, Livia Ann Trevino, Deborah Van Valkenburgh, Teresa Velarde, Bradley Whitford, Alicia Wollerton, Laurie Woolery, Annie Yee

PRODUCTIONS: *She Stoops to Folly* by Tom Murphy, *Raised in Captivity* by Nicky Silver, *Ballad of Yachiyo* by Philip Kan Gotanda, *Taming of the Shrew* by William Shakespeare, *New England* by Richard Nelson, *Arms and the Man* by George Bernard Shaw, *A Christmas Carol* by Charles Dickens, Adaptation, Jerry Patch, *The Things You Don't Know* by David Hollander, *The Interrogation of Nathan Hale* by David Stanley Ford, *Three Viewings* by Jeffrey Hatcher, *If We Are Women* by Joanna McClelland Glass, *A Mess of Plays by Chris Durang, La Posada Magica* by Octavio Solis

Henry DiRocco Photos

Richard Doyle, Matt Keeslar in
The Interrogation of Nathan Hale

Susannah Schulman, Cindy Katz in
The Taming of the Shrew

Jodi Thelen, Amanda Carlin, Howard Shangraw,
Robert Patrick Benedict in *A Mess of Plays by Chris Durang*

194

James Gammon, Ted Levine, Ethan Hawke in *Buried Child*

STEPPENWOLF THEATER COMPANY

Chicago, Illinois

Artistic Director, Randall Arney; Managing Director, Stephen Eich

BURIED CHILD by Sam Shepard; Director, Gary Sinise; Sets, Robert Brill, Costumes, Allison Reeds; Lighting, Kevin Rigdon CAST: Ethan Hawke, James Gammon, Ted Levine, Kellie Overbey, Lois Smith, Leo Burmester, Jim Mohr
AS I LAY DYING; Adapted by Frank Galati from the William Faulkner novel; Director, Mr. Galati; Set/Costumes, John Paoletti; Lighting, James F. Ingalls CAST: Cynthia Baker, Ian Barford, Christopher Bauer, Robert Breuler, Dana Eskelson, Neil Flynn, Marilyn Dodds Frank, Pat Healy, Steve Key, Jay Kiecolt-Wahl, Mariann Mayberry, Bill McGough, Nick Offerman, Jeff Perry, Robert Radkoff-Ek, Michael Sassone, Craig Spidle, Heidi Stillman, Marc Vann, Will Zahr
THE LIBERTINE by Stephen Jeffreys; Director, Terry Johnson; Sets, Derek Mclane; Costumes, Virginia C. Johnson; Lighting, Kevin Rigdon CAST: John Malkovich, Alan Wilder, Marc Vann, Steve Key, Mariann Mayberry, Lisa Nicholls, Ian Barford, Martha Plimpton, Si Osborne, Carole Gutierrez, Missi Pyle, Francis Guinan, Christopher Hainsworth, Pat Healy
SUPPLE IN COMBAT by Alexandra Gersten; Director, Max Meyer; Set, Narelle Sissons; Costumes, Laura Cunningham; Lighting, Kevin Rigdon CAST: Martha Lavey, John Mahoney, Linda Stephens, Ron Dean, David Alan Novak

Michael Brosilow Photos

Steve Kay, Marc Vann, John Malkovich
in *The Libertine*

195

VIRGINIA STAGE COMPANY

Norfolk, Virginia

Artistic Director, Charlie Hensley; Managing Director, Steven Martin; Marketing Director, Lori Schick

BLITHE SPIRIT by Noel Coward; Director, Charlie Hensley; Set, Dex Edwards; Costumes, Patricia Garel; Lighting, Liz Lee CAST: Deborah Stenard, Corinna May, David McCann, Richard Pelzman, Deborah Mayo, Betsy Palmer, Karla Hendrick
ONCE UPON THIS ISLAND; Music, Stephen Flaherty; Lyrics/Book, Lynn Ahrens; Director, Gerry McIntyre; Music Director, Kevin Wallace; Sets, Leonard Harman; Costumes, Howard Tsvi Kaplan; Lighting, Kenton Yeager CAST: Vanita Harbour, Michael Le Melle, John Eric Parker, Monica Pege, Stacey Russell, Sandye Smith, Dennis Stowe, Myra Lucretia Taylor, Dale E. Turner, Virginia Woodruff, Jim Weaver
HAMLET by William Shakespeare; Director, Charlie Hensley; Sets, Dex Edwards; Costumes, Susan E. Mickey; Lighting, Kenton Yeager CAST:Brad Paul Breckenridge, Adam R. Brown, Jonathan Brownlee, Lee Clodfelter, David DeBeck, David DeBesse, Shelley Delaney, Ed Hyland, Terry Jernigan, Deborah Kipp, Ethan Edward Marten, David McCann, Brett Porter, Scott Rollins, Connor Trinneer
A PENNY FOR THE GUY by Lanie Robertson; Director, Charlie Hensley; Sets, Chris Pickart; Costumes, Patricia Garel; Lighting, Liz Lee CAST: Ingrid MacCartney, Evan Bonifant, Ed Hyland
DEATHTRAP by Ira Levin; Director, Dex Edwards; Set, Rob Odorisio; Costumes, Patricia Garel; Lighting, Kenton L. Yeager CAST: Bruce Evers, Suzanna Hay, David DeBesse, Stefano Magaddino, Candy Aston-Dennis

Corinna May, David McCann in *Blithe Spirit* at at Virginia Stage Company

WAYSIDE THEATRE

Middletown, Virginia

Artistic Director, Christopher Owens; General Manager, Donna Johnson; Stage Manager, Kelly Mangis; Set Designer, Kevin Wall; Costume Designer, Dana Pinkston; Lighting Design, Kathleen Jackson; Musical Director, R. Mark Snedegar

LITTLE SHOP OF HORRORS; Music, Alan Menken; Lyrics, Howard Ashman; Director/Choreography, Ann Nieman CAST: Kim S. Goldfeder, Joshua Estrin, Joseph Parra, Joseph Beal, Herbert Mark Parker, Vincent Wares, Glenys Vargas, Suzanne Lindenblatt, Linda Chittick
NITE CLUB CONFIDENTIAL by Dennis Deal and Albert Evans; Director, Christopher Owens; Choreography, Ann Nieman CAST: Katherine Harber, Joseph Beal, Suzanne Lindenblatt, Joshua Estrin, Christopher Jackson
CHARLEY'S AUNT by Brandon Thomas; Director, Michael Haney CAST: Charlie Schroeder, Patrick Holland, Joseph Beal, Grant Neale, Vincent Wares, Dana Bate, Johanna Gerry, Kaleo Bird, Katherine Harber, Martha Libman, Leigh Anderson
GREETINGS by Tom Dudzick; Director, Christopher Owens CAST: Bruce Barney, Julie Mazzarella, Kathleen Goldpaugh, Dana Bate, Clark Middleton
TEN LITTLE INDIANS by Agatha Christie; Director, Christopher Owens CAST: Vincent Wares, Tamara Johnson, Jill Macy, Bruce Barney, Joseph Parra, Bruce Edward Barton, Bill Molesky, Dana Bate, Julie Mazzarella, Tod Williams, Leigh Anderson
DR. JEKYLL AND MISS HYDE by David DeBoy; Director, Christopher Owens CAST: Jill Macy, Bill Molesky, Bruce Barney, Tamara Johnson, Joseph Parra, Kathryn Dixon, Tod Williams, Kaleo Bird

John Westervelt Photo

Kim S. Goldfeder, Joshua Estrin in
Litt le Shop of Horrors at Wayside Theatre

NATIONAL TOURING COMPANY HIGHLIGHTS

AIN'T MISBEHAVIN'

Songs, Fats Waller; Based on an idea by Murray Horowitz and Richard Maltby Jr.; Director/Choreography, Arthur Faria; Set, John Lee Beatty; Costumes, Bob Mackie; Lighting, Pat Collins; Musical Director, William Foster McDaniel; Sound, Peter Fitzgerald; Presented by Pace Theatrical Group, Magic Promotions and Theatricals and Manny Kladitis in association with The Sterling/Winters Company; Press, Chris Boneau~Adrian Bryan-Brown

CAST
RUTH POINTER ANITA POINTER JUNE POINTER
EUGENE BARRY-HILL MICHAEL-LEON WOOLEY

A new production of the 1978 musical.
Joan Marcus Photos

Ruth Pointer in *Ain't Misbehavin'*

CAROUSEL

Music, Richard Rodgers; Lyrics/Book, Oscar Hammerstein; Director, Nicholas Hytner; Choreography, Sir Kenneth MacMillan, Jane Elliott; Sets/Costumes, Bob Crowley; Lighting, Paul Pyant; Sound, Steve Canyon Kennedy; Musical Director, Kevin Farrell; Stage Manager, Michael J. Passaro; Presented by Columbia Artists Management, Center Theatre Group, Jujamcyn Theatre Productions and Theatre Under the Stars in association with The Troika Organization and PACE Theatrical Group; Press, Anita Dloniak

CAST: Patrick Wilson (Billy), Sarah Uriarte (Julie), Sherry D. Boone (Carrie), Sean Palmer (Enoch), Rebecca Eichenberger (Nettie), Brett Rickaby (Jigger), Kate Buddeke, William Metzo, Dana Stackpole, Joseph Woelfel, Kristenelle Coronado, B.J. Crockett, Jasminn Ricketts

A new production of the 1945 musical drama.

Patrick Wilson, Sarah Uriarte in *Carousel*

DAMN YANKEES

Music/Lyrics, Richard Adler and Jerry Ross; Book, George Abbott and Douglas Wallop; Book Revisions/Director, Jack O'Brien; Choreography, Rob Marshall; Sets, Douglas W. Schmidt; Costumes, David C. Woolard; Lighting, David F. Segal; Sound, Jonathan Deans; Musical Director, Robert Hirschhorn; Presented by Workin' Man Films and PACE Theatrical Group; Press, Peter Cromarty/Theresa Burton

CAST: Jerry Lewis (Apllegate), Valerie Wright (Lola), David Elder (Joe Hardy), Susan Bigelow (Meg), Linda Gabler (Gloria), Dennis Kelly (Joe Boyd), Robert Lambert, Joseph R. Sicari, Jamie Ross, Amy Ryder, Mark Chmiel, Louis D. Giovannetti, Ned Hannah, R. Bradley Anderson, Ricky Armstrong, Karen Babcock, Bill Brassea, Bruce Anthony Davis, Michael Duran, Mark Esposito, John-Michael Flate, Mylinda Hull, Rod McCune, Amelia Prentice, Julie Prosser, Jill Slyter, Lyn Vaux

A new production of the 1955 musical comedy.
Carol Rosegg Photos

Jerry Lewis in *Damn Yankees*

J. G. Hertzler, Roddy McDowall in *Dial M for Murder*

Valerie Wright in *Damn Yankees*

DIAL M FOR MURDER

By Frederick Knott; Director, Edward Hastings
CAST: Roddy McDowall, Nancy Allen, John James, J.G. Hertzler

A new production of the 1952 mystery.

Shauna Hicks, Ralph Maccio in *How to Succeed in Business*

HOW TO SUCCEED IN BUSINESS WITHOUT REALLY TRYING

For creative credits see "Broadway-From Past Seasons" section; Tour Direction, Des McAnuff in association with Judy Minor; Musical Director, Randy Booth; Stage Manager, Susan Green; Presented by Dodger Productions and John F. Kennedy Center for the Performing Arts

CAST: Ralph Macchio (Finch), Shauna Hicks (Rosemary), Richard Thomsen (Bigley), Susan Fletcher (Smitty), Roger Bart (Frump), Pamela Blair (Hedy), Clif Thorn, Danny Rutigliano, Michael McEachran, John Deyle, Adam Turner, Lorna Shane, Tina Fabrique, Christopher Mixon, Paul Dobie, Blaine Mastalir, Jay Poindexter, Michael Cone, Jessica Sheridan, Wydetta Carter, Carol Lee Meadows

A new production of the 1961 musical comedy.

Joan Marcus Photos

AN INSPECTOR CALLS

By J.B. Priestley; Director, Stephen Daldry; Design, Ian MacNeil; Lighting, Rick Fisher; Stage Manager, Dan Hild; Presented by Noel Pearson, The Shubert Organization, Capital Cities/ABC, in association with Jospeh Harris; Press, Viator Associates

CAST: Susan Kellermann (Sybil), Kaye Kingston (Edna), Philip LeStrange succeeded by Stacy Keach (Arthur), David Andrew Macdonald (Gerald), Jane Fleiss (Sheila), Harry Carnahan (Eric), Sam Tsoutsouvas succeeded by John Lantz, Curt Hostetter, Kenneth Craham (Inspector Goode), Jeffrey Force succeeded by Zachary Freed (Boy)

A new production of a 1945 thriller.

J. P. Dougherty, Kelly Ebsary

LES MISERABLES

For creative credits see "Broadway-From Past Seasons" section; Tour Directors, John Caird and Trevor Nunn; Associate Director/Executive Producer, Richard-Jay Alexander; Musical Director, Robert S. Gustafson; Stage Managers, Gregg Kirsopp, Jim Badrak, Thom Shilling; Press, Bill Miller/Kevin Gerstein

CAST: Frederick C. Inkley succeeded by William Solo (Jean Valjean), David Masenheimer succeeded by Richard Kinsey (Javert), Anne Torsiglieri succeeded by Jacquelyn Piro (Fantine), Angela Pupello succeeded by Gina Feliccia, Jessica-Snow Wilson, Caren Lyn Manuel (Eponine), Barbara Russell succeeded by Jodie Langel (Cosette), Hayden Adams succeeded by Tom Donoghue (Marius), Gary Mauer succeeded by Robert Vernon (Enjolras), Gina Ferrall succeeded by Kelly Ebsary (Madame Thenardier), J.P. Dougherty (Thenardier), Eric Bennyhoff, Charles Bergell, William Paul Michals, Michael Oberlander, Jim Price, Todd Zamarripa, Brian Lynch, Mary Chesterman, Dave Hugo, Kelly Briggs, Ron Sharpe, Daniel Eli Friedman, Allison Briner, Anne Bueltman, Jessica Sheridan, Traci Lyn Thomas, Eileen Tepper, Lucy Vance, Joanna Young, Ashley Michelle Tisdale, Joanna Howard, Dave Hugo, Simon Pearl, Tre Roy

Tour opened in the Tampa Bay Performing Arts Center on November 30, 1988 and still touring into 1996.
Joan Marcus Photos

Anne Torsiglieri

200

Dedee Lynn Magno, Annalise Jone Wong

Dedee Lynn Magno, Matt Bogart

Thom Sesma

MISS SAIGON

For creative credits see "Broadway-From Past Seasons" section; Tour Director, Nicholas Hytner; Exexcutive Producers, Richard-Jay Alexander, Fred Hanson; Musical Director, Paul Raiman; Stage Manager, Lois Griffing; Press, Bill Miller/Janine Fawcett, Kevin Gerstein

CAST: Thom Sesma (Engineer), Matt Bogart (Chris), Deedee Lynn Magno (Kim), Cristina Paras succeeded by Alex Lee Tano (Kim for matinees), C.C. Brown (John), Anastasia Barzee (Ellen), Michael K. Lee (Thuy)Ciana Kikumi Calos-Nakano or Annalise Jane Wong (Tam), Michael John Balzarett, Kathlyn Lai Ling Ho (succeeding Tams), Sala Iwamatsu, Kristi Tomooka, Cristina Ablaza, Blythe Matsui, Jennifer O., Say Gan, Mary Ann Hu, Joyce Bautista, Alex Lee Tano, Charlene Carabeo, Richard Bassin, Jon E. Brandenberg, Will Chase, Cliftton Hall, Kurt Andrew Hansen, Damon Hill, Christopher Lee Michaels, Robb Edward Morris, J.T. Moye, Robert Orosco, Raymond Patterson, Rusty Reynolds, Amada Labez Cacho, Andrew Djang, Devanand N. Janki, Orville Mendoza, Moni Veluz, David Katei, Edmund A. Nalzaro, Jee Teo, Andrea Rivette, Brian Keith Fisher, Matt Jankowski, Melanie May Po, Robert Tatad

Tour opened in Seattle's Paramount Theatre on March 29, 1995 and still touring May 31, 1996.

Joan Marcus Photos

201

THE PHANTOM OF THE OPERA

For creative credits see "Broadway-From Past Seasons" section; Director, Harold Prince; Musical Director, Glenn Langdon; Stage Manager, Elisabeth Farwell; Press, Bill Miller

CAST: Grant Norman (Phantom), Adrienne McKeown succeeded by Diane Fratantoni (Christine), Sylvia Rhyne succeeded by Susan Facer (Christine at matinees), John Schroeder (Raoul), Geena L. Jeffries succeeded by Kelly Cae Hogan, Marilyn Caskey (Carlotta), David Cryer (Firmin), Roger E. DeWitt (Andre), Rebecca Judd, Paul Jacobsen, Ray Friedeck, Ilene Bergelson, Diana Gonzalez, John Dewar, Mark Agnes, Paul Berkolds, William R. Park, Stephen Len White, Jere Torkelsen, T.J. Myers, Keith Heinmann, james Conlin, Richard Toda, Tommy Schumacher, Cheryl Majercik, Martha Cares, Ann Hallbrook, Ann McMann, Gabrielyn Watson, Gloria Hodes, Emily Addona, Ursula Edwards, Elizabeth Nackley, Kristi Patricia, Laurie Volny, Michelle Lucci, Larry Adams, Fred Rose, Julie Schmidt

Tour opened in Seattle's Fifth Avenue Theatre on December 13, 1992 and still touring into 1996.

Joan Marcus Photos

WEST SIDE STORY

Music, Leonard Bernstein; Lyrics, Stephen Sondheim; Book, Arthur Laurents; Based on a conception of Jerome Robbins; Director/Choreography, Alan Johnson based on Robbins; Sets, Campbell Baird; Costumes, Irene Sharaff; Lighting, Nataska Katz; Sound, Otts Munderloh; Musical Director, Donald Chan; Stage Manager, Martin Gold; Presented by Barry Brown, Marvin A. Krauss, Irving Siders and the Booking Office; Press, Browne Zukow/Charles Zukow

CAST: H.E. Geer succeeded by Scott Carollo (Tony), Marcy Harriell (Maria), Natascia A. Diaz (Anita), Jamie Gustis (Riff), Vincent Zamora (Bernardo), Al DeCristo, Bernie Passeltiner, Jonathan Miller, Brent Sexton, Diana Laurenson, Charlie Brumbly, Lucio Fernandez, Lee Cherry, Joshua Bergasse, Robert Wersinger, Joseph H. Moscato, Bob Richard, Kimberely Kimble, Dore Manasevit, Michael Martino, Jason Dougherty, Bryan Crawford, Shane Jacobsen, Bryon Easley, Gary D. Ferguson, Natasha Harper, Michelle DeJean, Greta Martin, Eileen Kaden, Christiane Farr

A new production of the 1957 musical drama.

Joan Marcus Photos

Right: John Schroeder, Adrienne McGwan

Center: Marcy Harriell
Scott Carollo
Left: *The Jets*

1996 THEATRE WORLD
(OUTSTANDING NEW TALENT)

JORDAN BAKER
of *Suddenly Last Summer*

MICHAEL MCGRATH
of *Swinging on a Star*

ALFRED MOLINA
of *Molly Sweeney*

JOOHEE CHOI
of *The King and I*

KAREN KAY CODY
of *Master Class*

TIMOTHY OLYPHANT
of *The Monogamist*

ADAM PASCAL
of *Rent*

VIOLA DAVIS
of *Seven Guitars*

KATE FORBES
of *The School for Scandal*

LOU DIAMOND PHILLIPS
of *The King and I*

BRETT TABISEL
of *Big*

DAPHNE RUBIN-VEGA
of *Rent*

Jane Alexander

Marcus D'Amico

Marcia Gay Harden

1944-45: Betty Comden, Richard Davis, Richard Hart, Judy Holliday, Charles Lang, Bambi Linn, John Lund, Donald Murphy, Nancy Noland, Margaret Phillips, John Raitt
1945-46: Barbara Bel Geddes, Marlon Brando, Bill Callahan, Wendell Corey, Paul Douglas, Mary James, Burt Lancaster, Patricia Marshall, Beatrice Pearson
1946-47: Keith Andes, Marion Bell, Peter Cookson, Ann Crowley, Ellen Hanley, John Jordan, George Keane, Dorothea MacFarland, James Mitchell, Patricia Neal, David Wayne
1947-48: Valerie Bettis, Edward Bryce, Whitfield Connor, Mark Dawson, June Lockhart, Estelle Loring, Peggy Maley, Ralph Meeker, Meg Mundy, Douglass Watson, James Whitmore, Patrice Wymore
1948-49: Tod Andrews, Doe Avedon, Jean Carson, Carol Channing, Richard Derr, Julie Harris, Mary McCarty, Allyn Ann McLerie, Cameron Mitchell, Gene Nelson, Byron Palmer, Bob Scheerer
1949-50: Nancy Andrews, Phil Arthur, Barbara Brady, Lydia Clarke, Priscilla Gillette, Don Hanmer, Marcia Henderson, Charlton Heston, Rick Jason, Grace Kelly, Charles Nolte, Roger Price
1950-51: Barbara Ashley, Isabel Bigley, Martin Brooks, Richard Burton, Pat Crowley, James Daley, Cloris Leachman, Russell Nype, Jack Palance, William Smithers, Maureen Stapleton, Marcia Van Dyke, Eli Wallach
1951-52: Tony Bavaar, Patricia Benoit, Peter Conlow, Virginia de Luce, Ronny Graham, Audrey Hepburn, Diana Herbert, Conrad Janis, Dick Kallman, Charles Proctor, Eric Sinclair, Kim Stanley, Marian Winters, Helen Wood
1952-53: Edie Adams, Rosemary Harris, Eileen Heckart, Peter Kelley, John Kerr, Richard Kiley, Gloria Marlowe, Penelope Munday, Paul Newman, Sheree North, Geraldine Page, John Stewart, Ray Stricklyn, Gwen Verdon
1953-54: Orson Bean, Harry Belafonte, James Dean, Joan Diener, Ben Gazzara, Carol Haney, Jonathan Lucas, Kay Medford, Scott Merrill, Elizabeth Montgomery, Leo Penn, Eva Marie Saint

1954-55: Julie Andrews, Jacqueline Brookes, Shirl Conway, Barbara Cook, David Daniels, Mary Fickett, Page Johnson, Loretta Leversee, Jack Lord, Dennis Patrick, Anthony Perkins, Christopher Plummer
1955-56: Diane Cilento, Dick Davalos, Anthony Franciosa, Andy Griffith, Laurence Harvey, David Hedison, Earle Hyman, Susan Johnson, John Michael King, Jayne Mansfield, Sara Marshall, Gaby Rodgers, Susan Strasberg, Fritz Weaver
1956-57: Peggy Cass, Sydney Chaplin, Sylvia Daneel, Bradford Dillman, Peter Donat, George Grizzard, Carol Lynley, Peter Palmer, Jason Robards, Cliff Robertson, Pippa Scott, Inga Swenson
1957-58: Anne Bancroft, Warren Berlinger, Colleen Dewhurst, Richard Easton, Tim Everett, Eddie Hodges, Joan Hovis, Carol Lawrence, Jacqueline McKeever, Wynne Miller, Robert Morse, George C. Scott
1958-59: Lou Antonio, Ina Balin, Richard Cross, Tammy Grimes, Larry Hagman, Dolores Hart, Roger Mollien, France Nuyen, Susan Oliver, Ben Piazza, Paul Roebling, William Shatner, Pat Suzuki, Rip Torn
1959-60: Warren Beatty, Eileen Brennan, Carol Burnett, Patty Duke, Jane Fonda, Anita Gillette, Elisa Loti, Donald Madden, George Maharis, John McMartin, Lauri Peters, Dick Van Dyke
1960-61: Joyce Bulifant, Dennis Cooney, Sandy Dennis, Nancy Dussault, Robert Goulet, Joan Hackett, June Harding, Ron Husmann, James MacArthur, Bruce Yarnell
1961-62: Elizabeth Ashley, Keith Baxter, Peter Fonda, Don Galloway, Sean Garrison, Barbara Harris, James Earl Jones, Janet Margolin, Karen Morrow, Robert Redford, John Stride, Brenda Vaccaro
1962-63: Alan Arkin, Stuart Damon, Melinda Dillon, Robert Drivas, Bob Gentry, Dorothy Loudon, Brandon Maggart, Julienne Marie, Liza Minnelli, Estelle Parsons, Diana Sands, Swen Swenson
1963-64: Alan Alda, Gloria Bleezarde, Imelda De Martin, Claude Giraud, Ketty Lester, Barbara Loden, Lawrence Pressman, Gilbert Price, Philip Proctor, John Tracy, Jennifer West

Michael Hayden

Audra Ann McDonald

James Woods

1964-65: Carolyn Coates, Joyce Jillson, Linda Lavin, Luba Lisa, Michael O'Sullivan, Joanna Pettet, Beah Richards, Jaime Sanchez, Victor Spinetti, Nicolas Surovy, Robert Walker, Clarence Williams III

1965-66: Zoe Caldwell, David Carradine, John Cullum, John Davidson, Faye Dunaway, Gloria Foster, Robert Hooks, Jerry Lanning, Richard Mulligan, April Shawhan, Sandra Smith, Leslie Ann Warren

1966-67: Bonnie Bedelia, Richard Benjamin, Dustin Hoffman, Terry Kiser, Reva Rose, Robert Salvio, Sheila Smith, Connie Stevens, Pamela Tiffin, Leslie Uggams, Jon Voight, Christopher Walken

1967-68: David Birney, Pamela Burrell, Jordan Christopher, Jack Crowder (Thalmus Rasulala), Sandy Duncan, Julie Gregg, Stephen Joyce, Bernadette Peters, Alice Playten, Michael Rupert, Brenda Smiley, Russ Thacker

1968-69: Jane Alexander, David Cryer, Blythe Danner, Ed Evanko, Ken Howard, Lauren Jones, Ron Leibman, Marian Mercer, Jill O'Hara, Ron O'Neal, Al Pacino, Marlene Warfield

1969-70: Susan Browning, Donny Burks, Catherine Burns, Len Cariou, Bonnie Franklin, David Holliday, Katharine Houghton, Melba Moore, David Rounds, Lewis J. Stadlen, Kristoffer Tabori, Fredricka Weber

1970-71: Clifton Davis, Michael Douglas, Julie Garfield, Martha Henry, James Naughton, Tricia O'Neil, Kipp Osborne, Roger Rathburn, Ayn Ruymen, Jennifer Salt, Joan Van Ark, Walter Willison

1971-72: Jonelle Allen, Maureen Anderman, William Atherton, Richard Backus, Adrienne Barbeau, Cara Duff-MacCormick, Robert Foxworth, Elaine Joyce, Jess Richards, Ben Vereen, Beatrice Winde, James Woods

1972-73: D'Jamin Bartlett, Patricia Elliott, James Farentino, Brian Farrell, Victor Garber, Kelly Garrett, Mari Gorman, Laurence Guittard, Trish Hawkins, Monte Markham, John Rubinstein, Jennifer Warren, Alexander H. Cohen (Special Award)

1973-74: Mark Baker, Maureen Brennan, Ralph Carter, Thom Christopher, John Driver, Conchata Ferrell, Ernestine Jackson, Michael Moriarty, Joe Morton, Ann Reinking, Janie Sell, Mary Woronov, Sammy Cahn (Special Award)

1974-75: Peter Burnell, Zan Charisse, Lola Falana, Peter Firth, Dorian Harewood, Joel Higgins, Marcia McClain, Linda Miller, Marti Rolph, John Sheridan, Scott Stevensen, Donna Theodore, Equity Library Theatre (Special Award)

1975-76: Danny Aiello, Christine Andreas, Dixie Carter, Tovah Feldshuh, Chip Garnett, Richard Kelton, Vivian Reed, Charles Repole, Virginia Seidel, Daniel Seltzer, John V. Shea, Meryl Streep, A Chorus Line (Special Award)

1976-77: Trazana Beverley, Michael Cristofer, Joe Fields, Joanna Gleason, Cecilia Hart, John Heard, Gloria Hodes, Juliette Koka, Andrea McArdle, Ken Page, Jonathan Pryce, Chick Vennera, Eva LeGallienne (Special Award)

1977-78: Vasili Bogazianos, Nell Carter, Carlin Glynn, Christopher Goutman, William Hurt, Judy Kaye, Florence Lacy, Armelia McQueen, Gordana Rashovich, Bo Rucker, Richard Seer, Colin Stinton, Joseph Papp (Special Award)

1978-79: Philip Anglim, Lucie Arnaz, Gregory Hines, Ken Jennings, Michael Jeter, Laurie Kennedy, Susan Kingsley, Christine Lahti, Edward James Olmos, Kathleen Quinlan, Sarah Rice, Max Wright, Marshall W. Mason (Special Award)

1979-80: Maxwell Caulfield, Leslie Denniston, Boyd Gaines, Richard Gere, Harry Groener, Stephen James, Susan Kellermann, Dinah Manoff, Lonny Price, Marianne Tatum, Anne Twomey, Dianne Wiest, Mickey Rooney (Special Award)

1980-81: Brian Backer, Lisa Banes, Meg Bussert, Michael Allen Davis, Giancarlo Esposito, Daniel Gerroll, Phyllis Hyman, Cynthia Nixon, Amanda Plummer, Adam Redfield, Wanda Richert, Rex Smith, Elizabeth Taylor (Special Award)

1981-82: Karen Akers, Laurie Beechman, Danny Glover, David Alan Grier, Jennifer Holliday, Anthony Heald, Lizbeth Mackay, Peter MacNicol, Elizabeth McGovern, Ann Morrison, Michael O'Keefe, James Widdoes, Manhattan Theatre Club (Special Award)

1982-83: Karen Allen, Suzanne Bertish, Matthew Broderick, Kate Burton, Joanne Camp, Harvey Fierstein, Peter Gallagher, John Malkovich, Anne Pitoniak, James Russo, Brian Tarantina, Linda Thorson, Natalia Makarova (Special Award)

1983-84: Martine Allard, Joan Allen, Kathy Whitton Baker, Mark Capri, Laura Dean, Stephen Geoffreys, Todd Graff, Glenne Headly, J.J. Johnston, Bonnie Koloc, Calvin Levels, Robert Westenberg, Ron Moody (Special Award)

1984-85: Kevin Anderson, Richard Chaves, Patti Cohenour, Charles S. Dutton, Nancy Giles, Whoopi Goldberg, Leilani Jones, John Mahoney, Laurie Metcalf, Barry Miller, John Turturro, Amelia White, Lucille Lortel (Special Award)

1985-86: Suzy Amis, Alec Baldwin, Aled Davies, Faye Grant, Julie Hagerty, Ed Harris, Mark Jacoby, Donna Kane, Cleo Laine, Howard McGillin, Marisa Tomei, Joe Urla, Ensemble Studio Theatre (Special Award)

1986-87: Annette Bening, Timothy Daly, Lindsay Duncan, Frank Ferrante, Robert Lindsay, Amy Madigan, Michael Maguire, Demi Moore, Molly Ringwald, Frances Ruffelle, Courtney B. Vance, Colm Wilkinson, Robert DeNiro (Special Award)

1987-88: Yvonne Bryceland, Philip Casnoff, Danielle Ferland, Melissa Gilbert, Linda Hart, Linzi Hately, Brian Kerwin, Brian Mitchell, Mary Murfitt, Aidan Quinn, Eric Roberts, B.D. Wong, Special Awards: Tisa Chang, Martin E. Segal.

1988-89: Dylan Baker, Joan Cusack, Loren Dean, Peter Frechette, Sally Mayes, Sharon McNight, Jennie Moreau, Paul Provenza, Kyra Sedgwick, Howard Spiegel, Eric Stoltz, Joanne Whalley-Kilmer, Special Awards: Pauline Collins, Mikhail Baryshnikov

1989-90: Denise Burse, Erma Campbell, Rocky Carroll, Megan Gallagher, Tommy Hollis, Robert Lambert, Kathleen Rowe McAllen, Michael McKean, Crista Moore, Mary-Louise Parker, Daniel von Bargen, Jason Workman, Special Awards: Stewart Granger, Kathleen Turner

1990-91: Jane Adams, Gillian Anderson, Adam Arkin, Brenda Blethyne, Marcus Chong, Paul Hipp, LaChanze, Kenny Neal, Kevin Ramsey, Francis Ruivivar, Lea Salonga, Chandra Wilson, Special Awards: Tracey Ullman, Ellen Stewart

1991-92: Talia Balsam, Lindsay Crouse, Griffin Dunne, Larry Fishburne, Mel Harris, Jonathan Kaplan, Jessica Lange, Laura Linney, Spiro Malas, Mark Rosenthal, Helen Shaver, Al White, Special Awards: *Dancing at Lughnasa* company, *Plays for Living.*

1992-93: Brent Carver, Michael Cerveris, Marcia Gay Harden, Stephanie Lawrence, Andrea Martin, Liam Neeson, Stephen Rea, Natasha Richardson, Martin Short, Dina Spybey, Stephen Spinella, Jennifer Tilly. Special Awards: John Leguizamo, Rosetta LeNoire.

1993-94: Marcus D'Amico, Jarrod Emick, Arabella Field, Adam Gillett, Sherry Glaser, Michael Hayden, Margaret Illman, Audra Ann McDonald, Burke Moses, Anna Deavere Smith, Jere Shea, Harriet Walter.

1994-95: Gretha Boston, Billy Crudup, Ralph Fiennes, Beverly D'Angelo, Calista Flockhart, Kevin Kilner, Anthony LaPaglia, Julie Johnson, Helen Mirren, Jude Law, Rufus Sewell, Vanessa Williams, Brooke Shields (Special Award)

Anna Carteret, David Yelland

Martin Shaw, Pennie Downie

in *An Ideal Husband* (Special Theatre World Award for entire company

THEATRE WORLD AWARDS

Presented in the Roundabout Theatre on Monday, May 20, 1996

Top: Mary Murfitt with her Cowgirls who provided musical entertainment; John Willis holding caricature that Patricia Elliott presented him from previous Theatre World recipients for his 80th birthday.
Below: Len Cariou, Linda Hart, Kevin Kilner, Tisa Chang, Paul Provenza, Carol Channing, Lou Diamond Phillips, Gregory Hines, Lindsay Duncan, John Davidson, Audra McDonald, Rosemary Harris
Third Row: Kate Forbes, Gregory Hines, Lindsay Duncan, Karen Kay Cody, Michael McGrath, Paul Provenza
Bottom: Rosemary Harris, Dulcie and Michael Denison, Len Cariou, Daphne Rubin-Vega, Jordan Baker,
Photos by Michael Viade, Jack Williams, Van Williams

Top: Paul Provenza, Tisa Chang, Brett Tabisel, Joohee Choi, Lee Gange for Timothy Olyphant, Viola Davis, Karen Kay Cody, Brett Tabisel, John Davidson, cast members of *An Ideal Husband*

Third Row: Audra McDonald, Ginger Montell for Alfred Molina, Viola Davis, Adam Pascal

Fourth Row: Abby Lewis, Rosetta LeNoire, Alice Playten, Patricia Elliott, Laurie Kennedy, SuEllen Estey, John Davidson, Christine Andreas

Bottom Row: William Atherton, John Simon, Carol Channing, Michael & Dulcie Denison, Gregory Hines, Lindsay Duncan, John Davidson, Audra McDonald, Patricia Elliott, Rosemary Harris, Daphne Rubin-Vega, Adam Pascal, Brett Tabisel

Photos by Carol Henderson, Michael Viade, Jack Williams, Van Williams

Pulitzer Prize Productions

1918–Why Marry?, 1919–no award, 1920–Beyond the Horizon, 1921–Miss Lulu Bett, 1922–Anna Christie, 1923–Icebound, 1924–Hell-Bent fer Heaven, 1925–They Knew What They Wanted, 1926–Craig's Wife, 1927–In Abraham's Bosom, 1928–Strange Interlude, 1929–Street Scene, 1930–The Green Pastures, 1931–Alison's House, 1932–Of Thee I Sing, 1933–Both Your Houses, 1934–Men in White, 1935–The Old Maid, 1936–Idiot's Delight, 1937–You Can't Take It with You, 1938–Our Town, 1939–Abe Lincoln in Illinois, 1940–The Time of Your Life, 1941–There Shall Be No Night, 1942–no award, 1943–The Skin of Our Teeth, 1944–no award, 1945–Harvey, 1946–State of the Union, 1947–no award, 1948–A Streetcar Named Desire, 1949–Death of a Salesman, 1950–South Pacific, 1951–no award, 1952–The Shrike, 1953–Picnic, 1954–The Teahouse of the August Moon, 1955–Cat on a Hot Tin Roof, 1956–The Diary of Anne Frank, 1957–Long Day's Journey into Night, 1958–Look Homeward, Angel, 1959–J.B., 1960–Fiorello!, 1961–All the Way Home, 1962–How to Succeed in Business without Really Trying, 1963–no award, 1964–no award, 1965–The Subject Was Roses, 1966–no award, 1967–A Delicate Balance, 1968–no award, 1969–The Great White Hope, 1970–No Place to Be Somebody, 1971–The Effect of Gamma Rays on Man-in-the-Moon Marigolds, 1972–no award, 1973–That Championship Season, 1974–no award, 1975–Seascape, 1976–A Chorus Line, 1977–The Shadow Box, 1978–The Gin Game, 1979–Buried Child, 1980–Talley's Folly, 1981–Crimes of the Heart, 1982–A Soldier's Play, 1983–'night, Mother, 1984–Glengarry Glen Ross, 1985–Sunday in the Park with George, 1986–no award, 1987–Fences, 1988–Driving Miss Daisy, 1989–The Heidi Chronicles, 1990–The Piano Lesson, 1991–Lost in Yonkers, 1992–The Kentucky Cycle, 1993–Angels in America: Millenium Approaches, 1994–Three Tall Women, 1995–Young Man from Atlanta, 1996–Rent

New York Drama Critics Circle Awards

1936–Winterset, 1937–High Tor, 1938–Of Mice and Men, Shadow and Substance, 1939–The White Steed, 1940–The Time of Your Life, 1941–Watch on the Rhine, The Corn Is Green, 1942–Blithe Spirit, 1943–The Patriots, 1944–Jacobowsky and the Colonel, 1945–The Glass Menagerie, 1946–Carousel, 1947–All My Sons, No Exit, Brigadoon, 1948–A Streetcar Named Desire, The Winslow Boy, 1949–Death of a Salesman, The Madwoman of Chaillot, South Pacific, 1950–The Member of the Wedding, The Cocktail Party, The Consul, 1951–Darkness at Noon, The Lady's Not for Burning, Guys and Dolls, 1952–I Am a Camera, Venus Observed, Pal Joey, 1953–Picnic, The Love of Four Colonels, Wonderful Town, 1954–Teahouse of the August Moon, Ondine, The Golden Apple, 1955–Cat on a Hot Tin Roof, Witness for the Prosecution, The Saint of Bleecker Street, 1956–The Diary of Anne Frank, Tiger at the Gates, My Fair Lady, 1957–Long Day's Journey into Night, The Waltz of the Toreadors, The Most Happy Fella, 1958–Look Homeward Angel, Look Back in Anger, The Music Man, 1959–A Raisin in the Sun, The Visit, La Plume de Ma Tante, 1960–Toys in the Attic, Five Finger Exercise, Fiorello!, 1961–All the Way Home, A Taste of Honey, Carnival, 1962–Night of the Iguana, A Man for All Seasons, How to Succeed in Business without Really Trying, 1963–Who's Afraid of Virginia Woolf?, 1964–Luther, Hello Dolly!, 1965–The Subject Was Roses, Fiddler on the Roof, 1966–The Persecution and Assassination of Marat as Performed by the Inmates of the Asylum of Charenton under the Direction of the Marquis de Sade, Man of La Mancha, 1967–The Homecoming, Cabaret, 1968–Rosencrantz and Guildenstern Are Dead, Your Own Thing, 1969–The Great White Hope, 1776, 1970–The Effect of Gamma Rays on Man-in-the-Moon Marigolds, Borstal Boy, Company, 1971–Home, Follies, The House of Blue Leaves, 1972–That Championship Season, Two Gentlemen of Verona, 1973–The Hot l Baltimore, The Changing Room, A Little Night Music, 1974–The Contractor, Short Eyes, Candide, 1975–Equus, The Taking of Miss Janie, A Chorus Line, 1976–Travesties, Streamers, Pacific Overtures, 1977–Otherwise Engaged, American Buffalo, Annie, 1978–Da, Ain't Misbehavin', 1979–The Elephant Man, Sweeney Todd, 1980–Talley's Folley, Evita, Betrayal, 1981–Crimes of the Heart, A Lesson from Aloes, Special Citation to Lena Horne, The Pirates of Penzance, 1982–The Life and Adventures of Nicholas Nickleby, A Soldier's Play, (no musical) 1983–Brighton Beach Memoirs, Plenty, Little Shop of Horrors, 1984–The Real Thing, Glengarry Glen Ross, Sunday in the Park with George, 1985–Ma Rainey's Black Bottom, (no musical), 1986–A Lie of the Mind, Benefactors, (no musical), Special Citation to Lily Tomlin and Jane Wagner, 1987–Fences, Les Liaisons Dangereuses, Les Misérables, 1988–Joe Turner's Come and Gone, The Road to Mecca, Into the Woods, 1989–The Heidi Chronicles, Aristocrats, Largely New York (Special), (no musical) 1990–The Piano Lesson, City of Angels, Privates on Parade, 1991–Six Degrees of Separation, The Will Rogers Follies, Our Country's Good, Special Citation to Eileen Atkins, 1992–Two Trains Running, Dancing at Lughnasa, 1993–Angels in America: Millenium Approaches, Someone Who'll Watch Over Me, Kiss of the Spider Woman, 1994–Three Tall Women, Anna Deavere Smith (Special), 1995–Arcadia, Love! Valour! Compassion!, Special Award: Signature Theatre Company, 1996–Seven Guitars, Molly Sweeney, Rent

American Theatre Wing Antoinette Perry (Tony) Award Productions

1948–Mister Roberts, 1949–Death of a Salesman, Kiss Me, Kate, 1950–The Cocktail Party, South Pacific, 1951–The Rose Tattoo, Guys and Dolls, 1952–The Fourposter, The King and I, 1953–The Crucible, Wonderful Town, 1954–The Teahouse of the August Moon, Kismet, 1955–The Desperate Hours, The Pajama Game, 1956–The Diary of Anne Frank, Damn Yankees, 1957–Long Day's Journey into Night, My Fair Lady, 1958–Sunrise at Campobello, The Music Man, 1959–J.B., Redhead, 1960–The Miracle Worker, Fiorello! tied with The Sound of Music, 1961–Becket, Bye Bye Birdie, 1962–A Man for All Seasons, How to Succeed in Business without Really Trying, 1963–Who's Afraid of Virginia Woolf?, A Funny Thing Happened on the Way to the Forum, 1964–Luther, Hello Dolly!, 1965–The Subject Was Roses, Fiddler on the Roof, 1966–The Persecution and Assassination of Marat as Performed by the Inmates of the Asylum of Charenton under the Direction of the Marquis de Sade, Man of La Mancha, 1967–The Homecoming, Cabaret, 1968–Rosencrantz and Guildenstern Are Dead, Hallelujah Baby!, 1969–The Great White Hope, 1776, 1970–Borstal Boy, Applause, 1971–Sleuth, Company, 1972–Sticks and Bones, Two Gentlemen of Verona, 1973–That Championship Season, A Little Night Music, 1974–The River Niger, Raisin, 1975–Equus, The Wiz, 1976–Travesties, A Chorus Line, 1977–The Shadow Box, Annie, 1978–Da, Ain't Misbehavin', Dracula, 1979–The Elephant Man, Sweeney Todd, 1980–Children of a Lesser God, Evita, Morning's at Seven, 1981–Amadeus, 42nd Street, The Pirates of Penzance, 1982–The Life and Adventures of Nicholas Nickleby, Nine, Othello, 1983–Torch Song Trilogy, Cats, On Your Toes, 1984–The Real Thing, La Cage aux Folles, 1985–Biloxi Blues, Big River, Joe Egg, 1986–I'm Not Rappaport, The Mystery of Edwin Drood, Sweet Charity, 1987–Fences, Les Misérables, All My Sons, 1988–M. Butterfly, The Phantom of the Opera, 1989–The Heidi Chronicles, Jerome Robbins' Broadway, Our Town, Anything Goes, 1990–The Grapes of Wrath, City of Angels, Gypsy, 1991–Lost in Yonkers, The Will Rogers' Follies, Fiddler on the Roof, 1992–Dancing at Lughnasa, Crazy For You, Guys & Dolls, 1993–Angels in America: Millenium Approaches, Kiss of the Spider Woman, 1994–Angels in America: Perestroika, Passion, An Inspector Calls, Carousel, 1995–Love! Valour! Compassion! (play), Sunset Boulevard (musical), Show Boat (musical revival), The Heiress (play revival), King and I (musical revival), 1996–Master Class (play), Rent (musical), A Delicate Balance (play revival), King and I (musical revival)

Above: Anthony Rapp, Adam Pascal
in *Rent*

Left: Jason Robards, Catherine Byrne
in *Molley Sweeney*

Right: Elaine Stritch, Rosemary Harris
in *A Delicate Balance*

Below: David Loud, Zoe Caldwell
in *Master Class*

Julie Andrews

Ray Aranha

Yolande Bavan

Julian Brightman

Joy Behar

Matthew
Broderick

BIOGRAPHICAL DATA ON THIS SEASON'S CASTS

ABELE, JIM. Born November 14, 1960 in Syracuse, NY. Graduate Ithaca Col. Debut 1984 OB in *Shepardsets*, followed by *The Cabbagehead, The Country Girl, Any Place But Here Jack, Godot Arrives, Edith Stein, Great Kahn, Gift of Spice People.*

ABUBA, ERNEST. Born August 25, 1947 in Honolulu, HI. Attended Southwestern Col. Bdwy debut 1976 in *Pacific Overtures*, followed by *Loose Ends, Zoya's Apartment, Shimada, OB in Sunrise, Monkey Music, Station J., Yellow Fever, Pacific Overtures, Empress of China, The Man Who Turned Into a Stick, Shogun Macbeth, Three Sisters, Song of Shim Chung, It's Our Town Too, Mishima Montage, Detectice Story, Chang Fragments.*

ADAMS, JANE. Born April 1, 1965 in Washington, DC. Juilliard graduate. Debut 1986 OB in *The Nice and the Nasty* followed by *Young Playwrights Festival*, Bdwy in *I Hate Hamlet*, for which she received a Theatre World Award, *The Crucible, An Inspector Calls, A Thousand Clowns.*

ADAMS, MALCOLM.Born Feb.21, 1962 in Cork, Ireland. Graduate U of Ireland. Debut 1992 OB in *Lovechild* followed by *Public Enemy, Da.*

ADKINS, DAVID. Born Nov.12, 1962 in Easton, MD. Attended Dartmouth, Juilliard. Bdwy debut in *St. Joan* (1993) followed by OB in *Sabina.*

ADLER, BRUCE. Born November 27, 1944 in NYC. Attended NYU. Debut 1957 OB in *It's a Funny World* followed by *Hard to be a Jew, Big Winner, The Golden Land, The Stranger's Return, The Rise of David Levinsky, On Second Avenue, Bdwy in A Teaspoon Every 4 Hours* (1971), *Oklahoma!* (1979), *Oh Brother!, Sunday in the Park with George, Broadway, Those Were the Days, Crazy for You, Du Barry Was a Lady (Encores).*

ALDRICH, JANET. (formerly Aldridge) Born October 16, 1956 in Hinsdale, IL. Graduate Umiami. Debut 1979 OB in *A Funny Thing Happened on the Way to the Forum* followed by *American Princess, The Men's Group, Wanted Dead or Alive, The Comedy of Errors, Prime Time Prophet*, Bdwy in *Annie* (1982), *The Three Musketeers, Broadway, Starmites, Lust.*

ALERS, YASSMIN. Born in NYC. Attended SUNY Purchase. Debut 1994 OB in *Bring in the Morning* followed by *Blocks, Lightning Park* Bdwy 1996 in *Rent*

ALESSI, CHRISTOPHER V. Born Dec.28, 1964 in Bemus Pt., NY. Graduate Mercyhurst College. Debut 1996 OB in *Brine County Wedding.*

ALEXANDER, ROBERT. Born December 16, 1967 in Portsmouth, Va. Attended SUNY/Purchase. Debut 1991 OB in *Raft of the Medusa* followed by *Grand Guignol, Barbed Wire, The Red Rose*

ALMEDIA, JOAN. Born Sept.19, 1973 in Cebu City, Philippines. Attended U of San Carlos, Centro EscolarU, Nassau Community Col. Bdwy debut 1995 in *Miss Saigon.*

ANDREWS, JULIE. Bom Oct.l, 1935 in Walton-on-Thames, England. Bdwy debut 1954 in *The Boy Friend* followed by *My Fair Lady,Camelot, Victor Victoria* OB 1993 in *Putting It Together.*

ANDREWS, SALLY. Born June 23, 1948 in Cleveland, OH. Attended RADA. Debut OB in *Feiffer's People* followed by *Winterset, Sherlock Holmes and the Speckled Band, Night Must Fall.*

ANTONY, JOHN. Born Oct.17, 1956 in Los Angeles, CA. Attended UCLA. Bdwy debut 1994 in *Passion* followed by *Pal Joey(Encores)*, OB in *Mata Hari*

ARANAS, RAUL. Born October 1, 1947 in Manilla, P.I. Graduate Pace U. Debut 1976 OB in *Savages* followed by *Yellow is My Favorite Color, 49, Bullet Headed Birds, Tooth of the Crime, Teahouse, Shepard Sets, Cold Air, La Chunga, The Man Who Turned into a Stick, Twelfth Night, Shogun Macbeth, Boutique Living, Fairy Bones, In the Jungle of Cities*, Bdwy in *Loose Ends* (1978), *Miss Saigon, King and I.*

ARANHA, RAY. Born May 1, 1939 in Miami, FL. Graduate Fl. A&M U, AADA, Bdwy debut 1987 in *Fences* OB in *Zooman and the Sign, The Shattering, Black Ink.*

ARBEIT, HERMAN O. Born April 19, 1925 in Brooklyn, NY. Attended CCNY, HB Studio, Neighborhood Playhouse. Debut 1939 OB in *The Golem* followed by *Awake and Sing, A Delicate Balance, Yentl the Yeshiva Boy, A Yank in Beverly Hills, Second Avenue Rag, Taking Steam, Christopher Blake, Black Forest, Loophole* Bdwy in *Yentl* (1975).

ARCARO, ROBERT. (a.k.a. Bob), Born Aug. 9, 1952 in Brooklyn, NY. Graduate Wesleyan U. Debut 1977 OB in *New York City Street Show*, followed by *Working Theatre Festival, Man with a Raincoat, Working One-Acts, Henry Lumpur, Special Interests, Measure for Measure, Our Lady of Perpetual Danger, Brotherly Love, I Am a Man, Brotherly Love.*

ARI, ROBERT/BOB. Born July 1, 1949 in NYC. Graduate Camegie-Mellon U. Debut 1976 OB in *The Boys from Syracuse* followed by *Gay Divorce, Devour the Snow, Carbondale Dreams, Show Me Where the Good TimesAre, CBS LivePicasso at the Lapin Agile, Twelfth Night.*

ASHLEY, ELIZABETH. Born Aug.30, 1939 in Ocala, FL. Attended Neighborhood Playhouse. Bdwy debut 1959 in *Highest Tree* followed by *Take Her She's Mine* for which she received a Theatre World Award, *Barefoot in the Park, Ring Round the Bathtub, Cat on a Hot Tin Roof, Skin of Our Teeth, Legend, Caesar and Cleopatra, Hide and Seek, Agnes of God, Garden District* OB in *Milk Train Doesn't Stop Here Anymore, When She Danced.*

ASPILLAGA, VANESSA. Born Sept.16, 1972 in Miami Beach, FL. Attended William Esper Studio. Debut 1996 OB in *Park in Our House.*

AUSTIN, IVY.Born Jan.19, 1958 in Brooklyn, NY. Graduate ColgateU. Bdwy debut 1986 in *Raggedy Ann* OB in *Candide(NYCO), Sweeney Todd, Merry Widow (NYCO), South Pacific(NYCO), Half a World Away, Beauty Part.*

AVIDON, NELSON. Bom February 23, 1957 in Bmoklyn, NY. Debut in *Second Avenue* followed by *The Green Death, Cheapside, Chee-Chee, Three Sisters, Unnatural Acts, Progress, l Am A Camera, Cereau.*

AVNER, JON. Bom June 24, 1953 in NYC. Graduate Syracuse U. St. John's U. Debut 1986 OB in *Murder on Broadway*, followed by *Radio Roast, Crimes of Passion,*
World of Sholem Aleichem, Penguin Blues, Rasputin, Sarah, Currents Turned Awry, Gift Horse, Like Two Eagles.

BADER, JOHN L. Born in Lincoln, NE. Graduate DrakeU. Debut 1992 in *Actor's Nightmare* followed by *Angel Street, White People.*

BAGDEN, RONALD. Born December 26, 1953 in Philadelphia, PA. Graduatc Temple U., RADA. Debut 1977 OB in *Oedipus Rex*, followed by *Oh! What a Lovely War, Jack, Gonza the Lancer, Dead Mother, The Home Show Pieces, Moose Mating* Bdwy in *Amadeus* (1980).

BAGNERIS, VERNEL. Born July 31, 1949 in New Orleans, LA. Graduate Xavier U. Debut 1979 OB in *One Mo' Time*, followed by *Staggerlee, Further Mo'*, *Jelly Roll Morton: A Me-Morial*, *Jelly Roll Morton: Hoo Dude, Jelly Roll, Slow Drag* all of which he wrote.

BAILEY, ADRIAN. Bom September 23, in Detroit, MI. Graduate U. Detroit. Bdwy debut 1976 in *Your Arms Too Short to Box with God*, followed by *Prince of Central Park Jelly's Lasr Jam, Smokey Joe's Cafe*, OB in *A Thrill a Moment, Johnny Pye*.

BAISAS, ROXANNE. Born in Columbus, OH. Graduate NYU. Debut 1990 OB in *And the Soul Shall Dance* followed by *Portrait of the Artist as Filipino*.

BAKER, JORDAN. Born Sept.11, 1958 in Manhattan. Graduate Smith, RutgersU. Debut 1994 OB in *Three Tall Women*, Bdwy debut 1995 in *Suddenly Last Summer*.

BAKER, DARRIN. Born May 7, 1965 in Toronto, Can. Attended Center for Actors. Bdwy debut 1994 in *Sunset Blvd.*

BAKER, DAVID AARON. Born August 14, 1963 in Durham, NC. Graduate U. Tex., Juilliard. Bdwy debut 1993 in *White Liars/Black Comedy* followed by *Abe Lincoln in Illinois, Flowering Peach, Moliere Comedies*, OB in *Richard III, 110 in the Shade* (NYCO), *Durang Durang, Oblivion Postpones, Blue Window*.

BALL, JERRY. Born December 16, 1956 in New Lexington, OH. Graduate Capitol U., NYU. Debut 1995 OB in *Buk-Life and Yimes of Charles Bukowski, Marlowe's Eye*.

BALLINGER, JUNE. Born November 15, 1949 in Camden, NJ. Attended Briarcliff Col. Debut 1980 OB in *Mr. Wilson's Peace of Mind*, followed by *Dona Rosita, A Man in the House, Human Nature, Sound Bytes, Like Two Eagles* Bdwy in *Pack of Lies*.

BAMMAN, GERRY. Born Scpt.18, 1941 in Independence, KS. Graduate XavierU, NYU. Debut 1970 OB in *Alice in Wonderland* followed by *All Night Long, Richard III, Oedipus Rex, Midsummer Night's Dream, He and She, Johnny on the Spot, Museum, Henry V, Our Late Night, Sea Gull, Endgame, Road, Nixon's Nixon* Bdwy in *Accidental Death of an Anarchist* (1984), *Execution of Justice, Uncle Vanya*.

BARBIERI, DESTA. Born Nov.26, 1964 in Palo Alto, CA. Graduate San Jose StateU. Bdwy debut 1995 in *Hello Dolly*.

BARBOUR, THOMAS. Born July 25, 1921 in New York City Graduate Princelon. Harvard. Bdwy debut 1968 in *Portrait of a Queen*. followed by *The Great White Hope. Scratch, Lincoln Mask, Kingdoms*, OB in *Twelfth Night, Merchant of Venice, Admirable Bashful, The Lady's Not for Burning, The Enchanted, Antony and Cleopatra, The Saintliness of Margery Kemp, Dr. Willy Nilly, Under the Sycamore Tree, Epitaphfor George Dillon, Thracian Horses, Old Glory, Sgt. Musgrave's Dance Nestless Bird, The Seagull, Wayside Motor Inn, Arthur, The Grinding Machine, Mr Siman, Sorrows of Frederick, Terrorists, Dark Ages, Royal Bob, Relatively Speakin'. Aristocrats, The Taming of the Shrew, The Perpetrator, Cerceau*.

BARON, EVALYN. Born Apr. 21, 1948 in Atlanta, GA. Graduate Northwestern U., U. Min. Debut 1979 OB in *Scrambled Feet*, followed by *Hijinks, I Can't Keep Running in Place, Jerry's Girls, Harvest of Strangers, Quilters, Splendora* Bdwy in *Fearless Frank* (1980), *Big River, Rages, Social Security, Les Miserables*.

BARRE, GABRIEL. Born August 26, 1957 in Brattleboro, VT. Graduate AADA. Debut 1977 OB in *Jabberwock* followed by *T.N.T., Bodo, The Baker's Wife, The Time of Your Life, Children of the Sun, Wicked Philanthropy, Starmites, Mistress of the Inn, Gifts of the Magi, The Tempest, Return to the Forbidden Planet, The Circle, Where's Dick?, Forever Plaid, Jacques Brel, Show Me Where the Good Times Art Marathon Dancing, El Greco, King James and the Indian* Bdwy in *Rags* (1986), *Starmites, Anna Karenina, Ain't Broadway Grand*.

BARRETT, TIM. Born Apr.21, 1956 in Norwalk, CT. Attended Forham. Debut 1980 OB in *Oedipus Cycle* followed by *Bronx*.

BARRIT, DESMOND. Born Oct.19, 1944 in Wales. Bdwy debut 1996 in *Midsummer Night's Dream*.

BARRON, DAVID. Born May 11, 1938 in Pilot Point, TX. Graduate BaylorU.Yale, UIll. Debut 1976 OB in *Fantasticks* followed by *Trouble in Tahiti, Sound of Music, Doll's House, Feathertop, Kiss Me Quick, Sweeney Todd, Lust,* Bdwy 1989 in *Sweeney Todd*.

BARTENIEFF, GEORGE. Born January 24, 1933 in Berlin, Ger. Bdwy debut 1947 in *The Whole World Over*, followed by *Venus Is, All's Well That Ends Well, Quotations from Chairman Mao Tse-Tung, The Death of Bessie Smith, Cop-Out, Room Service, Unlikely Heroes*, OB in *Walking in Waldheim, Memorandum, The Increased Difficulty of Concentration, Trelawny of the Wells, Charley Chestnut Rides the IRT, Radio (Wisdom): Sophia Part I, Images of the Dead, Dead End Kids, The Blonde Leading the Blonde, The Dispossessed, Growing Up Gothic, Rosetti's Apologies, On the Lam, Samuel Beckett Trilogy, Quartet, Help Wanted, A Matter of Life and Death, The Heart That Eats Itself, Coney Island Kid, Cymbeline, Better People, Blue Heaven, He Saw His Reflection, Sabina*

BARTLETT, PETER. Born August 28, 1942 in Chicago, IL. Attended Loyola U. LAMDA. Bdwy debut 1969 in *A Patriot for Me*, followed by *Gloria and Esperanza, Beauty and the Beast* OB in *Boom Boom Room, I Remember the House Where I was Born, Crazy Locomotive, A Thurber Carnival, Hamlet, Buzzsaw Berkeley, Learned Ladies, Jeffrey, The Naked Truth*.

BARTON, FRED. Born Oct.20, 1958 in Camden, NJ. Graduate Harvard. Debut 1982 OB in *Forbidden Bdwy* followed by *Miss Gulch Returns, Forbidden Hollywood*.

BARTON, MISCHA. Born Jan.24, 1986 in London. Debut 1995 OB in *Slavs!* followed by *Twelve Dreams, Where the Truth Lies*.

BASCH, PETER. Born May 11, 1956 in NYC. Graduate Columbia U. UC/Berkeley. Debut 1984 OB in *Hackers* followed by *Festival of One Acts, Marathon '92, The Cowboy The Indian and the Fervent Feminist, Marmalade Tears*.

BATEMAN, BILL. Born December 10 in Rock Island, IL. Graduate Augustana Col Debut 1974 OB in *Anything Goes*, followed by Bdwy in *Hello Dolly* (1978/1995), *Bring Back Birdie, Peter Pan* (1990/1991).

BATT, BRYAN. Bom March 1, 1963 in New Orleans, LA. Graduate Tulane U. Debut 1987 OB in *Too Many Girls*, followed by *The Golden Apple, Jeffrey*, Bdwy in *Starlight Express* (1987), *Sunset Blvd.*

BAVAN, YOLANDE. Born June 1, 1942 in Ceylon. Attended UColumbo. Debut 1964 OB in *Midsummer Night's Deam* followed by *Jonah, House of Flowers, Salvation, Tarot, Back Bog Beast Bait, Leaves of Grass, End of the War, Bald Soprano/Leader,* Bdwy in *Heathen, Snow White, Chronicle of a Death Foretold*.

BEACH, DAVID. Born February 20, 1964 in Dayton, OH. Attended Darmouth Col, LAMDA. Debut 1990 OB in *Big Fat and Ugly with a Moustache* followed by *Modigliani, Octoberfest, Pets, That's Life!* Bdwy in *Moon Over Buffalo* (1995).

BEAN, REATHEL. Bom Aug. 24, 1942 In Missouri. Graduate Drake U. OB in *America Hurrah, San Francisco's Burning, Love Cure, Henry IV, In Circles, Peace, Journey of Snow White, Wanted, The Faggot, Lovers, Not Back with the Elephants, The Art of Coarse Acting, The Trip Back Down, Hunting Cockroaches, Smoke on the Mountain,* Bdwy in *Doonesbury* (1983) *Big River, Inherit the Wind*.

BEECHMAN, LAURIE. Born April 4, 1954 in Philadelphia, PA. Attended NYU. Bdwy debut 1977 in *Annie*, followed by *Pirates of Penzance, Joseph and the Amazing Technicolor Dreamcoat* for which she received a Theatre World Award, *Cats, Les Misérables*, OB in *Some Enchanted Evening, Pal Joey in Concert, Songs with a View*.

BEHAR, JOY. Born October 7 in Brooklyn, NY. Graduate Queens Col, SUNY Stonybrook. Bdwy debut 1994 in *Comedy Tonight*, OB 1996 in *Food Chain*.

BELL, GLYNIS. Born July 30, 1947 in London, England. Attended Oakland U., AADA. Debut 1975 OB in *The Devils* followed by *The Time of Your Life, The Robber Bridegroom, Three Sisters, Sleep Deprivation Camber* Bdwy in *My Fair Lady*(1993).

BENEDICT, PAUL. Born Sept.17 in Silver City, NM. Graduate SuffolkU. Debut 1965 OB in *Live Like Pigs* followed by *Local Stigmatic, Play's the Thing, Cherry Orchard, It's Only a Play* Bdwy includes *Leda Had a Swan*(1968), *Bad Habits, Little Murders, White House Murder Case, Richard III*.

BENSON, PETER. Born June 19 in Stockholm, Sweden. Graduate WesleyanU. Debut 1987 OB in *Casting of Kevin Christian* followed by *Korea*, Bdwy 1996 in *State Fair*.

BERMAN, DONALD. Born Jan.23, 1954 in NYC. Graduate USyracuse. Debut 1977 OB in *Savages* followed by *Dona Rosita, Lady or the Tiger, The Overcoat, Steel on Steel, Visions of Kerouac, Normal Heart, Phantom Lady, Marathon '89, The Promise, Degas C'est Moi*.

BERRESSE, MICHAEL. Born August 15, 1964 in Holyoke, MA. Bdwy debut 1990 in *Fiddler on the Roof* followed by *Guys and Dolls, Damn Yankees, One Touch of Venus (Encores), Chicago*.

BESSETTE, MIMI. Born January 15, 1956 in Midland, Mi.Graduate TCU, RADA. Debut 1978 OB in *The Gifts vf the Magi*, followed by *Bugles at Dawn, On the 20th Century, Opal, Camila* Bdwy in *The Best Little Whorehouse in Texas*.

BETLEM, PAULA. Born Apr.23 in Rochester, NY. Graduate GeneseoSt.U. Debut 1996 OB in *Have a Nice Day*.

BEVERLEY, TRAZANA. Born Aug. 9, 1945 in Baltimore, MD. Graduate NYU. Debut 1969 OB in *Rules for Running*, followed by *Les Femmes Noires, Geronimo, Antigone, The Brothers, God's Trombones, Marathon '91,Sleep Deprivation Chamber* Bdwy in *My Sister My Sister, For Colored Girls Who Have Considered Suicide* for which she received a Theatre World Award, *Death and the King's Horseman* (LC), *The Crucible*.

BIENSKIE, STEPHEN. Born May 15 in NJ. Graduate MontclairU. Debut 1996 OB in *Zombie Prom* Other OB: *Koppelvision, There's a War Going On, Balm in Gilead*.

BIGLIN, TOM. Born Aug.24, 1967 in Woodhaven, NY. Graduate U of Penn. Debut 1996 OB in *Gender Wars* followed by *Measure for Measure*.

BILLECI, JOHN. Born April 19, 1957 in Brooklyn, NY. Graduate Loyola Marymount U. Debut 1993 OB in *3 by Wilder* followed by *As You Like It, SSS Glencairn, Twelfth Night, Goose and TomTom, Anatomy of Sound, Child's Christmas in Wales* Bdwy 1993 in *Wilder Wilder Wilder*.

BILLMAN, SEKIYA. Born in Culver City, CA. Graduate UCLA. Bdwy debut 1996 in *Miss Saigon*.

BIRKELUND, OLIVIA. Born April 26, 1963 in New York City. Graduate Brown U. Debut 1990 OB in *Othello*, followed by *Cowboy in His Underwear, Misanthrope, Aimee and Hope*

BIRNEY, REED. Born September 11, 1954 in Alexandria, VA. Attended Boston U. Bdwy debut 1977 in *Gemini* OB in *The Master and Margarita, Bella Figura, Winterplay, The Flight of the Earls, Filthy Rich, Lady Moonsong, Mr. Monsoon, The Common Pursuit, Zero Positive, Moving Targets, Spare Parts, A Murder of Crows, 7 Blowjobs, Loose Knot, The Undertaker, An Imaginary Life, The Family of Mann, Minor Demons, Dark Ride*.

BISHOP, KELLY (formerly Carole). Born Feb. 28, 1944 in Colorado Springs, CO. Bdwy debut 1967 in *Golden Rainbow*, followed by *Promises Promises, On the Town, Rachel Lily Rosenbloom, A Chorus Line, Six Degrees of Separation, Bus Stop* OB in *Piano Bar, Changes, The Blessing, Going to New England, Six Degrees of Separation, Pterodactyls*.

BLACK, RACHEL. Born September 15 in NYC. Attended U. Buffalo. Debut 1989 OB in *Land of Dreams*, followed by *The Fiflh Romance Language, Yiddle with a Fiddle, Rags, Christmas Carol*

BLACK, ROYANA. Born Mar.1, 1973 in Poughkeepsie, NY Bdwy debut 1984 in *Brighton Beach Memoirs*, OB in *Miami, Trinity Site, Columbus in the Age of Gold*.

BLAISDELL, NESBITT. Born December 6, 1928 in NYC. Graduate Amherst, Columbia U. Debut 1978 OB in *Old Man Joseph and His Family*, followed by *Moliere in Spite of Himself, Guests of the Nation, Chekov Sketch Book, Elba, Ballad of Soapy Smith, Custom of the Country, A Cup of Coffee, The Immigrant, Yokohama Duty, Quincy Blues, Wasp and Other Plays* Bdwy in *Cat on a Hot Tin Roof* (1990), *Abe Lincoln in Illinois*

BLANCHARD, BRUCE Born July 7, 1965 in Lebanon, OR. Graduate Humanities Western Baptist, Acting U of Miss. Debut OB 1992 in *Opal* followed by *Forever Plaid* Bdwy 1995 in *Hello Dolly*.

BLANCHARD, STEVE. Bom December 4, 1958 in York, PA. Attended UMd. *Bdwy debut 1984 in The Three Musketeers* followed by *Camelot, Christmas Carol* OB in *Moby Dick*.

BLAZER, JUDITH. Born October 22, 1956 in *Oh Boy!*, followed by *Roberta* in concert, *A Little Night Music, Company, Babes in Arms, Hello Again, Jack's Holiday, Louisana Purchase* Bdwy in *Me and My Girl, A Change in the Heir*.

BLOCH, SCOTTY. Born January 28 in New Rochelle, NY. Attended AADA. Debut 1945 OB in *Craig's Wife* followed by *Lemon Sky, Battering Ram, Richard III, In Celebration, An Act of Kindness, The Price, Grace, Neon Psalms, Other People's Money, Walking The Dead, EST Marathon '92, The Stand-In, Unexpected Tenderness, Brutality of Fact* Bdwy in *Children of a Lesser God* (1980).

BLOOM, TOM. Born Nov. 1, 1944 in Washington, D.C. Graduate Western MD Col., Emerson Col. Debut 1989 OB in *The Widow's Blind Date*, followed by *A Cup of Coffee, Major Barbara, A Perfect Diamond, Lips Together Teeth Apart, Winter's Tale* Bdwy in *Racing Demon* (1995).

BLUE, ARLANA. Bom November 15, 1948 in Passaic, NJ. Attended NY School of Ballet. Debut 1971 OB in *Fear of Love* followed by *Paranoia Pretty, Sgt. Pepper's Lonely Hearts Club Band, Life During Wartime, Ruby and Pearl*.

BOBBY, ANNE MARIE. Born December 12, 1967 in Paterson, NJ. Attended OxfordU. Debut 1983 OB in *American Passion* followed by *Class I Acts, Godspell, Progress, Groundhog, Misconceptions, Merrily We Roll Along, Black Ink* Bdwy in *The Human Comedy* (1984-also OB), *The Real Thing, Hurlyburly, Precious Sons, Smile, Black Comedy*.

BOCKHORN, CRAIG.Born May 30, 1961 in Manhattan, NYC. Graduate Emerson Col. Debut 1989 OB in *You Can't Think of Everything* followed by *Truth Teller, Third Millennium, As You Like It, Loveliest Afternoon of the Year, Women of Manhattan, Runyon on Wry, Bard Silly, Hope Zone,* Bdwy 1990 in *Prelude to a Kiss (*also OB).

BODLE, JANE. Born Nov. 12 in Lawrence, KS. Attended U. Utah. Bdwy debut 1983 in *Cats*, followed by *Les Miserables, Miss Saigon, Sunset Blvd*.

BOEHMER, J. PAUL. Born Oct.30, 1965 in Dayton, OH. Graduate So.MethodistU, U of Del. Bdwy debut 1996 in *An Ideal Husband*.

BOEVERS, JESSICA. Born Aug.25, 1972 in Highland Park, IL. Graduate Cincinnati Conserv of Music, U of Cinn. Bdwy debut 1994 in *Beauty and the Beast* followed by *A Funny Thing...*

BOGUE, ROBERT. Born Aug.27, 1964 in Minden, NE. Graduate Colorado Col. Debut 1991 *Nothing to Dream About* followed by *Adding Machine, Waiting for Lefty, The Undertakers, Hotel Universe*.

BOLDEN, KEN. Born Mar.2, 1959 in Cleveland, OH. Graduate London Acad of Music and Dramatic Art. Debut 1989 OB in *La Ronde* followed by *Dining Room, Oedipus at Colonus, Santiago*.

BOLES, ROBERT. Born July 27, 1953 in Cincinnatti, OH. Attended MemphisSt.U., AMDA. Debut 1984 OB in *Richard II* followed by *Pericles, To Feed Their Hopes, Zombies from the Beyond*.

BOLTON, JOHN (KEENE). Born December 29, 1963 in Rochester, NY. Graduate St. John Fisher Col. Debut 1991 OB in *Cinderella.*, Bdwy in *Damn Yankees* (1994), *How to Succeed...*

BONDOC, LEXINE. Born Oct.14, 1988 in NYC. Bdwy debut 1992 in *Miss Saigon* followed by *King and I*.

BONNELL, JAY. Born Apr.12, 1932 in Passaic, NJ. Graduate Seton HallU. Debut 1958 OB in *Member of the Wedding* followed by *Escape Me Never, Look After Lulu, Fire Brand, Shoestring Revue, Meeow, Tiny Tim and the Size Queen, Beautiful People*.

BOONRAI, KAILIP. Born Feb.24, 1989 in Elmhurst, NY. Bdwy debut 1993 in *Miss Saigon* followed by *King and I*.

BORAS, JOHN. Born Mar.19, 1964 in Bronx, NY. Debut 1996 OB in *Gender Wars*.

BORROMEO, LUNA. Born in NYC. Debut 1995 OB in *Rita's Resources*.

BOSCO, PHILIP. Born Sept. 26, 1930 in Jersey City, NJ. Graduate Catholic U. Credits: *Auntie Mame, Rape of the Belt, Ticket of Leave Man, Donnybrook, A Man for All Seasons, Mrs. Warren's Profession,* with LCRep in *A Great Career, In the Matter of J. Robert Oppenheimer, The Miser, The Time of Your Life, Camino Real, Operation Sidewinder, Amphitryon, Enemy of the People, Playboy of the Western World, Good Woman of Setzuan, Antigone, Mary Stuart, Narrow Road to the Deep North, The Crucible, Twelfth Night, Enemies, Plough and the Stars, Merchant of Venice, A Streetcar Named Desire, Henry V, Threepenny Opera, Streamers, Stages, St. Joan, The Biko Inquest, Man and Superman, Whose Life Is It Anyway?, Major Barbara, A Month in the Country, Bacchae, Hedda Gabler, Don Juan in Hell, Inadmissable Evidence, Eminent Domain, Misalliance, Learned Ladies, Some Men Need Help, Ah Wilderness!, The Caine Mutiny Court Martial, Heartbreak House, Come Back Little Sheba, Loves of Anatol, Be Happy for Me, Master Class, You Never Can Tell, Devil's Disciple, Lend Me a Tenor, Breaking Legs, Fiorello (Encores), An Inspector Calls, The Heiress, Moon Over Buffalo*.

BOSNIAK, SLOANE. Born Feb.18, 1950 in Schenectady, NY. Graduate Goucer Col., CatholicU. Debut 1986 OB in *Annie Wobbler* followed by *Night Must Fall*.

BOURNEUF, STEPHEN. Born Nov.24, 1957 in St.Louis, MO. Graduate St. LouisU. Bdwy debut 1981 in *Broadway Follies* followed by *Oh Brother, Dreamgirls*(1987), *Chorus Line, Legs Diamond, Prince of Central Park, Hello Dolly*(1995).

BOVE, ELIZABETH. Bom Sept. 30 in Melbourne, Australia. Graduate U. Tex. Debut 1986 OB in *Witness for the Prosecution*, followed by *House of Bernarda Alba, Country Girl, The Maids, Round & Peakheads, The Dream Cure, House of the Dog, Shadow Box, Kiss the Blarney Stone, Moon for the Misbegotten, No Exit, Madwoman of Chaillot, Box Office Poison, Fautus A Ritual*.

BOWMAN, LYNN. Born February 20, 1950 in Buffalo, NY. Graduate SUNY/Buffalo. Debut 1973 OB in *Prizewinning Plays* followed by *The Beggar's Opera, Dracula, Molly's Dream, The Shannon Doyle Incident, Say Darling*.

BRACCHITTA, JIM. Born February 27, 1960 in Brooklyn, NY. Graduate NYU. Bdwy debut 1989 in *Gypsy*, OB in *The Tennants of 3R, The Merchant of Venice, Rapunzel, Mock Doctor/Euridice, I Can Get it for You Wholesale, Scaring the Fish, Yong Playwrights '95*.

BRADLEY, BRAD. Born Dec.9, 1971 in San Diego, CA. Graduate USC. Bdwy debut 1995 in *Christmas Carol*, OB in *Cocoanuts*.

BRAUGHER, ANDRE. Born July 1, 1962 in Chicago, IL. Graduate StanfordU., Juilliard. Debut 1991 OB in *Way of the World, Twelfth Night, Much Ado About Nothing, Coriolanus, King John, Measure for Measure, Richard II, Henry IV*.

BRENNAN, JAMES. Born Oct. 31, 1950 in Newark, NJ. Bdwy debut 1974 in *Good News*, followed by *Rodgers and Hart, So Long, 1 74th Street, Little Me, I Love My Wife, Singin' in the Rain, 42nd Street, Me and My Girl,Crazy for You*, OB in *Juba*.

BRIGHTMAN, JULIAN. Born March 5 1964 in Philadelphia, Pa. Graduate U. PA. Debut 1987 OB in *1984*, followed by *Critic, Leaves of Grass*, Bdwy in *Peter Pan* (1990/1991), *Hello Dolly* (1995).

BROADHURST, KENT. Born Feb.4, 1940 in St. Louis, MO. Graduate UNe. Debut 1968 OB in *Fourth Wall* followed by *Design for Living, Marching Song, Heartbreak House, Dark of the Moon, Hunchback of Notre Dame, Cold Sweat, April Snow, Early One Evening at the Rainbow Bar and Grill, After-Play*, Bdwy 1983 in *Caine Mutiny Court-Martial*.

BROCK, LEE. Born July 1, 1959 in Denver, CO. Graduate UOk. Debut 1994 OB in *Ghost in the Machine* followed by *Trust, Living Proof, By the Sea*

BRODERICK, MATTHEW. Born Mar. 21, 1963 in New York City. Debut 1981 OB in *Torch Song Trilogy*, followed by *The Widow Claire, A Christmas Memory*, Bdwy 1983 in *Brighton Beach Memoirs* for which he received a Theatre World Award, followed by *Biloxi Blues, How to Succeed...*(1995).

BROOKS, AVERY. Born Oct.2 in Evansville, Ind. OB in *The Offering, A Photograph, Are You Now..., Spell #7*, Bdwy in *Paul Robeson* (1988/95).

BROGGER, IVAR. Born January 10 in St. Paul, MN. Graduate U, Minn. Debut 1979 OB in *In The Jungle of Cities*, followed by *Collected Works of Billy the Kid, Magic Time, Cloud 9, Richard III, Clarence, Madwoman of Chaillot, Seascapes with Sharks and Dancer, Second Man, Twelfth Night, Almost Perfect Up 'N' Under, Progress, Juno, Madwoman of Chaillot, The Beauty Part* Bdwy in *Macbeth* (1981), *Pygmalion* (1987), *Saint Joan, Blood Brothers*.

BROMKA, ELAINE. Born Jan. 6 in Rochester, NY. Graduate Smith Col. Debut 1975 OB in *The Dybbuk*, followed by *Naked, Museum, The Son, Inadmissible Evidence, The Double Game, Cloud 9, Light Up the Sky, No One Will Be Immune* Bdwy in *Macbeth* (1982), *Rose Tattoo* (1995).

BROOKES, JACQUELINE. Born July 24, 1930 in Montclair, NJ. Graduate U. Iowa, RADA. Bdwy debut 1955 in *Tiger at the Gates*, followed by *Watercolor, Abelard and Heloise, A Meeting at the River*, OB in *The Cretan Woman* (1954) for which she received a Theatre World Award, *The Clandestine Marriage, Measure for Measure, The Duchess of Malfi, Ivanov, 8 Characters in Search of an Author, An Evening's Frost, Come Slowly Eden, The Increased Difficulty of Concentration, The Persians, Sunday Dinner, House of Blue Leaves, Owners, Hallelujah, Dream of a Black-listed Actor, Knuckle, Mama Sang the Blues, Buried Child, On Mt. Chimorazo, Winter Dancers, Hamlet, Old Flames, The Diviners, Richard II, Vieux Carre, Full Hookup, Home Sweet Home/Crack, Approaching Zanzibar, Ten Blocks on the Camino Real, Listening, Sand, Seascape, Elsa's Goodbye*.

BROWN, ANTHONY M. Born July 14, 1962 in Springfield, VA. Graduate FlStU., Juilliard. Debut 1993 OB in *Jeffrey* followed by *Mother and Child*, Bdwy 1995 in *School for Scandal*.

BROWN, ROBIN LESLIE. Born Jan. 18, in Canandaigua, NY. Graduate LIU. Debut 1980 OB in *The Mother of Us All*, followed by *Yours Truly, Two Gentlemen of Verona, Taming of the Shrew, The Mollusc, The Contrast, Pericles, Andromache, Macbeth, Electra, She Stoops to Conquer, Berneice, Hedda Gabler, A Midsummer Night's Dream, Three Sisters, Major Barbara, The Fine Art of Finesse, Two by Schnitzler, As You Like It, Ghosts, Chekhov Very Funny, Beaux Strategem, God of Vengeance, Good Natured Man, Twelfth Night, Little Eyolf, Ventian Twins, King Lear, Doll's House, Antigone*.

BRUMMEL, DAVID. Born November 1, 1942 in Brooklyn, NY. Bdwy debut 1973 in *The Pajama Game*, followed by *Music Is, Oklahoma!*, OB in *Cole Porter, The Fantasticks, Prom Queens Unchained, Camilla*.

BRYDON, W. B. Born September 20, 1933 in Newcastle, Eng. Debut 1962 OB in *The Long the Short and the Tall*, followed by *Live Like Pigs, Sgt. Musgrave's Dance, The Kitchen, Come Slowly Eden, The Unknown Soldier and His Wife, Moon for the Misbegotten, The Orphan, Possession, Total Abandon, Madwoman of Chaillot, The Circle, Romeo and Juliet, Philadelphia Here I Come, Making History, Spinoza, Mme. MacAdam Traveling Theatre, Last Sortie, Juno and the Paycock* Bdwy in *The Lincoln Mask, Ulysses in Nighttown, The Father*.

BRYGGMAN, LARRY. Born Dec. 21, 1938 in Concord, GA. Attended CCSF, Am. Th. Wing. Debut 1962 OB in *A Pair of Pairs*, followed by *Live Like Pigs, Stop You're Killing Me, Mod Donna, Waiting for Godot, Ballymurphy, Marco Polo Sings a Solo, Brownsville Raid, Two Small Bodies, Museum, Winter Dancers, Resurrection of Lady Lester, Royal Bob, Modern Ladies of Guanabacoa, Rum and Coke, Bodies Rest and Motion, Blood Sports, Class 1 Acts, Spoils of War, Coriolanus, Macbeth, Henry IV Parts 1 and 2, The White Rose, Nothing Sacred, As You Like It, New England* Bdwy in *Ulysses in Nighttown* (1974), *Checking Out, Basic Training of Pavlo Hummel, Richard III, Prelude to a Kiss* (also OB), *Picnic*.

BUCKLEY, CANDY.Born March10 in Albuquerque, MN.Graduate TCU, UTx, Trinity. Debut 1994 OB in *Petrified Prince, Funnyhouse of a Negro*.

BUELL, BILL. Born Sept. 21, 1952 in Paipai, Taiwan. Attended Portland State U. Debut 1972 OB in *Crazy Now*, followed by *Declassee, Lorenzaccio, Promenade, The Common Pursuit, Coyote Ugly, Alias Jimmy Valentine, Kiss Me Quick, Bad Habits, Groundhog, On the Bum, Picasso at the Lapin Agile* Bdwy in *Once a Catholic* (1979), *The First, Welcome to the Club, The Miser, Taking Steps*.

BULLOCK, ANGELA. Born July 5 in NYC. Graduate Hunter Co. Debut 1993 OB in *Washington Square Moves*, followed by *John Brown, Window Man, June and Jean in Concert*

BULOS, YUSEF. Born September 14, 1940 in Jerusalem. Attended American U., AADA. Debut 1965 OB with *American Savoyards* in rep, followed by *Saints, The Trouble with Europe, The Penultimate Problem of Sherlock Holmes, In the Jungle of Cities, Hermani, Bertrano, Duck Variations, Insignificance, Panache, Arms and the Man, The Promise, Crowbar, Hannah 1939, Strange Feet, Hyacinth Macaw, Henry V, Golden Boy* Bdwy in *Indians* (1970), *Capt. Brassbound's Conversion*.

BURK, TERENCE. Born Aug. 11, 1947 in Lebanon, IL. Graduate S. IL. U. Bdwy debut 1976 in *Equus*, OB in *Religion, The Future, Sacred and Profane Love, Crime and Punishment*.

BURNETT, CAROL. Born Apr.26, 1935 in San Antonio, TX. Attended UCLA. Bdwy debut 1959 in *Once Upon a Mattress* (also OB) for which she received a Theatre World Award, followed by *Fade Out-Fade In, Moon Over Buffalo*.

BURNS, ANDREA. Born Feb.21 1971 in Miami, FL. Attended Boston Conserv. Debut 1995 OB in*Songs for a New World* followed by*Bring In the Morning*.

BURRELL, FRED. Born Sept. 18, 1936. Graduate UNC, RADA. Bdwy debut 1964 in *Never Too Late*, followed by *Illya Darling, Cactus Flower, On Golden Pond, Inherit the Wind* OB in *The Memorandum, Throckmorton, Texas, Voices in the Head, Chill Queen, The Queen's Knight, In Pursuit of the Song of Hydrogen, Unchanging Love, More Fun Than Bowling, Woman without a Name, Sorrows of Fredrick, Voice of the Prairie, Spain, Democracy and Esther, Last Sortie, Rough/Play, Life is a Dream, Taming of the Shrew, Twelfth Night, Modest Proposal, Oedipus at Colonus, A Hamlet, 3 in the Back 2 in the Head, True Crimes*.

BURRELL, TERESA/TERRY. Born February 8, 1952 in Trinidad, W.I Attended Pace U. Bdwy debut 1977 in *Eubie!*, followed by *Dreamgirls, HonkyTonl Nights,Swinging on aStar* OB in*That Uptown FeelingThey Say It's Wonderful,GeorgeWhite'sScandals,Just So, AndtheWorld Goes 'Round*.

BURSTEIN, DANNY. Born June 16, 1964 in NYC. Graduate U. Cal/San Diego. Moscow Art Theatre. Debut 1991 OB in *The Rothschilds, Weird Romance, Merrily We Roll Along, All in the Timing* Bdwy in *A Little Hotel on the Side* (1992), *The Sea Gull, Saint Joan, Three Men on a Horse, Flowering Peach, Company, DuBarry Was a Lady* (Encores).

BURSTYN, ELLEN. Born December 7, 1932 in Detroit, MI. Attended Actors Studio. Bdwy debut 1957 (as Ellen MacRae) in *Fair Game*, followed by *Same Time Next Year, 84 Charing Cross Road, Shirley Valentine, Shimada, Sacrilege* OB in *Three Sisters, Andromeda II, Park Your Car in Harvard Yard*.

BURTON, ARNIE. Born Sept. 22, 1958 in Emmett, ID. Graduate U. Ariz. Bdwy debut 1983 in *Amadeus*, OB in *Measure for Measure, Major Barbara, Schnitzler One Acts, Tartuffe, As You Like It, Ghosts, Othello, Moon for the Misbegotten, Twelfth Night, Little Eyolf, Mollusc, Venetian Twins, Beaux Stratagem, King Lear, Winter's Tale, When Ladies Battle*.

BURTON, KATE. Born September 10, 1957 in Geneva, Switz. Graduate Brown U., Yale. Bdwy debut 1982 in *Present Laughter*, followed by *Alice in Wonderland, Doonesbury, Wild Honey, Some Americans Abroad, Jake's Women,Company* OB in *Winners* for which she received a 1983 Theatre World Award, *Romeo and Juliet, The Accrington Pals, Playboy of the Western World, Measure for Measure, London Suite*

BUSHMANN, KATE. Born October 6, 1961 in Ft.Smith, AR.Graduate Stephens Col. Debut 1992 OB in *Move It and It's Your's*, followed by-*Roleplay, Let Us Now Praise Famous Men, Comeback, Hail to the Chief, Glory Girls*.

BUTLER, BRUCE. Born March 11, 1954 in Clanton, NC. Graduate NC Central U. Debut 1983 OB in *Street Scene*, followed by *Freedom Days, Just a Night Out, North 17th St*

BUTLER, KERRY. Born in Brooklyn. Graduate Ithaca. Bdwy debut 1993 in *Blood Brothers* followed by *Beauty and the Beast*.

BUTTERFIELD, CATHERINE. Born February 5 in NYC. Graduate SMU. Debut 1983 OB in *Marmalade Skies*, followed by *Bobo's Birthday, Joined at the Head, Snowing at Delphi, Where the Truth Lies*.

CABOT, CHRISTINA. Born Dec.16, 1969 in NYC. Graduate NYU. Debut 1990 OB in *Midsummer Night's Dream* followed by *King Lear*.

CAIN, WILLIAM. Born May 27, 1931 in Tuscaloosa, AL. Graduate U. Wash., Catholic U. Debut 1962 OB in *Red Roses for Me*, followed by *Jericho Jim Crow, Henry V, Antigone, Relatively Speaking, I Married an Angel in Concert, Buddha, Copperhead, Forbidden City, Fortinbras*, Bdwy in *Wilson in the Promise Land* (1970), *You Can't Take It with You, Wild Honey, The Boys in Autumn, Mastergate, A Streetcar Named Desire The Heiress, Delicate Balance*.

CALAMIA, MARC. Born in New Orleans, LA. Graduate NYU. Debut 1996 OB in *The Skriker*.

CALAHAN, JAMIE. Born Aug.8, 1963 in Brighton, MA. Graduate SUNY Potsdam, Brooklyn College, Yale Drama. Debut 1995 OB in *Hardhats* followed by *Cardenio, Young Goodman Brown, Waiting for Godot*.

CALDWELL, ZOE. Born September 14, 1933 in Melbourne, Aust. Attended Methodist Ladies Col. Bdwy debut 1965 in *The Devils*, followed by *Slapstick Tragedy* for which she received a Theatre World Award, *Prime of Miss Jean Brodie, Creation of the World and Other Business, Medea* (1982), *Master Class* OB in *Colette, Dance of Death, Long Day's Journey into Night, A Perfect Ganesh*.

CALLAWAY, LIZ. Born Apr. 13, 1961 in Chicago, IL. Debut 1980 OB in *Godspell*, followed by *The Matinee Kids, Brownstone, No Way to Treat a Lady, Marry Me a Little, 1-2-3-4-5*, Bdwy in *Merrily We Roll Along* (1981), *Baby, The Three Musketeers, Miss Saigon, Cats, Fiorello(Encores)*.

CALNAN, ALLIE. Born Apr.21, 1984 in NYC. Debut 1994 OB in *He Saw His Reflection* followed by *Oz*, Bdwy 1996 in *Inherit the Wind*.

CAMACHO, BLANCA. Bom Nov. *19, 1956* in New York City. Graduate NYU,Debut 1984 in *Sarita*, followed by *Maggie Magalita, Salon, You Can Come Back. Belk Monde, Danny and the Deep Blue Sea, Born to Rumba!, Inkarri's Return, In the Land of Giants*.

CAMP, JOANNE. Born Apr. 4, 1951 in Atlanta, GA. Graduate Fl. Atlantic U., Geo. Wash. U. Debut 1981 OB in *The Dry Martini*, followed by *Geniuses* for which she received a Theatre World Award, *June Moon, Painting Churches, Merchant of Venice, Lady from the Sea, The Contrast, Coastal Disturbances, The Rivals, Andromache, Electra, Uncle Vanya, She Stoops to Conquer, Hedda Gabler, The Heidi Chronicles, Importance of Being Earnest, Medea, Three Sisters, A Midsummer Night's Dream, School for Wives, Measure for Measure, Dance of Death, Two Schnitzler One-Acts, Tartuffe, Lips Together Teeth Apart, As You Like It, Moon for the Misbegotten, Phaedra, Little Eyolf, Beaux Strategem, King Lear, Life Is a Dream, Winter's Tale, When Ladies Battle*, Bdwy in *The Heidi Chronicles* (1989), *Sisters Rosensweig*.

CAMPBELL, ALAN. Born Apr.22, 1957 in Homestead, FL. Graduate UMiami. Debut 1982 OB in *Boogie-Woogie Rumble of a Dream Deferred* followed by *Almost a Man, On Shiloh Hill*, Bdwy in *Sunset Blvd.* (1994).

CAMPBELL, AMELIA. Born Aug. 4, 1965 in Montreal, Can. Graduate Syracuse U. Debut 1988 OB in *Fun*, followed by *Member of the Wedding, Tunnel of Love, Five Women Wearing the Same Dress, Wild Dogs, Intensive Care, Wasp and Other Plays* Bdwy in *Our Country's Good* (1991), *A Small Family Business, Translations*.

CAMPBELL, COLIN. Born Jan.24, 1962 in Seattle, WA. Attended NYU. Debut 1982 OB in *Rabbit Ears* followed by *Real O'Brien, Her Hair, Norman Conquests, Titus Andronicus, Macbeth, Hamlet, Gambler, Baptists, Fashion Police, Bana Creme Pie, Baptists*.

CANNIS, MICHAEL. Born May 13, 1957 in Miami, FL. Graduate UCLA. Debut 1990 OB in *Savage in Limbo* followed by *Dreamtime, Currents Turned Awry, The Party, Half & Half, Danger of Strangers, Salesmen Don't Ride Bicycles, Down Dark Deceptive Streets, Minor Demons*.

CANOVA, DIANA. Born June 1, 1953 in West Palm Beach, FL. Attended LACC. Bdwy debut 1981 in *They're Playing Our Song* followed by *Company*(1995), OB 1985 in *Breaks*.

CANTONE, MARIO. Born Dec.9, 1959 in Boston, MA. Graduate Emerson Col. Bdwy debut 1995 in *Love! Valour! Compassion!* followed by *Tempest*.

CAPONE, VINCENT ANTHONY. Born Dec.30, 1972 in Staten Island, NY. Bdwy debut 1995 in *Mixed Emotions*.

CARHART, TIMOTHY. Born December 24, 1953 in Washington, DC. Graduate U.Ill. Debut 1984 OB in *The Harvesting*, followed by *Ballad of Soapy Smith, Hitchhikers, Highest Standard of Living, Festival of 1-Acts, By the Sea*, Bdwy in *A Streetcar Named Desire* (1992).

CARIOU, LEN. Bom Sept. 30. 1939 in Winnipeg, Can. Bdwy debut 1968 in *House of Atrew*, followed by *Henry V, Applause* for which he received a Theatre World Award, *Night Watch, A Littk Night Music, Cold Storage, Sweeney Todd, Dance a Littk Closer, Teddy and Alice, The Speed of Darkness*, OB in *A Sorrow Beyond Dreams, Upfrom Paradise, Master Class, Day Six, Measurefor Measure, Mountain, Papa*.

CARLIN, CHET. Born Feb.23, 1940 in Malverne, NY. Graduate Ithaca Col., CatholicU. Bdwy debut 1972 in *Evening with Richard Nelson*, OB in *Under Gaslight, Lou Gehrig Did Not Die of Cancer, Graffitti, Crystal and Fox, Golden Honeymoon, Arms and the Man, Arsenic and Old Lace, The Father, Comedy of Errors, Never the Sinner, Emperor Charles, Oedipus at Colonus, The Red Rose*.

CARPENTER, WILLIE C. Born Aug.9, 1945 in Eutaw, AL. Graduate Ohio St.U. Debut 1985 OB in *Rude Times* followed by *A Cup of Coffee, Sleep Deprivation Chamber*, Bdwy 1987 in *Musical Comedy Murders of 1940*.

CARTER, CAITLIN. Born February 1 in San Francisco, CA. Graduate Rice U., NC School of Arts. Bdwy debut 1993 in *Ain't Broadway Grand* followed by *Chicago, Victor Victoria*.

CARTER, DIXIE. Born May 25, 1939 in McLemoresville, TN. Graduate Memphis St.U. Debut 1963 OB in *Winter's Tale* followed by *Carousel, Merry Widow* and *King and I* (LC), *Sextet, Jesse and the Bandit Queen* for which she received a Theatre World Award, *Fathers and Sons, A Couple of White Chicks, Taken in Marriage, Buried Inside Extra*, Bdwy 1976 in *Pal Joey* followed by *Master Class*.

CARTERET, ANNA. Born Dec.11 in Bangalare, India. Bdwy debut 1996 in *An Ideal Husband*.

CASPER, JEFF. Born May 27, 1963 in Syracuse, NY. NYU Graduate. Debut 1995 OB in *Awake and Sing* followed by *Beau Defeated*

CASTREE, PAUL. Born in Rockford, IL. Graduate U. IL. Debut 1992 OB in *Forever Plaid*, Bdwy in *Grease* (1994).

CEBALLOS, RENE M. Bom Apr. 7, 1953 in Boston, MA. Attended San Fran. U. Bdwy debut 1977 in *A Chorus Linc*, followed by *Dancin', Cats, Dangerous Games, Grand Hotel, Chronicle of a Death Foretold*. OB in *Tango Apasionado, Shriker*.

CELLARIO, NARIA. Born June 19, 1948 in Buenos Aires, Arg. Graduate Ithaca Col. Bdwy debut 1975 in *Royal Family* followed by OB in *Fuge in a Nursery, Declassee, Equinox, Flatbush Faithful, Our Lady of Tortilla, Half Desrted Streets, George Washington Slept Here, Black Hat Karma, Inkarris Reutrn, Forever in My Heart*.

CHALFANT, KATHLEEN. Born January 14, 1945 in San Francisco, CA. Graduate Stanford U. Bdwy debut 1975 in *Dance with Me*, followed by *M. Butterfly, Angels in America, Racing Demon* OB in *Jules Feiffer's Hold Me, Killings on the Last Line, The Boor, Blood Relations, Signs of Life, Sister Mary Ignatius Explains it All, Actor's Nightmare, Faith Healer, All the Nice People, Hard Times, Investigation of the Murder in El Salvador, 3 Poets, The Crucible, The Party, Iphigenia and øther Daughters, Cowboy Pictures, Twelve Dreams, Henry V, Endgame*.

CHALFY, DYLAN. Born June 22, 1970 in Sarsota, FL. Debut 1994 OB in *Blood Guilty* followed by *Cross Your Heart*, Bdwy 1995 in *Rose Tattoo*.

CHALSMA, MELISSA. Born Oct.4, 1968 in Columbus, OH. Graduate Oberlin Col., U of Deleware. Bdwy debut 1995 in *Hamlet*, OB in *Moonlight, Modest Proposal*.

CHAMBERLIN, KEVIN. Born November 25, 1963 in Baltimore, MD. Graduate Rutgers U., Debut 1990 OB in *Neddy*, followed by *Smoke on the Mountain*, Bdwy in *My Favorite Year* (1992), *Abe Lincoln in Illinois, One Touch of Venus(Encores)*.

CHANDLER, DAVID. Born February 3, 1950 in Danbury, CT. Graduate Oberlin Col. Bdwy debut 1980 in *The American Clock* followed by *Death of a Salesman, Lost in Yonkers*, OB in *Made in Heaven, Black Sea Follies, The Swan, Watbanaland, Phaedra, Slavs!, Working Title*.

CHANDLER, REX. (Paul Fow). Born Aug.14, 1966 in Shelby Township, MI. Debut 1996 OB in *Making Porn*.

CHANG, JOHN. Born Dec.19, 1985 in Wuxi, China. Bdwy debut 1996 in *King and I*.

CHANG, MENG-CHEN. Born Sept.18, 1972 in Hoinchu, Taiwan. Graduate Juilliard. Bdwy debut 1996 in *King and I*.

CHANNING, CAROL. Born Jan.31, 1921 in Seattle WA. Attended Bennington Col. Bdwy debut 1941 in *No for an Answer* followed by *Let's Face It, Proof through the Night, Lend an Ear* for which she received a

Theatre World Award, *Gentlemen Prefer Blondes, Wonderful Town, The Vamp, Show Girl, Hello Dolly* (1964/1978/1995), *Four on a Garden, Lorelei.*

CHAPLAIN, HILARY. Born June 17, 1956 in Boston, MA. Graduate Hampshire Col. Debut 1988 OB in *Largely New York* (CC), Bdwy 1995 in *The Tempest.*

CHAPPELL, KANDIS. Born July 9, 1947 in Milwaukee, WS. Graduate San Diego St.U. Bdwy debut 1989 in *Rumours* followed by *Getting Away with Murder.*

CHARLTON, WILLIAM. Born in Vilenza, Italy. Graduate U. Col., LAMBDA. Debut 1989 OB in *Third Time Lucky,* followed by *Pericles, The Catalyst, Treasure Island.*

CHASTAIN, DON. Born Sept.2 in Oklahoma City, OK. Attended OklahomaU. Debut 1960 OB in *Parade* followed by *Floyd Collins* Bdwy in *No Strings.*

CHEN, TINA. Born Nov.2 in Chung King, China. Graduate BrownU. Debut 1972 OB in *Maid's Tragedy* followed by *Family Devotions, Midsummer Night's Dream, Empress of China, Year of the Dragon, Tropical Tree, Madame de Sade, Arthur and Leila, Chang Fragments,* Bdwy in *King and I, Love Suicide at Schofield Barracks.*

CHENG, KAM. Born Mar. 28, 1969 in Hong Kong. Attended Muhlenberg Col. Bdwy debut 1991 in *Miss Saigon* followed by *King and I.*

CHIASSON, GILLES. Born Nov.1, 1966 in Muskegou, MI. Graduate U of Mich. Debut 1992 OB in *Goundhog,* Bdwy 1996 in *Rent.*

CHIBAS, MARISSA. Born June 13, 1961 in NYC. Graudate SUNY/Purchase. Debut 1983 OB in *Asian Shade,* followed by *Sudden Death, Total Eclipse, Another Antigone, Fresh Horses, Fortune's Fools, Overtime* Bdwy in *Brighton Beach Memiors* (1984), *Abe Lincoln in Illinois.*

CHOI, JOOHEE. Born Mar.19, 1968 in Seoul, Korea. Attended ColumbiaU., Juilliard. Bdwy debut 1996 in *King and I* for which she received a Theatre World Award.

CHRISTIAN, KARL. Born Nov.25 in Windham, CT. Graduate SyracuseU. Bdwy debut 1994 in *Beauty and the Beast* followed by *Miss Saigon.*

CHRISTOPHER, DONALD. Born May 16, 1939 in Terre Haute, In. Graduate Ind. State U. Debut 1992 OB in *First the Supper* followed by *Rose and Crown.*

CLARK, BRYAN E. Born Apr.5, 1929 in Louisville, KY. Graduate Fordham U. Bdwy debut 1978 in *History of the American Film* followed by *Bent, Grown-Ups, On Golden Pond,* OB in *Winning Isn't Everything, Put Them All Together, Red Rover, Paradise Lost, Clarence, Step Out of Line, Madwoman of Chaillot, The Circle, Preservation Society.*

CLARKE, RICHARD. Born January 31, 1933 in England. Graduate U. Reading. With LCRep in *St. Joan* (1968), *Tiger at the Gates, Cyrano de Bergerac,* Bdwy in *Conduct Unbecoming, The Elephant Man, Breaking the Code, The Devils Disciple M. Butterfly, Six Degrees of Separation, Two Shakespearean Actors, Arcadia, Racing Demon* OB in *Old Glory, Trials of Oz, Looking Glass, Trelawney of the Wells, Fair Country.*

CLOSE, GLENN. Born May 19, 1947 in Greenwich, CT. Graduate William & Mary Col. Bdwy debut 1974 with Phoenix Co. in *Love for Love, Member of the Wedding,* and *Rules of the Game,* followed by *Rex, Crucifer of Blood, Barnum, The Real Thing, Benefactors, Death and the Maiden, Sunset Blvd.,* OB in *The Crazy Locomotive, Uncommon Women and Others, Wine Untouched, Winter Dancers, Singular Life of Albert Nobbs, Joan of Ark at the Stake, Childhood.*

CLOW, JAMES. Born April 15, 1965 in White Plains, NY. Graduate Syracuse U. LAMDA. Debut 1992 OB in *Juno,* Bdwy in *Blood Brothers* (1993) followed by *Company* (1995).

CODY, KAREN KAY. Born FEb.28, 1958 in Seattle, WA. Bdwy debut 1996 in *Master Class* for which she received a Theatre World Award.

COHEN, LYNN. Born August 10 in Kansas City, Mo. Graduate Northwestern U. Debut 1979 OB in *Don Juan Comes Back From the Wars* followed by *Getting Out, The Arbor, Cat and the Canary, Suddenly Last Summer, Bella Figura, The Smash, Chinese Viewing Pavillion, Isn't It Romatic, Total Eclipse, Angelo's Wedding, Hamlet, Love Diatribe, A Couple with a Cat, XXX Love Acts, Model Apt.* Bdwy in *Orpheus Descending* (1989).

COLEMAN, ROSALYN. Born July 20, 1965 in Ann Arbor, MI. Graduate Harvard U., Yale Drama. Bdwy debut 1990 in *Piano Lesson* followed by *Mule Bone, Seven Guitars,* OB 1992 in *Destiny of Me.*

COLL, IVONNE. Born November 4 in Fajardo, PR. Attended UPR, LACC. Debut 1980 OB in Spain 1980 followed by *Animals, The Wonderful Ice Cream Suit, Cold Air, Fabiola, Concerto in Hi-Fi, Quintuplets, A Burning Beach, The Promise, Blood Wedding, La Puta Vida, Pancho Diablo,* Bdwy in *Goodbye, Fidel* (1980), *Shakespeare on Broadway:Macbeth, As You Like It, Romeo and Juliet, Chronicle of a Death Foretold.*

COLLINS, MICHAEL. Born Aug.4, 1969 in Chattanooga, TN. Graduate U of Alabama. Debut 1995 OB in *The Window* followed by *In an Infinite Universe.*

COMLEY, BONNIE. Born in Mass.Graduate Emerson Col. Debut 1988 OB in *Noo Yawk Tawk* followed by *Fortune's Fools.*

CONE, MICHAEL. Born Oct.7, 1952 in Fresno, CA. Graduate UWash. Bdwy debut 1980 in *Brigadoon* followed by *Christmas Carol,* OB in *Bar Mitzvah Boy, The Rink, Commedia Tonite!*

CONNELL, JANE. Born Oct. 27, 1925 in Berkeley, CA. Attended U. Cal. Bdwy debut in *New Faces of 1956* followed by *Drat! The Cat!, Mame* (1966/83), *Dear World, Lysistrata, Me and My Girl, Lend Me a Tenor, Crazy For You, Moon Over Buffalo* OB in *Shoestring Revue, Threepenny Opera, Pieces of Eight, Demi-Dozen, She Stoops to Conquer, Drat!, Real Inspector Hound, Rivals, Rise and Rise of Daniel Rocket, Laughing Stock, Singular Dorothy Parker, No No Nanette in Concert.*

CONOLLY, PATRICIA. Born Aug.29, 1933 in Tabora, E. Africa. Attended U. Sydney. With APA in *You Can't Take It With You, War and Peace, School for Scandal, Wild Duck, Right You Are, We Comrades Three, Pantagleize, Exit the King, Cherry Orchard, Misanthrope, Cocktail Party, Cock-a-doodle Dandy* followed by *Streetcar Named Desire, Importance of Being Earnest, The Circle, Small Family Business, Real Inspector Hound/15 Minute Hamlet, Heiress, Tartuffe:Born Again* OB in *Blithe Spirit, Woman in Mind.*

CONROY, FRANCES. Born in 1953 in Monroe, GA. Attended Dickinson Col., Juilliard, Neighborhood Playhouse. Debut 1978 OB with the Acting Co. in *Mother Courage, King Lear, The Other Half* followed by *All's Well That Ends Well, Othello, Sorrows of Stephen, Girls Girls Girls, Zastrozzi, Painting Churches, Uncle Vanya, Romance Language, To Gillian on Her 37th Birthday, Man and Superman, Zero Positive, Bright Room Called Day, Lips Together Teeth Apart, Booth, Last Yankee, Three Tall Women, Arts and Leisure* Bdwy in *Lady from Dubuque* (1980), *Our Town, Secret Rapture* (also OB), *Some Americans Abroad* (also OB), *Two Shakespearian Actors, In the Summer House, Broken Glass.*

CONROY, JARLATH. Born September 30, 1944 in Galway, Ire. Attended RADA. Bdwy debut 1976 in *Comedians,* followed by *The Elephant Man, Macbeth, Ghetto, The Visit, On the Waterfront,* OB in *Translations, The Wind that Shook the Barley, Gardenia, Friends, Playboy of the Western World, One-Act Festival, Abel & Bela/Architect, The Matchmaker, Henry V*

COOK, VICTOR TRENT. Born Aug.19, 1967 in NYC. Debut 1976 OB in *Joseph and the Amazing Technicolor Dreamcoat* followed by *Haggadah, Moby Dick, Romance in Hard Times,* Bdwy in *Don't Get God Started* (1988), *Starmites* (also OB), *Smokey Joe's Cafe.*

COOPER, CHUCK. Born November 8, 1954 in Cleveland, OH. Graduate Ohio U. Debut 1982 OB in *Colored People's Time,* followed by *Riff Raff Revue, Primary English Class, Break/Agnes/Eulogy/Lucky, Avenue X,* Bdwy in *Amen Corner* (1983), *Someone Who'll Watch Over Me, Getting Away with Murder.*

COOPER, MARILYN. Born December 14, 1936 in NYC. Attended NYU. Bdwy in *Mr. Wonderful, West Side Story, Brigadoon, Gypsy, I Can Get It for You Wholesale, Hallelujah Baby, Golden Rainbow, Mame, A Teaspoon Every 4 Hours, Two by Two, On the Town, Ballroom, Woman of the Year, The Odd Couple, Cafe Crown, Fiorello(Encores), One Touch of Venus(Encores),* OB in *The Mad Show, Look Me Up, The Perfect Party, Cafe Crown, Milk and Honey, Petrified Prince.*

CORBALIS, BRENDAN. Born March 19, 1964 in Dublin, Ire. Graduate NYU. Debut 1988 OB in *April Snow* followed by *Indians of Venezuela, Finding the Sun, Beekeeper's Daughter, Food Chain.*

CORBO, GEORGINA. Born September 21, 1965 in Havana, Cuba. Attended SUNY/Purchase. Debut 1988 OB in *Ariano,* followed by *Born to Rumba, Mambo Louie and the Dancing Machine, Ghost Sonata, You Can't Win, Dog Lady, The Bundle, Family Affair.*

CORCORAN, JAY. Born Oct.16, 1958 in Boston, MA. Graduate CatholicU., HarvardU. Debut 1985 OB in *Caligula* followed by *Why to Refuse, Jerker, Play, Party* and wrote *The Fey* and *The Christening.*

CORDDRY, ROBERT. Born Feb.4, 1971 in Weymouth, MA. Graduate U.Mass Amherst. Debut 1994 OB in *Manchurian Candidate* followed by *What Doesn't Kiss Us.*

CORSAIR, BILL. Born September 5, 1940 in Providence, RI. Debut 1984 OB in *Ernie and Arnie,* followed by *In the Boom Boom Room, The Constituent, New Jersey/New York The Loophole.*

COSGRAVE, PEGGY. Born June 23, 1946 in San Mateo, CA. Graduate San Jose Col., CatholicU. Debut 1980 OB in *Come Back to the Five and Dime Jimmy Dean* followed by *Sandbox*, Bdwy in *The Nerd* followed by *Born Yesterday, Shadow Box, Garden District.*

COSTEN, RUSSELL. Born May 15, 1945 in Boston, MA. Graduate St. JohnsU. Bdwy debut 1970 in *J.B.* OB in *Caligula, Danton's Death, Othello, Birthday Party, Three Musketeers, Mary Tudor, Arsenic and Old Lace, Gigi, Beggar of Borough Park.*

COULLET, RHONDA. Born Sept.23, 1945 in Tampa, FL. Graduate UFl. Debut 1973 OB in *Merchant of Venice* followed by *Ghost Dance, Look We've Come Through, Arms and the Man, Isadora Duncan Sleeps with the Russian Navy, Arthur, Winter Dancer, Prevalence of Mrs. Seal, Jane Avril, Cowgirls*, Bdwy in *Royal Family* (1975), *Philadelphia Story, I'm Not Rappaport.*

COUNTRYMAN, MICHAEL. Born Sept. 15, 1955 in St. Paul, MN. Graduate Trinity Col., AADA. Debut 1983 OB in *Changing Palettes*, followed by *June Moon, Terra Nova, Out!, Claptrap, The Common Pursuit, Woman in Mind, Making Movies, The Tempest, Tales of the Lost Formicans, Marathon '91, The Stick Wife, Lips Together Teeth Apart, All in the Timing, The Ashfire, Where the Truth Lies*, Bdwy in *A Few Good Men* (1990), *Face Value, Holiday.*

COURTNEY, TOM. Born Feb.25, 1937 in Hull, Eng. Graduate RADA. Bdwy debut 1977 in *Otherwise Engaged* followed by *The Dresser, Uncle Vanya*, OB in *Moscow Station.*

COVER, BRADFORD. Born Jan.26, 1967 in NYC. Graduate DenisonU, UWis. Debut 1994 OB in *King Lear* followed by *Beaux Strategem, Venetian Twins, Oedipus at Colonus, Mrs. Warren's Profession, Winter's Tale, Life Is a Dream, When Ladies Battle, Antigone*

COX, VEANNE. Born Jan.19, 1963 in Virginia. Bdwy debut in *Smile*(1986) followed by *Company*, OB in *Nat'l Lampoon's Class of '86, Flora the Red Menace, Showing Off, Food Chain.*

COX, RICHARD. Born May 6, 1948 in NYC. Yale U. graduate. Debut 1970 OB in *Saved* followed by *Fugs, Moonchildren, Alice in Concert, Richard II, Fishing, What a Man Weighs, The Family of Mann*, Bdwy in *The Sign in Sidney Brustein's Window, Platinum, Blood Brothers, Apple Doesn't Fall.*

CRISP, QUENTIN. Born Dec.25, 1908 in Carshalton, Eng. Debut 1978 OB in *Evening with Quentin Crisp* followed by *Importance of Being Earnest, Lord Alfred's Lover, Murder at Rutherford House, Sherlock Holmes and the Speckled Band.*

CRISWELL, KIM. Bom July 19, 1957 in Hampton, VA. Graduate U.Cinn. Bdwy debut 1981 in *The First*, followed by *Nine, Baby, Stardust, 3 Penny Opera*, OB in *Sitting Pretty, 50 Million Frenchmen, Girls Night Out, I Married an Angel.*

CRIVELLO, ANTHONY. Born Aug. 2, 1955 in Milwaukee, WI. Bdwy debut 1982 in *Evita* followed by *The News, Les Miserables, Kiss of the Spiderwoman* OB in *Juniper Tree, Camila.*

CROFT, PADDY. Born in Worthing, England. Attended Avondale Col. Debut 1961 OB in *The Hostage* followed by *Billy Liar, Live Like Pigs, Hogan's Goat, Long Day's Journey into Night, Shadow of a Gunman, Pygmalion, The Plough and the Stars, Kill, Starting Monday, Philadephia Here I Come!, Grandchild of Kings, Fragments, Same Old Moon*, Bdwy in *Killing of Sister George, Prime of Miss Jean Brodie, Crown Matrimonial, Major Barbara.*

CROMWELL, KEITH A. Born July 5, 1963 in Tripoli, Lybia, No.Africa. Graduate James MadisonU. Debut 1993 OB in *Whoop-Dee-Doo.*

CROSBY, B. J. Born Nov.23, 1952 in New Orleans, LA. Bdwy debut 1995 in *Smokey Joe's Cafe.*

CROSSLEY, HOWARD. Born Feb.16, 1955 in Rotherham, S.Yorkshire, Eng. Bdwy debut in *Midsummer Night's Dream* (1996).

CRUIKSHANK, HOLLY. Born June 18, 1973 in Scottsdale, AZ. Attended No.Carolina School of Arts. Bdwy debut in *Hello Dolly* (1995).

CSIZMADIA, DAVID. Born June 7, 1963 in Detroit, MI. Graduate Eastern MichU, UNo.Carolina/Chapel Hill. Debut 1991 OB in *Sympathetic Affections* followed by *Carpool.*

CUERVO, ALMA. Born August 13, 1951 in Tampa, Fl. Graduate TulaneU. Debut 1977 OB in *Uncommon Women and Others* followed by *A Foot in the Door, Put Them All Together, Isn't It Romantic?, Miss Julie, Quilters, The Sneaker Factor, Songs on a Shipwrecked Sofa, Uncle Vanya, The Grandma Plays, The Nest, Secret Rapture, Christine Alberta's Father, Music from Down the Hall, Donahue Sisters, 3 in the Back 2 in the Head*, Bdwy in *Once in a Lifetime, Bedroom Farce, Censored Scenes from King Kong, Is There Life After High School?, Ghetto, Secret Rapture.*

CUMPSTY, MICHAEL. Born in England. Graudate UNC. Bdwy debut 1989 in *Artist Descending a Staircase* followed by *La Bete, Timon of Athens, Translations, Heiress, Racing Demon* OB in *The Art of Success, Man and Superman, Hamlet, Cymbeline, The Winter's Tale, King John, Romeo and Juliet, All's Well That Ends Well.*

CUNNINGHAM, EADWARD J. Born June 19, 1951 in Oragne, NJ. Graduate Rhode Island College. Debut 1978 OB in *Fool's Passage* followed by *Bathtub, Cornbury, Of Mice and Men, From These Two*

CUNNINGHAM, JOHN. Born June 22, 1932 in Auburn, NY. Graduate Yale, Dartmouth U. OB in *Love Me a Little, Pimpernel, The Fantasticks, Love and Let Love, The Bone Room, Dancing in the Dark, Father's Day, Snapshot, Head Over Heels, Quartermaine's Terms, Wednesday, On Approval, Miami, Perfect Party, Birds of Paradise, Naked Truth, Cheever Evening, Camping with Henry and Tom, Sylvia*, Bdwy in *Hot Spot* (1963), *Zorba, Company, 1776, Rose, The Devil's Disciple, Six Degrees of Separation* (also OB), *Anna Karenina, The Sisters Rosensweig, Allegro(Encores).*

CUNNINGHAM, T. SCOTT. Born December 15 in Los Angeles, CA. Graduate NC School of Arts. Debut 1992 OB in *Pterodactyls*, followed by *Takes on Women, Stand-In, Don Juan in Chicago, Wally's Ghost, New England*, Bdwy 1995 in *Love! Valour! Compassion!, Tartuffe: Born Again.*

CURLESS, JOHN. Born Sept. 16 in Wigan, Eng. Attended Central Schl. of Speech. NY debut 1982 OB in *The Entertainer,* followed by *Sus, Up 'n' Under, Progress, Prin, Nightingale, Absent Friends, Owners/Traps*, Bdwy in *A Small Family Business* (1992), *Racing Demon, King and I.*

CURTIN, CATHERINE. Born in NYC. Graudate Pinceton U. Bdwy debut 1990 in *Six Degrees of Separation*. OB in *Gulf War, Making Book, Orphan Muses, Aimee and Hope.*

CURTIS, KEENE. Born Feb. 15, 1925 in Salt Lake City UT. Graduate U. Utah. Bdwy debut 1949 in *Shop at Sly Corner*, with APA in *School for Scandal, The Tavern, Anatole, Scapin, Right You Are, Importance of Being Earnest, Twelfth Night, King Lear, Seagull, Lower Depths, Man and Superman, Judith, War and Peace, You Can't Take It with You, Pantaglieze, Cherry Orchard, Misanthrope, Cocktail Party, Cock-a-Doodle Dandy, and Hamlet, A Patriot for Me, The Rothschilds, Night Watch, Via Galactica, Annie, Division Street, La Cage aux Folles,White Liars/Black Comedy*, OB in *Colette, Ride Across Lake Consequence, Cocktail Hour.*

CYPHER, JON. Born Jan.13, 1932 in Brooklyn. Graduate UVt. Bdwu debut in *The Disenchanted* (1958) followed by *Jennie, Night of the Iguana, Man of La mancha, Sherry, Great White Hope, 1776, Coco, Big*, OB in *Great Western Union, The Wives.*

DAILY, DANIEL. Bom July 25, 1955 in Chicago, IL. Graduate Notre Dame, U. Wash. Debut 1988 OB in *Boy 's Breath*, followed by *A Ronde, Iron Bars, Chekhov Very Funny, Macbeth, As You Like It, Free Zone, Scarlet Letter, Two Nikita.*

DAKIN, LINNEA. Born Mar.21, 1972 in Kansas, City, Kan. Graduate U of Hartford. Bdwy debut in *State Fair* (1996).

d'AMBOISE, CHARLOTTE. Born May 11, 1964 in Manhattan, NYC. Bdeubt 1980 OB in *Tennis Game* Followed by Bdwy in *Cats* (1984), *Song and Dance, Carrie, Jerome Robbins' Bdwy, Damn Yankees, Company.*

DANNEHL, DAVID. Born Oct.4, 1950 in Washington, D.C. Attended Appalachain St.U., Graduate Cal.St./Northridge. Bdwy debut in *Show Boat*(1994).

DANNER, BLYTHE. Born Feb.3, 1944 in Philadelphia, PA. Graduate Bard Col. Debut 1966 OB in *The Infantry* followed by *Collision Course, Summertree, Up Eden, Someone's Comin' Hungry, Cyrano, Miser* for which she received a 1969 Theatre World Award, *Twelfth Night, New York Idea, Much Ado about Nothing, Love Letters, Sylvia, Moonlight*, Bdwy in *Butterflies are Free, Betrayal, Philadelphia Story, Blithe Spirit, Streetcar Named Desire.*

DANO, PAUL FRANKLIN. Born June 19, 1986 in NYC. Bdwy Debut in *Month in the Country*(1995) followed by *Christmas Carol, Inherit the Wind.*

DANSON, RANDY. Born April 30, 1950 in Plainfield NJ. Graduate Carnegie-Mellon U. Debut 1978 OB in *Gimme Shelter*, followed by *Big and Little, The Winter Dancers, Time Steps, Casualties, Red and Blue, The Resurrection of Lady Lester, Jazz Poets at the Grotto, Plenty, Macbeth, Blue Window, Cave Life, One-Act Festival, Mad Forest, Triumph of Love, The Treatment, Phaedra, Arts & Leisure.*

DANZINGER, MAIA. Born Apr.12, 1950 in NYC. Attended NYU. Bdwy debut 1973 in *Waltz of the Toreadors*, OB in *Total Eclipse, Milk of Paradise, Rachel Plays, Kill, Madwomen of Chaillot, Beauty Part, Measure for Measure.*

DARLOW, CYNTHIA. Born June 13, 1949 in Detroit, MI. Attended NCSch of Arts, Penn State U. Debut 1974 OB in *This Property Is Condemned* followed by *Portrait of a Madonna, Clytemnestra, Unexpurgated Memoirs of Bernard Morgandigler, Actor's Nightmare, Sister MaryIgnatius Explains.., Fables for Friends, That's It Folks!, Baby with the Bath Water, Dandy Dick, Naked Truth, Cover of Life, Death Deying Acts*, Bdwy in *Grease* (1976), *Rumors, Prelude to a Kiss* (also OB).

DAVENPORT, COLLEEN. Born Sept.2, 1958 in Beloit, KS. Graduate LaSt.U Debut 1983 OB in *The Seagull* followed by *New York Works '87, Dalton's Back, Great Kahn, Last of the Spice People*.

DAVID, KEITH. Born May 8, 1954 in NYC, Julliard Graduate. Debut 1979 OB in *Othello*, followed by *The Haggadah, Pirates of Penzance, Macbeth, Coriolanus, Titus Andronicus*, Bdwy in *Jelly's Last Jam* (1992), *Seven Guitars*.

DAVIDGE, DONNA. Born Jan.15, 1955 in Stamford, CT. Graduate UNH, Loma LindaU, Neighborhood Playhouse. Debut 1989 OB in *Two Girls on a Porch* followed by *Postmarks, Hotline, Trash City and Death, Fools in the West, Down Dark Deceptive, Streets, Bubbling*.

DAVIDSON, JACK. Born July 17, 1936 in Worcester, MA. Graduate BostonU. Debut1968 OB in *Moon for the Misbegotten*, followed by *Big and Little, Battle of Angels, A Midsummer Night's Dream, Hot L Baltimore, Tribute to Lili Lamont, Ulysses in Traction, Lulu, Hey Rube!, In the Recovery Lounge, Runner Stumbles, WinterSigns, Hamlet, Mary Stuart, Ruby Ruby Sam Sam, The Diviners, Marching to Georgia,Hunting Scenes from Lower Bavaria, Richard II, Great Grandson of Jedediah Kohler, Buck, Time Framed, Love's Labour's Lost, Bing and Walker, After theDancing in Jericho, Fair Country*, Bdwy in *Capt. Brassbound's Conversion* (1972), *Anna Christie, The Price, Shimada*.

DAVIDSON, JOHN. Born Dec.13, 1941 in Pittsburgh, PA. Graduate DennisonU. Bdwy debut in *Foxy* (1964) followed by *Oklahoma* (CC) for which he received a Theatre World Award, *State Fair*.

DAVIS, BRUCE ANTHONY. Born March 4, 1959 in Dayton, OH. Attended Juilliard. Bdwy debut 1979 in *Dancin'*, followed by *Big Deal, A Chorus Line, High Rollers, Damn Yankees, Chicago*, OB in *Carnival*.

DAVIS, HOPE. Born March 23, 1964 in Englewood, NJ. Graduate Vassar Col. Debut 1991 OB in *Can-Can* followed by *Goodnight Desdemona, Pterodactyls, Arts and Leisure, Measure for Measure, Food Chain*, Bdwy in *Two Shakespearean Actors* (1991).

DAVIS, VIOLA. Born Aug.11, 1965 in St. Matthews, So.Carolina. Graduate, Rhode Island Col., Juilliard. Debut 1992 OB in *As You Like It* followed by *House of Lear*, Bdwy in *Seven Guitars* (1996) for which she received a Theatre World Award.

DAVYS, EDMUND C. Born Jan. 21, 1947 in Nashua, NH. Graduate Oberlin Col. Debut 1977 OB in *Othello*, Bdwy in *Crucifer of Blood* (1979), *Shadowlands, A Small Family Business, The Show-off, St. Joan, Three Men on a Horse, Ideal Husband*.

DEAL, FRANK. Born October 7, 1958 in Birmingham, AL. Attended Duke U. Debut 1982 OB in *The American Princess* followed by *Richard III, Ruffian on the Stair, A Midsummer Night's Dream, We Shall Not All Sleep, The Legend of Sleepy Hollow, Three Sisters, The Triangle Project, One Neck, Window Man, Othello, Junk Bonds, Dark Ride*.

DEAN, DAVID JOHN. Graduate GeorgetownU. Debut 1993 OB in *Earl Ollie Austin & Ralph* followed by *God's Country, Native Son, Strangers in the Land of Canaan*.

DEASY, MARIA. Born Oct.3 in Rochester, NY. Graduate BrownU. Debut 1991 OB in *The Crucible* followed by *Female Dilemma*.

DEE, RUBY. Born Oct.27, 1923 in Cleveland, OH. Graduate Hunter Col. Bdwy debut in *Jeb* (1946) followed by *Anna Lucasta, Smile of the World, Long Way Home, Raisin in the Sun, Purlie Victorious, Checkmates*(1988), OB in *World of Sholom Aleichem, Boesman und Lena, Wedding Band, Hamlet, Take It from the Top, Checkmates* (1995).

DEEP, MICHAEL. Born June 12, 1954 in Macon, GA. Graduate MercerU. Debut 1979 OB in *Ragged Trousered Philanthropists* followed by *Engaged, Bring Mother Down*.

DE LA PENA, GEORGE. Born in NYC in 1956. Performed with Am. Bal. Th. before Bdwy debut 1981 in *Woman of the Year* followed by *On Your Toes, Red Shoes, Chronicle of a Death Foretold*.

DENISE, CAROL. Born in Akron, OH. Attended AkronU. Bdwy debut in *Will Rogers Follies* (1993) followed by *Ain't Bdwy Grand*, OB in *Time and the Wind*.

DENISON, MICHAEL. Born Nov.1, 1915. Graduate Oxford. Bdwy debut in *Ideal Husband* (1996).

DePINA, SABRINA. Born Apr.23, 1969 in NYC. Attended AADA. Debut 1985 OB in *Long Time Since Yesterday* followed by *Six Characters in Search of an Author, Black Girl*.

DeSHIELDS, ANDRE. Born January 12, 1946 in Baltimore, MD. Graduate U. Wis. Bdwy debut 1973 in *Warp*, followed by *Rachel Lily Rosenbloom, The Wiz, Ain't Misbehavin'* (1978/1988), *Haarlem Nocture, Just So, Stardust*, OB in *2008-1/2 Jazzbo Brown, The Soldier's Tale, The Little Prince, Haarlem Nocturne, Sovereign State of Boogedy Boogedy, Kiss Me When It's Over, Saint Tous, Ascension Day, Casino Paradise, The Wiz, Angel Levine, Ghost Cafe......*

DESMOND, DAN. Born July 4, 1944 in Racine, Wis. Graduate UWis, YaleU, Bdwy debut 1981 in *Morning's at 7* followed by *Othello, All My Sons, Rumors*, OB in *Perfect Diamond, The Bear, Vienna Notes, On Mt. Chimborazo, Table Settings, Moonchildren, Festival of 1-Acts, Marathon '88, Death Defying Acts*.

DEVLIN, JAY. Born May 8, 1929 in Ft. Dodge, IA. OB in *The Mad Show, Little Murders, Unfair to Goliath, Ballymurphy, Front Page, Fasnacht Day, Bugles at Dawn, A Cood Yearfor the Roses, Crossing the Bar, Murder of Crows, Fesaval of 1-Acts, Finding Rose*, Bdwy in *King of Hearts* (1978)

DeVRIES, MICHAEL. Born January 15, 1951 in Grand Rapids, Ml. Graduate U. Wash. Debut *1987* OB in *Ready or Not*, Bdwy in *Grand Hotel (1989), Secret Garden, Hello Dolly*(1995).

DiBENEDETTO, JOHN. Born Oct.9, 1955 in Brooklyn, NYC. Attended Hunter Col., HB Studio. Debut 1979 OB in *Prisoners of Quai Dong* followed by *Greatest of All Time, Apple Crest, Tales of Another City, Out at Sea, Heartdrops, Good Woman of Setzuan, Squeeze, Drunken Boat, Venus Dances Nightly, Not a Single Blade of Grass, Flashpoint, Sea Gull, Bruno's Donuts, Happy Birthday America, Full Circle, Across Arkansas, Jurlyburly, Wedding, Candide, Unrecognizable Characters, Secret Sits in the Middle, Wolf at the Door, Ruby and Pearl*.

DILLON, MIA. Born July 9, 1955 in Colorado Springs, CO. Graduate Penn State U. Bdwy debut 1977 in *Equas*, followed by *Da, Once a Catholic, Crimes of the Heart, The Corn is Green, Hay Fever, The Miser*, OB in *The Crucible, Summer, Waiting for the Parade, Crimes of the Heart, Fables for Friends, Scenes from La Ve de Boheme, Three Sisters, Wednesday, Roberta in Concert, Come Back Little Sheba, Venna Notes, George White's Scandals, Lady Moonsong, Mr. Monsoon, Almost Perfect, The Aunts, Approximating Mother, Remembrance, Lauren's Whereabouts, New England*.

DISHY, BOB. Born in Brooklyn, NYC. Graduate Syracuse U. Bdwy debut 1955 in *Damn Yankees* followed by *Can-Can, Flora the Red Menace, Something Different, Goodbye People, A Way of Life, Creation of the World and Other Business, American Millionaire, Sly Fox, Murder at Howard Johnson's, Grownups, Cafe Crown, Tenth Man*, OB in *When the Owl Screams, Wrecking Ball, By Jupiter, Unknown Soldier and His Wife, What's Wrong with This Picture?, Short Play Series, The Cowboy, The Indian and the Fervent Feminist, The Shawl*.

DIVENY, MARY. Born in Elmira, NY. Attended Elmira Col., AADA. Bdwy debut 1946 in *The Playboy of the Western World*, followed by *Crime and Punishment, Life with Mother*, OB in *The Matchmaker, Marvin 's Room, Arts & Leisure*.

DIXON, ED. Born Sept. 2, 1948 in Oklahoma. Attended U. Okla. Bdwy in *The Student Prince*, followed by *No No Nanette, Rosalie in Concert, The Three Musketeers, Les Miserables, Cyrano: The Musical*, OB in *By Bernstein, King of the Schnorrers, Rabboni, Hunchback of Notre Dame, Moby Dick, Shylock, Johnny Pye and the Foolkiller, America's Sweetheart*.

DIXON, MacINTYRE. Born December 22, *1931* in Everett, Ma. Graduate Emerson Col. Bdwy debut 1965 in *Xmas in Las Vegas*, followed by *Cop-Out, Story Theatre, Metamorphosis, Twigs, Over Here, Once in a Lifetime, Alice in Wonderland, 3 Penny Opera, A Funny Thing...*(1996), *Tempest*, OB in *Quare Fellow, Plays for Bleecker Street, Stewed Prunes, The Cat's Pajamas, Three Sisters, 3 X 3, Second City, Mad Show, Meow!, Lotta, Rubbers, Conjuring an Event, His Majesty the Devil, Tomfoolery, A Christmas Carol Times and Appetites of Toulouse-Lautrec, Room Service, Sills and Company, Little Murders Much Ado about Nothing, A Winter's Tale, Arms and the Man, Hamlet, Pericles, Luck Plauck Virtue*.

DIXON, OLIVER. Born Dec.9 in Colquitt, GA> Graduate FlSt.U. Bdwy debut in *Caine Mutiny Court-Martial* (1983) followed by OB in *Nightmare Alley, Nikita*.

DODDS, MAGAN. Born Feb.15, 1970 in Walnut Creek, CA. Graduate Juilliard. Bdwy debut in *School for Scandal* (1995) followed by OB in *English Made Simple/Ancient History*.

DON, CARL. Born Dec.15, 1916 in Vitebsk, Russia. Attended Western ReserveU. Bdwy debut in *Anastasia*(1954) followed by *Romanov and Juliet, Dear Me the Sky Is Falling, The Relapse, Tenth Man, Zalmen, Wings*, OB in *Richard III, Twelfth Night, Winterset, Arms and the Man,*

Between Two Thieves, He Who Gets Slapped, Jacobowsky and the Colonel, Carnival, The Possesed, Three Acts of Recognition, The Golem, Cafe Crown, Picasso at the Lapin Agile

D'ONOFRIO, VINCENT. Born June 30, 1959 in Brooklyn, NY. Bdwy debut in *Open Admissions* (1984), OB in *Tooth of Crime*.

DONOHOE, ROB. Born Dec.25, 1950 in Bossier City, LA. Graduate E.NewMxU., AmThArts. Debut 1987 OB in *Long Boat* followed by *Last Resort, Leave It to Jane* Bdwy in *Christmas Carol* (1995).

DOWNING, VIRGINIA. Bom Mar.7 in Washington, DC. Anended Bryn Mawr. Bdwy debut in *Father Malachy's Miracle* (1937), followed by *Forward the Heart, The Cradle Will Rock, A Gift of Time, We Have Always Lived in a Castle, Arsenic and Old Lace,* OB in *Juno and the Paycock, Man with the Golden Arm, Palm Tree in a Rose Garden, Play with a Tiger, The Wives, The Idiot, Medea, Mrs. Warren's Profession, Mercy Street, Thuder Rock, Pygmalion, First Week in Bogota, Rimers of Eldritch, Les Blancs, Shadow of a Gunman, All the Way Home, A Winter's Tak, Billy Liar, Shadow and Substance, Silent Catastrophe, Ernest in Love, Night Games, A Frog in His Throat, All That Fall, Richard III, Aimee and Hope.*

DRISCOLL, ANDREW. Born July 11, 1974 in Peoria, IL. Graduate AMDA. Debut 1995 OB in *Oedipus Private Eye* followed by *Slain in the Spirit,* Bdwy in *Miss Saigon* (1995).

DUDLEY, CRAIG. Born Jan. 22, 1945 in Sheepshead Bay, NY. Graduate AADA, Am.Th.Wing. Debut 1970 OB in *Macbeth,* followed by *Zou, I Have Always Believed in Ghosts, Othello, War and Peace, Dial "M" for Murder, Misalliance, Crown of Kings, Trelawny of The Wells, Ursula's Permanent.*

DUELL, WILLIAM. Bom August 30, 1923 in Corinth, NY. Attended Il. Wesleyan Yale. OB 1962 in *Portrait of the Artist as a Young Man/Barroom Monks,* followed by *A Midsummer Night's Dream, Henry IV, Taming of the Shrew, The Memorandum Threepenny Opera, Loves of Cass Maguire, Romance Language, Hamlet, Henry IV (I & 11), On the Bum,* Bdwy in *A Cook for Mr. General, Ballad of the Sad Cafe, Ilya Darling, 1776, Kings, Stages, Inspector General, Marriage of Figaro, Our Town, A Funny Thing...*(1996).

DUMAINE, REBECCA. Born Apr.1, 1970 in Albany, NY. Graduate DukeU. Debut 1996 OB in *One Way Street.*

DUNCAN, LINDSAY. Born Nov.7, 1950 in Edinburgh, Scotland. Attenede Central School of Speech/Drama, London. Debut 1982 OB in *Top Girls* followed by Bdwy in *Les Liasons Dangereuse* for which she received a 1987 Theatre World Award, *Midsummer Night's Dream.*

DUNLOP, TOM. Born Jan.14, 1961 in Waterbury, CT. Graduate BrownU, Juilliard. Debut 1989 OB in *Macbeth* followed by *Midsummer Night's Dream, King John, Misalliance.*

DURANG, CHRISTOPHER. Bom January 2, 1949 in Montclair, NJ. Graduate Harvard, Yale. Debut 1976 OB in *Das Lusitania Songspiel* followed by *Hotel Play, Sister Mary Ignatius Explains It All, Birthday Present, Marriage of Bette and Boo, Laughing Wild, Ubu, Putting It Together, A Christmas Memory, Chris Durang & Dawne.*

DURNING, CHARLES. Born Feb.28, 1923 in Highland Falls, NY. Attended Columbia, NYU. Bdwy in *Poor Bitros, Drat the Cat, Pousse Cafe, Happy Time, Indians, That Championship Season, Knock Knock, Cat on a Hot Tin Roof* (1990), *Inherit the Wind,* OB in *Two by Saroyan, Child Buyer, Album of Gunter Grass, Huui Huui, Invitation to a Beheading, Lemon Sky, Henry VI, Happiness Cage, Hamlet, In the BoomBoom Room, Au Pair Man.*

DYBAS, JAMES. Born Feb.7, 1944 in Chicago, IL. Bdwy debut in *Do I Hear a Waltz* (1965) followed by *George M, Via Galactica, Pacific Overtures, Sunset Blvd.*

DYLEWSKI, CHRIS. Born July 11, 1967 in Hartford, CT. Attended NYU. Debut 1987 OB in *Waiting for Lefty* followed by *Grand Guinol, Life Is a Dream.*

EBERSOLE, CHRISTINE. Born Feb.21, 1953 in Park Forest, IL. Attended AADA. Bdwy debut in *Angel Street* (1976) followed by *I Love My Wife, On the 20th Century, Oklahoma, Camelot, Harrigan and Hart, Getting Away with Murder,* OB in *Green Pond, Three Sisters, Geniuses.*

EDA-YOUNG, BARBARA. Born Jan.30, 1945 in Detroit, MI. Bdwy debut in *Lovers and Other Strangers* (1968) followed by LC's *Time of Your Life, Camino Real, Operation Sidewinder, Kool Aid, Streetcar Named Desire,* OB in *The Hawk, The Gathering, The Terrorists, Drinks before Dinner, Shout Across the River, After Stardive, Birdbath, Crossing the Crab Bebula, Maiden Stakes, Come Dog Come Night, Two Character Play, Mensch Meier, Glory in the Flower, Goodbye Freddy, A Rosen by Any Other Name, After Crystal Night, Slavs.*

EDDLEMAN, JACK. Born Sept.7, 1933 in Millsap, TX. Attended UTulsa, UMKC. Bdwy debut in *Shinbone Alley* (1957) followed by *Carousel*(CC), *Oh Captain, Camelot, Hot Spot, Girl Who Came to Supper, Oh What a Lovely War, My Fair Lady*(CC), OB in Diversions, *Lend an Ear, Great Scott, Jacques Brell is Alive..., Swan Song, A Perfectly Weill Evening, Greenwillow.*

EDELMAN, GREGG. Born Sept. 12, 1958 in Chicago, IL. Graduate Northwestern U. Bdwy debut 1982 in *Evita,* followed by *Oliver!, Cats, Cabaret, City of Angels, Falsettos, Anna Karenina, Passion, Fiorello (Encores), Out of This World (Encores),* OB in *Weekend, Shop on Main Street, Forbidden Broadway, She Loves Me, Babes in Arms, Make Someone Happy, Greetings, Standing By.*

EGAN, JOHN TRACY. Born July 10, 1962 in NYC. Graduate SUNY/Purchase, Attended Westchester Comm Col. Debut 1990 OB in *Whatnot*

EHLINGER, MARY. Born August 17 in Green Bay, Wi. Graduate St. Norbert Col.
LSU. Debut 1989 OB in *Oil City Symphony,* followed by *Return of the Forbidden*
Planet Cowgirls.

EICHE, JEFFREY D. Born Mar.28, 1955 in San Diego, CA. Graduate San DiegoStU. Debut 1983 OB in *Taming of the Shrew* followed by *Nude with Violin, As You Like It, Engaged.*

EIGENBERG, DAVID M. Born May 17, 1964 in Manhasset, NY. Graduate AADA. Debut 1989 OB in *Young Playwright's Festival/Finnagan's Funeral Parlor & Ice Cream Shop,* followed by *The My House Play, EST Marathon '92, Tunnel of Love, Paradise, Generation X,Black Ink,* Bdwy in *Six Degrees of Separation* (1990, also OB).

EIS, MARK. Born June 18, 1964 in Schenectady, NY. Graduate SUNY/Albany, UNCarolina. Debut 1994 OB in *Oh What a Lovely War* followed by *Botticelli, Romeo and Juliet, Measure for Measure, Titus Andronicus, Edith Wharton's Manhattan.*

EISENBERG, NED. Born January 13, 1957 in NYC. Attended Acl. Inst. of Arts. Debut 1980 OB in *Time of the Cuckoo* followed by *Our Lord of Lynchville, Dream of a Blacklisted Actor, Second Avenue, Moving Targets, Claus, Titus Adronicus, Saturday Morning Cartoons, Antigone in NY, Green Bird,* Bdwy 1995 in *Pal Joey*(Encores).

ELDER, DAVID. Born July 7, 1966 in Houston, TX. Attended U. Houston. Bdwy debut 1992 in *Guys and Dolls* followed by *Beauty and the Beast.*

ELKINS, ELIZABETH. Born July 24, 1967 in Ft. Lauderdale, FL. Debut 1991 OB in *Blue Window* followed by *Lion in the Streets.*

ELLIS, AUNJANUE. Born 1969 in San Francisco, CA. Graduate U of Evansville, Juilliard. Bdwy debut in *The Tempest* (1995-also OB).

EMERY, LISA. Born January 29 in Pittsburgh, PA. Graduate Hollins Col. Debut 1981 OB in *In Connecticut,* followed by *Talley & Son, Dalton's Back, Growaups!, The Matchmaker, Marvin's Room, Watbanaland, Monogomist, Curtains,* Bdwy in *Passion* (1983), *Burn This, Rumors.*

EMICK, JARROD. Born July 2, 1969 in Ft. Eustas, VA. Attended S. Dakota State U. Bdwy debut 1990 in *Miss Saigon* followed by *Damn Yankees* for which he received a 1994 Theatre World Award. OB in *America's Sweetheart.*

EMMETT, ROBERT/BOB. Born Sept. 28, 1921 in Monterey, CA. Attended U. Cal., Neighborhood Playhouse. Bdwy credits include *Peter Gynt* (1951), *Two on the Aisle, Mid-Summer,* OB in *Knight of the Burning Pestle, Madam Will You Walk, Eye of the Beholder, Doll's House, The Visit, King James and the Indian.*

ENDERS, CAMILLA. Born Sept.6, 1967 in Boston, MA. Graduate Oberlin Col. U of London. Debut 1995 in *Sylvia*(u/s) followed by *Ivanov.*

ENGLISH, ROBERT. Born Oct.18, 1965 in Queens, NYC. Graduate NorthwesternU. Debut 1995 OB in *Doll's House* followed by *The Idiot, Brothers Karamazov, Antigone, Winter's Tale.*

EPPERSON, JOHN. Born 1956 in Hazelburst, MS. Debut 1988 OB in *I Could Go on Lypsynching,* followed by *The Fabulous Lypsinka Show. Lysinka! A Day in the Life!, As I Lay Lip-Synching.*

ERRICO, MELISSA. Born March 23, 1970 in NYC. Graduate Yale U. BADA. Bdwy debut in *Anna Karenina* (1992) followed by *My Fair Lady*(1994), *Call Me Madam (Encores), One Touch of Venus (Encores),* OB in *After Crystal Night, Spring Awakening.*

ESHELMAN, DREW. Born October 12, 1946 in Long Beach, CA. Graduate Shimer Col., Am. Cons. Th. Broadway debut 1992 in *Les Miserables.*

ESPINOZA, AL. Born Aug.18, 1968 in Oriente, Cuba. Graduate So. MethodistU, Yale Drama. Bdwy debut in *Sacrilege* (1995) followed by *Getting Away with Murder.*

ESPINOZA, BRANDON. Born August 9, 1982 in Queens, NYC. Bdwy debut 1993 in *The Will Rogers Follies* followed by *Les Miserables, Big*.

ESPOSITO, GIANCARLO. Bom April 26, 1958 in Copenhagen, Den. Bdwy debut in *Maggie Flynn* (1968) followed by *Me Nobody Knows, Lost in the Stars, Seesaw, Merrily We Roll Along, Don't Cet God Started, 3 Penny Opera, Sacrilege*, OB in *Zooman and the Sign* for which he received a 1981 Theatre World Award, *Keyboard, Who Loves the Dancer, House of Ramon Iglesias, Do Lord Remember Me, Balm in Gilead, Anchorman, Distant Fires, The Root, Trafficking in Broken Hearts*.

ESTERMAN, LAURA. Born April 12 in NYC. Attended Radcliffe Col., LAMDA. Debut 1969 OB in *The Time of Your Life*, followed by *Pig Pen, Carpenters, Ghosts, The Sea Gull, Rubbers, Yankees 3 Detroit 0, Golden Boy, Out of Our Father's House, The Master and Margarita, Chinchilla, Dusa, Fish Stas and Vi, A Midsummer Night's Dream, The Recruiting Officer, Oedipus the King, Two Fish in the Sky, Mary Barnes, Tamara, Marvin's Room, Edith Stein, Curtains, Yiddish Trojan Women*, Bdwy in *Waltz of the Toreadors, The Show-off*.

ESTEY, SUELLEN. Born Nov. 21 in Mason City, IA. Graduate Stephens Col., Northwestern U. Debut 1970 OB in *Some Other Time*, followed by *June Moon, Buy Bonds Buster, Smile Smile Smile, Carousel, Lullaby of Broadway, I Can't Keep Running, The Guys in the Truck, Stop the World..., Bittersuite—One More Time, Passionate Extremes, Sweeney Todd, Love in Two Countries, After the Ball*, Bdwy in *The Selling of the President* (1972), *Barnum, Sweethearts in Concert, Sweeney Todd* (1989), *State Fair*.

EVANS, DANIEL. Born July 31, 1973 in South Wales. Graduate Guildhall School of Music/Drama. Bdwy debut in *Midsummer Night's Dream* (1996),

EVANS, HARVEY. Born Jan. 7, 1941 in Cincinnati, OH. Bdwy debut 1957 in *New Girl in Town*, followed by *Annie Get Your Gun, Nash at 9, West Side Story, Redhead, Gypsy, Anyone Can Whistle, Oklahoma, Hello Dolly!, George M!, Our Town, The Boy Friend, Follies, Barnum, Damn Yankees, La Cage aux Folles, Damn Yankees, Sunset Blvd., Sunset Blvd.*, OB in *The Rothschilds, Sextet, Annie Warbucks*.

EWIN, PAULA. Born Dec.6, 1955 in Warwick, Rhode Island. Attended King's College/Wilkes-Barre, PA, Graduate Rhode Island College. Debut 1991 OB in *Necktie Breakfast* followed by *As You Like It, Lion in the Streets, Baptists*.

FABEL, KYLE. Born Nov.24, 1970 in Chicago, IL. Graduate MarquetteU, NYU. Debut OB 1996 in *English Made Simple*.

FACTORA, MARSHALL. Born Aug.19 in the Philippines. Graduate USt.Thomas, NYU. Debut 1990 OB in *The Wash* followed by *Rita's Resources, Tibet Does Not Exist, Caucasian Chalk Circle*.

FARLEY, LEO G. Born Oct.30, 1950 in Flushing, NY. Graduate Queensboro Comm Col. Debut 1986 OB in *Rimmers of Eldrich* followed by *Convulsions, Necktie Breakfast, Under Control, Visiting Oliver, Killer Joe*.

FAUGNO, MAX. Born Mar.2, 1975 in NYC. Attends NYU. Debut 1994 OB in *One Flew Over the Cukoo's Nest* followed by *The Beautiful People*.

FAUVELL, TIM. Born Aug.2, 1961 in Queens, NYC. Attended Hunter Col. Debut 1978 OB in *Sojourner Truth* followed by *King of the Schnorrers*, Bdwy in *Grease* (1979) followed by *Joseph and the...Dreamcoat, Sondheim Celebration at Carnegie Hall, State Fair*.

FAYE, PASCALE. Born January 6, 1964 in Paris, France. Bdwy debut in *Grand Hotel*(1991) followed by *Guys and Dolls, Victor Victoria*.

FELDSHUH, TOVAH. Born Dec. 28, 1953 in New York City. Graduate Sarah Lawrence Col., U. Minn. Bdwy debut 1973 in *Cyrano*, followed by *Dreyfus in Rehearsal, Rodgers and Hart, Yentl* for which she received a Theatre World Award, *Sarava, Lend Me a Tenor*, OB in *Yentl the Yeshiva Boy, Straws in the Wind, Three Sisters, She Stoops to Conquer, Springtime for Henry, The Time of Your Life, Children of the Sun, The Last of the Red Hot Lovers, Mistress of the Inn, A Fierce Attachment, Custody, Six Wives, Hello Muddah Hello Faddah, Best of the West, Awake and Sing, Tovah: Out of Her Mind, Tovah in Concert*.

FIERSTEIN, HARVEY. Born June 6, 1954 in Brooklyn, NY. Graduate Pratt Inst. Debut 1971 OB in *Pork*, followed by *International Stud, Figures in a Nursery, Haunted Host, Pouf Positive, This Is Not Going to Be Pretty*, Bdwy in *Torch Song Trilogy* (1982) for which he won a Theatre World Award, *Safe Sex* (also OB).

FIGUEROA, RONA. Born March 30, 1972 in San Francisco, CA. Attended UC/Santa Cruz. Bdwy debut in *Miss Saigon* (1993).OB in *Caucasain Chalk Circle*.

FILANI, MARIANNE. Born May 18, 1968 in Casablanca, Morocco. Bdwy debut in *Chronicle of a Death Foretold* (1995). OB in *Dancing on Her Knees*.

FINCH, SUSAN. Born Aug.30, 1959 in Germantown, PA. Attended Juilliard. Debut 1986 OB in *Orchards* followed by *Fair Fight, Sisters Dance*.

FINKEL, BARRY. Bom Jul. 21, 1960 in Philadelphia PA. Attended TempleU. AMDA. Debut 1986 OB in *Have I Got a Girl for You*, followed by *Cowboy, A Funny Thing..., Lust*, Bdwy in *Late Nite Comic* (1987).

FIRE, NORMA. Born June 9, 1937 in Brooklyn, NY. Graduate Brooklyn Col. Debut 1982 OB in *3 Acts of Recognition*, followed by *Merry Wives of Windsor, Henry V, It's All Talk, Macbeth, The Mysteries?, Wally's Ghost*.

FISCHER, LORI. Born Mar.17, 1963 in Moline, IL. Graduate BelmontU. Debut 1996 OB in *Cowgirls*.

FISHER, MARY BETH. Born in Plainfield, NJ. Graduate RutgersU, Debut 1978 OB in *Are You Now or Have You Ever Been?* followed by *Extremities, Radical Mystique*, Bdwy in *Night of the Iguana* (1996).

FITZPATRICK, ALLEN. Born January 31, 1955 in Boston, MA. Graduate U. Va. Debut 1977 OB in *Come Back Little Sheba* followed by *Wonderful Town, Rothschilds, Group One Acts, Jack's Holiday, Mata Hari*, Bdwy in *Gentlemen Prefer Blondes*(1995).

FLANAGAN, KIT. Born July 6 in Pittsburgh, PA. GRaduate NorthwesternU. Debut 1979 OB in *Diary of Anne Frank* followed by *Evening with Dorothy Parker, Still Life, Cloud 9, Alto Part, Step Out of Line, Goodbye Freddy, Wonder Years, Nine*, Bdwy in *All My Sons* (1987).

FLANAGAN, PAULINE. Born June 29, 1925 in Sligo, Ire. Debut 1958 OB in *Ulysses in Nighttown*, followed by *Pictures in the Hallway, Later, Antigone, The Crucible, The Plough artd the Stars, Summer, Close of Play, In Celebration, Without Apologies, Yeats, A Celebration, Philadelphia Here I Come!, Grandchild of Kings, Shadow of a Gunman, Juno and the Paycock*, Bdwy in *God and Kate Murphy, The Living Room, The Innocents, The Father, Medea, Steaming, Corpse, Philadelphia Here I Come* (1994)

FLEMING, EUGENE. Born Apr. 26, 1961 in Richmond, VA. Attended NC Sch of Arts, Bdwy in *Chorus Line* followed by *Tap Dance Kid, Black and Blue, High Rollers, DuBarry Was a Lady(Encores), Swinging on a Star*, OB in *Voorhas, Dutchman, Ceremonies in Dark Old Men, Freefall*.

FLETCHER, SUSANN. Born September 7, 1955 in Wilmington, DE. Graduate Longwood Col., Bdwy debut in *Best Little Whorehouse in Texas* (1980), followed by *Raggedy Ann, Jerome Robbins' Broadway, Goodbye Girl, Guys and Dolls*, OB in *Homo Americanus, Stairway to Heaven, Any Place But Here*.

FLOCKHART, CALISTA. Born Nov.11 in Stockton, IL. Graduate RutgersU. Debut 1989 OB in *Beside Herself* followed by *Bovver Boys, Mad Forest, Wrong Turn at Lungfish, Sophistry, All for One, The Loop, The Imposter*, Bdwy in *Glass Menagerie* (1994) for which she received a Theatre World Award.

FLYNN, J. LEE. Born Dec.13, 1937 in Long Lake, NY. Graduate Ithica Col. Debut 1984 OB in *Selma* followed by *State Fair*.

FORBES, KATE. Born Oct.10, 1963 in Athens, GA. Graduate Sarah Lawrence Col., NYU. Debut 1994 OB in *Doll's House* followed by *Othello*, Bdwy in *School for Scandal* (1995) for which she received a Theatre World Award, *Inherit the Wind*.

FORD, BARRY. Born Mar.27, 1933 in Oakland, CA. Graduate CalStU. Debut 1972 OB in *Ruddigore* followed by *Devil's Disciple, Nymph Errant, After You've Gone, Trial of Adam Clayton Powell, Heartbreak House, Tiny Tim and the Size Queen*.

FORMAN, KEN. Born September 22, 1961 in Boston, MA. Attended NYU. Debut 1985 OB in *Measure for Measure*, followed by *Rosencrantz and Guildenstern Are Dead, Macbeth, I Stand Before You Naked, Romeo and Juliet, 3 by Wilder, As You Like It, SS Glencairn, Goose and Tom Tom, Twelfth Night, Anatomy of Sound, Ends of the Earth, Child's Christmas in Wales*, Bdwy in *Wilder Wilder Wilder* (1983).

FORSYTHE, JOHN. Born Jan.29, 1918 in Penn's Grove, NJ. Bdwy debut in *Yankee Point* (1942) followed by *Vickie, Winged Victory, Yellow Jack, It Takes Two, All My Sons, Mister Roberts, Teahouse of the August Moon, Weekend, Sacrilege*.

FOSTER, HERBERT. Born May 14, 1936 in Winnipeg, Can. Bdwy in *Ways and Means, Touch of the Poet, Imaginary Invalid, Tonight at 8:30, Henry V, Noises Off, Me and My Girl, Lettice and Lovage, Timon of Athens, Government Inspector, Sacrilege, Getting Away with Murder* OB in *Afternoon Tea, Papers, Mary Stuart, Playboy of the Western World, Good Woman of Setzuan, Scenes from American Life, Twelfth Night, All's Well That Ends Well, Richard II, Gifts of the Magi, Heliotrope Bouquet, Troilus and Cressida*.

FOWLER, BETH. Born November 1, 1940 in New Jersey. Graduate Caldwell Col. Bdwy debut 1970 in *Gantry* followed by *A Little Night Music, Over Here, 1600 Pennsylvania Avenue, Peter Pan, Baby, Teddy and Alice, Sweeney Todd* (1989), *Beauty and the Beast*, OB in *Preppies, The Blessing, Sweeney Todd*.

FOWLER, CLEMENT. Born December 27, 1924 in Detroit, MI. Graduate Wayne State U. Bdwy debut 1951 in *Legend of Lovers* followed by *The Cold Wind and the Warm, The Fragile Fox, The Sunshine Boys, Hamlet* (1964), *Richard II, Inherit the Wind*, OB in *The Eagle Has Two Heads, House Music, The Transfiguration of Benno Blimpie, The Inheritors, Paradise Lost, The Time of Your Life, Children of the Sun, Highest Standard of Living, Cymbeline, The Chairs, Venetian Twins*.

FOY, HARRIETT D. Born August 24, 1962 in New Bern, NC. Graduate HowardU. Debut 1993 OB in *Fire's Daughters* followed by *Mr. Wonderful, Struttin', Trinity, Inside Out, Trojan Women:A Love Story*

FRANCIS-JAMES, PETER. Born Sept. 16, 1956 in Chicago, IL. Graduate RADA. Debut 1979 OB in *Julius Caesar*, followed by *Long Day's Journey into Night, Antigone, Richard II, Romeo and Juliet, Enrico IV, Cymbeline, Hamlet, Learned Ladies, 10th Young Playwrights Festival, Measure for Measure, Amphitryon, Troilus and Cressida*.

FRANKLIN, NANCY. Born in NYC. Debut 1959 OB in *Buffalo Skinner* followed by *Power of Darkness, Oh Dad Poor Dad..., Theatre of Peretz, 7 Days of Mourning, Here Be Dragons, Beach Children, Safe Place, Innocent Pleasures, Loves of Cass McGuire, After the Fall, Bloodletters, Briar Patch, Lost Drums, Ivanov*, Bdwy in *Never Live Over a Pretzel Factory* (1964), *Happily Never After, The White House, Charlie and Algernon*.

FRASER, ALISON. Bom July 8, 1955 in Natick, MA. Attended Camegie-Mellon, Boston Consv. Debut 1979 OB in *In Trousers*, followed by *March of the Falsettos, Beehive, Four One- Act Musicals, Tales of Tinseltown, Next Please!, Up Against It, Dirtiest Show in Town, Quarrel of Sparrows, The Gig, Cock-a-Doodle Dandy, Swingtime Canteen, Oh That Wily Snake, America's Sweetheart*, Bdwy in *Mystery of Edwin Drood* (1986), *Romance Romance, Secret Garden, Tartuffe: Born Again*

FREEMAN, JONATHAN. Born February 5, 1950 in Bay Village, OH. Graduate Ohio U. Debut 1974 OB in *The Miser* followed by *Bil Baird Marionette Theatre, Babes in Arms, Confessions of Conrad Gerhardt, Bertrano, Clap Trap, In a Pig's Valise*, Bdwy in *Sherlock Holmes* (1974), *Platinum, 13 Days to Broadway, She Loves Me, How to Succeed.*.

FRENCH, ARTHUR. Born in New York City and attended Brooklyn Col. Debut 1962 OB in *Raisin' Hell in the Sun*, followed by *Ballad of Bimshire, Day of Absence, Happy Ending, Brotherhood, Perry's Mission, Rosalee Pritchett, Moonlight Arms, Dark Tower, Brownsville Raid, Nevis Mountain Dew, Julius Caesar, Friends, Court of Miracles, The Beautiful LaSalles, Blues for a Gospel Queen, Black Girl, Driving Miss Daisy, The Spring Thing, George Washington Slept Here, Ascension Day, Boxing Day Parade, A Tempest, Hills of Massabielle, Treatment, As You Like It, Swamp Dwellers, Tower of Burden, Henry VI, Black Girl*, Bdwy in *Ain't Supposed to Die a Natural Death, The Iceman Cometh, All God's Chillun Got Wings, The Resurrection of Lady Lester, You Can't Take It with You, Design for Living, Ma Rainey's Black Bottom, Mule Bone, Playboy of the West Indies*.

FREYTAG, BETSY. Born Dec.17, 1963 in Cincinnatti, OH. Graduate DePaulU, DenisonU, Bdwy debut in *Night of the Iguana* (1996).

FRIED, JONATHAN. Born March 3, 1959 in Los Angeles, CA. Graduate Brown U., U. Cal/San Diego. Debut 1986 OB in *1951* followed by *Dispatches from Hell, Richard II, Marathon Dancing, Sleep Deprivation Chamber*.

FRIED, THEODORE. Born in Ft. Wayne, IN. Graduate Carnegie MellonU, Manhattan Sch Music. Bdwy debut in *Master Class* (1996).

FRIEL, MICHAEL. Born Feb.2, 1950 in Philadelphia, PA. Attended Allentown Col., Graduate VillanovaU. Debut 1987 OB in *Teddy Roosevelt*, Bdwy in *Master Class* (1995).

FUGARD, ATHOL. Born June 11, 1932 in Middleburg, SoAfrica. Attended UCapeTown. Bdwy debut (as actor) in *Blood Knot* (1985), OB 1988 in *Road to Mecca* followed by *Valley Song* all of which he wrote.

FULLER, PENNY. Born in 1940 in Durham, NC. Attended NorthwesternU. Bdwy in *Barefoot in the Park* (1965) followed by *Cabaret, Richard II, As You Like It, Henry IV, Applause, Rex*, OB in *Cherry Orchard, Three Viewings, New England*.

FURTH, ALEX. Born Jan.8, 1967 in Caracas, Venezela. Graduate NortheasternU. OB in *Piano Stories, All Hack and No Jab, Bomber Jackets*.

FYFE, JIM. Born Sept.27, 1958 in Camden, NJ. Graduate Allentown Col. Bdwy debut in *Biloxi Blues* (1985) followed by *Legs Diamond, Artist Descending a Staircase, A Thousand Clowns*, OB in *Remedial English, Moonchildren, Privates on Parade*.

GAGE, AMY. Born Jan.2, 1972 in Plainfield, NJ. Graduate CCM. Bdwy debut in *State Fair* (1996).

GAINES, BOYD. Born May 11, 1953 in Atlanta, GA. Graduate Juilliard. Debut 1978 OB in *Spring Awakening*, followed by *A Month in the Country* for which he received a Theatre World Award, BAM Theatre Co.'s *Winter's Tale, The Barbarians*, and *Johnny on a Spot, Vikings, Double Bass, The Maderati, Extra Man, Comedy of Errors, The Shawl*, Bdwy in *The Heidi Chronicles* (1989-also OB), *Show-Off, She Loves Me, Company* (1995).

GAINES, DAVIS. Born in Orlando, FL. Graduate FlStU. Bdwy debut in *Camelot* (1980) followed by *Phantom of the Opera, Boys from Syracuse (Encores)*, OB in *Death of Von Richthofen* (1982) followed by *Forbidden Bdwy, She Loves Me, New Moon* (NYCO), *1-2-3-4-5, Assassins*.

GALARNO, BILL. Born Mar.1, 1938 in Saginaw, MI. Graduate MiStU. Debut 1962 OB in *Natahan the Wise* followed by *Merry Wives of Windsor*, Bdwy in *Sound of Music*(CC-1967) followed by *Abe Lincoln in Illinois*.

GALLARDO, EDGARD. Born June 10 in Puerto Rico. Graduate UPR. Bdwy in *Chronicle of a Death Foretold* (1995).

GALLAGHER, HELEN. Born in 1926 in Brooklyn, NY. Bdwy debut in *Seven Lively Arts* (1947) followed by *Mr. Strauss Goes to Boston, Billion Dollar Baby, Brigadoon, High Button Shoes, Touch and Go, Make a Wish, Pal Joey, Guys and Dolls, Finian's Rainbow, Oklahoma, Bus Stop, Portofino, Sweet Charity, Mame, Cry for Us All, No No Nanette, A Broadway Musical, Sugar Babies*, OB in *Hothouse, Tickles by Tucholsky, Misanthrope, I Can't Keep Running in Place, Red Rover, Tallulah, Flower Palace, Tallulah Tonight, Riders to the Sea*.

GAMPEL, CHRIS (C.M.) Born Feb.19, 1921 in Montreal, Can. Bdwy debut in *Flight into Egypt* (1950) followed by *Capt. Brassbound's Conversion, Richard II, St. Joan, Waltz of the Toreadors, No Exit, The Crucible, Compulsion, Firstborn, Girl Who Cam to Supper, Front Page*, OB in *Spoon River, Samson Agonistes, Measure for Measure*.

GAMACHE, LAURIE. Born September 25, 1959 in Mayville, ND. Graduate Stephens Col. Bdwy debut in *Chorus Line* (1982) followed by *Red Shoes*, OB in *Cocoanuts*.

GAMMON, JAMES. Born Apr.20, 1940 in Newman, IL. Debut 1978 OB in *Curse of the Starving Class* followed by *Lie of the Mind, Simpatico*, Bdwy in *Buried Child* (1996).

GARRISON, DAVID. Born June 30, 1952 in Long Branch, NJ. Graduate BostonU. Debut 1976 OB in *Joseph and the Amazing Technicolor Dreamcoat* followed by *Living at Home, Geniuses, It's Only a Play, Make Someone Happy, Family of Mann, I Do I Do* (1996), Bdwy in *A History of the American Film* (1978), *A Day in Hollywood/A Night in the Ukraine, Pirates of Penzance, Snoopy, Torch Song Trilogy, One Touch of Venus (Encores)*.

GASTON, LYDIA. Born Apr.15, 1959 in NYC. Bdwy debut in *Jerome Robbins' Bdwy* (1990) followed by *Shogun, Miss Saigon, Red Shoes, King and I*, OB in *Rita's Resources* (1995) followed by *Cambodia Agonistes*.

GAYSUNIS, CHERYL. Born January 8, in Westminster, CA. Graduate Otterbein Col. Bdwy debut 1991 in *La Bete* followed by *Moliere Comedies, Ideal Husband* OB in *Finding the Sun* (1994), *An Enraged Reading, Fragments*.

GEIER, PAUL. Born Aug.7, 1944 in NYC. Graduate Pratt Inst. Debut 1980 OB ib *Family Business* followed by *Women in Shoes, Johnstown Vindicator, No Time Flat, Marathon '90, Sleep Deprivation Chamber*, Bdwy in *Lunch Hour* (1981).

GELLER, MARC. Born July 5, 1959 in Rhode Island. Debut 1981 OB in *Butterflies are Free* followed by *As Is, Marat/Sade, Equus, Cloud 9, Orphans, Bomber Jackets, Faustus, Box Office Poison*.

GERARD, TOM. Born October 10, 1947 in Newark, NJ. Graduate SyracuseU. Debut 1970 OB in *The Drunkard* followed by *Better Living, A Better Life, Alexander Plays*, Bdwy in *Grease* (1974).

GIAMATTI, MARCUS. Born Oct.31, 1961 in New Haven, CT. Graduate Bowdoin Col. Debut 1989 OB in *Measure for Measure* followed by *Italian American Reconciliation, All This and Moonlight, Durang Durang, Brutality of Fact*.

GILBERT, TONY. born Mar. 22 in Roanoke, VA. Graduate WA. Debut 1983 OB in *Robber Bridegroom* followed by *Sweeney Todd, Manhattan Class 1 Acts, Sheba*, Bdwy in *Oliver!* (1984), *Sweeney Todd*.

GILLESPIE, ROBERT. Born Nov.9, 1933 in Lille, France. Attended RADA, Graduate LondonU. Bdwy debut in *Midsummer Night's Dream* (1996).

GILLAN, TONY. Born Aug. 15, 1963 in NYC. Attended Queens Col., California Inst. Debut 1990 OB in *Rosetta Street* followed by *Oblivion Postponed*, Bdwy in *Conversations with My Father* (1992).

GIONSON, MEL (DUANE). Born February 23, 1954 in Honolulu, HI. Graduate U. HI. Debut 1979 OB in *Richard II*, followed by *Sunrise, Monkey Music, Behind Enemy Lines, Station J, Teahouse, A Midsummer Night's Dream, Empress of China, Chip Shot, Manoa Valley, Ghashiram, Shogun, Macbeth, Life of the Land, Noiresque, Three Sisters, Lucky Come Hawaii, Henry IVParts I & 2, Working I -Acts '91, School for Wives, How He Lied to Her Husband, Village Wooing, King Lear.*

GIORDANO, ANDREW. Born June 11, 1969 in Boston, MA. Attended Boston Consv., Westminster Choir Col. Bdwy debut in *Sunset Blvd.* (1996).

GIORDANO, JONATHAN MICHAEL. Born Jan.20, 1986 in Brooklyn, NY. Debut 1994 OB in *Odd Potato*, followed by *Captured Claus, Sheba*, Bdwy in *King and I* (1996).

GIRARDEAU, FRANK. Born Oct. 19, 1942 in Beaumont, TX. Attended Rider Col. Debut 1972 OB in *22 Years*, followed by *The Soldier, Hughie, An American Story, El Hermano, Dumping Ground. Daddies, Accounts, Shadow Man, Marathon '84, Dennis, Marathon '89, Marathon '90, Talking Pictures, Night Seasons, Carpool, Promised Land.*

GLEASON, LAURENCE. Born November 14, 1956 in Utica, NY. Graduate Utica Col. Debut 1984 OB in *Romance Language* follwed by *Agamemnon, Country Doctor, The Misanthrope, The Sleepless City, Electra, Morning Sond, Like To Live, Macbeth, 3 by Wilder, As You Like It, S.S. Glencairn, Twelfth Night, Goose and Tom Tom, Anatomy of Sound, Ends of the Earth, Child's Christmas in Wales,* Bdwy in *Wilder Wilder Wilder* (1993).

GLENN, SCOTT. Born Jan.26, 1942 in Pittsburgh, PA. Graduate Wm & Mary Col. Bdwy debut in *Impossible Years* (1965) followed by *Burn This*, OB in *Collision Course, Angelo's Wedding, Dark Rapture.*

GLEZOS, IRENE. Born June 15, in Washington, DC. Graduate Catholic U. Debut OB in *Modigliani* followed by *Last Good Moment of Lily Baker, Antigone, The Rose Tattoo, Top Girls, Lie of the Mind, Barbed Wire.*

GLOVER, JOHN. Born Aug.7, 1944 in Kingston, NY. Attended TowsonStCol. Debut 1969 OB in *Scent of Flowers* followed by *Government Inspector, Rebel Women, Treats, Booth, Criminal Minds, Fairy Garden, Digby, Oblivion Postponed*, Bdwy in *Selling of the President, Great God Brown, Don Juan, Visit, Chemin de Fer, Holiday, Importance of Being Earnest, Frankenstein, Whodunit, Design for Living, Love! Valour! Compassion!* (also OB), *Tartuffe: Born Again.*

GLOVER, SAVION. Born Nov. 19, 1973 in Newark, NJ. Bdwy debut in *Tap Dance Kid* (1984) followed by *Black and Blue, Jelly's Last Jam, Bring in Da Noise Bring in Da Funk* (also OB).

GOEKU, AI. Born Dec.20, 1972 in Los Angeles, CA. Bdwy debut in *Miss Saigon* (1994).

GOING, JOANNA. Born July 22, 1963 in Washington, DC. Graduate Emerson Col., AADA. Bdwy debut in *Flowering Peach* (1994), OB in *Women and Wallace, Pricipality of Sorrows.*

GOLDEN, LEE. Born Mar.15, 1939 in Philadelphia, PA. Debut 1995 OB in *Lust.*

GOLDES, JOEL. Born Sept.28, 1963 in Carmel, CA. Graduate UCal/Irvine. Debut 1993 OB in *News in Revue* followed by *3 By Wilder, Mourning Becomes Electra, Edward II, A Greater Good,*

GOLDSMITH, MERWIN. Born Aug.7, 1937 in Detroit, MI. Graduate UCLA, Old Vic. Bdwy debut 1970 in *Minnie's Boys* followed by *The Visit, Chemin de Fer, Rex, Leda Had a Little Swan, Trelawney of the Wells, Dirty Linen, 1940's Radio Hour, Slab Boys, Me and My Girl, Ain't Broadway Grand*, OB in *Naked Hamlet, Chickencoop Chinaman, Real Life Funnies, Wanted, Rubbers and Yanks, Chinchilla, Yours Anne, Big Apple Messengers, La Boheme, Learned Ladies, An Imaginary Life, Little Prince, Beau Jest, After-Play, Louisianna Purchase, Beauty Part.*

GOLDWYN, TONY. Born May 20, 1960 in Los Angeles, CA. Graduate Brandeis U., LAMDA. Debut 1985 OB in *Digby* followed by *Messiah, Sum of Us, Spike Heels*, Bdwy in *Lady in the Dark(Encores-1994), Holiday.*

GOODMAN, LORRAINE. Born Feb.11, 1962 in Bronx, NYC. Graduate PrincetonU. Debut 1985 OB in *Very Warm for May*, Bdwy in *Mystery of Edwin Drood* (1987), *Master Class.*

GOODNESS, JOEL. Born Jan. 22, 1962 in Wisconsin Rapids, WI. Graduate U. Wisc. Debut 1991 OB in *Custody*, followed by *Georgy*, Bdwy in *Crazy for You* (1992).

GOODWIN, AARON. Born Nov. 8, 1966 in Macon, GA. Graduate Furman U. Debut 1991 OB in *Macbeth* followed by *Fridays, Tales from Hollywood, God's Country, Greetings, Good.*

GORDON, JOSHUA DEAN. Born Oct.4, 1971 in Boston, MA. Graduate Kenyon Col. Debut 1996 OB in *Life Is a Dream.*

GORDON, MARK ALAN. Born Aug.22, 1960 in Columbus, OH. Graduate NiagaraU. OhioU. Debut 1991 OB in *Ambrosia* followed by *King James and the Indian, Giggle and Scream, Oscar over There, Math and Aftermath, True Crime, King James and the Indian.*

GORMAN, MARK. Born Sept.1, 1967 in Roanoke, VA. Graduate RadfordU. Debut 1996 OB in *Sleep Deprivation Chamber.*

GORNEY, KAREN LYNN. Born January 28, 1945 in Los Angeles, CA. Graduate Carnegie Tech, Bradeis U. Debut 1972 OB in *Dylan* followed by *Life on the Third Rail, Academy Street, Unconditional Communication, Something to Eat, Curved Ladder, Love Museum, King John, Hamlet*

GOTLIEB, BEN. Born June 27, 1954 in Kfar Saba, Israel. Attended RADA, CUNY, Brooklyn Col. Bdwy debut in *Dogg's Hamlet/Cahoot's Macbeth* (1979) OB in *Kohlhass, Relatively Speaking, The Underlings, Match Made in Heaven, Oklahoma Samovar, The Misanthrope.*

GOTTSCHALL, RUTH. Born April 14, 1957 in Wilmington, DE. Bdwy debut in *Best Little Whorehouse in Texas*(1981) followed by *Cabaret, Legs Diamond, Prince of Central Park, Goodbye Girl, A Funny Thing...*(1996).

GRAAE, JASON. Born May 15, 1958 in Chicago, IL. Graduate Cincinnati Consv. Debut 1981 OB in *Godspell*, followed by *Snoopy, Heaven on Earth, Promenade, Feathertop, Tales of Tinseltown, Living Color, Just So, Olympus on My Mind, Sitting Pretty in Concert, Babes in Arms, The Cat and the Fiddle, Forever Plaid, A Funny Thing Happened on the Way to the Forum, 50 Million Frenchmen, Rodgers and Hart Revue, Hello Muddah Hello Faddah, All in the Timing, I Married an Angel,* Bdwy in *Falsettos* (1993), *Grand Night for Singing*(also OB).

GRACE, GINGER. Born in Beaumont, TX. Graduate U. Tex, Penn State U. Debut 1981 OB in *Peer Gynt* followed by *Wild Oats, Ghost Sonata, Cherry Orchard, Faust, Hamlet, The Oresteia, Mourning Becomes Electra, Beaux Defeated.*

GRAFF, LAURIE. Born May 25, 1956 in NYC. Graduate SUNY/Binghamton. Debut 1983 OB in *In the Boom Boom Room* followed by *Talk about Love, Tiny Tim Is Dead.*

GRAFF, RANDY. Born May 23, 1955 in Brooklyn, NY. Graduate Wagner Col. Debut 1978 OB in *Pins and Needles*, followed by *Station Joy, A...My Name Is Alice, Once on a Summer's Day*, Bdwy in *Sarava, Grease, Les Miserables, City of Angels, Falsettos, Laughter on the 23rd Floor, Moon Over Buffalo.*

GRANT, KATHRYN/KATE. Born Jan. 5, 1955 in Philadelphia, PA. Graduate Juilliard. Debut OB in *Month in the Country* (1979) followed by *Spring Awakening, Talley's Folly, American Clock, The Bundle, Family Affair.*

GRANT, SEAN. Born July 13, 1966 in Brooklyn, NY. Attended NC School of Arts. Bdwy debut in *Starlight Express* (1987) followed by *Prince of Central Park, Goodbye Girl, DuBarry Was a Lady(Encores)*, OB in *Bring in the Morning.*

GRAVITTE, DEBBIE SHAPIRO. Born September 29, 1954 in Los Angeles, CA. Graduate LACC. Bdwy debut in *They're Playing Our Song* (1979) followed by *Perfectly Frank, Blues in the Night, Zorba, Jerome Robbins' Broadway, Ain't Broadway Grand, Les Miserables*, OB in *They Say It's Wonderful, New Moon in Concert, Louisianna Purchase.*

GRAY, CHARLES. Born July 15, 1960 in Annapolis, MD. Attended TowsonStU. Bdwy debut 1995 in *Grease.*

GRAY, DULCIE. Born Nov.20, 1920 in Kuala Lumpur, Malaysia. Acting since 1939 in Europe, made Bdwy debut in *Ideal Husband* (1996).

GREEN, ELIZABETH. Born Nov.9, 1963 in Madison, OH. Graduate ShenandoahU. Debut 1992 OB in *Anyone Can Whistle* followed *Anything Cole*, Bdwy in *Allegro(Encores-1994), Hello Dolly* (1995).

GREEN, GARY. Born Sept.28, 1951 in Topeka, KA. Graduate PittsburghStU. Debut 1981 OB in *Under Cover* followed by Bdwy in *Master Class* (1996).

GREEN, LAWRENCE. Born July 18 in Boulder, CO. Graduate UWash., Juilliard. Debut 1988 OB in *King John*, followed by *Much Ado about Nothing, Hamlet, Black Eagles, Good.*

GREENFIELD, MARK. Born Mar.12, 1963 in Queens, NYC. Graduate Antioch Col. Debut 1995 OB in *I Giullardi Di Piazza* followed by *Where I'm Headed, Round Trip.*

GREENSPAN, DAVID. Born 1956 In Los Angeles, CA. OB in *Phaedra, Education of Skinny Spyz, Boys in the Band, Moose Mating.*

GREGG, CLARK. Born April 2, 1962 in Boston, MA. Graduate NYU. Debut 1987 OB in *Fun* followed by *The Detective, Boy's Life, Three Sisters, Old Boy, Nothing Sacred, The Imposter*, Bdwy in *A Few Good Men* (1990).

GREY, JOEL. Born Apr.11, 1932 in Cleveland, OH. Attended Cleveland Playhouse. Bdwy debut 1951 in *Borscht Capades* followed by *Come Blow Your Horn, Stop the World I Want to Get Off, Half a Sixpence, Cabaret* (1966/1987/1995), *George M!, Goodtime Charley, Grand Tour*, OB in *Littlest Revue, Harry Noon and Night, Marco Polo Sings a Solo, Normal Heart, Greenwich Village Follies*.

GRIER, DAVID ALAN. Born June 30, 1955 in Detroit, MI. Graduate UMi., YaleU. Bdwy debut in *The First*(1981) for which he received a Theatre World Award, followed by *Dreamgirls, One Touch of Venus (Encores)*, OB in *Soldier's Play, Richard III, The Merry Wives of Windsor.*

GRIESEMER, JOHN. Born December 5, 1947 in Elizabeth, NJ. Graduate Dickinson Col., URI. Debut 1981 OB in *Turnbuckle*, followed by *Death of a Miner, Little Victories, Macbeth, A Lie of the Mind, Kate's Diary, Little Egypt, EST Marathon 93, Woyzeck, Born Guilty*, Bdwy in *Our Town* (1989), *Abe Lincoln in Illinois, Inherit the Wind.*

GRIFFITH, KRISTIN. Born September 7, 1953 in Odessa, TX. Graduate Juilliard. Bdwy debut 1976 in *Texas Trilogy*, OB in *Rib Cage, Character Lines, 3 Friends, 2 Rooms, A Month in the Country, Fables for Friends, The Trading Post, Marching in Georgia, American Garage, A Midsummer Night's Dream, Marathon '87, Bunker Reveries, On the Bench, EST Marathon '92 and '93, The Holy Terror, Black, Bonds of Affection, Crocodiles in the Potomac.*

GRIMES, TAMMY. Born January 30, 1934 in Lynn, MA. Attended Stephens College, Neighborhood Playhouse. Debut 1956 OB in *Littlest Revue* followed by *Clerambord, Molly Trick, Are You Now Or..., Father's Day, A Month in the Country, Sunset, Waltz of the Toreadors, Mlle. Colombe, Tammy in Concert, After the Ball, Stories of Women*, Bdwy in *Look After Lulu* (1959) for which she received a Theatre World Award, *The Unsinkable Molly Brown, Private Lives, High Spirits, Rattle of a Simple Man, The Only Game in Town, Musical Jubilee, California Suite, Tartuffe, Pal Joey in Concert, 42nd Street, Orpheus Descending.*

GRIZZARD, GEORGE. Born Apr.1, 1928 in Roanoke, Rapids, VA. Graduate UNC. Bdwy debut in *All Summer Long* (1954) followed by *Desperate Hours, Happiest Millionaire* for which he received a Theatre World Award, *The Disenchanted, Big Fish Little Fish, APA 1961-62, Who's Afraid of Virginia Woolf, Glass Menagerie, You Know I Can't Hear You When the Water's Running, Noel Coward's Sweet Potato, Gingham Dog, The Inquest, Country Girl, Creation of the World and Other Business, Crown Matrimonial, Royal Family, California Suite, Man and Superman, Delicate Balance* (1996), OB in *Beach House, Another Antigone.*

GROENENDAAL, CRIS. Born Feb. 17, 1948 in Erie, PA. Attended Allegheny Col., ExeterU. Bdwy debut in *Sweeney Todd* (1979)followed by *Sunday in the Park with George, Brigadoon, Desert Song, South Pacific* (LC), *Phantom of the Opera, Passion, A Funny Thing...*(1996), OB in *Francis, Sweethearts in Concert, Oh Boy, No No Nanette in Concert, Sitting Pretty, The Cat and the Fiddle, Broadway Classics at Carnegie Hall.*

GROENER, HARRY. Born September 10, 1951 in Augsburg, Germany, Graduate U. Washington. Bdwy debut in *Oklahoma!* (1979) for which he received a Theatre World Award, followed by *Oh, Brother!, Is There Life After High School, Cats, Harrigan 'n' Hart, Sunday in the Park with George, Sleight of Hand, Crazy for You*, OB in *Beside the Seaside, Twelve Dreams, Picasso at the Lapin Agile.*

GROSSMAN, HENRY. Born October 11, 1938 in New York City. Attended Actors Studio. Debut 1961 OB in *The Magistrate*, followed by *Gafileo, Musical: Madame Bovary*, Bdwy in *Grand Hotel* (1989).

GUTTMAN, RONALD. Born August 12, 1952 in Brussels, Belg. Graduate Brussels U. Debut 1986 OB in *Coastal Disturbances*, followed by *Modigliano, Free Zone, Escurial, Liliom, Philanthropist, Funky Crazy Bugaloo Boy, No Exit, Sabina, Price of Madness*, Bdwy in *Coastal Disturbances* (1987).

HADLEY, JONATHAN. Born May 6, 1964 in Charlotte, NC. Graduate NC Sch. of Arts. Debut 1993 OB in *Theda Bara and the Frontier Rabbi* followed by *Cincinnati Saint, Prime Time Prophet, Mayor Musicals, Sheba.*

HAGEN, UTA. Born June 11, 1919 in Goettingen, Ger. Bdwy debut in *The Seasgull* (1938) followed by *Happiest Years, Key Largo, Vickie, Othello, Streetcar Named Desire, Country Girl, St. JOan, Whole World Over, In Any Language, Magic and the Loss*, CC's *Angel Street* and *Tovarich, Who's Afraid of Virginia Woolf?, Cherry Orchard, Charlotte, You Never Can Tell*, OB in *Month in the Country, Good Woman of Setzuan, Mrs. Warren's Profession, Mrs. Klein.*

HAINES, MERVYN JR. Born Aug.20, 1933 in Newark, NJ. Attended AADA. With NYSF in *All's Well That Ends Well, Measure for Measure, Richard III, Henry VI*, with LCRep in *King Lear, Cry of Players, Henry* (1969), *Hamlet, King John.*

HALL, DAVIS. Born April 10, 1946 in Atlanta, Ga. Graduate NorthwesternU. Bdwy debut 1973 in *Butley*, followed by *Dogg's Hamlet and Cahoot's Macbeth*, OB in *The Promise, The Team, Dreamboats, The Taming of the Shrew, Donkey's Years, Love's Labour's Lost, Betrayal, The Travelling Squirrel, Gunmetal Blues, Measure for Measure, Entertaining Mr. Sloane.*

HALL, STEVE. Born June 4, 1958 in Washington, DC. Attended NC-SchArts. Bdwy debut in *Marlowe* (1981) followed by OB in *T.N.T., Collette Collage, Conrack, Hanged Man.*

HALSTEAD, CAROL. Born Sept.12 in Hempstead, NY. Graduate FlStU., ACT. Debut 1992 OBin*The Mask* followed by *Bats, Margo's Party.*

HALSTON, JULIE. Born December 7, 1954 in New York. Graduate Hofstra U. Debut OB 1985 in *Times Square Angel*, followed by *Vampire Lesbians of Sodom, Sleeping Beauty or Coma, The Dubliners, Lady in Question, Money Talks, Red Scare on Sunset, I 'll Be the Judge of That, Lifetime of Comedy, Honeymoon Is Over, You Should Be So Lucky, This Is Not Going to Be Pretty.*

HAMILTON, JOSH. Born in NYC. Attended BrownU. OB in *Women and Wallace, Korea, As Sure As You Live, Four Corners, Eden Cinema, A Joke, Sons and Fathers, Wild Dogs, Suburbia, Wonderful Time.*

HANDLER, EVAN. Born Jan. 10, 1961 in NYC. Attended Juilliard. Debut 1979 OB in *Biography A Game*, followed by *Striker, Final Orders, Marathon '84, Found a Peanut, What's Wrong with This Picture?, Bloodletters, Young Playwrights Festival, Human Nature, Marathon '91, Big Al, Time on Fire, Grey Zone*, Bdwy in *Solomon's Child* (1982), *Biloxi Blues, Brighton Beach Memoirs, Broadway Bound, Six Degrees of Separation*(also OB), *I Hate Hamlet.*

HANKET, ARTHUR. Born June 23, 1934 in Virginia. Graduate UVA, FlStU. Debut 1979 OB in *Cuchculain Cycle*, followed by *Boys Next Door, In Perpetuity throughout the Universe, L'ilusion, White Collar, Heaven on Earth, One Act Festival, Kingitsh, Love and Anger, One-Act Festival, Amphitryon, Oh That Wiley Snake.*

HARADA, ANN. Born February 3, 1964 in Honolulu, HI. Attended Brown U. Debut 1987 OB in *1-2-3-4-5* followed by *Hit the Lights!, America Dreaming, Dog and His Master*, Bdwy in *M. Butterfly* (1988).

HARDING, JAN LESLIE. Born in 1956 in Cambridge, MA. Graduate Boston U. Debut 1980 OB in *Album*, followed by *Sunday Picnic, Buddies, The Lunch Girls, Marathon '86, Traps, Father Was a Peculiar Man, A Murder of Crows, David's Red-Haired Death, Strange Feet, Impassioned Embraces, Storm Patterns, Bondage, My Head was a Sledgehammer, Bremen Freedom, Shades of Grey, I've Got the Shakes, Swoop, Cats and Dogs, Hell's Kitchen Sink.*

HARMON, JENNIFER. Born Dec.3, 1943 in Pasadena, Ca. Attended UMs. With APA in *Right You Are, You Can't Take It with You, War and Peace, Wild Duck, School for Scandal*, OB in *The Effect of Gamma Rays on Man-in-the-Moon Marigolds, Hot L Baltimore, Leamed Ladies, Holly and the Ivy, In Perpetuity throughout the Universe, Macbeth.*

HARPER, VALERIE. Born Aug.22, 1940 in Suffern, NY. Bdwy in *Li'l Abner, Destry Rides Again, Take Me Along, Wildcat, Subways are for Sleeping, Something Different, Story Theatre, Metamorphosis*, OB in *Death Defying Acts.*

HARPOLD, WILLIAM AARON. Born July 1, 1971 in Buckhannon, WV. Graduate Carnegie-Mellon U. Debut 1993 OB in *The Survivor* followed *Finding Rose, Admissions*, Bdwy in *Picnic* (1994).

HARRINGTON, DELPHI. Born Aug.26 in Chicago, IL. Graduate NorthwesternU. Debut 1960 OB in *Country Scandal* followed by *Moon for the Misbegotten, Baker's Dozen, The Zykovs, Character Lines, Richie, American Garage, After the Fall, Rosencrantz and Guildenstern Are Dead, Good Grief, Hay Fever, Madwoman od Chaillot, Too Clever by Half, Beauty Part*, Bdwy in *Thieves* (1974), *Everything in the Garden, Romeo and Juliet, Chapter Two, Sea Gull.*

HARRIS, JARED. Born 1962 in London. Attended DukeU. OB in *Henry IV, Tis Pity She's a Whore, King Lear, Ecstacy,*

HARRIS, ROSEMARY. Born Sept.19, 1930 in Ashby, Eng. Attended RADA. Bdwy debut 1952 in *Climate of Eden* for which she received a Theatre World Award, followed by *Troilus and Cressida, Interlock, The Disenchanted, The Tumbler, with APA in The Tavern, School for Scandal, The Sea Gull, Importance of Being Earnest, War and Peace, Man and Superman, Judith and You Can't Take It with You, Lion in Winter, Old Times, Merchant of Venice, Streetcar Named Desire, Royal Family, Pack of Lies, Hay Fever, An Inspector Calls, Delicate Balance*, OB in *New York Idea, Three Sisters, The Sea Gull.*

HASSON, ANN. Born in Ireland. Graduate UCol.Dublin, LAMDA. Bdwy debut in *Midsummer Night's Dream* (1996).

HASTED, VICTORIA. Born June 15, 1963 in London, Eng. Bdwy debut in *Ideal Husband* (1996).

 Timothy Carhart

 Diana Canova

 Mario Cantone

 Dixie Carter

 Paul Castree

 Rene Ceballos

 Keene Curtis

 B.J. Crosby

 Craig Dudley

 Carol Denise

 David Elder

 Melissa Errico

 Jarrod Emick

 Laura Esterman

 Jonathan Freeman

 SuEllen Estey

 Boyd Gaines

 Marianne Filali

 Davis Gaines

 Lori Fischer

 David Garrison

 Mary Beth Fisher

 Charles Gray

 Pauline Flanagan

 Josh Hamilton

 Lydia Gaston

 Page Johnson

 Ann Hasson

 Joe Joyce

 Victoria Hasted

225

HATTAN, MARK. Born Mar.21, 1952 in Portland, OR. Graduate UVa. Debut 1975 OB in *Our Father* followed by *Maggie Flynn, Ferocious Kisses, Kid Champion, Two Cities, Two Nikita*

HAWKINS, TRISH. Born Oct.30, 1945 in Hartford, CT. Attended Radcliffe, Neighborhood Playhouse. Debut 1970 OB in *Oh!Calcutta!* followed by *Iphigenia, Hot l Baltimore* for which she received a 1973 Theatre World Award, *him, Come Back Little Sheba, Battle of Angels, Mound Builders, The Farm, Ulysses in Traction, Lulu, Hogan's Folly, Twelfth Night, A Tale Told, Great Grandson of Jedediah Kohler, Time Framed, Levitations, Love's Labour's Lost, Talley & Son, Tomorrow's Monday, Caligula, Quiet in the Land, Road Show, Why We Have a Body,Wolf at the Door*, Bdwy in *Some of My Best Friends* (1977), *Talley's Folly*.

HAWLEY, LYNN. Born November 12, 1965 in Sharon, CT. Graduate Middlebury Col. Debut 1992 OB in *Woyzeck* followed by *Owners, The Illusion, Truth Teller, Golden Boy, Venus, Truth Teller.*

HEALD, ANTHONY. Born August 25 1944 in New Rochelle, NY. Graduate MichStU. Debut 1980 OB in *Glass Menagerie*, followed by *Misalliance* for which he received a Theatre World Award, *The Caretaker, The Fox, Quartermaine's Terms, Philanthropist, Henry V, Digby, Principia Scriptoriae, Lisbon Traviata, Elliot Loves, Pygmalion, Lips Together Teeth Apart*, Bdwy in *Wake of Jamey Foster* (1982), *Mnrriage of Figaro, Anything Goes, Small Family Business, Love! Valour! Compassion!, Inherit the Wind.*

HEARN, GEORGE. Born June 18, 1934 in St. Louis, MO. Graduate Southwestern Col. OB in *Macbeth, Antony and Cleopatra, As You Like It, Richard III, Merry Wives of Windsor, Midsummer Night's Dream, Hamlet, Horseman Pass By, The Chosen*, Bdwy in *A Time for Singing, Changing Room, An Almost Perfect Person, I Remember Mama, Watch on the Rhine, Sweeney Todd, A Doll's Life, Whodunit, Cage aux Folles, Ah!Wilderness!, Ghetto, Meet Me in St. Louis, Sunset Blvd.*

HEBERT, RICH. Born Dec.14, 1956 in Quincy, MA. Graduate BostonU. Debut 1978 OB in *Rimers of Eldritch* followed by *110 in the Shade, Dazy, Easy Money, Ballad of SamGrey*,Bdwy in *Rock 'n' Roll: First 5000 Years*(1982), *Cats, Les Miserables, Sunset Blvd.*

HECHT, PAUL. Born Aug.16, 1941 in London, Eng. Attended McGillU. OB in *Sjt. Musgrave's Dance, Macbird, Phaedra, Enrico IV, Coriolanus, Cherry Orchard, Androcles and the Lion, Too Clever by Half, London Suite, Moonlight*, Bdwy in *Rosencrantz and Guildenstern Are Dead, 1776, Rothschilds, Ride Across Lake Constance, Great God Brown, Don Juan, Emperor Henry IV, Herzl, Caesar and Cleopatra, Night and Day, Noises Off.*

HECKART, EILEEN. Born Mar.29, 1919 in Columbus, OH. Graduate OhioStU. Debut 1942 OB in *Tinker's Dam* followed by *Eleemosynary, Northeast Local*, Bdwy in *Our Town, They Knew What They Wanted, The Traitor, Hilda Crane, In Any Language, Picnic* for which she received a Theatre World Award, *Bad Seed, View from the Bridge, Dark at the Top of the Stairs, Invitation to a March, Pal JOey, Everybody Loves Opal, And Things That Go Bump in the Night, Barefoot in the Park, You Know I Can't Hear You When the Water's Running, Mother Lover, Butterflies Are Free, Veronica's Room, Ladies at the Alamo, Cemetary Club.*

HEINZ, LEE. Born Apr.29 in Warren, OH. Graduate Vassar Col. WayneStU, OxfordU. Debut 1985 OB in *Daddy and Sue at the Beach* followed by *Halloween, Here Everything Still Floats, Mamet Women, Old Bachelor, Mamet Women*, Bdwy in *Peter Pan*(1980).

HELLER, ADAM. Born June 8, 1960 in Englewood, NJ. Graduate NYU. Debut 1984 OB in *Kuni-Leml*, followed by *The Special, Half a World Away, Encore!, Mererily We Roll Along*, Bdwy in *Les Miserables* (1989), *Victor Victoria.*

HENRITZE, BETTE. Born May 23 in Betsy Layne, KY. Graduate U. TN. OB in *Lion in Love, Abe Lincoln in Illinois, Othello, Baal, A Long Christmas Dinner, Queens of France, Rimers of Eldritch, Displaced Person, Acquisition, Crime of Passion, Happiness Cage, Henry VI, Richard III, Older People, Lotta, Catsplay. A Month in the Country. The Golem, Daughters, Steel Magnolias, All's Well That Ends Well*, Bdwy in *Jenny Kissed Me* (1948), *Pictures in the Hallway, Giants Sons of Giants, Ballad of the Sad Cafe, The White House, Dr. Cook's Garden, Here's Where I Belong, Much Ado about Nothing, Over Here, Angel Street, Man and Superman, Macbeth* (1981), *Present Laughter, The Octette Bridge Club, Orpheus Descending, Lettice and Lovage, On Borrowed Time, Hedda Gabler, Uncle Vanya, Inherit the Wind.*

HENRY, DIANA. Born Feb.25, 1968 in New Haven, IN. Graduate MiamiU, RutgersU. Debut 1995 OB in *Buddah* followed by *Prelude and Liebestod.*

HENSLEY, DALE. Born April 9, 1954 in Nevada, MO. Graduate Southwest MO. State U. Debut 1980 OB in *Annie Get Your Gun*, Bdwy in *Anything Goes* (1987), *Guys and Dolls* (1992), *Sunset Blvd.*

HEREDIA, WILSON JERMAINE. Born 1972 in Brooklyn. OB in *New Americans, Popal Vu, The Tower*, Bdwy in *Rent* (1996-also OB).

HIBBARD, DAVID. Born June 21, 1965. Graduate OhioStU. Debut 1989 OB in *Leave It to Jane* followed by *Chess, Forbidden Bdwy Strikes Again*, Bdwy in *Cats* (1993).

HICKS, RODNEY. Born Mar.28, 1974 in Philadelphia, PA. Attended MansfieldU. Debut 1994 OB in *Bring in the Morning* followed by *Blocks, Lotto, Chaos*, Bdwy in *Rent* (1996).

HIGLIN, DAVID.Born Aug.9, 1952 in San Bernadino, CA. Graduate Stephens Col. Bdwy Debut in *Heartland* (1981), OB in *Brooklyn Bridge, Of Mice and Men.*

HILL, ERIN. Born February 13, 1968 in Louisville, Ky. Graduate Syracuse U. Debut 1991 OB in *Return to the Forbidden Planet* followed by *Rent, True Crimes.*

HILL, KEVIN. Born Mar.29, 1968 in Waltham, MA. Debut 1995 OB in *Party.*

HILLNER, JOHN. Born November 5, 1952 in Evanston, IL. Graduate Deniston U. Debut 1977 OB in *Essential Shepard*, followed by *To Whom It May Concern, At Home, Let 'Em Rot, The Proposition*, Bdwy in *They're Playing Our Song, Little Me, Woman of the Year, Crazy for You, Company.*

HIRSCH, JUDD. Born March 15, 1935 in NYC. Bdwy debut 1966 in *Barefoot in the Park* followed by *Chapter Two, Talley's Folly, I'm Not Rappaport* (also OB)*Conversations with My Father*, OB in *On the Necessity of Being Polygamous, Scuba Duba, Mystery Play, The Hot L Baltimore, Prodigal, Knock Knock Life and/or Death, Talley's Folly, The Sea Gull, Below the Belt.*

HIRSCH, VICKI. Born Feb.22, 1951 in Wilmington, DE. Graduate UDel., VillanovaU. Debut 1985 OB in *Black County Crimes* followed by *Casualties, Mr. Universe, Working Magic, Tempest, Twelfth Night.*

HOCK, ROBERT. Born May 20, 1931 in Phoenixville, PA. Yale Graduate. Debut 1982 OB in *The Caucasian Chalk Circle* followed by *Adding Machine, Romeo and Juliet, Edward II, Creditors, Two Orphans,Macbeth, Kitty Hawk, Heathen Valley, Comedy of Errors, Phaedra, The Good Natur'd Man, Oedipus the King, Game of Love and Chance, Twelfth Night, Mrs. Warren's Profession, Oedipus at Colonus, King Lear, Beaux Stratagem, Life Is a Dream, Doll's House,Antigone*, Bdwy in *Some Americans Abroad* (1990).

HODGES, BEN. Born September 17, 1969 in Morristown, TN. Graduate Otterbein Col. Debut OB 1992 in *Loose Ends* followed by *Hysteria, Beyond Therapy.*

HOEBEE, MARK S. Born July 2, 1960 in NYC. Graduate Northwestern U. Bdwy debut in *Jerome Robbins Broadway* (1989), followed by *Street Scene* (NYCO), *Nick and Nora, Victor Victoria.*

HOFHEIMER, CHARLIE. Born Apr.17, 1981 in Detroit, MI. Bdwy debut 1995 in *On the Waterfront.*

HOLLIS, TOMMY. Born March 27, 1954 in Jacksonville, TX. Attended Lon Morris Col., U. Houston. Debut 1985 OB in *Diamonds*, followed by *Secrets of the Lava Lamp, Paradise, Africanus Instructus, Colored Museum*, Bdwy in *Piano Lesson* (1990) for which he received a Theatre World Award, *Seven Guitars.*

HOLM, CELESTE. Born Apr.29, 1919 in NYC. Attended UCLA, U. Chicago. Bdwy debut 1938 in *Gorianna*, followed by *Time of Your Life, Another Sun, Return of the Vagabond, 8 O'Clock Tuesday, My Fair Ladies, Papa Is All, All the Comforts of Home, Damask Cheek, Oklahoma!, Bloomer Girl, She Stoops to Conquer, Affairs of State, Anna Christie, King and I, His and Hers, Interlock, Third Best Sport, Invitation to a March, Mame, Candida, Habeas Corpus, Utter Glory of Morrissey Hall, I Hate Hamlet, Allegro in Concert*, OB in *Month in the Country, Paris Was Yesterday, With Love and Laughter, Christmas Carol, The Brooch*

HOLMES, DENIS. Born June 7, 1921 in Coventry, Eng. Graduate LAMDA. Bdwy debut in *Troilus and Cressida* (1955) followed by *Homecoming, Merchant of Venice, Moliere Comedies, Hamlet, Ideal Husband*, OB in *Dandy Dick*(1987).

HOLMES, RICHARD. Born March 16, 1963 in Philadelphia, PA. Graduate Gettysburg Col., NY. Debut 1990 OB in *Richard III*, followed by *Othello, Shadow of a Gunman, Mr. Parnell, Christina Alberta's Father, Yeoman of the Guard*, Bdwy in *Saint Joan* (1993), *Timon of Athens, Government Inspector.*

HOOVER, PAUL. Born June 20, 1945 in Rockford, II. Graduate Pikeville Col.. Pittsburgh Sem. Debut 1980 OB in *Kind Lady*, followed by *Prizes, As You Like It, Bonds of Affection.*

HORMAN, NICHOLAS. Born Dec.22, 1944 in Honolulu, HI. Graduate Oberlin Col., Yale. Bdwy debut in *The Visit* (1973) followed by *Chemin de Fer, Holiday, Love for Love, Rules of the Game, Member of the Wedding, St. Joan, Moose Murders,* OB in *Ice Age, Marco Polo, Artichoke, Looking-Glass, Dining Room, A Private View, Bonhoeffer 1945.*

HOSHKO, JOHN. Born July 28, 1959 in Bethesda, MD. Graduate USo-Cal. Bdwy debut 1989 in *Prince of Central Park* followed by *Gentlemen Prefer Blondes, Sunset Blvd.,* OB in *Two by Two.*

HOSMER, GEORGE. Born Sept.4, 1941 in Essex, NY. Attended USC, UMd., UHeidelberg, HB Studio. Debut 1970 OB in *I'm Getting My Act Together..., Bonds of Affection.*

HOTY, TONY. Born September 29, 1949 in Lakewood, OH. Attended Ithaca Col., U. WVA., Debut 1974 OB in *Godspell* (also Bdwy 1976) followed by *Joseph and the Amazing Technicolor Dreamcoat, Robin Hood, Success and Succession, The Root, Requiem for a Heavyweight,* Bdwy in *Gypsy* (1989).

HOXIE, RICHMOND. Born July 21, 1946 in NYC. Graduate Dartmouth Col., LAMDA. Debut 1975 OB in *Straw for an Evening* followed by *The Family, Landscape with Waitress, 3 from the Marathon, The Slab Boys, Vivien, Operation Midnight Climax, The Dining Room, Daddies, To Gillian on Her 37th Birthday, Dennis, Traps, Sleeping Dogs, Equal Wrights EST Marathon '93, Dolphin Project, Rain, Slice of Life.*

HUBER, KATHLEEN. Born March 3, 1947 in NYC. Graduaute U. Cal. Debut 1969 OB in *Scent of Flowers,* followed by *Virgin and the Unicorn, Constant Wife, Milestones, Tamara, Romeo and Juliet, Richard III, Sisters Rosensweig.*

HUFF, NEAL. Born in NYC. NYU Graduate. Debut 1992 OB in *Young Playwrights Festival* followed by *Joined at the Head, Day the Bronx Died, Macbeth, House of Yes, Class 1-Acts, Saturday Mourning Cartoons, Troilus and Crssida, Tempest*

HUFFMAN, FELICITY. Born Dec.9, 1962 in Westchesyter, NY. Graduate NYU, AADA, RADA. Debut 1988 OB in *Boys' Life,* followed by *Been Taken, Grotesque Lovesongs, Three Sisters, Shaker Heights, Jolly, Cryptogram, Stories of Women in Love, Dangerous Corner,* Bdwy in *Speed the Plow* (1988).

HULKOWER, ELLEN. Born Sept.6, 1963 in Long Island, NY. Graduate RutgersU. Debut 1992 OB in *Zel Rebels* followed by *Hamlet, Penthesilea, Jumping Off the Fridge, Las Rafaelas.*

HUNT, ANNETTE. Born January 31, 1938 in Hampton, Va. Graduate Va. Intermont Col. Debut 1957 OB in *Nine by Six,* followed by *Taming of the Shrew, Medea, Anatomist, The Misanthrope, The Cherry Orchard, Electra, Last Resort, The Seducers, A Sound of Silence, Charades, Dona Rosita, Rhinestones, Where's Charley?, The White Rose of Memphis, M. Amilcar, The Sea Gull, Rutherford & Son, Lemonmade, A Greater Good,* Bdwy in *All the Girls Came Out to Play* (1972).

HUNT, ROBERT. Born July 16. Attended WeberStU., RooseveltU. Debut 1996 OB in *Have a Nice Day.*

HUNTER, JAMES. Born Aug.16, 1943 in London. Attended LAMDA. Bdwy debut in *Loot* (1968), OB in *Dance Card.*

HUNTER, KIM. Born Nov.12, 1922 in Detroit, MI. Attended Actors Studio. Bdwy debut in *Streetcar Named Desire* (1947) followed by *Darkness at Noon, The Chase, Children's Hour, Tender Trap, Write Me a Murder, Weekend, Penny Wars, The Women, To Grandmother's House We Go,* OB in *Come Slowly Eden, All is Bright, Cherry Orchard, When We Dead Awaken, Territorial Rites, Faulkner's Bicycle, Man and Superman, Murder of Crows, Eye of the Beholder, The Visit*

HURT, MARY BETH. Born September 26, 1948 in Marshalltown, IA. Attended U. Iowa, NYU. Debut 1972 OB in *More Than You Deserve,* followed by *As You Like It, Trelaway of the Wells, The Cherry Orchard, Love for Love, Member of the Wedding, Boy Meets Girl, Secret Service, Father's Day, Nest of the Wood Grouse, The Day Room, Secret Rapture, Othello, One Shoe Off, Arts and Leisure, Oblivion Postponed,* Bdwy in *Crimes of the Heart* (1981), *The Misanthrope, Benefactors.*

IERARDI, ROBERT. Born Nov.4, 1961 in Southington, CT. Debut 1987 OB in *The Trial* followed by *Hamlet, Three Sisters, The Rehearsal, Importance of Being Earnest, Rockland County No Vaudeville.*

IRVING, GEORGE S. Born Nov. 1, 1922 in Springfield, MA. Attended Leland Powers Sch. Bdwy debut 1943 in *Oklahoma!* followed by *Call Me Mister, Along Fifth Avenue, Two's Company, Me and Juliet, Can-Can, Shinbone Alley, Bells Are Ringing, The Good Soup, Tovarich, A Murderer Among Us, Alfie, Anya, Galileo, Four on a Garden, An Evening with Richard Nixon, Irene, Who's Who in Hell, All over Town, So Long 174th Street, Once in a Lifetime, I Remember Mama, Copperfield, Pirates of Penzance, On Your Toes, Me and My Girl, Cinderella,* OB in *Rosalie in Concert Pal Joey in Concert Mexican Hayride, Louisiana Purchase*

IRWIN, BILL. Born April 11, 1950 in Santa Monica, CA. Attended UCLA, Clown Col. Debut 1982 OB in *Regard of Flight* followed by *The Courtroom, Waiting for Godot,* Bdwy in *5-6-7-8 Dance* (1983), *Accidental Death of an Anarchist, Regard of Flight, Largely New York, Fool Moon, Tempest*

IRWIN, TOM. Born June 1, 1956 in Peoria, IL. Graduate IllStU. Debut 1984 OB in *Balm in Gilead* followed by *New England.*

ISHEE, SUZANNE. Born October 15 in High Point, NC. Graduate UNC., Manhattan School of Music. Bdwy debut in *Show Boat* (1983) followed by *Mame, La Cage aux Folles, Phantom of the Opera,* OB in *Lust.*

ISOLA, KEVIN. Born Jan.27, 1970 in Ft. Irwin, CA. Graduate DukeU., NYU. Debut 1995 in *Wasp and Other Plays* followed by *Venus.*

IVES, DONALD. Born October 25, 1962 in Salem, MO. Attended Southwest MO. State, Webster Col., Southern IL. U. Bdwy debut in *Camelot*(1993), *Hello Dolly* (1995).

IVEY, DANA. Born August 12 in Atlanta, GA. Graduate Rollins Col., LAMDA. Bdwy debut in *Macbeth* (LC-1981), followed by *Present Laughter, Heartbreak House, Sunday in the Park with George, Pack of Lies, Marriage of Figaro, Indiscretions,* OB in *Call from the East, Vivien, Candida, Major Barbara, Quartermaine's Terms, Baby with the Bath Water, Driving Miss Daisy, Wenceslas Square, Love Letters, Hamlet, Subject Was Roses, Beggars in the House of Plenty, Kindertransport.*

IVEY, JUDITH. Born September 4, 1951 in El Paso, TX. Bdwy debut in *Bedroom Farce* (1979) followed by *Steaming, Hurlyburly, Blithe Spirit, Park Your Car in Harvard Yard,* OB in *Dulsa Fish Stas and Vi, Sunday Runners, Second Lady, Mrs. Dally Has a Lover, Moonshot and Cosmos, A Fair Country.*

JACKSON, ANNE. Born Sept. 3, 1926 in Allegheny, PA. Attended Neighborhood Playhouse. Bdwy debut in *Signature* (1945) followed by *Yellow Jack, John Gabriel Borkman, Last Dance, Summer and Smoke, Magnolia Alley, Love Me Long, Lady from the Sea, Never Say Never, Oh Men! Oh Women!, Rhinoceros, Luv, The Exercise, Inquest, Promenade All, Waltz of the Toreadors, Twice Around the Park, Cafe Crown* (also OB), *Lost in Yonkers, Flowering Peach,* OB in *The Tiger and the Typist, Marco Polo Sings a Solo, Diary of Anne Frank, Nest of the Wood Gouse, Madwoman of Chaillot, In Persons Stories of Women in Love.*

JACKSON, ERNESTINE. Born Sept. 18 in Corpus Christie, TX. Graduate Del Mar Col., Juilliard. Debut 1966 in *Show Boat* (LC), followed by *Finian's Rainbow, Hello Dolly!, Applause, Jesus Christ Superstar, Tricks, Raisin* for which she received a Theatre World Award, *Guys and Dolls, Bacchae,* OB in *Louis, Some Enchanted Evening, Money Notes, Jack and Jill, Black Girl, Brownstone, Sophie, Broadway Jukebox, Island Memories, Sheba.*

JACKSON, KIRK. Born Feb. 8, 1956 in Albany, NY. Graduate Binghamton U., Yale U. Debut 1990 OB in *Stirrings Still* followed by *Bremen Freedom, The Secret Lives of Ancient Egyptians, Underground Soap, Heartbreak House, Untitled Lindberg, Listen to Me, Inktomi, The Almond Seller, Necropolis, Private Property, Apocrypha, Storm Patterns, Quills,* Bdwy in *Love!Valour!Compassion!*(1995).

JACOBSON, NAOMI. Born July 21, 1956 in Philadelphia, PA. Attended UC San Diego, Graduate TempleU. Debut 1996 OB in *Scenes from an Execution.*

JACOBSON, PETER. Born Mar.24, 1965 in Chicago, IL. Graduate BrownU, Juilliard. Debut 1992 OB in *Comedy of Errors* followed by *Hot Keys, Two Noble Kingsmen, Love's Labours Lost, Four Dogs and a Bone, Compleat Wrks of Wllm Shkspr, The Workroom, Picasso at the Lapin Agile.*

JAKUBOWSKI, ZANIZ. Born in the UK. Graduate AmCol/Switzerland. Debut 1995 OB in *Ecstacy.*

JANKI, DEVANAND. Born Nov.20, 1969 in London, Ontario, Can. Attended AMDA. Debut 1991 in *Promise Land,* Bdwy in *Cats* (1992) followed by *King and I* (1996).

JBARA, GREGORY. Born Sept. 28, 1961 in Wayne, Michigan. Graduate U. MI., Juilliard. Debut 1986 OB in *Have I Got a Girl for You, Serious Money, Privates on Prarade, Forever Plaid,* Bdwy in *Serious Money* (1988), *Born Yesterday* (1989), *Damn Yankees* (1994), *Victor Victoria.*

JENKINS, DANIEL. Born Jan. 17, 1963 in NYC. Attended Columbia U. Bdwy debut 1985 in *Big River* followed by *Angels in America, Big,* OB in *Feast Here Tonight, Young Playwrights Festival, Triumph of Love, Johnny Pye and the Foolkiller.*

JENNINGS, ALEX. Born May 10, 1957 in Upminster, Essex, England. Graduate WarwickU, Bristol Old Vic ThSch. Bdwy debut 1996 in *Midsummer Night's Dream.*

JENNINGS, KEN Born Oct. 10, 1947 in Jersey City, NJ. Graduate St. Peter's .Col. Bdwy debut 1975 in *All God's Chillun Got Wings*, followed by *Sweeney Todd* for which he received a 1979 Theatre World Award, *Present Laughter, Grand Hotel, Christmas Carol*, OB in *Once on a Summer's Day, Mayor, Rabboni, Gifts of the Magi, Carmilla, Sharon, Mayor, Amphigory, Shabbatai*.

JOHANSON, DON. Born October 19, 1952 in Rock Hill, SC. Graduate USC. Bdwy debut 1976 in *Rex* followed by *Cats, Jelly's Last Jam, Best Little Whorehouse in Texas Goes Public, Christmas Carol*, OB in *The American Dance Machine*.

JOHNSON, DAVID CALE. Born Dec.28, 1947 in El Paso, TX. Attended AmConsvTh. Bdwy debut in *Shenandoah* (1975) followed by *My Fair Lady* (1981), *Doll's Life, Human Comedy*, OB in *True Crimes*.

JOHNSON, JEREMY. Born Oct. 2, 1933 in New Bedford, MA. Graduate CCNY, Columbia U. Debut 1975 OB in *Moby Dick*, followed by *Anna Christie, Harrison Texas, Romeo and Juliet, Much Ado about Nothing, Merchant of Venice, Winter's Tale, Bob's Butch Bar*.

JOHNSON, MEL, JR. Born Apr.16, 1949 in NYC. Graduate HofstraU. Debut 1972 OB in *Hamlet* followed by *Love! Love! Love!, Shakespeare's Cabaret, Peanut Man, The Lottery, Spell #7, Do Lord Remember Me, Venus*, Bdwy in *On the 20th Century, Eubie, The Rink, Big Deal*.

JOHNSON, PAGE. Born Aug. 25, 1930 in Welch, WV. Graduate Ithaca Col. Bdwy 1951 in *Romeo and Juliet*, followed by *Electra, Oedipus, Camino Real, In April Once* for which he received a Theatre World Award, *Red Roses for Me, The Lovers, Equus, You Can't Take It with You, Brush Arbor Revival*, OB in *The Enchanted Guitar, 4 in 1, Journey of the Fifth Horse*, APA's *School for Scandal, The Tavern*, and *The Seagull*, followed by *Odd Couple, Boys in the Band, Medea, Deathtrap, Best Little Whorehouse in Texas, Fool for Love, East Texas*.

JOHNSON, TINA. Born October 27, 1951 in Wharton, TX. Graduate N. TX State U. Debut 1979 OB in *Festival* followed by *Blue Plate Special, Christina Alberta's Father, Just So*, Bdwy in *Best Little Whorehouse in Texas, South Pacific* (NYCO/LC), *State Fair*.

JOHNSTON, NANCY. Born Jan. 15, 1949 in Statesville, NC. Graduate Carson Newman Col., UNC/Greensboro. Debut 1987 OB in *Olympus on My Mind*, followed by *Nunsense, Living Color, White Lies, You Can Be a New Yorker Too, Splendora*, Bdwy in *Secret Garden, Allegro(Encores)*.

JOHNSTON, RON. Born July 17, 1937 in Hot Springs, Ark. Graduate TCU, Hunter, Brandeis. Debut 1961 OB in *Hi Paisano, Merton of the Movies*, Bdwy in *Wild Honey* (1987), *Born Yesterday*

JONES, CHERRY. Born Nov. 21, 1956 in Paris, TN. Graduate Carnegie-Mellon. Debut 1983 OB in *The Philanthropist*, followed by *He and She, The Ballad of Soapy Smith, The Importance of Being Earnest, I Am a Camera, Claptrap, Big Time, A Light Shining in Buckinghamshire, The Baltimore Waltz, Goodnight Desdemona, And Baby Makes 7, Desdemona*, Bdwy in *Stepping Out* (1986), *Our Country's Good, Angels in America, The Heiress, Night of the Iguana*.

JONES, JEN. Born March 23, 1927 in Salt Lake City, UT. Debut 1960 OB in *Dreams Under the Window* followed by *Long Voyage Home, Diff'rent, The Creditors, Look at Any Man, I Knock at the Door, Pictures in the Hallway, Grab Bag, Bo Bo, Oh Dad Poor Dad, Henhouse, Uncle Vanya, Grandma's Play, Distance from Calcutta, Good*, Bdwy in *Dr. Cook's Garden* (1967), *But Seriously, Eccentricities of a Nightingale, Music Man* (1980), *Octette Bridge Club*.

JONES, PATRICIA. Born Oct.30 in Tacoma, WA. Graduate UNC, Nat'l Th Consv. Bdwy debut in *Indiscretions* (1995) followed by *Buried Child*, OB in *When Ladies Battle* (1995), *Winter's Tale, Life Is a Dream*.

JONES, SIMON. Born July 27, 1950 in Wiltshire, Eng. Attended Trinity Hall. NY debut 1984 OB in *Terra Nova* followed by *Magdalena in Concert, Woman in Mind Privates on Parade*, Bdwy in *The Real Thing* (1984), *Benefactors, Getting Married Private Lives, Real Inspector Hound/5 Minute Hamlet, School for Scandal*.

JORDAN, DAVID. Born Mar.6, 1957 in Raleigh, NC. Graduate SUNY/Oswego. Debut 1982 OB in *Death of Von Richtofen* followed by *Bells Are Ringing, A Musical: Madame Bovary*.

JOYCE, JOE. Born November 22, 1957 in Pittsburgh, PA. Graduate Boston U. Debut 1981 OB in *Close Enough for Jazz*, followed by *Oh Johnny!, They Came from Planet Mirth, Encore!, You Die at Recess, Forever Plaid, Pageant*, Bdwy in *Swinging on a Star*.

JUE, FRANCIS. Born Sept.29, 1963 in San Francisco, CA. Graduate Yale. Debut 1984 OB in *Pacific Overtures* followed by *Timon of Athens, King Lear, Language of Their Own, Richard II*, Bdwy in *M.Butterfly* (1989).

KANE, CAROL. Born June 18, 1952 in Cleveland, OH. Bdwy in *Prime of Miss Jean Brodie, The Tempest, Macbeth* (LC), *Effect of Gamma Rays on Man-in-the-Moon Marigolds* (1978), OB in *Lucky Spot, Debutante Ball, In-Betweens, Wasp and Other Plays*.

KANE, JOHN. Born Aug.29, 1920 in Davenport, IA. Attended St.Ambrose Col. Bdwy debut in *Three's a Family* (1944) followed by *Marcus in the High Grass, Ding Dong Bell, Uncle Willy, The Visit, Midsummer Night's Dream*, OB in *Hooray It's a Glorious Day, Ludwig*.

KANTOR, KENNETH. Born Apr. 6, 1949 in the Bronx, NYC. Graduate SUNY, Boston U. Debut 1974 OB in *Zorba*, followed by *Kiss Me Kate, A Little Night Music, Buried Treasure, Sounds of Rodgers and Hammerstein, Shop on Main Street, Kismet, The Fantasticks, Colette Collage, Snow White, Philemon*, Bdwy in *The Grand Tour* (1979), *Brigadoon* (1980), *Mame* (1983), *The New Moon* (NYCO/LC), *Me and My Girl, Guys and Dolls* (1992), *A Funnt Thing...*(1996).

KATIMS, ROBERT. Born April 22, 1927 in Brooklyn, NYC. Attended Brooklyn Col. Debut 1953 OB in *The Penguin* followed by *The Invasion of Aratooga, Shmulnik's Waltz, On the Wing, No Conductor, Teibele and Her Demon, The Shawl*.

KATZMAN, BRUCE. Born December 19, 1951 in NYC. Graduate Ithaca Col. Yale U. Debut 1990 OB in *Richard III* followed by *Othello, Sylvia*, Bdwy in *The Crucible* (1991), *A Little Hotel on the Side*.

KEAL, ANITA. Born in Philadelphia, PA. Graduate SyracuseU. Debut 1956 OB in *Private Life of the Master Race* followed by *Brothers Karamazov, Hedda Gabler, Witches Sabbath, Six Characters in Search of an Author, Yes MY Darling Daughter, Speed Gets the Poppy, You Don't Have to Tell Me, Val Christie and Others, Do You Still Believe the Rumoor?, Farmyard, Merry Wives of Scarsdale, Exiles, Fish Riding Bikes, Haven, The Affair, Mother Bickerdyke, Made in Heaven, Brandley & Beth, Carbondale Dreams, Aimee and Hope, Finding Rose*, Bdwy in *M. Buuterfly* (1989).

KEELER, WILLIAM. Born Sept.14, 1943 in Topeka, Kan. Graduate San Jose StU, U of Cal/Santa Barbara. Debut 1991 OB in *Learned Ladies* followed by *Candide, Picasso at the Lapin Agile*.

KELLNER, CATHERINE. Born Oct. 2, 1970 in NYC. Graduate Vassar Col., NYU. Debut 1994 OB in *Escape from Happiness* followed by *Troilus and Cressida*.

KELLY, DAREN. Born in Burbank, CA. Graduate UC/Irvine. Debut 1974 OB in *Breadwinner* followed by *Ivanov*, Bdwy in *Deathtrap* (1978) followed by *Woman of the Year, Crazy for You*.

KELLY, KRISTEN LEE. Born 1968. OB in *Loved Less, Blaming Mom, Apollo of Bellac*, Bdwy in *Rent* (1996-also OB).

KELLY, RITAMARIE. Born Sept.18, 1959 in Camden, NJ. Attended AdelphiU. Debut 1986 OB in *Have I Got a Girl for You* followed by *Mamet Women*.

KENNEDY, LAURIE. Born Feb. 14, 1948 in Hollywood, CA. Graduate Sarah Lawrence Col. Debut 1974 OB in *End of Summer*, followed by *Day in the Death of Joe Egg, Ladyhouse Blues, he and she, The Recruiting Officer, Isn't It Romantic, Master Builder, Candida, 2, Preservation Society*, Bdwy in *Man and Superman* (1978) for which she received a Theatre World Award, *Major Barbara, Angels in America*.

KENYON, LAURA. Born Nov. 23, 1948 in Chicago, IL. Attended USC. Debut 1970 OB in *Peace* followed by *Carnival, Dementos, Trojan Women, Have I Got a Girl for You, Desire, Hunchback of Notre Dame, Ballad of June Cool, Splendora*, Bdwy in *Man of La Mancha* (1971), *On the Town, Nine*.

KEPROS, NICHOLAS. Born November 8, 1932 in Salt Lake City, UT. Graduate U. UT, RADA. Debut 1958 OB in *Golden Six*, followed by *Wars and Roses, Julius Caesar, Hamlet, Henry IV, She Stoops to Conquer, Peer Gynt, Octaroon, Endicott and the Red Cross, Judas Applause, Irish Hebrew Lesson, Judgment in Havana, The Millionairess, Androcles and the Lion, The Redempter, Othello, Times and Appetites of Toulouse-Lautrec, Two Fridays, Rameau's Nephew, Good Grief, Overtime, Measure for Measure* Bdwy in *Saint Joan* (1968/1993), *Amadeus, Execution of Justice, Timon of Athens, Government Inspector*.

KERNER, NORBERTO. Born July 19, 1929 in Valparaiso, Chile. Attended Piscator Workshop, Goodman Theatre. Debut 1971 OB in *Yerma*, followed by *I Took Pananma, F.M. Safe, My Old Friends, Sharon Shashanovah, Blood Wedding, Crisp, The Great Confession, Cold Air, Don Juan of Seville, Human Voice, Ox Cart*, Bdwy in *Chronicle of a Death Foretold* (1995).

KILEAR, B. PAUL. Born July 9, 1923 in New Castle, PA. Graduate U of Chicago. Bdwy debut 1955 in *Inherit the Wind* , OB in *Tempest* (1993) follwed by *Wedding Portrait, Flowers for Algernon, Heart of Dearkness, The Captive, Timon of Athens, Waves Frozen, King Lear*.

KIM, DANIEL DAE. Born August 4, 1968 in Korea. Graduate Haverford Col. Debut 1991 OB in *Romeo and Juliet* followed by *Love Letters from a Student Revolutionary, A Doll House., School for Wives, Chang Fragments*.

KIM, TAEWON. Born July 8, 1966 in Seoul, Korea. Graduate Juilliard, Peabody Consv. Bdwy debut in *King and I* (1966).

KNAUER, IAN. Born June 6, 1968 in Toledo, OH. Graduate U of Mich. Bdwy debut in *State Fair* (1996).

KNIGHT, EZRA. Born July 7, 1962 in Atlanta, GA. Debut 1995 OB in *Othello* followed by *King Lear*.

KNUDSON, KURT. Born Sept.7, 1936 in Fargo, ND. Attended NDStU, UMiami. Debut 1976 OB in *Cherry Orchard* followed by *Geniuses, Room Service, Without Apologies,* Bdwy in *Curse of an Aching Heart* (1982), *Sunday in the Park with George, Take Me Along, Beauty and the Beast*.

KOENIG, JACK. Born May 14, 1959 in Rockville Centre, NY. Graduate ColumbiaU. Debut OB 1991 in *Grand Finale* followed by *Misalliance, Cymbeline, American Plan, Mad Forest, Not about Heroes, Trip to the Beach*.

KOTLER, JILL. Born Oct.3, 1952 in Chicago, IL. Graduate USC. OB in *The Piagkies, Goatman, Willie, Play with an Ending, Sh-Boom, Etiquette, Heart That Eats Itself, Hail to the Chief*.

KOUO, THOMAS C. Born Sept.25, 1972 in Albany, NY. Graduate BinghamtonU. Bdwy debut in *Miss Saigon*(1995).

KRAFT, KEVIN. Born July 30, 1968 in Abington, PA. Graduate USC. Bdwy debut in *A Funny Thing...*(1996).

KRAKOWSKI, JANE. Born September 11, 1968 in New Jersey. Debut 1984 OB in *American Passion*, followed by *Miami, A Little Night Music,* Bdwy in *Starlight Express* (1987), *Grand Hotel, Face Value, Company* (1995),*One Touch of Venus(Encores), Tartuffe: Born Again*.

KRAMER, JOEL. Born July 1, 1943 in The Bronx, NYC. Graduate Queens Col., UMich. Debut 1963 OB in *St. Joan of the Stockyards* followed by *Playboy of the Western World, Measure for Measure, Man Who Corrupted Hadleyburg, Call me madam, Castaways, Esther, Bodo,* Bdwy in *Animals* (1981), *Getting Away with Murder*.

KUBALA, MICHAEL. Born February 4, 1958 in Reading, PA. Attended NYU. Bdwy debut 1978 in *A Broadway Musical* followed by *Dancin', Woman of the Year, Marilyn, Jerome Robbins' Broadway, Crazy for You,* OB in *Double Feature* (1981).

KUDISCH, MARC. Born Sept.22, 1966 in Hackensack, NJ. Attended FlAtlanticU. Debut 1990 OB in *Tamara* followed by *Quiet on the Set, Beauty Part,* Bdwy in *Joseph and the..Dreamcoat*(1994), *Beauty and the Beast, Chicago(Encores)*.

KUNZE, ERIC P. Born May 22, 1971 in Oceaside, CA. Graduate USIC/San Diego, UC/Irvine. Bdwy debut in *Les Miserable* (1992) followed by *Miss Saigon, Damn Yankees*.

KURTZ, MARCIA JEAN. Born in The Bronx, NYC. Juilliard graduate. Debut 1966 OB in *Jonah,* followed by *American Hurrah, Red Cross, Muzeeka, Effect of Gamma Rays..., Year Boston Won the Pennant, The Mirror, The Orphan, Action, The Dybbuk, Ivanov, What's Wrong with This Picture?, Today I Am a Fountain Pen, Chopin Playoffs, Loman Family Picnic, Human Nature, When She Danced, The Workroom, The Cowboy the Indian and the Fervent Feminist, Extensions, Credo, Hell's Kitchen Sink,* Bdwy in *The Chinese and Dr. Fish* (1970), *Thieves, Execution of Justice*

KUSS, RICHARD. Born July 17, 1927 in Astoria, NY. Attended Ithica, Col.Debut 1951 in *Mother Said No* followed by *Maid's Tragedy, Winning Isn't Everything, Picasso at the Lapin Agile,* Bdwy in *J.B., Wait Until Dark, Solitaire/Double Solitaire, Golda, Loves of Cass McGuire, Bacchae, John Gabriel Borkman*.

LaCHANZE. Born December 16, 1961 in St. Augustine, FL. Attended Morgan State U., Philadelphia Col. Bdwy debut in *Uptown It's Hot* (1986), followed by *Dreamgirls* (1987), *Once on This Island* (also OB) for which she received a 1991 Theatre World Award, *Out Of This World (Encores), Company*.

LACHOW, STAN. Born December 20, 1931 in Brooklyn, NY. Graduate Roger Williams Col. Debut 1977 OB in *Come Back, Little Sheba* followed by *Diary of Anne Frank, Time of the Cuckoo, Angelus, The Middleman, Charley Bacon and Family, Crossing the Bar, Today I Am a Fountain Pen, Substance of Fire,* Bdwy in *On Golden Pond* (1979), *Sisters Rosensweig, Apple Doesn't Fall*.

LACY, FLORENCE. Born July 22, 1948 in mCKeesport, PA. Graduate Pittsburgh Playhouse. Bdwy debut in *Hello Dolly* (1978) for which she received a Theatre World Award, followed by *Grand Tour, Les Miserables, Hello Dolly* (1995), OB in *Elizabeth and Essex*.

LACY, TOM. Born Aug. 30, 1933 in NYC. Debut 1965 OB in *Fourth Pig,* followed by *The Fantasticks, Shoemakers Holiday, Love and Let Love, The Millionairess, Crimes of Passion, Real Inspector Hound, Enemies, Flying Blind, Abel & Bela/Archtruc,* Bdwy in *Last of the Red Hot Lovers* (1971), *Two Shakesperean Actors, Timon of Athens, Government Inspector, Holiday*.

LAGE, JORDAN. Born Feb. 17, 1963 in Palo Alto, CA. Graduate NYU. Debut 1988 OB in *Boy's Life,* followed by *Three Sisters,Virgin Molly, Distant Fires, Macbeth, Yes But So What?, Blue Hour, Been Taken, The Woods, Five Very Live, Hot Keys, As Sure as You Live, The Arrangement, The Lights, Shaker Heights, Missing Persons, Blaming Mom, Night and Her Stars, Dangerous Corner,* Bdwy in *Our Town* (1989).

LaGIOIA, JOHN. Born Nov. 24, 1937 in Philadelphia, PA Graduate TempleU. OB in *Keyhole, Lovers in the Metro, Cherry Orchard, Titus Andronicus, Henry VI, Richard III, A Little Madness, Rubbers, Right You Are, Pavlo Hummel, Brotherly Love,* Bdwy in *Henry V* (1969), *Gemini, Doubles, On Borrowed Time* (1991).

LAINE, CLEO. Born Oct.28, 1927 in Southall, Eng. Bdwy debut in *Mystery of Edwin Drood* for which she received a Theatre World Award, OB in *Great Songs*.

LAMB, MARY ANN. Born July 4, 1959 in Seattle, WA. Attended Neighborhood Playhouse. Bdwy debut in *Song and Dance* (1985), followed by *Starlight Express, Jerome Robbins' Broadway, Goodbye Girl, Fiorello! (Encores), Out of Thsi World(Encores), Pal Joey(Encores), A Funny Thing...*(1996).

LAMISON, TAMIKA. Born May 26, 1961 in Richmond, VA. Graduate AmericanU, HowardU. Debut 1984 OB in *Tower of Burden* followed by *For Colored Girls.*.

LANDER, JOHN-MICHAEL. Born January 17 in Hamilton, OH. Attended U. Cal./Irvine, Wright State U. Debut 1989 OB in *Adam and the Experts,* followed by *Custody, Bob's Butch Bar.*

LANDFIELD, TIMOTHY. Born Aug.22, 1950 in Palo Alto, CA. Graduate Hampshire Col. Bdwy debut in *Tartuffe* (1977) followed by *Crucifer of Blood, Wild Honey, Rumors, Company,* OB in *Actor's Nightmare, Sister Mary Ignatius Explains It All..., Charlotte Sweet, Flight of the Earls*.

LANDRIEU, NELSON ROBERTO. Born July 6, 1949 in Montevideo, Uruguay. Graduate AADA. Bdwy debut in *Chronicle of a Death Foretold* (1995), OB in *Ceremony for a Black Man, Happy Birthday Mama, Yepeto*.

LANE, NATHAN. Born Feb. 3, 1956 in Jersey City, NJ. Debut 1978 OB in *A Midsummer Night's Dream,* followed by *Love, Measure for Measure, Claptrap, Common Pursuit, In a Pig's Valise, Uncounted Blessings, Film Society, Lisbon Traviata, Bad Habits, Lips Together Teeth Apart,* Bdwy in *Present Laughter* (1982), *Merlin, Wind in the Willows, Some Americans Abroad, On Borrowed Time, Guys and Dolls, Laughter on the 23rd Floor, Love!Valour!Compassion'(alsoOB), A Funny Thing...*(1996).

LANG, MARK EDWARD. Born May 2 in NYC. Graduate Vassar Col. Debut 1986 OB in *In Their Own Words* followed by *Initiation Rites, Milestones, Midsummer Night's Dream, Julius Caesar, The Tempest, Radical Roots, Mary Stuart, Dark of the Moon, Jim the Lionhearted*.

LANGE, ANN. Born June 24, 1953 in Pipestone, MN. Attended Carnegie-Mellon U. Debut 1979 OB in *Rats Nest,* followed by *Hunting Scenes from Lower Bavaria, Crossfire, Linda Her and the Fairy Garden, Little Footsteps, 10th Young Playwrights Festival, Jeffrey, Family of Mann, 12 Dreams,*Bdwy in *The Survivor* (1981), *Heidi Chronicles, Holiday*.

LANSBURY, DAVID. Born Feb.25, 1961 in NYC. Attended Conn. Col., Circle in the Sq Th Sch, Central Sch of Speech/Drama, London. Debut 1989 OB in *Young Playwrights Festival* followed by *Advice from a Caterpillar, Progress, Hapgood, Principality of Sorrows,* Bdwy in *Heidi Chronicles* (1990).

LaPAGLIA, ANTHONY. Born Jan.31, 1960 in Adelaide, Aust. College Grad/B.A. degree. Debut 1987 OB in *Bouncers* followed by *On the Open Road, Mere Mortals, Northeast Local,* Bdwy 1995 in *Rose Tattoo* for which he received a Theatre World Award.

LARSEN, LIZ. Born Jan. 16, 1959 in Philadelphia, PA. Attended Hofstra U. SUNY/Purchase. Bdwy debut in *Fiddler on the Roof*(1981), followed by *Starmites, A Little Night Music, (NYCO/LC), Most Happy Fella, Damn Yankees, DuBarry Was a Lady(Encores)* OB in *Kuni Leml, Hamlin, Personals, Starmites, Company, After These Messages, One Act Festival, Loman Family Picnic, Teibele and Her Demon, America's Sweetheart*.

LAUREN, JULIE. Born in NYC. Graduate Dartmouth Col., Neighborhood Playhouse. Debut 1993 OB in *The Survivor* followe by *Ryan Interview, A Hamlet*.

LAURENT, WENDELL. Born Dec.1, 1961 in New Orleans, LA. Graduate LoyolaU. Debut 1992 OB in *You're a Good Man Charlie Brown* followed by *My Sister Eileen, Holy Ghosts, Maderati*.

LAWRENCE, TASHA. Born January 31, 1967 in Alberta, Can. Graduate UGuelph. 1992 OB in *Loose Ends*, followed by *Cowyboy in His Underwear, Ten Blocks on the Camino Real, 3 by Wilder, Who Will Carry the Word?, Anatomy of Sound, Goose and Tom Tom, Killing of Sister George*, Bdwy in *Wilder Wilder Wilder* (1993).

LEARY, DAVID. Born Aug.8, 1939 in Brooklyn, NY. Attended CCNY. Debut 1969 OB in *Shoot Anything That Moves* followed by *Macbeth, Plough and the Stars, Emigres, Sus, Before the Dawn, Whistle in the Dark*, Bdwy in *National Health, Da, Lady from Dubuque, Piaf*.

LEASK, KATHERINE. Born Sept.2, 1957 in Munich, Ger. Graduate SMU. Debut 1988 OB in *Man Who Climbed the Pecan Trees* followed by *Cahoots, Melville Boys, Amphitryon, The Imposter*.

LEE, DARREN. Born June 8, 1972 in Long Beach, CA. Bdwy debut in *Shogun*(1990), followed by *Miss Saigon, Victor Victoria*, OB in *Petrified Prince*(1994), *Chang Fragments*.

LEE, MICHAEL. Born June 5, 1973 in Brooklyn, NYC. Graduate StanfordU. Bdwy debut in *Miss Saigon* (1996).

LEE, SAMANTHA ROBYN. Born Dec.14, 1983 in NYC. Debut 1994 OB in *South Pacific* followed by *Oliver, Big* (1996).

LEE, TOM (formerly Tom Lee Jones). Born Sept.15, 1946 in San Saba, TX. Graduate Harvard. Bdwy debut in *Patriot for Me* (1969) followed by *4 on a Garden, Ulysses in Nighttown*, OB in *Blue Boys, True West, LaMama 2000*.

LEEDS, JORDAN. Born Nov. 29,1961 in Queens, NYC. Graduate SUNY/Binghamton. Bdwy debut in *Les Miserables* (1987) followed by *Sunset Blvd.*, OB in *Beau Jest, Angel Levine*.

LENOX, ADRIANE. Born Sept. 11, 1956 in Memphis, TN. Graduate Lambuth Col. Bdwy debut in *Ain't Misbehavin* (1979), followed by *Dreamgirls*, OB in *Beehive, Merrily We Roll Along, America Play, Identical Twins from Baltimore, Venus*.

LEONARD, ROBERT SEAN. Born February 28, 1969 in Westwood, NJ. Debut 1985 OB in *Sally's Gone She Left Her Name*, followed by *Coming of Age in Soho, Beach House, Young Playwrights Festival-And the Air Didn't Answer, When She Danced, Romeo and Juliet, Pitching to the Star, Good Evening, Great Unwashed, Principality of Sorrows, Below the Belt*, Bdwy in *Brighton Beach Memoirs* (1985), *Breaking the Code, Speed of Darkness, Candida, Philadelphia Here I Come, Arcadia*.

LEONARDO, LOUIE. Debut 1995 OB in *Bomber Jackets* followed by *Carmen's Community*.

LEUNG, KEN. Born Jan.21, 1970 in NYC. Graduate NYU. Debut 1994 OB in *Ghost in the Machine* followed by *Admissions*.

LEWIS, MARCIA. Born Aug. 18, 1938 in Melrose, MA. Attended UCinn. OB in *Impudent Wolf, Who's Who Baby, God Bless Coney, Let Yourself Go, Romance Language, When She Danced, Big City Rhythms, Greenwillow*, Bdwy in *Time of Your Life, Hello Dolly!, Annie, Rags, Roza, Orpheus Descending, Gypsy* (1991), *Grease, Chicago*.

LIFF, SPENCER. Born Feb.6, 1985 in Phoenix, AZ. Bdwy debut in *Big*(1996).

LIMA, PAUL. Born Feb. 5, 1961 in Ithaca, NY. Graduato AADA. Debut 1987 OB in *Deathmarch*, followed by *Idiot's Delight, Fanny's First Play, Archbishop's Ceiling, Threepenny Opera, The Rnack, Three Sisters, Romeo and Juliet, White Boys Can't Rap, Something Rotten in Denmark, Sisters Dance*.

LINARES, CARLOS. Born July 26, 1954 in El Salvador, C.A. Attended Lehman Col. Debut 1988 OB in *Senora Carrar's Rifles*, followed by *Tafpoletigermosquitos at Mulligan's, Contract*.

LINN-BAKER, MARK. Born June 17, 1954 in St. Louis, MO. Attended Yale. Bdwy debut in *Doonesbury*(1985) followed by *Face Value, Laughter on the 23rd Floor, A Funny Thing...*(1996), OB in *All's Well That Ends Well, Othello, Alice in Concert*.

LINNEY, LAURA. Born Feb. 5, 1964 in NYC. Graduate BrownU, Juilliard. Debut 1990 OB in *Six Degrees of Separation*, followed by *Beggars in the House of Plenty, The Seagull: The Hamptons 1990, Sight Unseen* for which she received a Theatre World Award, Bdwy in Six *Degrees of Separation* (1990), *Sea Gull, Holiday*.

LISH, BECCA. Born Dec.26, 1959 in San Francisco, CA. Graduate Yale. Debut 1991 OB in *Bella Belle of Byelorussia* followed *Down the Stream, Joined at the Head*, Bdwy in *Holiday* (1995).

LITTLEFORD, BETH. Born July 17, 1968 in Nashville, TN. Attended Swarthmore Col. Graduate New School. Debut 1996 OB in *This Is Where I Get Off* followed by *Chicago City Limits, Brutality of Fact*.

LIVELY, DeLEE. Born Nov.27 in Houston, TX. Bdwy debut in *Chorus Line* followed by *Grand Hotel, Smokey Joe's Cafe*.

LIZZUL, ANTHONY JOHN. Born Jan.11 in The Bronx, NYC. Graduate NYU. Debut 1977 OB in *Cherry Orchard* followed by *The Prophets, Lady Windermere's Fan, Revenger's Tragedy, Twelfth Night, Night Talk, Butterfingers Angel, Consulting Adults, Hyde Park, Heartbreak House*.

LOAR, ROSEMARY. Born in NYC. Attended UOhio, UOre. Bdwy debut in *You Can't Take It with You* (1984) followed by *Chess, Cats, Sunset Blvd.*, OB in *Encore, Sally in concert, Chess*.

LoBUONO, DAN. Born Aug.11, 1964 in Cincinnati, OH. Attended U of Cin. Bdwy debut in *Hello Dolly* (1995).

LOESSER, EMILY. Born lune 2, 1965 in New York City. Graduate NorthwesternU. Debut 1988 OB in *Secret Garden*, followed by *Together Again for the First Time, The Witch, Follies, Yiddle with a Fiddle, Music in the Air in concert, Swingtime Canteen, Greenwillow*, Bdwy in *The Sound of Music* (LC/90), *Inherit the Wind*.

LOMBARD, MICHAEL. Born Aug. 8, 1934 in Brooklyn, NYC. Graduate Brooklyn Col., Boston U. OB in *King Lear, Merchant of Venice, Cages, Pinter Plays, La Turista, Elizabeth the Queen, Room Service, Mert and Phil, Side Street Scenes, Angelo's Wedding, Friends in High Places, What's Wrong with This Picture?, Another Time*, Bdwy in *Poor Bitos* (1964), *The Devils, Gingerbread Lady, Bad Habits, Otherwise Engaged, Awake and Sing, Nick & Nora, Timon of Athens, Government Inspector*.

LONDEREE, TERRY. Born June 9, 1947 in Lynchburg, VA. Graduate William & Mary. Debut 1989 OB in *Cheri* followed by *Of Mice and Men*.

LONG, JODI. Born in New York City. Graduate SUNY/Purchase. Bdwy debut in *Nowhere to Go But Up* (1963) followed by *Loose Ends, Bacchae, Getting Away with Murder*, OB in *Fathers and Sons, Family Devotions, Rohwer, Tooth of the Crime, Dream of Kitamura, Midsummer Night's Dream, Madame de Sade, Thc Wash*.

LOOMIS, ROD. Born Apr.21, 1942 in St. Albans, VT. Graduate BostonU. BrandeisU. Debut 1972 OB in *Two if by Sea* followed by *You Never Know, Uncle Vanya*, Bdwy in *Sunset Blvd.*

LOPEZ, DIEGO. Born Jan.19, 1977 in NY. Bdwy debut in *Night of the Iguana* (1996).

LOPEZ, PRISCILLA. Born Feb. 26, 1948 in The Bronx, NY. Bdwy debut in *Breakfast at Tiffany's* (1966) followed by *Henry Sweet Henry, Lysistrata, Company, Her First Roman, Boy Friend, Pippin, Chorus Line* (also OB), *Day in Hollywood/Night in the Ukraine, Nine*, OB in *What's a Nice Country Lik You..., Key Exchange, Buck, Extremites, Non Pasquak, Be Happyfor Me, Times and Appetites of oulouse-Lautrec, Marathon '88, Other Peopk's Money, Antigone in NY*.

LORITE, FRANCISCO. Born Aug.11, 1969 in Spain. Graduate Northeastern. Debut 1996 OB in *Bomber Jackets*.

LOVCI, MARC. Born June 27, 1968 in Las Vegas, NV. Graduate U of Neb. Debut 1996 OB in *Zombie Prom*.

LOVEJOY, DEIRDRE. Born June 30, 1962 in Abilene, Tx. Graduate U.Evansville, NYU. Debut 1988 OB in *Midsummer Night's Dream* followed by *Henry IV Part 1, Hannah 1939, Machinal, Alice in Wonderland, Don Juan, Preservation Society*. Bdwy in Six *Degrees of Separation* (1991).

LOVEMAN, LENORE. (a.k.a. Lenore Koven) Born February 23, 1934 in Brooklyn, NY. Attended Columbia U., SUNY. Debut 1954 OB in *Miss Julie*, followed by *Two by Linney, Cafe Crown, The Return, Subways Hallways Rooftops, Where Memories Are Magic and Dreams Invented, World of Sholem Aleichem, Backward Glance of Edith Wharton, Academy Street, Greetings, Unorthodox Behaviour, Dance Card*, Bdwy in *Checking Out* (1976).

LOW, MAGGIE. Born Apr.23, 1957 in Nyack, NY. Debut 1982 OB in *Catholic School Girls* followed by *Action, Thoughts Modern, Candle in the Window, LaMama 2000*.

LOWE, FRANK. Born June 28, 1927 in Appalachia, VA. Attended Sorbonne. Debut 1952 OB in *Macbeth*, followed by *Hotel De Breney, The Lady's Not for Burning, Fox Trot on Gardiner's Bay, As You Like it, A Sleep of Prisoners, Cymbeline, Did Elvis Cry!, Man with a Raincoat, Donkey's Years, Ring Round the Moon!, Moon for the Misbegotten, Twelfth Night, Titus Andronicus, Henry VI, Measure for Measure*.

LUCKINBILL, LAURENCE. Born Nov. 17. 1938 in Ft. Smith, AR. Graduate U. Ark. Catholic U. Bdwy debut in *Man for All Seasons*(1962) followed by *Beekman Place, Poor Murderers, Meeting by the River, Shadow Box, Chapter 2, Past Tense, Dancing in the End Zone*, OB in *Oedipus Rex, There's a Play Tonight, The Fantasticks, Tartuffe, Boys in the Band, Horesman Pass By, Memory Bank, What the Butler Saw, Alpha Beta, Prayer for My Daughter, Life of Galileo, Lyndon Johnson, Unfinished Stories, Fair Country*.

LUDWIG, JAMES W. Born Nov.16, 1967 in Subic Bay Naval Base, PI. Graduate UMi, UWash. Debut 1995 OB in *jon & jen* followed by *Louisiana Purchase.*

LUDWIG, SALEM. Born Jul. 31, 1915 in Brooklyn, NY. Attended Brooklyn Col. Bdwy debut in *Mirack in thc Mountains* (1946) followed by *Camino Real, Enemy of the People, All You Need Is One Good Break, Inherit the Wind, Disenchanted, Rhinoceros, Three Sisters, Zulu and the Zahda, Moonchildren, American Clock, Month of Sundays,* OB in *Brothers Karamazov, Victim, Troublemaker, Man of Destiny, Night of the Dunce, Corner of the Bed, Awake and Sing, Prodigal Babylon, Burnt Flower Bed, Friends Too Numerous to Mention, After the Fall, What's Wrong with This Picture?, Spinoza, The Shawl.*

LUM, ALVIN. Born May 28. 1931 in Honolulu, HI. Attended UHi. Debut 1969 OB in *In the Bar of a Tokyo Hotel,* followed by *Pursuit of Happiness, Monkey Music, Flowers and Household Gods, Station J, Double Dutch, Teahouse, Song for a Nisei Fisherman, Empress of China, Manos Valley, Hot Sake, Friends,* Bdwy in *Lovely Ladies Kind Gentlemen* (1970), *Two Gentlemen of Verona, City of Angels, Chu-Chem* (also OB).

LuPONE, PATTI. Born Apr.21, 1949 in Northport, NY. Graduate Julliard. Debut 1972 OB in *School for Scandal* followed by *Women Beware Women, Next Time I'll Sing to You, Beggars Opera, Scapin, Robber Bridegroom, Edward II, The Woods, Edmond, America Kicks Up Its Heals, Cradle Will Rock,* Bdwy in *Water Engine*(1978), *Working, Evita, Oliver!, Accidental Death of an Anarchist, Anything Goes, Pal Joey(Encores), Patti LuPone on Bdwy, Master Class.*

LYLES, LESLIE. Born in Plainfield, NJ. Graduate Monmouth Col., Rutgers U. Debut 1981 OB in *Sea Marks,* followed by *Highest Standard of Living, Vanishing Act, I Am Who I Am, The Arbor, Terry by Terry, Marathon '88, Sleeping Dogs, Nebraska, My House Play, Life during Wartime, Angel of Death, Sam I Am, The Workroom, Dark Ride, Brutality of Fact,* Bdwy in *Night and Day* (1979), *Hide and Seek, Real Thing, Garden District.*

LYNCH, BARRY. Born 1960 in Dublin, Ire. Bdwy debut 1996 in *Midsummer Night's Dream.*

LYNDECK, EDMUND. Born Oct.4, 1925 in Baton Rouge, LA. Graduate MontclairStCol., FordhamU. Bdwy debut in *1776* (1969) followed by *Sweeney Todd, Doll's Life, Merlin, Into the Woods, Artist Descending a Staircase,* OB in *King and I*(JB), *Mandragola, Safe Place, Amoureuse, Piaf: A Remembrance, Children of Darkness, Kill, The Interview, I Married an Angel.*

LYONS, CAPPY. Born in Boston, MA. Graduate MarquetteU, Boston St Col. OB in *The Warrior, Androcles and the Lion, Joslyn Circle, Overtones, Town Meeting, The Trail, Dolores, Fen, Harry Sears Relives New Years 1991, Adding Machine, Cerceau.*

MacDONALD, ALFREDO. Born Mar.8, 1969 in Chicago, IL. Bdwy debut in *Night of the Iguana* (1996).

MACHT, GABRIEL. Born Jan.22, 1972 in The Bronx, NYC. Graduate Carnegie Mellon. Debut 1995 OB in *Picasso at the Lapin Agile.*

MacINTYRE, MARGUERITE. Born in Detroit, MI. Graduate U. S. Cal., RADA. Debute 1988 OB in *Some Summer Night,* followed by *Weird Romance, Awakening of Spring, Annie Warbucks, Mata Hari,* Bdwy in *City of Angels* (1991).

MACKLIN, ALBERT. Born November 18, 1958 in Los Angeles, CA. Graduate StanfordU. Debut 1982 OB in *Poor Little Lambs* followed by *Ten Little Indians, Anteroom, Finding Donis Anne, Library of Congress, Howling in the Night, Fortinbras, The Houseguests, Dog Opera, Jeffrey, Hide Your Love Away, Wally's Ghost,* Bdwy in *Doonesbury*(1983) followed by *Floating Light Bulb, I Hate Hamlet.*

MacMILLAN, ANN. Born Apr.7, 1942 in Scotland. Attended RADA. Debut 1970 OB in *Merry Wives of Windsor* followed by *Winslow Boy, Learned Ladies, The Housekeeper, Ivanov.*

MacNICHOL, KATIE. Born Apr.11 in Portland, ME. Graduate NYU. Bdwy debut in *Two Shakespearean Actors* (1992),OB in *Food Chain*(1996).

MacVITTIE, BRUCE. Born Oct. 14, 1956, in Providence, RI. Graduate BostonU. Bdwy debut in *American Buffalo* (1983) followed by OB in *California Dog Fight, The Worker's Life, Cleveland and Halfway Back, Marathon '87, One of the Guys, Young Playwrights '90, Darker Purpose, Body of Water, Darp Ride, Golden Boy, Dark Rapture.*

MAIER, CHARLOTTE. Born Jan. 29, 1956 in Chicago, IL. Graduate Northwestern U. Debut 1984 OB in *Balm in Gilead* followed by *Gunplay, Last Girl Singer,* Bdwy in *Abe Lincoln in Illinois* (1993), *Picnic* (1984)*Delicate Balance.*

MAILER, KATE. Born Aug.18, 1962 in NY. Graduate BrownU. Debut 1988 OB in *Cherry Orchard* followed by *Nine Armenians, Glasses, My Plait, More Basketcases, Night Must Fall, Motherless Children*

MAKKENA, WENDY. Born in New York City. Attended Juilliard; danced with NYC Ballet. OB debut 1982 in *Divine Fire,* followed by *Wedding Presence, The Rivals, Taming of the Shrew, Loman Family Picnic, Birthday Party, Mountain Language, Prin, American Plan, The Shawl,* Bdwy in *Pygmalion* (1987). *Lend Me a Tenor.*

MALAS, SPIRO. Born Jan. 28,1933 in Baltimore, MD. Graduate Towson State U. Bdwy debut 1992 in *Most Happy Fella,* for which he received a Theatre World Award, OB in *Oklahoma!,* (NYCO/LC), followed by *Johnny Pye and the Foolkiller, Milk and Honey, Golden Boy.*

MANGANO, NICK. Born Oct.22, 1958 in Brooklyn, NY. Attended HofstraU. Bdwy debut in *Oh Calcutta* (1981), OB in *Coyote Bleeds.*

MANHEIM, CAMRYN. Born March 8, 1961 in Caldwell, NJ. Graduate U. Cal./Santa Cruz, NYU. Debut 1987 OB in *Stella* followed by *Alice in Wonderland, Henry IV Parts I & II, Woyzeck, St. Joan of the Stockyards, Two Gentlemen of Verona, Triumph of Love, Missing Persons, Wake Up I'm Fat, Sin.*

MANN, TERRENCE. Born in 1951 in Kentucky. Graduate N.C. Sch. Of Arts. Bdwy debut in *Barnum*(1980) followed by *Cats, Rags, Les Miserables, Jerome Robbins' Broadway, Beauty and the Beast, Christmas Carol, Getting Away with Murder,* OB in *Night at the Fights, Queen's Diamond, Assassins.*

MANSON, ALAN. Born in NYC. Bdwy debut in *Journey to Jerusalem* (1940) followed by *This Is the Army, Call Me Mister, Southern Exposure, Angel Kiss Me, Ponder Heart, Maybe Tuesday, Tenth Man, Gideon, Nobody Loves an Albatross, Funny Girl, A Place for Polly, 40 Carats, No Hard Feelings, Broadway Bound,* OB in *Dr. Jekyll and Mr. Hyde, Midsummer Night's Dream, Oh Say Can You See L.A.?, Other Man, Endgame.*

MANSOURI, MAIRE. Born Dec.8, 1965 in Teheran, Iran. Graduate U of Cal/Irvine. Debut 1995 OB in *Caucasian Chalk Circle* followed by *Duel of Angels, Road, Portrait of An Artist.*

MARCEAU, YVONNE. Born July 13, 1950 in Chicago, IL. Graduate UUtah. Bdwy debut in *Grand Hotel* (1989) followed by OB in *American Ballroom Theatre*

MARCHIONDA, ANTHONY, JR. Born Mar.25, 1959 in Youngstown, OH. Graduate YoungstownStU. Debut 1993 OB in *Second Annual Heart of Texas Eczema Telethon.*

MARGULIES, DAVID. Born Feb. 19, 1937 in NYC. Graduate CCNY. Debut 1958 OB in *Golden Six,* followed by *Six Characters in Search of an Author, Tragical Historie of Dr. Faustus, Tango, Little Murders, Seven Days of Mourning, La Analysis, An Evening with the Poet Senator, Kid Champion, The Man with the Flower in His Mouth, Old Tune, David and Paula, Cabal of Hypocrites, The Perfect Party, Just Say No, George Washington Dances, I'm with Ya Duke, The Treatment,* Bdwy in *Iceman Cometh* (1973), *Zalmen or the Madness of God, Comedians, Break a Leg, West Side Waltz, Brighton Beach Memoirs, Conversations with My Father, Angels in America, A Thousand Clowns.*

MARIE, JEAN. Born Dec.14, 1968 in Mountainside, NJ. Attended FordhamU. Bdwy debut in *Crazy for You*(1992).

MARINEAU, BARBARA. Born Aug. 22 in Detroit, MI. Graduate W. MI. U. Bdwy debut in *Shenandoah*(1977) followed by *Best Little Whorehouse in Texas, Beauty and the Beast, Christmas Carol,* OB in *I'm Getting My Act Together* (1981), *Bittersuite, Witch of Wall Street, Our American Cousin, Silas.*

MARKS, KENNETH. Born Feb. 17, 1954 in Harwick, PA. Graduate UPenn., LehighU. Debut 1978 OB in *Clara Bow Loves Gary Cooper,* followed by *Canadian Gothic, Time and the Conways, Savoury Meringue, Thrombo, Fun, 1-2-3-4-5, Manhattan Class I Acts, Bright Room Called Day, Pix, Sabina,* Bdwy in *Dancing at Lughnasa* (1992).

MARQUETTE, CHRISTOPHER. Born Oct. 3, 1984 in Stuart, FL. Bdwy debut in *An Inspector Calls* (1994) followed by *Christmas Carol.*

MARSHALL, AMELIA. Born Apr. 2, 1958 in Albany, GA. Graduate U. TX. Debut 1982 OB in *Applause,* followed by *Group One Acts, Minor Demons,* Bdwy in *Harrigan 'n' Hart* (1985), *Big Deal.*

MARSHALL, DONNA LEE. Born Feb.27, 1958 in Mt. Holly, NJ. Attended AADA. Debut 1987 OB in *By Strouse* followed by *Human Comedy, Sidewalkin', Charley's Tale,* Bdwy in *Pirates of Penzance, Christmas Carol, Big.*

MARTIN, COLIN. Born Mar.19, 1963 in Chicago Heights, IL. Graduate Carnegie-MellonU., Attended Macalester Col. Debut 1996 OB in *Virgins and Other Myths.*

MARTIN, GEORGE N. Born Aug. 15, 1929 in NYC. Bdwy debut in *Wilson in the Promise Land* (1970) followed by *The Hothouse, Plenty , Total Abandon, Pack of Lies, Mystery of Edwin Drood, The Crucible, Little Hotel on the Side, Broken Glass, On the Waterfront, Racing Demon,* OB in *Painting Churches, Henry V, Springtime for Henry.*

MARTIN, JESSE L. Born in 1969. Bdwy in *Timon of Athens, Government Inspector, Rent* (also OB), OB in *Arabian Nights.*

MARTIN, MICHAEL X. Born Oct.18, 1954 in San Jose, CA. Graduate Santa ClaraU. Debut 1991 OB in *Fantasticks* followed by *Jack's Holiday, Bed and Sofa, Greenwillow,* Bdwy in *Les Miserables* (1993) followed by *Anyone Can Whistle*(CH), *Christmas Carol.*

MARTIN, RICKY. Born 1972 in Puerto Rico. Bdwy debut in *Les Miserables* (1996).

MARTIN, RUDOLF. Born July 31, 1967 in Berlin, Ger. Attended FreieU/Berlin Debut 1995 in *Food Chain.*

MARTINS, TOM. Born July 28, 1970 in Fall River, MA. Graduate Marymount Manhattan Col. Debut OB 1995 in *Baptists.*

MARVEL, ELIZABETH. Born 1970 in Fullerton, CA. Graduate Juilliard. Debut 1995 OB in *Silence Cunning Exile* followed by *Henry V, Arts and Leisure, King Lear.*

MASON, JACKIE. Born June 9, 1934 in Sheboygan, WI. Bdwy debut in *Teaspoon Every Four Hours* (1969) followed by *World According to Me, Jackie Mason Brand New, Politically Incorrect, Love Thy Neighbor.*

MASTERS, ANDREA. Born Nov.16, 1949 in Chicago, IL. Attended Mills Col., ColumbiaU. Debut 1975 OB in *Long Valley* followed by *Justice, Little Eyolf, Six Characters in Search of an Author,* Bdwy in *Basic Training of Pavlo Hummel* (1977).

MASTRANTONIO, MARY ELIZABETH. Born Nov.17, 1958 in Chicago, IL. Attended UIll. Bdwy debut in *West Side Story* (1980) followed by *Copperfield, Oh Brother, Human Comedy, Marriage of Figaro,* OB in *Henry V, Christmas Carol, Measure for Measure, The Knife, Twelfth Night, Northeast Local.*

MASTRO, MICHAEL(formerly Mastrototaro). Born May 17, 1962 in Albany, NY. Graduate NYU. Debut 1984 OB in *Victoria Station,* followed by *Submarines, Naked Truth/Name Those Names, Darker Purpose, Hot Keys, Crows in the Cornfield, City, Escape from Happiness, Naked Faith, Alone But Not Lonely,* Bdwy in *Love!Valour!Compassion!* (1995).

MASTRONE, FRANK. Born Nov. 1, 1960 in Bridgeport, CT. Graduate CentralStU. Bdwy debut in *Phantom of the Opera* (1988) followed by *Big.*

MATSON, JILL. Born in Torrance, CA. Bdwy debut in *Crazy for You* (1993) followed by *Big.*

MATSUSAKA, TOM. Born Aug. 8 in Wahiawa, Hl. Graduate MichStU. Bdwy debut in *Mame* (1968) followed by *Ride the Winds, Pacific Overtures, South Pacific,* OB in *Agamemnon, Chu Chem, Jungle of Cities, Santa Anita '42, Extenuating Circumstances, Rohwer, Teahouse, Song of a Nisei Fisherman, Empress of China, Pactfic Overtures* (1984), *Eat a Bowl of Tea, Shogun Macbeth, The Imposter, Privates, Lucky Come Hawaii, Caucasian Chalk Circle.*

MAU, LES J.N. Born Jan.8, 1954 in Honolulu, HI. Graduate U of HI. Debut 1983 OB in *Teahouse* followed by *Empress of China, Eat a Bowl of Tea, Lucky Come Hawaii, Wilderness, Pacific Overtures, New Living Newspaper, Geniuses, Friends, Dog and His Master.*

MAURO, JASON. Born May 26, 1973 in Bethpage, LI (NY). Debut 1995 OB in *Party.*

MAYER, JERRY. Born May 12, 1941 in NYC. Debut 1968 OB in *Alice in Wonderland,* followed by *L'Ete, Marouf, Trelawny of the Wells, King of the Schnorrers, Mother Courage, You Know Al, Goose and Tom-Tom, The Rivals, For Sale, Two Gentlemen of Verona, Julius Caesar, A Couple with a Cat, Silence Cunning Exile, Henry VI, Greater Good,* Bdwy in *Much Ado about Nothing* (1972), *Play Memory.*

MAZZIE, MARIN. Born October 9, 1960 in Rockford, IL. Graduate W. MI. U. Debut 1983 OB in *Where's Charley?, And the World Goes Round, I Married an Angel, Trojan Women,* Bdwy in *Big River* (1986) *Passion.*

McARDLE, ANDREA. Born Nov. 5, 1963 in Philadelphia, PA. Bdwy debut in *Annie* (1977) for which she received a Theatre World Award, followed by *Starlight Express, Les Miserables, State Fair,* OB in *They Say It's Wonderful.*

McCANN, CHRISTOPHER. Born Sept. 29, 1952 in New York City. Graduate NYU. Debut 1975 OB in *The Measures Taken,* followed by *Ghosts, Woyzeck, St. Joan of the Stockyards, Buried Child, Dwelling in Milk, Tongues, 3 Acts of Recognition, Don Juan, Michi's Blood, Five of Us, Richard III, The Golem, Kafka Father and Son, Flatbush Faithful, Black Market, King Lear, Virgin Molly, Mad Forest, Ladies of Fisher Cove, The Lights, Grey Zone.*

McCARREN, PAUL. Born Jan.19, 1943 in Yonkers, NY. Graduate FordhamU. Debut 1979 OB in *Second Thoughts* followed by *Love's Labour's Lost, Rescuers.*

McCARTHY, JEFF. Born Oct.16, 1954 in Los Angeles, CA. Graduate Amer. Consv. Bdwy debut 1982 in *Pirates of Penzance* followed by *Zorba*(1983), *Beauty and the Beast,* OB in *Gifts of the Maji, On the 20th Century, Sisters Rosensweig.*

McCARTHY, KEVIN. Born Feb.15, 1914 in Seattle, WA. Attended UMn. Bdwy debut in *Abe Lincoln in Illinois* (1938) followed by *Flight to the West, Winged Victory, Truckline Cafe, Joan of Lorraine, Death of a Salesman, Anna Christie, Deep Blue Sea, Red Roses for Me, Day the Money Stopped, Two for the Seasaw, Advise and Consent, Something about a Soldier, Three Sisters, A Warm Body, Cactus Flower, Happy Birthday Wanda June, Poor Murderer, Alone Together, Sacrilege,* OB in *The Children, Rapists, Harry Outside.*

McCARTY, CONAN. Born Sept. 16, 1955 in Lubbock, 1-X. Attended U.S. Cal., AADA/West. Debut 1980 OB in *Star Treatment,* followed by *Beyond Therapy, Hemy IV Part 1, Titus Andronicus, Man Who Shot Lincoln, Madwoman of Chaillot, Dark Rapture,* Bdwy in *Macbeth* (1988), *A Few Good Men.*

McCLANAHAN, MATT. Born July 1st in Kenmore, NY. Graduate SUNY/Purchase. Debut 1988 OB in *Psycho Beach Party,* followed by *Vampire Lesbians of Sodom, A Little Night Music, Balancing Act, Forever Plaid, Hearts and Voices, Zombies from the Beyond,* Bdwy in *Les Miserables* (1992).

McCLARNON, KEVIN. Born Aug. 25, 1952 in Greenfield,lN. Graduate ButlerU,LAMDA. Debut 1977 OB in *The Homecoming* followed by *Heaven's Gate, Winter's Tale, Johnny on a Spot, The Wedding, Between Daylight and Boonville, Macbeth, The Clownmaker, Cinders, Ballad of Soapy Smiith, Better Days, The Showoff,* Bdwy in *Inherit the Wind* (1996).

McCRADY, TUCKER. Born September 24, 1965 in Sewanee, TN. Graduate HarvardU, Juilliard. Bdwy debut in *Camelot* (1993) followed by OB in *Sherlock Holmes and the Speckled Band, Ballad of Little Joe.*

McCULLOH, BARBARA. Born Mar.5 in Washington, D.C. Attended Col. of William & Mary, UMd. Debut 1984 OB in *Up in Central Park* followed by *Kuni-Leml, On the 20th Century, 1-2-3-4-5, Life Forms,* Bdwy in *King and I* (1996).

McDONALD, AUDRA ANN. Born July 3, 1970 in Berlin, Ger. Graduate Juilliard. Debut OB 1989 in *Man of La Mancha,* followed by Bdwy in *Secret Garden*(1991), *Carousel* (1994) for which she received a 1994 Theatre World Award, *Master Class.*

McDONIEL, NANCY. Born Feb.6, 1950 in Henderson, NV. Graduate SWMo.StU., WayneStU. OB includes *Grandma Sylvia's Funeral* (1995), *Bob Funk, Blackberry Frost, Touch My Face, Pie Supper, Blackout.*

McGIVER, BORIS. Born Jan. 23, 1962 in Cobleskill, NY. Graduate Ithaca Col., SUNY/Cobleskill, NYU. Debut 1994 OB in *Richard II* followed by *Hapgood, Troilus and Cressida.*

McGOWAN, TOM. Born July 26, 1959 in Neptune, NJ. Graduate Yale, HofstraU. Debut 1988 OB in *Coriolanus,* followed by *Winter's Tale, One of the All-Time Greats, Food Chain,* Bdwy in *La Rete* (1991).

McGRATH, MATT. Born June 11, 1969 in NYC. Attended FordhamU. Bdwy debut in *Working* (1978) followed by *Streetcar Named Desire,* OB in *Dalton's Back* (1989), *Amulets Against the Dragon Forces, Life During Wartime, The Old Boy, Nothing Sacred, The Dadshuttle, Fat Men in Skirts, A Fair Country.*

McGRATH, MICHAEL. Born Sept.25, 1957 in Worcester, MA. Debut 1988 OB in *Forbidden Bdwy* followed by *Cocoanuts, Forbidden Hollywood, Louisiana Purchase,* Bdwy in *My Favorite Year* (1992), *Goodbye Girl, DuBarry Was a Lady (Encores), Swinging on a Star* for which he received a 1996 Theatre World Award.

McGUINESS, MICHAEL JOHN. Born May 13, 1961 in Corning, NY. Graduate NYU. Debut 1985 OB in *Brand* followed by *Frankenstein, Wakefield/Chester Mystery Play Cycle, Frankenstein, Richard II, Andromache, She Stoops to Conquer, All's Well That Ends Well, Three Sisters, Midsummer Night's Dream, Medea, Importance of Being Earnest, Detective Story.*

McKECHNIE, DONNA. Born in November 1944 in Detroit, MI. Bdwy debut in *How to Succeed in Business* (1961) followed by *Promises Promises, Company, On the Town, Music! Music!, A Chorus Line, Fiorello(Encores), State Fair,* OB in *Wine Untouched, Cut the Ribbons, Annie Warbucks.*

McKEE, LONETTE. Born July 22, 1955 in Detroit, MI. Bdwy debut in *The First* (1981) followed by *Show Boat*(1983/1995).

McLACHLAN, RODERICK. Born September 9, 1960 in Detroit, MI. Graduate Northwestern U. Bdwy debut in *Death and the King's Horseman* (LC-1987) followed by *Our Town, Real Inspector Hound, Saint Joan, Timon in Athens, Government Inspector, Holiday,* OB in *Madame Bovary, Julius Caesar, Oh Hell!, Hauptmann, Make Up Your Mind.*

McLAUGHLIN, ELLEN. Born Nov.9, 1957 in Cambridge, MA. Graduate Yale U. Debut 1991 OB in *A Bright Room Called Day* followed by *Blue Window,* Bdwy in *Angels in America.*

McMILLAN, LISA. Born May 28, 1955 in Oregon. Juilliard graduate. Debut 1980 OB in *City Junket* followed by *Identical Twins from Baltimore*, Bdwy in *Moose Murders*(1983).

McNIGHT, SHARON. Born Dec. 18 in Modesto, CA. Graduate SanFranStCol. Debut 1987 OB in *Murder at the Rutherford House* followed by *Looney Experience, Sophie Tucker Song Book*, Bdwy in *Starmites* (1989) for which she received a Theatre World Award.

MEDEIROS, JOSEPH. Born May 8, 1984 in Modesto, CA. Bdwy debut in *Big* (1996).

MEDINA, AIXA M. ROSARIO. Born July 5, 1965 in Rio Piedras, PR. Graduate UPR. Bdwy debut in *Victor Victoria* (1995).

MEINDL, ANTHONY. Born Jan.14, 1970 in LaPorte, IN. Graduate CalStU., U of London. Debut 1995 OB in *Titus Andronicus* followed by *Like a Brother, Party*.

MEISLE, KATHRYN. Born June 7 in Appleton,WI. Graduate Smith Col., UNC/Chapel Hill. Debut 1988 OB in *Dandy Dick* followed by *Cahoots, Othello, As You Like It* (CP), *Brutality of Fact*, Bdwy in *Racing Demon* (1995).

MEISNER, VICKI. Born Aug. 2, 1935 in NYC. Graduate Adelphi Col. Debut 1958 OB in *Blood Wedding*, followed by *The Prodigal, Shakuntala, Nathan the Wise, Decathlon, Afternoon in Las Vegas, Beauty Part, Trelawny of the Wells, Rimers of Eldritch, Mothers and Daughters, Heartbreak House*.

MELANCON, CORINNE. Born March 13 in Buffalo, NY. Attended Niagara U. Debut 1984 OB in *Up in Central Park*, Bdwy in *Me and My Girl* (1986), *My Fair Lady* (1993), *Big*.

MELLOR, STEPHEN. Born Oct. 17, 1954 in New Haven, CT. Graduate Boston U. Debut 1980 OB in *Paris Lights*, followed by *Coming Attractions, Plenty, Tooth of the Crime, Shepard Sets, A Country Doctor, Harm's Way, Brightness Falling, Terminal Hip, Dead Mother, Murder of Crows, Seven Blowjobs, Pericles, The Illusion, Hyacinth Macaw, Careless Love, Teibele and Her Demon, Terminal Hip, Strange Feet, Dream Express, Nixon's Nixon*, Bdwy in *Big River* (1985).

MENDILLO, STEPHEN. Born Oct. 9, 1942 in New Haven, CT. Graduate Colo. Col., Yale U. Debut 1973 OB in *Nourish the Beast*, followed by *Gorky, Time Steps, The Marriage, Loot, Subject to Fits, Wedding Band, As You Like It, Fool for Love, Twelfth Night, Grotesque Lovesongs, Nowhere, Portrait of My Bikini, Country Girl, Last Yankee, Ivanov, Black Ink*, Bdwy in *National Health* (1974), *Ah! Wilderness, View from the Bridge, Wild Honey, Orpheus Descending, Guys and Dolls*.

MERCOUFFER, THEA. Born Mar.26, 1966 in Romania. Graduate UofWA., PennSt. Debut 1996 OB in *Always Together*.

MERLIN, JOANNA. Born July 15 in Chicago, Il. Attended UCLA. Debut 1958 OB in *Breaking Wall*, followed by *Six Characters in Search of an Author, Rules of the Game, Thistle in My Bed, Canadian Gothic American Modern, Family Portrait, Brooklyn Trojan Women, Yiddish Trojan Women*, Bdwy in *Becket* (1961) *A Far Country, Fiddler on the Roof, Shelter, Uncle Vanya, The Survivor, Solomon's Child*.

METTNER, JERRY. Born Aug. 21, 1958 in Detroit, MI. Bdwy debut in *Present Laughter* (1982), OB in *Confessional* (1983), *Look Back in Anger, Jerusalem Mountain, 3 by Wilder, Somewhere I Have Never Traveled, Eye of the Beholder, Cinoman and Rebeck, Live Witness, Edward II, A Greater Good*.

MICHIE, WILLIAM D. Born July 6, 1959 in Omaha, NE. Graduate Macalester, SMU. Debut 1990 in *Romeo and Juliet* followed by *Richard III, Coriolanus, Cardenio*.

MIGLIORE, BILL. Born July 23, 1970 in Massachusetts. Debut 1990 OB in *Dreamer Examines His Pillow*.

MILLENBACH, GEORGE. Born Aug. 24, 1953 in Toronto, Can. Graduate U. Toronto. Debut 1982 OB in *Cinderella*, followed by *As You Like It, Cricket on the Hearth, Ceremony in Bohemia, Lion in Winter, Little Lies, What the Butler Saw, The Rehearsal, Habeas Corpus*.

MILLER, ANDREW. Born May 25 in Racine, WI. Attended UofIL, Royal Nat'l Th Studio. Debut 1995 OB in *Blue Man Group:Tubes* followed by *A Hamlet, Macbeth*.

MILLER, BETTY. Born Mar.27, 1925 in Boston, MA. Attended UCLA. OB in *Summer and Smoke, Cradle Song, La Ronde, Plays for Bleeker St., Desire Under the Elms, The Balcony, Power and the Glory, Beaux Stratagem, Gandhi, Girl on the Via Flammia, Hamlet, Summer, Before the Dawn, Curtains*, Bdwy in *You Can't Take It with You, Right You Are, Wild Duck, Cherry Orchard, Touch of the Poet, Eminent Domain, Queen and the Rebels, Richard III*.

MILLER, JOSH. Born Dec.1, 1973 in West Palm Beach, FL. Attended AMDA. Debut 1994 OB in *Fantasticks*.

MILLER, MADELINE. Born Apr.4, 1945 in NYC. Attended AMDA. Bdwy debut in *Bajour* (1964) followed by *Apple Doesn't Fall*, OB in *Slow Dance on the Killing Gound*.

MILLS, ELIZABETH. Born August 3, 1967 in San Jose, CA. Attended San Jose StateU. Bdwy debut in *Ain't Broadway Grand* (1993) followed by *Crazy for You, DuBarry was a Lady (Encores)*.

MINOT, ANNA. Born in Boston, MA. Attended Vassar Col. Bdwy debut in *The Strings My Lord Are False* (1942) followed by *Russian People, The Visitor, Iceman Cometh, Enemy of the People, Love of Four Colonels, Trip to Bountiful, Tunnel of Love, Ivanov*, OB in *Sands of the Niger, Gettin Out, Vieux Carre, State of the Union, Her Great Match, Rivals, Hedda Gabler, All's Well That Ends Well, Tarfuffe, Good Natur'd Man, Little Eyolf, Beaux Stratagem, Doll's House*.

MIRABAL, LORI BROWN. Born Jan.15, 1959 in Nashville, TN. Attended Juilliard, Manhattan Sch Music, Graduate Uof Memphis. Bdwy debut in *Showboat* (1996).

MISTRETTA, SAL. Born Jan.9, 1945 in Brooklyn, NYC. Graduate Ithaca Col. Bdwy debut in *Something's Afoot*(1976) followed by *On the 20th Century, Evita, King and I, Sunset Blvd.*, OB in *Charley's Tale, Education of Hyman Kaplan*.

MITCHELL, ALETA. Born in Chicago. Graduate UIowa, YaleU. Bdwy debut in *Ma Rainey's Black Bottom* (1984), OB in *Approaching Zanzibar, Night Sky, Marvin's Room, Crystal Stairs, Young Playwrights Festival*,

MITCHELL, GREGORY. Born December 9, 1951 in Brooklyn, NY. Graduate Juilliard, Principle with Eliot Feld Ballet before Bdwy debut in *Merlin*(1983) followed by *Song and Dance, Phantom of the Opera, Dangerous Games, Aspects of Love, Man of La Mancha* (1992), *Kiss of the Spider Woman, Chronicle of a Death Foretold*, OB in *Kicks*(1961),*One More Song One More Dance, Young Strangers, Tango Apasionado*.

MITZNER, RONIT. Born July 25, 1973 in Haifa, Israel. Graduate UofMI. Debut 1996 OB in *Zombie Prom*.

MIYATA, KENJI. Born Aug.4, 1984 in Osaka, Japan. Bdwy debut in *King and I* (1996).

MOGENTALE, DAVID. Born December 28, 1959 in Pittsburgh, PA. Graduate Auburn U. Debut 1987 OB in *Signal Season of Dummy Hoy*, followed by *Holy Note, Killers, Battery, Necktie Breakfast, Under Control, 1 Act Festival, Charmer, Killer Joe., Breast Men*.

MOLASKEY, JESSICA. Born in Waterbury, CT. Bdwy debut in *Oklahoma* (1980), *Chess, Cats, Les Miserables, Crazy for You, Tommy*, OB in *Weird Romance* (1991), *Songs for a New World*.

MOLINA, ALFRED. Born May 24, 1953 in London, Eng. Debut 1996 OB in *Molly Sweeney* for which he received a Theatre World Award.

MONFERDINI, CAROLE.Born in Eagle Lake, TX. Graduate NoTxStU. DEbut 1973 OB in *The Foursome* followed by *The Club, The Alto Part, Goodbye Freddy, Comeback, Full Gallop, Glory Girls*.

MONK, DEBRA. Born February 27, 1949 in Middletown, OH. Graduate Frostburg State Col., Southern Methodist U. Bdwy debut in *Pump Boys and Dinettes*(1982) followed by *Prelude to a Kiss, Redwood Curtain, Picnic, Company*, OB in *Young Playwrights Festival, A Narrow Bed, Oil City Symphony, Assassins, Man in His Underwear, Innocents Crusade, Three Hotels, Death Defying Acts*.

MONTANO, ROBERT. Born April 22 in Queens, NYC. Attended AdelphiU. Bdwy debut in *Cats* (1995) followed by *Chita Rivera + Two, Legs Diamond, Kiss of the Spider Woman*, OB in *The Chosen* (1987), *The Torturer's Visit, How Are Things in Costa del Fuego?, Picture Perfect, Young Playwrights Festival*.

MOORE, CRISTA. Born September 17 in Washington, DC. Attended Am. Ballet Th. Schl. Debut 1987 OB in *Birds of Paradise* followedby *Rags, Marathon '93, Long Ago and Far Away*, Bdwy in *Gypsy* (1989) for which she received a Theatre World Award, *110 in the Shade* (LC/NYCO), *Cinderella* (LC/NYCO), *Crazy For You, Wonderful Town*(NYCO), *Big*.

MOORE, DANA. Born in Sewickley, PA. Bdwy debut in *Sugar Babies*(1982) followed by *Dancin', Copperfield, On Your Toes, Singin' in the Rain, Sweet Charity, Dangerous Games, Chorus Line, Will Rogers Follies, Pal Joey*(Encores), OB in *Petrified Prince, Camila*.

MOORE, JUDITH. Born Feb.12, 1944 in Princeton,WVa. Graduate IndU. Debut 1971 OB in *The Drunkard* followed by *Ten by Six, Boys from Syracuse, The Evangelist, Miracle of the Month, Midsummer Nights, Petrified Prince, Lust*, Bdwy in *Sunday im the Park with George* (1984-also OB), *Into the Woods*.

MOORE, MAUREEN. Born August 12, 1951 in Wallingford, CT. Bdwy debut in *Gypsy*(1974) followed by *Moonie Shapiro Songbook, Do Black Patent Leather Shoes Really Reflect Up?, Amadeus, Big River, I Love My Wife, Song and Dance, Les Misérables, Amadeus, Jerome Robbins' Broadway, A Little Night Music* (NYCO), *Falsettos, Sunset Blvd.* OB in *God* spell, Unsung Cole, By Strouse, First Lady Suite.

MORALES, MARK. Born Nov.9, 1954 in NYC. Attended TrentonStU, SUNY/Purchase. Debut 1978 OB in *Coolest Cat in Town* followed by *Transposed Heads*, Bdwy in *West Side Story*(1980), *Cats, Sunset Blvd.*

MORAN, DAN. Born July 31, 1953 in Corcoran, CA. Graduate NYU. Debut 1977 OB in *Homebodies*, followed by *True West, Pericles, Merchant of Venice, The Vampires, Sincerely Forever, The Illusion, Class 1-Acts, Dark Rapture,* Bdwy in *Month in the Country*(1995).

MORAN, MARTIN. Born December 29, 1959 in Denver, CO. Attended StanfordU., AmConsvTh. Debut 1983 OB in *Spring Awakening,* followed by *Once on a Summer's Day, 1-2~3~4~5, Jacques Brel Is Alive* (1992), *Bed and Sofa, Floyd Collins* Bdwy in *Oliver!·*(1984), *Big River, How to Succeed.*.(1995).

MORELOCK, CHRISTOPHER. Born Nov.6, 1973 in Morristown, TN. Graduate Carson Newman Col. Debut 1996 OB in *Rock Around the Clock.*

MORENO, RITA. Born Dec.11, 1931 in Humacao, PR. Bdwy debut in *Skydrift* (1945) followed by *West Side Story, Sign in Sidney Brustein's Window, Last of the Red Hot Lovers, National Health, The Ritz, She Loves Me, Wally's Cafe, Odd Couple,* OB in *Size of the World, Afterplay.*

MORFOGEN, GEORGE. Born March 30, 1933 in New York City. Graduate Brown U., Yale. Debut 1957 OB in *Trial of D. Karamazov,* followed by *Christmas Oratorio, Othello, Good Soldier Schweik, Cave Dwellers, Once in a Lifetime, Total Eclipse, Ice Age, Prince of Homburg, Biography: A Game, Mrs. Warren's Profession, Principia Scriptoriae, Tamara, Maggie and Misha, Country Girl, Othello, As You Like It* (CP), *Uncle Bob, Henry V, Hope Zone,* Bdwy in *Fun Couple* (1962), *Kingdoms, Arms and the Man, An Inspector Calls.*

MORGAN, CASS. Born Apr.15 in Rochester, NY. Attended AdelphiU. Debut 1984 OB in *La Boheme* followed by *Another Paradise, The Knife, Catfish Loves Anna, Feast Here Tonight, Can Can, Merrily We Roll Along, Inside Out, Floyd Collins,* Bdwy in *Hair*(1969), *Pump Boys and Dinettes, Human Comedy, Beauty and the Beast.*

MORITSUGU, KIKI. Born March 24, 1966 in Montreal, Can. Attended George Brown Col. Bdwy debut in *Shogun: The Musical*(1990).

MORRIS, JAY HUNTER. Born 1970 in Paris, TX. Attended Juilliard. Bdwy debut in *Master Class* (1995).

MORSE, ROBERT. Born May 18, 1931 in Newton, MA. Bdwy debut in *The Matchmaker* (1955) followed by *Say Darling* for which he received a Theatre World Award, *Take Me Along, How to Suc c eed in Business ..., Sugar, So Long 1 74th Strret, Tru, DuBarry was a Lady (Encores),* OB in *More of Loesser, Eileen in Concert.*

MOSES, BURKE. Born in NYC. Graduate Carnegie-Mellon U. Debut 1986 OB in *Wasted,* followed by *Way of the World,* Bdwy in *Most Happy Fella*(NYCO), *Guys and Dolls* (1993), *Beauty and the Beast,* for which he received a 1994 Theatre World Award, *DuBarry was a Lady (Encores).*

MOSTEL, JOSHUA. Born December 21, 1946 in NYC. Graduate BrandeisU. Debut 1971 OB in *The Proposition,* followed by *More Than You Deserve, The Misanthrope, Rocky Road, Boys Next Door, Perfect Diamond,* Bdwy in *Unlikely Heroes, American Millionaire, Texas Trilogy, 3 Penny Opera, My Favorite Year, Flowering Peach, Getting Away with Murder.*

MOTLEY, BYRON. Born June 26 in Kansas City, MO. Graduate USC. Bdwy debut in *Patti LuPone on Bdwy* (1995).

MOZER, ELIZABETH. Born Nov.17, 1960 in Jamaica, NY. Graduate SUNY/Brockport. Debut 1986 OB in *Funny Girl,* Bdwy in *Dangerous Games* (1989), *Victor Victoria.*

MUELLER, JULIA. Born Apr.16, 1961 in Ft. Lee, NJ. Graduate Dartmouth Col. DEbut 1987 OB in *Come Blow Your Horn* followed by *Requiem for a Heavyweight.*

MULLALLY, MEGAN. Born Nov. 12, 1958 in Los Angeles, CA. Attended Northwestern U. Bdwy debut in *Grease*(1994) followed by *How to Succeed...*(1995).

MUNIZ, MARCOS. Born Apr.17, 1969 in Rochester, NY. Attended AADA. Debut 1996 OB in *Bomber Jackets.*

MURAOKA, ALAN. Born August 10, 1962 in Los Angeles, CA. Graduate UCLA. Bdwy debut 1988 in *Mail,* followed by *Shogun: The Musical, My Favorite Year, Miss Saigon, King and I*(1996).

MURFITT, MARY. Born Mar.29, 1954 in Kansas City, MO. Graduate Marymount Col. Debut 1987 OB in *Oil City Symphony* for which she received a Theatre World Award, *Cowgirls.*

MURPHY, DONNA. Born March 7, 1959 in Corona, NY. Attended NYU. Bdwy debut in *They're Playing Our Song*(1979) followed by *Human Comedy*(also OB), *Mystery of Edwin Drood, Passion, King and I* (1996),

OB in *Francis, Portable Pioneer and Prairie Show, Little Shop of Horrors, A ... My Name is Alice, Showing Off, Privates on Parade, Song of Singapore, Hey Love, Hello Again, Twelve Dreams.*

MURPHY, KAREN. Born Aug.11, 1958 in White Plains, NY. Attended Boston Consv., UMA. Debut 1989 OB in *Forbidden Bdwy* followed by *Hysterical Blindness, Greenwillow.* Bdwy in *Christmas Carol* (1994).

MURPHY, ROSEMARY. Born Jan.13, 1927 in Munich, Ger. Attended Neighborhood Playhouse, Actors Studio. Bdwy debut in *Tower Beyond Tragedy*(1950) followed by *Look Homeward Angel, Death of Bessie Smith, Butterflies Are Free, Ladies at the Alamo, Cheaters, John Gabriel Borkman, Coastal Disturbances*(also OB), *Devil's Disciple, Delicate Balance,* OB in *Are You Now or Have You Ever Been?, Learned Ladies, Uncommon Women and Others, The Arbor, Cold Sweat, Night of the Iguana.*

MURRAY, BRIAN. Born October 9, 1939 in Johannesburg, SA. Debut 1964 OB in *The Knack,* followed by *King Lear, Ashes, Jail Diary of Albie Sachs, Winter's Tale, Barbarians, The Purging, Midsummer Night's Dream, Recruiting Officer, Arcata Promise, Candide in Concert, Much Ado about Nothing, Hamlet, Merry Wives of Windsor, Travels with My Aunt, Entertaining Mr. Sloane, Molly Sweeney,* Bdwy in *All in Good Time* (1965), *Rosencrantz and Guildenstern Are Dead, Sleuth, Da, Noises Off, Small Family Business, Black Comedy, Racing Demon.*

MURTAUGH, JAMES. Born October 28, 1942 in Chicago, IL. Debut OB in *The Firebugs* followed by *Highest Standard of Living, Marathon '87, Other People's Money, Marathon '88, I Am a Man, Wreck on the 5:25, Elegy for a Lady, Beauty Part, No One Will Be Immune,* Bdwy in *Two Shakespearean Actors* (1991).

NAKAMURA, MIDORI. Born in Missoula, MT. Graduate YaleU. UChicago. Debut 1991 OB in *Piece of My Heart* followed by *King Lear, Madame de Sade, Prometheus Bound, Kokoro.*

NASTASI, FRANK. Born Jan. 7, 1923 in Detroit, MI. Graduate Wayne U. NYU. Bdwy debut in *Lorenzo* (1963) followed by *Avanti,* OB in *Bonds of Interest, One Day More, Nathan the Wise, Chief Things, Cindy, Escurial, Shrinking Bride, Macbird, Cakes with the Wine, Metropolitan Madness, Rockaway Boulevard, Scenes from La Vie de Boheme, Agamemnon, Happy Sunset Inc., 3 Last Plays of O'Neill, Taking Steam, Lulu, Body! Body!, Legend of Sharon Shashanova, Enrico IV, Stealing Fire, Mourning Becomes Electra, Beautiful People.*

NAUFFTS, GOEFFREY. Born Feb.3, 1961 in Arlington, MA. Graduate NYU. Debut 1987 OB in *Moonchildren,* followed by *Stories from Home, Another Time Anothet Place, The Alarm, Jerusalem Oratorio, The Survivor, Spring Awakening, Summer Winds, Saturday Mourning Cartoons,* Bdwy in *A Few Good Men* (1989).

NAUGHTON, GREG. Born June 1, 1968 in New Haven, CT. Graduate Middlebury Col., LAMDA. Debut 1994 OB in *Dogg's Hamlet Cahoot's Macbeth* followed by *Jack's Holiday, Golden Boy, Scenes From an Execution.*

NAUGHTON, JAMES. Born December 6, 1945 in Middletown, CT. Graduate Brown U., Yale. Debut 1971 OB in *Long Day's Journey into Night* for which he received a Theatre World Award, followed by *Drinks before Dinner, Losing Time,* Bdwy in *I Love My Wife, Whose Life Is It Anyway?, City of Angels, Four Baboons Adoring the Sun, Chicago.*

NELSON, MARK. Born September 26, 1955 in Hackensack, NJ. Graduate Princeton U. Debut 1977 OB in *The Dybbuk,* followed by *Green Fields, The Keymaker, Common Pursuit, Cabaret Verboten, Flaubert's Latest, Picasso at the Lapin Agile,* Bdwy in *Amadeus* (1981), *Brighton Beach Memoirs, Bilaxi Blues, Broadway Bound, Rumors, A Few Good Men.*

NEUBERGER, JAN. Born Jan. 21 1953 in Amityville, NY. Attended NYU. Bdwy debut in *Gypsy*(1974) followed by *Change in the Heir, Big,* OB in *Silk Stockings, Chase a Rainbow, Anything Goes, A Little Madness, Forbidden Broadway, After These Messages, Ad Hock, Rags, Christina Alberta's Father, All in the Timing.*

NEVARD, ANGELA. Born March 19, 1963 in Montreal, Can. Graduate Skidmore Col. Debut 1988 OB in *Faith Hope and Charity,* followed by *3 by Wilder, Macbeth, The Balcony, Harm's Way, Judgment Day, Tartuffe, Morning Song, Who Will Carry the Word, Sea Plays, Twelfth Night, Camino Real, As You Like It, Goose and TomTom, Child's Christmas in Wales, Ends of the Earth,* Bdwy in *Wilder Wilder Wilder* (1993).

NEVINS, KRISTINE. Born October 9, 1951 in Champaign, IL. Graduate KanStateU. Debut 1986 OB in *Charley's Tale,* followed by *Starmites, Kiss Me Ouick before the Lava Reaches the Village, Midsummer Nights, A Mind Is a Terrible Thing to Lose, Say Darling.*

NEWMAN, PHYLLIS. Born Mar.19, 1935 in Jersey City, NJ. Attended West ReserveU. Bdwy debut in *Wish You Were Here* (1953) followed by *Bells Are Ringing, First Impressions, Subways Are for Sleeping, Apple Tree, On the Town, Prisoner of Second Ave., Madwoman of Central Park West, Miami, Bdwy Bound,* OB in *I Feel Wonderful, Make Someone Happy, I Married an Angel, I'm Getting My Act Together, Red Rivers, The New Yorkers, Food Chain.*

NEWMAN, RONNIE. Born in Brooklyn, NYC. Graduate Brooklyn Col. Debut 1970 OB in *Universal Nigger* followed by *Water Hen, Eternal Love, Appear and Show Cause, Like Two Eagles,* Bdwy in *Strider* (1979-also OB).

NGAI, BRANDON MARSHALL. Born June 7, 1987 in Queens, NYC. Bdwy debut in *Miss Saigon* (1992) followed by *King and I* (1996).

NICHOLAW, CASEY. Born October 6, 1992. Attended UCLA. Debut 1986 OB in *Pajama Game* followed by *Petrifeid Prince,* Bdwy in *Crazy for You* (1992), *Best Little Whorehouse Goes Public, Victor Victoria.*

NOONAN, JIMMY. Born Jan.31, 1958 in Massapequa Pk, NY. Bdwy debut in *An Inspector Calls* (1994).

NORRIS, BRUCE. Born May 16, 1960 in Houston, TX. Graduate Northwestern U. Bdwy debut in *Biloxi Blues* (1985), OB in *Midsummer Night's Dream, Wenceslas Square, The Debutante Ball, What the Butler Saw, Life During Wartime, Arabian Nights, Sin.*

NOURI, MICHAEL. Born Dec.9, 1945 in Washington, D.C. Debut 1964 OB in *The Crucible* followed by *Booth,* Bdwy in *40 Carats* (1968), *Victor Victoria.*

OBERLANDER, MICHAEL. Born Aug. 25, 1960 in Newark, NJ. Graduate Carnegie-Melon U. Debut 1985 OB in *The Crows,* followed by *The Misanthrope, Dracula, Georgy, Paradise Re-Lost, Promised Land, Family Obligations, The Survivor, Twelfth Night.*

O'GORMAN, HUGH. Born June 11, 1965 in NYC. Graduate CornellU, UWash. Debut 1991 OB in *The Tempest* followed by *Cloud 9, Taming of the Shrew, Time of Your Life, Yiddish Trojan Women,* Bdwy in *Translations*(1995).

OJEDA, PERRY LAYLON. Born Apr.25, 1968 in Tecumseh, MI. Graduate UofMI. Debut 1991 OB in *Jekyll and Hyde* followed by *Cute Boys...Prove How Good They Are, Geneology, Ben and Jerry, The Trick, Cafe Boys,* Bdwy in *Blood Brothers* (1994).

O'KARMA, ALEXANDRA. Born Mar.28, 1948 in Cincinnati, OH. Graduate Swarthmore Col. Debut 1976 OB in *Month in the Country* followed by *Warbeck, Flea in Her Ear, Knitters in the Sun, The Beethoven, Clownmaker, Minor Demons.*

O'KELLY, AIDEEN. Born in Dalkey, Ireland. Member Dublin's Abbey Theatre. Bdwy debut in *A Life* (1980) followed by *Othello,* OB in *Killing of Sister George, Man Enough, Resistance, Remembrance, Somewhere I Have Never Traveled, Same Old Moon*

OLLEN, SINJE. Born Dec.4, 1967 in Saarbruecken, Ger. Graduate Stella Adler Consv. Debut 1994 OB in *Reel to Real,* Bdwy in *Night of the Iguana* (1996).

OLYPHANT, TOMOTHY. Born May 20 in Honolulu, HI. Attended USC. OB includes *Jimmy and Evelyn, Joe's Not Home, The Monogamist* for which he received a 1996 Theatre World Award.

OMILAMI, AFEMO. Born Dec.13, 1950 in Petersburg, VA. Graduate NYU, Attended Morehouse. Debut 1982 OB in *Livingston and Sechele* followed by *Nest of the Woodgrouse, Por'Knockers.*

O'NEILL, MICHELLE. Born April 26 in Bend, OR. Graduate UUtah, Juilliard. Bdwy debut in *Abe Lincoln in Illinois* (1993) followed by *Heiress.*

OPPENHEIMER, ALAN. Born Apr.23, 1930 in NYC. Graduate Carnegie-MellonU, Neighborhood Playhouse. Debut OB in *I Am a Camera* (1956), Bdwy in *Sunset Blvd.*(1994).

O'REILLY, CIARAN. Born March 13, 1959 in Ireland. Attended Carmelite Col., Juilliard. Debut 1978 OB in *Playboy of the Western World,* followed by *Summer, Freedom of the City,Fannie, Interrogation of Ambrose Fogarty, King Lear, Shadow of a Gunman, Mary Month of May, I Do Not Live Like Thee Dr. Fell, Plough and the Stars, Yeats: A Celebration, Philadelphia Here I Come, Making History, Mme. MacAdam Traveling Theater, Au Pair Man, Same Old Moon, Whistle in the Dark.*

OREM, SUSAN. Born June 15, 1949 in Ellizabeth, NJ. Graduate NYU. Debut 1979 OB in *Big Bad Burlesque,* followed by *Christopher Blake, Rise and Rise of Daniel Rocket, How He Lied to Her Husband, Two Nikita.*

ORESKES, DANIEL. Born in NYC. Graduate U. PA., LAMDA. Debut 1990 OB in *Henry IV,* followed by *Othello, 'Tis Pity She's a Whore, Richard II, Henry VI, Troilus and Cressida, Quills,* Bdwy in *Crazy He Calls Me* (1992).

O'SULLIVAN, ANNE. Born February 6, 1952 in Limerick City, Ire. Debut 1977 OB in *Kid Champion,* followed by *Hello Out There, Fly Away Home, The Drunkard, Dennis, Three Sisters. Another Paradise, Living Quarters, Welcome to the Noon, Dreamer Examines His Pillow, Mama Drama, Free Fall, Magic Act, Plough and the Stars, Marathon '88, Bobo's Guns, Marathon '90, Festival of 1 Acts, Marathon '91, Murder of Crows, Cats and Dogs.*

OVERBEY, KELLIE. Born November 21, 1964 in Cincinnati, OH. Graduate Northwestern U. Debut 1988 OB in *Debutante Ball,* followed by *Second Coming, Face Divided, Melville Boys,* Bdwy in *Buried Child* (1996).

OYSTER, JIM. Born May 3, 1930 in Washington, DC. OB in *Coriolanus, Cretan Woman, Man and Superman, Fallen Angels, The Underlings, Traveler in the Dark,* Bdwy in *Cool World* (1960), *Hostile Witness, Sound of Music, Prime of Miss Jean Brodie, Who's Who in Hell, Mrs. Dally Has a Lover, Romulus, Holiday.*

PACHECO, GIL. Born May 9, 1944 in NYC. Debut 1967 OB in *Pins and Needles* followed by *Waiting for Lefty, Journey's End, Swallows, Dog Lady, No More Bingo at the Wake, Minor Demons.*

PAIGE, ELAINE. Born 1951 in England. Bdwy debut in *Sunset Blvd.* (1996).

PALZERE, EMMA. Born June 15, 1962 in Manchester, CT. Graduate Emerson Col. Debut 1991 OB in *Born in the R.S.A.,* followed by *Montage, Rimers of Eldritch, Live from the Milky Way.*

PANKOW, JOHN. Born 1955 in St. Louis, MO. Attended St. Nichols Sch. of Arts. Debut 1980 OB in *Merton of the Movies* followed by *Slab Boys, Forty Deuce, Hunting Scenes from Lower Bovaria, Cloud 9, Jazz Poets at the Crotto, Henry V, North Shore Fish, Two Gentlemen of Verona, Italian American Reconciliation Aristocrats, Ice Cream with Hot Fudge, EST Marathon '92, Tempest(CP),* Bdwy in *Amadeus* (1981), *The Iceman Cometh, Serious Money.*

PARK, STEPHANIE. Born Aug.11, 1967 in Framingham, MA. Graduate Carnegie-Mellon. DEbut OB in *Song of Singapore,* Bdwy in *Getting Away with Murder* (1996).

PARKER, ELLEN. Born September 30, 1949 in Paris, Fr. Graduate Bard Col. Debut 1971 OB in *James Joyce Liquid Theatre,* followed by *Uncommon Women and Others, Dusa Fish Stas and Vi, Day in the Life of the Czar, Fen, Isn't It Romantic?, Winter's Tale, Aunt Dan and Lemon, Cold Sweat, Heidi Chronicles, Absent Friends, Joined at the Head, Entertaining Mr. Sloane,* Bdwy in *Equus, Strangers, Plenty.*

PARKER, MARY-LOUISE. Born Aug. 2, 1964 in Ft. Jackson, SC. Graduate NC. Sch of Arts. Debut 1989 OB in *Art of Success* followed by *Babylon Gardens, EST Marathon '92, Four Dogs and a Bone,* Bdwy in *Prelude to a Kiss* (1990-also OB) for which she received a 1990 Theatre World Award, *Bus Stop.*

PARKER, SARAH JESSICA. Born March 25, 1965 in Nelsonville, OH. Bdwy debut in *Annie* (1978), OB in *The Innocents, One-Act Festival, To Gillian on Her 37th Birthday, Broadway Scandals of 1928, Heidi Chronicles, Substance of Fire, Sylvia.*

PARKER, TIMOTHY BRITTEN. Born 1962 in Nelsonville, OH. Bdwy debut in *The Innocents* (1976) followed by *Runaways, The Vist, Rent* (also OB), OB in *Summer Winds, Machinal, Cherry Orchard, Chelsea Walls, Suffering Colonel, Night and Her Stars,*

PARKS, KATHERINE. Born May 11, 1946 in Louisville, KY. Graduate Stephens Col., UMo. Debut 1978 OB in *Old Man Joseph and his Family* followed by *Moliere in spite of Himself, Feelers, The Mask, Margo's Party.*

PARLATO, DENNIS. Born March 30, 1947 in Los Angeles, CA. Graduate Loyola U. Bdwy debut 1979 in *Chorus Line,* followed by *The First, Chess,* OB in *Becket, Elizabeth and Essex, The Fantasticks, Moby Dick, The Knife, Shylock, Have I Got a Girl for You, Romance! Romance!, The Earl, Violent Peace, Traveler in the Dark, Hello Again, Jack's Holiday, Down by the Ocean, Aimee and Hope.*

PASCAL, ADAM. Born 1968 in Woodbury, NY. Bdwy debut in *Rent* (1996-also OB).

PASEKOFF, MARILYN. Born Nov. 7, 1949 in Pittsburgh, PA. Graduate BostonU. Debut 1975 OB in *Godspell* followed by *Maybe I'm Doing It Wrong, Professionally Speaking. Forbidden Broadway, Showing off, Forbidden Broadway 1990, Forbidden Broadway 1991, Shmulnik's Waltz, Yiddish Trojan Women,* Bdwy in *Godspell* (1976), *Odd Couple* (1985).

PATERSON, JOSEPH. Born June 22, 1964 in London, Eng. Attended LAMDA. Bdwy debut in *Hamlet* (1995).

Eric Kunze

Cherry Jones

Nathan Lane

Patricia Jones

Michael K. Lee

Laurie Kennedy

Robert Sean
Leonard

Taewon Kim

Michael Mastro

Samantha Robyn
Lee

Matt McGrath

Patti LuPone

Josh Miller

Mary Elizabeth
Mastrantonio

Mark Morales

Jill Matson

Martin Moran

Carole Monferdini

Mark Nelson

Debra Monk

Bruce Norris

Donna Murphy

Afemo Omilami

Jan Neuberger

Austin Pendleton

Angela Nevard

Rafael Petlock

Sarah Jessica
Parker

Richard Roland

Pamela Payton-
Wright

PATTERSON, JAY. Born Aug.22 in Cincinnatti, OH. Attended OhioU. Bdwy debut in *K-2* (1983), OB in *Caligula, Mound Builders, Quiet in the Land, Of Mice and Men, Domino, Early One Evening, Tempest, Doll House, The Misanthrope.*

PAUL, GUY. Born September 12, 1949 in Milwaukee, WI. Attended UMinn. Debut 1984 OB in *Flight of the Earls*, followed by *Frankenstein, The Underpants, Oresteia, Ever Afters, Oh Baby Oh Baby, Of Blessed Memory, Candida,* Bdwy in *Arms and the Man*(1985), *Wild Honey, Rumors, Private Lives, King and I* (1996).

PAYTON-WRIGHT, PAMELA. Born Nov.1, 1941 in Pittsburgh, PA. Graduate Birmingham So.Col., RADA, Bdwy debut in *Show-Off* (1967) followed by *Exit the King, Cherry Orchard, Jimmy Shine, Mourning Becomes Electra, Glass Menagerie* (1975), *Romeo and Juliet, Night of the Iguana, M. Butterfly, Garden District,* OB in *Effect of Gamma Rays..., The Crucible, The Seagull, Don Juan, In the Garden.*

PEDI, CHRISTINE. Born Oct.24 in Yonkers, NY. Graduate FordhamU. Debut 1993 in *Forbidden Bdwy.*

PEERCE, AHRRY. Born Feb.21, 1952 in Detroit, MI. Graduate UMi., Goodman Sch. Debut 1982 OB in *Little Murders* followed by *Anatol, Songs of Paradise, Double Identity.*

PELLEGRINO, SUSAN. Born June 3, 1950 in Baltimore, MD. Attended CCSan Francisco, CalStU. Debut 1982 OB in *Wisteria Trees,* followed by *Steel on Steel, Master Builder, Equal Wrights, Come as You Are, Painting Churches, Marvin's Room, Glory Girls, Minor Demons,* Bdwy in *Kentucky Cycle* (1994).

PENDLETON, AUSTIN. Born March 27, 1940 in Warren, OH. Debut 1962 OB in *Oh Dad Poor Dad...,* followed by *Last Sweet Days of Isaac, Three Sisters, Say Goodnight Gracie, Office Murders, Up from Paradise, The Overcoat, Two Character Play, Master Class, Educating Rita, Uncle Vanya, Serious Company, Philotetes, Hamlet, Richard III, What about Luv?, Sorrows of Frederick, The Show-Off, Jeremy Rudge, Sophistry, The Imposter,* Bdwy in *Fiddler on the Roof* (1964), *Hail Scrawdyke, Little Foxes, American Millionaire, The Runner Stumbles, Doubles.*

PENNINGTON, GAIL. Born October 2, 1957 in Kansas City, MO. Graduate SMU. Bdwy debut in *Music Man* (1980) followed by *Can-Can, America, Little Me* (1982), *42nd Street, Most Happy Fella, Christmas Carol,* OB in *Baker's Wife.*

PEREZ, LAZARO. Born December 12, 1945 in Havana, Cuba. Bdwy debut in *Does A Tiger Wear a Necktie?* (1969) followed by *Animals, Streetcar Named Desire* (1992), *Chronicle of a Death Foretold,* OB in *Romeo and Juliet, 12 Angry Men, Wonderful Years, Alive, G.R. Point, Primary English Class, Man and the Fly, Last Latin Lover, Cabal of Hypocrites, Balm in Gilead, Enrico IV.*

PEREZ, LUIS. Born July 28, 1959 in Atlanta, GA. With Joffrey Ballet before Bdwy debut in *Brigadoon* (LC-1986), followed by *Phantom of the Opera, Jerome Robbins' Broadway, Dangerous Games, Grand Hotel, Man of La Mancha* (1992), *Ain't Broadway Grand, Chronicle of a Death Foretold,* OB in *Wonderful Ice Cream Suit, Tango Apasionada.*

PEREZ, MIGUEL. Born September 7, 1957 in San Jose, CA. Attended Natl. Shakespeare Consv. Debut 1986 OB in *Women Beware Women,* followed by *Don Juan of Seville, Cymbeline, Mountain Language, Birthday Party, Hamlet, Henry IV Parts 1 & 2, Arturo Ui, The Merry Wives of Windsor,* Bdwy in *Tempest* (1995)

PERLMAN, BONNIE. Born Sept. 9, 1953 in Baltimore. MD. Graduate NYU. Bdwy debut in *Prince of Central Park* (1989), OB in *Say Darling.*

PERLMAN, MACE. Born July 31, 1963 in NYC. Graduate StanfordU. Debut 1994 OB in *Venetian Twins.*

PERLMAN, RON. Born Apr. 13 1950 in NYC. Graduate Lehman Col., UMinn. Debut 1976 OB in *Architect and the Emperor of Assyria,* followed by *Tartuffe, School for Buffoons, Measure for Measure, Hedda Gabler,* Bdwy in *Teibele and Her Demon* (1979), *A Few Good Men, Bus Stop.*

PESCE, VINCE. Born Dec. 3, 1966 in Brooklyn NY. Bdwy debut in *Guys and Dolls* (1993), *Victor Victoria,* OB in *Hunchback of Notre Dame.*

PETERSEN, ERIKA. Born Mar.24, 1949 in NYC. Attended NYU. Debut 1963 OB in *One Is a Lonely Number* followed by *I Dreamt I Dwelt in Bloomingdale's, F. Jasmine Addams, The Dubliners, P.S. Your Cat Is Dead, The Possessed, Murder in the Cathedral, Further Inquiry, State of the Union, Brand, Frankenstein, Death and the King's Horesman, Case of Kasper Meyer.*

PETERSON, PATRICIA BEN. Born Sept. 11 in Ponland, OR. Graduate Pacific LutheranU. Debut 1985 OB in *Kuni Leml,* followed by *The Chosen, Grand Tour, Yiddle with a Fiddle,* Bdwy in *Into the Woods* (1989), *Company.*

PETLOCK, RAFAEL. Born Sept.23, 1974 in Sarasota, FL. Debut 1994 OB in *Andrew My Dearest One.*

PEVSNER, DAVID. Born Dec. 31, 1958 in Skokie, IL. Graduate CarnegieMellonU. Debut 1985 OB in *A Flash of Lightning* followed by *Rags, Rag on a Stick and a Star, Party,* Bdwy in *Fiddler on the Roof* (1990).

PFISTERER, SARAH. Born Oct.13 in Beloit, WI. Graduate NorthwesternU. Bdwy debut in *Show Boat* (1996).

PHILLIPS, ANGIE. Born in Denison, TX. Graduate NYU. Debut 1991 OB in *Bright Room Called Day* followed by *Way of the World, Suppliant Women, The Treatment, Midsummer Night's Dream, Golden Boy, Dark Ride, Many and Lo, 15 Minute Hamlet, The Skriker.*

PHILLIPS, ARTE. Born Feb. 13, 1959 in Astoria, Queens, NYC. Attended Baruch Col. Bdwy debut in *Grand Hotel*(1990) followed by *Victor Victoria.*

PHILLIPS, LOU DIAMOND. Born Feb.17, 1962 in Subic Bay Naval Air Station, Philippines. Graduate UofTexas/Arlington. Bdwy debut in *King and I* (1996) for which he received a 1996 Theatre World Award.

PHILLIPS, MacKENZIE. Born Nov.10, 1959 in Alexandria, VA. Bdwy debut in *Grease* (1996).

PHILLIPS, SIAN. Born in Carmarthenshire, Wales. Graduate UWales, RADA. Bdwy debut in *An Inspector Calls* (1995).

PHOENIX, ALEC. Born Sept.9, 1964 in Bristol, Eng. Graduate Swarthmore Col., Juilliard. Debut 1992 OB in *Henry V,* followed by *Love's Labour's Lost, Merry Wives of Windsor, A Hamlet,* Bdwy in *Timon of Athens* (1993), *Government Inspector.*

PHOENIX, REGGIE. Born Sept.11, 1960 in NYC. Attended Brooklyn Col. Debut 1980 OB in *Lion and the Jewel* followed by *Homeseekers, Angel Levine,* Bdwy debut in *Chorus Line* (1983).

PIDGEON, REBECCA. Born Oct.25, 1965 in Edinburgh, Scotland. Attended RADA. Debut 1992 OB in *Oleanna* followed by *Dangerous Corner.*

PIECH, JENNIFER (LYNN). Born Jan.25, 1967 in Camden, NJ. Graduate College of William & Mary. Debut 1995 OB in *Lust.*

PIERCE, LINDA. Born Oct.18, 1946 in Tennesse. Graduate UNC. Debut 1995 OB in *Night and Her Stars.*

PINE, LARRY. Born March 3, 1945 in Tucson, AZ. Graduate NYU. Debut 1967 OB in *Cyrano,* followed by *Alice in Wonderland, Mandrake, Aunt Dan and Lemon, Taming of the Shrew, Better Days, Dolphin Project, Treasure Island, Preservation Society,* Bdwy in *End of the World* (1984), *Angels in America, Bus*

PINKINS, TONYA. Born May 30, 1962 in Chicago Il. Attended Carnegie-Mellon U. Bdwy debut in *Merrily We Roll Along* (1981) followed by *Jelly's Last Jam, Chronicle of a Death Foretold,* OB in *Five Points, Winter's Tale, An Ounce of Prevention, Just Say No, Mexican Hayride, Young Playwrights '90, Approximating Mother, Merry Wives of Windsor.*

PITTU, DAVID. Born April 4, 1967 in Fairfield, CT. Graduate NYU. Debut 1987 OB in *Film is Evil: Radio is Good,* followed by *Five Very Live, White Cotton Sheets, Nothing Sacred, Stand-In, The Lights, Three Postcards, Dangerous Corner,* Bdwy in *Tenth Man*(1989).

POCHOS, DEDE. Born Apr.27, 1960 in Lake Forest, IL. Graduate UPa. Bdwy debut in *Wilder Wilder Wilder* (1993), OB in *Midsummer's Night Dream, Macbeth, Tomorrow Was War, Judgment Day, Tartuffe, Who Will Carry the Word?, As You Like It, Anatomy of Sound, Child's Christmas in Wales.*

POE, RICHARD. Born Jan. 25, 1946 in Portola, CA. Graduate USanFran., U. Cal/Davis Debut 1971 OB in *Hamlet,* followed by *Seasons Greetings, Twelfth Night, Naked Rights, Approximating Mother, Jeffrey,* Bdwy in *Broadway* (1987), *M. Butterfly, Our Country's Good, Moon Over Buffalo.*

PONTING, DAVID. Born Apr.16, 1936 in Denizes, Eng. Graduate UofBristol, Uof London, SyracuseU. Bdwy debut in *Gentlemen Prefer Blondes* (1995).

POPE, PEGGY. Born May 15, 1929 in Montclair, NJ. Attended Smith Col. Bdwy in *Docror's Dilemma, Volpone, Rose Tarroo, Harvey, School for Wives, Dr. Jazz,* OB in *Muzeeka, House of Blue Leaves, New Cirl in Town, Romeo and Juliet, Wasp and Other Plays.*

POPE, STEPHANIE. Born April 8, 1964 in NYC. Debut 1983 OB in *Buck Stops Here,* followed by *Shades of Harlem, Watermellon Rinds,* Bdwy in *Big Deal* (1986), *Jelly's Last Jam, Kiss of the Spiderwoman, A Funny Thing...*(1996).

PORTER, ADINA. Born Feb.18, 1963 in NYC. Attended SUNY/Purchase. Debut 1988 OB in *Debutante Ball* followed by *Inside Out, Tiny Mommie, Footsteps in the Rain, Jersey City, The Mysteries?, Aven U' Boys, Silence Cunning Exile, Girl Gone, Dancing on Moonlight, Saturday Mourning Cartoons, Venus.*

PORTER, BILLY. Born Sept. 21, 1969 in Pittsburgh, PA. Graduate Carnegie-Mellon U. Debut 1989 OB in *Romance in Hard Times* followed by *Merchant of Venice, Songs for a New World*. Bdwy in *Miss Saigon*(1991), *Five Guys Named Moe, Grease*.

POSEY, LEAH. Born Oct.28, 1953 in Laurens, SC. Debut 1981 OB in *Little Murders* followed by *Danny and the Deep Blue Sea, Belles, More Than Madness, Bible Burlesque, Nightwalking, Baptists*.

POTTS, MICHAEL. Born Sept.21, 1962 in Brooklyn, NY. Graduate ColumbiaU, Yale Drama. Debut 1993 in *Playboy of the West Indies* followed by *America Play, Rent, Overtime*.

POWELL, JANE. Born Apr.1, 1929 in Portland, Ore. Bdwy debut in *Irene* (1974), OB in *After-Play* (1996).

PRATT, SEAN. Born Dec. 26, 1965 in Oklahoma City, OK. Graduate Santa Fe Col. BADA. Debut OB 1993 in *Good Natur'd Man*, followed by *Phaedra, Widowers Houses, Oedipus the King, Game of Love and Chance, Twelfth Night, Winter's Tale, Life Is a Dream*.

PREDOVIC, DENNIS. Born Sept.14, 1950 in Cleveland, OH. Graduate OhioU. Debut OB in *Other People's Money*, Bdwy in *Night of the Iguana* (1996).

PRESTON, CARRIE. Born 1967 in Macon, GA. Graduate Juilliard, UofEvansville, IN. Bdwy debut in *Tempest* (1995), OB in *In No Man's Land*.

PRESTON, WILLIAM. Born Aug. 26, 1921 in Columbia, PA. Graduate PennStU. Debut 1972 OB in *We Bombed in New Haven*, followed by *Hedda Gabler, Whisper into My Good Ear, Nestless Bird, Friends of Mine, Iphigenia in Aulix, Midsummer, Fantasticks, Frozen Assets, The Golem, Taming of the Shrew, His Master's Voice, Much Ado about Nothing, Hamlet, Winter Dreams, Palpitations, Rumor of Glory, Killers, Not Partners, Rumor of Glory, Great Shakes, The Bacchae, Holy Ghosts, Of Mice and Men, Authenticating Whelmley*, Bdwy in *Our Town* (1988).

PRINCE, FAITH. Born Aug. 5, 1957 in Augusta, GA. Graduate UCinn. Debut 1981 OB in *Scrambled Feet*, followed by *Olympus on My Mind, Groucho, Living Color, Bad Habits, Falsettoland*, Bdwy in *Jerome Robbins' Broadway* (1989), *Nick & Nora, Guys and Dolls* (1992), *Fiorello(Encores), What's Wrong with This Picture, DuBarry Was a Lady (Encores)*.

PROVENZA, PAUL. Born July 31, 1957 in NYC. Graduate UPenn., RADA. Debut OB 1988 in *Only Kidding*, for which he received a Theatre World Award, followed by *Aryan Birth, Picasso at the Lapin Agile*.

PUDENZ, STEVE. Born Sept.25, 1947 in Carroll, IA. Graduate IIa. Debut 1980 OB in *Dona Rosita* followed by *Dick Deterred, Lifelines*, Bdwy in *Hello Dolly* (1995).

QUINN, MICHAEL Born Aug.23, 1963 in The Bronx, NYC. Graduate FredoniaStU. Bdwy debut in *Hello Dolly* (1995).

QUINN, PATRICK. Born Feb. 12, 1950 in Philadelphia, PA. Graduate TempleU. Bdwy debut in *Fiddler on the Roof* (1976) followed by *Day in Hollywood/Night in the Ukraine, Oh, Coward!, Lend Me a Tenor, Damn Yankees, Beauty and the Beast*, OB in *It's Better with a Bank, By Strouse, Forbidden Broadway, Best of Forbidden Broadway, Raft of Medusa, Forbidden Broadway's 10th Anniversary, A Helluva Town, After the Ball*.

QUINN, TARYN. Born July 29, 1959 in Hamilton, OH. Attended WittenbergU., Actors Studio. Debut 1979 OB in *Pudding Lake, Holy Junkie, Savage in Limbo, Danger of Strangers, Place Where Love Is, Half and Half, Fish in a Chimney, Environmental, Down Dark Deceptive Streets*.

QUINTERO, JOE. Born Aug. 27, 1969 in Paterson, NJ. Graduate RutgersU. Debut 1993 OB in *Boiler Room* followed by *Washington Square Moves, Park in Our House, Inkarri's Return, In the Land of Giants*.

RACLEFF, OWEN. Born July 16, 1934 in NYC. Graduate ColumbiaU. LondonU. Bdwy debut in *Piaf* (1977) OB in *The Lesson* (1978), *Catsplay, Arms and the Man, Escoffier: King of Chiefs, New Way to Pay Old Debts, Samson Agonistes, Enter Laughing, Jew of Malta, Sunday Promenade, Impropriety*.

RAEBECK, LOIS. Born in W. Chicago, IL. Graduate PurdueU. Debut 1986 OB in *Rule of Three* followed by *Cork, Between Time and Timbuitu, Women in the Family, All's Well That Ends Well, Necktie Breakfast, Hour of the Dog, Single and Proud*.

RAGSDALE, WILLIAM. Born Jan.19, 1961 in El Dorado, AK. Graduate Hendrix Col. Bdwy debut in *Biloxi Blues* (1985) followed by *Getting Away with Murder*, OB in *Blind Spot, Step Lively and Watch the Closing Doors, Briarpatch*.

RAITER, FRANK. Born Jan. 17, 1932 in Cloquet, MN. Yale graduate. Bdwy debut in *Cranks* (1958) followed by *Dark at the Top of the Stairs, J.B., Camelot, Salome, Sacrilege*, OB in *Soft Core Pornographer, Winter's Tale, Twelfth Night, Tower of Evil, Endangered Species, Bright Room Called Day, Learned Ladies, 'Tis Pity She's A Whore, Othello, Comedy of Errors, Orestes, Marathon Dancing, Sudden Devotion*.

RAMBARAN, DOMINIC. Born in Baltimore, MD. Graduate NorthwesternU, Attended Carnegie Mellon. Bdwy debut in *Showboat* (1995).

RANDALL, TONY. Born Feb. 26, 1920 in Tulsa, OK. Attended Northwestern, Columbia, Neighborhood Playhouse. Bdwy debut in *Antony and Cleopatra* (1947) followed by *To Tell You the Truth, Caesar and Cleopatra, Oh Men! Oh Women!, Inherit the Wind, Oh! Captain!, UTBU, M. Butterfly, A Little Hotel on the Side, 3 Men on a Horse, Government Inspector, School for Scandal*.

RANDELL, PATRICIA. Born Mar.18 in Worcester, MA. Graduate BostonU. Debut 1995 OB in *Durang Durang* followed by *Waiter Waiter, The Shattering*.

RANDELL, RON. Born Oct. 8, 1920 in Sydney, Aus. Attended St. Mary's Col. Bdwy debut in *Browning Version* (1949)followed by *Harlequinade, Candide, World of Suzie Wong, Sherlock Holmes, Mrs. Warren's Profession, Measure for Measure, Bent, Brigadoon* (CC), *School for Scandal*, OB in *Holy Places, Aper You've Gone, Patrick Pearse Motel, Maneuvers, Swan Song, Man for All Seasons, Rosencrantz and Guildenstern Are Dead, M. Amilcar*.

RANDLE, ROBERT. Born Nov.24 in El Paso, TX. Graduate ArizonaSt. Debut 1988 OB in *HMS Pinafore* followed by *Student Prince, Forever Plaid, Pirates of Penzance, Lady in the Dark*, Bdwy in *Hello Dolly* (1995).

RAPP, ANTHONY. Born Oct.26, 1971 in Joliet, IL. Bdwy debut in *Little Prince and the Avaitor* (1981) followed by *Precious Sons, Six Degrees of Separation* (also OB), *Rent* (also OB), OB in *Youth Is Wasted, Destiny of Me, Family Animal, Reproducing Georgia, Prosthetics and the Twenty-Five Thousand Dollar Pyramid, Making of Edward III, Sophistry, Trafficking in Broken Hearts, Raised in Captivity*.

RASCHE, DAVID. Born Aug. 7, 1944 in St. Louis, MO. Graduate Elmhurst Col, U. Chicago. Debut 1976 OB in *John*, followed by *Snow White, Isadora Duncan Sleeps with the Russian Navy, End of the War, A Sermon, Routed, Geniuses, Dolphin Position, To Gillian on Her 37th Birthday, Custom of the Country, Country Girl, Marathon '91, No One Will Be Immune*, Bdwy in *Shadow Box* (1977), *Loose Ends, Lunch Hour, Speed-the-Plow, Mastergate, Christmas Carol*.

RAYNER, MARTIN. Born Aug.1, 1949 in Ryde, Eng. Attended London Drama Studio. Debut 1995 OB in *Travels with My Aunt* followed by *Cardenio*.

REBHORN, JAMES. Born Sept. 1, 1948 in Philadelphia, PA. Graduate WittenbergU. ColumbiaU. Debut 1972 OB in *Blue Boys* followed by *Are You Now.., Trouble with Europe, Othello, Hunchback of Notre Dame, Period of Adjustment, The Freak, Half a Lifetime, Touch Black, To Gillian on Her 37th Birthday, Rain, Hasty Heart Husbandry, Isn't It Romantic?, Blind Date, Cold Sweat, Spoils of War. Marathon 88, Ice Cream with Her Fudge, Life during Wartime, Innocents Crusade, On the Bum, Oblivion Postponed*, Bdwy in *I'm Not Rappaport, Our Town* (1989) .

REDDY, HELEN. Born Oct.25, 1941 in Melbourne, Australia. Bdwy debut in *Blood Brothers* (1995).

REED, BOBBY. Born Sept. 26, 1956 in NYC. Attended AMDA. Debut 1975 OB in *Boy Meets Boy*, followed by *Hunchback of Notre Dame, Der Ring Got Farblon Jet, Big Hotel, Christmas Carol, At Home with the TV, White Cotton Sheets, How to Write a Play, Polly's Panic Attack*.

REED, RONDI. Born Oct. 26, 1952 in Dixon, IL. Graduate IlStU. Bdwy debut in *Grapes of Wrath* (1990) followed by *Rise and Fall of Little Voice*, OB in *Picasso at the Lapin Agile*.

REINER, ALYSIA. Born July 21, 1970 in Gainesville, FL. Graduate Vassar. Debut 1993 OB in *Bye Bye Blackbird* followed by *Single and Proud*.

REINKING, ANN. Born Nov.10, 1949 in Seattle WA. Attended Joffrey Sch, HB Studio. Bdwy debut in *Cabaret* (1969) followed by *Coco, Pippin, Over Here* for which she received a Theatre World Award, *Goodtime Charley, Chorus Line, Chicago* (1975/1996), *Dancin', Sweet Charity* (1986), OB in *One More Song One More Dance, Music Moves Me*.

RETHKE, LAURELLE. Born Aug.26, 1969 in Omaha, NE.Attended Perf Artists Musical Th Consv/Dallas. Debut 1993 in *String Theory* followed by *Henry and June, Topper, Loves' labour's Lost, One Step, What Everyone Knows But Me*.

REVASCH, ABIGAIL. Born Oct.20, 1968 in NYC. Graduate NorthwesternU. Debut 1996 in *Grey Zone*.

RHOADS, KURT. Born Oct. 17, 1957 in Columbus, GA. Graduate EastIllU, UChicago, Goodman School. Debut 1992 OB in *Othello* followed by *Good Natur'd-Man, Them That's Got, Case of Kaspar Mayer*.

RICHARDS, PENELOPE. Born Jan.16, 1948 in Columbus, OH. Debut 1973 OB in *Smith* followed by *Voices Insistent Voices*.

RICHARDSON, LEE. Born Sept.11, 1926 in Chicago, IL. Graduate Goodman Th. Debut 1952 OB in *Summer and Smoke* followed by *St. Joan, Volpone, American Dream, Bartleby, Plays for Bleecker Street, Merchant of Venice, King Lear, Thieves Carnival, Waltz of the Toreadors, Talented Tenth, Ivanov,* Bdwy in *Legend of Lizzie* (1959), *Lord Pengo, House of Atreus, Find Your Way Home, Othello, Jockey Club Stakes, Devil's Disciple, Getting Married.*

RICKABY, BRETT. Born Dec.15, 1964 in Minneapolis, MN. Graduate UMn/Duluth, NYU. Debut 1990 OB in *Richard III* followed by *Two Gentlemen of Verona, The Workroom, Dream of Wealth, Richard III, Dracula, All's Well That Ends Well, Carnal Knowledge,* Bdwy in *Glass Menagerie*(1994).

RIDEOUT, LEENYA. Born Mar.22, 1969 in Missoula, MT. Graduate Uof Colorado. Debut 1996 OB in *Cowgirls.*

RIGBY, TERENCE. Born Jan.2, 1937 in Birmingham, Eng. Graduate RADA. Bdwy debut in *The Homecoming* (1967) followed by *No Man's Land, Hamlet,* OB in *Richard III.*

RILEY, ERIC. Born March 22, 1955 in Albion, MI. Graduate UMich. Bdwy debut in *Ain't Misbehavin'*(1979) followed by *Dreamgirls, Ain't Misbehavin'* (1988), *Once on This Island*(also OB),*Christmas Carol,* OB in *Weird Romance.*

RIPLEY, ALICE. Born December 14, 1963 in San Leandro, CA. Graduate Kent State U. Bdwy debut in *Tommy* (1993) followed by *Sunset Blvd.*

RITCHIE, MARGARET. Born May 31 in Madison, WI. Graduate UWi, NYU. Debut 1981 OB in *Last Summer at Bluefish Cove,* followed by *Who's There?, All Souls Day, Days and Nights of an Ice Cream Princess, Two by Horton Foote, Delicate Dangers, Rose and Crown.*

RITZ, MELISSA. Born July 28 in Bristol, TN. Graduate UGeorgia, UTenn. OB in *Bubbling, Triumph of the West, One Act Festival, Gentle Lion, Dream St.*

ROBARDS, JASON. Born July 26, 1922 in Chicago, IL. Attended AADA. Bdwy debut 1947 with *D'Oyly Carte Co.,* followed by *Stalag 17, The Chase, Long Day's Journey into Night* for which he received a Theatre World Award, *The Disenchanted, Toys in the Attic, Big Fish Little Fish, A Thousand Clowns, Hughie, The Devils, We Bombed in New Haven, Country Girl, Moon for the Misbegotten, Touch of the Poet, You Can't Take It With You, Iceman Cometh, Month of Sundays, Ah Wilderness!, Long Day's Journey into Night* (1988), *Christmas Carol, Park Your Car in Harvard Yard,* OB in *American Gothic*(1953), *Iceman Cometh, After the Fall, But for Whom Charlie, Long Day's Journey into Night, Moonlight, Molly Sweeney.*

ROBBINS, REX. Born in Pierre, SD. Bdwy debut in *One Flew over the Cuckoo's Nest* (1964) followed by *Scrarch, Changing Room, Gypsy*(1974), *Comedians, An Almost Perfect Person, Richard III, You Can't Take It with You, Play Memory, Six Degrees of Separation, Sisters Rosensweig,* OB in *Servant of Two Masters, The Alchemist, Arms and the Man, Boys in the Band, Memory of Two Mondays, They Knew What They Wanted, Secret Service, Boy Meets Girl, Three Sisters, The Play's The Thing, Julius Caesar, Henry IV Part 1, Dining Room, Urban Blight, Deja Revue, Ballad of Little Jo.*

ROBERTS, DARCIE. Born Dec.12, 1973 in Pomona, CA. Bdwy in *Crazy for You* (1993).

ROBERTS, LANCE. Born Dec.18 in NYC. Attended TuftsU. Debut 1981 in *March of the Falsettos* followed by *Me Nobody Knows, Forbidden Hollywood,* Bdwy in *The First* (1981).

ROBERTS, TONY. Born October 22, 1939 in NYC. Graduate NorthwesternU. Bdwy debut in *Something about a Soldier* (1962) followed by *Take Her She's Mine, Last Analysis, Never Too Late, Barefoot in the Park, Don't Drink the Water, How Now Dow Jones, Play It Again Sam, Promises Promises, Sugar, Absurd Person Singular, Murder at the Howard Johnson's, They're Playing Our Song, Doubles, Brigadoon* (LC), *South Pacific* (LC), *Love Letters, Jerome Robbins' Broadway, Sisters Rosensweig, Sea Gull, Victor Victoria,* OB in *Cradle Will Rock, Losing Time, Good Parts, Time Framed, Normal Heart, 4 Dogs and a Bone.*

ROBINS, LAILA. Born March 14, 1959 in St. Paul, MN. Graduate UWi., Yale. Bdwy debut in *The Real Thing* (1984) OB in *Bloody Poetry, Film Society, For Dear Life, Maids of Honor, Extra Man, Merchant of Venice, Mrs. Klein.*

ROBINSON, HAL. Born in Bedford, IN. Graduate InU. Debut 1972 OB in *Memphis Store Bought Teeth* followed by *From Berlin to Broadway, Fantasticks, Promenade, Baker's Wife, Yours Anne, Personals, And a Nightingale Sang, Old Wicked Songs,* Bdwy in *On Your Toes* (1983), *Broadway, Grand Hotel, Nick & Nora.*

ROBINSON, ROGER. Born May 2, 1941 in Seattle, WA. Attended USC. Bdwy debut in *Does a Tiger Wear a Necktie?* (1969) followed by *Amen Comer, Iceman Cometh, Seven Guitars,* OB in *Walk in Darkness, Jericho-Jim Crow, Who's Got His Own, Trials of Brother Jero, The Miser, Interrogation of Havana, Lady Day, Do Lord Remember Me, Of Mice and Men, Middle of Nowhere, Measure for Measure, The Tempest.*

RODGERS, ELISABETH S. Born Jan.8, 1964 in Houston, TX. Graduate PrincetonU. OB 1989 in *Loving Dutch* followed by *Guilty Innocence, White Water, Richard Foreman Trilogy, Gender Wars.*

RODRIGUEZ, AL D. Born Mar.5, 1963 in NYC. Graduate LIU. Debut 1981 OB in *Who Collects the Pain?* followed by *Charge It Please, Born to Rumba, English Only Restaurant, Caucasian Chalk Circle, Young Playwrights Festival.*

RODRIGUEZ, ENRICO. Born July 18, 1980 in Warren, MI. Bdwy debut in *Big* (1996).

ROGERS, DIANA. Born Feb.5, 1952 in Cincinnati, OH. Bdwy debut in *Les Miserables* (1994).

ROGERSON, DAVID A. (previously Gus). Born Nov.14, 1961 in Boston, MA. Graduate Dartmouth Col. Debut 1990 OB in *Show Must Go On* followed by *Big Al, Grey Zone, Henry V,* Bdwy in *Six Degrees of Separation*(1990-also OB), *Face Value.*

ROLAND, RICHARD. Born Aug.28, 1968 in NYC. Graduate DensionU. Debut 1992 OB in *Forever Plaid* followed by *Fantasticks, Zombie Prom, Cocoanuts.*

ROSAGER, LARS. Born Mar.21, 1956 in San Francisco, CA. Attended UofCal/Santa Cruz. Bdwy debut in *42nd St.*(1980) followed by *Cabaret,* OB in *American Ballroom Theater*

ROSE, CANDICE. Born Jan.24, 1974 in Los Angeles, CA. Attended BostonU, Trinity Rep Consv. Debut 1996 OB in *Gender Wars.*

ROSS, TYLEY. Born Nov.11, 1970 in Windsor, Ontario, Can. Graduate Canterbury. Bdwy debut 1996 in *Miss Saigon*(1996).

ROTHMAN, JOHN. Born June 3, 1949 in Baltimore, MD. Graduate WesleyanU, Yale. Debut 1978 OB in *Rats Nest* followed by *Impossible H.L. Mencken, Buddy System, Rosario and the Gypsies, Italian Straw Hat, Modern Ladies of Guanabacoa, Faith Hope Charity, Some Americans Abroad, EST Marathon '92, Death Defying Acts,* Bdwy in *End of the World...* (1984), *Some Americans Abroad.*

ROTHSTEIN, JON. Born July 15, 1970 in Philadelphia, PA. Bdwy debut in *Ghetto* (1989), OB in *Golden Boy, Treasure Island, Scenes from an Execution.*

ROWAN, RICHARD. Born June 7, 1965 in NYC. Graduate NorthwesternU. Debut 1992 OB in *News in Revue* followed by *Doctor in Spite of Himself.*

ROZNOWSKI, ROBERT. Born July 16, 1963 in Baltimore, MD. Graduate Point Park Col., OhioStU. Debut 1992 OB in *Lightin' Out* followed by *Young Abe Lincoln, Identical Twins from Baltimore.*

RUBINSTEIN, JOHN. Born Dec. 8, 1946 in Los Angeles. Attended UCLA. Bdwy debut in *Pippin* (1972) for which he received a Theatre World Award, followed by *Children of a Lesser God, Fools, Soldier's Tale, Caine Mutiny Court Martial, Hurlyburly, M. Butterfly, Getting Away with Murder,* OB in *Rosencrantz and Guildenstern Are Dead, Urban Blight, Love Letters, Princess Ida.*

RUBIN-VEGA, DAPHNE. Born Nov.18, 1968 in Panama. Bdwy debut in *Rent* (1996 also OB) for which she received a Theatre World Award.

RUNOLFSSON, ANNE. Born in Long Beach, CA. Attended UCLA. Bdwy debut in *Les Miserables* (1989) followed by *Aspects of Love, Cyrano, Victor Victoria.*

RUSH, SUSAN. Born Nov.17, 1943 in Mansfield, PA. Graduate MansfieldStCol., UAz. Debut 1970 OB in *The Drunkard* followed by *Splendora,* Bdwy in *Knickerbocker Holiday*(1977), *Guys and Dolls, Gentlemen Prefer Blondes*(1995).

RYAN, STEVEN. Born June 19, 1947 in New York City. Graduate BostonU, U. Minn. Debut 1978 OB in *Winning Isn't Everything,* followed by *The Beethoven, September in the Rain, Romance Language, Love's Labour's Last, Love and Anger, Approximating Mother, Merry Wives of Windsor, Unexpected Tenderness, Minor Demons,* Bdwy in *I'm Not Rappaport* (1986), *Guys and Dolls* (1992), *On the Waterfront.*

RYAN, THOMAS JAY. Born Aug.1, 1962 in Pittsburgh, PA. Graduate Carnegie-Mellon. Debut 1992 OB in *Samuel's Major Problem* followed by *Egypt, My Head was a Sledgehammer, Robert Zucco, Dracula, Venus.*

RYNN, MARGIE. Born in Princeton, NJ. Graduate UCal/Berkeley, ULA. Debut 1988 OB in *Autobahn* followed by *Bed Experiment, Suite Sixteen, Les Miserables, Paradise Is Closing Down.*

SAGE, ALEXANDRIA. Born June 25, 1968 in San Francisco, CA. Graduate Yale U. Debut 1993 OB in *Ceremony of Innocence,* followed by *Fragments, The Co-Op, Jacob's Blanket, Lion in the Streets.*

SAITO, JAMES. Born March 6, 1955 in Los Angeles, CA. Graduate UCLA. Debut 1988 OB in *Rashomon,* followed by *Day Standing on Its Head, Ripples in the Pond, Wilderness, Friends.*

SALAMANDYK, TIM. Born Feb.25, 1967 in Minneapolis, MN.Graduate Illinois WesleyanU. Debut 1996 OB in *Food Chain.*

SALATA, GREGORY. Born July 21, 1949 in NYC. Graduate Queens Col. Bdwy debut in *Dance with Me* (1975) followed by *Equus, Bent,* OB in *Piaf: A Remembrance, Sacraments, Measure for Measure, Subject of Childhood, Jacques and His Master, Androcles and the Lion, Madwoman of Chaillot, Beauty Part.*

SALVATO, LAURA JANE. Born Feb.2 in NY. Graduate PrincetonU. Debut 1993 OB in *Fruits and Nuts* followed by *2000 Miles, Sensivity Training, Pandora, Angel of Mercy.*

SALVATORE, JOHN. Born Nov.13, 1961 in Rockville Center, NY. Attended AdelphiU. Bdwy debut in *Chorus Line* (1986) followed by *Hello Dolly,* OB in *Pageant.*

SANCHEZ, JAIME. Born Dec. 19, 1938 in Rincon, PR. Attended Actors Studio. Bdwy debut in *West Side Story* (1957) followed by *Oh Dad Poor Dad, Midsummer Night's Dream, Richard III,* OB in *The Toilet/Conerico Was Here to Stay* for which he received a Theatre World Award, *Ox Cart, The Tempest, Merry Wives of Windsor, Julius Caesar, Coriolanus, He Who Gets Slapped, State without Grace, Sun Always Shines for the Cool, Othello, Elektra, Domino, The Promise, Rising Sun Falling Star, Academy Street, Written and Sealed, Dog and His Master.*

SANCHEZ, JAIME. Born December 19, 1938 in Rincon, PR. Attended Actors Studio. Bdwy debut 1957 in *West Side Story,* followed by *Oh Dad Poor Dad, A Midsummer Night's Dream, Richard III,* OB in *The Toilet/Conerico Was Here to Stay* for which he received a Theatre World Award, *The Ox Cart, The Tempest, Merry Wives of Windsor, Julius Caesar, Coriolanus, He Who Gets Slapped, State without Grace, The Sun Always Shines for the Cool, Othello, Elektra, Domino, The Promise, Rising Sun Falling Star, Academy Street, Written and Sealed.*

SANDERS, JACKIE. Born July 17, 1967 in Thornston, GA. Graduate BrenauU, AMDA. Debut 1994 OB in *Judy at the Stonewall Inn* followed by *Swingtime Canteen, Cowgirls.*

SANTIAGO, DOUGLAS. Born July 4, 1972 in Rio Piedras, PR. Debut 1995 OB in *Simpson St.*

SANTIAGO, SAUNDRA. Born April 14, 1957 in NYC. Graduate U. Miami, SMU. Bdwy debut in *View from the Bridge* (1983) followed by *Chronicle of a Death Foretold,* OB in *Road to Nirvana, Spike Heels, Hello Again.*

SANTIAGO-HUDSON, RUBEN. Born 1957 in Lackawanna, NY. Attended SUNY/Binghamton, WayneStU. Debut OB in *Soldier's Play* followed by *Measure for Measure, East Texas Hot Links, Ceremonies in dark Old Men,* Bdwy in *Jelly's Last Jam* (1992), *Seven Guitars.*

SAPOFF, ROBERT. Born July 9, 1955 in Newark, NJ Graduate RutgersU. Debut 1996 OB in *Cocoanuts.*

SARNO, JANET. Born Nov. 18, 1933 in Bridgeport, CT. Graduate SCTC, YaleU. Bdwy debut in *Dylan* (1963) followed by *Equus, Knockout, Apple Doesn't Fall,* OB in *Six Characters in Search of an Author, Who's Happy Now, Closing Green, Fisher, Survival of St. Joan, The Orphan, Mama's Little Angels, Knuckle Sandwich, Mar/on Brando Sat Here, Last Summer at Bluef sh Cove, Brass Birds Don't Sing, Money Talke, Fayebird.*

SATTA, STEVEN. Born Dec. 25, 1964 in The Bronx, NYC. Graduate NYU. Debut 1991 OB in *Macbeth,* followed by *Chekhov Very Funny, Family, Affair, The Bundle,* Bdwy in *Little Hotel on the Side* (1992).

SAUNDERS, ALONZO. Born June 18, 1972 in Birmingham, AL. Graduate AMDA. Bdwy debut in *Showboat* (1995).

SCHAFER, SCOTT. Born Aug.26, 1958 in Chicago, IL. Graduate DePaulU. Debut 1980 ob in *Aphrodite: The Witch Play* followed by *Babes in Toyland, Sally, Beauty Thing,* Bdwy in *Raggedy Ann* (1986).

SCHRAMM, DAVID. Born Aug.14, 1946 in Louisville, KY. Attended Western KyU. Juilliard. Debut 1972 OB in *School for Scandal* followed by *Lower Depths, Women Beware Women, Mother Courage, King Lear, Duck Variations, Cradle Will Rock, Twelfth Night, Palace of Amateurs,* Bdwy in *Three Sisters, Next Time I'll Sing to You, Edward II, Measure for Measure, Robber Bridegroom, Bedroom Farce, Goodbye Fidel, The Misanthrope, Tartuffe: Born Again.*

SCHREIBER, LIEV. Born Oct. 4, 1967 in San Francisco, CA. Graduate Hampshire Col., Yale U., RADA. Debut 1992 OB in *Goodnight Desdemona Good Morning Juliet* followed by *Tempest(CP), Moonlight,* Bdwy in *In the Summer House* (1993).

SCHULTZ, ARMAND. Born May 17, 1959 in Rochester, NY. Graduate NiagaraU., Catholic U. Debut OB 1988 in *Coriolanus* followed by *Crystal Clear, Titus Andronicus, Tower of Evil, Richard III, Sight Unseen, King Lear, Where the Truth Lies.*

SCHULTZ, CAROL. Born February 12 in Chicago, IL. Graduate Case Western Reserve U., U. Ill. Debut 1982 OB in *Peer Gynt,* followed by *The Cherry Orchard, King Lear, Ghost Sonata, Doll's House, Antigone,* Bdwy in *Abe Lincoln in Illinois* (1993).

SCOTT, GEORGE C. Born Oct. 18, 1927 in Wise, VA. Attended UMo. Debut 1957 OB in *Richard III* for which he received a Theatre World Award, followed by *As You Like It, Merchant of Venice, Children of Darkness, Desire Under the Elms, Wrong Turn at Lungfish,* Bdwy in *Comes a Day, Andersonville Trial, The Wall, General Seegar, Little Foxes, Plaza Suite, All God's Children Got Wings, Uncle Vanya, Death of a Salesman, Sly Fox, Tricks of the Trade, Present Laughter, Boys in Autumn, On Borrowed Time, Inherit the Wind.*

SCOTT, JOHN. Born July 20, 1967 in Lafayette, IN. Graduate NC School of Arts, AMDA. Debut 1989 OB in *Babes in Toyland,* Bdwy in *110 in the Shade* (NYCO/LC), *My Fair Lady* (1993), *State Fair.*

SCOTT, KEVIN. Born Dec.10, 1928 in Oakland, CA. Bdwy debut in *Wish You Were Here* (1952) followed by *Carnival in Flanders, Almost Crazy,* OB in *Ralph Roister Doister, Senseless.*

SCOTT, SERET. Born Sept.1, 1949 in Washington, DC. Attended NYU. Debut 1969 OB in *Slave Ship* followed by *Ceremonies in Dark Old Men, Black terror, Dream, One Last Look, My Sister My Sister, Weep Not for Me, Meetings, The Brothers, Eyes of the American, Remembrances/Mojo, Tapman, Burning Beach, Human Nature, Alexander Plays,* Bdwy in *For Colored Girls...*

SEAMON, EDWARD. Born Apr. 15, 1937 in San Diego, CA. Attended San Diego St Col. Debut 1971 OB in *Life and Times of J. Walter Smintheus* followed by *The Contractor, The Family, Fishing, Feedlot, Cabin 12, Rear Column, Devour the Snow, Buried Child, Friends, Extenuating Circumstances, Confluence, Richard II, Great Grandson of Jedediah Kohler, Marvelous Gray, Time Framed, Master Builder, Fall Hookup, Fool for Love, The Harvesting, Country for Old Men, Love's Labour's Lost, Caligula, Mound Builders, Quiet in the Land, Talley & Son, Tomorrow's Monday, Ghosts, Or Mice and Men, Beside Herself, You Can't Think of Everything, Tales of the Last Formicans, Love Diatribe, Empty Hearts, Sandbox, Winter's Tale,* Bdwy in *The Trip Back Down* (1977), *Devour the Snow, American Clock.*

SELDES, MARIAN. Born Aug. 23, 1928 in NYC. Attended Neighborhood Playhouse. Bdwy debut in *Media* (1947) followed by *Crime and Punishment, That Lady, Town Beyond Tragedy, Ondine, On High Ground, Come of Age, Chalk Garden, Milk Train Doesn't Stop Here Anymore, The Wall, Gift of Time, Delicate Balance, Before You Go, Father's Day, Equus, The Merchant, Deathtrap,* OB in *Different, Ginger Man, Mercy Street, Isadora Duncan Sleeps with the Russion Navy, Painting Churches, Gertrude Stein and Companion, Richard II, The Milk Train Doesn't Stop..., Bright Room Called Day, Another Time, Three Tall Women.*

SETLOCK, MARK. Born June 26, 1968 in Cleveland, OH. Graduate KentStU., AmRepTh/Harvard. Debut 1995 OB in *Don Juan in Chicago,* Bdwy in *Rent* (1996).

SETRAKIAN, MARY. Born in San Francisco, CA. Graduate StanfordU., New England Consv. Debut 1990 OB in *Hannah, 1939,* followed by *Colette Collage, New York Romance,* Bdwy in *Hello Dolly* (1995).

SEVERS, WILLIAM. Born Jan. 8, 1932 in Britton, OK. Attended Pasadena Playhouse, Columbia Col. Bdwy debut in *Cut of the Axe* (1960) followed by *On Borrowed Time* (1991), OB in *Moon Is Blue, Lulu, Big Maggie, Mixed Doubles, The Rivals, Beaver Coat, Twister, Midnight Mass, Gas Station, Firebugs, Fellow Travelers, Iowa Boys, Carpool.*

SHANNON, MARK. Born Dec. 13, 1948 in Indianapolis, In. Attended UCin. Debut 1969 OB in *Fortune and Men's Eyes,* followed by *Brotherhood, Nothing to Report, When You Comin' Back Red Ryder?, Serenading Louie, Three Sisters, K2, Spare Parts, Lips Together Teeth Apart, Tales from Hollywood, Lonely Planet.*

SHARIF. Born Apr.26, 1982 in Queens, NYC. Debut 1989 OB in *Black Spectrum Theatre* followed by *Man Women Dinosaur, Good Times are Killing Me, Young Playwrights Festival.*

SHEA, JERE. Born June 14, 1965 in Boston, MA. Graduate Boston College, NYU. Debut 1992 OB in *As You Like It* followed by *Overtime, I Married an Angel,* Bdwy in *Guys and Dolls* (1992), *Passion,* for which he received a 1994 Theatre World Award.

SHEARA, NICOLA. Born May 23 in NYC. Graduate USyracuse. Debut 1975 OB in *Another Language,* followed by *Sananda Sez, All the Way Home, Inadmissible Evidenc e, Another Part of the Forest, Working One Ac ts, Undying Love, Price of Madness,* Bdwy in *Grapes of Wrath* (1990).

SHELLEY, CAROLE. Born Aug. 16,1939 in London, Eng. Bdwy debut in *Odd Couple* (1965) followed by *Astrakhan Coat, Loot, Noel Coward's Sweet Potato, Hay Fever, Absurd Person Singular, Norman Conquests, Elephant Man, The Misanthrope, Noises Off, Stepping Out, The Miser, Show Boat,* OB in *Little Murder, Devil's Disciple, Play's the Thing, Double Feature, Twelve Dreams, Pygmalion, Christmas Carol, Jubilee in Concert, Waltz of the Toreadors, What the Butler Saw, Maggie and Isha, Later Life, Destiny of Me, Lady in the Dark in Concert, Cabaret Verboten, Richard II, London Suite.*

SHENKEL, LES. Born May 20, 1944 in Brooklyn, NYC Attended Rider Col., AADA. Debut 1969 ob in *Fantasticks* followed by *Time of Harry Harass, Coiled Spring, Moon and Mongols, The Occupation.*

SHERIDAN, CLARENCE M. Born Mar.19, 1958 in Fond du Lac, WI. Graduate UAz. Bdwy debut in *Hello Dolly* (1995).

SHERMAN, JON. Born July 16, 1972 in NYC. Graduate Middlebury Col. Debut 1996 OB in *Scenes from an Execution.*

SHEW, TIMOTHY. Born Feb.7, 1959 in Grand Forks, ND. Graduate MillikinU., UMich. Debut 1987 OB in *The Knife,* Bdwy in *Les Miserables, Guys and Dolls, Sunset Blvd.*

SHINICK, KEVIN. Born Mar.19, 1969 in Rockville Center, NY. Bdwy debut in *Sea Gull* (1992) followed by *St. Joan, Timon of Athens, Gov't Inspector, School for Scandal.*

SHIPLEY, SANDRA. Born Feb.1 in Rainham, Kent, Eng. Attended New Col. of Speech and Drama, LondonU. Debut 1988 OB in *Six Characters in Search of an Author* followed by *Big Time, Kindertransport, Venus,* Bdwy in *Indiscretions* (1995).

SHULL, RICHARD B. Born Feb. 24, 1929 in Evanston, Il. Graduate StUIowa. Debut 1953 OB in *Coriolanus,* followed by *Purple Dust, Journey to the Day, American Hamburger League, Frimbo, Fade the Game, Desire under the Elms, Marriage of Betty and Boo, Front Page* (LC), *One of the All-Time Greats, Sausage Eaters,* Bdwy in *Black-eyed Susan* (1954), *Wake Up Darling, Red Roses for Me, I Knock at the Door, Pictures in the Hallway, Have I Got a Girl for You, Minnie's Boys, Goodtime Charley, Fools, Oh, Brother!, Ain't Broadway Grand, Victor Victoria.*

SIMMONS, J.K. (formerly Jonathan). Born Jan 9, 1955 in Detroit, MI. Graduate UMinn. Debut 1987 OB in *Birds of Paradise,* followed by *Dirty Dick, Das Barbecu, Joseph and Mary,* Bdwy in *Change in the Heir* (1990), *A Few Good Men, Peter Pan* (1990/1991), *Guys and Dolls, Laughter on the 23rd Floor.*

SIMS, BARBARA CAREN. Born June 17 in Ft. Worth, TX. Graduate UHouston. Debut OB in *Trip to Bountiful* followed by *Night Seasons, Laura Dennis, Hope Zone.*

SISTO, ROCCO. Born February 8, 1953 in Bari, Italy. Graduate UIl., NYU. Debut 1982 OB in *Hamlet,* followed by *Country Doctor, Times and Appetites of Toulouse-Lautrec, Merchant of Venice, What Did He See, Winter's Tale, The Tempest, Dream of a Common Language, Tis Pity She's a Whore, Mad Forest, Careless Love, All's Well That Ends Well, The Illusion, Merry Wives of Windsor, Quills, Overtime,* Bdwy in *Month in the Country* (1995).

SITLER, DAVID. Born April 7, 1957 in Harrisburg, PA. Graduate Franklin-Marshall Col., Catholic U. Debut 1991 OB in *Necktie Breakfast,* followed by *Blues for Mr. Charlie,The Hollow,* Bdwy in *An Inspector Calls* (1994).

SKINNER, EMILY. Born June 29, 1970 in Richmond, VA. Graduate Carnegie-MellonU. Bdwy debut 1994 in *Christmas Carol,* OB in *Watbanaland.*

SKOWRON, JEFF. Born July 7, 1973 in Johnstown, PA. Graduate PennSt. Debut 1995 OB in *The Occupation* followed by *Crackerbox Kids, Zombie Prom.*

SLEZAK, VICTOR. Born July 7, 1957 in Youngstown, OH. Debut 1979 OB in *Electra Myth* followed by *Hasty Heart, Ghosts, Alice and Fred, Window Claire, Miracle Worker, Talk Radio, Marathon '88, One Act Festival, Briar Patch, Appointment with a High Wire Lady, Sam I Am, White Rose, Born Guilty, Naked Truth, Ivanov,* Bdwy in *Any Given Day* (1993), *Garden District.*

SLOMAN, JOHN. Born June 23, 1954 in Rochester, NY. Graduate SUNY/Genasco. Debut 1977 OB in *Unsung Cole,* followed by *Apple Tree, Romance in Hard Times, The Waves, An Elephant Never Forgets, Hit the Lights!, Mayor,* Bdwy in *Whoopee!* (1979), *1940's Radio Hour, Day in Hollywood/A Night in the Ukraine, Big.*

SLUTSKER, PETER. Born Apr.17, 1958 in NYC. Graduate UMi. Bdwy debut in *On Your Goes* (1983) followed by *No Way to Treat a Lady, Coconuts.*

SMITH, DEREK. Born Dec. 4, 1959 in Seattle, WA. Juilliard Graduate. Debut 1985 OB in *Cruise Control,* followed by *Ten by Tennessee, Traps,*

Hyde in *Hollywood,Sylvia, Dark Rapture, Green Bird,* Bdwy in *Timon of Athens* (1993), *Government Inspector.*

SMITH, LOIS. Born Nov. 3, 1930 in Topeka, KS. Attended UWV. Bdwy debut in *Time Out for Ginger* (1952) followed by *Young and the Beautiful,Wisteria Trees, Glass Menagerie, Orpheus Descending, Stages, Grapes of Wrath, Buried Child,* OB in *Midsummer Night's Dream, Non Pasquale, Promenade, LaBoheme, Bodies Rest and Motion, Gus and Al, Measure for Measure, Spring Thing, Beside Herself, Sam I Am, Dog Logic, Paradise.*

SMITH-CAMERON, J. Born September 7 in Louisville, KY. Attended Florida State U. Bdwy debut in *Crimes of the Heart* (1982) followed by *Wild Honey, Lend Me a Tenor, Our Country's Good, Real Inspector Hound, 15 Minute Hamlet,* OB in *Asian Shade, The Knack, Second Prize: Two Weeks in Leningrad,Great Divide, Voice of the Turtle, Women of Manhattan, Alice and Fred, Mi Vida Loca, Little Egypt, On the Bum, Traps/Owners,Desdemona, NakedTruth, Don JuaninChicago,BlueWindow.*

SNOW, NORMAN. Born Mar.29, 1950 in Little Rock, AR. Graduate Juilliard. Debut 1972 OB in *School for Scandal* followed by *Lower Depths, Hostage, Timon of Athens, Cymbeline, U.S.A., Women Beware Women, One Crack Out, Winter's Tale, The Wedding, Johnny on a Spot, She Stoops to Conquer, Fantod, Midsummer Night's Dream,* Bdwy in *Three Sisters* (1973), *Measure for Measure, Beggar's Opera, Next Time I'll Sing to You, Macbeth, Scenes and Revelations, School for Scandal.*

SOLARI, MATTHEW. Born Mar.28, 1968 in Atlantic City, NJ. Graduate NYU. Debut 1995 OB in *Triumph of the West.*

SOMMER, JOSEF. Born June 26, 1934 in Griefswald, Ger. Graduate CamegieTechU. Bdwy debut in *Othello* (1970) followed by *Children Children, Trial of the Catonsville 9, Full Circle, Who's Who in Hell, Shadow Box, Whose Life Is It Anyway?, Racing Demon,* OB in *Enemies, Merchant of Venice, The Dog Ran Away, Drinks before Dinner, Lydie Breeze, Black Angel, Lady and the Clarinet, Love Letters on Blue Paper, Largo Desolato, Hamlet, Later Life, Hapgood.*

SOPHIEA, CYNTHIA. Born Oct.26, 1954 in Flint, MI. Bdwy debut in *My Fair Lady* (1981) followed by *She Loves Me, Victor Victoria,* OB in *Lysistrata, Sufragette, Golden Apple, Winter's Tale, Petrified Prince.*

SOREL, THEODORE/TED. Born Nov.14, 1936 in San Francisco, CA. Graduate Col. of the Pacific. Bdwy debut in *Sly Fox* (1977) followed by *Horowitz and Mrs. Washington, Little Family Business, School for Scandal,* OB in *Arms and the Man, Moon Mysteries, Call from the East, Hedda Gabler, Drinks before Dinner, Tamara, The Matchmaker.*

SPAISMAN, ZYPORA. Born Jan. 2, 1920 in Lublin, Poland. Debut 1955 OB in *Lonesome Ship,* followed by *My Father's Court, Thousand and One Nights, Eleventh Inheritor, Enchanting Melody, Fifth Commandment, Bronx Express, Melody Lingers On, Yoshke Musikant, Stempenya, Generation of Green Fields, Ship, Play for the Devil, Broome Street America, Flowering Peach, Riverside Drive, Big Winner, Land of Dreams, Father's Inheritance, At the Crossroads, Stempenyu, Mirele Efros, Double Identity.*

SPECHT, PATTI. Born Aug.13, 1954 in San Diego, CA. Graduate OhioStU. Debut 1979 OB in *Svengali* followed by *Pearl of Great Price, Two* by Horton Foote, *Riders to the Sea.*

SPELLMAN, KERRIANNE. Born Jan.7, 1966 in NJ. Graduate AMDA. Bdwy debut in *Les Miserables* (1993), OB in *Cover of Life* (1994)

SPIEGEL, BARBARA. Born Mar. 12 in NYC. Debut 1969 in LCRep's *Camino Real, Operation Sidewinder* and *Beggar on Horseback,* OB in *Disintegration of James Cherry, Feast for Fleas, Museum, Powder, The Bleachers, Nightshift, Cassatt, Rope Dancers, Friends Too Numerous to Mention, Bronx Dreams, Green Fields, Festival of I-Acts, What's Wrong with This Picture?, Jewish Wife, Where Do We Go from Here?, Those Summer Nights, Circus, SWAK, World without Men, The Bleachers, Miami Stories, Beau Jest, Food Chain.*

SPINELLA, STEPHEN. Born Oct. 11, 1956 in Naples, Italy. Graduate NYU. Debut 1982 OB in *Age of Assassins* followed by *Dance for Me Rosetta, Bremen Coffee, Taming of the Shrew, L'Illusion, Burrhead, Love!Valour!Compassion!, Troilus and Cressida,* Bdwy in *Angles in America* (1993) for which he received a Theatre World Award.

SPORE, RICHARD. Born March 23, 1948 in Chicago, IL. Debut 1982 OB in *Frances Farmer Story* followed by *Counselor-at-Law, Troilus and Cressida, Motions of History, Henry IV, Comedy of Errors, Woyzeck, Under the Kerosene Moon, Polly's Panic Attack.*

SPYBEY, DINA. Born Aug.29, 1965 in Columbus, OH. Graduate OhStateU,Rutgers. Debut 1993 OB in *Five Women Wearing the Same Dress* for which she received a Theatre World Award, followed by *Girl Gone, Dates and Nuts, Don Juan in Chicago, The Shawl.*

STADLEN, LEWIS J. Born March 7,1947 in Brooklyn, NY. Attended Stella Adler Studio. Bdwy debut in *Minnie's Boys* (1970) for which he received a Theatre World Award, followed by *Sunshine Boys, Candide, Odd*

Couple, Laughter on the 23rd Floor, A Funny Thing...(1996), OB in *Happiness Cage, Heaven on Earth, Barb-A-Que, Don Juan and Non Don Juan, Olympus on My Mind, l-2-3-4-5, S. J. Perelman in Person, The My House Play.*

STANEK, JIM. Born Aug.5, 1971 in Havre de Grace, MD. Graduate Carnegie MellonU. Bdwy debut in *Indiscretions* (1995) followed by *A Funny Thing...*(1996).

STANLEY, FLORENCE. Born July 1 in Chicago. Graduate NorthwesternU. Debut 1960 OB in *Machinal* followed by *It's Only a Play, Mexican Hayride,* Bdwy in *Glass Menagerie*(1965), *Fiddler on the Roof, Safe Place, Prisoner of Second Ave., Secret Affairs of Mildred Wild, What's Wrong with This Picture?*(also OB), *Apple Doesn't Fall.*

STANTON, ROBERT. Born March 8, 1963 in San Antonio, TX. Graduate George Mason U., NYU. Debut 1985 OB in *Measure for Measure,* followed by *Rum and Coke, Cheapside, Highest Standard of Living, One Act Festival, Best Half-Foot Forward, Sure Thing, Emily, Ubu, Casanova, Owners/Traps, Visits from Mr. Whitcomb, All in the Timing, Cheever Evening, Overtime,* Bdwy in *Small Family Business* (1992).

ST.CLAIR, BART. Born Mar.11, 1971 in Baltimore, MD. Graduate Harvard. Debut 1995 OB in *By Jupiter* followed by *Topper.*

STEIN-GRAINGER, STEVEN. Born Oct.17, 1958 in Chicago, IL. Graduate N.IllU, AmConsvMusic. Bdwy debut 1994 in *Sunset Blvd.*

STEINHARDT, LEE. Born Sept.4, 1959 in Philadelphia, PA. Graduate Brooklyn Col., NYU, ACT. Debut 1986 OB in *Beautiful Truth* followed by *Twelfth Night, Stranger on the Road to Jericho, M Club, Tell Veronica, The Hollow.*

STEPHENS, LANNYL. Born Apr.20 in Lafayette, LA. Graduate UTx/Austin, AmerConsvTh. Debut 1990 OB in *Love in Two Countries* followed by *First Night, Cather Country, Tonight at 8:30, New Yorkers, Eulogy/Lucky Nurse, They Shoot Horses..., Off Key* Bdwy in *My Favorite Year* (1992), *Moon Over Buffalo.*

STERN, CHERYL. Born July 1, 1956 in Buffalo, NY. Graduate NorthwesternU. Debut 1984 OB in *Daydreams,* followed by *White Lies, Pets, That's Life!*

STERNER, STEVE. Born May 5, 1951 in NYC. Attended NYCC. Bdwy debut in *Clothes for a Summer Hotel* (1980) followed by *Oh Brother!,* OB in *Lovesong, Vagabond Stars, The Fabulous 50's, My Heart is in the East, Mandrake, The Special, Let It Ride, Encore!, Yiddle with a Fiddle, That's Life!, Cincinnati Saint, Double Identity.*

STEVENS, JODI. Born Apr.24 in Summit, NJ. Graduate PennSt. Debut OB in *My Name Is Pablo Picasso* followed by *27 Wagons Full of Cotton, Antigone, Meet Him, Bodyshop, Cardenio, Gender Wars.*

STEVENS, WESLEY. Born Apr. 6, 1948 in Evansville, IN. Graduate U.Va., OhStU. Debut 1978 OB in *Othello* followed by *Importance of Being Earnest, Candida, Platanov, But Most/v Because It's Raining, Comedy of Erro/s, Measure for Measure, Like a Brother.*

STEVENSON, JAMES. Born Nov.18, 1930 in NYC. Graduate Vanderbilt. Bdwy debut in *Goodbye Again* (1957) followed by *The Wall, Don't Drink the Water, Forty Carats, Hello Dolly,* OB in *Once Upon a Mattress* (1959), *Seascape.*

STEWART, GWEN. Born Sept.5, 1963 in Newark, NJ. Debut 1986 OB in *Mama I Want to Sing* followed by *God's Creation, Suds, Oedipus Private Eye,* Bdwy in *Starmites* (1989), *Truly Blessed, Rent.*

STEWART, PATRICK. Born July 13, 1940 in Mirfield, Eng. Attended Bristol Old Vic Sch. Bdwy debut with RSC in *Midsummer Night's Dream* (1971) followed by *Christmas Carol, Tempest.*

STILLER, JERRY. Born June 8, 1931 in NYC. Graduate USyracuse. Debut 1953 OB in *Coriolanus* followed by *Power and the Glory, Golden Apple, Measure for Measure, Taming of the Shrew, Carefree Tree, Diary of a Scoundrel, Romeo and Juliet, As You Like It, Two Gentlemen of Verona, Passione, Prairie/Shawl, Much Ado about Nothing, After-Play,* Bdwy in *The Ritz* (1975), *Unexpected Guests, Passione, Hurlyburly* (also OB), *3 Men on a Horse, What's Wrong with This Picture?*

STOLARSKY, PAUL. Born Feb. 18, 1933 in Detroit, MI. Graduate. WayneStateU. U.Mich. Debut 1972 OB in *Bluebird* followed by *Let Yourself Go Rocket to the Moon, D, My Mother My Father and Me, Me and Molly, Shlemiel the First, Rachel Plays, Model Apt.*

STONE, JESSICA. Born July 30, 1970 in Rochester, NY. Attended Barnard Col. Bdwy debut in *Grease* (1994) followed by *How to Succeed...*

STOUT, MARY. Born April 8, 1952 in Huntington, WVa. Graduate MarshallU. Debut 1980 OB in *Plain and Fancy* followed by *Sound of Music, Crisp, Christmas Carol, Song for a Saturday, Prizes, Golden Apple, Identical Twins from Baltimore,* Bdwy in *Copperfield* (1981), *Change in the Heir, My Favorite Year.*

STRAM, HENRY. Born Sept. 10, 1954 in Lafayette, IN. Attended Juilliard. Debut 1978 OB in *King Lear,* followed by *Shout and Twist, Cradle Will Rock, Prison-made Tuxedos, Cinderella/Cendrillon, Making of Americans, Black Sea Follies, Eddie Goes to Poetry City, Bright Room Called Day, Mind King, On the Open Road, My Head was a Sledge Hammer, Christina Alberta's Father, All's Well that Ends Well, Jack's Holiday, Dancing on Her Knees, Troilus and Cressida, Henry V, Grey Zone.*

STRAUSS, JANE. Born in Philadelphia, PA. Graduate USoFl. Bdwy debut in *Oliver* (1984), OB in *Sheba.*

STRITCH, ELAINE. Born Feb.2, 1925 in Detroit, MI. Bdwy debut in *Loco* (1946) followed by *Made in Heaven, Angel in the Wings, Call Me Madam, Pal Joey, On Your Toes, Bus Stop, Sin of Pat Muldoon, Goldilocks, Sail Away, Who's Afraid of Virginia Woolf?, Wonderful Town*(CC), *Company, Love Letters, Show Boat*(1994), *Delicate Balance,* OB in *Private Lives, Rogers and Hart Revue.*

STROMAN, GUY. Born Sept. 11, 1951 in Temil, TX. Graduate Tex. ChristianU. Bdwy debut in *Peter Pan* (1979) followed by *Annie,* OB in *After the Rain, Berlin to Broadway, Jerome Moross Revue, Close Your Eyes, Juno and the Paycock, Clory Hallelujah!, To Whom It May Concern, A/dersgate '88, Forever Plaid, America's Sweetheart.*

STRUTHERS, SALLY. Born July 28, 1948 in Portland, OR. Attended Pasadena Playhouse. Bdwy debut in *Wally's Cafe* (1981) followed by *Odd Couple* (1985), *Grease.*

STUART, IAN. Born May 25, 1940 in London, Eng. Debut 1971 OB in *Misalliance,* followed by *Count Dracula, Jack the Ripper Review, Accrington Pals, The Foreigner, Doctor's Dilemma, Romeo and Juliet,* Bdwy in *Caesar and Cleopatra (1977), Run for Your Wife, Racing Demon.*

STUART, TOM. Born Mar.19, 1970 in Berkeley, CA. Graduate AADA. Debut 1994 OB in *Fantasticks* followed by *Dames at Sea, Maurice, Grass Harp, Party,* Bdwy in *Christmas Carol* (1995).

SULLIVAN, K.T. Born Oct. 31, 1953 in Coalgate, OK. Graduate OklaU. Bdwy debut in *3 Penny Opera* (1989) followed by *Gentlemen Prefer Blondes*(1995), OB 1992 in *A..My Name Is Still Alice, Splendora.*

SURRENCE, KATYA. Born Sept.21, 1959 in Los Angeles, CA. Attended Santa Monica Col. Debut 1995 OB in *American Ballroom Theatre.*

SUSSMAN, MATTHEW. Born March 8, 1958 in NYC. Graduate BrownU, YaleU. Debut 1981 OB in *Steel on Steel, Grey Zone,* Bdwy in *Angels in America* (1993).

SUTTILE, ROBERT. Born Aug.9, 1958 in Brooklyn, NYC. Attended AADA. Debut 1980 OB in *Arsenic and Old Lace* followed by *Wait Until dark, Man Who Came to Dinner, Taming of the Shrew.*

SWAIN, ELIZABETH. Born Aug.6, 1941 in England. Bdwy debut in *The Crucible* (1968) followed by *Charley's Aunt, Crown Matrimonial, Sherlock Holmes,* OB in *Tango, Quilling of Prue, Scenes from an Execution.*

TABISEL, BRETT. Born Sept.14, 1982 in NYC. Bdwy debut in *Big* (1996) for which he received a 1996 Theatre World Award.

TACKABERRY, CELIA. Born Sept.17 in St. Louis, MO. Bdwy debut in *Day in Hollywood Night in the Ukraine* (1980) followed by *Sweet Charity,* OB in *Desk Set* (1984), *Cocoanuts.*

TAKASE, KAZUKI. Born Sept.8, 1959 in Tikyo, Japan. Graduate CCNY. Debut 1983 OB in *Teahouse* followed by *Sleepless City, The Tower, Salonika.*

TALBERTH, KENNETH. Born June 22, 1956 in Boston, MA. Graduate New York University. Debut 1981 OB in *Total Eclipse,* followed by *Henry IV Part I, The Misanthrope, Stray Dog Story, Winter's Tale, After the Rain, King Lear, Emperor of the Moon, Lucky Man.*

TARANTINA, BRIAN. Born March 27, 1959 in New York City. Debut 1980 OB in *Innocent Thoughts and Harmless Intentions* followed by *Time Framed, Fables for Friends, Balm in Gilead, V & V Only, Portrait of My Bikini, Shades of Grey,* Bdwy in *Angels Fall,* for which he received a 1983 Theatre World Award, *Biloxi Blues, Boys of Winter, Sacrilege.*

TATUM, BILL Born May 6, 1947 in Philadelphia, PA. Graduate Catawba Col. Bdwy debut in *Man of La Mancha* (1971), OB in *Missouri Legend, Time of the Cuckoo, Winner Take All, Last Girl Singer, Say Darling.*

TAYLOR, ANDY. Born Oct. 3 in Eugene, OR. Graduate Oberlin Col., UMon. Debut 1990 OB in *Romeo and Juliet,* followed by *Rodgers and Hart, On The Open Road, Juno, Painting it Red, Christina Alberta's Father, Golden Boy,* Bdwy in *One Touch of Venus* (Encores-1996*), Moon Over Buffalo.*

TAYLOR, CANDACE. Born Oct.4 in Washington, DC. Graduate NorthwesternU. Debut 1994 OB in *Young Playwrights Festival* followed by *Antigone.*

| Douglas Santiago | Christine Pedi | Mark Setlock | Patricia Ben Peterson | Sharif | Sarah Pfisterer |

| Kevin Shinick | Siân Phillips | Peter Slutsker | Angie Phillips | Jim Stanck | Adina Porter |

| Tom Stuart | Mary Setrakian | Andy Taylor | Carole Shelley | Jim True | Sandra Shipley |

| Walter Willison | Sally Struthers | Ray Willis | Celia Tackaberry | Marc Wolf | Maxine Taylor-Morris |

| Marc Jason Wong | Leslie Uggams | John Woodson | Joyce Van Patten | Ben Wright | Karen Ziemba |

243

TAYLOR, MYRA. Born July 9, 1960 in Ft. Motte, SC. Graduate Yale U. Debut 1985 OB in *Dennis*, followed by *The Tempest, Black Girl, Marathon 86, Phantasie, Walking the Dead, I Am a Man, Marathon Dancing, Come Down Burning*, Bdwy in *A Streetcar Named Desire, Mule Bone, Chronicle of a Death Foretold*.

TAYLOR, SCOTT. Born June 29, 1962 in Milan, TN. Attended MisStU. Bdwy in *Wind in the Willows* (1985), followed by *Cats, Crazy for You, Victor Victoria*.

TAYLOR-MORRIS, MAXINE. Born June 26 in NYC. Graduate NYU. Debut 1977 OB in *Counsellor-at-Law*, followed by *Manny, Devil's Disciple, Fallen Angels, Billy Liar, Unc/e Vanya, What the Butler Saw, Subject Was Roses, Goodnight Grandpa, Thirteenth Chair, Comedy of Errors, Second Avenue, One Act Festival, Midsummer, Broken English*.

TEMPERLEY, STEPHEN. Born July 29, 1949 in London, England. Attended AADA. Debut 1968 OB in *Invitation to a Beheading*, followed by *Henry IV Parts I & II, Up Against It*, Bdwy in *Crazy for You* (1992).

TESTA, MARY. Born June 4, 1955 in Philadelphia, PA. Attended URI. Debut 1979 OB in *In Trousers* followed by *Company, Life Is Not a Doris Day Movie, Not-So-New Faces of 1982, American Princess, Mandrake, 4 One-Act Musicals, Next, Please!, Daughters, One-Act Festival, The Knife, Young Playwrights Festival, Tiny Mommy, Finnegan's Funeral and Ice Cream Shop, Peter Breaks Through, Lucky Stiff, 1-2-3-4-5, Scapin, Hello Muddah Hello Faddah, Broken English*, Bdwy in *Barnum* (1980), *Marilyn, The Rink, A Funy Thing...*(1996).

THOLE, CYNTHIA. Born Sept.21, 1957 in Silver Springs, MD. Graduate ButlerU. Debut 1982 OB in *Nymph Errant*, Bdwy in *42nd St.*(1985), *Me and My Girl, Meet Me in St. Louis, Nick & Nora, Christmas Carol*.

THORNTON, ANGELA. Born in Leeds, Eng. Attended Webber-Douglas Sch Bdwy debut in *Little Glass Clock* (1956) followed by *Nude with Violin, Present Laughter, Hostile Witness, Pygmalion* (1987), *Racing Demon, An Ideal Husband*, OB in *Mousetrap, Big Broadcast, Mary Barnes, What the Butler Saw*.

THURSTON, TODD. Born May 29, 1956 in Baltimore, MD. Graduate UWa/Seattle. Debut 1985 OB in *She Loves Me* followed by *Camila*.

TIRELLI, JAIME. Born March 4, 1945 in NYC. Attended U. Mundial, AADA. Debut 1975 OB in *Rubbers, Yanks 3 Detroit 0* followed by *Sun Always Shines on the Cool, Body Bags, Bodega, Blade to the Heat*, Bdwy in *In the Summer House* (1993), *Chronicle of a Death Foretold*.

TOLENTINO, YOLANDA. Born Dec.31 in Agana, Guam. Graduate San FranStU, SUNY/Binghamton. Bdwy debut in *King and I* (1996).

TOMEI, MARISA. Born Dec. 4, 1964 in Brooklyn, NY. Attended BostonU, NYU. Debut 1986 OB in *Daughters*, for which she received a Theatre World Award followed by *Class 1 Acts, Evening Star, What the Butler Saw, Marathon '88, Sharon and Billy, Chelsea Walls, Summer Winds, Comedy of Errors, Fat Men in Skirts, Slavs!, Dark Rapture*.

TOREN, NICHOLAS. Born July 26, 1973 in Portland, OR. Graduate Middlebury Col. Debut 1996 OB in *Scenes from an Execution*.

TORMEY, JOHN. Born Aug.4, 1937 in Willimantic, CT. Graduate BostonU. Bdwy debut in *Beg Borrow or Steal* (1960) followed by *Bajour, Marat/Sade, Mike Downstairs, Our Town*, OB in *Ten by Six, Carpool*.

TOY, CHRISTINE. Born Dec. 26, 1959 in Scarsdale, NY. Graduate Sarah Lawrence Col. Debut 1982 OB in *Oh Johnny!*, followed by *Pacific Overtures, Genesis, Festival of One Acts, Balancing Act, Merrily We Roll Along, Tokyo Can Can*.

TREADWELL, TOM. Born May 7, 1955 in Seattle, WA. Debut 1982 OB in *Silver on Silver* followed by *Elephant Piece, Camilla, Madame Bovary: The Musical, Wizard of Oz, Mata Hari*.

TRESE, JANE/JANIE (SELL). Born Oct.1, 1940 in Detroit, MI. Attended UDetroit. Debut 1966 OB in *Mixed Doubles* followed by *Dark Horses, Dames at Sea, By Bernstein, God Bless You Mr. Rosewater, Sidewalkin*, Bdwy in *George M, Irene, Over Here* for which she received a Theatre World Award, *Pal Joey, Happy End, I LOve My Wife, Moon Over Buffalo*.

TRUCCO, ED. Born June 3, 1963 in NYC. Attended HB Studio. Debut 1988 OB in *Ariano* followed by *Boiler Room, Royal Affair, Blond Man*.

TRUE, JIM. Born July 31, 1966 in Greenwich, CT. Attended Northwestern U. Bdwy debut 1990 in *Grapes of Wrath*, followed by *Philadelphia Here I Come!, Buried Child*.

TRURO, VICTOR. Born Feb.7, 1940 in Boston, MA. Graduate Harvard, ColumbiaU, AADA. DEbut 1975 OB in *Crack* followed by *After the Revolution, Broken Borders, Tribe of the People, SWAK, God's Country*.

TULL, PATRICK. Born July 28, 1941 in Sussex, England. Attended LAMDA. Bdwy debut in *Astrakhan Coat* (1967) followed by *The Crucible, Master Builder, Getting Married, Ten Little Indians, The Tamer*

Tamed, Brand, Frankenstein, What the Butler Saw, She Stoops to Conquer, Art of Success, Ivanov.

TULLY, EDWARD. Born June 2, 1965 in NYC. Attended NYU. Debut 1992 OB in *Una Pooka* followed by *Twelfth Nigh, Driving By Numbers, Admissions*.

TUTHS, EVELYN. Born Sept.2, 1959 in Rockville Centre, NY. Graduate Brockport StU. Debut 1990 OB in *By and for Havel* followed by *Dark and Mr. Stone, La Mama 2000*

TURK, BRUCE. Born December 27, 1962 in California. Graduate Northwestern U. Debut 1994 OB in *Titus Andronicus* followed by *Green Bird*

UBARRY, HECHTER. Born September 25, 11946 in NYC. Bdwy debut 1965 in *Royal Hunt of the Sun*, followed by *Man of La Mancha* (1970/72/77/92), OB in *Romance Language*, Chum Chem, *Inkaarri's Return, In the Land of Giants*.

UGGAMS, LESLIE. Born May 25, 1943 in NYC. Bdwy debut 19647 in *Hallelujah Baby!* for which she received a Theatre World Award, followed by *Her First Roman, Blues in the Night, Anything Goes*, OB in *Black Girl*.

UMBERGER, ANDY. Born February 21, 1957 in Portsmouth, VA. Graduate VaComU. Debut 1986 OB in Rainbow followed by *The Man of the Ninties, What Do They Want from Me*, Bdwy in *City of Angels* (1991), followed by *Company*.

UTLEY, BYRON. Born November 4, 1954 in Indianapolis, IN. Attended UDC. Bdwy debut 1977 in *Hair*, followed by *Reggae, Big Deal, Rent*, OB in *Bones, The Trojan Women, Sweet Will Shakespeare, Transposed Heads, Death and the King's Horseman, A Better Life*.

VALENTINE, JAMES. Born February 18, 1933 in Rockford, IL. Attended U. London, Central School in London. Bdwy debut 1958 in *Cloud 7*, followed by *Epitaph for George Dillon, Duel of Angels, Ross, Caesar and Cleopatra, The Importance of Being Earnest, Camelot*, (1980,1981,1993), *Alice in Wonderland, Moon Over Buffalo*.

VAN ARK, JOAN. Born June 16, 1943 in NYC. Attended YaleU, Actors Studio. Bdwy debut 1965 in *Barefoot in the Park* followed by *School for Wives* for which she received a 1971 Theatre World Award, *Rules of the Game*, OB in *3 Tall Women*(1995).

VAN PATTEN, JOYCE. Born March 9, 1934 in Kew Gardens, NY. Bdwy debut 1941 in *Popsy* followed by *This Rock, Tomorrow the World, The Perfect Marriage, The Wind is 90, Desk Set, A Hole in the Head, Murder at the Howard Johnson's, I Ought to Be in Pictures, Supporting Cast, Brighton Beach Memoirs, Rumors, Jake's Women*, OB in *Between Two Thieves, Spoon River Anthology, The Seagull, A Fair* OB in *Rush Limbaugh in Night School*.

VAN ZANDT, NED. Ft. Worth, TX, Mar. 24, 1956. Attended NYU, UCLA. Debut OB in 1973 in *A Boy Named Dog*, followed by *Concerning the Effects of Trimethylchloride, The Alexander Plays*.

VARON, CHARLIE. Born November 11, 1958 in NYC. Debut 1995.

VAUGHAN, MELANIE. Born September 18 in Yazoo City, MS. Graduate LaStateU. Bdwy debut 1976 in *Rex* followed by *Sunday in the Park with George, On the 20th Century, Music Is, Starlight Express, The Most Happy Fella* (1992), OB in *Canterbury Tales, Big City Rhythms*.

VENNEMA, JOHN C. Born August 24, 1948 in Houston, TX. Graduate Princeton U., LAMA, Bdwy debut 1976 in *The Royal Family*, followed by *The Elephant Man, Otherwise Engaged, Racing Demon*, OB in *Loot, Statements after an Arrest, The Biko Inquest, No End of Blame, In Celebration, Custom of the Country, The Basement, A Slight Ache, Young Playwrights Festival, Danday Dick, Nasty Little Secrets, Mountain, Light Up the Sky, Joined at the Head, Quarrel of Sparrows, The Illusion, After-Play*

VEREEN, BEN. Born October 10, 1946 in Miami, FL. Debut 1965 OB in *Prodigal Son*, Bdwy in *Sweet Charity, Golden Boy, Hair, Jesus Christ Superstar* for which he received a Theatre World Award, *Pippin, Grind, Jelly's Last Jam, A Christmas Carol.*.

VINCENT, A. J. Born May 26 in Darby, PA. Attended NYU, MarquetteU., TempleU. Debut 1987 OB in *Psycho Beach Party* followed by *Did You Ever Go to PS 43?, Girls We Have Known, Vampire Lesbians of Sodom, Lust*, Bdwy in *The Will Rogers Follies* (1993).

VIRTA, RAY. Born June 18, 1958 in L'Anse, MI. Debut 1982 OB in *Twelfth Night*, followed by *The Country Wife, The Dubliners, Pericles, Tartuffe, The Taming of the Shrew, No One Dances, Jacques and His Master, Progress, Snowing at Delphi, The Eye of the Beholder, King Lear*, Bdwy in *The School for Scandal*.

VIVIANO, SAL. Born July 12, 1960 in Detroit, MI. Graduate E.III.U. Debut 1985 OB in *Hot Times and Suicide* followed by *The Fantasticks, Miami, RomancelRomance, Hamlet: The Opera*, Broadway *Jukebox, Catch Me If I Fall, Weird Romance, Beau Jest, From This Day On*, Bdwy in *The Three Musketeers* (1984), *Romance/Romance*, *City of Angels*, *Falsettos*.

VLASTNIK, FRANK. Born May 30, 1965 in Pru, IL. Graduate Illinois Wesleyan U. Bdwy debut 1996 in *Big*.

VOGEL, DAVID. Born October 19, 1922 in Canton, OH. Attended U. PA. Bdwy debut 1984 in *Ballet Ballads* followed by *Gentlemen Prefer Blondes*, *Make a Wish*, *Desert Song*, OB in *How to Get Rid of It*, *The Fantasticks*, *Miss Stanwyck Is Still in Hiding*, *Marya*, *She Loves Me*, *The Male Animal*, *The Mind Is a Terrible Thing to Lose*, *Say Darling*.

WAARA, SCOTT. Born June 5, 1957 in Chicago, IL. Graduate SMU. Debut 1982 OB in The Rise of Daniel Rocket, followed by The Dining Room, Johnny Pye and the Foolkiller, Gifts of the Magi, Falsettoland, 50 Million Frenchmen, Joseph & Mary, DuBarry Was a Lady in Concert, Bdwy in The Wind in the Willows (1985), Welcome to the Club, City of Angels, The Most Happy Family.

WACHTEL, EMILY. Born March 8, 1965 in NYC. Sarah Lawrence Col., Neighborhood Playhouse. Debut Off 1995 in *Golden Boy*.

WADE, ADAM. Born Mar. 17, 1935 in Pittsburgh, PA. Attended VaStateU. Debut 1976 OB in *My Sister My Sister*, followed by *Shades of Harlem*, *Falling Apart*, *The War Party*, *Staggerlee*, *Lifetimes*, *Burner's Frolic*, *Black Girl*.

WAITE, JOHN THOMAS. Born Apr. 19, 1948 in Syracuse, NY. Attended SyracuseU. Debut 1976 OB in *The Fantasticks*, followed by *Measure for Measure*, Bdwy in *Amadeus* (1982).

WALBYE, KAY. Born Ft. Collins, CO. KansasStU. Debut 1984 OB in *Once on a Summer's Day* followed by *The Majestic Kid*, Bdwy 1989 in *Run for Your Wife*, followed by *The Secret Garden*, *The Rose Tattoo*.

WALDRON, MICHAEL. Born Nov. 19, 1949 in West Orange, NJ. Graduate ColumbiaU. Debut 1979 OB in *Mary* followed by *Dulcy*, *Romance Is*, *New Faces of '52*, *What Comes After Ohio?*, *The Cocoanuts*, Bdwy in *Baby* (1983).

WALKER, FREDI. Born Oct. 2, 1962 in St. Louis, MO. Attended NYU. Appeared OF in *Welcome to the Moon*, *God is a Guess What?*, *Brewsie's Willie*, *Georgy*, *Cinderella*, Bdwy debut 1996 in *Rent*.

WALKER, SYBYL. Born April 30 in Chicago, IL. Graduate SMU. Debut 1991 OB in *From the Mississippi Delta*, Bdwy in *The Tempest*.

WALLACH, ROBERTA. Born July 13, 1938 in NYC. Attended Sarah Lawrence Col., Neighborhood Playhouse. Debut 1978 OB in *The Diary of Anne Frank*, followed by *Second Avenue*, One Act Festival, *The Model Apt*.

WALLNAU, COLLEEN SMITH. Born June 28, 1948 in Trenton, NJ. Graduate Emerson Col., Trenton St., RutgersU. Debut OB 1992 in *Thru Darkest Ohio*, followed by *Romeo and Juliet*, *On the Verge*, Bdwy in *Crazy for You* (1994).

WALSH, BARBARA. Born June 3, 1955 in Washington, DC. Attended Montgomery Col. Bdwy debut 1982 in *Rock 'n' Roll: The First 5000 Years*, followed by *Nine*, *Falsettos*, *Blood Brothers*, *Big* OB in *Forbidden Broadway*, *Hello Again*, *Camila*.

WALSH, ELIZABETH. Born Oct. 12, in Puerto Rico. Graduate U.Wis, U. Mass. Debut 1987 OB in *Mademoiselle Colombe*, followed by *She Loves Me*, *Frankie*, *Love in Two Countries*, *DuBarry Was a Lady in Concert*

WALSH, NANCY. Born Jan. 5, 1965 in Greenfield, MA. Graduate U. Conn, SMU. Debut 1991 OB in *Sabina and Lucretia*, followed by *William Shakespeare's The Red Rose*, *Rescuers*.

WALTER, WENDY. Born Nov. 13, 1961 in Dallas, TX. U. of Ks. Bdwy debut 1994 in *Sunset Blvd*.

WANG, LUOYONG. Born Dec. 24, 1958 in Luoyong, China. Graduate Shanghai Drama Inst., Boston U. Bdwy debut 1995 in *Miss Saigon*, OB in *Fulei and Fuchong*.

WARING, WENDY. Born Dec. 7, 1960 in Melrose, MA. Attended Emerson Col., Debut 1987 OB in *Wish You Were Here*, Bdwy in *Legs Diamond* (1988), *Will Rogers Follies*, *Crazy for You*.

WARMFLASH, STUART. Born June 27, 1949 in NYC. Graduate NYU. Debut 1970 OB in *The Lady from Maxim's*, followed by *Secret Service*, *Boy Meets Girl*, *Let Me Finish!*, *A Map and a Cap*, *Owning the Knuckleball*.

WARREN, DAVID. Born in Huntington, NY. Graduate Columbia Col. Debut 1992 OB in *Trudy and Paul Come to the Rescue*, followed by *Coming Through*, *Acts of Contrition*.

WATSON, BECKY. Born in Wooster, OH. Graduate Kent St., Florida St. U., U. of AL. Debut 1996 OB in *The Cocoanuts*.

WATT, GREGORY. Born in Framingham, MA, Mar. 28, 1963. Graduate U.of MI, Amer. Conserv. Th. Debut Bdwy 1994 in *Blood Brothers*, OB in *Party*.

WEEMS, ANDREW. Born July 18, 1961 in Seoul, S. Korea. Graduate Brown U., U. California. Debut 1993 OB in *A Quarrel of Sparrows*, followed by *Marathon Dancing*, *Mud Angel*, *A Midsummer Night's Dream*, *The Dolphin Position*, *Green Bird*.

WEIL, SEAN. Born May 28, 1961 in The Bronx, NYC. Attended Sienna College. Debut 1991 in Nebraska, followed by Heart of Earth, Dalton's Back, Superman is Dead, Performance, Troy.

WEINCEK, DAVID. Born June 10, 1965 in Naperville, IL. Graduate NYU. Debut OB 1988 in *Don Juan in Vegas*, followed by *The Dressing Room*, *American Scrapbook*, *Taming of the Shrew*, *Flaming Idiots*, *Party*.

WEISS, JEFF. Born in 1940 in Allentown, PA. Debut 1986 OB in Hamlet, followed by *Front Page*, *Casanova*, *Hot Keys*, *Henry V*, *The Wallenberg Mission*, Bdwy in *Macbeth*, (1988), *Our Town*, *Mastergate*, *Face Value*, *Real Inspector Hound/15 Minute Hamlet*, *Carousel* (1994).

WELLS, CHRISTOPHER. Born June 18, 1955 in Norwalk, CT. Graduate Amherst Col. Debut 1981 OB in *Big Apple Country* followed by *Broadway Jukebox*, *Savage Amusement*, *Overrules*, Heart of Darkness, Ancient History, One Act Festival, Bdwy 1985 in *Harrigan 'n' Hart*, Broadway, *Teddy and Alice*, *Crazy for You*.

WEMITT, MONICA M. Born May 19, 1956 in Pittsfield, MA. OB in *Rebel/The James Dean Musical*, Bdwy in *Three Men on a Horse*, *Hello Dolly!*

WENCKER, LEIGH-ANNE. Born June 16 in St. Louis, MO. Graduate Webster U. Debut 1993 Bdwy in *Crazy for You*.

WEST, JENNIFER. Born Sept. 22, 1939 in Ft. Smith, AK. Attended CCLA. Debut OB in *Dutchman* for which she received a Theatre World Award, followed by *After the Fall* (LCRep), *Diamond Orchid*, *Malcolm*, *Harold*, and *Sondra* (OB), *Hemingway Hero*, *Tiger at the Gates* (LCRep), Bdwy in *Sunset Blvd*.

WESTENBERG, ROBERT. Born October 26, 1953 in Miami Beach, FL. Graduate U. California/Fresco. Debut 1981 OB in *Henry IV Part I*, followed by *Hamlet*, *Death of von Richthofen*, *3 Birds Alighting on a Field*, Bdwy in *Zorba* (1983), for which he received a Theatre World Award, *Sunday in the Park with George*, *Into the Woods*, *Les Miserables*, *Secret Garden*, *Abe Lincoln in Illinois*, *Christmas Carol*, *Company*.

WESTON, CELIA. Born in South Carolina. Attended Salem Col., NC School of Arts. Bdwy debut 1979 in *Loose Ends*, followed by *Garden District*, OB in *Bargains*, *Laura Dennis*.

WESTON, DOUGLAS. Born January 13, 1960 in London, England. Graduate Princeton U. RADA. Debut 1991 OB in *Whitestones*, followed by *Working Title*, Bdwy in *Blood Brothers* (1993).

WEYERS, MARIUS. Born Feb. 3, 1945 in Johannesburg, South Africa. Debut 1996 OB in *Valley Song*.

WHITE, DANA. Born Mar. 5, 1930 in Flint, MI. Attended Carroll Col. Appeared in *Tea and Sympathy*, *The Happiest Millionaire*, *Love Me Little*, *Engaged*.

WHITE, RICHARD. Born Aug. 4, 1953 in Oak Ridge, TN. Graduate Oberlin Col.Bdwy debut 1979 in *The Most Happy Fella*, followed by *Brigadoon*, *South Pacific*, *The Desert Song*, OB in *Elizabeth and Essex*, *Frankie*, *Topper*.

WHITTHORNE, PAUL. Born Feb. 17, 1970 in Tucson, AZ. Graduate Juilliard Sch. Bdwy debut 1995 in *The Tempest*, OB in *Orestes: I Murdered My Mother* (1996).

WHITTON, MARGARET. (formerly Peggy). Born November 30 in Philadelphia, PA. Debut 1973 OB in *Baba Goya*, followed by *Arthur*, *Nourish the Beast*, *Another Language*, *Chinchilla*, *Othello*, *The Art of Dining*, *One Tiger to a Hill*, *Henry IV Parts 1 and 2*, *Don Juan*, *My Uncle Sam*, *Aunt Dan and Lemon*, *Ice Cream and Hot Fudge*, *The Merry Wives of Windsor*, *Silence Cunning Exile*, *Three Viewings*, *New England*, Bdwy in *Steaming* (1982), *The Apple Doesn't Fall*.

WIDDOES, KATHLEEN. Born Mar.21, 1939 in Wilmington, DE. Attended Paris Theatre de Natoons. Bdwy debut 1958 in *The Firstborn* followed by *World of Suzy Wong*, *Much Ado about Nothing*, *Importance of Being Earnest*, *Brighton Beach Memoirs*, *Hamlet*, OB in *Three Sisters*, *The Maids*, *You Can't Take It with You*, *To Clothe the Naked*, *World War 2*, *Beggars Opera*, *As You Like It*, *Midsummer Night's Dream*, *Hamlet*, *Tower of Evil*, *Truth Teller*, *Moonlight*.

WIEST, DIANNE. Born March 28, 1948 in Kansas City, MO. Attended U. MD. Debut 1976 OB in *Ashes*, followed by *Leave it to Beaver is Dead*, *The Art of Dining*, for which she received a 1980 Theatre World Award, *Bonjour La Bonjour*, *The Three Sisters*, *Serenading Louie*, *Other Places*, *Hunting Cockroaches*, *After the Fall*, *Square One*, *Don Juan in Hell* (in concert), *The Shawl*, Bdwy in *Frankenstein* (1981), *Othello*, *Beyond Therapy*, *In the Summer House*.

WILKOF, LEE. Born June 25, 1951 in Canton, OH. Graduate U. Cinn. Debut 1977 OB in *Present Tense*, followed by *Little Shop of Horrors*, *Holding Patterns*, *Angry Housewives*, *Assassins*, *Born Guilty*, *Treasure Is-*

land, *Golden Boy,* Bdwy in *Sweet Charity* (1986), *The Front Page, She Loves Me.*

WILKS, ELAYNE. Born Sept. 25, 1933 in Bronx, NY. Graduate Adelphi U., NYU. Debut OB 1995 in *Babyluv.*

WILLEY, CHARLES.Born Sept. 18, 1956 in Abington, PA. Graduate Syracuse U. Debut OB 1991 in *Necktie Breakfast* followed by *Battery, Single and Proud, Holy Note, The Firebugs, Blue Window, Lion in the Streets.*

WILLIAMS, CARLA RENATA. Born Sept. 16, 1961 in Cherry Point, NC. Graduate Howard U. Debut OB 1992 in *The Balmyard,* Bdwy in *How to Succeed in Business...* (1995).

WILLIAMS, DATHAN B. Born Oct. 30, 1960 in Washington, DC. Graduate Wheeling Jesuit Col, WV U. Bdwy debut 1994 in *Showboat.*

WILLIAMSON, NICOL. Born Sept. 14, 1938 in Hamilton, Scotland. Bdwy debut 1965 in *Inadmissible Evidence,* followed by *Plaza Suite, Hamlet, Uncle Vanya, Macbeth, The Real Thing, I Hate Hamlet, Jack: A Night on the Town with John Barrymore,* OB in *Nicol WIlliamson's Late Show, Inadmissible Evidence, The Entertainer.*

WILLIAMS, RUTH. Born January 25, 1954 in Baltimore, MD. Graduate U. Md. Bdwy debut 1981 in Annie, followed by *Smile, Guys and Dolls,* OB in *Preppies, Bodo, A Helluva Town, DuBarry Was a Lady in Concert.*

WILLIS, SCOTT. Born Nov. 9, 1956 in Eldorado, IL. Graduate Murray St. U. Debut 1981 OB in *Something for the Boys,* followed by *Damn Yankees, Encore, Sing Me Sunshine,* Bdwy in *State Fair.*

WILLISON, WALTER. Born June 24, 1947 in Monterey Park, CA. Bdwy debut 1970 in *Norman Is That You?,* followed by *Two by Two,* for which he received a Theatre World Award, *Wild and Wonderful, Celebration of Richard Rodgers, Pippin, Tribute to Joshua Logan, Tribute to George Abbott, Grand Hotel, A Christmas Carol,* OB in *South Pacific in Concert, They Say It's Wonderful, Broadway Scandals of 1928* and *Options,* both of which he wrote, *Aldersgate '88.*

WILLS, RAY. Born Sept. 14, 1960 in Santa Monica, CA. Graduate WichitaStU., BrandeisU. Debut 1988 OB in *Side by Side by Sondheim,* followed by *Kiss Me Quick, Grand Tour, The Cardigans, The Rothschilds, Little Me, A Backers Audition, All in the Timing,* Young Playwrights Festival, Bdwy in *Anna Karenina* (1993), *Big.*

WILNER, LORI. Born July 17, 1959 in NYC. Graduate SUNY/Binghamton. Debut 1985 OB in *Hannah Senesh,* followed by *The Witch, Hannah 1939, Milk and Honey, The Yiddish Trojan Women,* Bdwy 1990 in *Those Were the Days.*

WILSON, ELIZABETH. Born Apr. 4, 1925 in Grand Rapids, MI. Attended Neighborhood Playhouse. Bdwy debut 1953 in Picnic, followed by *The Desk Set, Tunnel of Love, Big Fish Little Fish, Sheep on the Runway, Sticks and Bones, Secret Affairs of Mildred Wild, The Importance of Being Earnest, Morning's at Seven, You Can't Take It With You, A Delicate Balance,* OB in *Plaza Suite, Eh?, Little Murders, Good Woman of Setzuan, Uncle Vanya, Threepenny Opera, All's Well That Ends Well, Taken in Marriage, Salonika, Anteroom.*

WILSON, MARY LOUISE. Born Nov. 12, 1936 in New Haven, CT. Graduate Northwestern U. Bdwy debut 1963 in Hot Spot, followed by *Flora the Red Menace, Criss-Crossing, Promises Promises, The Women, The Gypsy, The Royal Family, The Importance of Being Earnest, Philadelphia Story, Fools, Alice in Wonderland, The Odd Couple, Prelude to a Kiss,* OB in *Our Town, Upstairs at the Downstairs, Threepenny Opera, A Great Career, Whispers on the Wind, Beggar's Opera, Buried Child, Sister Mary Ignatius Explains It All, Actor's Nightmare, Baby with the Bathwater, Musical Comedy Murders of 1940, Macbeth, Flaubert's Latest, Full Gallop.*

WING, VIRGINIA. Born November 9 in Marks, MS. Graduate MissCol. Debut 1989 OB in *Two by Two* followed by *Food and Shelter, Cambodia Agonistes, America Dreaming, Caucasian Chalk Circle.*

WINN, KATY. Born in 1944 in Washington, DC. Graduate Boston U. Bdwy debut 1969 in *Three Sisters,* followed OB by *Hamlet, Knuckle, Tell Me Something I Don't Really Know.*

WINSTON, CONNIE. Born Sept. 26, 1962 in Baltimore, MD. Graduate SUNY/New Paltz, Emerson Col. OB in *Transformations, The Arden Party, Black Elvis, A Greater Good.*

WINTHER, MICHAEL. Born Feb. 1, 1962 in San Francisco, CA. Graduate Williams Col. Debut 1988 OB in *Tony 'n' Tina's Wedding,* followed by *Forever Plaid,* Bdwy 1989 in *Artist Descending a Staircase.*

WIPF, ALEX. Born in Brooklyn, NY. Graduate Brooklyn Col, Neighborhood Playhouse. Bdwy debut 1972 in *An Evening with Richard Nixon,* followed by *6 Rms Riv Vu, Da, Fearless Frank, To Grandmother's House We Go, Victor/Victoria,* OB in *Poppie Nongena, The Majestic Kid.*

WOLF, MARC. Born July 16 in NYC. Graduate Williams Col. OB debut 1996 in *Party.*

WONG, MARC JASON. Born Feb. 20, 1970 in Houston, TX. Graduate U of CA/San Diego. Debut OB in 1996 in *Dog and His Master.*

WOODMAN, BRANCH. Born Aug.31, 1962 in Upland, CA. Attended Chaffee Col., CalStU/Fullerton. Debut 1989 OB in *Out of This World,* Bdwy 1994 in *Crazy for You.*

WOODS, CAROL. Born November 13, 1943 in Jamaica, NY. Graduate Ithaca Col. Debut 1980 OB *One Mo' Time,* followed by *Blues in the Night, Encores: One Touch of Venus,* Bdwy in *Grind* (1985), *Big River, Stepping Out, The Crucible, A Little Hotel on the Side, The Goodbye Girl.*

WOODSON, JOHN. Born May 12, 1950 in Des Moines, IA. Attended NC Schl. of Arts. Debut 1990 OB in *King Lear,* followed by *The Sorrows of Frederick, Democracy and Esther, Henry V,* Bdwy in *Medea.*

WORKMAN, JASON. Born Oct. 9, 1962 in Omaha, Neb. Attended UKy., Goodman Bdwy debut 1989 in *Meet Me in St. Louis,* for which he received a Theatre World Award followed by *Damn Yankees*(1994), OB in *Haunted Host, Safe Sex, Music in the Air in concert, Bed & Sofa.*

WORLEY, JO ANN. Born Sept.6, 1937 in Lowell, IN. Attended CCLA, Pasadena Playhouse. Bdwy debut 1961 in *Billy Barnes Revue* followed by *Prince of Central Park, Grease* (1994), OB in *That Thing at the Cherry Lane, Hotel Passionata, Mad Show, Second City Revue.*

WRIGHT, AMY. Born April 15, 1950 in Chicago, IL. Graduate Beloit Col. Debut 1977 OB in *The Stronger* followed by *Nightshift, Hamlet, Miss Julie, Slacks and Tops, Terrible Jim Fitch, Village Wooing, The Stronger, Time Framed, Trifles, Words from the Moon, Prin, Born Guilty,Mrs. Klein,* Bdwy in *5th of July,* (1980), *Noises off.*

WRIGHT, BEN. Born Sept. 3, 1969 in Indianapolis, IN. Graduate NYU, Indiana U. Debut OB 1985 in *Paradise,* Bdwy in *Into the Woods* (1987), followed by *State Fair.*

WRIGHT, JEFFREY. Born in Washington, DC, 1966. Attended Amherst College. Bdwy debut 1993 in *Angels in America,* followed by *Bring in da Noise Bring in da Frunk,* OB in *King Lear.*

WROE, CRAIG. Born Apr. 8, 1958 in Los Angeles, CA. Graduate Loyola U., Catholic U. Debut 19489 OB in *The Tempest,* followed by *Othello, Measure for Measure, Two, The Alexander Plays*

WYLIE, JOHN. Born Dec. 14, 1925 in Peacock, TX. Graduate No. TX St. Univ.Debut 1987 OB in *Lucky Spot,* followed by *Life is a Dream, The Winter's Tale, The Venetian Turn,* Bdwy in *Born Yesterday* (1989), *Grand Hotel.*

WYMAN, NICHOLAS. Born May 18, 1950 in Portland, ME. Graduate Harvard U.Bdwy debut 1975 in *Very Good Eddie,* followed by *Grease, The Magic Show, On the 20th Century, Whoopee!, My Fair Lady* (1981), *Doubles, Musical Comedy Murders of 1940, Phantom of the Opera,* OB in *Paris Lights, When We Dead Awaken, Charlotte Sweet, Kennedy at Colonus, Once on a Summer's Day, Angry Housewives, The Hunchback of Notre Dame, Brimstone, 3 in the Back 2 in the Head.*

WYNKOOP, CHRISTOPHER. Born December 7, 1943 in Long Branch, NJ. Graduate AADA. Debut 1970 OB in *Under the Gaslight,* followed by *And So to Bed Cartoons for a Lunch Hour, Telecast, Fiorello!, The Aunts, Moonlight,* Bdwy in *Whoopee!* (1979) *City of Angels, Anna Christie.*

YAKER, JAMES. Born Jan. 29, 1972 in NYC. Graduate Wesleyan U. OB debut 1996 in *The Food Chain.*

YALUN, JEFF. Born June 18, 1991 in Bronx, NY. Bdwy debut 1995 in *Miss Saigon* followed by *The King and I.*

YANO, YOSHI. Born Nov. 10, 1959 in Gifu, Japan. Graduate Kyoto Industrial U. OB in *In My Father's House, Twilight Crane.*

YING, YAN. Born Oct. 5, 1969 in Shanghai, China. Bdwy debut 1996 in *The King and I.*

YOSHIOKA, KAYOKO. Born Aug. 3, 1965 in Osaka, Japan. Bdwy debut 1994 in *Cats* followed by *Carousel, The King and I.*

YULIN, HARRIS. Born November 5, 1937 in California. Attended USC. Debut 1963 OB in *Next Time I'll Sing to You,* followed by *A Midsummer Night's Dream, Troubled Waters, Richard III, King John, The Cannibals, A Lesson from Aloes, Hedda Gabler, Barnum's Last Life, Hamlet, Mrs. Warren's Profession, Don Juan in Hell* (in concert), *Arts and Leisure,* Bwdy in *Watch on the Rhine* (1980), *The Visit.*

YUEN, LISA. Born Jan. 27, 1972 in Mountain View, CA. Graduate UCLA. Bdwy debut 1995 in *Miss Saigon.*

ZAGNIT, STUART. Born Mar. 28 in New Brunswick, NJ. Graduate Montclair St. Col. Debut 1978 OB in *The Wager,* followed by *Manhattan Trasnference, Women in Tune, Enter Laughing, Kuni Leml, Tatterde-*

malion, Golden Land, Little Shop of Horrors, Lucky Stiff, Grand Tour, Majestic Kid, Made in Heaven, Encore!, A Trip to the Beach.

ZALABAK, MARISA. Born Mar. 1, 1958 in Elmhurst, IL. Graduate AADA. Debut 1984 OB in *The Ballad of Soapy Smith*, followed by *Original One Acts, The Bear, Domino Courts, Toys in the Attic, Yours Truly, Night with Guests, Right You Are If..., The Maderati.*

ZALOOM, JOE. Born July 30, 1944 in Utica, NY. Graduate Catholic U. Bdwy debut 1972 in *Capt. Brassbound's Conversion,* followed by *Kingdoms,* OB in *Nature and the Purpose of the Universe, Plot Counter Plot, Midsummer Night's Dream, Madrid Madrid, Much Ado About Nothing, Cymbeline, Tamara, The Taming of the Shrew, King Lear.*

ZARAGOZA, GREGORY. Born Aug. 23, 1954 in San Jose, CA. Graduate San Jose St., UCalBerkeley, NYU. Bdwy debut 1988 in *Macbeth,* OB in *Two Cities.*

ZARRIELLO, WILLIAM. Born Aug. 18, 1963 in Mountain View, CA. Graduate CalifStU/Sacramento. Debut 1992 OB in *Dear World* followed by *The Triumph of the West.*

ZAY, TIM. Born August 13, 1952 in Cleveland, OH. Graduate U. Cincinnati. Debut 1988 OB in *Moby Dick,* followed by *This One Thing I Do, The Rover, Teibele and Her Demon, Let Us Now Praise Famous Men, Rescuers.*

ZELLER, MARK. Born Apr. 20, 1932 in NYC. Attended NYU. Bdwy debut 1956 in *Shangri-La,* followed by *Happy Hunting, Wonderful Town* (CC), *Saratoga, Ari, Chu Chem, Fiddler on the Roof* (1990), OB in *Candle in the Wind, Margaret's Bed, Freud,Kuni Leml, Lies My Father Told Me, Big Block Party, Chu Chem, Metesky.*

ZERKLE, GREG. Born Aug. 19, 1957 in Wisconsin. Graduate Univ. of WI. Bdwy in *Into the Woods, The Secret Garden, Grand Hotel,* OB in *Sherlock Holmes & the Red-Headed League, Bittersuite, Richard II.*

ZICKEL, MATHER. Born in NYC. Graduate NYU. Debut OB 1996 in Cardenio.

ZIEMBA, KAREN. Born Nov. 12, 1957 in St. Joseph, MO. Graduate UAkron. Debut 1981 OB in *Seesaw,* followed by *I Married an Angel, Sing for Your Supper, 50 Million Frenchmen, And the World Goes Round, 110 in the Shade* (NYCO/LC), *A Grand Night for Singing, I Do! I Do!,* Bdwy in *Crazy for You* (1994), *Allegro in Concert, Crazy for You.*

ZIMMERMAN, LEIGH. Born Mar. 28, 1969 in Stoughton, WI. Attended Fordham U. Bdwy debut 1991 in *The Will Rogers Follies* followed by *Crazy for You.*

ZISKIE, KURT. Born April 16, 1956 in Oakland, CA. Graduate Stanford U., Neighborhood Playhouse. Debut 1985 OB in *A Flash of Lightning,* followed by *Ulysses in Nighttown, Three Sisters,* Marathon '92, *Cincinnati Saint, Beaux Stratagem, King Lear, A Doll's House, Antigone,* Bdwy in *Broadway* (1987).

ZOBEL, RICHARD. Born June 5, 1952 in West Chester, PA. Attended Temple U. Debut 1979 OB in *The Taming of the Shrew,* followed by *All''sWell That Ends Well, Big Apple Messenger, The Country Girl, Below the Belt,* Bdwy in *Nuts* (1980).

ZORICH, LOUIS. Born February 12, 1924 in Chicago, IL. Attended Roosevelt U. OB in *Six Characters in Search of an Author, Crimes and Crimes, Henry V, Thracian Horses, All Women Are One, The Good Soldier Schweik, Shadow of Heroes, To Clothe the Naked, A Memory of Two Mondays, They Knew What They Wanted, The Gathering, True West, The Tempest, Come Day Come Night, Henry IV Parts I & 2, The Size of the World,* Bdwy in *Becket, Moby Dick, The Odd Couple, Hadrian Vll, Moonchildren, Fun City, Goodtime Charley, Herzl, Death of a Salesman, Arms and the Man,The Marriage of Figaro, She Loves Me.*

Thomas Anderson

Tony Azito

Martin Balsam

Vivian Blaine

Jeremy Brett

Peter Carew

OBITUARIES
(June 1, 1995-May 31, 1996)

JOHN ABBOTT, 90, London-born actor, died May 24, 1996. After London stage work beginning in 1934, he appeared on Bdwy in *He Who Gets Slapped, Montserrat* and *Waltz of the Toreadors*.

THOMAS CHARLES ANDERSON, 90, California-born actor, died Jan.12, 1996 in Englewood, NJ after a stroke. A pioneering black actor, he was in Bdwy's *Great White Hope, Native Son* and *Hello Dolly* with Pearl Bailey. He was asst. director on Orson Welles' all-black *Macbeth*. Survived by his wife and a sister.

MAXENE ANDREWS, 79, of the Andrews Sisters vocal group, died Oct.21, 1995 in Hyannis, MA. of a heart attack. Popular in the 1930s/40s, she made her Bdwy debut with sister Patty in *Over Here* (1974). Just prior to her death she appeared in Off-Bdwy's *Swingtime Canteen*.

TONY AZITO, 46, NYC-born actor, died May 26, 1995 in NYC of AIDS. Nominated for a Tony for the 1980 *Pirates of Penzance*, his other Bdwy shows included *Happy End* and *Mystery of Edwin Drood*. OB included *Red White and Black* (1971), *Players Project, Secrets of the Citizens Correction Committee, Threepenny Opera, Buskers* and *Twelfth Night*. Survived by his mother, sister and three brothers.

WARD BAKER, 72, Texas-born director, died Oct.31, 1995 in Paris, TX. He directed *The Fantasticks* in 1960 and watched it become the world's longest running musical. Survived by three daughters and grandchildren.

MARTIN BALSAM, 76, NYC-born actor, died Feb.13, 1996 in Rome, Italy. He won a Tony for Bdwy's *You Know I Can't Hear You When the Water's Running*. NYC debut in *Pot Boiler* followed by *Ghost for Sale, Closing Door, Sundown Beach, Macbeth, Rose Tattoo, Camino Real, Wedding Breakfast, Middle of the Night, Porcelain Year* and *Cold Storage*. Well known also for film and tv, he is survived by actress daughter Talia Balsam.

VIVIAN BLAINE, 74, New Jersey-born performer, died Dec.9, 1995 in Manhattan of heart failure. Creator of the delightful Miss Adelaide in *Guys and Dolls* (1950), she also played the role onscreen and in a 1966 City Center revival. Other Bdwy includes *Hatful of Rain, Say Darling, Enter Laughing, Company* and *Zorba* (1984).

RALPH BLANE (HUNSECKER), 81, songwriter/performer, died Nov.13, 1995 in Broken Arrow, Okla., the town where he was born. With partner Hugh Martin, he wrote songs for *Best Foot Forward* (1941) and the beloved *Meet Me in St. Louis,* the 1944 film adapted for Bdwy in 1989. Working solo, he wrote music and lyrics for *Three Wishes for Jamie.* As a performer he appeared in *New Faces of 1936* and *Louisiana Purchase.* Survived by his son.

JEREMY BRETT, 59, English actor, died Sept.12, 1995 in London of heart failure. Best known for his television portrayal of Sherlock Holmes, his Bdwy debut in *Troilus and Cressida* (1956) with the Old Vic was followed by *Macbeth, Richard II, Romeo and Juliet, The Deputy, Dracula* and *Aren't We All?*. Survived by a son from his first marriage to actress Anna Massey.

PHYLLIS BROOKS, 80, Idaho-born actress, died Aug.1, 1995 in Cape Neddick, ME. Bdwy included *Stage Door*(1936), *Panama Hattie* and *Road Trip*. Survived by two sons, two daughters, a brother and grandchildren.

PETER CAREW. 73, Pennsylvania-born actor, died Aug.9, 1995 in Paramus, NJ of a heart attack. On Bdwy in *Great White Hope* (1969) his Off-Bdwy included *Coffee House*(1948), *Street Scene, Ah Wilderness, Antigone, Waiting for Lefty, 12 Angry Men, Falling from Heaven, Go Show Me a Dragon, Stage Affair, King of the Whole Damned World, Purple Canary, Kiss Mama, View from the Bridge, He Who Gets Slapped, Istanbul, Thunder Rock, Monsters* and *Dazy.*

ROSALIND CASH, 56, New Jersey-born actress, died Oct.31, 1995 in Los Angeles of cancer. Bdwy in *Wayward Stork* (1966) followed by many Off-Bdwy shows including *Fiorello, June-bug Graduates Tonight, To Bury a Cousin, Song of the Lusitanian Bogey, Kongi's Harvest, Ceremonies in Dark Old Men, Evening of One Acts, Man Better Man, The Harangues, Day of Absence, Brotherhood, Charlie was Here, King Lear, Boesman and Lena* and *16th Round*(1980). An original member of the Negro Ensmble Company, she is survived by a sister and two brothers.

ALEXANDER CLARK, 94, NYC-born actor, died Sept.30, 1995. NYC theatre included *Merton of the Movies, Excess Baggage, Biography, Too True to be Good, Victoria Regina, Abe Lincoln in Illinois, Margin for Error, In Time to Come, Sheppy, Legend of Lovers, Captains and the Kings, Calculated Risk, Brigadoon(CC), Carousel(CC), Life with Father(CC)* and *The Show-Off.*

MICHAEL CLAKINS, 47, Illinois-born actor, died Oct.16, 1995. Off-Bdwy included *Sisters of Mercy* (1973), *Love! Love! Love!, Lifesongs* and *Gifts of the Magi.*

JOHN CRAVEN, 79, NYC-born actor, died Nov.24, 1995 in Salt Point, NY. He created the role of George Gibbs in the original Bdwy *Our Town* (1938). Other Bdwy included *Happiest Days, Delicate Story, Two on an Island, They Knew What They Wanted* and *Village Green*. Prior to acting, he worked as a stage manager for *Babes in Arms*. Survived by his wife, two sons, a daughter and grandchildren.

JULIA ASLER FOSHKO, 97, actress, died June 3, 1995 in Englewood, NJ. The last surviving member of the theatrical Adler clan (including Stella and Luther), she started as a child performer in the Yiddish theatre with her family. Bdwy roles started in the 1920s and included *Merchant of Venice, Rosa Machree* and *Awake and Sing* (1939) in a part originated four years earlier by her sister Stella. Her last major NYC appearance was in City Center's *Tovarich* (1952). Survived by a daughter and grandchildren.

RICHARD EDWARD FRANK, 42, Boston-born actor, died Sept.3, 1995 in Los Angeles of AIDS. NYC stage included *Sring Awakening, Hamlet* (Kevin Kline) and *Misanthrope*. Survived by his parents and sister.

| Rosalind Cash | Kevin John Gee | Harry Guardino | Tom Helmore | Barton Heyman | Phyllis Hyman |

KEVIN JOHN GEE, 40, California-born actor, died Aug.3, 1995 in NYC of pneumonia. Bdwy iluded *Anything Goes*. Off-Bdwy included *Helen* (1977), *Boticelli, Tropical Tree, Prime Time, Wedding of the Siamese Twins* and *Hot Keys*. Survived by his mother and sister.

HARRY GUARDINO, 69, NYC-born actor, died July 17, 1995 in Palm Springs, CA. of lung cancer. Known for both drama and musicals including the 1964 cult favorite *Anyone Can Whistle* and *Woman of the Year* (1981), other NYC stage included *End as a Man, Hatful of Rain, Natural Affection, Rose Tattoo* and *Seven Descents of Myrtle*. Survived by his wife, three sons, a daughter, 2 brothers, 2 sisters and a grandson.

ALBERT HARRIS, 51, artistic director, died Mar.1, 1996 in NYC of lymphoma. Artistic Director of Off-Bdwy's Theatre Off Park, he presented this season's Rodgers & Hart series. He leaves a legacy of carefully re searched and restored versions of classic musicals. He worked on Bdwy's *Stardust* (1986) and directed Off-Bdwy's *Madamoiselle Colombe, Poker Session, Promenade* (revival) and *Lovesong*. Survived by his father, a sister and brother.

TOM HELMORE, 91, London born actor, died Sept.12, 1995 in Longboat Key, FL. After working in British stage and film he made his Bdwy debut in *No Time for Comedy* (1939) followed by *Day Before Spring, You Never Can Tell, Clutterbuck, Legend of Sarah, Love and Let Love, High Ground, The Winner, One Eye Closed, Dark Is Light Enough, Debut, Mary Mary, The Playroom* and Off-Bdwy's *House of Flowers* (1968). He also acted as standby to Rex Harrison during the original run of *My Fair Lady*. Survived by a daughter.

BARTON HEYMAN, 59, Washington, DC-born actor, died May 15, 1996. Bdwy included *Indians* (1969), *Trial of the Catonsville 9, Talent for Murder, Doll's House* and Off-Bdwy's *Midsummer Night's Dream, Sleep, Phantasmagoria Historia, Enclave, Henry V, Signs of Life, Crack, Private View, Night Hank Williams Died* and *Him*.

PHYLLIS HYMAN, 45, Philadelphia-born singer/actress, committed suicide June 30, 1995 in NYC. She received a Theatre World Award for her Bdwy debut in *Sophisticated Ladies* (1981). Other Bdwy included *Dreamgirls*.

JOHNNY JOHNSTON, 81, St.Louis-born singer/actor, died Jan.6, 1996. Known mostly as a singer, he was the male lead in the Bdwy musical *A Tree Grows in Brooklyn*.

GEORGE KEANE, 78, Mass.-born actor, died Oct.10, 1995. Bdwy included *Hamlet* (1938), *Richard II, Henry IV, Moon is Down, Othello, Lifeline, Park Avenue, Brigadoon, Love Me Long*.

GENE KELLY (Eugene Curran Kelly), 83, Pittsburgh-born dancer/singer/actor/director/ choreographer, died Feb.2, 1996 in Beverly Hills, CA after a series of strokes. A movie legend for his screen work, he originated *Pal Joey* (1940) on Bdwy. He made his Bdwy debut in *Leave It To Me* (1938) with Mary Martin. In 1958 he directed the Bdwy musical *Flower Drum Song*. Survived by his third wife, two daughters, a son and grandchildren.

CLINTON KIMBROUGH, 63, actor, died Apr.9, 1996. Bdwy included *Look We've Come Through* (1961), *After the Fall, But For Whom Charlie, The Changeling, Incident at Vichy* and Off-Bdwy's *Our Town* and *Camino Real*.

TOM KINDLE, 47, St.Louis-born actor, died Feb.12, 1996. He appeared in Off-Bdwy's *The Soldier* (1973).

NANCY LaMOTT, 43, singer, died Dec.13, 1995 of cancer. In addition to her solo singing engagements and albums, she contributed vocals to *Best Little Whorehouse Goes Public*. Survived by her husband.

WILLIAM LARSEN, 68, Louisiana-born actor, died Jan.21, 1996. Bdwy included *Ballad of Sad Cafe, Half a Sixpence, Funny Girl, Halfway Up a Tree, There's a Girl in My Soup, Dear World, Cat on a Hot Tin Roof*. Off-Bdwy included *The Crucible, Fantasticks, Legend of Lovers, Twelfth Night, The Tavern, Lower Depths, School for Scandal, Troilus and Cressida* and *Murderous Angels*.

JONATHAN LARSON, 35, White Plains, NY-born composer, died Jan.25, 1996 in his NYC apartment of an aortic aneurysm. He died following the final dress rehearsal for his landmark musical *Rent* which was scheduled to being previews at New York Theatre Workshop the next day. The first preview was cancelled and the company sang the score for Mr. Larson's friends and family instead. *Rent* became a smash, moving to Broadway and winning the Pulitzer Prize, Tony Award and many other honors. Previous Off-Bdwy scores were *Superbia, Tick Tick...Boom!* and *J.P. Morgan Saves the Nation*. Survived by his parents and a sister.

RODHA LAWRENCE, 71, Mass.-born singer/actress, died July 30, 1995 in Sherman Oaks, CA of pulmonary fibrosis. Bdwy included the original *Oklahoma, Carousel* and Off-Bdwy's *The Hostage, The Way to San Jose* and *The Homefront Blues*. Survived by her husband, daughter and brother.

VIVECA LINDFORS, 74, Swedish-born actress, died Oct.25, 1995 in Uppsala Sweden where she was performing, of rheumatoid arthritis. After starting in movies, she made her Bdwy debut in *I've Got Sixpence* followed by *Anastasia, King Lear* and *Postmark Zero*. Off-Bdwy included *Miss Julie, Pal Joey* (CC), *Cuba Si, Guns of Carrar, Dance of Death, I am a Woman* and *Gypsy Swede*. Survived by her son, actor Kristoffer Tabori, another son, a daughter and grandchildren.

PAUL LIPSON, 82, Brooklyn-born actor, died Jan.3, 1996. Best known for many performances in *Fiddler on the Roof* (1964/76/81), often as Tevye, he also appeared in Bdwy's *Lily of the Valley* (1942), *Heads or Tails, Detective Story, Remains to Be Seen, Carnival in Flanders, I've Got Sixpence, The Vamp, Bells Are Ringing, Fiorello, Sound of Music* and Off-Bdwy's *Deep Six Briefcase, Inn at Lydia* and *Golden Boy*.

KATHERINE LOCKE, 85, Russian-born actress, died Sept.12, 1995 in Los Angeles of a brian tumor. A big hit in Bdwy's *Having a Wonderful Time* (1937), other Bdwy included *Hamlet* (Maurice Evans), *Fifth Column* and *Clash By Night*. Survived by her husband, son and daughter.

JEFFREY LYNN, 89, Mass.-born actor, died Nov.24, 1995. Bdwy included *Slight Case of Murder* (1935), *Stick-in-the-Mud, Cyrano de Bergerac, Brother Rat, The Long Days, Lo and Behold, Caine Mutiny Court Martial, Two for the Seesaw, Call on Kuprin, Critic's Choice, Mary Mary* and *Dinner at Eight* (1966).

Gene Kelly

William Larsen

Viveca Lindfors

Paul Lipson

Carmen Matthews

Butterfly McQueen

CARMEN MATTHEWS, 84, Philadelphia-born actress, died Aug.31, 1995 in West Redding, CT. Bdwy included *Henry IV*(1938), *Hamlet, Richard II, Harriet, Cherry Orchard, The Assassin, Man and Superman, Ivy Green, Courtin' Time, My Three Angels, Holiday for Lovers, Night Life, Lorenzo, The Yearling, Delicate Balance, I'm Solomen, Dear World, Ring Round the Bathtub, Ambassador, Copperfield, Morning's at 7*and Off-Bdwy's *Sunday in the Park with George.*

LARRY MAXWELL, 43, actor, died Dec.7, 1995 in Laurelton, OH. A member of Charles Ludlam's Ridiculous Theatre, his many Off-Bdwy credits included *Le Bourgeois Avant-Garde, How to Write a Play, Act and the Actor, Aboriginal Sin, No Damn Good* and *Dark Shadows.* Survived by his companion, mother and a brother.

FRANK MAYA, 45, NYC-born performance artist, died Aug.7, 1995 in Manhattan of AIDS. One of the first openly gay male comics, he had solo shows Off-Bdwy including *Paying for the Pool*(1993), *Frank Maya Talks, Get Out of the House* and *Unauthorized Biography: An Outing for the Whole Family.* He also was a cast member of *Chang in a Void Moon.* Survived by his companion, three sisters, two brothers and his parents.

TOM McDERMOTT, 83, actor, died Mar.6, 1996 in Manhattan of prostate cancer. Bdwy roles included *Three Sisters* with Katharine Cornell and Judith Anderson, *Best Man, Tiger at the Gates, Macbeth* and *Mastergate*(1989). Off-Bdwy included *Billy Budd, Hogan's Goat* and *Rosencrantz and Guildenstern are Dead.* He was active in regional theatre and film for most of his life. Survived by his wife, son, two daughters and grandchildren.

BUTTERFLY McQUEEN, 84, Florida-born actress, died Dec.22, 1995 in Augusta, Georgia after being critically burned in a fire in her cottage. Best known for her film role as Prissy in *Gone With the Wind,* she started her stage career in 1937 with *Brown Sugar* and *Brother Rat .* Other Bdwy included *What a Life, Swingin' the Dream, 3 Men On a Horse* and *Front Page.* Off Bdwy included *School for Wives,* the musicals *Athenian Touch* and *Curley McDimple.* She devoted her later years to the African-American community.

JOHN MEGNA, 42, NYC-born actor, died Sept.4, 1995 in Los Angeles of AIDS. As a youngster, he created the role of Rufus in Bdwy's *All the Way Home* (1960). In the 1962 film *To Kill a Mockingbird,* he played Dill. Survived by two sisters and a brother.

GRACE MICELI, 81, Cleveland-born costumer, died Nov.14, 1995 in Manhattan. Her credits included *Fiddler on the Roof, Cabaret, She Loves Me, The Wiz, Beauty and the Beast* and this season's *Hello Dolly.* Survived by her sister Maria Brizzi, also a costumer.

ESTHER MUIR, 92, actress, died Aug.1, 1995 in Mt. Kisco, NY. Bdwy roles started in the 1920s with *Greenwich Village Follies, Earl Carroll Vanities, International Revue* and *My Girl Friday!*(1929). Married to Busby Berkely (1929-31) and later to composer/producer Sam Coslow, she worked in many films. Survived by actress daughter Jacqueline Coslow and grandchildren.

DAVID OPATOSHU, 78, Bronx-born actor, died Apr.30, 1996. Bdwy included *Night Music*(1940), *Clinton Street, Man of Tomorrow, Me and Molly, Flight into Egypt, Reclining Figure, Silk Stockings, Once More with Feeling, The Wall, Bravo Giovanni, Lorenzo, Does a Tiger Wear a Necktie?.* Off- Bdwy included *Yoshe Kalb, Big Winner.*

JOHN PATRICK, 90, Kentucky-born playwright, committed suicide Nov.7, 1995 in Delray Beach, FL. Author of the Pulitzer-Prize winning *Teahouse of the August Moon* (1953) his other plays included *Curious Savage, Love Is a Time of Day* and *The Hasty Heart* He also wrote many films.

ILKA TANYA PAYAN, 53, Santo Domingo-born born actress, died Apr.6, 1996. Off-Bdwy included *Respectful Prostitute* (1969), *Francesco Cenci, Effect of Gamma Rays..., Blood Wedding, Miss Margarida's Way, Bitter Tears of Petra von Kant, The Servant, Parting Gestures* and *Our Lady of the Tortilla.*

WYMAN PENDLETON, 79, Rhode Island-born actor, died June 1, 1995. Bdwy included *Tiny Alice*(1964), *Malcolm, Quotations from Chairman Mao, Happy Days, Henry V, Othello, There's One in Every Family, Cat on a Hot Tin Roof, Scenes and Relevations* and *Prelude to a Kiss.* Off-Bdwy included *Gallow's Humor, American Dream, Zoo Story, Corruption in the Palace of Justice, Giant's Dance, Child Buyer, Butler and Egg Man, Albee Directs Albee, Dance for Me Simeon, Mary Stuart, Collyer Brothers, Period Piece, Bold Stroke for a Wife, Hitch-Hikers, Waltz of the Toreadors, Time of the Cukoo, Stopping the Desert.*

SAMUEL D. RATCLIFFE, 50, Florida-born scriptwriter/actor, died Dec.14, 1995 in Manhattan of AIDS. Starting in the chorus of *Fiddler on the Roof* his NYC performances included Matt in *Fantasticks* and the lead in Bdwy's *Hurry Harry.* He then began to write and became a leading writer for daytime tv. Survived by his companion, Jeffrey Hayenga, his parents and three sisters.

WILLIAM ROERICK, NYC-born actor, died Nov.30, 1995 in Monteray, MA. from a car accident. Bdwy debut in *Romeo and Juliet* (1935) followed by *St. Joan, Hamlet* (Gielgud), *Our Town, Importance of Being Earnest, Land Is Bright, Autumn Hill, This Is the Army, Magnificent Yankee, Tonight at 8:30, The Heiress, Medea, Macbeth, Burning Glass, Right Honorable Gentleman, Marat/Sade, Homecoming, We Bombed in New Haven, Elizabeth the Queen(CC), Waltz of the Toreadors, Night of the Iguana, The Merchant* and *Happy New Year.* Off-Bdwy included *Madam Will You Walk, Cherry Orchard, Come Slowly Eden, Passage to E.M. Forster, Trials of Oz* and *Close of Play.* In addition to film and tv acting, he wrote two plays, *Happiest Years* and *Passage to E.M. Forster.* Survived by a sister.

MADGE SINCLAIR, 57, actress, died Dec.20, 1995 in Los Angeles of leukemia. NYC stage included *Wedding of Iphigenia* (1971) at the NY Shakespeare Festival. In addition to film and television, she worked in Los Angeles theatre. Survived by her husband, sons, mother and sister.

ROBERT STEPHENS, 64, English actor, died Nov.12, 1995 in London after recent liver and kidney transplants. Best known for his work in England, Bdwy included *Epitaph for George Dillon* (1958). In 1963 Laurence Olivier invited him to join England's National Theater Company where he did memorable work until self-destructive behavior hurt his career. In the 1990s he re-established himself with the Royal Shakespeare Company and was knighted. Once married to actress Maggie Smith, he is survived by his fourth wife and four children including actor Toby Stephens.

Ika Tanya Payan

Wyman Pendleton

Sam Stoneburner

Benay Venuta

Janet Ward

Jack Weston

SAM STONEBURNER, 66, Virginia-born actor, died Nov.29, 1995. Bdwy included *Different Times* (1972), *Bent, Macbeth* (1981), *The First* and *Six Degrees of Separation* (also OB). Off Bdwy included *Ernest in Love* (1960), *Foreplay, Anyone Can Whistle, Twilight Cantata, Flaubert's Latest* and *Little White Lies*.

KAY STROZZI, 96, actress, died Jan.18, 1996 in New Rochelle, NY. Bdwy included *Crown Prince* (1927), *Heavy Traffic, Silent Witness* and *St. Helena* (1936) with Maurice Evans. She toured with Ethel Barrymore and worked on radio and tv.

LYLE TALBOT (LYLE HENDERSON), 94, Pittsburgh-born actor, died Mar.5, 1996 in San Francisco, CA. Best known for character work in fi-olm and tv, his stage work included Bdwy's *Seperate Rooms* and toring shows. Survived by two sons, two daughters and grandchildren.

GENEVIEVE TOBIN, 93, NYC-born actress, died July 31, 1995 in Pasadena, CA. Bdwy included *Little Old New York* (1920), *Dear Sir, Murray Hill* and *Fifty Million Frenchman* (1929). She went to Hollywood and appeared in many films in the 1930s. Survived by her sister.

DANIEL E.TYRA, 58, Kentucky-born actor, died July 5, 1995 in NYC. Off-Bdwy included *Hogan's Goat, Where People Gather, Americana Pastoral* and *Enemy of the People*. Survived by his companion.

BENAY VENUTA (Benvenuta Rose Crooke), 84, San Francisco-born actress, died Sept.1, 1995 in Manhattan of lung cancer. A mainstay of Bdwy musicals, she debuted in 1935 by replacing Ethel Merman in *Anything Goes*. Other Bdwy included *Orchids Preferred, Kiss the Boys Goodbye, By Jupiter, Nellie Bly, Hazel Flagg, Copper and Brass, Dear Me the Sky Is Falling, Carousel* (1965), *Annie Get Your Gun* (1966) and *Romantic Comedy*. Off Bdwy included *Quarter for the Ladies Room*. She also worked in film and nightclubs, painted and made sculptures. Survived by two daughters and grandchildren.

IRA WALLACH, 83, playwright, died Dec.2, 1995 in NYC following a stroke. His Bdwy and Off-Bdwy plays included *Sticks and Stones, Phoenix 55, Sleep We Must, Drink to Me Only, Smiling the Boy Fell Dead* and *Absence of a Cello*. He wrote screenplays and novels. Survived by his wife and a daughter.

JANET WARD, 70, NYC-born actress, died Aug.2, 1995 in Manhattan after a heart attack. Bdwy included *Dream Girl* (1945), *Anne of a Thousand Days, Detective Story, King of Friday's Men, Middle of the Night, Miss Lonelyhearts, J.B.,Cheri, The Egg, Play with a Tiger, Impossible Years* and *Of Love Remembered*. Off-Bdwy included *Chapparal, The Typists, The Tiger, Summertree, Dream of a Blacklisted Actor, Crusing Speed 600 MPH, One Flew Over the Cukoo's Nest* (1971), *Love Gotta Come by Saturday Night, Home Is the Hero, Love Death Plays, Olympic Park, Hillbilly Wives, Q.E.D.* and *Yellow Dog Contract*. She also worked in film and tv.

DAVID WARRILOW, 60, English actor, died Aug.17, 1995. Off-Bdwy included *Red Horse Animation* (1970), *Penguin Touquet, A Piece of Monologue, Three Plays by Samuel Beckett, Messiah, Golden Windows* and *Zangezi*.

JACK WESTON, 71, Cleveland-born actor, died May 3, 1996. Bdwy includes *Season in the Sun* (1950), *South Pacific, Bells Are Ringing, California Suite, The Ritz, Cheaters, Floating Light Bulb, Tenth Man*. Off-Bdwy included *Baker's Wife* and *Measure for Measure*. The actor, popular in both comedy and drama, was also a familiar figure in films and tv.

MARY WICKES (Mary Isabelle Wickenhauser), 85, St.Louis-born actress, died Oct.22, 1995 in Los Aneles, CA. Perhaps best known for Miss Preen, the nurse in *Man Who Came to Dinner* (1939)-a role she also played in the film version, she was active in stage, film and tv for more than 50 years. Bdwy included *Farmer Takes a Wife* (1934), *One Good Year, Spring Dance, Stage Door, Swing Your Lady, Father Malachy's Miracle, Hitch Your Wagon, Too Much Johnson, Danton's Death, George Washington Slept Here, Jackpot, Dark Hammock, Hollywood Pinafore, Apple of His Eye, Park Avenue, Town House* and *Oklahoma* (1979).

INDEX

Hudson, Duffy, 167
Hudson, Scott, 114
Huey, Tom, 191
Huff, Neal, 23, 94, 227
Hughes, Allen Lee, 97, 108, 168
Hughes, Douglas, 92
Hughes, Julie, 67
Hughes, Liam, 164
Hughes, Mick, 102
Hugo, Dave, 200
Hugo, Katie, 165
Hugo, Victor, 71
Hugot, Marceline, 185
Hull, Bryan, 77
Hull, Mylinda, 198
Humphrey, Nina, 100, 185
Humphreys, Tom, 78
Hune, Michael, 181
Hunter, JoAnn M., 70, 189
Hunter, Kim, 108, 154, 169, 227
Hunter, Michael, 191
Hunter, Tim, 169, 190
Hunter, Timothy, 75, 139
Hunter, Todd, 165
Huntington Theatre Company, 42, 179
Huntington, Crystal, 58, 97, 120
Huntington, John, 96
Huntley, Paul, 12, 36
Hurd, Michelle, 37
Hurrell, Robert, 108, 143
Hurston, Zora Neale, 164
Hurt, Mary Beth, 52, 103, 227
Hussong, Cristina, 181
Husted, Patrick, 159, 167
Huston, Charles, 38
Hutchins, Ron J., 184
Hutchinson, Jeffrey, 103, 174
Hutter, Mark, 188
Hyatt, Jeffrey, 78
Hyde, William York, 46
Hyland, Ed, 196
Hyman, Julie, 84
Hyman, Phyllis, 207, 249
Hyman, Yehuda, 165
Hyslop, David, 62, 69

Hytner, Nicholas, 72, 165, 197, 201
I Love You, You're Perfect, Now Change, 182-183
IBIS Supper Club, 112
Ibsen, Henrik, 98, 163, 167-168, 178, 185, 188, 192
Identical Twins From Baltimore, 109
If We Are Women, 172, 194
IgLoo, 109
Imperioli, Michael, 109
In The Loneliness Of The Cotton Fields, 85
Inchaustegui, Adriana, 143, 185
Inconstant Lovers, The, 85
Indiscretions, 82
Ingalls, James F., 38, 91, 164, 166, 174, 181, 195
Inge, William, 36
Ingermann, Ivan, 187
Ingram, Carol A., 47
Ingram, Jack, 66
Ingram, Kenny, 190
Ingram, Michael H., 66
Inherit The Wind, 45-47
Inkley, Frederick C., 71, 200
Innvar, Christopher, 21, 99
Inskeep, Carter Mac, 107
INTAR Hispanic American Arts Center, 7, 127, 143, 157
Intar Theatre, 78, 114, 117, 136-137, 152,
International Dragfest Group, 111
Interrogation Of Nathan Hale, The, 194
Intrieri, Anita, 177
Invisible Circus, The, 171, 181
Irby-Ranniar, Scott, 190
Irish Repertory Theatre, 88
Irish, Fred, 28
IRT's New Directions Theatre, 110
Irving, Alicia, 76
Irwin, Bill, 22, 94, 227
Irwin, Robin, 190
Irwin, Tom, 93, 227
Isaacs, Pamela, 167

Isenegger, Nadine, 65
Ishee, Suzanne, 110, 227
Isola, Kevin, 95-96, 227
Israel, Robert, 161
Ives, David, 35, 87, 100, 167, 182
Ives, Donald, 16, 227
Ivey, Judith, 47, 91, 227
Iwamatsu, Sala, 194, 201
J.P. Morgan Saves The Nation, 108
Jack A Night On The Town With John Barrymore, 53
Jackowitz, Michael, 115
Jackson, Chris, 113
Jackson, Christopher, 108, 143, 196
Jackson, Dana Leigh, 66
Jackson, Ernestine, 89, 207, 227
Jackson, Gregory, 187
Jackson, Jeffrey J., 167
Jackson, Kathleen, 196
Jackson, Kirk, 97, 227
Jackson, R. Wade, 18
Jackson, Richard II, 167
Jackson, Robert Jason, 104, 185
Jacobs, Amy, 51, 131, 143
Jacobs, Craig, 69
Jacobs, David, 69, 160
Jacobs, Douglas, 193
Jacobs, Jim, 69
Jacobs, Max, 177
Jacobs, Tammy, 71
Jacoby, Marc, 73
Jacoby, Mark, 74, 207
Jaeck, Kathryn, 184
Jaeck, Scott, 38
Jaffe, Brian, 112
JaJuan, Kimberly, 43
Jakubowski, Zaniz, 111, 227
Jalenak, Natalie, 191
James, Brian d'Arcy, 99
James, Elmore, 64
James, Jeffrey, 81, 165
James, John, 198
James, Judy, 66, 108, 176
James, Peter Francis, 94, 96, 132, 168
James, Terry, 184

James, Toni-Leslie, 7, 23, 94, 96, 135, 170
Jameson, John, 167
Jamieson, Dawn, 46
Jampolis, Neil Peter, 39, 182
Janis, Peter, 77, 119
Janki, Devanand N., 48, 201
Janney, Allison, 93
Jar The Floor, 180
Jarreau, Al, 69
Jarrett, Bella, 107
Javore, James, 110, 179
Jayes, Catherine, 85
Jbara, Gregory, 21, 227
Jean, Marie, 67, 231
Jefferies, Annalee, 191
Jefferies, Clint, 108
Jeffreys, Stephen, 195
Jeffryes, Timothy, 112
Jellison, John, 67, 173
Jellsion, John, 67
Jenkins, Beerly, 72
Jenkins, Daniel, 56-57, 227
Jenkins, Jackie, 112, 131
Jenkins, Richard, 86
Jenkins-Evans, Hollis, 159
Jenks, Barbara, 186
Jennings, Alex, 44, 47, 227
Jennings, Byron, 92, 147
Jennings, Ken, 66, 207, 228
Jennings, Regi, 81
Jensen, Robert, 165
Jernigan, Terry, 196
Jewish Repertory Theatre, 89
Jimenez, Robert, 46
Jinaro, Jossara, 160
Jo-Ann, Ebony, 135, 163-164, 170
Jochim, Keith, 167, 192
Johanson, Don, 66, 228
Johanson, Robert, 190
John F. Kennedy Center for the Performing Arts, 44, 48, 70, 199
John Frost and the Adelaide Festival Centre, 48
John Houseman Theatre, 110, 113, 121, 130, 142, 152
Johnson, Alan, 105, 202
Johnson, Bernard, 113
Johnson, Bill, 112

Mowery, Rusty, 65
Moyer, Allen, 63, 95, 103
Moynihan, David, 168
Mozer, Elizabeth, 21, 234
Ms. Cinderella, 184
Muir, Esther, 250
Muir, Keri, 164
Muir, Kiri-Lyn, 74
Muirhead, Janice, 182
Mulamba, Gwendolyn, 191
Mulay, Denene, 190
Mulcahy, Andy, 111
Mulcahy, John, 190
Mulero, Javi, 181
Mulheren, Michael, 84, 99
Mulhern, Leonard A., 79
Mull, Kathe, 88
Mullally, Megan, 69-70, 234
Mullins, Melinda, 164
Mullins, Paul, 187
Munderloh, Otts, 15, 67, 90, 202
Mundinger, Matthew T., 12, 38
Munier, Leon, 77
Muniz, Marcos, 101, 234
Munoz, Rodney, 100
Munson, Kristabelle, 114
Mura, Mark La, 98
Muraoka, Alan, 48, 234
Murin, David, 167, 182
Murlin, Michele, 165
Murphy, Karen, 35, 66, 148, 234
Murphy, Kelly, 177
Murphy, Thomas, 88
Murphy, Tom, 194
Murray, Brian, 30-31, 139, 234
Murray, Sharon, 193
Murray, Stephen, 107
Murtaugh, James, 87, 130, 137, 147, 234
Museum Of Contemporary Art, The, 109
Musser, Tharon, 165
Muzio, Gloria, 8, 142
MVineyard Entertainment, 116
Mwine, Ntare, 170, 182
Myers, Beverly, 47
Myers, Don, 39, 112

Myers, Eileen, 87, 105, 124, 129, 145, 153
Myers, Mary, 104
Myers, Scott, 30
Myers, Troy, 35, 43
Myler, Randal, 159, 168
Nabel, Bill, 64
Nachamie, Stephen, 190
Nadal, Harry, 101, 107
Nadoolman, Deborah, 160
Nagel, Maryann, 168, 177
Nagel, Richard, 182
Nakagawa, Jon, 105
Nakahara, Ron, 94, 110, 126, 153
Nakamura, Midori, 23, 94, 234
Nakasone, Aiko, 58, 97
Nakauchi, Paul, 48
Naked Eye, The, 161
Nakuuchi, Paul, 48
Napier, John, 65, 71-72, 76
Napolitano, Nicole, 66
Narita, Rob, 108
Naro, Thomas V., 23
Naro, Tom, 94
Nash, Earl, 105
Nash, Ogden, 43
Nash, Ron, 93-94
Nason, Brian, 149, 182
Natale, David, 188
Natel, Jean-Marc, 71
Nathan, Fred, 65
Nathanson, Gary, 163
National Actors Theatre, 29, 46
Naughton, James, 63, 131, 207, 234
Naughton, Naomi, 65, 141
Nave, Bill, 112
Neale, Grant, 125, 196
Near, Timothy, 167
Necastro, Neil, 112
Nederlander, James L., 44, 139
Nehring, Larry, 177
Neil, Kevin, 72
Nelson, Edward J., 30
Nelson, J. A., 78
Nelson, John, 168
Nelson, Lee Mark, 81, 95

Nelson, Mark, 47, 81, 95, 123, 234, 236
Nelson, Richard, 18, 34, 93, 128, 148, 176, 182, 194, 216
Nelson, Tim Blake, 92, 94
Neofitou, Andreane, 71-72
Nesbit, Pat, 163
Nessen, Doug Van, 96
Neuberger, Jan, 56, 190, 234, 236
Neufeld, Jane E., 42
Neufeld, Mary, 111, 151
Neufeld, Peter, 65
Neuman, Jani, 165
Neuwirth, Bebe, 63
New England, 93, 132, 194
New Federal Theatre, 110, 129, 150
New Georges, 107, 114
New Jersey Shakespeare Festival, 187
New York Shakespeare Festival, 23, 55, 94
New York Theatre Workshop, 58, 97
New Yorkers, The, 184
New, David, 174, 184
Newcomb, James, 194
Newfield, Anthony, 163
Newman, Evan J., 66, 190
Newman, Molly, 168
Newman, Phyllis, 115, 235
Newman, Randy, 181
Newsome, Paula, 192
Ngai, Brandon, 47-48, 235
Nicholaw, Casey, 21, 235
Nicholls, Lisa, 195
Nichols, Jackie, 191
Nichols, Robert, 81
Nicholson, Betsy, 74
Nicholson, William, 186
Nicklaus, Jill, 65
Nicks, Tom, 28
Nicola, James C., 97
Niebuhr, Mark, 114, 135, 187,191
Nielsen, Kristine, 135, 142, 182
Nielson, Scott, 194
Nieman, Ann, 196
Niemtzow, Annette, 115

Nieves, Mazerati, 111
Night Of The Iguana, The, 38
Niko Associates, 16, 21, 29, 46
Nimoy, Lenoard, 50
Nimura, Megan, 193
Nine, 190, 210
Nishikawa, Lane, 189, 194
Nite Club Confidential, 196
Nixon's Nixon, 92
Nixon, April, 47, 75
Nixon, Cynthia, 185, 207
Nixon, Morgan A., 167
Noah, James, 164
Noble, Adrian, 44
Noel, Craig, 188-189
Nolan, James Michael, 182
Nolan, Kathleen Kund, 185
Nolan, Mike, 92
Nolan, Robert, 71
Nolen, Timothy, 73
Nolte, Bill, 167
Noone, James, 46, 78, 93, 147, 166, 176, 189
Nordan, Lewis, 192
Nordberg, Steven Philip, 160
Nordli, Robin Goodrin, 162
Nordlinger, Sharon, 159
Noritoshi, Yamamoto, 94
Norris, Bruce, 103, 235-236
Norris, William J., 186
Norrup, Christina Marie, 165
Northeast Local, 90
Norton, Jim, 194
Nothing Forever, 97
Noto, Lore, 77
Nottage, Lynn, 105
Nouri, Michael, 20-21, 235
Novak, David Alan, 195
Novak, Elizabeth, 168, 179, 192
Novice, Ken, 188
Novikoff, Garry, 108, 143
Nude Nude Totally Nude, 96
Null, Panchali, 74
Nunn, Trevor, 65, 71, 76, 200
Nystuen, Sally, 171, 177
Nyswaner, Ron, 103
O'Brien, Adale, 159
O'Brien, Jack, 37, 188, 198

Schmiel, William F., 192
Schoeffler, Paul, 190
Schon, Bonnie, 165
Schonberg, Claude-Michel, 71-72
School For Scandal, The, 28-29, 177, 205
School For Wives, The, 110
Schramm, David, 63, 240
Schreiber, Liev, 94, 102, 240
Schreier, Dan Moses, 23, 94-95, 99
Schroeder, Charlie, 196
Schrot, Richard A., 186
Schuberg, Carol, 187
Schuette, James, 96-97, 99, 107, 124, 159
Schulman, Craig, 71
Schulman, Susan L., 67
Schulman, Susan, 41
Schulman, Susannah, 194
Schulte, Mark, 111
Schultz, Armand, 95, 150, 240
Schultz, Carol, 98, 192, 240
Schultz, Joseph, 177
Schwab, Kaipo, 167
Schwab, Norm, 28
Schwartz, Clifford, 56, 66
Schwartz, Erica, 99
Schwartz, Gary, 165
Schwartz, Robert Joel, 98
Schwarz, Kristen, 167
Schworer, Angie L., 32, 67
Scotland Road, 192
Scott, Brian, 159
Scott, Bryan, 193
Scott, Christopher, 77, 113, 181
Scott, Ernie, 33
Scott, George C., 45-46, 206, 240
Scott, Harold, 14, 33
Scott, James, 167, 177, 192
Scott, John, 41, 240
Scott, Klea, 94
Scott, Michael Lee, 41
Scott, Michael, 74
Scott, Patrick, 193
Scott, Rodney, 108
Scott, Seret, 104, 153, 164, 182, 240

Scott, Sherie Rene, 69, 181
Scribe, Eugene, 98
Scrofano, Paula, 184
Scruggs, S.J., 161
Scully, David, 162
Scurria, Anne, 86
Seacat, James, 159
Seader, Richard, 18
Seagull, The, 191
Seale, Petie Trigg, 182
Sears, Joe, 167
Seascape, 116
Seasmon, Edward, 98
Sebastian, Kim, 32
Secada, Jon, 32, 69
Second Stage Theatre, 103
Seery, Florie, 7
Segal, David F., 93, 198
Seitz, John, 84, 120
Sekacz, Ilona, 44
Sclig, Paul, 87
Sella, Robert, 182
Seller, Jeffrey, 58
Sellon, Kim, 64
Selner, Jenny, 193
Selverstone, Katy Wales, 97
Semmelman, Jim, 16
Seng, Sonya, 180
Sept, Doug, 160
Seraphim, 108, 146
Serendipity Productions, 107
Screys, Jacques, 85
Sergel, Christopher, 179, 192
Serotsky, Aaron, 167
Serrano, Nestor, 23, 94
Setlock, Mark, 58, 132, 240, 243
Setrakian, Mary, 16, 240, 243
Setterfield, Valda, 96, 166
Seven Guitars, 42-43, 160, 165, 179, 204
Seweryn, Andrzej, 85
Seyd, Richard, 160
Seymour Hoffman, Philip, 96, 185
Seymour, Caroline, 96, 99, 111
Shadowlands, 186
Shaffer, Anthony, 159
Shaffer, Diane, 24
Shaiman, Marc, 15

Shakespeare, William, 23, 44, 94-95, 98, 116, 118, 125, 132, 135, 144-145, 149, 155-157, 159-162, 164, 174, 177-179, 181-182, 187-188, 191, 194, 196, 245
Shales, Geoff, 101
Shalwitz, Howard, 97
Shamash, Beba, 108, 118
Shamblin, Jack, 96
Shane, Lorna, 47, 69, 199
Shange, Ntozake, 110, 170
Shangraw, Howard, 194
Shannon, Mark, 86, 240
Shannon, Sarah Solie, 64
Shapiro, Mel, 187
Shapiro, Steve, 163
Sharkey, Joe, 87
Sharp, Monti, 105
Sharpe, Ron, 184, 200
Shatraw, David, 168
Shatto, Bart, 159
Shaw, George Bernard, 112, 125, 148, 162, 167, 171, 173, 192, 194
Shaw, Martin, 62, 207
Shay, Michele, 42, 160, 165, 179
Shaya, Carol, 77
Shayne, Tracy, 73
She Loves Me;, 167, 192
She Stoops To Folly, 194
Shca, Jere, 93, 207, 240
Shea, Matt, 177
Shearer, Andy, 12, 34, 38, 42, 61, 102, 121
Sheba, 89, 140
Sheehan, Mary C., 41
Sheehy, Alison, 30
Sheehy, Catherine, 164
Sheets, J.C., 71
Shelley, Carole, 74, 241, 243
Shelton, Raymond, 47
Shenkman, Ben, 92, 96, 113
Shenoy, Nandita, 89
Shepard, Matthew, 64
Shepard, Sam, 61, 129, 161, 195
Sheredy, Bernie, 192
Sheridan, Clarence M., 16, 241

Sheridan, Jessica, 71, 199-200
Sheridan, Richard Brinsley, 29, 177-178
Sherin, Mimi Jordan, 159, 161, 164
Sherman, Geoffrey, 186
Sherman, Jason, 92
Sherman, Jonathan Marc, 106
Sherman, Keith, 18, 113-114, 118, 131, 136, 145
Sherman, Loren, 96, 100, 182
Sherman, Lori, 106
Sherman, Richard M., 81
Sherman, Robert B., 81
Sherman, Stanley Allan, 77
Sherwood, Tony, 165
Shevelove, Burt, 51
Shilling, Thom, 200
Shimmer, 88
Shimono, Sab, 194
Shine, Kevin, 110
Shiner, David, 22
Shinick, Kevin, 29, 241, 243
Shipley, Sandra, 96, 241, 243
Shire, David, 56
Shively, Sarah, 191
Shore, Gregg David, 112
Shore, Sammy, 84
Shortt, Paul, 167
Show Boat, 32, 47, 74,
Shubert Organization, 23, 65, 199
Shull, Richard B., 21, 241
Sicari, Joseph R., 198
Siccardi, Arthur, 21, 29, 56, 76
Sickle, Luke, 159, 173
Sicuso, Tony, 108, 143
Sidney Productions, 112
Sieber, Christopher, 181
Siebert, Jeff, 72
Siebert, Ronald H., 163
Siedenburg, Charlie, 30, 90, 145
Siegel, David, 70
Siegel, June, 113
Siff, Helen, 77

288